The Negotiator's Desk Reference

Volume 2

Published by DRI Press, an imprint of the
Dispute Resolution Institute at Mitchell Hamline School of Law

Dispute Resolution Institute
Mitchell Hamline School of Law
875 Summit Ave, St Paul, MN 55105
Tel. (651) 695-7676
© 2017 DRI Press. All rights reserved.
Printed in the United States of America.
Library of Congress Control Number: 2017936301
ISBN 978-0982794647

Mitchell Hamline School of Law in Saint Paul, Minnesota has been educating lawyers for more than 100 years yet remains committed to innovation to respond to the changing legal market. Featuring more enrollment options than any law school in the country, Mitchell Hamline is committed to accessibility and offers a curriculum rich in advocacy and problem solving. The law school's Dispute Resolution Institute, consistently ranked in the top five dispute resolution programs by U.S. News & World Report, offers more than 30 alternative dispute resolution courses each year in a wide variety of domestic and international programs, including certificate programs in arbitration law and practice, problem solving, and conflict resolution, and is the home of DRI Press. For information on other DRI Press publications, visit http://open.mitchellhamline.edu/dri_press/

The Negotiator's Desk Reference

Chris Honeyman
Andrea Kupfer Schneider
Editors

DRI Press
Saint Paul, Minnesota

ANNOTATED TABLE OF CONTENTS: VOLUME 2

water, air and fire—and relate each concept to the heart and mind of negotiators. It turns out that aesthetics are a clue to much that's going on at the back of our counterparts' minds, and our own. We will negotiate better if we take due account of the wisdom they offer. This chapter should be read in conjunction with the same authors' Part Two, in which they argue for a contemporary negotiation application of the ancient concept of alchemy.

The authors here pursue the logic of their Part One chapter further. Showing how negotiators tend to concentrate on a limited range of skills and stimuli, while overlooking others, they argue that the ancient concept of *alchemy* works in conjunction with modern concepts of neuroscience to unlock a whole series of aesthetics-derived, embodied strategies and approaches. These, they contend, make it possible to advance "stuck" negotiations in which progress is stalled, as well as to improve a whole range of less complex negotiation processes.

The author reviews the life work of one of negotiation's most famous scholars, and reveals a wholly new observation. Roger Fisher, she argues, did not understand negotiation as primarily something that happens in the shadow of the law. Rather, based on his years thinking about international conflict, Fisher offered a theory of negotiation as a form of legal ordering and, by extension, a theory of law as a form of negotiation—one with enduring relevance for dispute resolution today.

Is there such a thing as a generally reliable theory of negotiation? Is there even a coherent definition of what negotiation is? And if not, how are we to make sense of a field that produces so many examples in so many settings? Lande has studied a wide variety of texts and sources, and sets out to pull them into, if not a single coherent range, at least a recognizable matrix.

This chapter serves as the overview to all of the chapters on the use of different media and technology as part of negotiation. How do we make sense of all our options? The authors argue that knowing your own "default", while understanding your counterpart and the context, is crucial. Being able to choose wisely among the different modes requires careful consideration of the advantages and disadvantages that go along with each of these. This chapter can usefully be read in conjunction with Thompson, Ebner, and Giddings on Nonverbal Communication, as well as with the technology chapters—particularly, Ebner's chapters on Email, Texting, and Videoconferencing.

Email is typically the first technology people think of when they start to imagine negotiating using a computer. By now, this is a common practice, at least for parts and phases of a typical negotiation. Yet few practitioners or students pause to consider how the technology affects what is said, how it is said, and when and how it is heard. Reviewing what is now a substantial body of research, the author finds seven major challenges in negotiating via e-mail, most of which are as yet poorly understood. He goes on to provide practical advice on each one.

"Never!" That's the typical reply, says the author, when he queries a negotiator about negotiating through text messages. Not so fast, Ebner says—look closely at how your day goes and how your various forms of communication fit together, and you may well find yourself already handling part of that traffic via text. Furthermore, he says, in the future you can expect to use this medium more, as more and more of your counterparts depend on it. Yet negotiating via text is significantly different even from email negotiation. Ebner walks you through the assets, and the liabilities.

Here, Ebner addresses a tool which has crept up on negotiators. Videoconferencing for negotiation was first hailed long ago with certain expectations: high quality video at high cost, to be used for negotiation between business teams in expensively equipped conference rooms. But now, these conditions are largely supplanted by widespread use of lower-resolution videoconferencing tools such as Skype and other low-to-no-cost programs, of varying quality and reliability. As one result, people now find themselves, routinely, in face-to-face negotiations with people whose faces cannot be seen very clearly. The social effects go far beyond this, too—concerns about who might be listening out of camera view, and other privacy and confidentiality issues, combine with widely varying levels of comfort with this technology to create a significant likelihood of a mismatch between parties who do not trust, or cannot manage, the technology or the setting equally. Ebner provides a matrix of considerations that apply to nonverbal communication in video conferencing, and another to help a negotiator understand the particular features and risks of using video.

Here, the author follows up on his Email and Text negotiating chapters, both of which discuss technology which by now have become quite generic. This chapter is different: Ebner here describes representative examples of a burgeoning class of proprietary programs, which individually address one or another situation or problem a negotiator may have. Together, they form an expanding array of electronic helpers – and merely hint at what may be available not far into the future. It is increasingly evident, as a result, that keeping up with the field is no longer simply a matter of reading; learning new programs as they come along is virtually guaranteed to become more and more essential.

In the next decade, lawyers' roles will change dramatically because of the expansion of online dispute resolution (ODR). As technology increasingly pervades professional life, demand for efficient negotiation tools and software-supported dispute resolution processes can also be expected to grow. The authors discuss how lawyers' practice is changing as a result of the advent of high technology specific to their field, and outline both the uses and risks for lawyers that are associated with a whole series of specific platforms and programs that are increasingly being used to transact or settle cases online and offline, including in courts. Finding the technologies to be constantly evolving and disruptive of existing practice, the authors nevertheless conclude that lawyers have little option but to learn, use and advise their clients about these platforms. They point out that some of the new technologies promise to obviate a great deal of unrewarding work, to speed up possible resolution and, if designed appropriately, to enhance fairness and access to justice, reinforcing the negotiation field's strong interest in "process pluralism".

So many successive generations of people have remarked on how they don't understand the next generation that it's now become a cliché. Yet the "digital generation" does represent a departure from years of assumptions of how people will typically get and process information, how they understand the world, and how many different things they ought to expect to do at the same time. Newell reviews the research on the digital generation's ability to maintain sustained attention over time, and finds that, yes, there is a difference. Multitasking—defended by many as an efficient way to process multiple concurrent streams of information—has been exposed as something of a myth. And there are other prices paid for assuming that one can handle multiple digital forms of communication, from cognitive overload to neurological changes. Yet communication technology is here to stay, Newell says: we have to learn how to handle it. She offers a succession of techniques for reclaiming and holding attention.

Section XII. Organizations and Teams 216

This chapter analyzes the research on what individuals accomplish, when compared to teams in which the members have differentiated functions. Not surprisingly, the teams turn out to be able to handle more information more accurately more of the time. But of course, that's not the whole story. The authors, who include two advisors to professional sports teams, use examples from professional sports to show where you might want a team to negotiate, and where it makes sense to use an individual.

The authors discuss the surprising shortage of research on how organizations negotiate or plan to negotiate, when the work is considered on a broader than individual level. They contrast this with evidence that certain organizations have profited enormously, and even become dominant players in their markets, largely by adopting and enforcing one consistent style and approach to negotiation, one which supports in every detail the organization's overall strategy. They argue that building on this evidence represents a potentially huge strategic opportunity for organizations which have not yet tackled consistency of purpose and of execution across all of their relationships with suppliers, employees and other stakeholders. They note, however, that the results of such consistency are not always attractive to the outside observer.

The author earned his living for many years mediating between 20,000 scientists and working with interdisciplinary research teams. Reflecting on his career, Gadlin finds himself valuing disagreement (at least sometimes) more than agreement. Especially among scientists or other people who must think and work in teams, disagreement can spur new thinking. Developing this theme, Gadlin finds that the maintenance of *productive* disagreement has its own principles, and is at the heart of professional practice in an increasing number of occupations and settings which depend on developing new intellectual property.

To many who are frustrated with ill-organized, expensive, catch-as-catch-can approaches to handling entirely predictable conflict, dispute system design has seemed a logical, socially productive way of planning to reduce the costs of conflict, and effectuating justice on a larger scale. Amsler shows how this is not always the case, beginning with an analysis of how Boston lawyers on all sides effectively conspired to keep the pattern and practice of abuse of children in the Roman Catholic Church quiet for decades. This was a *system* at work—there is no denying it. Thus questions of justice and accountability arise at the outset when analyzing or, even more important, planning any dispute resolution system. Amsler lays out the criteria and makes proposals for how to design and effectuate a system that is not only systematic, but requires *justice*.

In several distinct domains of conflict—heavy construction, international relations and U.S. labor relations—there are by now highly sophisticated and widely-adopted techniques for anticipating future conflict. If not ensuring outright that there will be only minimal such conflicts, these techniques at least encourage the conflicts which inevitably follow the formation of a new relationship to be handled with a minimum of time, cost and stress to all involved. For the most part, the evidence is that these systems work. Surprisingly, however, most other industries and domains have yet to adopt anything comparable. The authors analyze the history and the sources of resistance, and offer a new strategy toward wider adoption and adaptation of these proven tools.

The authors, who include unimpeachable experts on boxing, review what actually happens in the ring and in the frequently unspoken dialogue between the boxers, the referee, and the fight doctor. They find negotiation behavior routinely taking place in this most unlikely of environments. They explain why, and also show the price that is paid in injury, and sometimes a life, when the referee or the doctor gets the subtle signals wrong.

The authors use case studies from three highly dissimilar environments to unpack the negotiating differences that apply when the parties are many, the stakes are high, and the situation is unstable.

How can you-the-negotiator ensure that your client is really on board? Nolan-Haley argues that by paying more attention to "informed consent" not only before, but again at intervals during a negotiation, and taking care to reaffirm this as the process reaches agreement, agents will not only better serve their clients but reach better, more lasting agreements. Yet revisiting the subject, years after the 2008 financial shocks demonstrated the degree to which large institutions were ignoring these principles, she finds strong evidence that lawyers and other professionals with a duty to their clients have badly failed them. As a result, she concludes that if your attorney *isn't* asking you the hard questions, it's in your interest to ask the attorney why not. This chapter should be read in conjunction with Wade's Shadow of the Tribe.

Your case is complicated; it involves specialized knowledge, and without some help, the judge probably won't understand it and the jury certainly won't. Furthermore, your chances of negotiating a settlement depend on getting some degree of shared understanding with the other side of what the facts are. So you've hired your expert, and the other side has hired its expert—and now the experts themselves are locked in combat. Could you avoid this next time? In the meantime, what do you do now? Wade analyzes your options at every stage, and shows how even when the experts have delivered black-versus-white reports of the facts, you can still salvage the situation. This chapter should be read in conjunction with Adler on Negotiating Facts.

Many believe that in negotiations as elsewhere, facts are the bedrock, the only things that can be firmly ascertained and then relied on, in a shifting universe of personalities, perceptions and preferences. Adler, steeped in the mediation of scientific disputes, begs to differ. Facts in science are routinely challenged. Factual disagreement is also at the heart of many public policy disputes, and cannot be successfully papered over by focusing either on interests or positions. Yet after years of experimentation, public policy negotiators and mediators have made considerable progress in developing systems and structures for uncovering the assumptions and data that underlie many difficult disputes. This makes it possible to address fact-driven disputes more productively—and the technology now exists to do this on a wider scale. Adler shows how. This chapter should be read in conjunction with Wade on Dueling Experts.

Section XV. Making Conflicts Less Intractable

Peter Coleman and Robert Ricigliano
In the first of a trilogy on complex cases, the authors estimate that far beyond the usual categories people think of as "intractable"—such as international, race relations or major environmental conflicts—about 5% of disputes of virtually all kinds actually fit this pattern. The authors review why this is, and outline a series of techniques developed in recent years for handling conflict of the worst kind, in any domain. This chapter should be read in conjunction with Coleman, Redding & Fisher's "Intractable 1 and 2" chapters.

Peter Coleman, Nicholas Redding and Joshua Fisher
In the second chapter of our complex-case trilogy, the authors summarize recent findings from complexity science and dynamical systems theory, showing how the new insights provide the possibility of innovative levers for change. Their key findings are presented as a set of five guidelines. This follows the more general explanation in Coleman and Ricigliano on Getting in Sync and is also closely related to the next chapter, Influencing Intractable Conflicts, which also presents a set of five guidelines: this time, for actually working on a conflict which, on the surface, appears impossible to influence.

Peter Coleman, Nicholas Redding and Joshua Fisher
The final chapter of our complex-case trilogy describes techniques developed in recent years which promise greater effectiveness in the admittedly frustrating process of actually tackling an intractable conflict. It should be read not only in conjunction with Understanding Intractable Conflicts by the same authors and Getting in Sync by Coleman and Ricigliano, but also in conjunction with McDonald on Kashmir, in which a retired U.S. Ambassador describes what he actually did when drawn into working on the long-standing Kashmir problem.

Stuart Kirschner and Jack J. Cambria
Let's say you've finished this book and would like to use some of it. But what about your more hardheaded colleagues, team members or other audiences? Using their experience in training the highly skeptical police officers of the New York City Police Department, psychologist Stuart Kirschner and longtime (2001-2015) NYPD Hostage Negoti-

ation Team commander Jack Cambria discuss the design of training for a potentially resistant audience.

In the first of two chapters, the author argues that the relationship between religion and conflict is widely oversimplified. Recent and careful social science research has demonstrated that, contrary to the assumptions of some people, religion most often increases its adherents' ability to relate positively to others—and this can include adherents of another religion or none at all. In contrast, he reviews the research on extreme religious militancy, including the evidence on suicide and other violent attackers, and concludes that the most careful researchers have universally found that these actions are not principally propelled by religion itself, but by other factors. In his next chapter, Seul proceeds to analysis of how religion can help to transform conflict, and how it can be consciously invoked toward that purpose.

In the second of two chapters on religion and conflict, Seul reviews the research on religious prosociality, and the ability of religion to help people relate positively to others, and to help resolve conflict. He offers examples of specific strategies to encourage cooperative behavior when working with religious stakeholders in a conflict.

Only rarely is the public privileged to track a major negotiation and see up close whether the theories actually get put into practice. A multitude of other chapters in the book are implicated here as Ambassador John McDonald talks about the prevailing assumptions, the intractable conflict, and a breakthrough move toward progress in the decades-old conflict between India and Pakistan over Kashmir. Because so few practitioners at this level have undertaken to write down what they actually did, we have elected to preserve the original 2006 text largely intact, with only a few clarifying changes. The McDonalds' updated (2016) assessment follows. [This chapter stands particularly as a practical illustration, by a consummate practitioner, of the principles explained by Coleman et al., in Intractable 1 and 2, as well as Adler's Protean Negotiator. For another view of how the field's theories apply, or do not, in a difficult environment, this chapter could be read in conjunction with NDR: Kaufman & Blanchot, *Theory Meets Reality*]

Section XVI. Getting It Done (Strategies)   594

90. Making Deals about Power Sharing   595
John Wade

Power-sharing is an intrinsic element of many negotiations, particularly those which involve some kind of continued interaction in the future. The need to provide for future decisions to be made without resort to open conflict creates a series of questions, about who will make each decision or type of decision, what the criteria will be, and what essential or ancillary conditions might apply. Clear thinking is essential, and here Wade offers a gradation in 13 steps from total power held by one party to total power held by the other. Somewhere along the 11 steps in between, perhaps, is your best solution to your particular problem in negotiating today, for what must happen next week or next year.

91. The Uses of Ambiguity   609
Chris Honeyman

The reality sinks in: everybody's now trying to reach an agreement, but on some fundamental things, the parties *really* don't agree. Some of those involved see themselves as reasonable people, others are Standing On Principle without any thought of what that will mean in practice. Is there anything you can do to get this dispute over with before it spirals completely out of control? Yes, says Honeyman: you can allow, or even consciously design in, a bit of ambiguity here and there. Doing this knowledgeably can preserve your principles, while allowing for an agreement that works well enough for an imperfect world. This can be read with Moffitt's chapter on Contingent Agreements and Wade's on the Final Gap.

92. Contingent Agreements   619
Michael Moffitt

What if you and the other side have very different views of the future? Should this make it harder to achieve an agreement? In fact, as Moffitt explains, these different views can provide exactly the lubricant needed for the gears to mesh. Contingent agreements can help negotiators move toward an overall agreement, even (or particularly) when they disagree. As one of several chapters discussing particular techniques for use when things get sticky, it should be read in conjunction with Wade's chapter on the Final Gap and Honeyman's on Ambiguity.

93. Crossing the Final Gap   627
John Wade

It's three o'clock in the morning. You've been negotiating or mediating since 9 a.m. and everybody is exhausted. Each side has made more concessions that it really thinks it should have had to, and the gap between the parties has narrowed to millimeters. But there it has stuck, and will stay stuck unless you do something new. Every sophisticated negotiator or experienced mediator has a personal answer to this problem, a private stock of a few gambits, often tried and sometimes successful. But John Wade has the longest list we have ever seen, 16 techniques in all. Not one of them works all the time; but together they can materially improve your batting average.

One of the clear roles of negotiators, mediators, lawyers, managers, parents and human beings is to attempt to re-open "jammed" negotiations. Lawyers, negotiators, managers and mediators are paid to be competent, even expert, at recommencing communications and negotiations which have reached a stalemate or a tense stand-off. Yet many otherwise competent professionals find this difficult. This chapter sets out seventeen common strategies used by the most skilled "problem-solvers" to re-open negotiations between deadlocked disputants.

So, you finally have a deal! How can you make the deal stick? This straightforward chapter shows why deals regularly fall apart, and provides specific advice on what you can do in order to increase the likelihood that *your* agreement will survive the slings and arrows of outrageous fortune.

How's your negotiation going? Would using a mediator perhaps be helpful? This chapter shows why and when mediation can help negotiators reach an agreement. It also explains the different types of mediation goals, and how each of those goals can affect the process. This should be read in conjunction with Honeyman on Working with Mediators.

Perhaps you've reached the point in the negotiation where it's time to bring in a third party. This chapter helps you make wise choices about whom to hire as a mediator. It's designed to help the negotiator understand how mediators actually operate, and to be aware of the skill set and biases within which any given mediator *must* operate. This should be read in conjunction with Love and Stulberg on The Uses of Mediation.

One of the U.S.'s most experienced mediators here discusses a striking difference between his own view of one critical feature of practice, and that of most of his peers. Most high-end litigators and their clients, he argues, have found most mediators to be anything but transparent as to their own thinking processes, even while pressing the parties to be more transparent about theirs. Brazil discusses the pluses and minuses of this way of working, offering his own take on transparency as an alternative. Delving further into the motivations, however, he concludes ultimately that his own practice is a bit less transparent than he thought—more "gray box" than either black or translucent box. The resulting reflection stands as one of the most transparent discussions of a mediator's motivations and methods offered by a prominent practitioner.

In a thought-provoking book, Mayer analyzed new roles that experienced mediators and other conflict specialists might play, and suggested that they think more broadly about how they can best assist disputants. Here, he focuses specifically on how negotiators can enlist these specialists as allies instead of as third party neutrals. Just for openers, this could help you to get a complex negotiation framed properly, or to approach the other side in ways that will put them in the right frame of mind. But a decade after first analyzing the possible roles, Mayer has extended the reach of the underlying idea to a long list of "ally" roles which today often go unfilled—to the negotiator's and principals' disadvantage.

You're about to start negotiating in a language where you can't even read the alphabet. What to do? This chapter is essential for anyone about to engage in a negotiation involving multiple languages—which could include many "domestic" negotiations in Singapore or Chicago or London or Paris. Kaufman explores how translators are neither perfectly neutral third parties, nor part of a team (contrary to common assumptions). She then shows how they are often powerful and autonomous actors in the negotiation, and demonstrates how important it is to think about the use of interpreters *before* the day they are hired.

Negotiation, mediation, and arbitration—the three major practice areas of ADR—have become so mainstream that many argue that the "A" of ADR, which historically has stood for "alternative," no longer applies. But modern ADR originally developed as a set of practices outside the mainstream, intended in large part to promote social transformation and empower individuals. Reynolds argues that these activist roots of ADR should not be forgotten, and in fact should spur new research and pedagogy around activism, community organizing, social movements, and other "extralegal" approaches to changing law and society.

IN VOLUME ONE:

2.   **Learning How to Learn to Negotiate**   13
Scott Peppet and Michael Moffitt
At the outset of a book with many new ideas, this chapter can help the reader *implement* what you are about to read. Analyzing research on how we can learn to learn, the authors provide specific advice to negotiators and negotiation trainers. For those whose students—or colleagues—are more hardheaded than most, this chapter should be read in conjunction with Captive Audience by Kirschner and Cambria.

3.   **Integrative and Distributive Bargaining**   33
Rishi Batra
The distinction between integrative and distributive negotiation is one of the baseline innovations of our field's modern development. Any number of other concepts simply cannot be understood until its lessons have been absorbed. Here, the author walks the reader through the all-important basics of this key element of understanding of negotiation: why "creating value" and claiming it represent competing goals; how these relate to the negotiator's personality; how they affect the process as it unfolds - and how, in the end and despite obstacles, they must be *integrated*, if a good result is to be reached.

4.   **Style and Culture in Negotiation**   43
Eko Yi Liao
Even at a basic level, a negotiator's effort to understand how her own style works and how it might mesh or collide with the style of a counterpart is not only essential, but usefully illustrated in conjunction with cultural differences. Liao uses Chinese examples to show how individual styles work and don't work in common combinations, in Western as well as Asian settings.

This chapter should be read in conjunction with Abramson on Good Practices, Styles and Tricks, and Batra on Integrative and Distributive Bargaining.

Abramson points out that the term "style" in our field has two distinct connotations, because someone's conflict style and their negotiation style can be different. He first recommends clearly analyzing and understanding your personal conflict style. Then he unpacks "good practices", tactics and tricks as three key features of negotiation style to show, quite apart from questions of morality, how a negotiation style that does not account for your own conflict style will be less effective. At the same time, Abramson says, you need to invest effort in understanding your counterpart's negotiation choices, especially use of tactics and tricks, when fashioning your own effective negotiation style. This chapter should be read in conjunction with Liao on Style and Culture, Craver on Distributive Negotiation and Batra on Integrative and Distributive Negotiation.

Interest-based negotiation, transformative approaches to mediation, and other relatively recent and enlightened doctrines have created wide enthusiasm among negotiators and negotiation students. They continue, however, to bump regularly into forms of "reality" that are less appealing. In particular, there is no practical way to ensure that you will find yourself dealing only with people who have the same progressive worldview towards joint gains that you may have. In this chapter, a veteran teacher dispassionately dissects no less than 28 different varieties of "hard bargaining", and describes how to defend yourself in each case (or even, for those so inclined, how to prosecute these techniques.)

The authors argue that a negotiation cannot be understood by looking at its *substance* alone: a three-dimensional view that takes into equal account the negotiation's *people* and its *process* is essential to make head or tail of it. In turn, mapping these three dimensions onto a negotiator's mind set begins to make it possible for the negotiator to see where and how he or she might change things, rather than reflexively responding to the other's impetus, or narrowly pursuing a set strategy that may not be working.

Not all negotiators are capable of seeing the world in multiple dimensions, shifting their responses according to different needs, and accepting uncertainty with good grace. But the best negotiators do this routinely. Adler shows why, particularly in conflicts and transactions that involve people and groups with different world frames or cultures, it becomes essential to be able to shape-shift, like the Greek god Proteus. This is not a charade—it is responsiveness. And it can be learned.

   The economists' traditional and convenient concept of human beings as rational actors who pursue self-interest has by now been thoroughly amended, if not debunked. But how the complicating factors, including gender, culture, emotion, and cognitive distortions, actually work in our brains has been elusive until more recently. Lately, however, neuroscience has begun to make inroads toward a better understanding of many of these factors. This chapter describes one large piece of the puzzle: the evolution of human beings' brains into those of a highly interdependent, social species.

   To be truly effective, negotiators must try to influence their counterparts not only through substantive offers, but also through engaging their attitudes and thinking patterns. This need has been analyzed (and, increasingly, taught) mostly in terms of empathy. Here, the authors suggest that empathy is separate from a broader construct, which they term social intuition. This skill, they contend, gives a negotiator the ability to have an impact on the entire negotiation interaction. Yet it requires attention not only to developing empathy, but also nonverbal communication abilities, as well as several other elements. In an effort to make a difficult skill more accessible, they suggest dividing its learning into three elements, structured quite differently from previous discussions: understanding first the self, then the other, and then the elements of "bridging" between these two.

   Contrary to what might be expected from common usage, people's creativity and their flexibility rely on entirely different structures in the brain. Here, a brain researcher describes the recent findings of neuroscience in relation to both qualities. Jendresen shows how the experience of aging (sadly) robs *everyone* of some degree of mental flexibility. The good news is, the brain can be trained for both flexibility and creativity, and your brain will adapt, altering itself physically to respond to your needs.

   The author, a physician specializing in emergency medicine, finds his work replete with negotiations of all kinds, many of them demanding compassion. Finding similarities to police hostage negotiation work, O'Shea reviews the neuroscience involved, and concludes that professionals of any kind who must demonstrate compassion at work can pay a price in their own peace of mind, or at an extreme, even in their ability to continue to do the job at all, when the demands exceed their time and ability to recharge their batteries of compassion. Most insidiously, the author finds hidden curricula in the training of his profession, and of others, which militate against the professional ever adopting a compassionate enough attitude to really suffer stress – or to do the job properly.

    Have you ever been in a negotiation where you (or the other side) seem to be acting instinctively, but perhaps not helpfully? Have you wondered what was going on inside your counterpart? Deutsch summarizes how psychological theory applies to basic negotiation, and explains how negotiators' internal conflicts affect them and everybody else in the room. In a coda about our global community, he adds an analysis of how powerful individuals' internal conflicts have increasingly played out with disastrous consequences on the world stage.

    It's all but routine for a negotiator leaving a meeting to mutter under her breath concerning the perceived mental health issues of someone on the other side. Unfortunately, the research now demonstrates that such suspicions may not always be unreasonable. Mental health issues, it turns out, do not prevent people from assuming and holding high status in many kinds of organizations, so you may be negotiating with borderline mentally ill people with some regularity. Furthermore, we know that high-stress situations like the death of a family member, divorce or job changes, which often lead to negotiations, can trigger mental illness. Here, a psychologist and a lawyer (and sister and brother) analyze the most common types of mental illness, and tell you what to expect from each of the types you are most likely to encounter in negotiations. Crucially, they also provide recommendations as to how to deal with the reality of each type of mental illness.

    Can you both trust and distrust the other side? In fact, we often do exactly that. Lewicki provides practical advice on dealing with trust and distrust in each interaction. Of particular importance to negotiators facing troubled relationships, this chapter shows how distrust is not merely a mirror image of trust: it actually works quite differently. Effective negotiators must learn both to build trust and to manage distrust. This chapter should be read in conjunction with Tinsley, Cambria and Schneider on Reputations; Lewicki-'s chapter on Repairing Trust; and Cristal on No Trust.

    Of course trust is important to build, and maintain. Yet inevitably, trust is sometimes violated. Here, Lewicki analyzes what happens in the wake of a trust violation, and offers prescriptions for a meaningful attempt to rebuild it. This chapter should be read in conjunction with Tinsley, Cambria and Schneider on Reputations; Lewicki's chapter on Trust and Cristal's on No Trust.

    In the final chapter of our trilogy on trust, its development and repair, a "pracademic" with significant experience of high stakes conflicts assesses situations where it is not practicable even to try to build or rebuild trust—and yet a deal must be made, whether with a political enemy, former spouse or labor union leader. For these situations, Cristal offers an alternative paradigm of three elements: allowing for the emotional component of "freedom to hate"; replacing for working purposes the concept of trust with that of respect; and building trust in the process rather than in the good faith of the other side. These steps, he argues, can make some of the most difficult negotiations workable.

Time was when a Formica plaque could often be found on the desk of a certain type of negotiator. It said "Yea, when I walk through the Valley of the Shadow of Death I shall fear no evil, for I am the meanest son of a bitch in the valley." But is it really to your advantage to have a reputation as one of the junkyard dogs of negotiation? The authors approach the question from three very different starting points. Tinsley summarizes the research on reputation in controlled settings. Schneider turns to real-life reputations of lawyers in action. Finally, Cambria shows how the life-and-death negotiations which characterize the work of the New York Police Department's Hostage Negotiation Team have led to a new understanding of reputation. This chapter should be read in conjunction with Lewicki on Trust and Hollander-Blumoff on Relationships.

Is "I'm sorry" the hardest phrase to say? Does it matter whether you mean it? This essay examines the critically important issue of apology, and how and when an apology can be helpful or harmful in a negotiation. Reviewing the latest empirical work, the authors discuss the purpose, type and timing of an apology, to ensure that any apology given accomplishes its goals. Note that they find that an apology offered cynically or casually may be worse than none at all. This chapter is closely related to Toussaint and Waldman on Forgiveness.

How many negotiations are reduced to a numbers game by the unthinking responses of professional negotiators who don't recognize what is really at stake for their clients? How many negotiators frame what "should" be achieved in the negotiation, conveniently getting around the fact that the agent can't be paid one-third of an apology? Here, a lawyer and a psychologist together examine the evidence that forgiveness may be the single most desirable negotiation outcome in many situations, when measured by the physical and mental health of those involved—but that a lockstep push toward forgiveness in all disputes is neither possible, nor desirable. This chapter should be read in conjunction with Brown & Robbennolt on Apology.

The author argues that relationships in negotiation can be simultaneously over- and under-valued. She locates a significant stream of argument to the effect that relationships should be developed almost for their own sake, or at least with an eye to long-term and repeated dealings—and finds another that focuses on the short term and implicitly if not explicitly devalues relationships. The author contends that there is a reasonably moral and thoroughly practical view in between. Arguing that there is nothing wrong with admitting that one's goals in a negotiation may fall somewhat short of true friendship or deep mutual understanding, Hollander-Blumoff notes that it is still productive and well worth the effort to form *some* level of connection with the other party. Even this modest step can smooth the rough edges, develop better information for the use of both parties, and make more agreements, and more creative agreements, possible.

In today's world, intergroup conflict transcends time and space as we face problems that affect multiple generations. Wade-Benzoni discusses how intergenerational contexts push the boundaries of more traditional conceptions of negotiations to include the reconciliation of conflicting interests between parties who may not exist contemporaneously. Furthermore, research on intergenerational conflict challenges the dichotomy between "self" and "other" interest. This chapter should be read in conjunction with Welsh on Fairness.

When you set out to negotiate with someone, how do you evaluate what you're really trying to achieve? Is it an unfocused want; something better than your BATNA; or anything you can get that's above your reservation price? Schneider analyzes research showing that a conscious choice of goal helps you come out with more. Four keys to this are "making your reach a little longer than your arm"; setting goals you can justify in public without laughing or lying; making them specific; and paying real attention to goals which can't be expressed in a number. It's also helpful not to take yourself too seriously. Finally, Schneider argues that we need to get used to disappointment in order to achieve true success.

Why is it that attractive or well-liked people tend to do better in negotiation? Guthrie explains how persuasion in negotiation works differently from persuasion in court. The psychology behind six different factors that tend to influence people is described: liking, social proof, commitment and consistency, reciprocity, authority, and scarcity all have consequences. Guthrie offers practical tips, exploring how lawyers and other negotiators can use these phenomena to influence their counterparts in negotiation.

We know instinctively that not everyone is persuaded by the same set of facts or the same type of argument. Shestowsky explains the two different types of audiences we typically face in a negotiation, and provides pointers on how to persuade in the way that will be most effective to each audience. This chapter should be read in conjunction with Perceptions & Stories by Heen & Stone and Getting your Way by Guthrie.

standing, based on Carl Rogers' theories in clinical psychology. This approach can change speakers' attitudes, making them more complex and less extreme, and help promote more integrative solutions. The authors outline specific tools to help us all become better listeners.

31. **What Negotiators Can Learn from Modern Sales Theory**
    Ava J. Abramowitz
    For many negotiators, a self-concept of professionalism seems to militate against learning from sales, a field they appear to devalue. Yet sales is the central setting of negotiation for all sorts of firms, particularly when what is sold is a complex and high-end service, or multimillion-dollar equipment. Not surprisingly, since sales is also the lifeblood of these firms' survival, there has been a great deal of research and theorizing about it. In the best of selling, it turns out, forceful statements are largely replaced by thoughtful questions about every aspect of the customer's needs. Here, Abramowitz takes a classic of sales theory and shows how it applies to negotiation in many other domains.

32. **Facing Off across the Table: Negotiators' Facial Features Affect the Agreements They Reach**
    Kathleen O'Connor and Margaret Ormiston
    Does your face determine your fortune at the bargaining table? Some of us profoundly hope not; but O'Connor and Ormiston review work from economics, psychology, and organizational behavior, and find three categories of facial features that *have* been found to make a difference. Each of these facial features has a unique and important effect in negotiation. In particular, these facial features affect how counterparts perceive negotiators.

33. **Non-Verbal Communication in Negotiation**
    Jeff Thompson, Noam Ebner and Jeff Giddings
    The authors first review the research indicating that what most negotiating advice focuses on—what should be said or written, and how, and when—amounts to about 7% of communication. The other 93% is nonverbal....and is mostly ignored by proponents of better negotiation. They then set out to remedy this situation by analyzing different modes of nonverbal communication, and offering a matrix of ways to understand it, and employ it more consciously and more effectively.

Section VII. Ethics and Morality

34. **Moral Character and Trustworthiness in Negotiations**
    Taya Cohen
    The author considers character as a key element in building trust. Yet she finds moral character to be a phenomenon somewhat independent of the "calculus-based" and "identification-based" concepts of trust discussed elsewhere in this volume by Roy Lewicki. Cohen argues that individuals can be assessed as having high or low moral character, and that high moral character is justly rewarded with the trust of others.

35. **Negotiation Ethics**
    Art Hinshaw
    Morals, rules, or law? The author shows how ethics in negotiation can be viewed through any of these three lenses—but they produce different results. So, how to decide, when it's your case and your reputation at stake? Hinshaw works through a series of social norms, showing how people with

different personality profiles tend to opt for one norm over another. He then uses these norms to demonstrate how a negotiator can assess whether a counterpart has opted for a cooperative approach, or a competitive or even a deceitful one. This is followed by analysis of how the rules applicable specifically to attorneys affect a lawyer's possible choices, and in turn, a brief tour of the applicable and overarching law. In the end, however, Hinshaw concludes that the best advice overall for even a lawyer-negotiator is to listen closely to his or her own personal sense of ethics—and follow it.

     Your dilemmas as a negotiator fall into two basic sets, "what's possible?" and "what's right?" The first is treated by many chapters in this book. Here, from his philosopher's background, Gibson writes about the influence of morality on negotiations, and how we can think more clearly about what's the right thing to do. This chapter should be read in conjunction with Carrie Menkel-Meadow's chapter on The Morality of Compromise.

     As negotiators seek to apply the legal and professional considerations that govern ethical decisions, they will inevitably be impacted by psychological factors. The authors review the research on "bounded ethicality" and find that even people who try to behave ethically can be led astray by psychological phenomena that cause them to unconsciously downplay and rationalize improper actions. Negotiators and organizations that are aware of this problem, however, can take steps outlined in the chapter to prevent themselves from inadvertently acting unethically. This chapter should be read in conjunction with Hinshaw on Ethics, Cohen on Moral Character, and Rule on Online Ethics.

     In all of negotiation there is no bigger trap than "fairness." Welsh explains why: among multiple models of fairness, people tend to believe that the one that applies *here* is the one that happens to favor *them*. This often creates a bitter element in negotiation, as each party proceeds from the unexamined assumption that its standpoint is the truly fair one. Welsh argues that for a negotiation to end well, it is imperative for both parties to assess the fairness of their own proposals from multiple points of view, not just their instinctive one—and to consider the fairness of their *procedures* as well as of their substantive proposals.

     The authors argue that better outcomes result when negotiations incorporate principles of justice. They review evidence that when negotiators seek justice for *all* parties, in both the process and outcome senses of the term, the outcomes are more likely to be actually implemented. The authors contend that in major negotiations in particular, such as international conflicts, it has proven to be possible to get the parties to think about different concepts of justice and fairness, which allow in turn for a richer discussion of what should be done. This pays dividends far into the future. This chapter should be read in conjunction with Welsh on Fairness.

In this chapter, a leading expert on online negotiation and dispute resolution considers the new ethical challenges wrought by his field. Rule finds that the advent of technology as a routine element in all sorts of negotiations has introduced new questions about impartiality, competence, cost, accessibility, confidentiality, privacy, and even the possibility of systemic biases being built into software code. As yet, he argues, few negotiators are thinking about or even aware of most of these factors. Yet they increasingly affect how your case will be handled.

With America's increasingly multicultural population, the ability to recognize that race still matters is an important factor in negotiations. This chapter attempts to capture an important chunk of the literature that identifies the unique experience for black persons in negotiation, and makes some suggestions to address these challenges. Because of its focus on cultural impacts of negotiating while being black, this chapter can usefully be read in conjunction with Bee Chen Goh's chapter on negotiating under Chinese culture, Gale Miller's on Codes of Culture, and Kaufman and Blanchot on Theory Meets Reality.

It's no longer rare for negotiators based in a Western culture and instinctively applying Western concepts to find themselves in dealings with people who start from a very different cultural frame of reference. Goh, a Chinese-Malaysian law professor working in Australia, deconstructs the typical errors that negotiators unfamiliar with Chinese culture can be expected to make. This chapter should be read in conjunction with Miller on Codes of Culture, Kaufman and Blanchot on Theory Meets Reality as well as Michael Green's on Negotiating while Black; together, they can provide you with a fast tour that will provide some hints as to what you might encounter in still other cultures—and, perhaps, in less familiar parts of your own culture.

By now, it's widely discussed that men and women tend to negotiate differently. But what does this mean in practice? Are women always disadvantaged? And what can be done to improve the gender gaps typically seen in negotiation outcomes? The authors review decades of experimental research and make a series of recommendations—both for individuals, and for organizations which increasingly see it as in their own interest to ensure fair handling of employee and other negotiations.

Culture, Miller argues, has become a widely recognized element in negotiation at many levels. Yet he finds that this has failed to clarify how culture actually works, because culture means so many things to so many people that invoking the concept is as likely to confuse as to enlighten negotiators. The author argues for making a distinction between three different orientations to culture. They range from treating culture as widely shared values and practices of large groups and societies (which the author calls "encompassing codes"), to focusing on the distinctive social realities created in social interactions in small groups ("small group codes"). Between these extremes, he says, is the "multiple codes" orientation, which stresses the diversity of values and practices shared within cultural communities. Miller contends that understanding these three codes can help any negotiator decode what is really going on.

Do the theories and best practices now widely understood among negotiators actually hold up, when exposed to a culture and setting very different from those in which they originated? The authors track Blanchot's experiences in a Francophone African country, and find evidence that when given such a cultural stress test, some of our field's most cherished theories do not help. It is even possible that standard approaches and remedies, applied in the wrong place, may cause active harm.

Every negotiation has a rhythm to it—whether lyrical, musical or mechanical. The rhythm regulates a progression which, once understood, can help you realize where you stand at any given moment. Here, Zartman outlines the process and the typical steps that negotiations must work through.

How do you know when it's time to get serious about negotiating? When is a deal ready to be made? In the settlement of civil disputes, we often see parties expensively delaying negotiations, even waiting for mediation till they're on the proverbial courthouse steps. Is there a science to this? From the perspective of international relations, Zartman analyzes the issue of ripeness and demonstrates when it's time to settle.

Before metaphor and underneath framing lies the structure in which you find yourself negotiating. Because the structural elements are often buried, they can go unremarked. But many times, there is a *choice* of structure, or dispute domain, within which you may be able to pursue your negotiation. The authors use two particular domains of negotiation to explain how this works....and how you might foresee a need to switch to another process. This chapter should be read in conjunction with Gross on Arbitration's Shadow.

Plea bargaining accounts for the disposition of a significant majority of criminal cases. Indeed, without this kind of negotiation, either the judicial and criminal prosecution systems would have to be radically enlarged, or they would collapse completely. Yet misunderstanding of how these negotiations work is rife. Alkon describes plea-bargaining's varieties, its frequently severe constraints (which surprisingly affect prosecutors almost as badly as the defense), and outlines its potential to do better—with some relatively modest reengineering.

"Bargaining in the shadow of the law" is a famous phrase that by now has passed into negotiators' and particularly lawyers' subconscious. Yet as the backdrop for setting norms and expectations in negotiation, case law has been largely supplanted in recent years by a plethora of standardized, unilateral contracts which propel anyone with a subsequent grievance toward a private, confidential arbitration proceeding—and increasingly bar such individual parties not only from airing their concerns in court, but from joining with others similarly situated in a class action. The result has profound consequences for many who are trying to negotiate redress for all sorts of contract violations. This chapter should be read in conjunction with Miller & Dingwall on Dispute Domains.

The authors started with a "natural experiment", involving a canceled flight and the resulting competition for the last seat on the last remaining plane out: in the real world, which negotiator gets that seat? Years of further study have combined with years of further sad experience, in which the authors increasingly found themselves grappling with customer service agents with routinized training and scripts for how to deal with dissatisfied customers, in one industry after another. Here, they survey the state of play across a wide range of environments which have now adopted such playbooks—and provide suggestions for how *you* can play in turn, with ingenious and effective responses.

Preface to Volume 2

For any reader who is holding Volume 2 but has not seen Volume 1, a brief note here may be helpful. The *Negotiator's Desk Reference* is intended as the most comprehensive reference in its field, and also as an unusually versatile teaching tool; but it did not arrive at these roles in one step. The underlying project has been running for the best part of fifteen years, and has had a number of phases and publications.

We formed the *Canon of Negotiation Initiative* (www.convenor.com/canon-of-negotiation.html) in 2003, initially to see if there was a substantial quantity of research that might be applicable beyond the specific domain (law, public policy, business and international relations, at first) that had originated each piece. The results have been far beyond what we expected. The initiative is described in the Preface to Volume 1, but if you don't have ready access to that, you will find it among the "public" pages at our Web edition, at www.ndrweb.com.

The short version of a quite complex venture is that over the years of the *Canon* initiative, we have published first a full special issue of the *Marquette Law Review;* then, what stood for more than a decade as the most thorough reference in our field (*The Negotiator's Fieldbook*, published by the American Bar Association in 2006); and now this book, which supersedes the *Fieldbook*. The present book updates approximately 40 of the *Fieldbook* chapters and adds approximately 60 completely new ones. The Web edition (free to buyers of both print volumes or of the full Kindle edition) includes a third "update" volume, to be filled gradually. It also includes a search engine which covers all the content; this is provided instead of a static index, since by its nature an index does not respond to updates. The search function is open to readers who purchase only one of the print volumes.

The *Canon of Negotiation Initiative* has also produced a number of articles, but more important, it led to a "spinoff" project which was itself ambitious and deserves specific mention here. *Rethinking Negotiation Teaching* (2007-2013) produced a four-volume book series, as well as several special issues of journals. It can be found (and all of its book chapters can be downloaded free in PDF) at www.convenor.com/rethinking-negotiation-teaching.html .

In all of this work we have had the privilege of working closely with an unequalled array of our field's best thinkers, both practical and academic. Our long-term institutional partners have been Marquette Law School, the Section of Dispute Resolution of the American Bar Association, and Mitchell Hamline Law School. They are described and our gratitude expressed more thoroughly in the Preface and Acknowledgements in Volume 1. Here we will simply thank them once again.

Chris Honeyman and Andrea Kupfer Schneider, Editors

Section X: The Hidden Ideas that Power Our Field

Volume 2 begins with The Hidden Ideas that Power Our Field. The first of these, but perhaps not the best hidden, is metaphor. (Metaphor is all around us, it's the oxygen in our intellectual atmosphere.) Following our chapter on metaphor is one on why, when we consider whether or not to negotiate (and how), we are making moral choices as well as practical ones.

Of course, illustrating hidden ideas is problematic, or they wouldn't be hidden: the next chapter discusses literature as a rich source of examples and explanations. Yet many ideas don't reduce themselves easily to writing, and the following two chapters explore ground-breaking ideas of how aesthetics, particularly ideas of beauty and alchemy, can be used to open up negotiating possibilities that remain invisible if only the standard approaches are used.

The final two chapters of Section X return to ideas that have definitely been expressed in text, but not necessarily understood: the core ideas of one of the field's founders, and the "jungle" of competing negotiation theories.

ℭ 52 ℬ

The Road to Hell is Paved with Metaphors

Howard Gadlin, Andrea Kupfer Schneider
& Chris Honeyman

Editors' Note: Metaphors are so deeply embedded in our minds that they are, to a large extent, how we think. This creates an enormous trap for negotiators, as they not only tend to start out with metaphors for conflict handling that derive from war, but tend not to notice their assumptions. Yet metaphor can be the key to a solution, as well as the central problem. The authors argue that developing a holistic understanding is the essential element in using metaphor creatively—that, and avoiding letting a metaphor creep up on us, like a thief in the night.

When one talks about meaning in human communication, inevitably one must talk about metaphor. Students of negotiation looking to understand what conflicts are really about have discovered the importance of metaphor (Cohen 2003; Jones and Hughes 2003; Docherty 2004). This work

Howard Gadlin retired after serving for 18 years as Ombudsman at the National Institutes of Health. Before that he was University Ombudsperson and director of the UCLA Conflict Mediation Program and co-director of the Center for the Study and Resolution of Interethnic/Interracial Conflict. Earlier he was Ombudsperson and Professor of Psychology at the University of Massachusetts, Amherst. Currently he is studying the dynamics of scientific collaborations and developing approaches to address conflicts among scientists. He is co-author of *Collaboration and Team Science: A Field Guide* and author, among other writings, of *Bargaining in the Shadow of Management; Conflict, Cultural Differences, and the Culture of Racism*; and *Mediating Sexual Harassment*.
Andrea Kupfer Schneider is a Professor of Law at Marquette University Law School and is the director of Marquette's nationally-ranked dispute resolution program. Professor Schneider has written numerous books, book chapters and articles on negotiation skills and styles, dispute system design, international conflict, and gender and negotiation. She was named the Outstanding Scholar by the ABA Section of Dispute Resolution for 2017.
Chris Honeyman is managing partner of Convenor Conflict Management, a consulting firm based in Washington, DC. He is co-editor of *The Negotiator's Desk Reference* and five other books, and author of over 90 published articles, book chapters and monographs. He has directed a 25-year series of research-and-development programs, advised many academic and practice organizations, and served as a mediator, arbitrator and in other neutral capacities in more than 2,000 disputes.

has been inspired by the research and writings of George Lakoff (1999) and his colleagues, who have demonstrated that much of abstract thinking is dependent upon metaphor, and that we can more fully grasp how someone understands a matter, and the emotions associated with that understanding, through a careful examination of the metaphors by which they describe it. Even on the most bare-bones practical level, it turns out, an awareness of metaphor is important to any negotiator who hopes to jog someone out of an unproductive pattern of thinking.

The interest in metaphors parallels in some respects the interest in framing; both are concerned to explicate how disputants understand their own disputes, how they see those with whom they are in dispute, and how they experience the dispute resolution processes through which they address the disputes. This interest is, again, more than academic; people who work regularly with people in conflict learn very quickly that there is typically much more to a conflict than there appears to be at first. Aristotle wrote about the dual nature of metaphor when giving advice on rhetoric and how to craft persuasive arguments. He noted that metaphors can be incredibly helpful and persuasive when used appropriately and yet could be seen as deviations from clear language. As we outline below, certain metaphors *can* help disputants see the other side or see the dispute differently. At the same time, there is a danger of exacerbating the most antagonistic and destructive elements of conflict.

When these disputes are in the legal framework, the metaphors for the adversary system contribute even more to the danger of competitive and destructive assumptions. Famed jurist Benjamin Cardozo wrote close to 100 years ago, "Metaphors in law are to be narrowly watched, for starting as devices to liberate thought, they end often by enslaving it." (Berkey v. Third Ave 1926) As Cardozo noted, common metaphors in law, from piercing the corporate veil to the wall of separation between church and state, can lead to sloppy rather than careful thinking. In negotiation, the danger is perhaps even greater where we are unconsciously using metaphors to set the emotional tone of the negotiation, define the relationship, and outline the rules.

Common Metaphors in Conflict

Metaphors often are used to describe the parties in conflict, the structure of the conflict and the potential strategies used. Perhaps the most common (and overused) metaphor in conflict is war. We are fighting, my lawyer is my knight in shining armor or gladiator, and my arguments will demolish them. We attack weak points, we parry their thrusts, and we hope our iron-clad arguments are right on target. We can adopt a "take no prisoners" attitude.

Another common metaphor for negotiation is sports or games. We play for our team or we are in a boxing match. We might lay our cards on the table, go to the mat, or play hardball. Or sometimes we are in the animal kingdom where it is a "dog eat dog" world or a zoo and we are trying to herd cats.

Yet other less competitive metaphors exist, and are used. Sometimes we say that we are "working through" the problem, or building a bridge to the other side, almost invoking an engineering or production-management view of the world. Arguments can be structured and rebuilt. We might have a toolbox of options. If we are "hammering out our differences," it connotes that we are in the mechanic's shop trying to find ways of "repair," but working together. (The phrase is metaphorically distinguished from another use of similar language, in which the parties are hammering each other—or in which even mediators have been known to refer to hammering a party.)

Arts-related metaphors also offer a different window. Are the parties painting a picture or even on the same canvas? Can they weave an argument? Perhaps their conversation is more like a dance (waltz or tango) where we are trying to dance to the same beat or listen to the same tune. [These metaphors are growing. See NDR: LeBaron & Alexander, *Alchemy* and NDR: Alexander & LeBaron, *Beauty*]

And we could move the dispute to the outdoors where the negotiators are on a journey (perhaps needing some guidance.) There might be speed bumps and detours before we reach our destination. Of course not all alternative metaphors are helpful. Imagine mountain climbing as a metaphor where parties "ratchet" themselves upwards to a "precipice" from which they need help "climbing down." (Of course, you could always jump!)

Finally, we can think about metaphors for conflict resolution. John Paul Lederach analogized peace agreements to temporary antacids. Are we trying to get parties to take medicine for their own good? Or are conflicts like fruit where they need to ripen [NDR: Zartman, *Timing*] in order to be properly harvested? All of these metaphors give us insight into how the parties see themselves and their potential strategies. In the rest of this chapter, we outline how understanding these different metaphors can help illuminate the parties' assumptions in emotions, relationships, and rules, and then also help us shift them to more productive ones.

Metaphor as Reflecting Emotion

Every negotiator faces two realities about what they hear: people don't always mean what they say; people don't always say what they mean. Perhaps paradoxically, the astute negotiator is able to recognize this while still finding a way to take people at their word; or at least, to understand them *from* their words. We attend to metaphors in communication because they provide some link to understanding, in two ways. First, metaphors reflect the feelings that are a part of how people think about the dispute; second, they provide a way to go from what people say to what they mean to say. Of course the connotations of, and associations to, the metaphors people use when describing their conflicts often reveal as much about the emotional impact of the conflicts as it does about how they think about it. Think of the connotations to the term "war" as opposed to those to the term "dance." (War as stress, dance as energy, sports as fun are merely some of the connotations a negotiator might employ; each metaphor has many more, and an astute negotiator can bend the metaphor in an appropriate direction.)

Although metaphor can help us recognize factors that might make people reluctant to tell a full story, it is especially useful in orienting us toward two features of people's thinking that we often confront when working with conflict. The first is succinctly described by Jones and Hughes: "humans are feeling beings with thoughts and not thinking beings with feelings." (Jones and Hughes, 2003) Every negotiator has had the experience of realizing how thoroughly the issues in a dispute are infused with emotions, sometimes even while the parties deny that this is the case. The second is that much of our cognitive process proceeds outside of our conscious awareness. Note that in speaking about thought processes as "unconscious" we are using the term in a somewhat different way than did Freud, who was referring to what we think of as "irrational" aspects of thinking. [NDR: Deutsch, *Internal Conflict*] The "unconscious" thinking that Lakoff and others examine is what we ordinarily think of as "rational." Daniel Kahneman's groundbreaking work on judgement and decision making reveals in great detail how much of our seemingly rational decision making is actually intuitive and emotional. (Kahneman, 2011)

In part because of these realities, in recent years conceptions of negotiation have expanded beyond the notion of the self-centered, rational pursuit of self-interest through distributive bargaining. The ideal of the rational actor has been challenged both by the recognition that emotions are intrinsically tied up with thoughts and by the realization that much thinking goes on outside the scope of conscious awareness. This recognition also has opened up ideas about the negotiation process. We are now alert to the fact that negotiations are always about more than the pursuit of interests; they are also about identity and about relationships. The key to understanding these dimensions of what a negotiation is "really" about resides in the stories that people tell about the conflicts or issues that bring them into the negotiation as well as how they describe the negotiation process itself. [NDR: Heen & Stone, *Perceptions & Stories*]

There are two major ways in which negotiators can benefit from understanding and attending to metaphor. One has to do with how we interpret what we hear; the other has to do with how we intervene. While using a person's metaphors as a means to interpret where the person is coming from is obviously very important, the question of what one does with what one learns from the metaphor is not straightforward. As Jones and Hughes make clear, metaphors help us see and feel both what a party feels about something *and* how the party thinks about it, and that how they feel and how they think are intrinsically interwoven. The old advice of separating the feelings from the issues, if it ever was believed, is clearly off base. If we follow Jones and Hughes, the feeling cannot be separated from the "thinking about" because the thinking contains the feelings within it (Jones and Hughes 2003).

Metaphors can be used to help a party express directly what is only being expressed indirectly. One of the authors, for instance, worked for some time with a deeply disturbed person who was experiencing a wide range of workplace performance and relationship problems. In every one of the mediating conversations, while her words were about work-related matters, the metaphors were about neglect and abuse. It was not until these metaphors were brought to her attention that she was able to move toward a framing of the various issues in ways that were amenable to being addressed successfully.

In another instance a person whose long-term collaborator had terminated their partnership interpreted every proposal for working out the details of their separation as proof of a desire to humiliate her, as if working through an ugly divorce. Only after she was able to discuss in detail that it was the dissolution itself that had been painful and humiliating for her were the parties able to agree on the terms of their separation.

Metaphor as a Reflection of Relationship

The disputing parties' use of metaphor can help us better appreciate how they understand and experience the negotiation process, as well as how they understand and experience the conflict and their relationship with their counterpart. If, in talking about the conflict, they are using words with combat connotations, it suggests that perhaps the parties see all interactions with the other person as acts of war. Most likely this means they see the negotiation in terms of winning and losing.

The war metaphor also alerts us to the fact that the conflict has very high stakes; people may feel that their very identity is at stake. For the negotiator this is a sign that she must carefully explore, through questioning, what the conflict means to the disputants. On the other hand, if the war metaphors have emerged only in their discussion of the negotiation process and not in their accounts of the reasons they have come to negotiation, the parties can take the war metaphor as an indicator of apprehension about the process of negotiation.

Recognizing the metaphor that is guiding the parties' orientation toward the negotiation process always presents the negotiator with a tactical decision point—whether to work with the other party's metaphors, or to introduce a different metaphor that might help re-orient him or her. When working with people who are divided by deep enmity and longstanding rivalry, one of the authors often talks early on (but after they have described their conflict and its history) about establishing the terms of a cease-fire or a truce. Doing this honors their war metaphor, but orients them towards a different outcome than the one with which they arrived, i.e. win/lose.

At other times, a metaphorical expression that introduces a greater transformation than in the example above might be used, one that helps to reframe the conflict itself and not just the negotiation process. For example, when people describe how they are always fighting at work and are unable to cooperate, it may become appropriate to comment on how *well choreographed* their conflict appears. In this case the dance metaphor, by referring to the synchronization of movements that choreography produces, points directly to the sort of "cooperation" that is required between people who sustain a conflict over time—and undermines the idea that they are unable to cooperate. In recent years the dance metaphor has become the basis of a new line of inquiry, which is already leading to an expanded array of related metaphors, not to mention physical—yes, physical—methods for enlarging the possible ways of addressing a wide variety of negotiations. (LeBaron, MacLeod and Acland 2013)

The judicious use of a new metaphor can also allow the negotiator or mediator to articulate what the disputants may not be able to state directly. Sometimes when participants in a failed collaboration are exchanging accusations of blame and describing each other's inability to change, one can ask whether they have ever thought about divorce. Introducing a divorce metaphor in a workplace dispute can give permission for the disputants to discuss their problems in a new way. With parties who have not been able to articulate the depths of their enmity and the breadth of their incompatibility, such a framing is often a relief, both because it acknowledges dimensions of the conflict they have only alluded to and because it alleviates the fear that to resolve their dispute means they are going to have to become friends.

Metaphor as a Reflection of the Rules of Engagement

Sometimes metaphors can reflect the underlying assumptions that the parties are making about the negotiation process. If they see the conflict in terms of winning and losing they are likely to be on the lookout for dirty tactics ("All's fair in love and war") and highly suspicious of communications from the other person. Of course the person who sees a negotiation as war might also justify withholding crucial information and disguising their true intent. (Consider how many stories from war glorify deception tactics—from the Trojan Horse to D-Day. In a war metaphor, deception is not unethical, it is accepted practice.) When, for example, a negotiator talks about negotiation as poker, it seems to imply that bluffing will be part of that negotiator's repertoire *and that we, the other side, ought to know that.* Bluffing is, after all, acceptable and expected in the game of poker. Since not every negotiator assumes that those are the rules of the game, unpacking this metaphor and realizing its ramifications can be crucial if you were expecting a more candid exchange.

In sports, we assume that the teams are relatively equal, that the score starts at 0-0, and that, even after a loss, the score starts the next day again at 0-0. We can draw the metaphor out even further talking about "an even playing field" and how any team can win on "any given day." It is unclear that these assumptions apply to most negotiations, however, where the parties are not balanced and are unable to start each negotiation, regardless of how the last interaction went, at a new starting place. Yet if the negotiator on the other side seems to be talking about her "team" and the game of negotiation, that will reflect some important values about negotiation that would be good for us to know. Each of these metaphors, and many others, helps clarify the assumptions that each party has about the "rules of the game" and the negotiation interaction.

Among the other metaphors are some that are quite specialized, and to be used only sparingly. One of the authors, for instance, used to spend a great deal of time mediating between extremely liberal public-sector unions and thoroughly conservative rural county and school boards. The boards were dominated by farmers, who tended toward metaphors of individualism and self-reliance. This had its comic aspect, to anyone with a smattering of knowledge about the complicated government farm price support system, from which many farmers suffer while some do rather well. More than once, a particularly recalcitrant board member who enjoyed membership in the latter camp would find the mediator making an apparently offhand remark, usually to someone else entirely, about "farming the federal government." But those occasions had to be very selectively chosen.

Recognizing Our Own Metaphors

It is important to note here that negotiators must at least try to be aware of the metaphors that reflect and inform their own understanding of the conflict. We must recognize that the very language that is used to describe the negotiation process can frame and shape the interaction and substantive content of the negotiation between the parties. Someone who is using a dance metaphor might herself be "out of step" with the other party. Dance often has connotations of intimacy, and one party might find such a framing inappropriate for their situation, especially if lack of trust is a major issue. Sometimes a negotiator or mediator is able to help the other party adopt his or her governing metaphor for the process, but there are circumstances where metaphor mismatch is partly responsible for failure of the process.

One can easily imagine an introduction to a negotiation or mediation process in which a mediator and the parties "negotiate," implicitly or explicitly, which metaphor will govern the process. One of the authors recently conducted a mediation session in which one party began by asking that his concerns about possible retaliation by his supervisor be addressed before the group discussed substantive matters, while the supervisor asserted that it was critically important for him that the other party affirm his trust in him so that they could be partners in problem solving. The employee was very uncertain of his ability to stand up to the supervisor. Clearly, the mediation meant something different, and raised different issues, for the two parties. They were not able to make any progress until, in a private caucus, the mediator talked with the supervisor about coaching the employee about how to help the employee be stronger in his dealings with the supervisor. The concept of "coach" changes the underlying metaphor from "hierarchy" (boss/underling) to "team." In this metaphor, a player can be a star. But because a coach still tells a player what to do, this metaphor is also widely accepted in management. It was, indeed, readily adopted, and as the supervisor changed his stance from boss to coach, the interactions between the two were transformed.

Of course, there is no reason to assume that there will only be one governing metaphor—interactions can go from dancing to warfare and back and forth many times. In one such mediation, one of the authors gave a fairly standard interest-based negotiation introduction at the outset of the mediation to four scientists involved in a complex dispute concerning, among other things, the use of space and facilities in a shared laboratory. They had brought the dispute to an ombudsman because it had become a battle that was quite personal and was undermining their ability to do their scientific work. Recognizing how suspicious they had become of one another, the ombudsman suggested that as scientists, they might think of taking a stance of curiosity toward each other's statements and positions, rather than the adversarial stance they had assumed in their daily interactions. One of the scientists promptly brightened, looking as if he had been freed from himself, and said "Curiosity? I can do that." Science as metaphor was introduced, in this case, as a deliberate attempt to move them away from their description of a battle over space, not by challenging their battle metaphor but by substituting curiosity for opposition and tapping into the one passion that was certain to re-orient them toward what they all wanted—to "do science." But the session proceeded under the orientation provided by the guidance of *two* governing metaphors, scientific inquiry and interest-based bargaining. Instead of attacking each other's statements they began to ask questions of one another. While it was not a love-fest, they were able to work out a quite satisfactory arrangement, one that held together for years.

It is important to recognize that metaphorical communication need not be verbal. One of the authors was once working with the new director of a small biomedical research program that had been fraught with conflict since the departure of the former director (a man highly revered by all). The new director, a thoughtful, intellectual and culturally refined man, was one of those scientists who is not especially tuned in to the fine points of human interaction, and was not able to describe in useful detail the nature of the problems being experienced within his group. Earlier conversations with him, however, had revealed his deep appreciation and knowledge of classical music. In our caucus, while haltingly discussing the situation in his group and the impact of losing their leader, the mediator suggested that perhaps Mozart's requiem would be an appropriate piece to capture the feeling of the group. Almost instantly the scientist replied no; the Mozart would not be appropriate; but the Haydn requiem would be. He then proceeded to explain what it was about that piece of music that more accurately reflected the sense of mourning he experienced with his group than did the Mozart. That was exactly the breakthrough needed to develop a plan for intervention with his team.

Metaphor as Tool for Mediators Too

This story illustrates how a mediator can use metaphor not only as a tool to understand a situation but also to intervene in it. The use of metaphors that differ from those employed by the disputants can help to reorient the parties toward the negotiation/mediation process and help reframe the parties' understanding of the conflict and the issues in dispute. This is an especially important point because the terms by which disputants describe their conflicts raise complex challenges to mediator neutrality. Among the guiding principles of mediation is the belief that parties to a dispute ought to be able to speak for themselves and play an active role in deciding what would be an acceptable resolution of a dispute. In a negotiation, what people say is the primary raw material with which negotiators work. On the one hand it is crucially important for mediators to understand how the disputants understand a conflict. On the other hand, we know that we cannot take literally the stories disputants tell us about their conflicts.

Working effectively requires some degree of interpretation, and metaphor provides one of the most reliable pathways to interpretations that can be helpful to the participants, because we are working with their own words even as we move beyond their stated understanding of the situation. If we were to understand the conflict in the same terms as the disputants do, even if they agree with each other, then we would become, to some degree, co-participants in the conflict rather than independent interveners. Neutrality and fairness *require* that we understand the dispute in terms other than those stated by the disputants, while still being anchored in their understandings. Identifying and understanding the metaphors used by the disputants is the single most important step we can take toward helping the disputants reframe the dispute in ways that are true to the full meaning of the dispute to them.

Of course this forces us to confront the fact that mediators are interveners, with the active rather than passive metaphors that term embodies. All mediators intervene in disputes by attempting, at various times, to influence (or help) people to alter the way they interact and speak with each other, the ways they understand and feel about the issues in a dispute, and the possible solutions they can imagine. Even the "transformative" mediators, who assert that the mediator should not "try to influence how problems are defined and how solutions are chosen," discuss the value of a party realizing better what matters to her, being able to listen and communicate better, being able to see a situation differently. The trick is to find a use of language that accurately reflects what the parties are experiencing (as you understand it from how they have described it to you, and recognizing the paradox created by this if you are trying to avoid excessively influencing them) but at the same time introduces enough of a different perspective that it allows the parties to go beyond their initial descriptions and positions. The beauty of a creative use of metaphor as intervention is in its ability to stay true enough to the disputants' metaphors that they still recognize what you are talking about, while introducing something novel enough to allow them to reconfigure their own feelings and thinking into a new framework.

Conclusion

The current attention to metaphor is part of the natural expansion of the repertoire of conceptual tools by which negotiations can be understood and directed. This expansion, in turn, reflects an increase in the degree to which negotiators and mediators are incorporating into their work conceptual approaches and methods of intervention developed in other areas of research and professional practice. This shift has been described as "process pluralism," the recognition that different varieties of conflict require different conceptual frameworks and different modes of intervention.

It might also be that these developments reflect a fundamental shift in the way we think about conflict, negotiation and mediation, a movement away from reductionist conceptualizations toward a more holistic approach. From this perspective it becomes easier to recognize that the dynamics of conflict can only be understood within the context of the disputants' lives—the multiplicity of identities that define them, the full range of their relationships, and the institutions within which they are embedded. With more attention to and greater skill with metaphor, we have better tools to appreciate the motivating factors behind the verbiage, and will be in a better position to help people negotiate effectively—or to negotiate with them more effectively ourselves.

Ironically, just as we seem to be moving toward more holistic understanding of matters such as conflict and empathy, research has turned our attention to another sort of reductionism: neuroscience. The stimulus for this was the discovery of so-called empathy neurons, neurons that appear to fire in a very similar way when a person undertakes a particular action or observes someone else taking that same action. Almost immediately, there was a flurry of popular articles suggesting that activity in particular parts of the brain that were linked to compassion, followed by suggestions that perhaps those who lack or are lower in compassion, like psychopaths, simply suffered from some sort of deficient functioning in those parts of the brain. [NDR: O'Shea, *Compassion*]

To make things even more interesting, neuroscientists with an interest in language and cognitive functioning have begun to study metaphor, looking for the underlying physiological processes that allow humans to understand metaphorical discourse. (Sapolsky, 2010). Sapolsky, a prominent neuroscientist and neurosurgeon, asks "What are we to make of the brain processing literal and metaphorical versions of a concept in the same brain region? Or that our neural circuitry doesn't cleanly differentiate between the real and the symbolic?" Note the parallel between the observations on the processing of metaphor and the way the brain seems to respond in the same way to taking an action or observing that action by another.

While we acknowledge how tremendously interesting and potentially important this research is, we will not at this time join those rushing to use this research to draw inferences about what is "really going on" in conflict, empathy and conflict resolution. Reductionism is always tempting, especially in the face of great complexity. And we take holistic comfort in a paper titled "Metaphors in Cognitive and Neurosciences: Which impact have Metaphors on scientific theories and models?" (Goschler 2007). The paper explores the various metaphors that are used in the neuroscience literature itself, and moves us away from reductionist literalism back to a more holistic appreciation of metaphor.

And for all the reasons stated above, a holistic understanding remains the only kind of understanding that will enable us to use metaphor, and interpret it, to best advantage. Metaphor is, as we have pointed out, all around us. Of all people, negotiators can least afford to have metaphor, like a thief in the night, creep up on them unawares.

References

Berkey v. Third Ave. Ry. Co., 155 N.E. 58, 61 (N.Y.1926).

Cohen, J. 2003. Adversaries? Parties? How about Counterparts? On Metaphors in the Practice and Teaching of Negotiations and Dispute Resolution. *Conflict Resolution Quarterly* 20: 433-40.

Docherty, J. 2004. Narrative, Metaphors, and Negotiations. *Marquette Law Review* 87: 847-51.

Goschler, J. 2007. Metaphors in Cognitive and Neurosciences: Which Impact have Metaphors on scientific theories and models? metaphorik.de 12 (online journal).

Jones, W. and S. Hughes. 2003. Complexity, Conflict Resolution, and How the Mind Works. *Conflict Resolution Quarterly* 20: 485-94.

Kahneman, D. 2011. *Thinking Fast and Slow*. New York: Farrar, Straus and Giroux.

Lakoff, G. and M. Johnson. 1999. *Philosophy in the Flesh*. New York: Basic Books.

Lederach, J.P. 2005. *The Moral Imagination: The Art and Soul of Building Peace*. New York: Oxford University Press.

Menkel-Meadow, C., L. Love, A. K. Schneider and J. Sternlight. 2005. *Dispute Resolution: Beyond the Adversarial Model*, 2d edn. New York: Aspen.

Sapolsky, R. 2010. This is Your Brain on Metaphors, *The Stone* https://opinionator.blogs.nytimes.com/2010/11/14/this-is-your-brain-on-metaphors/

☙ 53 ❧

The Morality of Compromise

Carrie Menkel-Meadow

Editors' Note: Does how we negotiate reflect or shape our character, or both? Does choosing to negotiate have moral implications? What are the ethical and moral implications of making the assumption that negotiation is inappropriate? Here, Menkel-Meadow notes that not all negotiation is based in the idea of compromise, and discusses the ethical and moral underpinnings of our choices in negotiation—choices we may ignore we are making, but cannot avoid making. Compromise, in some cases, may be more moral and appropriate than not to negotiate at all.

> The art of compromise,
> Hold your nose and close your eyes.
> *Lin-Manuel Miranda,* The Room Where It Happens, lyrics from Hamilton: The Musical (2015)

> The compromise process is a conscious process in which there is a degree of moral acknowledgement of the other party.
> *Martin Goldin,* The Nature of Compromise, at 16

> You can't always get what you want, but if you try sometimes, you get what you need.
> *The Rolling Stones,* You Can't Always Get What You Want (1969)

> All government—indeed every human benefit and enjoyment, every virtue and every prudent act—is founded on compromise and barter.
> *Edmund Burke* (1775)

Carrie Menkel-Meadow is Chancellor's Professor of Law and Political Science, University of California, Irvine and A.B. Chettle Professor of Law, Dispute Resolution and Civil Procedure at Georgetown University Law Center. She has published over 10 books and 200 articles in the fields of conflict and dispute resolution. She has received three honorary doctorates, and has taught and practiced mediation, restorative justice, negotiation, conflict resolution and ethics in 26 countries, and on all seven continents. She has been a conflict consultant to the World Bank, UN, International Red Cross and the U.S. Federal Judicial Center, as well as to many court systems and public and private organizations.

Introduction: The Meanings and Measures of Compromise

Why does compromise in law, politics and philosophy have such a bad name, when in family and relationship settings we are told that compromise is a good thing? Compromise is a concept with different and often conflicting definitions and value valences in different settings. For those in philosophy and politics, compromise connotes a giving up of pure principle and commitment to rights and truth, demonstrating weakness or lack of integrity (Benjamin 1990; Luban 1985: 411). In contrast, in relationships we are told to compromise to consider the needs and interests of the other. We give up something to someone else because we value something beyond the particular issue or dispute we are having about something, such as the relationship itself or an agreement, policy or decision. The "morality" of compromise requires a consideration of when it is "good" (right, correct, just, or fair) to compromise and when it might be "wrong" to compromise (Margalit 2010; Mnookin 2010). *Different contexts* clearly produce different assessments of the morality of compromise.

Compromise as a concept assumes that one is conceding something to someone else, usually in order to achieve some goal—any agreement (e.g. contract, treaty, legislation, policy, or decision of more than one person), or simply to end a conflict or dispute—a peace agreement, perhaps to preserve a relationship or to avert or end conflict. It has come to connote a relinquishment of something that one really believes in or values. *Principles* are philosophically "higher" and more valued than pragmatic decisions to forego something of value in order to agree to accomplish something else. Compromise is achieved when parties concede something to each other, either mutually and reciprocally or unilaterally or unequally. Compromises may or may not be symmetrical or equal in what is foregone, given up or traded, resulting in ethical concerns about power imbalances in the process that usually governs how compromises are made—negotiation (Menkel-Meadow, Schneider and Love 2013).

It is not a compromise when parties in conflict arrive at an agreement that meets their needs, either through a new or creative solution to their conflict, or by a fairly agreed to negotiation and allocation of their interests (Menkel-Meadow 1984). Sometimes agreements are reached that are contingent, to be revisited when facts or conditions change, or when an agreed to process is used to resolve conflicts—these situations also are not compromises, strictly speaking, because parties may gain from engaging in the negotiation process and come to a new understanding of what their interests are, as well as recognizing the value of reaching a jointly achieved agreement, as contrasted with reaching no agreement at all by insisting on their claimed principles (usually an

impasse results when "true" principles conflict or the *res* being negotiated is scarce and cannot be shared or divided).

Some political scientists (Gutmann and Thompson 2010), philosophers (Kuflick 1979; Golding 1979; Benjamin 1990; Margalit 2010) and
negotiation theorists (Menkel-Meadow 2006; Menkel-Meadow 2010;
Menkel-Meadow 2011) have argued that instead compromise should be
valued as both intrinsically and pragmatically justified because it allows
agreements to be made, actions to be taken, and decisions to be made,
when not agreeing might be worse than making an agreement which is a
compromise. Further, *compromise may be morally valuable*, because it
actually demonstrates respect for and recognition of other human beings
(Golding 1979; Cohen 2001). Successful politicians (practical people)
have long lauded the use of compromise to get things done, from
Machiavelli (1532) to, most recently, President Obama, who has urged
even dedicated social and legal reformers to listen and sit down with the
other side, as Martin Luther King, Jr. did with President Lyndon Johnson in order to produce the United States Civil Rights Act of 1964
(Obama 2016; Shapiro 2013).

For some, compromise is not possible, or is unethical or immoral
when the interests or conflicts among or between people are not equally
legitimate (Margalit 2010; Benjamin 1990). Thus, an effort to balance or
equate that which is incommensurable in order to reach agreements is
not an ethical compromise. Compromises that result in great harm,
cruelty or inhumane consequences (consider Chamberlain's concessions
to Hitler at Munich) are evaluated after the fact as being wrong, but may
have been considered instrumentally expedient at the time they were
made (Margalit 2010). Thus, evaluating the morality of compromise
contains a *temporally* complex element of assessment, either at the time
of reaching the compromise or when its effects and consequences can be
measured at a later time.

Compromise includes both the processes by which agreements are
reached, such as negotiation, mediation and even arbitration and adjudication, and the substantive agreement itself. Consider King Solomon's
story of potentially "splitting the baby" with two mothers claiming ma-
ternity—to split the baby in two would clearly harm the baby and be a
terrible outcome, but King Solomon's process of announcing his intention to do so allowed the true mother to emerge (she who would not
allow her child to be split in two)—was this an arbitration or a very clever
mediation? Recently, and very unusually, the United States Supreme
Court refused to decide an important and contested matter and returned
a case to the lower courts for the parties to seek an "accommodation" of
conflicting interests (religious employer insurance benefits of employee
reproductive (contraception) on health benefits under the American
Affordable Health Care Act (*Zubik vs. Burwell* 2016). If the parties do
not agree here (and elsewhere) it is also possible that a compromise
ruling can occur by a *command decision* or a court or other deci-

sion-maker. Consider the parent who cuts a piece of cake in two and orders two children to share it (a classic "split the difference" solution of an item, Brams and Taylor 1996), or a court that allocates property, money or personal rights in a shared, not binary, manner (as in divorce and joint child custody decisions). Thus, the morality of compromise concerns itself with both *how we make agreements* with others and then, *what we actually agree to—processual*, as well as *substantive* ethical assessments.

This essay reviews the arguments made about when compromise is potentially ethically questionable, but also when compromise is ethically superior to no agreement at all.

What is Unethical about Compromise?

The classic ethical objection to compromise is that it is a foregoing of principle—that which is philosophically, politically, morally or personally "right" and "true." We say that one should not compromise one's principles, those things we believe in, because it is those moral and political beliefs that are constitutive of who "we" (nation, organization, group, team, or person) are—how we define ourselves and our reasoned *integrity*. Thus, Chamberlain should not have conceded sovereignty of Poland to Hitler in the hope of preventing war, Alexander Hamilton should not have offered to move the first US capital away from his home of New York, the Constitutional framers should never have allowed slavery to continue when drafting the first US Constitution (Levinson 2011) in order "to form and preserve the American union" and new nation, and Republicans (in the US) should never agree to tax increases (believing as party principle that taxes should be low and government spending should be minimalist).

Under this conception of what is wrong with compromise, it is assumed that principles are rational (agreed to by any thinking person), morally correct, or strongly believed as a matter of self-constitution of a group or identity (values, beliefs or religious, political or emotional commitments). There are right and good conceptions of how to behave or think, and fault and wrongness should be assessed and condemned. In this view, there is a notion that the "good" is knowable, objective, rational and essentially, at its core, universal. Consider the traditional conceptions of fault (wrong behavior resulting in liability) in tort law or breach of contract. The fault lines, so to speak, are clear and must be policed, to maintain order in a world, society, institution, organization or family. Our integrity, worth and values are what constitute us, and we must be morally consistent to be true and right, both in our individual selves and in the polities, organizations and societies in which we live. These ideas are based on *ideal* conceptions of what we should be as human beings and of the groups that human beings create for their identities and self-governance.

How we actually behave and assess ourselves, however, is often a different matter—thus compromise is both a *philosophical and sociological* concept, though many philosophers cling to the notion that a basic morality is or should be universal and not culturally variable, as in a Platonic or Rawlsian ideal of right-thinking, moral language, and ultimately, judgment of behavior (Mikhail 2011; Benjamin 1990). [NDR: Gibson, *Ethical Bedrock*]

Compromises are considered unethical on a *behavioral or process* basis when agreements are coerced, forced or achieved through the exercise of unequal power—the unconscionable contract or the victor's peace treaty (e.g. Versailles after World War I). This, of course, assumes that in crafting agreements or decisions, the less powerful have alternatives to walk away or not make the agreement. Although it may be "unethical" or undesirable to agree to give up something under threat of force, there may be no choice in some settings, and it might be preferable to many to live with an unethical compromise than to die by principle. Whether the more powerful party is content to live with a coerced agreement is another matter, which demonstrates that the assessment of the ethicality of a compromise or agreement is not necessarily symmetrical or universal. The assessments of the morality of compromise, once again, are *variable, contextual* and *not universal, but situational.* The morality of compromise can be assessed from the perspectives of *all sides* to an agreement—the behavior of all parties, as well as the substantive agreement they reach—or by assessing what *each party does on its own part* to create, craft or concede to the compromise (use of force, coercion, threat, empathy, fairness or necessity).

What is Unethical about *Not* Compromising?

Pragmatic Justifications for Compromise: To Get Something Done

It may, in fact, be unethical, immoral, or at least, ill advised not to compromise, in many circumstances. As the political and practical theorist Edmund Burke (1775) has opined, most successful human interaction is the product of "compromise and barter" or the negotiated trading of interests. At the most pragmatic level, we would not have family relationships, legislation, governmental policies, any economic relations, or international treaties if we did not have a process of traded and bargained for exchanges, many of which involve one or both parties conceding something to each other for the greater benefit that the agreement or relation itself affords the parties. In their recent plea for *more compromise* in American politics, political scientists and philosophers Amy Gutmann and Dennis Thompson have argued that movement forward in political legislation and social policy is only achieved when parties of conflicting political values approach each other with *mutual respect, willing to engage in mutual sacrifice, and a respect for the good faith values and intentions of their political opponents* (Gutmann and Thompson 2010). As relevant case studies, many commentators have pointed to successful forms of legislation that were achieved by compromises of conventional political party commitments (such as the Tax Reform Act of 1986, the Civil Rights Act of 1964 and, to a much lesser extent, the Affordable Health Care Act of 2010) in which political parties "traded" such interests as deductions, tax rates, characterizations of legal liability, remedies and choice versus mandates, with varying (and often inconsistent, less pure) subsidies and definitions of legal terms. While attempting to provide different solutions for the public good, political legislation (derogatively called "sausage") often provides an array of incentives and disincentives for different public and private interests to participate in the greater good (e.g. generation of public revenues, health care insurance and even the creation of new legal rights). Political legislation and public policy, with hotly contested differences of principles and ideas about how best to structure a society, can *only* be accomplished by allowing some, if not all, contestants of principle to gain at least some of what they want, both substantively and remedially. As President Obama recently said in a speech on listening and compromise, it is better to get something and then try to improve on it in iterative negotiations than to get nothing at all (speaking of his efforts in policing reform, as well as health care policy, Obama 2016).

More Precise Justice

Despite the binary (and assumed to be "principled") nature of most legal actions, over the years many legal scholars have also argued that compromise or some form of less brittle (win-lose) result may actually effectuate a more "precise justice." (Coons 1980, 1963; Sunstein, 1995; Menkel-Meadow 1984; Schatzki 1972). Legal standards and remedies of comparative negligence, *quantum meruit*, joint child custody, joint and several liability, creditor workouts in bankruptcy, and jury nullification are just a few examples of places where the law and legal process now recognize that "winner take all" outcomes often do not reflect either factual or legal reality when there are equal rights on both sides (parental custody), mixed or indeterminate causation, or competing concerns between policy setting and justice in individual cases (consider good faith purchasers for value who acquire title from a thief). Or, there are competing legal principles from which one might have to choose one over the other, where it might make more sense to find an accommodation between two or more equally important policy concerns—as in certainty and commitment of contracts and impossibility of performance, or equal distribution, or "equitable" or "redistributive" justice concerns (Sinai and Alberstein 2015).

When we have legal, policy or scientific doubt it might make more sense to split the epistemological difference and craft agreements and solutions that do not cut with too sharp a knife. As a form of compromise, mediated agreements now often are *contingent*, allowing revisiting the agreement when conditions change, or data and empirical study demonstrate consequences and actual effects of decisions made, often with the need to change commitments to accomplish particular ends: consider the use of "adaptive management" and tax subsidies, graduated incentives and penalties in some in environmental disputes, annuities in tort settlements, and transitional justice reforms that must take into account the past and the future, punishment and reconciliation (Menkel-Meadow 2015). Many legal problems, like bankruptcy and legal tort or contract claims, now require more subtle apportionment of liability and redress than simple or principled winner takes all solutions.

Although legal policies are intended to govern for the many, and contracts and agreements only for those who are parties to a negotiated agreement, the tensions between what is right for the many (as a matter of a priori rule setting) and just or fair (in the actual moment of execution of duties and promises) for those in a particular situation often requires a more subtle use of discretion and flexibly tailored making and enforcement of legal and governmental obligations. Thus, the ongoing tension in law between rule of law/equal treatment, and factual variation and discretion/judgment, presents the need for the more tailored making and execution of law that entails compromise as a more elastic form of human decision making.

Humanistic Justification

When parties are in conflict over the right and the good in general terms, it is far easier to speak of unethical compromises (how can one compromise on such values as "one should not kill"?) than the kinds of disputes that occur more readily in everyday life. Since even such basic principles as "thou shalt not kill" have been "compromised" with justifiable exceptions, such as "except in self-defense," or when the other (fetus, animal) is not regarded as a rights-bearing entity, it is clear that more contestable principles or human needs may require some accommodation. Some moral theorists, political scientists and negotiation scholars now have articulated an even more powerful justification for compromise—the recognition of the "other" with whom we might differ on our conceptions of the good (Hampshire 2000) as a sentient, rights bearing, human being who should be listened to, respected and from whom we might learn something and have our own views and yes, principles, modified. Compromise, then, may be ethically required, as a human value of empathy or recognition of the other, on both processual (listening, taking account of) and substantive (if you really care so much about that, then I will let you have some of it, if you will let me have some of what I need) grounds. Compromise has its own morality of *reciprocity and fellow-feeling*. This form of compromise suggests that where there are scarce resources we should learn to share them, if we are all humans inhabiting the world of scarce resources; with no clear, fair, just or accurate way of allocating those resources and when they are not scarce, we should engage each other in participatory and negotiated forms of consented to allocation. Compromise, as an ethical value in itself, promotes other good ethical concerns—sharing, consent and fairness (a value sometimes in opposition to the more draconian "justice" ("just-us").

The Morality of Compromise—Considerations and Issues

While many condemn the assumed concessions to principle made when agreements are made somewhere "in the middle," or when the weak are forced to give up to the powerful, or the minority to the majority (in conventional politics), this conception of compromise is thin and unrealistic. Agreements don't always require compromise ("I like the icing, my brother likes the cake so we can cut the cake horizontally and both of us have what we want" *is* not the vertical, get-only-half cut of a compromise solution to a conflict). True communication and exploration of each party's needs and interests can explore complementary, not always conflicting, interests, so that exchanges or trades or joint and creative activity can produce agreements where no one has to "give something up" in order to reach an agreement. Furthermore, in situations of repeat interactions (iterative games in game theory, repeat play in real politics) compromises may also alternate and use temporal agreements to produce multiple occasions for interaction, contingent improvement of agreements and outcomes, and opportunities for learning and revision.

Assessment of the morality of compromise cannot be made as a universal or uniform value (Compromis/Compromise 2004). What is compromised (from what principles or endowments) is highly situational—depending, for example, on pre-war, during war, or after war for diplomatic and political agreements, and the nature of the conflict itself (scarce resources vs. sharable resources) and the relationship of the parties to each other (personal, familial, one-off or ongoing). Where there is doubt (from a factual, legal or moral basis) about what is "right" or "true," temporary, intermediate or other non-firm outcomes or agreements can resolve the immediate dispute, allow more time for investigation, and allow the parties to proceed to more subtle action later. Sometimes compromise is literally the precise or called for *just* or *fair* solution (e.g. shared custody of children, shared use of resources, allocations of scarce resources, alternating uses, multiple actions rather than one) allowing other values, like balancing of interests, resolution of ambiguity, humility, peace and contingency to trump certainty, brittleness and non-reviewability of outcomes.

Yes, there are "rotten compromises" (Margalit 2010) when agreements do great harm or injustice to people on one side of an agreement, and there are "devils" (Mnookin 2010) with whom we should not negotiate because we may not be able to trust them or verify their good faith in doing what they say they will do. But almost any human action, including so called principled actions, court decisions, executive commands or freely consented-to contracts, may turn out later to have consequences that were unintended, harmful to some of the parties or yes, just plain wrong. The unjust continuation of slavery in American history was facilitated by both constitutional compromises and political compromises (the Missouri Compromise in allocating free and slave states), but principled legal rulings (*Brown v. Board of Education* 1954) which proclaimed "right principles" did not fully facilitate the integration of the races in American education or civil life, and some have argued that a more fully honest and more incremental (compromising?) longer engagement over remedies might have led to greater acceptance and legitimacy of basic principles of equality (Seul 2004).

The search for some form of compromise or meeting of the minds of multiple parties to a conflict or dispute may itself be intrinsically valuable. In that search, parties grant each other the respect of understanding and listening to what each values as they attempt to both settle differences between and among themselves, and craft new solutions to difficult social, legal, and even moral problems—e.g. abortion and right to life disputes (Podziba 2011). When our parents tell us to share and compromise with our siblings they may be imparting an important message of human co-existence—learn to listen and work with your rival, for ultimately you may need to work with those with whom you have conflicts (both ideational and material) in order for both of you to live and prosper. We should learn to consider in the morality of compromise not only when we *should not compromise* to preserve our integrity and basic principles, but when we *should compromise* as a matter of human humility, fallibility and the possibility that we may not be the only one who is morally, politically or socially "right".

References

Benjamin, M. 1990. *Splitting the Difference: Compromise and Integrity in Ethics and Politics.* Lawrence, KS: University Press of Kansas.

Brams, S. and A. D. Taylor. 1996. *Fair Division: From Cake-Cutting to Dispute Resolution.* New York: Cambridge University Press.

Brown v. Board of Education of Topeka, 347 U.S. 483 (1954).

Burke, E. 1775. *Speech on the Conciliation of America 1775.* Available online at http://blog.gaiam.com/quotes/authors/edmund-burke/9589 (last accessed July 5, 2016).

Cohen, J. R. 2001. When People are the Means: Negotiating with Respect. *Georgetown Journal of Legal Ethics* 14: 739-802.

Compromis/Compromise. 2004. *Information Sur les Sciences Sociales* 43: 131-305.

Coons, J. E. 1963. Approaches to Court Imposed Compromise: The Uses of Doubt and Reason. *Northwestern Law Review* 58: 750-794.

Coons, J. E. 1980. Compromise as Precise Justice. *California Law Review* 68: 250-262.

Golding, M. P. 1979. The Nature of Compromise. In *Nomos: Compromise in Ethics, Law and Politics*, edited by J. R. Pennock and J. W. Chapman. New York: New York University Press.

Gutmann, A. and D. Thompson. 2010. The Mindsets of Political Compromise. *Perspectives on Politics* 8(4): 1125-1143.

Gutmann, A. and D. Thompson. 2014. *The Spirit of Compromise: Why Governing Demands it and Campaigning Undermines It*. Princeton, NJ: Princeton University Press.

Hampshire, S. 2000. *Justice as Conflict*. Princeton, NJ: Princeton University Press.

Kuflik, A. 1979. Morality and Compromise. In *Nomos: Compromise in Ethics, Law, and Politics*, edited by J. R. Pennock and J. W. Chapman. New York: New York University Press.

Levinson, S. 2011. Compromise and Constitutionalism. *Pepperdine Law Review* 38(5): 821-844.

Luban, D. 1985. Bargaining and Compromise: Recent Work on Negotiation and Informal Justice. *Philosophy and Public Affairs* 14(4): 397-416.

Machiavelli, N. 1961. *The Prince*, edited by G. Bull. New York: Penguin Press.

Margalit, A. 2010. *On Compromise and Rotten Compromises*. Princeton, NJ: Princeton University Press.

Menkel-Meadow, C. 2015. Process Pluralism in Transitional/Restorative Justice: Lessons from Dispute Resolution for Cultural Variations in Goals Beyond Rule of Law and Democracy Development (Argentina and Chile). *International Journal of Conflict Engagement and Resolution* 3(1): 3-32.

Menkel-Meadow, C. 2006. The Ethics of Compromise. In *The Negotiator's Fieldbook*, edited by A. K. Schneider and C. Honeyman. Washington, DC: American Bar Association.

Menkel-Meadow, C. 2010. Compromise, Negotiation, and Morality. *Negotiation Journal* 26: 483-499.

Menkel-Meadow, C. 2011. The Variable Morality of Constitutional (and Other) Compromises: A Comment on Sanford Levinson's Compromise and Constitutionalism. *Pepperdine Law Review* 38: 903-914.

Menkel-Meadow, C. 1984. Toward Another View of Legal Negotiation: The Structure of Problem Solving. *UCLA Law Review* 31: 754-842.

Menkel-Meadow, C. and M. Wheeler (eds). 2004. *What's Fair: Ethics for Negotiators*. San Francisco, CA: Jossey Bass.

Menkel-Meadow, C., A. K. Schneider and L. Love. 2013. *Negotiation: Processes for Problem Solving*, 2nd edn. New York: Wolters Kluwer Law & Business.

Mikhail, J. 2011. *Elements of Moral Cognition: Rawls' Linguistic Analogy and the Cognitive Science of Moral and Legal Judgment*. New York: Cambridge University Press.

Mnookin, R. 2010 *Bargaining with the Devil: When to Negotiate, When to Fight*. New York: Simon & Schuster.

Obama, B. 2016. Listening and Compromise Speech, Graduation Address. *Howard University, May 7, 2016*. Available online at https://www.whitehouse.gov/briefing-room/speeches-and-remarks (last accessed July 5, 2016).

Podziba, S. 2011. *Civic Fusion: Mediating Polarized Public Disputes*. Washington, DC: ABA Press.

Schatzki, G. 1972. NLRB Resolution of Contract Disputes Under Section 8(A)(5). *Texas Law Review* 50(2): 225-265.

Seul, J. R. 2004. Settling Significant Cases. *Washington Law Review* 79: 881-968.

Shapiro, I. 2013. *The Last Great Senate: Courage and Statesmanship in Times of Crisis*. New York: Public Affairs.

Sinai, Y. and M. Alberstein. 2015. Court Arbitration by Compromise: Rethinking Delaware's State Sponsored Arbitration Case. *Cardozo Public Law and Policy and Ethics Journal* 13(3): 739-764.

Sunstein, C. 1995. Incompletely Theorized Agreements. *Harvard Law Review* 108(7): 1733-1772.

Zubik v. Burwell, 578 U.S. ---- (2016)

C3 54 8O

Literature and the Teaching of Negotiation

David Matz

Editors' Note: The author, a veteran teacher of the field, found himself wondering how to address the subtler concepts necessary to teach an advanced course, in ways that would get students to think more deeply about the possibilities and limitations of their work. He discovered that literature provided a potential answer. Here, Matz discusses more than a dozen books and other writings he has found particularly insightful in teaching negotiation, and shows how each contributes to a rounded view of what negotiation can and cannot do.

Thirteen Days in September, by Lawrence Wright, (2014) is a magnificent book. Also troubling. It is magnificent in the way it dramatizes the clash of histories in the negotiation at Camp David in 1978. The drama featured three strong-willed leaders: Jimmy Carter, Anwar Sadat, and Menachem Begin. The three produced an agreement between Israel and Egypt that has stayed stable for over 35 years despite hurricane-strength forces in the region. Wright's is the fullest, even the deepest, account of what "really" happened in this much-studied negotiation. It is also a model for how to write about any negotiation.[1]

The book is troubling because it is dominated by dynamics which the conflict resolution literature mostly ignores. These dynamics were crucial to the existence of the negotiation, to the impasse that defined most of it, to its breakthroughs, and to the agreement it finally reached. These dynamics were driven by will-power, by a commitment to honor, by the temptations and pitfalls of courage, by vivid memories, by the fear of failure, by lifelong habits of struggle with menacing enemies, by perceptions of politics infused with violence, by the feelings that go with the exercise of power and the pains of frustration, and by the mystery at the heart of much negotiating: what can change one's own mind, and what

---

David Matz has been teaching negotiation for forty years, and has also practiced extensively as a mediator and consultant. He has taught in graduate programs in conflict resolution, programs for the elderly, law schools, divinity schools, high schools, grade schools, and programs for at least eight professions. He has taught on four continents, live and on line. He needs to do something new. Hence this essay.

can change the mind of the Other. Wright's book suggests that these feelings are not just background to the negotiation. They *are* the negotiation. They are what drive the negotiators. Enacting these feelings is what negotiators do.

Both the strength of this book and its troubling implications drew my attention while I was engaged in a several-year project to design and teach an advanced negotiation course. How does advanced relate to introductory? Is there content to the idea that it is "advanced," as distinguished from being just "more?" This essay focuses on the reasoning I have been using to answer these questions, and describes the structure and readings I am working with now.

Wright's book has had two kinds of impact on my thinking. First it has made me wonder why so little of the conflict resolution literature seems relevant to what he describes at Camp David. More on that below. Second, I have realized that although the book takes the form of a heavily documented work of history, it had the effect on me that literary art does. It gave me an understanding of how Camp David *felt* to the major players. The book focuses on what these players brought to the process, how the players and their different histories interacted, and what those interactions felt like to the players. It gave me a feeling for the players' sense of possibility, and for the way in which this changed through the process. It is the experience of being a negotiator that Wright captures, and it is his art to make the reader feel that experience. Halfway through the book, therefore, I was only mildly surprised to learn that, before he wrote the book, Wright had already written a play about the same topic (Camp David 2014).

The book helped focus for me the question: Might there be other artists whose work would illuminate the negotiating process in ways that our usual hortatory and empirical approaches do not? Might there be important aspects of negotiating that we have been missing in our teaching which literary approaches might make accessible for students? Novels, stories, plays, and poems specialize in opening experience to the reader and providing an emotional understanding. The basic point, that fiction enhances empathy, will of course be old news to any reader of novels. Indeed, there is also a body of experimental work that tries to give fiction-induced empathy an identifiable shape. Mar and Oatley (2008) have summarized that research and begun to elaborate a theory. "Literary narratives...offer models or simulations of the social world via abstraction, simplification and compression. Narrative fiction also creates a deep and immersive simulative experience of social interactions for readers. This simulation facilitates the communication and understanding of social information and makes it more compelling, achieving a form of learning through experience. (This can) facilitate the understanding of others who are different from ourselves and can augment our capacity for empathy and social inference." (Mar and Oately 2008: 173).

Of course, I am hardly the first person to seek to broaden the focus for negotiation students. John Paul Lederach is interested in "who we are and how we are in the world," and he engages many of the same questions I do (Lederach 2005: viii). Donna Hicks (2011) tells of deeper parts of our humanity through a lens she calls dignity. David Hoffman (2011) uses a model of conflicting parts of self (*Mediation, Multiple Minds, and Managing the Negotiation Within*) that provides a comprehensible picture that students can use. Bernard Mayer (2004) pioneered this thinking in *Beyond Neutrality*, identifying aspects of human nature, especially in a negotiating setting, that our literature has tended to ignore. Jay Rothman has focused on identity as a way to look more deeply into the lives of negotiators. Michelle LeBaron has taught a course at George Mason University on Theories of the Person, to help students get outside their assumptions and be aware of philosophical choice points that would otherwise be unnoticed. Even traditional negotiation texts are aware of realities not well addressed by our toolbox. Malhotra and Bazerman (2007) title one chapter "Negotiating Rationally In An Irrational World." Thompson (2011) uses the title *The Mind and Heart of the Negotiator*. And Raiffa's (1985) classic text is entitled *The Art and Science of Negotiation*. Each of these excellent texts, however, is better at pointing to the non-rational, noncalculating aspects of negotiating than at giving students much awareness of what those aspects *feel like*, and how those feelings impact what we do as negotiators.

Over the last several years, therefore, I have focused the development of an advanced negotiation course on these questions: What is the experience of negotiating, and how can an awareness of that experience enhance our ability as negotiators?

This has generated for me a set of sub-questions.

- How does empathy work in a setting of conflict and competition?
- What is the relationship between being more aware of the experience of the Other and being aware of one's own experience?
- In contrast with an introductory course that focuses on how to change the views of the Other, can we focus also on how to change our own views?
- Can negotiators become more aware of the roles of memory and aspiration in a particular negotiation? How do the past and future interact in creating our sense of the present?
- What goes into decisions about what to settle for or when the negotiation should end?
- What is the feeling of being accountable to someone not at the table?
- The point of negotiation is to produce change. Can literary fiction help us understand the experience of change as it occurs in our own mind or in the mind of the Other?

- All negotiators contend with the difference between what a party shows to the Other, and what the party actually experiences.

How can literature help negotiators cope with those differences? A basic structure of my advanced course now is based on a triangulation: what is my experience, what is the experience of fictional characters, and what is the experience of the negotiating Other? Does my awareness of each of these enhance an awareness of the other two?

What follows here is an annotated list of materials on which I draw in making a syllabus; some I have used and some I intend to use. The supply of potentially useful literature is, of course, endless. I organize the readings into these categories:

- Focus on the inner life of self and Other. No link to a negotiation.
- Focus on the inner life, with reference to a negotiation.
- Focus on negotiator behavior, encouraging the student to infer an inner life from that.
- Compare the inner life of a negotiator as inferred by a student, with the same done by an artist.
- Students create negotiating lives by writing fiction.

The Readings

Focus on the Inner Life. No Link to Negotiation.

Albert Camus, *The Stranger*, pp 50-59 (1989). We are inside Meursault's head just before he kills the stranger. There is an account of thinking and feeling, an awareness of light and heat, a perception of the victim, an inner atmosphere. The focus is on the immediate present, and the number of things happening in a moment. After discussion I ask students to take a few minutes at home to write about their felt experience even as they write. I then ask students to send me and their classmates their comments. Class discussion focuses on the links between inner and outer experience, on the varieties of student experience resulting from the same assignment, on how other parts of their lives (previous writing assignments, desire to please the teacher, time pressure to get this done) impact what they write, how accurate the writing is to their "true" experience. Then we go back to Camus: what is the relationship of Meursault's experiencing self to his action; what is the impact of the situation on Meursault's feelings? What is the impact of the Other on how he feels? And finally I ask about the students' feelings about Meursault: can they connect with his feelings? Are they drawn into his feelings? What is their feeling about his feeling? The goal is to raise awareness of the inner life, to begin forming a vocabulary to allow it to be shared, to notice the limits of that vocabulary, and to emphasize the relationship of the inner and outer life.

Shakespeare, _Hamlet_, "To Be or Not To Be" soliloquy and the following scene with Ophelia, the king, Polonius. (Act 3, Scene 1) (1603). This too offers an account of a mind under great pressure. One question throughout: is Hamlet mad? For Hamlet in the soliloquy, the suicide-question is one of evidence and reason, combined with one of temperament: how long should I put up with this? In the following scene, Hamlet's behavior is different: Ophelia interprets it as madness, the King is not so sure. What accounts for the difference in the way he presents himself in the soliloquy and the way he presents himself to Ophelia? Why does she interpret his comments differently than the king does? Does the difference derive from their different histories, ages, or relations to Hamlet? Does it have to do with what they, or we, mean by madness? Do we feel for, with, Hamlet? Ophelia? How to describe those feelings?

Arthur Miller, _Death of a Salesman_ (1949). I ask the students to see the whole play on DVD. This play, too, is about different experiences of madness, about the relationship of reason and feeling, and about the question of when one should stop trying. One focus is the difficulty for the players in hearing each other, contrasted with how clearly we hear their outer and inner voices. Why is it so difficult for them to hear each other? What forces them finally to do so? How does each character experience the intense interactivity among the players? If we feel the pain the players feel, does that help us understand the kind of prison each is in? What would it take to break out? Miller makes a lot of Willy Loman being a salesman. In what way does being a negotiator feel like being a salesman?

David Grossman, _To The End of the Land_ (2008). There is a brilliant two-page scene (pp 597-600) which requires me to provide a lot of background. It is worth the preparation time because the selection captures with pain and humor the raging inner voices of an Israeli mother, furious that her two wonderful sons have been "nationalized" by the government into the army and into a hostile, suspicious frame of mind. The author contrasts her inner fury with her cheery-mom-voice, attempting to make normal with words and a salad what she feels as simultaneously sane and insane. I ask the students for their feelings about the mother, and what impact her inner and outer life has on the atmosphere of the kitchen and on the sons. Can they identify occasions when they have played the mother's role of conflicted inner and outer life, and can they identify occasions when someone else in their presence was playing the mother's role?

Emily Dickinson, _Hope Is the Thing with Feathers_ (1891). This poem has produced a much richer conversation than I expected. Students argued that hope is a more powerful force than the poet seems to credit, and also that hope is dangerous and subject to manipulation. Some were put off by her rather cheery take. They were surprisingly conflicted. When I asked that they describe what hope has felt like to them, several very moving stories came forth, in none of which did hope play a purely positive role.

Allegra Goodman, *Apple Cake* (2014). This two-page story is blunt about the unreliability of memory. It raises the paradox that we know of this unreliability and we act nonetheless as if this were not true. The story encourages us to ponder the problem of working with another person who is confronting the same paradox.

Focus on the Inner Life, with Reference to a Negotiation.

Rae Armantrout, *Negotiations* (1947).[2]
The best part
is when we're tired
of it all
in the same degree,

a fatigue we imagine
to be temporary,
and we lie near each other,
toes touching.

What's done is done,
we don't say,
to begin our transaction

each letting go of something
without really
bringing it to mind

until we're lighter,
sicker,
older

and a current
runs between us
where our toes touch.

It feels unconditional.

Remember this, we don't say:
The Little Mermaid
was able to absorb
her tail,

refashion it
to form legs.

This means that
everything's negotiable

and that everything is played out
in advance

in secret.

This poem is a stretch in the way any good poem is a stretch. Why does the author call this "negotiations?" Does she mean the same thing we do? Do our categories, such as competition and collaboration make the slightest sense here? When each lets go of something, are those concessions? There are two references to "we don't say." Why don't we say it? Is that mermaid a poet's way of reframing? How does the mermaid make everything negotiable? Poets love to put a sting in the tail: Who is in on the secret and who is not? How can something be negotiable and "played out in advance?" How do past and future work together here?

Marc Ross, *The Cultural Contestation of Ethnic Conflict* (2007). This is a scholarly study of the role of symbols in conflict. i.e. of fictions. The things themselves (monuments, battles, flags) are the carriers of stories and the shorthand for values: they are the tools we use to achieve what Ross calls our "drive for meaning." One might think of them as "group art." Ross says they are a way of linking past and present, individual and group. They can be the source of energy for stamina, for explaining the taking of risks, for being courageous. The meanings attached to symbols do evolve over time. Can they be intentionally changed? I ask students to think of symbols they have encountered in their own negotiations and how they have worked.

Focus on Negotiator Behavior, Encouraging the Student to Infer an Inner Life from That.

Lee Blessing, *A Walk in the Woods* (1988). There are a few artistic efforts intended to engage the reader and audience with the thinking and feeling of the participants in a negotiation. A Walk in the Woods is a play available on DVD. It is a "private" conversation between two participants in an arms control negotiation, and juxtaposes an innocent but learning American negotiator with an experienced, not completely cynical, Russian negotiator. The parties are explicitly trying to understand each other, and it is their feelings of success and failure that most draw in the observer. The parties are aware of the power of the organizational and political context to make personal communication nearly, though perhaps not completely, impossible. One way to understand this play is to see negotiation as a prison, with the drama residing in the parties' awareness of the risks of breaking out. The play may be about a conflict that no negotiation can resolve, and what it feels like to live with that limit. It thus raises issues of stamina and hope, and what makes them so difficult.

Lawrence Wright, *Thirteen Days in September* (2014). (Book), ***Camp David*** (2014). (Play). The strength of the book rests in the power of the complex clashes. The strength of the play, with only a sketch of the background, rests in the impact of the negotiating on deeply felt characters. The play is most moving (I have read it, not seen it) in the scenes between Carter and Rosalynn where their ambitions and their love are exposed and strained; and in the scenes in which Begin, under tremendous pressure from many sides, and especially from Carter, struggles and struggles, and then changes his mind about the Sinai. These are dramas of courage, and particularly the fear that goes with it.

Genesis (Chapter 23:1-20). Abraham negotiates with Efron for the purchase of a plot of land in which to bury his wife. In the way of the Bible, a close reading renders the negotiation exceptionally strange, and in that strangeness lies an opening to engagement with the inner life of both Abraham and Efron. For one thing, this is a reverse negotiation: Abraham wants to pay more; Efron wants to take less. Indeed, one wonders why there needs to be a negotiation at all. God has already promised this land to the Jews; why negotiate for that which God has promised? Both sides seem to assume that a transaction for money will be somehow more binding, serious, legally significant. Is it relevant that Abraham is burying the mother of all the Jews to follow? Since the Bible was written as a history, is the goal of the authors to be a retrospective legitimating of Abraham's ownership of land that is contested to this day? A further oddity is that although Abraham and Efron argue over the price (Abraham says he wants to buy the land and Efron initially says he wants to give it away), in Hebrew they use the same verb. So, what is this negotiation "about?" Was either of them using the negotiation process to test the Other? The Bible tells us of an active audience of Efron's people. Was either negotiator playing to that audience? With what goal? Did both negotiators know what was at stake for himself, for the Other? Is Abraham concerned for honor? Is Efron eager to make money (some interpretations say the price he finally asks is exorbitant) or is he also concerned for honor? How do principles, or values, relate to material benefit in a negotiation? Is it important to know? When?

Charles Portis, *True Grit* (1968). There is an excellent scene of a teenage girl besting an adult in a negotiation. Her legal case is not strong, but she uses the threat of outlasting him and embarrassing him in public to get what she wants. I ask the students to imagine the inner life of the man and why he caves. Neither the book nor the movie give much to go on about his inner life, but by painting her negotiating techniques so clearly, they enable the reader to empathize well with the man's problem.

John Lukacs, *The Duel* (2001). This is a brilliant historical take on Churchill's decision not to negotiate with Hitler in 1940. Using many documents and much historical imagination, Lukacs focuses on what Churchill was thinking. The author also quotes a number of others, who worked with Churchill, about the feelings he displayed, and about how those feelings impacted his reasoning. Churchill's contemporaneous writings show how clearly he knew what was at stake. Though the reader knows how it turned out, one is still drawn into the turmoil and pain of the decision.

Tamara Wittes, ed., *How Israelis and Palestinians Negotiate* (2005). These passages emphasize the role of national memory in negotiating. They give students an opportunity to compare a scholarly effort to read the mind and feelings of negotiating parties with the use of fictional materials to do the same job. The reading also raises the question of how national memory, beyond personal memory, can impact even the most worldly negotiators. But it raises the reverse question as well: When can negotiators overcome the communal memory? Comparing the Wittes materials with those in the Wright book, and perhaps even more dramatically in Wright's play or Blessing's play, students can engage with individuals wrestling with this question.

Compare the Inner Life of a Negotiator as Inferred by a Student, with the Same Done by an Artist.

Sheldon Stern, *The Week the World Stood Still* (2005)(Cuban Missile Crisis); **Anthony Page (Director), *The Missiles of October*** (1974). Stern's book is almost a transcript of the meetings of JFK and his advisors at the time of the Cuban missile crisis; the movie is a depiction of the same set of events. I ask the students to read portions of Stern and to imagine the inner lives of the key players and write that up; then I ask them to watch the DVD and contrast what the director/performers have created. How do the two paths differ in creating the inner life of negotiators?

A variation on this last exercise asks the question: how do different intellectual tools differ in the way they give us access to the inner life of the Other? I give out the write-ups of a social psychology experiment. It describes patterns of behavior the researchers have discovered, after which the researchers speculate about why people behave that way. I ask: How is that speculation different from what negotiators do when they infer meaning from the behaviors of the Other? How is that speculation different from what Arthur Miller did when he wrote of the inner life of Willy Loman?

Students Create Negotiating Lives by Writing Fiction.

Toward the end of the term I give the students two unpublished stories, each about one of two parties in an ordinary salary negotiation. Each focuses on the inner life of a negotiator, and how the behavior of the Other impacts that inner life. Class discussions have produced a burst of engagement with the characters. I focused on the question: What relationship do you see between the inner lives and the negotiating moves they make? This produced a rich discussion about the differences between what we as readers (and writers) know of the inner lives of the negotiators, what the negotiators know of themselves and of the Other, and what the negotiators might be able to know if they tried to learn.

Then I assign the task of writing their own stories, either entirely fictional or fictionalized versions of real negotiating. For a number of students this assignment is a breakthrough. They explore with gusto and imagination the complexity and ambiguity that go with the inner life of one of their negotiators. But they have a more difficult time employing the same imaginative energy for both parties. They find empathizing with the other side difficult, and this leads to thoughtful conversation about why this should be so, and what it might mean about empathizing with both sides in a real negotiation. Why is standing in the shoes of the Other difficult?

How Useful is Any of This in Improving One's Success as a Negotiator?

Expanding The Focus.

Introductory negotiation courses tend to focus on a set of tools created from a viewpoint analogous to that of a GPS: how can we help the student choose the right way to get from here to there? It is tool-and-goal oriented, and a major goal is to change the mind of the Other.

This advanced course is premised on the idea that in order to be an effective negotiator a student needs to focus not only on the use of (e.g.) a sword, but also on who is using it. It maintains the emphasis on individual players, and it assumes their capacity to have a large impact on the outcome. But this approach puts emphasis on the lives of the players, and how those lives impact the way the players see and make their choices. It gives high status to the use of imagination and to the sophisticated use of inference.

Studying negotiation through the lens of fiction raises questions about, for example, ambiguity. Wright's book can be read to show that the heart of the negotiation resides in how the players feel and cope with ambiguity. But neither the book nor the course provides rules of thumb on "what to do in case of ambiguity." What the study of experiencing ambiguity can provide includes stories or templates for coping; it can also provide cautionary lessons about problems that can arise, and it can alert one to errors one can make, especially errors that see clarity where the reality is ambiguous. This approach suggests that there is value in taking time to learn about the ways in which ambiguity is experienced by the Other and by oneself, whether in pre-negotiation homework or in the topics one focuses on at the table.

Reading Minds.

A premise of this course is that it is possible for negotiators to understand the thinking and feeling of the Other. This is hardly a trouble-free premise.

To start, there is the substantial literature about the human propensity to misunderstand what is going on in the Other. Projection and the fundamental attribution error have been well documented, as has Kahneman's observation that we are prone to great certainty despite the radically inadequate data we use to reach that certainty. (Kahneman 2011)

Add to these difficulties the special circumstance of negotiation in which the honesty of expressed feeling and thinking is inevitably suspect at almost all times. At the heart of all negotiation are uncertainty and power, each of which undermines both candor and understanding.

In other words, urging students to aim at understanding the inner life of self and Other sounds like a way of urging them to make more mistakes.

Despite these cautions, Kahneman's work, and common experience, make clear that there is in all of us a powerful drive to act as if we understand the inner life of the Other and of ourselves. Much of negotiating is based on predicting the behavior of Other and self. We believe that an understanding of the inner life of Other and self will provide additional dots which, when connected with the dots provided by behavior, will give us a better picture for predicting Other's behavior. So the question is not whether students will create fully accurate interpretations of the Other's inner life, or their own, but whether we can help them do this better. And this sharpens the focus on what is "advanced" about this course.

Conclusion: A Critique of the "Tools" View of Negotiation Learning

All of the above leads to two questions: What does it mean to call this an advanced course? What is its relationship to an introductory course?

One might think of this advanced course as a critique of the typical introductory course. The Wright book suggests that when we study up close what negotiators really do, we find that they don't always use the tools we invent and advocate. The dominating energies in Wright's drama have little to do with creating and claiming value, or cooperating and collaborating, or positions and interests, or problem-solving, or neutral principles, or zones of agreement, or aspiration levels. Wright's account might suggest that the parties simply hadn't discovered the value of our tools categories, or it might mean that Wright had not discovered it. His index makes no reference to any conflict resolution text.

Or it might mean that the tools in the introductory course were not used because they didn't meet the parties' needs as they perceived them. What the Wright book and what the memoirs of many negotiators suggest is that there are dynamics inherent in negotiation that are powerfully experienced by all negotiators. Not all of those dynamics are pretty (e.g. a desire for revenge); but the negotiators must cope with them. These dynamics are the result of the interaction of the inner life of each participant with the lives of all the others. Do we understand what happens in real negotiations? Do we understand what dynamics negotiators inevitably face? Do we understand the experience of being a negotiator? How many full and detailed accounts do we have of what goes on in a negotiation, and how often do we use such accounts in teaching and research? A clue about the relationship of tools to negotiating dynamics is provided when Wright tells the story of one of Carter's aides (the Secretary of State) asking Roger Fisher for some negotiating advice. Fisher suggested the single text procedure. Carter adopted the idea, and then used it as a mallet to bludgeon each of the parties, and to encourage acceptance of each of his drafts.

Of course, Camp David One is easily defined as far from the typical negotiation: world stage, existential issues, experienced political leaders, huge historical pressures focusing on one moment. I would, however, hypothesize that if an author of Wright's talent were to make the same commitment to a divorce negotiation or a commercial negotiation, the resulting study, describing the inner lives of participants, would be rather close in complexity and dynamics to what we see at Camp David.

Learning the inner life of an Other and of one's self is a lifelong challenge. Negotiating provides a framework in which doing it better can have discernible benefits. Literary fiction can help students use their imaginations to do this better.

Notes

[1] Carter is usually thought of a mediator at Camp David, and he certainly tried to bring Begin and Sadat to an agreement. But his behavior day by day looked much more like that of a negotiator, sometimes one on one, sometimes part of a three cornered negotiation. For this essay I am focusing on the negotiating rather than mediating.
[2] I want to thank Howard Gadlin for calling this poem to my attention.

References

Armantrout, R. 1947. *Negotiations.*
Blessing, L. 1988. *A Walk in the Woods.* Dramatists Play Service.
Camus, A. 1989. *The Stranger,* translated by M. Ward. New York: Cambridge University Press.
Dickinson, E. 1891. *Hope is the thing with feathers.*

Goodman, A. 2014. Apple Cake. In *The New Yorker*: 74-81.

Grossman, G. 2008. *To the End of the Land*. Tel Aviv: Publishing House.

Hicks, D. 2011. *Dignity, The Essential Role It Plays in Resolving Conflict*. New Haven: Yale University Press.

Hoffman, D. A. 2011. Mediation, Multiple Minds, and Managing the Negotiation Within. *Harvard Negotiation Law Review* 16: 297-328.

Kahneman, D. 2011. *Thinking Fast and Slow*. New York: Farrar, Staus and Giroux.

Lederach, J. P. 2005. *Moral Imagination, The Art and Soul of Building Peace*. Boston: Oxford University Press.

Lukacks, J. 2001. *The Duel: The Eighty-Eight Day Struggle Between Churchill and Hitler*, 1st edn. United States: Yale University Press.

Maholtra, D. and M. H. Bazerman. 2007. *Negotiation Genius*. New York: Bantam.

Mar, R. A. and K. Oatley. 2008. The Function of Fiction is the Abstraction and Simulation of Social Experience. *Perspectives on Psychological Science* 3: 173-192.

Mayer, B. S. 2004. *Beyond Neutrality: Confronting the Crisis in Conflict Resolution*. Jossey-Bass: San Francisco.

Miller, A. 1949. *The Death of a Salesman*. New York.

Portis, C. 1968. *True Grit*. New York: Overlook Press.

Raiffa, H. 1985. *The Art and Science of Negotiation*, revised edn. Boston: Harvard University Press.

Ross, M. 2007. *Cultural Contestation in Ethnic Conflict*. Boston: Cambridge University Press.

Shakespeare. 1603. *Hamlet*.

Stern, S. 2005. *The Week the World Stood Still*. Stanford University Press: Stanford, CA.

The Missiles of October. Directed by Anthony Page. 1974. Los Angeles, CA: Viacom Productions.

Thompson, L. L. 2011. *The Mind and Heart of the Negotiator*, 5th edn. New Jersey: Prentice Hall.

Wittes, T.C. ed., 2005. *How Israelis and Palestinians Negotiate*. Washington, D.C.: United States Institute of Peace.

Wright, L. 2014. *Camp David*. (Unpublished).

Wright, L. 2014. *Thirteen Days in September: The Dramatic Story of the Struggle for Peace*. New York: Knopf Doubleday.

ɔʒ 55 ଞ

Aesthetics in Negotiation:
Part One—Four Elements

Nadja Alexander & Michelle LeBaron

Editors' Note: At least in the West, negotiators have mostly assumed that the arts have little or nothing to do with their work. Not so, say the neuroscientists, in increasingly persuasive recent work. Here, the authors review that research, and place it in context of ancient wisdom. They draw a line through the classicists' four elements—earth, water, air and fire—and relate each concept to the heart and mind of negotiators. It turns out that aesthetics are a clue to much that's going on at the back of our counterparts' minds, and our own. We will negotiate better if we take due account of the wisdom they offer. This chapter should be read in conjunction with the same authors' Part Two, in which they argue for a contemporary negotiation application of the ancient concept of alchemy.

Nadja Alexander is Academic Director at the Singapore International Dispute Resolution Academy, and Visiting Professor of Law at Singapore Management University. An award-winning (2011, 2007, 1997) author and educator, Nadja also works as a policy adviser and conflict intervener in diverse dispute resolution settings. Her work on cross-border and cross-cultural conflict embraces interdisciplinary approaches to deepen conflict engagement. Nadja has been appointed Honorary Professor at The University of Queensland, Australia, and Senior Fellow of the Dispute Resolution Institute at Mitchell Hamline School of Law in the United States. Her books include *International and Comparative Mediation; Global Trends in Mediation; Negotiation: Strategy Style Skills,* and *The EU Mediation Handbook.*

Professor **Michelle LeBaron** is a conflict transformation scholar/practitioner at the University of British Columbia Allard School of Law whose work is animated by creativity, culture and interdisciplinarity. She has done seminal work in many types of conflicts including intercultural, international, family, organizational and commercial, exploring how arts help shift intractable conflicts. She is a fellow at the Trinity College Long Room Hub Arts and Humanities Research Institute in Dublin and holds a Wallenberg Fellowship at the Stellenbosch Institute for Advanced Studies, South Africa. Her books include *The Choreography of Resolution: Conflict, Movement and Neuroscience; Conflict Across Cultures: A New Approach for a Changing World; Bridging Cultural Conflicts;* and *Bridging Troubled Waters.*

Introduction

From Sun Tzu's *Art of War* to Fisher and Ury's *Getting to Yes*, negotiation advice is widely available. Each publication offers a window on the subject, drawing from particular theories of human nature and change. They serve a variety of ends and address a number of possible avenues to improving negotiation that vary according to context, culture and discipline. The publications explain strategy, structure and skills; they promise efficiency, effectiveness or success. What they do not provide is insight into the essential roles that beauty and nature—aesthetic elements—play in negotiation. Overlooked through lenses that accent utility and orderliness, beauty and natural metaphors introduce a range of sensual, embodied ways that our human thirst for belonging and for feeling moved is implicated in negotiation. When these ideas are introduced to the corpus of work on negotiation, the importance of intuition and relational capacities comes into focus. Negotiation becomes more vivid and compelling; fields of possibility appear that were unavailable via more analytic ways of imagining negotiation processes.

Throughout this chapter, we tap into a significant 21st century vein of scientific, philosophical and aesthetic work that underlines ways we are all interconnected, portraying humans as porous beings with the ability for agency and mutual, multidirectional influence. What we previously believed as real—Cartesian duality of mind and body and separateness between individuals and objects—is a fast-fading myth. (Damasio 1994; BenZion 2010) This significant shift in thinking has profound implications for our approach to negotiation.

We follow a discussion of aesthetics and beauty with an exploration of how four elements—earth, water, air and fire—can assist with the project of expanding our effectiveness as negotiators. We examine how these elements help us to better build awareness—of ourselves, of other negotiators and of the context within which negotiation interactions unfold. By developing greater awareness of beauty and nature, negotiators can better navigate the emergent and complex nature of the negotiation process itself.

Art as Vehicle for Aesthetic Engagement in Negotiation

One place that beauty and nature come together is through art. Art in its many forms is essentially about encounter. As Victor Hugo wrote about music, art expresses that which cannot be said and about which it is impossible to be silent. As a form of aesthetic engagement, art embraces and stimulates senses and perceptions beyond cognitive analysis. Arts practices activate our complementary capacities for seeing beyond the visible, hearing beyond words and touching both the formless fears and inspiring possibilities that constitute figure and ground in negotiation. To the extent that negotiation writing draws on dated scientific frames, it either excludes these capacities altogether because they are not scientifically valid, or colonizes them into "optional extras" which, while non-essential, may be grudgingly admitted to serve utilitarian functions. However, as indicated earlier, science has seismically shifted, revealing evidence supporting the potency of arts-based approaches to decision-making, conflict resolution and negotiation. These insights invite beauty and nature into our thinking about negotiation.

Art is much more than an optional extra or an instrumental modality; it provokes or invites, posing questions without easy answers to the viewer or listener who gives it her attention. When used as a focus for dialogue, art comes alive, surfacing questions and complexities that simply do not arise in the course of more didactic forms of negotiation education. As part of her graduate coursework in negotiation, one of the authors has many times taken classes to the Hirshhorn Museum of Modern Art in Washington, DC. Standing in front of Anish Kapoor's *At the Hub of Things*, a concave, egg-like structure in vivid Prussian blue, students' dialogues on negotiation become subtler and layered, venturing into the complexities of perception, perspective, standpoint and representation. The intense color of the piece and its resemblance to a womb or a burial chamber evoke a myriad of sensed, felt phenomena: the unknown, the feminine aspect of presence and the transitory nature of all human relations. For some, it is inviting. For others, it evokes fear. These felt experiences become a canvas on which dialogue about the roles of fear, uncertainty and risk in negotiation are engaged with increasing nuance.

At the Hub of Things
(Kapoor: 1987)

Studies in neuroscience explain the contagion of the sensed and felt experience, and how feelings can move between us without our being consciously aware of the exchange. This process begins at birth and is made possible by mirror neurons in the brain, which fire up and "mirror" the physical signals of another. A wealth of data demonstrates that when we observe others experiencing emotions, our own brains engage the same neural circuits that are active in "the other"—the basis of empathy. (Gallese 2005; Singer 2006) Through the activation of mirror neurons, these "shared representations" allow us to experience vicariously what is felt and expressed by someone else. This phenomenon helps to explain how we can be transported to the place of our deepest fears by a painting or moved to tears by a dance performance, and how we can have empathy for people we encounter without ever speaking to them. It explains how we can invite beauty into our negotiation worlds by connecting with others—and vice versa.

Art grounds us in a collective understanding that mystery is always a part of negotiation; no analytic framework is powerful enough to account for all the dimensions present in any human communication. Anchored by these exchanges and observations, students approach their negotiations with a spirit of inquiry and appreciation for the ways that aesthetic engagement amplifies self-and-other awareness. It is as if the parts of each of us that long for beauty and connection with something greater than ourselves are drawn out through engaging with the visual art, introducing spaciousness and a larger grid into our interactions and our sense of self.

Sophists and other relativist philosophers may challenge the existence and the endurance of beauty, arguing that meaning depends on the frame of the perceiver. While we agree that beauty is indeed in the eye of the beholder, we also see the element of subjectivity as crucial—for it opens the door to our souls and helps us perceive the vital process of meaning-making as we link our experiences with our values, and the values and experiences of others. The art critic Frederick Turner wrote that beauty is "the highest integrative level of understanding and the most comprehensive capacity for effective action. It enables us to go with, rather than against, the deepest tendency or theme of the universe." (Brooks 2016)

Meaning, or the knowability of a situation, typically depends on what is represented, how it is framed and by whom. (Scarry 2001) Elaine Scarry argues that beauty is essential to understanding the power of framing, and to seeing the differences and the gaps that inevitably exist among negotiators. Dismissing arguments made against beauty in recent decades as being too subjective and unwieldy, she contends that beauty presses us toward a greater concern for justice. Taking inspiration from a wide range of thinkers from Homer to Simone Weil to Iris Murdoch, Scarry argues for the revival of beauty in our intellectual work as well as in our engagement with each other.

Responses to beauty, according to Scarry, are events of profound significance for individuals and societies because they make diffuse concepts like fairness and justice available to the full spectrum of our senses. Beauty, she asserts, stops and transfixes us, filling us with a "surfeit of aliveness". In this process, we are transported from a focus on ourselves, and our attention encompasses others and the wider world, including ideas of ethical fairness. We experienced this phenomenon when we asked a group of experienced negotiators to draw "home". The drawings conveyed nuanced feelings and sensory components of home that would have been impossible to capture in words alone and grounded our ongoing work in potent shared images.

This is the essence of reflexive negotiation practice. We literally find ourselves standing on new, more stable ground as we reflect and grow, as stability is generated by awareness of interdependence and of the effects of our actions on others and our social world. Taken together, these levels and dimensions of awareness help us as negotiators to open up to the multiple subtle sources of information that lead to deeper insights and more successful outcomes. (Scarry 2001)

Infusing arts engagement into negotiation education does not mean ignoring or neglecting other aspects of negotiation theory. Traditional approaches to negotiation and negotiation education are filtered through concepts that accentuate logic and reason. Logic and reason are useful in negotiation, but are not reliable maps of the entire territory. They are always culturally situated, and—in traditional approaches to negotiation—actually distort understandings when they are taken as complete and sufficient. It is for this reason that we have advocated in previous writing for experiential, aesthetic components to be integrated into problem-solving education and practice. This integration can accent either problem-solving or aesthetics, but is more potent than when the two are separated. For example, an activity as simple as introductions in a new learning setting can be infused with aesthetic dimensions by asking each person to use gesture to embody their attitude to conflict. At the end of an intensive day, learners can be invited to give a "weather report" that conveys something of their current state. From the "weather reports", a wealth of information proceeds: are group members calm or agitated; are they feeling open and relaxed, or defensive against what might feel threatening? Are they in a fog or does the atmosphere they bring into the room with them feel spacious and clear? This information can be used to fine-tune teaching and learning plans, and it gives learners the opportunity to convey a range of sensations associated with learning that do not confront or risk losing face, yet do communicate multiple layers of experience. Another way to describe this approach is that it combines the mimetic with the rational.

Logical analysis can be located in a wider, more useful map when negotiation is seen through a mimetic lens. Walter Benjamin, Jacques Derrida and others define mimetic activity in social practice and interpersonal relations as something that goes beyond rational models to emphasize the body, emotions, the senses and temporality. (Kelly 1998: 234) In this sense, the mimetic incorporates the aesthetic, emphasizing that there is always a gap between a phenomenon and a representation of that phenomenon.

Aesthetic approaches to negotiation draw our attention to the gap itself, to what is not known and therefore is not reducible to a framework or rational analysis. This is one aspect of the potency of art in negotiation education: it presents gaps and diverse interpretations; it accentuates ambiguity and the elusive nature of truth. An example comes from an exploration of the nature of fairness designed by one of us. Economists, lawyers and other scholars had traveled from around the world to negotiate understandings of the elusive concept of fairness. One of the activities involved participants working silently in small groups to create fairness installations. Each group had a range of natural materials from the forest and the beach: feathers, small stones, moss, twigs, beach glass, stalks of bamboo, shells. They negotiated in silence, composing sculptures from the elements they had been given that somehow spoke to the fairness theme. Once the pieces were complete, we all walked around to view them in silence. Only then was the group assigned to select an item from their installation to trade with another group, and to designate a representative to negotiate the trade. One group assigned "Pat", the only African American scholar in the group of white European-origin scholars, to try to trade a small pebble for the only eagle feather in the room, which crowned another group's sculpture. Pat was unsuccessful, and the experience led to a very emotional dialogue about the unconscious choice made by the group to ask the only person of color in the room to try to trade something trivial for something substantial. Power, historical disadvantage and unconscious positioning to maintain privilege were all discussed in ways made far more nuanced by the gap in realization that had just played out.

Just as Picasso said, "We all know that art is not truth. Art is a lie that makes us realize truth, at least the truth that is given us to understand", those attending the fairness atelier left with new realizations about the truths of unfairness and fairness that remain wired in our consciousness. (Picasso Speaks 1946: 270-271) Beauty, on the other hand, was famously equated with truth by John Keats in his poem *Ode to a Grecian Urn*. Perhaps it is this capacity of beauty that art reaches for.

To ground our understanding of negotiation in the aesthetic domain is to be aware of the importance of gaps. In art, truth— insofar as truth exists—is the gap between the map (the artwork) and the territory (what has been painted or represented). In negotiation, gaps exist between one negotiator's perceptions and another's; between one model of best practice and an alternative way of constructing effectiveness. Gaps also exist between each person's particular construction of a negotiation—what is seen as salient, necessary and possible—and the issues involved. Fundamental gaps also exist between the negotiators themselves. When we encounter gaps, the four classic elements of earth, water, air and fire can function as resources to help us bridge them because they are themselves carriers of beauty just as landscapes and seascapes are beautiful. These elements deepen our journey of discovery with beauty and its potential to transform our embodied experiences of negotiation. We begin, as mortals must, on the ground.

Earth: The Grounded Negotiator

What is the first thing a negotiator does when preparing to engage with another? Some would say we should first "ground" ourselves, clearing the mind of other tasks and generally coming into our physical center. When an electrical circuit is grounded, it protects users from dangerous exposure if electrical insulation fails. Grounding gives the current a place to go, a place that absorbs its energy without damaging things around it. Humans ground using variable means including physical and imaginal practices that may produce some of the same protective effects. To be grounded is to feel a connection with our core, to have a strong and rooted sense of ourselves. By extension, as we ground, we may also feel a connection to the earth, with its powerful properties of stability, creativity and coalescing. When we are in a grounded state, we are less susceptible to being upset by unpleasant emotions or unexpected tactics; we react with more equanimity.

Earth as an Aesthetic Dimension of Negotiation

When we ground ourselves before entering a negotiation, we literally embrace a bigger sensory world, one that widens our apertures and increases our perceptive and reflexive abilities. Doing so embeds a spirit of inquiry into negotiation processes by importing vitality into the often-narrowed worlds in which negotiations occur. For example, imagine that prior to negotiating, parties were invited to walk silently in a nearby woodland, to notice and later share an image from their walk that speaks to their aspirations for the process. As they share, aesthetic pleasure associated with these images infuses the negotiation process, heightening imagination and possibility rather than the more bounded rational thought that is usually accented. Such an approach is reflected in Lee Blessing's 1988 play, *A Walk in the Woods*. It tells the tale of two arms negotiators who develop a personal relationship while searching for a breakthrough in the formal talks, while walking "informally" through the woods during year-long negotiations in Switzerland. And so it was that the scholars who designed the Oslo negotiation process to bring together Israeli and Palestinian negotiators in the 1990s chose a remote, rural Norwegian setting. They built in time for nature, such as walks in the woods, and time and space for contemplation surrounded by natural beauty. Through these walks, they experienced what South Africans call *Ubuntu*: seeing in others a reflection of self and of our interdependence. We literally exist *through* each other.

How might the element of earth help negotiators practice *Ubuntu* and infuse aesthetic sensibilities into processes? Do our negotiating experiences engage the senses in beautiful ways? If we struggle to imagine this, then what would need to happen for beauty to be a part of the landscape of our negotiations? A few suggestions follow.

Applications for Reflexive Negotiation Practice

By invoking natural images and their associated beauty as we "ground" ourselves before negotiation, we may experience not only more self-awareness, but increased resonance with others and nature itself. This builds the foundation for reflexive practice. Reflexive practice involves being attuned and able to make sense of complex and dynamic experiences in interacting with our surroundings. It also means making sense of an experience beyond our own worldview, with awareness of the social, political, theoretical, intellectual and psychological context in which experiences occur. It is both a meta-analysis and a micro-focus, reflecting on reflecting, or thinking about thinking—this is what happened, this might be why it happened (in context), this is how I came to understand it in the way that I do, and this is one of the ways that I can modify it or change how I will perceive it in the future. (Cunliffe 2001; Lam et al. 2007; Alexander, Howieson and Fox 2015)

Drawing upon the element of earth, we can become more grounded as negotiators and increase our capacity to contribute to successful negotiation outcomes in these and other ways:

- Invite nature into negotiations. Choose a natural setting such as a park or rural setting. Integrate time for engaging with nature into the negotiation. Something as simple as a walk after lunch can help to reconnect us to our centers. It can also sow the seeds of transformation from an "us and them" to a collective "us" as we share the experience of enjoying the gifts of nature.
- In preparing for negotiations, we can deepen our understanding of our counterparts and how they view the subject-matter of the negotiation by getting to know their art—visual art, stories, music or dance. Aesthetically-inspired preparation for negotiation broadens and deepens our perspective of the negotiation landscape and those inhabiting it. Equally, doing so can contribute to new language and new ways of talking about issues, paving the way for creative inspiration to infuse talks.
- Look to a variety of art forms—music, painting, dance, song and others—to strengthen the common ground we stand on as negotiators, and to build foundations for identifying, understanding, and beginning to bridge the inevitable negotiation gaps.

Not only can these approaches help connect across gaps, they can bring everyone involved to deeper presence with each other. As scholar and filmmaker Cynthia Cohen points out, aesthetic experiences are "intensely felt human apprehensions of the world, engendered by nature and certain human-made forms and processes." (Cohen 2015) Cohen elaborates that these experiences are rooted in reciprocity arising between the forms and the perceptual capabilities and sensibilities of perceivers. As an essential component of aesthetic experience, reciprocity is both a justification for linking aesthetics to negotiation, and a resonance between the two. Neither form works well without it.

The importance of reciprocity and mutuality across aesthetic experience and negotiation leads us to the next element: water. Water connotes flow, fluidity and clarity, all of which involve reciprocity.

Water: The Fluid Negotiator

If negotiation is grounded in an aesthetic ethic, how does a process unfold? Which possibilities arise that are not visible from more traditional vantage points? A reciprocal negotiation process creates a flow between the parties as they encounter a more comprehensive standpoint—perhaps a perspective larger than their own—and find a way to dissolve into it. When it works, parties find themselves holding a larger world, putting things on a bigger grid, and trying in partnership to find a way into a positive momentum or flow.

Of course, negotiation is never static. As Andrea Schneider and Jennifer Brown (2013) demonstrate with their Dynamic Negotiating Approach Diagnostic (DYNAD), negotiation styles are always in motion. Competitive, entrenched positions may transform into collaborative flow. Avoidance may shift into competition. These shifts tend to follow the "emotional tenor" of a negotiation. (Schneider and Brown 2013) The parallels to water are startling. Not only does water have the ability to change external form from liquid to gas or solid, water in its liquid form also has the ability to change the structure of its molecules. Research (which remains controversial) suggests that the structure of water changes according to external influences including emotions. According to Masaru Emoto's work, positive emotions facilitate the creation of exquisitely structured water molecules that generate beauty. (Emoto 2007) Negative emotions generate broken, weak, unattractive molecular patterns. It seems that the molecular structure of water can and does continually change. Parallels to the neuroscientific concept of emotional contagion, discussed previously, are immediately apparent.

Water as an Aesthetic Dimension of Negotiation

Our discussion about water and the human condition moves beyond a mere analogy once we contemplate the fact that our bodies consist primarily of water. We are water. We can freeze and be blocked; we can pretend to disappear like gas; or we can flow into one another as liquid water does when the river meets the ocean. As the structures of water molecules alter, adapting to their surrounding environments, so do we. Positive, constructive, and empathetic emotions from our negotiation counterpart may increase our receptivity to their interests and help us generate new, elegant neural pathways, which, in turn, yield new ways to problem-solve not previously imagined. This is the social brain in action, examined in more detail below as well as elsewhere in this book. [NDR:

Crampton, *Social Brain*] The social brain has the qualities of water—fluid yet robust; strong yet yielding; open to connection yet stable in its own identity. It has the capacity to know, and fill, the gaps. The openness and vulnerability of the social brain might just help us and our negotiation counterpart get closer to filling gaps with beauty—on both molecular and mental levels.

Italian architect Carlo Scarpa became famous for his use of gaps in architecture. One of his notable works, the *Fondazione Querini Stampalia*, is a testament to the power of designing strategic gaps to invite the outside in and the inside out, to create contrasts and tensions, and a different sense of "space". Designer Alan Fletcher, exploring why space is important, writes: "[s]pace is substance. Cézanne painted and modelled space. Giacometti sculpted by *'taking the fat off space'*. Mallarmé conceived poems with absences as well as words. Ralph Richardson asserted that acting lay in pauses... Isaac Stern described music *as 'that little bit between each note—silences which give the form.'* The Japanese have a word (ma) for this interval which gives shape to the whole. In the West we have neither word nor term. A serious omission." (Fletcher 2001: 370)

It is enlightening to apply this "philosophy of gaps" to the world of negotiation. In the West, we are preoccupied with filling up space, and tend to over-rely on words to convey meanings. As negotiators, we use talk to convene, structure, order and identify issues and uncover common ground. The works of these artists and architects highlight the potential power of using gaps to create spaces in which both negotiators, relieved of pressure to fill spaces, can explore, innovate and diversify. When gaps are filled in a synergistic way, we speak of entering a state of "flow". When we enter this state, it is as if unpredictable beauty has taken over. Beauty has been invited into the room.

This awareness of our bodies as spacious and fluid helps us imagine and then experience a state of flow. Recall a point in a past negotiation when things began to move with positive momentum. Effort was reduced, and things fell into place with relative ease. Now reflect on the precursors of that flow state. What helped it come about? What aesthetic textures accompanied it? Did it feel smooth, soft, elastic or fluid? What experiences can you imagine that would help you touch into and then incorporate a route into a flow state so that you can access it more easily?

The above questions are designed to take your attention into your body, where memories and feelings are experienced as physical sensations. Often, these physical sensations are just below conscious awareness; they only grab our attention when they turn into pain or irritation. But tuning into them is a very helpful thing to do in the midst of negotiation; they give us important clues about our state, our comfort level with the way things are proceeding, and what we need to feel safe and engaged going forward.

The flow state can emerge from two elements meeting each other. There is a complementarity, a fusion of beauty that draws many people to the seashore, for example. Irish philosopher John O'Donohue wrote about this meeting place this way: "Unlike the land, which is fixed in one place, the sea manifests freedom: she is the primal dance, a dance that has always moved to its own music. The wild divinity of the ocean infuses the shore with ancient sound. Who can tell what secrets she searches from the shoreline? What news she whispers to the shore in the gossip or urgent wavelets? This is a primal conversation. The place where absolute change rushes against still permanence, where the urgency of Becoming confronts the stillness of Being, where restless desire meets the silence and serenity of stone. Beyond human seeing and knowing, the meeting of ocean and shoreline must be one of the places where the earth almost breaks through to word." (O'Donohue 2003: 129)

Here, O'Donohue captures the transformative potential of water when it meets earth. Related to this idea, John Paul Lederach reminds us that we can imagine a range of different results in any negotiation process, and that our capacity to do so increases when we see ourselves as a part of a web of relations. (Lederach 2005) Recognizing interconnections with other bodies—and constellations of felt experiences within and amongst them—is an important step toward empathy, requiring both fluidity and a grounded sense of our own identity.

Applications for Reflexive Negotiation Practice

Reflexive practice requires an awareness of the fluid nature of one's experiences and the ways that meaning evolves through interaction with others and in the negotiation context. As negotiators, we can increase capacities for reflexive practice in these ways:

- To increase awareness of self, ask: How am I attuned to my physical sensations and spatial relations (physiological dimension of awareness) within my own body (proprioception)?
- To increase awareness of others, ask: How attuned am I to the quality of physical presence of my counterpart in relation to me?
- To increase awareness of context, notice: What is the atmosphere like when the negotiation flows? How fluid are the roles and relationships (including power relations) among the parties and others within the larger network of relations and social contexts? Reflect on the role that culture might play in this. Movement is an excellent way to shift uneasy intercultural dynamics when things feel stuck.

To shift from a stuck place to flow, shift modes of operating. If analyzing, check what is being sensed. If sitting still, take a walk. If stuck on one issue, try another. If trying hard to see, listen. If locked in the business mode of the office, move way from a "business as usual" location. If overwhelmed by talking, take time for silence, breaks and meditative time. If stuck on the horns of a dilemma, focus on a different part of the beast. If taking issues too seriously, infuse sessions with an appropriate amount of playfulness. And, for those of us who still listen to LPs, we know that when the needle gets stuck, we need to move it either back or forward to the beginning of the track or to another song. When we do this, the air is again filled with music. This brings us to the third element: air.

Air: The Spacious Negotiator

So far, we have explored the interplay of earth and water as sources of aesthetic wisdom for negotiators. And we have looked to how aesthetic elements to help us navigate the gaps between representations and meaning. As illustrated previously, gaps exist—and can be bridged—between individual negotiators. But they also exist within individual negotiators. [NDR: Deutsch, *Internal Conflict*] This brings us to the element of air and the spaciousness of identity. Before examining identity, let us consider how the element of air relates to spaciousness.

Air comes from the Latin word meaning "high". The element of air reminds us that we can get above a problem, seeing it from a bigger view or in a more spacious way. In air, we have the possibility of ascent to a vantage point above the confining entanglements of practical existence with its many challenges. Air releases the hidden spirit in matter; it opens the possibility that we are more than we think. This brings us to a discussion of identity.

Air as an Aesthetic Dimension of Identity in Negotiation

Why do we relate identity to the element of air? Because identity is ephemeral; it changes and is difficult to fully describe or understand. Think of it this way: if you had to describe your identity briefly, how would you do so? If you were asked to convey something about your identity to someone you had just met without using words, what would you do? If you were communicating your identity to someone from your own group (according to factors like religion, demography, gender, ability, sexual orientation, etc.), how would you do so differently than if you were describing your identity to someone from another group? Identity is something that seems clear until you try to capture it; then it can slip through your fingers like air. The quote below from Jiddu Krishnamurti points toward the multiple levels of identity within and beyond in each human being:

> The distance to the stars is much less than the distance within ourselves. The discovery of ourselves is endless, and it requires constant inquiry, a perception which is total, an awareness in which there is no choice. This journey is really an opening of the door to the individual

in his relationship with the world. (Krishnamurti 2012: 243)

Walt Whitman poetically addresses this theme, asking, "Do I contradict myself? Very well, then I contradict myself, I am large, I contain multitudes." (Whitman 1891) Through the element of air, we can clearly see where there are gaps, the ways that paradoxes and polarities co-exist, and when authenticity is present. As negotiators, we get a little bit closer to finding what it is that moves and motivates us. We may get a glimpse into our souls: those places where our bedrock of being has its foundation, even as we see only its manifestations in the air of human interactions.

While we often think about identity in a static sense, nothing could be further from the truth. Identity moves. It darts and ducks. It slides and shifts, eliding in the thin air of our awareness. Our identity calibrates and calculates with every moment of every encounter. There are many aspects to identity—race, gender, socio-economic class, regional and educational background, religious and philosophical beliefs, and numerous kinds of intelligences and abilities, to name but a few. Each of these characteristics plays a part in shaping how we view ourselves, how we as negotiators perceive, experience, make sense of and react to one another, and how we experience ourselves contextually.

Of course, no single inner identity characteristic operates in isolation. When different aspects of our identity clash, these contradictions can generate an inner impasse. This state of stasis, with associated emotional and embodied tensions, can block our ability to negotiate at the level of mastery, or beauty. When it is particularly intense, neuroscientists label such a blockage "emotional hijacking", in which the rational and emotional parts of our brain cease operating in concert as team players, and input from the rational brain center is inhibited. Clear thinking is hijacked and cortisol is released into the blood as a way of managing the physiological experience of stress, while emotions flood the brain and trigger flight-or-fight responses. [NDR: Jendresen, *Creativity* and NDR: Lee & Shanahan, *Martial Arts*]

Recall a time when a negotiation was not going well, when your anxiety or discomfort was increasing. Although it might not be comfortable, try to remember what it was like for you. How did you feel physiologically: Were you flushed or perspiring? Was your heart pounding? Did you feel a knot in your stomach or a pain in your neck? How would you describe your emotions—anxious, angry, disappointed? Were you thinking negative thoughts about yourself or others, such as, "You idiot, I knew you weren't up to it"? What did you say? How did your internal dissembling affect your behavior and the course of interactions?

In confrontational and stressful situations, we are all susceptible to a flood of emotions and an overdose of cortisol. It is therefore crucial to be mindful of your body's emotional warning signs that tell you that you are hurtling towards a heightened state of tension, frustration or anger. Some people will experience an increased heart rate and flushed face; others will report muscle tension or abdominal discomfort associated with changed blood flow.

So, when you are engaged in a negotiation about something that has negative associations for you, be on your guard for emotional hijacking. When emotions are triggered through neural pathways associated with extremely vivid experiences recalled in great emotional and somatic-sensory detail, this activation can occur very rapidly. Before we know it, our bodies and our minds are stuck right back in the argument from last week or the childhood trauma. Neuro-imaging studies show the speed of emotional hijacking, which can happen below conscious awareness—33 milliseconds are all that is needed for our brains to respond to emotional stimuli. (Allen, Fonagy and Bateman 1998: 120) Unfortunately, while emotional hijacking can occur very quickly, it takes longer to recover from such a release of hormones—more than 20 minutes may be needed to recover a state of inner attunement (1,200,000 milliseconds).

Defusing action is needed because the embodied aspect of emotions cannot be wished away. When we hurt emotionally, we hurt physically. Brain imaging has also demonstrated that the degree of perceived unfairness we feel (for example, feeling unappreciated at work or unfairly treated by your supervisor) correlates with increased neural activity in the insula cortex region. This is same area of the brain that is activated when we feel pain. Ouch! In other words, unfairness hurts. Experiencing unfairness, and emotions generally, is a whole-body phenomenon. Scientifically, what is needed at these moments of heightened, self-protective activation is to engage negative feedback loops to reduce stress-associated brain activity. (Spencer, Fox and Day 2004) As these loops are engaged, attunement and synergy are again open as possibilities.

Attunement cannot be seen, yet it is a powerful force, just as the wind is powerful. Negotiation is more beautiful when we are aware of our inner terrains and notice when we or others are blown off course. It is almost always unproductive to continue engaging when tempers escalate and blaming, negative words hang in the air. Take a break, name what is happening, do some deep, meditative breathing, or find another way to change the climate of the negotiation. When you are able to do so, stress-associated brain activity will gradually lessen. In a state of calm, perspective returns, and the beauty we associate with proportionality and balance is again possible.

Finally, we explore how the properties of the air element can infuse negotiation processes with more beauty. Air, with its association with clarity and quickness, reminds us not to cloud the atmosphere amongst negotiators with judgments and preconceptions. Staying open to the needed sustenance of oxygen, we infuse our work with the resources of respect and curiosity, thus facilitating more rapid and satisfying progress. Aware of the physical ways our intuition communicates to us, we learn to be more aware of what exists that we cannot touch. As we hone our intuition, we increase our capacity to discern unseen dynamics and to act in ways that respond to the unseen essence of disagreements.

Applications for Reflexive Negotiation Practice

When reflecting on past negotiations, it's useful to ponder an experience of getting stuck in an impasse. Connecting air with identity, ask: How often have *I* posed the greatest obstacle to moving a negotiation forward? If my inner identities are locked in positional battle, is there space to breathe? Is there a pathway open to my grounded center? Can I see beyond my narrow trajectory? Do I have peripheral vision; do I feel very small? If so, then no matter how much I might try to make myself bigger including loud posturing or shouting, I remain small. The greatness of a negotiator lies with her ability to step into and embrace the vastness of her identity—an identity that recognizes that it is at once grounded in a sense of self, and at the same time continually evolving, as it moves into hitherto uninhabited spaces connected to others and to our inner worlds.

Drawing on the element of air, we can improve our capacity for reflexive negotiation practice in the following ways:

- To increase self-awareness, ask: What do our responses to beauty reveal about ourselves?
- To increase awareness of others, ask: Which experiences have I had with my counterpart that have shown me her complexity, or ways that she sees beyond what is in front of us?
- To increase awareness of context, ask: Which aspects of what is around me are beautiful? How can I bring more beauty in our midst? What could be different about this situation?

Drawing upon the element of air, we can become more intuitive as negotiators. [NDR: Schneider & Ebner, *Social Intuition*] Applying intuition can be lightning quick, revealing a close sister to the element of air in negotiations: fire.

Fire: The Dynamic Negotiator

Fire illuminates and cleanses. Replete with kinetic energy, it is dynamic, unpredictable and often beautiful. It can also be destructive, leaving charred remains in its wake. Fire is also contagious: when it occurs in one area, it easily catches nearby. Fire is often invoked by those describing negotiations, and not usually in positive ways.

Fire as an Aesthetic Dimension of Negotiation

How can negotiation be as dynamic as fire, and as energized, without causing great damage? How can we harness our passions for justice, fairness and possibility, even in the face of potentially dangerous consequences if we do not? One example, recent at the time of this writing, gives us some guidance. The 2015 Paris climate talks were multi-party negotiations where a lot was at stake. Now that we know unequivocally that human actions are causing potentially catastrophic climate chaos, there is international urgency to negotiate coordinated action. Yet complex negotiations between parties some of whom, in other contexts, may literally be firing weapons at each other, is difficult indeed. One of the ways that negotiations were successfully concluded was via an African process called an *indaba*. In this process, parties work in small groups, naming their bright-line boundaries not to be crossed. They are also tasked with naming places where progress is possible. During the Paris talks, multiple *indabas* occurred all through the days and nights, ultimately generating a contagious flame of momentum that led to a successful agreement. (Rathi 2015)

In what other ways does fire connect negotiation with beauty? Mary Catherine Richards had some powerful insights into this question as she, a few years before her death, was writing a chapter on conflict called *Separating and Connecting: The Vessel and the Fire*. (Richards 1998) She encountered great difficulty in writing about conflict, which surprised her because her work as a potter and educator had put her in the midst of many conflicts. She felt challenged to write about conflict in a way that was not watered down, but addressed its true dynamism, complexity and paradoxical gifts as an engine of change and a possible vehicle of destruction. Though Richards was reaching for a holistic way of writing about conflict, the words seemed too wooden, too thin. Then, one night, she had a dream. In the dream, there was a large fire on the horizon, spreading toward her neighborhood. Forced to evacuate, she and a neighbor gathered up a few of the most precious of her pots and drove away. As they were leaving, they encountered a man they knew who came into the room with her pots and just stood there. Though they admonished him to leave, he remained.

Days later, when—in her dream—they were allowed to return, Richards went immediately into the charred remains of the room with her pots. To her surprise, they were still there intact. The only difference was that they were more beautiful than when she had left. And the man was also still standing where they had left him. When they asked him how this was so, he said, "Everything is still here. Only the color is deepened." As the pots stood in the intensity of the fire, their colors came out more strongly and with more nuance than before. From this dream, Richards found a way to describe one of the paradoxes of conflict: that if we can withstand its ferocity, it can burn away those things within and between us that keep us attached to "being right" rather than living in peace. As she writes:

> When color deepens, it adds both darkness and light to itself; it contains more color. Goethe said that color is "the sufferings of light". *The sufferings of light!* That is, what light undergoes, we undergo; as vessels, we are

> deepened by our capacities for darkness and for light. It
> is an inner light that wakes in the lustrous stone. It is
> our darkness, our guilt and guile and greed and hope-
> lessness that, undergone like a fire, may flame through
> our consciousness, through our sense of ourselves,
> deepening our capacities, changing into colored light.
> Though we may feel annihilated in the process, we are
> intact. (Richards 1998: 234)

As human beings, we have an incredible capacity to emerge out of the
ashes of conflict's blaze, shaken yet somehow stronger. Could it be that
our capacity for resilience is related to our ability to tap into the soul of
our collective humanness, which after the shared experience of savage
conflict, is left exposed, raw, vulnerable and accessible, in new ways?
(See Jones 2004, describing how *some* children recovered remarkably
well after horrifying experiences in the Bosnian civil war.)

Richards' work points to another Jungian idea, that of the shadow,
defined as "the guardian of the threshold." (Richards 1998: 232) Individually and collectively, we have shadows—those parts of ourselves or our
group that are dark and often unacknowledged. Worse, they can be projected onto others. In negotiation, when you accuse the other side of
inflexibility, stop and ask whether that intractability is reciprocal. When
you associate the other with negative traits, ask what you are not acknowledging about yourself that might be keeping the process stuck.
Psychologically, we tend to perform largely unconscious mental and
emotional gymnastics to situate ourselves positively and others in alternative, negative positions. But this human tendency may get in the way
in negotiation rather than facilitating progress. The wise negotiator is
willing to take a full-spectrum look at herself and others, recognizing
that all of us are vessels for darkness *and* light. Illuminated by this thinking, negotiation becomes a process where the sufferings of light can show
a way forward.

Applications for Reflexive Negotiation Practice

So far we have been speaking of reflexive practice as comprising three
elements:

- Awareness of self;
- Awareness of other; and
- Awareness of context.

Yet the further we journey, the more challenging it becomes to separate
concepts of self, other and context. Drawing on the element of fire, we
can enhance our reflexive capacity as negotiators through these and
other practices:

- Reflect on personal responses to fire, escalation, intensity. What
  do they tell us about ourselves? Use a negotiation diagnostic

instrument such as the DYNAD referred to earlier to map your emotional shifts as conflict heats up.

- Does the fire of conflict deepen our coloring? Does it reveal darker, less attractive sides of us? Have the courage to explore negative characteristics that surface in conflict. How do these aspects of ourselves inhibit the flow of relations and the spread of ideas in negotiation?
- Be on the lookout for the conditions that may ignite a fire of connection. For example, take a risk and share a personal vulnerability with the other negotiators, or suggest constellation work for the group.
- Fire moves quickly, as do opportunities for change. Watch for opportunities associated with intense dynamics in negotiation. How can I step into a fire and be a catalyst for constructive contagion?
- When the destructive path of fiery conflict has seemingly destroyed all hope of resolution, pause for a moment and take stock. Am I still intact? And the others? What has changed? Has the torching and scorching of my assumed order of things introduced more nuanced hues into the negotiation landscape? Can I see things that were previously hidden to me? Have power relations shifted and if so, how?

Getting Closer to Beauty

In his book, *Self and Soul*, Mark Edmundson argues that as children we dream of ideals such as goodness and beauty and that, as adults, we still yearn for these aspirational qualities. (Edmundson 2015) Why, then, do these qualities not imbue more negotiations?

It seems that we gradually lose the child-like art of play and inquiry, finding ourselves increasingly disconnected from beauty, replacing it with glamour or a more utilitarian focus. As Morgan reminds us, "Beauty is not glamour ... Glamour is a highly fickle and commercially driven enterprise that contributes to ... "the humdrum". It appears and disappears ... No one ever catches up to glamour." (Morgan 2003: 15) And it is this never-ending pursuit of glamour that makes us unwell as individuals and a society.

Contemporary writers from diverse disciplines bemoan what they see as a societal slide into complacency, conformity and consumerism. A condition called affluenza has been the subject of numerous books and a high-profile US court case, where it provided a successful defense in a case involving driving under the influence of alcohol, causing death. (Dart 2014) In their book, *Affluenza: The All-Consuming Epidemic*, John de Graaf and his colleagues define it as "a painful, contagious, socially transmitted condition of overload, debt, anxiety and waste resulting from the dogged pursuit of more." (De Graaf, Wann and Naylor

2001) Even when economies are doing well, Australian writers Clive Hamilton and Richard Denniss remind us that we are not becoming happier. They explain how affluenza leads to "psychological disorders, alienation and distress," with the result that people "self-medicate with mood-altering drugs and excessive alcohol consumption." (Hamilton and Denniss 2005: 170-180)

Edmundson describes how Americans abandoned the virtues of beauty and truth in exchange for pragmatism and small-mindedness. In a similar vein, Singaporean diplomat, lawyer and professor Tommy Koh opines that "Singapore has raised pragmatism to the level of a philosophy [...] Singapore stands against the beauty of ideas in favor of what works" (Kaplan 2014: 93).

But what if we envisaged the aspiration of beauty as essential to negotiation; couldn't beauty and pragmatism delight in each other's company? On the practical benefits of beauty, Edmundson suggests that "by committing to ideals, men and women can escape the alternating peaks and low points that the life of desire creates and live in a more continuously engaged and satisfying way"—and—we would add—in a more grounded way. (Edmundson 2015: 102) Because beauty is related to deeper needs for aesthetic meaning and belonging, it can be an antidote to affluenza. Reflecting on Australian society, Hamilton and Denniss describe a related antidote, "downshifting"—shifting priorities away from maximizing towards minimizing; away from consuming towards conserving; away from complacency towards caring. It's a move away from temptations of glamour and towards the call of beauty.

Howard Gardner makes an impassioned plea to bring beauty back to the classroom, asking what we should teach and what we should learn, if not truth, beauty and goodness? (Gardner 2011). Gardner suggests that beauty primarily arises from experiences of nature and the arts. He explores what makes an experience beautiful and concludes that it's not just about what you like. Rather, getting close to beauty is about studying yourself, what you value and why. For example, why might one person resonate with a contemporary urban landscape and another with an endless desert plain? Why does the face of a family member evoke beauty for their relatives, but not for others? According to Gardner, we could all do well to notice how we perceive beauty, in order to get to know ourselves in a richer, deeper way. He suggests that teachers can ask students to curate a portfolio of beauty based on their own lived experiences. As negotiation educators, we encourage students to create portfolios of beauty from their negotiation experiences, drawing on each of the four elements. This will not only infuse negotiation learning with aesthetic vibrancy, it can also help surface what is outside our conscious awareness.

Richards cautions us that outside conscious awareness can easily trip us up in conflict. (Richards 1998: 234) She goes on: "With mixed feelings we may discover that the part we play in Art and Beauty and Love is

Lucifer's mask." (Richards 1998: 235) What, then, are we to do as we seek to implement the ideas outlined in this chapter in ways that are honest and beautiful? Richards suggests engaging negotiation, and building capacity to negotiate, as an ongoing, emergent process. Conflict itself is a process through which our human natures may develop and mature. It is a tension between contrary impulses within and between us. As we learn to respect the intense fire of disagreement, introducing fluidity to our fiercely defended egos and embracing our quicker-than-air intuition, we find ourselves standing on new ground. It is the ground not of arrival, but of *becoming*. It is a ground of being that we can rely upon, for its composition is better understood than ever before in human history.

Combining the powerful new understandings of neuroscience with political awareness of standpoints, we move into self-reflexive possibility. Understanding ourselves as both actors in human systems and negotiators means acknowledging the multi-sensory encounters within and between us, and the elemental wisdom they offer. The arts and, in particular, embodied art forms and practices, open up ways for us to know ourselves more deeply and to negotiate our relations with others.

Conclusion

Richards writes eloquently of what we are reaching for:

> Nature tells us that we are self-directing, self-correcting organisms, who function therefore by a dynamic of polarities: in-breathing and out-breathing, sleeping and waking, expanding and contracting, seeking balance. Our inner development as persons comes about as we are able to bear the wholeness of these opposites, to experience them as mutually completing, as interdependent and interpenetrating, in some sense simultaneous. To see them, in other words, as *alive, moving and interweaving*, like the distinct yet interflowing rivers that course through the oceans. (Richards 1998: 233)

As Richards describes, beauty arises from integrating the elements that animate, connect and divide us. As we embrace beauty as central to negotiation, we gain a more dynamic understanding of our work that points the way to virtuosity and pleasure, and to more satisfying, full-spectrum outcomes. As aesthetic ingredients in negotiation are awakened, our negotiation processes will pulse with essential and beautiful texture, nuance and multi-dimensional possibilities.

References

Alexander, N., J. Howieson and K. Fox. 2015. *Negotiation: Strategy, Style, Skills.* Sydney: Lexis Nexis 2015.

Allen, J. G., P. Fonagy and A. W. Bateman. 2008. *Mentalizing in Clinical Practice.* Arlington, VA: American Psychiatric Publishing, Inc.

BenZion, G. 2010. Overcoming the Dyslexia Barrier: The Role of Kinesthetic Stimuli in the Teaching of Spelling. In *The Neurocognition of Dance: Mind, Movement and Motor Skills,* edited by B. Bläsing, M. Puttke and T. Schack. London: Psychology Press.

Brooks, D. 2016. When Beauty Strikes. *The New York Times, January 15, 2016* p. A31. Available online at http://www.nytimes.com/2016/01/15/opinion/when-beauty-strikes.html?_r=0 (last accessed August 3, 2016).

Cohen, C. 2015. Arts and Building Peace: Affirming the Basics and Envisioning the Future. *United States Institute of Peace: Making Peace Possible.* Available online at http://www.usip.org/insights-newsletter/arts-and-building-peace-affirming-the-basics-and-envisioning-the-future (last accessed August 3, 2016).

Cunliffe, A. L. 2001. Managers as Practical Authors: Reconstructing our Understanding of Management Practice. *Journal of Management Studies* 38: 351-371.

Damasio, A. 1994. *Descartes' Error: Emotion, Reason, and the Human Brain.* New York: Putnam.

Dart, T. 2014. Texas Teenager Suffering 'Affluenza' Avoids Jail for Second Time. *The Guardian, February 5, 2014.* Available online at http://www.theguardian.com/world/2014/feb/06/texas-teenager-affluenza-escapes-jail-second-time (Last accessed August 3, 2016).

De Graaf, J., D. Wann and T. H. Naylor. 2001. *Affluenza: The All-Consuming Epidemic.* San Francisco, CA: Berrett-Koehler Publishers, Inc.

Edmundson, M. 2015. *Self and Soul: A Defense of Ideals.* Cambridge, MA: Harvard University Press.

Emoto, M. 2007. *The Miracle of Water.* Hillsboro, OR: Beyond Words Publishing, Inc.

Fletcher, A. 2001. *The Art of Looking Sideways.* London: Phaidon Press.

Gallese, V. 2005. "Being like me": Self-Other Identity, Mirror Neurons, and Empathy. In *Perspectives on Imitation: From Neuroscience to Social Science,* edited by Hurley, S and Chater, N. Cambridge, MA: MIT Press.

Gardner, H. 2011. *Truth, Beauty and Goodness Reframed: Educating for the Virtues in the Age of Truthiness and Twitter.* New York: Basic Books.

Hamilton, C. and R. Denniss. 2005. *Affluenza: When Too Much Is Never Enough.* Australia: Allen & Unwin.

Jones, L. 2004. *Then They Started Shooting: Growing Up in Wartime Bosnia.* Cambridge, MA: Harvard University Press.

Kaplan, R. D. 2014. *Asia's Cauldron: The South China Sea and the End of a Stable Pacific.* New York: Random House.

Kapoor, A. 1987. *At the Hub of Things.* Available online at http://anishkapoor.com/66/at-the-hub-of-things (last accessed August 3, 2016).

Kelly, M (ed). 1998. Mimesis. *The Encyclopedia of Aesthetics, vol. 3.* Oxford: Oxford University Press.

Krishnamurti, J. 2012. Choiceless Awareness 1. From Madras, 7th Public Talk, December 1959. *Collected Works,* XI.

Lam, H. E. W. Deutsch, J. S. Eddes, J. K. Eng, N. King, S. E. Stein and R. Aebersold. 2007. Development and Validation of a Spectral Library Searching Method for Peptide Identification from MS/MS. *Proteomics* 7: 655-67.

Lederach, J. P. 2005. *The Moral Imagination: The Art and Soul of Building Peace.* New York: Oxford University Press.

O'Donoghue, J. 2003. *Divine Beauty: The Invisible Embrace.* Great Britain: Bantam Press.

Picasso Speaks The Arts, New York, May 1923. Reprinted in Alfred Hamilton Barr. 1946. *Picasso, fifty years of his art.* New York: Museum of Modern Art.

Rathi, A. 2015. This Simple Negotiation Tactic Brought 195 Countries to Consensus. *Quartz, December 12, 2015.* Available online at http://qz.com/572623/this-simple-negotiation-tactic-brought-195-countries-to-consensus-in-the-paris-climate-talks/. (last accessed May 3, 2016).

Richards, M. C. 1998. Separating and Connecting: The Vessel and the Fire. In *The Fabric of the Future: Women Visionaries Illuminate the Pathways to Tomorrow*, edited by M. J. Ryan. Berkeley, CA: Conari Press.

Scarry, E. 2001. *On Beauty and Being* Just. New Jersey: Princeton University Press.

Schneider, A. K. and J. G. Brown. 2013. Negotiation Barometry: A Dynamic Measure of Conflict Management Style. *Ohio State Journal on Dispute Resolution* 28(3): 557-580.

Singer, T. 2006. The Neuronal Basis and Otogeny of Empathy and Mind Reading: Review of Literature and Implications for Future Research. *Neuroscience and Behavioral Reviews* 30: 855-863.

Spencer, S. J., J. C. Fox and T. A. Day. 2004. Thalamic Paraventricular Nucleus Lesions Facilitate Central Amygdala Neuronal Responses to Acute Psychological Stress. *Brain Research* 997(2): 234-237.

Whitman, W. 1891. Song of Myself. In *Leaves of Grass*. Available online at http://whitmanarchive.org/published/LG/1891/poems/27 (last accessed August 4, 2016).

ↄ৪ **56** ৪ↄ

Aesthetics in Negotiation:
Part Two—The Uses of Alchemy

Michelle LeBaron & Nadja Alexander

Editors' Note: The authors here pursue the logic of their Part One chapter further. Showing how negotiators tend to concentrate on a limited range of skills and stimuli, while overlooking others, they argue that the ancient concept of alchemy works in conjunction with modern concepts of neuroscience to unlock a whole series of aesthetics-derived, embodied strategies and approaches. These, they contend, make it possible to advance "stuck" negotiations in which progress is stalled, as well as to improve a whole range of less complex negotiation processes.

In Part One, in this volume, we discussed the four classic elements —earth, water, air and fire—as paths via which beauty can infuse negotiation. Another way these four elements can be explored is through the organizing concept of alchemy. Alchemy, historically concerned with changing states and physical properties, including turning one substance into another, is essentially concerned with transformation. Given that

Professor **Michelle LeBaron** is a conflict transformation scholar/practitioner at the University of British Columbia Allard School of Law whose work is animated by creativity, culture and interdisciplinarity. She has done seminal work in many types of conflicts including intercultural, international, family, organizational and commercial, exploring how arts help shift intractable conflicts. She is a fellow at the Trinity College Long Room Hub Arts and Humanities Research Institute in Dublin and holds a Wallenberg Fellowship at the Stellenbosch Institute for Advanced Studies, South Africa. Her books include *The Choreography of Resolution: Conflict, Movement and Neuroscience*; *Conflict Across Cultures: A New Approach for a Changing World*; *Bridging Cultural Conflicts*; and *Bridging Troubled Waters*.

Nadja Alexander is Academic Director at the Singapore International Dispute Resolution Academy, and Visiting Professor of Law at Singapore Management University. An award-winning (2011, 2007, 1997) author and educator, Nadja also works as a policy adviser and conflict intervener in diverse dispute resolution settings. Her work on cross-border and cross-cultural conflict embraces interdisciplinary approaches to deepen conflict engagement. Nadja has been appointed Honorary Professor at The University of Queensland, Australia, and Senior Fellow of the Dispute Resolution Institute at Mitchell Hamline School of Law in the United States. Her books include *International and Comparative Mediation*; *Global Trends in Mediation*; *Negotiation: Strategy Style Skills*, and *The EU Mediation Handbook*.

negotiation—when optimal—may also yield transformation, we examine what alchemical concepts may have to offer here.

Alchemy has a long history, appearing in the myths and legends of ancient China and texts from Egypt dating back to 1900 BCE (Cockren 2016). Western ideas of alchemy, as a process that blends the four basic elements of earth, water, air and fire in different ways to create change and transformation, trace their origins to the Egyptian god, Hermes Trismegistus, with whom the ancient Emerald Tablet is associated (Conniff 2014). It also has roots in ancient Greek philosophy (Ball 2004) and Buddhist and Hindu teachings in India (Gurmet 2004). Centuries later, the Swiss psychologist Carl Jung associated alchemy with the process of individuation, integrating inner and outer aspects of our beings (Jung 1980). He imagined the four elements of earth, water, air and fire as symbolically associated with differentiation and transformation (Jung 1980).

Drawing on Jung's and others' work, this chapter explores how integrating understandings of alchemy via natural metaphors into negotiation can change our embodied experiences of processes, of each other and of negotiation outcomes themselves. We use the four elements—earth, water, air and fire—and their corresponding alchemical processes of *coagulatio, solutio, sublimatio* and *calcinatio* to open a path towards a deeper, more holistic and aesthetically-grounded understanding of negotiation. Just as humans individuate in the process of maturing in ways that are still not well understood, negotiators and negotiations may mature. An understanding of how alchemical processes help us think about the maturation process is the subject of this chapter.

Jungian Perspectives on Alchemical Processes and Individuation

According to Carl Jung, individuation involves the integration of internal and external elements toward maturation or, in his words, "coming to selfhood" (Jung 1966: 266). This individuation always has collective elements, as Jung acknowledged when he wrote: "As the individual is not just a single, separate being, but by his very existence presupposes a collective relationship, it follows that the process of individuation must lead to more intense and broader collective relationships and not to isolation" (Jung 1966: 266). Individuation both has predictable patterns, and is unique for each individual. Thus, normal babies learn to form sounds into words and walk within predictable bands of time, but the processes by which they do so are still not well understood. As we progress, individuation continues cognitively, emotionally and physically. Jung believed that individuation or self-realization continues throughout life as we become more and more able to integrate internal and external aspects of ourselves and the world into meaningful wholes.

Jung used alchemical processes associated with the four elements to describe the process of individuation, believing that the processes that alchemists of old pursued to change base metal to gold had psychic parallels. At the same time, given that historical alchemists—as far as we know—were not successful in changing base metals into gold, and that little definitive writing about their quests survives, it is not clear exactly what the sequences were or how they worked. This left Jung with the freedom to constellate alchemical processes in relation to individuation according to his intuition and experiences with psychoanalysis. Though his writing on the subject is complex and not fully developed during his lifetime, alchemy provides an intriguing way to think about individuation and, by extension, negotiation. From it, we take this treasure: *negotiation always involves combining elements in ways that we can explain* and *in ways that are mysterious.* Jungian ideas of alchemy help us peer with a bit more clarity into the mysteries.

Parallels between negotiation and the individuation process are fruitful to examine. As individuation involves integrating inner and outer aspects, so negotiation requires the same. While working with material dimensions of problems and potential solutions, our internal geographies are necessarily invoked. As discussed in Part One, these geographies serve us best when we are as aware of self and other as possible.

The four alchemical processes of *coagulatio, solutio, sublimatio* and *calcination* will each be described below, with discussions of how they might expand our awareness and thus our capacities for effective negotiation. Though each will be described in isolation for clarity's sake, it is in their combination that the alchemical processes are most potent.

Coagulatio: The Element of Earth

In coagulatio, the element of earth is central. It relates to things taking on solid form, or coalescing. This is the condition at the beginning of negotiation: people arrive with solid positions and clear ideas of what the optimal material outcome should be. When negotiation works well, other elements come in to unsettle the solidity of earth. Put differently, negotiating parties come into an attunement one with another that coagulates into a new form. This new ground becomes one from which the parties can proceed, one even more reliable because it is shared. In this way, *coagulatio* can happen many times in a single negotiation as breakthroughs occur and parties gradually come to establish a way of proceeding that coheres. One way that *coagulatio* has been pursued scientifically is through the phenomena of resonance and attunement.

Coagulatio *and Attunement*

Resonance is a physical phenomenon imaged by religious scholar Christopher Bache as "lateral bands of colored light stretching horizontally across a room" between people (Bache 2000: 178). Bache postulates that resonance is "always trying to happen" between people, giving examples of phase locking from chaos theory (Bache 2000: 178). "Phase locking," he writes, "occurs in nature when individual oscillating systems shift from a state of collective chaos to integrated resonance." (Bache 2000: 178) For example, when individual cells from the heart of a chicken embryo are separated, they beat erratically. If a number of the cells are brought back together, they begin to beat coherently in what is called phase lock. In humans, this phenomenon is obvious in choir singing, but also happens in subtler ways such as the synchronization of women's menstrual cycles when they live together.

When negotiation works well, do the parties come into resonance approaching phase lock? What role does attuning have in fostering collaboration? Two points here, from opposite directions. The U.S. military is well aware of the power of music and has used it frequently in recent engagements. Marco Accattatis explores relations between music and violence, commencing with the Homeric legend of the sirens, whose song killed anyone who heard it (Accattatis 2014: 2). He goes on to detail the use of round-the-clock hard rock and heavy metal music directed at the Papal refuge of General Manuel Noriega, Panama's military dictator who had fallen out of favor with Washington. Several other examples of the use of loud music to irritate, disorient and intimidate range from its use in the Branch Dividian siege in Waco, Texas to interrogations of detainees in Guantanamo Bay. In these instances, music is pressed into the service of destroying resonance within, and fragmenting connection and coherence, by preventing phase lock with others and disrupting connection with positive sensory anchors.

On the positive side, music was used in one of our negotiation classes by collaboration expert Hussein Janmohamed, who taught a group of twenty-five lawyers and other professionals a vocal round of devotional songs from diverse world religious traditions. We had spent four days studying and dialoguing together and the atmosphere had been warm and positive. At the end of thirty minutes with Hussein, something new had constellated. The music had brought an entirely different dimension of attunement, opening us up to the ground of our shared humanity, alive with the quality of wonder and shimmering with awe at the beauty generated through song.

The solid ground we stand on as negotiators, then, can be strengthened and made more robust by awareness of moments of *coagulatio* —literally, when things come together. While it may be difficult to imagine parties singing together in advance of or during a negotiation process, the imaginal challenge is worth taking. Perhaps a better question is to ask where parties can find trusted resonance in their midst. As was illustrated in our chapter on aesthetics and negotiation, the source of resonance often comes via arts and experiences that accent physical, sensory dimensions.

For example, a recent issue of the United States Institute of Peace newsletter *Insights* discusses arts in peacebuilding and negotiation as an idea whose time has come. The lead article advises negotiators with Russian counterparts to stop reading "jargon-filled scholarly analysis from those political science journals and to turn to works by Russian literary giants, such as Dostoyevsky, Tolstoy, and Solzhenitsyn" (Wood 2015: 1). According to the author, literature is the way to understand Russians and their leader, Vladimir Putin, because these artists illuminate Russia's worldview, nationalism, and endurance like nothing else can. Quoting Four-Star U.S. Admiral Stavridis, the article asserts that "[l]iterature is the true lens. If you want to understand the Russian mind, remember that no other culture esteems its writers more than Russia. Every Russian can—and frequently does—quote Pushkin, Tolstoy and Gogol; whereas you would be hard pressed to get a line of Whitman, Hemingway or Toni Morrison out of a typical American" (Wood 2015).

In South Africa, meanwhile, as a political prisoner, Nelson Mandela turned to the arts to incrementally build and nurture a collaborative negotiation spirit with his jailers, the then-apartheid government. During his 27 years in prison, Mandela learnt not only the language of his oppressors, he also familiarized himself with their poetry, their literature, their music and their rugby. He got to know the prison guards and—in some cases—their families. He learnt their stories. Negotiations ultimately led to his release from Robben Island prison and facilitated his rise to power as president of South Africa in 1994. Through the beauty of empathy and genuine engagement, Mandela was famously able to negotiate a new inclusive political climate for his country and avoid the bloody civil war that so many had assumed would be inevitable. Using alchemical language, Mandela invoked *coagulatio* in the form of newly grounded relations arising from his genius for empathy.

Arts practices are universal ways of invoking *coagulatio*, though different forms are accented in different cultures. Throughout the South African struggle, for example, the arts played vital roles in galvanizing people and transforming unfairness. South African Constitutional Court judge and anti-apartheid activist Albie Sachs explains the importance of guarding nuance and complexity in art: "In the case of a real instrument of struggle, there is no room for ambiguity: a gun is a gun is a gun, and if it were full of contradictions, it would fire in all sorts of directions and be useless for its purpose. But the power of art lies precisely in its capacity to expose contradictions and reveal hidden tensions—hence the danger of viewing it as if it were just another kind of missile-firing apparatus" (Gerhart and Glaser 2010: 696; Allen 2005). This passage reminds us that when art is instrumentalized, it can lose its power. Sachs also writes: "What are we fighting for but for the right to express our humanity in all its forms, including our sense of fun and capacity for love and tenderness and our appreciation of the beauty of the world?....Let us write better poems and make better films and compose better music" (Sachs 1998: 240, 247).

From Sachs' invitation, we take this: that we should not only infuse negotiation with aesthetic sensibilities because it will work better and more holistically (though we do believe this is true), but also for the sake of pleasure—and that is partly because the pleasure turns out to be *functional* in bringing about *coagulatio*. If, as negotiators, we feel more fully alive and secure in our capacities to relate one with another, our negotiations will actually be more grounded in reliable progress and good feeling. In addition, we will be better able to adopt another piece of South African wisdom, the idea of *Ubuntu*. Judge Sachs pleaded eloquently for mediators and negotiators to recognize the importance of *Ubuntu*—an African concept referring to the essence and interconnectedness of being human. *Ubuntu* can look very different in diverse contexts, but always involves engaging the senses (Sachs 2010).[1]

Applications for Reflexive Negotiation Practice

How does coagulatio inform negotiation practice? Above descriptions of attunement and resonance offer some ideas, as does our discussion of arts and *Ubuntu*. Negotiators may also:

- Watch for moments when things "gel" and find ways to signal or mark these so that collective experiences of *coagulatio* build;
- Emphasize interdependence as a reliable way to generate solid relational and substantive outcomes;
- Notice how experiences of time change in the course of negotiation, moving into *kairos* territory. As William Isaacs wrote: "The process of dialogue helps us to rediscover and appreciate *kairos*....People become quite reflective and aware of the conversation as taking place in time, but also lose track of it and begin listening more for the sense of meaning that is unfolding." (Isaacs 1999: 289-290) In other words, dialogue and negotiation help cultivate *coagulatio* as people begin to listen for shared meaning rather than focusing on advocating their preferred outcome.

Solutio: The Element of Water

Water is associated with the alchemical operation of *solutio*, turning a solid into a liquid. In many negotiation processes, this operation arises. Consider two people whose positions are very far apart. They come in feeling "solid" and "attached", and not only to their way of framing the issues and their perceptions of their counterparts. Along the way, resentments and enmities may dissolve, another aspect of *solutio*.

The ability of water to appear in different forms, namely gas, solid or liquid forms, resembles the variety of the human condition in conflict. Human responses to conflict may appear as:

- solid, fixed, entrenched positions which compete against one another (solidified water, ice);
- invisible ways of avoiding conflict or accommodating someone else's entrenched position (water as steam or gas);
- fluid responses characterized by flow, exploration, connection, movement (liquid water).

Solutio *in Negotiation*

This operation of *solutio* does not happen in every negotiation; sometimes parties come to an agreement or fail to do so, and leave with their "ground of being" unaltered. But negotiation is essentially about change, about finding a meeting place that dissolves some amenable aspects of our positions while still leaving us a reliable place to stand. It is also about affective change, yielding a fluidity of being that allows all parties more space and flexibility going forward, especially when there are ongoing family, business or community relations. As negotiation educators, we can help others see that all things are in flux, and that the opportunity to come to agreements and closure is to participate in that flux rather than merely standing on the edge of the flow. The words of a man who experienced *solutio* in a marital negotiation are illustrative: "I am at the center of a great city watching a vast stream of humanity pass by—individuals of every type and description. It's like the flow of a great river. I am fascinated." This man's experience of touching into a bigger grid in negotiation is classic *solutio*.

The operation of *solutio* is also germane to addressing impasse in negotiation. When things are stuck, referencing aesthetic experiences may be helpful. Once, when working with members of a group who needed to renegotiate their ways of working with each other following a merger, one of the authors invited everyone to draw their experience of their present relations. Pictures ranged from a sinking ship to a collapsing building to a placid lake with monsters beneath the surface, viscerally representing the intensity of upheaval shared by group members. Speaking from the pictures, participants framed their concerns aesthetically, inhabiting the gap between their frustration and their images of how to move forward. While concrete, the sensory images also introduced fluidity, as all of them depicted movement and many of them included water. This opened conversations about how to craft new systems and reclaim an experience of flow in the midst of unfamiliar configurations.

Later, while addressing leadership questions in the same organization, the participants were invited to find a physical, aesthetic way of representing their experiences. From a table full of various media and assorted materials, they chose multi-colored yarn which they wound around their leader to represent their experience of him being unavailable, immobilized by the demands of his new role. Seated in their midst with yarn spun all around him, he was viscerally able to articulate his

experience of trying to negotiate new sets of relations and job requirements while feeling tied down and held back by conflicting expectations
and the challenge of creating a new, hybrid culture out of two distinct
group norms and patterns. Everyone understood that the leader's main
need was mobility, and they were then able to problem-solve ways that
his maneuverability could be enhanced and made more available and
fluid. The operation of *solutio* was at work here as those involved found
new fluidity, beginning to relate to the problem as something amenable
to action.

The ability to create space allowing for movement and flow is an
essential aspect of creativity and problem-solving. We now know that our
brain is not a fixed piece of hardware but rather a malleable, adaptive
living organ that has the ability to transform its own function and structure. Research on neuroplasticity demonstrates how our beliefs can shift
our biology and change our brain anatomy (Lipton 2008). At the heart of
neuroplasticity is the principle that neurons that fire together wire together, while neurons that wire apart, stay apart (Beausoleil and
LeBaron 2013). This means that we create patterns and develop habits as
we repeat thoughts and behaviors. Over time, these become comfortable
superhighways that we drive along without conscious thought. We turn
to autopilot as we traverse the well-travelled terrain of neurons that have
fired together countless times. These patterns are not easy to shift: in
negotiations, such habits of thought lead us down the slippery slope of
positional posturing towards blockages and impasse. Yet it is possible to
bring movement into the brain. Here, the alchemic process of *solutio* is
at work again. Through conscious practice, we can discover spaces that
have fallen victim to our blind spots and link them into our active
neuro-grid of highways, major roads and T-junctions. By seeking out
opportunities to create different neural routes—as simple as taking a
different way to work every other day—we can begin to break limiting
patterns and create space for creativity to enter and thrive. Then, we
notice that T-junctions turn into intersections, and intersections into
roundabouts, as previously unnoticed opportunities appear in front of
us. Cul-de-sacs open up into new districts as we enter into a state of
biological flow with mind and body connected, operating in concert.

Movement in Negotiation: Solutio Mobilized

In negotiation, movement is fundamental. Without it, parties are
hard-pressed to reach agreements. Water flows around whatever is in its
path; it takes the shape of whatever container it is in, yet does not lose its
coherence. Movement-based experiences can therefore be useful in assisting negotiators to apprehend and incorporate flexibility, flow and
clarity into their approaches. They can help parties literally learn, in
embodied ways, how to move across continua or paradoxes. Finally, they
provide powerful anchors for mutuality and reciprocity, both of which

are central to aesthetic collaboration. Over the past several years, we have worked extensively with physical movement in negotiation education, finding that learners report dramatic shifts in their capacity to work with others arising from their experiences of this channel into *solutio* (LeBaron, MacLeod and Acland 2013).

Recent scientific discoveries bolster the case for movement as a way of teaching negotiation as they highlight the interconnection between physical and verbal expression. Both activities are located in Broca's area of the brain, where speech neural pathways overlay sensorimotor circuitry; apparently, linguistic forms of expression arose later in human brain evolution and are intricately interwoven with physical experience (Beausoleil and LeBaron 2013). These findings point to movement and gesture as early pre-verbal forms of expression, cognition and communication. And so we ask whether, "[w]hen we fell out of animal presence,... [was] dance our first language?" (O'Donohue 2003: 129). In evolutionary terms, we have vastly more experience with movement than with words, yet academic study has traditionally focused on the part of the brain with which life on Earth has had least experience; namely, the rational brain (or neocortex). This focus has led our attention away from our bodies, and has been cemented in place by Cartesian dualism, which privileges cognitive ways of knowing over physical wisdom.

Given millions of years communicating kinesthetically, it's not surprising that humans read body language better than verbal language. It's easier for others to lie to us with words than with their bodies because we intuitively and accurately read body language, detecting authenticity or a lack of it in our negotiation counterpart. We know this on a kinesthetic level, often below conscious awareness, when we experience intuition or the weird feeling in our stomach that something isn't quite right, although we can't think of a logical reason not to believe what they say.

Similarly, it must come as no surprise that babies communicate with body language long before they acquire the capacity for words. [NDR: Thompson et al., *Nonverbal*] How does an infant summon the capacity to shrug her shoulders to communicate "I don't know" (or "I want you to think that I don't know") or to hide something from you by putting it behind her back and distracting you with cute smiles and innocent blinks of the eye? These highly complex messages are physically practiced, refined and mirrored even before birth. What experience and wisdom must then repose in our collective corporeal selves! For movement is not the wisdom of one person but the pooled kinesthetic know-how and know-why of our genetic evolution. Thus, we see echoes of Jung's insight that individuation (and alchemical processes) are never only individual; they are always collective.

So how can we access *solutio* as part of alchemical knowing, and put it to work for us in negotiation? In a recent workshop for people working on conflicts with religious and political dimensions, dancer Margie Gillis used a number of physical metaphors in designing shared experiences.

For example, she asked participants to explore "yielding" and "resisting" in various movement activities. Gillis also helped participants learn to understand and navigate the gaps between themselves and other parties, and to welcome them as generative. As we moved, we began to physically understand the concept of "negative space" between and around us.

So connected are brain and body that dance (and other physical movement—see Honeyman and Parish 2013) has the ability to release us from mental habits when we feel locked in negotiation impasse. For example, dancing or walking through breathtaking nature can resonate with us at emotional and unconscious levels, thereby accessing and shifting the neural processes of firing and wiring, referred to previously. Dance has been explained as highly complex, synchronized body work facilitating social bonding (Beausoleil and LeBaron 2013). Taking that walk through nature or going dancing one evening in the midst of negotiations can transport us to surprising spaces that help transform perspectives and attitudes, surfacing insights and options not noticeable in the midst of conventional negotiations (Beausoleil and LeBaron 2013).

Another movement form helpful to negotiators is aikido. *Aikido* is increasingly used to assist learners to physically experience the differences between yielding and movement, and the counter-productive effect of resisting given its likelihood of eliciting a similar response in a counterpart (Ringer 2006; Palmer 2016). [See also NDR: Lee & Shanahan, *Martial Arts*] Practitioners physically learn to cultivate and inhabit "flow". Wendy Palmer, a well-known American aikido master, writes about the flow state as experienced via movement this way: "Most of us have experienced the phenomena often called the 'zone' or the 'flow state'. This happens when we have the experience of effort as we do an activity, then beginning to tire and backing off a bit, and suddenly the activity becomes easy, effortless. Often people will describe this as, 'something was coming through me/us'. This phrase, 'something was coming through me/us', points to the idea that the energy or inspiration came from outside our body—it came from the space or environment around us. This idea presupposes that space is not empty and our bodies are not solid. From a scientific point of view, our bodies consist of trillions of atoms. Atoms are primarily space with very small particles within that space; from this we deduce that we are not as solid as we sometimes feel. Indeed, we might say that the feeling of being solid is more of a belief than a fact" (Palmer 2016). Indeed, given that our bodies are primarily water, it makes sense that effectiveness in negotiation is really about learning to find flow.

Applications for Reflexive Negotiation Practice

While movement is a way of cultivating "flow" in negotiations, there are several other things negotiators can do, and ways they can pay attention to summon *solutio* into their processes. These include:

- Cultivate comfort with strong emotions. Strong emotions are always part of complex conflicts, and it is often true that hearing them helps dissolve bad feelings;
- Learn your inner geography in relation to flow states; when do you feel most able to give yourself to a process wholeheartedly? Try to include as many of these conditions in the processes you design as possible;
- Use water as an experience of fluidity and flow. Make paper sailboats and write your worst fears for a negotiation on them, then sail them away on a lake. Go swimming. Take a long drink. Look at a beautiful image of the sea while listening to its tidal rhythms. Water is restorative and inspiring.

Air: The Spacious Negotiator

So far, we have explored the interplay of the alchemical elements of earth and water as resources for negotiators. We have looked to notions of resonance and attunement to help us navigate the gaps between representations and meaning, and at moments of flow as ways of getting through tight spots.

We explored *coagulatio* and *solutio* in our previous sections, noting how they help us to (a) ground ourselves and enlarge the grid of our interactions, (b) feel alive and increase our capacity to connect with others, and (c) enter a state of flow. With the element of *sublimatio*, we enter the invisibility of air, asking about identity and other things that not solid yet are very real. In this section, we examine who we are as negotiators, and as human beings engaging in negotiation.

Sublimatio is related to the element of air which—as we know—is largely invisible. Air reminds us that things can move quickly and that many invisible things influence the course of negotiations. It is thus related to intuition and imagination. It is also related to being able to see ourselves as if from above, and from the perspectives of others. We begin by examining the internal aspects of our identities, which are always powerful and frequently invisible both to ourselves and others in negotiation.

German communication psychologist Friedemann Schulz von Thun refers to the multiple voices within us as members of our "inner team" (Pörksen and Schulz von Thun 2014: 92). He explains that, as in any collaborative group, the members of each person's individual inner team represent different views, perspectives, interests, characteristics and values. [See NDR: Deutsch, *Internal Conflict*] For example, I may have a strong value for loyalty, but this value can come into conflict with self- or ethical interest. Do I break confidentiality after a colleague in my law firm who is a valued member of a negotiating team confides in me about her drug addiction? If I don't, our clients, our firm and others may suffer. Yet, doing so requires me to violate my value of loyalty, as well as, perhaps, a specific promise. Thus, negotiating amongst members of the inner team is a primary act, a precondition to effective negotiation with another. Yet, it is always related to *sublimatio*, because others do not see this inner negotiation process taking place. [See also NDR: Deutsch, *Internal Conflict*] Mary Catherine Richards puts it this way:

> [It is important to get to know] one's inner family: for example, the fearful child, the scornful brother, the sorceress, the fanatical seeker, the possessive parent, who stand in the shadow and create difficulties. (Richards 1998: 232)

As members of our inner family or team interact with one another, and also with team members of other inner teams, encountering innumerable complex and emergent contextual factors, challenges necessarily arise. Richards advises that we learn to listen to all of these voices as far as we are aware and able, so that we find ourselves "peaceably at war, neither victorious nor defeated" (Richards 1998: 233). For it is in recognizing the insights of these different voices, in ourselves and others, that we are able to see more of a full spectrum. We begin to be able to look with more acuity and to see patterns more clearly, products of the process of *sublimatio*.

A related concept to the inner team or family is intersectionality, which "acknowledges an individual's multiple social identities, thus creating a more complete portrayal of the whole [embodied] person" (Wijeyesinghe and Jones 2014: 10). Intersectionality looks beyond the "additive" nature of multiple identity characteristics and instead focuses on the ways that different aspects of identity simultaneously and repeatedly encounter one another, generating unique gaps in motion (Goodman 2014: 99-108; Alexander, Howieson and Fox 2015). There will always be a gap between the experience that comes through "encounter" and the representations we create to understand and explain the encounters we have. Gaps create space for insights to emerge, for truth to be experienced, for embodied ways of knowing and being to be embraced, and for us to know and engage the artistry of flow in negotiation. *Sublimatio* is a practice of noticing gaps and insights for the gold they are in negotiation. It need not be only individual, it can also be collective.

Intersectionality explodes the illusion of separation—we cannot separate mind, body and soul, nor can we separate ourselves from one another. As human beings, we are designed to dance, to interact, with one another as whole porous beings—taking and giving, pulling and pushing, always influencing, always flowing—like water.

Daniel Goleman uses the term social intelligence to highlight the communicative nature of our senses—visual, auditory, kinesthetic, olfactory and gustatory—all of which offer pathways to who we are at this moment and who we are becoming in the next (Goleman 2006). In other words, we are continually noticing and adapting our behavior in relation to those around us. [NDR: Schneider & Ebner, *Social Intuition*] In part because of intersectionality, we are ineffective at predicting behavior. It is virtually impossible to know how the complex inner and outer senses will interrelate in any one person at any one time. And, despite our beliefs to the contrary, we are not consistent from moment to moment or setting to setting. Robert J. Lifton and others have criticized the notion of a stable personality in which our senses always interact in predictable ways, arguing that we are always changing and adapting within, with others and with our environments, in a condition he calls protean (Lifton 1993). [See also NDR: Adler, *Protean Negotiator*] The process of *sublimatio* is to be aware of this, to cease insisting that we or others remain unchanging, and to instead embrace the mystery of our unfolding.

Intersectionality and *sublimatio* therefore offer ways to think about our essential interconnectedness and porousness as human beings, and highlight the potential for rapid change as well as incremental shifts, both often beyond conscious effort. Peace scholar Louise Diamond once challenged a room full of graduate students to explain how change happens. Their explanations were somewhat ponderous, full of prescriptions and step-by-step progressions. After listening, she asked everyone whether they could recall a time in their lives when change happened very quickly. It turned out they could. Perhaps it was associated with a pivotal event (either global or personal) or with a surprising shift in a relationship. The element of air and the associated process of *sublimatio* remind us that things can happen slowly or with great rapidity. The world readers will be in when this chapter is published may be a very different one from the world that exists as we are writing it.

Applications for Reflexive Negotiation Practice

In addition to being aware of our inner teams and intersectionality as described above, the process of sublimatio reminds us to

- Be aware of and open to change that does not seem to have a clear antecedent, in ourselves and others. Notice dynamism and welcome intuition, yours and others';
- Consciously invoke imaginative ways of engaging, both in relation to negotiation processes and outcomes. Draw your magic solution and share it with a counterpart. Imagine a world when the problems you are negotiating are solved: how does it feel in your body? Can you bring some of that feeling into the negotiation itself as a way of introducing more spaciousness into the process? Spaciousness is always associated with the element of air;
- Suspend negotiating as usual and invite all present to "rise above" the process for a fixed time. What do you see? Where are

the strengths? What is precarious? How does the clarity of the view from above help you think about moving forward?

Calcinatio: The Element of Fire

Calcinatio is associated with the element of fire. Consider the many properties of fire: its warmth, coziness, beauty—and its destructive potential. *Calcinatio* tends to be associated with anger and resentment and with their potential to erupt into violence. As with each of the other processes, it is important to befriend *calcinatio* so that its violent potential can find form in ways that mobilize negotiation progress.

Calcinatio can be understood by imagining a tango. Each part of your body that interacts—embraces, melts, asserts—with each part of your partner's body generates an embodied relational identity experience that helps define you at that moment. Our embodied emotional identities have been studied by numerous neuroscientists starting with Antonio Damasio (Damasio and Damasio 1994; Damasio 1994). What we come to experience as our truest emotions or feelings are in fact interpretations of physical sensations or impulses to act generated through social interactions. These social interactions are always the product of multiple factors in context, and are influenced by mysterious and unseen forces as well. When we do the tango well, we literally yield to a state of union that contains our two wholes: we melt as we experience *calcinatio*.

This operation reminds us that we need to cultivate ways of standing in the fire of disagreement, both within and in the external world. One way of imaging effective negotiation, then, is as a state of attunement amongst members of our "inner team". Attunement opens the possibility of infusing our negotiation identity and processes with more nuanced texture, depth, tolerance for passion and flexibility. Remember that this attunement can shift quickly because of external events or the way a particular interaction stimulates an old wound, just as fire changes quickly. This is another reason that negotiators need the fire of *calcinatio*: fire lights, helping us see clearly and to "right" ourselves when we have been thrown off by what psychologists call a negative trigger. Consider, for example, the effect of seeing an image of a beloved family member when you have been feeling less than clear or anxious. It can bring you back into your body's home and back into attunement with your "inner team".

Calcinatio *and Attunement: Constellations at Work*

Another manifestation of the element of fire, with its capacity to move quickly and shift the landscape, is the process of systemic constellation work as pioneered by Insa Sparrer and others (Sparrer 2007). Just as fire consumes a territory touching everything in its wake, constellation processes become containers for dynamics to be seen and to shift in ways that are mysterious, yet effective. Constellation work offers an illustration of the curious experience of change that Diamond's students (referred to in the previous section) were not able to explain.

The theory and practice of systemic constellations offers an embodied approach to problem-solving that is fire-like in the speed and accuracy with which it unfolds. In this process, a person (client) who wishes to gain deep insights into a particularly challenging issue in a negotiation, selects any number of individuals (so-called representatives) to assist in creating a physical constellation that depicts the situation from the client's perspective. It is not necessary for the client to brief the representatives about the exact nature or details of the issue, although this may occur in some practices to varying extents. The client then physically directs the representatives to take positions in a way that depicts the current situation as he or she perceives it. The resulting constellation —the spatial arrangement of the representatives as a whole and the kinesthetically-felt reactions of the representatives to one another— reproduce the structure and dynamics of the situation (system) the client is describing. Following the initial placement, a series of interventions may be undertaken by the constellation leader (host) or the client to rearrange the spatial scene until the representatives feel better in the constellation and the client perceives the new geometrical arrangement as coherent. Finally, the client has time to absorb the rearranged scene, which, in turn, can lead to new insights, relationships and actions in response to the relations themselves.

One of the fascinating aspects of constellations is the importance of placing physical bodies in relation to each other in space. Over and over again, the system that representatives embody "catches fire" within them, and they report suddenly feeling something outside their own experience that relates to an element of the system or story they are representing. Through physical placement, constellation processes ignite representatives' embodied, affective experiences that reliably match the corresponding elements of a relational system, or the relevant parts of a client's story. Perhaps this phenomenon is less perplexing when we recall the scientific findings that debunk the two myths of separateness discussed earlier, the myth of separateness of mind and body and the myth of separateness of human beings. As we have seen, though we speak of feelings and rational thinking as if they are mutually exclusive, nothing could be further from the scientific truth. Woven tightly together in the finest of cerebral tapestries, effective negotiators and smart decision-makers do not see them as separate. Similarly, though we imagine ourselves as contained individuals, mirror neurons and other relational processes mean that we cannot shut our minds and bodies off from those around us.

Increasingly, systemic constellation work is being used in a range of settings, from organizational development to family therapy. Both of us have experienced it, and felt its potency to ignite understanding. Here is an account from one of us of a first encounter with it:

I had heard about constellation practice in Europe and was keen to see how the practice worked in action. A friend of mine told me about a constellation session where I could offer to be a representative in a constellation. Intrigued and excited, I went along. After a short introduction by the constellation host, we got started. The first client outlined her situation very briefly and then was invited to select representatives. As the second person to be selected, I was placed in a particular position in the room. I was a little nervous; I still didn't really know what was expected of me. Everyone said not to worry; just to embrace it...but I wasn't feeling really comfortable. Once all the representatives had been placed, the client hesitated. "She's not right", she said pointing at me, "Can I swap her?" It turns out that I was so consumed with my own performance that I had forgotten to inhabit my body and maintain my open and curious focus on the constellation. The client was absolutely correct—I was all wrong. Yet how could she know? Sheepishly, I went and sat down again. Someone next to me whispered that she had never seen a representative be replaced before. I wanted to disappear beneath the floor.

As the first constellation unfolded, I soon forgot myself and I was drawn deeply into its process. I saw vividly that constellation work asks us to be exquisitely present in our bodies and to our intuition, clearing our minds and hearts as we make ourselves available to the process.

Next time around, I was given another chance to be a representative. This time I was ready: relaxed, aware, and breathing deeply. At first we were told nothing about the client's situation, yet when asked what I was feeling, I could immediately talk about my physical sensations and the accompanying feelings of rejection and isolation that I was experiencing as a representative. "Yes", the client chimed in, "that's because of this incident and that relationship." How could I have known? It was as if I had breathed in spaciousness and embraced my porosity, thereby enhancing my capacity to connect with the process of calcinatio and inhabit a collective tableau. The constellation host invited the client to reposition me in the space; she came and guided me to another position with her hand on my back, this time not standing but sitting. The kinesthetic impact was immediate and powerful. It felt amazingly different. I could hardly believe how the dynamic we were inhabiting had caught fire amongst us. As a fire burns through a forest, the constellation took on its own shape, showing itself as system that could shift in space and time. When we had finished, I could not explain the transformation that had occurred. The client reported that the changes made gave her many insights into how to work with the real situation; it was as if the foliage had been stripped away and she could see the underlying structure of the forest more clearly.

According to Insa Sparrer, the key to transformation in physical constellations may be something pre-verbal, in line with scientific hypotheses presented earlier. Sparrer goes even further, suggesting that this pre-verbal something is somehow known collectively, even though this knowledge cannot be formulated verbally. Thus, it "catches" and is shared amongst us without conscious awareness, another illustration of *calcinatio*. Sparrer calls this phenomenon transverbal language and explains that it exists among representatives, and therefore goes beyond verbal and non-verbal language of individuals. It is not just about relational inter-representative insights, she explains; it is about relational systems as a whole, always more than the sum of their parts. While representatives may be asked how they are feeling and how rearrangements of the spatial geometry affect them, the perceptions they report relate to the client's situation rather than the representatives' subjective experiences. Somehow, in taking on the shape of the story, they literally inhabit it, in all of its affective, sensory dimensions. Constellation work makes the embodied wisdom of the collective accessible for the benefit of another (Sparrer 2007).

Applications for Reflexive Negotiation Practice

In addition to the constellation work described above, here are some other ways negotiators may infuse their work with the wisdom of *calcinatio*:

- Befriend anger in yourself and learn to relate to it, rather than resisting or retaliating when it is expressed by others. In three decades of training negotiators, we have become convinced that problems relating to anger thwart processes in multiple ways that could be ameliorated by this work;
- Learn to assess when the *calcinatio* property needed is a floodlight (to illuminate all corners of an issue) and when it is a candle (to softly, deftly move through tender terrain.) Both forms of calcinatio are powerful;

- Work within narrative and process redlines, or zones of safety, to prevent the destructive power of *calcinatio* from blocking or destroying negotiation progress.

Conclusion

As we have seen, the use of systemic constellations is one way to come closer to the ineffable gaps we have been discussing and, therefore, closer to alchemy. It literally offers a bridge between what we conventionally understand as knowable and unknowable. Further, it brings all of the elements together. While we have foregrounded its kinetic and illuminating *calcinatio* properties, constellation work literally involves finding new forms (*coagulatio*) that bring to the surface patterns that were previously invisible (*sublimatio*) and that dissolve preconceptions, initiating a new flow of understanding (*solutio*). Because the nascent work of constellations is just developing, there is much that is unknown. As such, it is an apt comparator for alchemy: both stress the imperatives of enactment and embracing mystery.

As constellation work demonstrates, we have the ability to move beyond metaphors and literally put ourselves in another negotiator's shoes. But it is more than this: we have the capacity to enter a collective embodied space, drawing on all four of the alchemical processes. So the self finds itself in the other and then connects to the wider contextual world in effortless and immediate transformation.

While our alchemical exploration ends here, there are many more applications to negotiation and conflict engagement that can be imagined. When a situation feels too hot (too much fire), we ask ourselves how properties associated with water might cool it down. If a negotiation feels as though it is wandering and off track (too much air), we consider how to bring more of the earth element into our midst. When things seem stuck (too much earth), we consider how to increase airy spaciousness, whether by taking a break or shifting focus. And when things are uncomfortably opaque or murky (too much water), we find ways to invoke the clarity of fire by breaking them into component parts or finding new ways to name our experiences.

The ancient process of alchemy, endlessly transforming earth, water, air and fire, offers us a dynamic understanding of negotiation practice that points the way to virtuosity and increased pleasure in processes, and to more satisfying, full-spectrum outcomes. As alchemy was used by Jung to refer to individuation, so it provides inspiration for negotiators to be alive to combinations of elements in ways that import multi-dimensional possibilities into negotiation.

Notes

[1] See also Phyllis Bernard (2013) as to the relationship between *Ubuntu* and the concept of *muntu*: "ubuntu translates the ineffable, transcendent muntu into understandable social norms that reinforce the bonds of the life force among community mem-

bers" (Bernard 2013: 177). In other words, negotiating from an awareness of Ubuntu is a way to coagulate connection.

References

Accattatis, M. 2014. *Music, Violence, and Militarism: A Study on the Reflexivity of Culture*. New Jersey: Rutgers University.

Alexander, N., J. Howieson and K. Fox. 2015. *Negotiation: Strategy, Style, Skill*. Sydney: Lexis Nexis 2015.

Ball, P. 2004. *The Elements: A Very Short Introduction*. Oxford: Oxford University Press.

Bache, C. M. 2000. *Dark Night, Early Dawn: Steps to a Deep Ecology of Mind*. New York: State University of New York Press.

Beausoleil, E. and M. LeBaron. 2013. What Moves Us: Dance and Neuroscience Implications for Conflict Approaches. *Conflict Resolution Quarterly* 31(2): 133-158.

Bernard, P. 2013. Muntu meets Mencius: Can Ancient Principles Guide Modern Negotiations on the Export of Africa's Natural Resources to China? In *Educating Negotiators for a Connected World*, edited by C. Honeyman, J. Coben and A. W.-M. Lee. St. Paul, MN: DRI Press.

Cockren, A. 2016. History of Alchemy. Available online at http://www.alchemylab.com/history_of_alchemy.htm (last accessed August 9, 2016).

Conniff, R. 2014. Alchemy May Not Have Been the Pseudoscience We All Thought It Was. *Smithsonian Magazine, February 14*. Available online at http://www.smithsonianmag.com/science-nature/alchemy-may-not-been-pseudoscience-we-thought-it-was-180949430/?no-ist (last accessed May 2, 2016).

Damasio, A and H. Damasio. 1994. Cortical Systems for Retrieval of Concrete Knowledge: The Convergence Zone Framework. In *Large-Scale Neuronal Theories of the Brain*, edited by C. Koch and J. L. Davis. Cambridge, MA: Massachusetts Institute of Technology.

Damasio, A. 1994. *Descartes' Error: Emotion, Reason, and the Human Brain*. New York: Putnam.

Gerhart, G. M. and C. L. Glaser. 2010. *From Protest to Challenge: A Documentary History of African Politics in South Africa, 1882-1990, Volume 6 — Challenge and Victory, 1980-1990*. Bloomington, IN: Indiana University Press.

Goleman, D. 2006. *Social Intelligence: The New Science of Human Relationships*. New York: Bantam Books.

Goodman, D. 2014. The Tapestry Model: Exploring Social Identities, Privilege, and Oppression from an Intersectional Perspective. In *Intersectionality & Higher Education: Theory, Research & Praxis*, edited by D. Mitchell (Jr.), C. Y. Simmons and L. A. Greyerbiehl. New York: Peter Lang Publishing.

Gurmet, P. 2004. "Sowa – Rigpa": Himalayan Art of Healing. *Indian Journal of Traditional Knowledge* 3(2): 212-218.

Honeyman, C. and R. Parish. 2013. Choreography of Negotiation: Movement in Three Acts. In *Choreography of Resolution: Conflict, Movement and Neuroscience*, edited by M. LeBaron, C. MacLeod and A. F. Acland. Washington, DC: American Bar Association.

Isaacs, W. 1999. *Dialogue: The Art of Thinking Together*. New York: Random House, Inc.

Jung, C. G. 1966. *Two Essays in Analytical Psychology, Volume 7: The Complete Works of C. G. Jung*, edited and translated by G. Adler and R. F. C. Hull. Princeton, NJ: Princeton University Press.

Jung, C. G. 1980. *Psychology and Alchemy, Volume 12: The Collected Works of C.G. Jung*, edited and translated by G. Adler and R. F. C. Hull. Princeton, NJ: Princeton University Press.

LeBaron, M., C. MacLeod and A. F. Acland. 2013. *The Choreography of Resolution*. Chicago, IL: American Bar Association.

Lifton, R. J. 1993. *The Protean Self: Human Resilience in an Age of Fragmentation*. Chicago, IL: The University of Chicago Press.

Lipton, B. H. 2008. *The Biology of Belief: Unleashing the Power of the Consciousness Matter & Miracles*. United Kingdom: Hay House, Inc.

O'Donoghue, J. 2003. *Divine Beauty: The Invisible Embrace*. Great Britain: Bantam Press.

Palmer, W. 2016. *Search Outside Yourself*. Leadership Embodiment: Embody Possibilities. Available online at http://www.embodimentinternational.com/search-outside-yourself-by-wendy-palmer/ (last accessed August 5, 2016).

Pörksen, B. and F. Schultz von Thun. 2014. *Kommunikation als Lebenskunst: Philosophie und Praxis des Miteinander-Redens*. Heidelberg: Carl-Auer Verlag.

Richards, M. C. 1998. Separating and Connecting: The Vessel and the Fire. In *The Fabric of the Future: Women Visionaries Illuminate the Pathways to Tomorrow*, edited by M. J. Ryan. Berkeley, CA: Conari Press.

Ringer, J. 2006. *Unlikely Teachers. Finding the Hidden Gifts in Daily Conflict*. Portsmouth, NH: OnePoint Press.

Sachs, A. 1998. Preparing Ourselves For Freedom. In *Writing South Africa: Literature, Apartheid, and Democracy*, 1970-1995, edited by D. Attridge and R. Jolly. Cambridge, UK: Cambridge University Press.

Sachs, A. 2010. Keynote Address, *National Mediation Conference*. Adelaide, Australia.

Sparrer, I. 2007. *Miracle, Solution and System: Solution-Focused Systemic Structural Constellations for Therapy and Organizational Change*, translated by S. W. F. Onn. Cheltenham, UK: Solutions Books.

Wijeyesinghe, C. L. and S. Jones. 2014. Intersectionality, Identity, and Systems of Power and Inequality. In *Intersectionality & Higher Education: Theory, Research, and Praxis*, edited by D. Mitchell (Jr), C. Y. Simmons and L. A. Greyerbiehl. New York: Peter Lang Publishing.

Wood, K. 2015. The Arts and Peacebuilding: An Emerging Approach. *United States Institute of Peace: Making Peace Possible*. Available online at http://www.usip.org/insights-newsletter/the-arts-and-peacebuilding-emerging-approach (last accessed August 5, 2016).

Negotiation as Law's Shadow:
On the Jurisprudence of Roger Fisher

Amy J. Cohen

Editors' Note: The author reviews the life work of one of negotiation's most famous scholars, and reveals a wholly new observation. Roger Fisher, she argues, did not understand negotiation as primarily something that happens in the shadow of the law. Rather, based on his years thinking about international conflict, Fisher offered a theory of negotiation as a form of legal ordering and, by extension, a theory of law as a form of negotiation—one with enduring relevance for dispute resolution today.

The *Physician's Desk Reference* provides medical practitioners with important contextual information, such as regulatory warnings, indications and contraindications, about the prescriptions they dispense to people in the world. This contribution to the *Negotiator's Desk Reference* follows suit. There is perhaps no more influential negotiation practitioner—with no more set of influential negotiation diagnoses and prescriptions—than Roger Fisher. Fisher's classic, *Getting to Yes*, co-authored with William Ury, has a circulation in the millions in more than 30 languages (Wheeler and Waters 2006). And as Fisher made clear in a response to a criticism of the book, he is far more concerned with "what intelligent people ought to do than with 'the way the world is'" (Fisher 1984: 120). That is, Fisher dispenses prescriptions, leaving it to others to make visible some of the embedded assumptions and normative commitments that underlie his advice—that is, to provide an expla-

Amy J. Cohen is professor of law at the Ohio State University Moritz College of Law, where she studies informal and formal dispute resolution, law and economic development, and the political economy of food. She is currently writing about negotiations in Indian food supply chains in the shadow of supermarket restructuring. Cohen has held visiting professorships at Harvard Law School, Osgoode Hall Law School, the University of Turin, and the West Bengal National University of Juridical Sciences, and fellowships from the Radcliffe Institute for Advanced Study, the Fulbright Program, and the American Institute of Indian Studies.

nation of the chemical constitution of the remedies on offer, if I may draw out this desk reference analogy just a bit more.

In the spirit of a reference work that aims to enable practitioners to consider when, why and under what conditions they should dispense a particular prescription, this short essay describes one foundational element of Fisher's negotiation advice. This element, perhaps surprisingly, is Fisher's theory of the function and purpose of law. Fisher, we shall see, understood negotiation as a form of legal ordering. What I thus call Fisher's "jurisprudence of negotiation" should help practitioners evaluate the normative desirability of negotiation—at least as Fisher understood it—not simply as a set of skills and techniques but rather as a kind of legal process applied to private and public conflicts across local, national, and transnational scales.

So what does Roger Fisher, an international lawyer and law professor as much as a world-famous theorist and practitioner of negotiation, think about law? From simply reading *Getting to Yes*, one might conclude that he thought about it very little. In *Getting to Yes*, law features in brief and sporadic ways. When Fisher and Ury describe objective criteria, they list "what a court would decide" alongside market value, scientific judgment, and tradition (Fisher, Ury, and Patton 1991: 85). What law is and whether it is a special or distinct criterion is not discussed. To the contrary, the list presents law as simply one tool among many—coequal with the market, various sources of authority, and private norms. Fisher's earlier work, however, suggests that he had an explicit theory of law as a special approach to conflict resolution—a theory left implicit in his later writings, but that, I argue, informed his practices of negotiation in important and intrinsic ways.

To make sense of how Fisher's theory of law evolved, it is worth revisiting some of the international jurisprudential debates of the 1960s of which Fisher was a part. Like many international legal scholars of his day, Fisher engaged a pressing legal question: why do states comply with law? To answer this question, he began by rejecting John Austin's classic theory of law as a command of the sovereign backed by force (Austin 1873; Fisher 1961: 1131). The Austinian view was marshaled by legal scholars who argued that international law is not "real" law that demands compliance. In a 1961 *Harvard Law Review* article, "Bringing Law to Bear on Governments," Fisher claimed it was "woolly thinking" to draw a sharp distinction between domestic law as real and international law as not. He argued that in practice, states regularly limit themselves via legal rules even in the absence of compelling sovereign force. This is because, Fisher ventured, of a mix of rational incentives and a moral commitment or belief in law. Law, he concluded, affects what states do when it serves states' interests and instantiates their beliefs.

At the same time, however, Fisher also challenged the realist international relations approach of Myres McDougal as overemphasizing or collapsing law into state policy (Fisher 1962). McDougal, Fisher's contemporary at Yale Law School, argued for a policy-oriented approach to international law that understood law not as a set of neutral rules and doctrines but rather as an authoritative form of decision-making used by states to advance particular values and policy ends (see, e.g., McDougal 1956). Fisher challenged this approach on intriguing and instrumental grounds. In his 1964 book chapter, "Intervention: Three Problems of Policy and Law," Fisher claimed that "the very question of how one ought to perceive the relationship between international law and international policy is itself a matter of policy" (Fisher 1964b: 3). He proceeded to argue that it is bad policy to order a world where anything that appears desirable as a matter of state policy could be law, as he read McDougal to argue. Instead, Fisher thought it better to preserve what he called a "non-McDougal" and more traditional, limited approach to law (Fisher 1964b: 4-5). If, as Fisher argued, the aim of an international lawyer is to persuade governments of what they ought to do, we should proceed *"as though"* law is a distinctive good with certain independent objective force (Fisher 1964b, 4; emphasis added).

For Fisher, law as a distinctive good (whether "as though" or real) made it a special problem-solving tool. Fisher explained that he rejected a rather technical instrumentalist idea of law as merely a means to a-chieve the statesman's ends, whatever they are. To the contrary, he thought law should help to shape the statesman's ends in the first instance. Our desires, he explained, are informed by what is considered lawful and thus legitimate: "goals are to be formulated, not found" and "law provides . . . a model of what it is that a statesman really ought to want" (Fisher 1979: 476).

So what is this model that the statesman ought to want and that law in a unique way provides? The answer in Fisher's words is: "a functioning system for coping with disputes before they become crises" (Fisher 1978: 22). In other words, Fisher argued that the ultimate expressive function of law is both popular and official faith in a system of procedural restraints as the best way to deal with conflict. (For more detail, he laid out these arguments in his 1969 book *International Conflict for Beginners*, with more added in his 1979 article "International Law: A Toolbox for the Statesman.")

Indeed, throughout his writing Fisher stressed that the special and distinct value of law was procedural, not substantive (and he didn't agonize much about drawing a process/substance distinction). Law does not solve substantive problems, he argued, it creates systems to manage them. For example, he wrote that "criminal law does not end crime; contract law does not stop broken contracts; tort law does not stop auto accidents. Law is not a way of ending problems, it is an orderly way of dealing with them" (Fisher 1979: 478-479). And likewise, "law is not a substitute for politics but rather a way of organizing social forces just as the rules of football are not a substitute for sporting skills but a way of structuring the contest. More fundamentally, law is not a way of bringing about an end to mistakes, disputes, misconduct, or crime; it is simply an orderly way of coping with such ills" (Fisher 1978: 24). It was in this sense that Fisher would conclude that "the best political strategy [for managing conflict] turns out to be a legal strategy" (Fisher 1979: 483).

There's more. As we have seen, like other legal scholars influenced by pragmatist and legal process ideas, Fisher described the distinctiveness of law as its procedural capacity for managing social problems. But he also saw in law a particular kind of pragmatic procedure. He argued that adjudication and the case method required what he called fractionation—that is, breaking up large and highly charged ideological claims into their "smallest components and dealing with them one at a time" (Fisher 1964a: 103). He argued in a 1964 article "Fractionating Conflict," that "little issues can be adjudicated," but big issues—that is, issues like democracy and communism, colonialism and independence—cannot (ibid., 91). Thus he wrote: "Viewed from this perspective, adjudication appears not as a process for settling big conflicts, but rather as one that is valuable because it tends to fragment conflict situations by cutting off and serving up for decision one small issue at a time" (ibid., 92). On the international plane, where states may not be bound by any compulsory form of adjudication, Fisher argued that the overarching task of the international lawyer is to persuade state actors to engage in a system of negotiation that is analogous to adjudication—a "system that can handle problems and make little disputes out of what might be big disputes" (Fisher 1979: 478). In practice, he explained, this could involve transforming a dispute that appears to be about ideology into discrete economic questions, or this could involve reframing disputes as not between nation states but rather as sets of smaller more discrete problems among different individuals, corporations, and other non-state actors—in a sense, privatizing conflict to make it easier to resolve.

At the same time, however, Fisher stressed that in negotiation, *just like in adjudication*, actors would not abandon their principles, but rather would use them to persuade others of their positions and work out accommodations among them. He wasn't particularly interested in questions of either legal indeterminacy or legal truth; he presumed there would always be conflicts of interest, conflicts of authority, and conflicts of ideology—the point was to manage these conflicts by designing a better process (see Alberstein 2002). Note that from this perspective there is no significant qualitative difference between international and domestic legal systems: both processes involve fractionating conflicts into component parts and then using principles to adjust and accommodate these parts. And perhaps more important, there is no significant qualitative difference between adjudication and *negotiation*.

Indeed, Fisher's early work on law and negotiation includes a rather striking and prescient transgression of the public/private divide. He saw public as much as private problems through a world of negotiation and mediation where consensual accommodations, adjustments, and agreements are the most practicable and desirable legal approach. Thus he opened *Getting to Yes* by talking about families, employees, businesses, consumers, and nations as entities that could all be sensibly lumped together in the same sentence for negotiation advice (Fisher, Ury and Patton 1991). But unlike other dispute resolution luminaries who were similarly challenging the public/private divide—Robert Mnookin's work around the same time is especially important—Fisher did not offer a theory of negotiation in the shadow of law (Mnookin and Kornhauser 1979). Nor did he offer a theory of a negotiated order without law (Ellickson 1991). Rather, based on his years thinking about international conflict, Fisher offered a theory of negotiation as a form of law and, by extension, a procedural theory of law as a form of negotiation—and one that was applicable to the most pressing problems of the day.

If this reading is correct, it has some important implications. Around the same time that Fisher and Ury wrote *Getting to Yes*, within the legal academy the field of negotiation and alternative dispute resolution (ADR) took a different turn. In response to the exigencies of civil justice and court reform at home rather than international crises abroad, ADR scholars came to speak in a different register—namely the Lon Fuller (1971; 1978) and Frank Sander (Sander and Goldberg 1994) inspired language of fitting the forum to the fuss. In this register, ADR scholars could more easily accept the conceptual premises of a critic like Owen Fiss, (1984; see also Cohen 2009) who claimed that there were *huge* institutional differences between adjudication and negotiation. In response, many ADR scholars offered to specify the conditions under which courts remained superior to ADR, and characteristically endorsed adjudication for conflicts deemed to involve the public's interest (see, e.g., Menkel-Meadow 1985; Susskind and Cruikshank 1987; Ury, Brett, and Goldberg 1988). ADR scholars thus wrested negotiation away from Fisher's rather grand if also workmanlike vision and returned it to a more modest, private sphere.

Today, these impulses are changing. This is in part because of the complementary work that is happening outside the field of ADR, positioning negotiation as a tool of public governance—for example deliberative democracy (see, e.g., Mansbridge 2009; see also Menkel-Meadow 2004) and democratic experimentalism (see, e.g., Dorf and Sabel 1998; Simon 2004) [See NDR: Adler, *Negotiating Facts*]. But there is also a shift that is bubbling up from the core, as negotiation theorists increasingly turn their sights to rapidly evolving and expanding fields such as consensus building (see, e.g., Susskind and Cruikshank 2006) and dispute systems design (see, e.g., Rogers et al. 2013). [NDR: Amsler, *Systems Design*] Or to put this point another way, in a world where states now share power with transnational corporations and social movements, and where problems regularly cross jurisdictional boundaries that defy sovereign control, negotiation is not simply a question of how individuals can pursue wealth-maximizing trades against the backdrop of preexisting legal rules. It is its own field and practice of legal governance (Cohen 2008). Practitioners may thus wish to consider whether they view negotiation strategies as normatively desirable regulatory and legal practices rather than simply neutral or apolitical tools. And if they do so, why? Revisiting Fisher's early jurisprudence suggests that negotiation, at least as Fisher defined it, embodies a particular understanding of the function and purpose of *law*: one that is highly procedural and that actively encourages the fragmentation of large or complete or incommensurable claims. This understanding is one that practitioners may or may not find compelling given the distributional questions and bargaining inequalities before them, but it is one that, following Fisher, they will likely increasingly engage and reproduce. Today, rather than negotiation in the shadow of the law we often have negotiation as law's shadow.

References

Alberstein, M. 2002. *Pragmatism and Law: From Philosophy to Dispute Resolution.* Burlington, VT: Dartmouth.

Austin, J. 1873. *Lectures on Jurisprudence, or, The Philosophy of Positive Law,* (ed. R. Campbell) London: J. Murray.

Cohen, A. J. 2008. Negotiation, Meet New Governance: Interests, Skills, and Selves. *Law and Social Inquiry* 33(2): 501-562.

Cohen, A. J. 2009. Revisiting *Against Settlement*: Some Reflections on Dispute Resolution and Public Values. *Fordham Law Review* 78(3): 1143-1170.

Dorf, M. C. and C. F. Sabel. 1998. A Constitution of Democratic Experimentalism. *Columbia Law Review* 98(2): 267-463.

Ellickson, R. C. *1991. Order Without Law: How Neighbors Settle Disputes.* Cambridge, MA: Harvard University Press.

Fisher, R. 1961. Bringing Law to Bear on Governments. *Harvard Law Review* 74(6): 1130-1140.

Fisher, R. 1962. Law and Policy in International Decisions. *Science* 135: 658-660.

Fisher, R. 1964a. Fractionating Conflict. In *International Conflict and Behavioral Science,* edited by R. Fisher. New York: Basic Books, Inc.

Fisher, R. 1964b. Intervention: Three Problems of Policy and Law. In *Essays on Intervention,* edited by R. J. Stanger. Ohio State University Press.

Fisher, R. 1969. *International Conflict for Beginners.* New York: Harper & Row.

Fisher, R. 1978. *Points of Choice.* Oxford: Oxford University Press.

Fisher, R. 1979. International Law: A Toolbox for the Statesman. *California Western International Law Journal* 9: 472-484.

Fisher, R. 1984. Comment on "The Pros and Cons of Getting to Yes." *Journal of Legal Education* 34: 120-124.

Fisher, R., W. Ury and B. Patton. 1991. *Getting to Yes: Negotiating Agreement Without Giving In,* 2nd ed. New York: Penguin.

Fiss, O. W. 1984. Against Settlement. *Yale Law Journal* 93(6): 1073-1090.

Fuller, L. L. 1978. The Forms and Limits of Adjudication. *Harvard Law Review* 92(2): 353-409.

Fuller, L. L. 1971. Mediation—Its Forms and Functions. *Southern California Law Review* 44(2): 305-339.

Mansbridge, J. 2009. *Deliberative and Non-Deliberative Negotiations.* Cambridge, MA: Harvard University, John F. Kennedy School of Government.

McDougal, M. S. 1956. Law as a Process of Decision: A Policy-Oriented Approach to Legal Study. *Natural Law Forum* 1(1): 53-72.

Menkel-Meadow, C. 1985. For and Against Settlement: Uses and Abuses of the Mandatory Settlement Conference. *UCLA Law Review* 33: 485-514.

Menkel-Meadow, C. 2004. The Lawyer's Role(s) in Deliberative Democracy, *Nevada Law Journal* 5: 347-369.

Mnookin, R. H. and L. Kornhauser. 1979. Bargaining in the Shadow of the Law: The Case of Divorce. *Yale Law Journal* 88(5): 950-997.

Rogers, N. H., R. Bordone, F. E. A. Sander and C.A. McEwen. 2013. *Designing Systems and Processes for Managing Disputes*. New York: Walters Kluwer Law & Business.

Sander, F. E. A. and S. B. Goldberg. 1994. Fitting the Forum to the Fuss: A User-Friendly Guide to Selecting an ADR Procedure. *Negotiation Journal* 10(1): 49-68.

Simon, W. H. 2004. Solving Problems vs. Claiming Rights: The Pragmatist Challenge to Legal Liberalism. *William and Mary Law Review* 46: 127-212.

Susskind, L. E. and J. L. Cruikshank. 1987. *Breaking the Impasse: Consensual Approaches to Resolving Public Disputes*. New York: Basic Books.

Susskind, L. E. and J. L. Cruikshank. 2006. *Breaking Robert's Rules: The New Way to Run Your Meeting, Build Consensus, and Get Results*. New York: Oxford University Press.

Ury, W. L., J. M. Brett and S. B. Goldberg. 1988. *Getting Disputes Resolved: Designing Systems to Cut the Costs of Conflict*. San Francisco: Jossey-Bass.

Wheeler, M. and M. J. Waters. 2006. The Origins of a Classic: Getting to Yes Turns Twenty-Five. *Harvard Negotiation Law Review* 22(4): 475-481.

๛ 58 ๛

Taming the Jungle of Negotiation Theories

John Lande

Editors' Note: Is there such a thing as a generally reliable theory of negotiation? Is there even a coherent definition of what negotiation is? And if not, how are we to make sense of a field that produces so many examples in so many settings? Lande has studied a wide variety of texts and sources, and sets out to pull them into, if not a single coherent range, at least a recognizable matrix.

You are probably familiar with the fable of the seven blind men and the elephant. Each man touches a different part of the elephant, such as the trunk, tusk, or ear, and is convinced that he knows the true nature of the beast. Of course, the moral of the story is that the whole animal reflects a combination of all their perspectives.

Theoretical analysis of negotiation is like seven tribes describing animals in a jungle ecosystem. Unlike a single elephant species, negotiation ranges from children swapping toys on a playground to lengthy multi-national processes producing detailed treaties—and everything in between. Unlike a small number of individuals describing elephants, there are numerous negotiation theorists who belong to various disciplines including anthropology, business, communication, crisis intervention, economics, labor, law, international relations, organizational behavior, political science, psychology, and sociology, among others. Although there are different disciplinary "tribes," they "intermarry" so that negotiation theory in any of the disciplines includes features of others.

This chapter surveys theoretical literature about negotiation from various disciplines to identify the range of issues they address. I surveyed recent books that focused specifically on negotiation, excluding books

John Lande is the Isidor Loeb Professor Emeritus at the University of Missouri School of Law and former director of its LLM Program in Dispute Resolution. He received his J.D. from Hastings College of Law and his Ph.D in sociology from the University of WisconsinMadison. He began mediating in 1982 in California. His work focuses on dispute systems design and legal education, and he has been honored by the CPR Institute. The ABA published the second edition of his book *Lawyering with Planned Early Negotiation: How You Can Get Good Results for Clients and Make Money.*

that were primarily practice guides. This chapter does not include all significant issues or analyze any of the issues in detail, but I hope it is a useful way to explain why the whole field looks so different to different people, and will provide a summary of major issues addressed by contemporary negotiation theorists.

This chapter demonstrates that, although there is considerable overlap between the texts, there is nothing approaching a consensus about the structure and content of negotiation theory or even a definition of negotiation. (Of course, the book this chapter appears in might be viewed as an attempt, at least, at a truly rounded view.) Even in the thirteen books I reviewed that were devoted to negotiation generally, including eight legal texts, the structure and content varied dramatically. Table 1 is a general framework synthesizing the content of the books in this survey and it provides an outline for this chapter.

In General
- Definition of Negotiation
- Disputes, Transactions, and Decision Making
- Complexity, Uncertainty, and Risk
- Theoretical Perspectives

Negotiation Structure and Process
- Motivations, Goals, and Interests
- Negotiation Models
- Alternatives to Negotiated Agreement and Bargaining Zone
- Criteria of Success
- Stages of Negotiation
- Negotiation Strategy and Planning
- Information Bargaining
- Escalation, Impasse, and Failure to Agree
- Overcoming Barriers to Agreement
- Legal and Ethical Constraints

Individual Negotiators
- Individual Qualities and Skills
- Identity
- Perception, Cognition, and Emotion

Negotiation Relationships
- In General
- Reputations
- Agents, Teams, and Leadership
- Multiple Parties and Coalitions
- Negotiation Audiences

Negotiation Interactions
- Communication Modes
- Communication Units and Sequences
- Trust
- Fairness and Justice
- Power and Influence

Table 1. General Framework of Negotiation Issues

In General

Definition of Negotiation

Nine of the thirteen general negotiation books included definitions of negotiation (including one book that provided three definitions from different sources). Of these eleven definitions, five indicated that negotiation is interpersonal (i.e., involving two or more people) (Goldman and Rojot 2003; Rau, Sherman and Peppet 2006; Gifford 2007; Korobkin 2014; Lewicki, Saunders and Barry 2015), and five indicated that it involved communication (Goldman and Rojot 2003; Spangle and Isenhart 2003; Rau, Sherman and Peppet 2006; Folberg and Golann 2011; Lewicki, Saunders and Barry 2015). Four books indicated that negotiators were interdependent as they could not achieve their goals without the others (Rau, Sherman and Peppet 2006; Folberg and Golann 2011; Korobkin 2014; Menkel-Meadow, Schneider and Love 2014) and four books indicated that the negotiators had differing interests (Rau, Sherman and Peppet 2006; Carrell and Heavrin 2008; Korobkin 2014; Lewicki, Saunders and Barry 2015). Other definitions stated that negotiation involves matters of common concern (Gifford 2007), reasoned discussion and problem-solving processes (Spangle and Isenhart 2003), shared understandings (Spangle and Isenhart 2003), efforts to reach agreement (Rau, Sherman and Peppet 2006), goals of coordinating behavior or allocating scarce resources (Korobkin 2014) or changing people's relationships with others or objects (Goldman and Rojot 2003).

Some of these factors are trivial or problematic as definitional elements. For example, since people do not negotiate with themselves or negotiate without communicating, it seems unnecessary to include them in a definition. Although people often have differing interests when they negotiate, this is not necessarily the case, such as when they are not aware of each other's interests. Similarly, people may be able to accomplish certain goals without others, but negotiation may enhance the process or outcome. Certainly, negotiation does not always involve reasoned discussion or problem-solving. This analysis shows that there is no general theoretical consensus about the essential nature of negotiation and that some conceptions are problematic.

Disputes, Transactions, and Decision Making

Theorists often distinguish between negotiation of disputes and transactions (Mnookin, Peppet and Tulumello 2000). In a dispute, parties begin negotiation with different claims or understandings about past events. In deal-making, parties seek to make a transaction and typically do not begin the process with claims against each other. Michael Carrell and Christina Heavrin (2008) suggest a third category, decision-making negotiation, where individuals and/or entities jointly decide on a course of action other than resolving disputes or planning transactions.

Complexity, Uncertainty, and Risk

Negotiation is an extremely complex phenomenon. Although the simplest negotiations involve only two individuals, one issue, and a short timeframe, many negotiations involve organizational entities that engage in internal negotiation as well as negotiation with other parties; multiple parties and issues; and processes that last for extended periods. Negotiation involves processes within individual negotiators, social-psychological dynamics between negotiators, and broad contextual factors such as social roles, norms, values, stereotypes, rules, communication media, resource differentials, technical complexity, political situations, stakeholder constituencies, audiences, and epistemologies (Olekalns and Adair 2013).[1]

The complexity of negotiation situations contributes to negotiators' uncertainty. As a result of the complexity, parties have difficulty processing information and emotions, understanding the reality of the situation, and gathering information about counterparts' interests and intentions. Negotiators often use heuristics to simplify their analysis and decision-making (Olekalns and Adair 2013). They may also deal with uncertainty by using formal decision analysis to manage their risks by estimating the likelihood of various outcomes (Mnookin, Peppet and Tulumello 2000).

Theoretical Perspectives

Negotiation theory is derived from multiple disciplines including the following theoretical perspectives. Identity theory is based on symbolic interaction and society's shaping of social behavior. Social interaction theory focuses on individuals' perceptions, expectations, and skills based on symbols, rules, and values. Field theory focuses on systemic forces creating psychological climates affecting individuals' cognition and behavior. Human needs theory asserts that everyone has biological and social needs driven by their emotions and values. Rational choice theory assumes that people's behavior reflects choices driven by desires to maximize gains and minimize losses. Transformation theory analyzes how struggles are fundamentally transformed in the process of conflict. Mutual gains theory grows out of rational choice and human needs theories and posits that negotiators reach agreement because they believe that it is better for them than not reaching agreement (Spangle and Isenhart 2003; Olekalns and Adair 2013). This is not an exhaustive accounting of theories underlying negotiation, but it illustrates the wide range of factors affecting negotiation.

Negotiation Structure and Process

Motivations, Goals, and Interests

The structure of negotiation is defined by the configuration of the negotiators' motives. The basic structure is illustrated by the "dual concerns" model, which analyzes negotiation based on the combination of negotiators' concern for their own outcomes and concern for their counterparts' outcomes. Negotiators use a "contending" strategy when they are highly concerned about their own outcomes and have little concern about counterparts' outcomes. Conversely, they use a "yielding" strategy when they have little concern for their own outcomes and high concern for counterparts' outcomes. They use a "problem-solving" strategy when they are concerned both about their own and counterparts' outcomes. There is "inaction," or no real negotiation, when they are unconcerned about either party's outcomes. A more complex variation of this model contemplates negative interest, i.e., a desire for some harm. This model includes negative approaches identified as martyr, masochist, sado-masochist, sadist, and competitive strategies depending on the combination of the party's concerns. Positive approaches in this model are called altruistic, cooperative, or individualistic corresponding to the yielding, problem-solving, and contending labels (Carnevale and De Dreu 2006).

These orientations reflect the perspective of a single negotiator. The structure becomes more complicated when considering the motivations of counterparties, negotiation agents, team members, leaders, constituents, and audiences, among others.

Peter J. Carnevale and Carsten K. W. De Dreu (2006) developed a taxonomy of five types of motivations. Aspirations are the desired negotiation outcomes. Social motivations are the preferences about distribution of outcomes, as illustrated by the dual concern model. Identity motivations reflect desired images resulting from negotiation, such as being strong or respectable. Epistemic motivations are desires for understanding about the issues and negotiators' interests. Initiation motivation are the motivations at the outset of negotiation. Negotiators often have multiple motivations and the strength and priority of particular motivations may change over time.

Goals are negotiators' conscious and intentional "needs, wants, purposes, desires, predispositions, and motives" (Carnevale and De Dreu 2006: 55). Negotiators have interests, which they may not be aware of or seek to satisfy. For example, negotiators may have an interest in maintaining good relationships with their counterparties but may not recognize or try to satisfy those interests.

Negotiation Models

Much negotiation theory embodies two general models of negotiation based on the dual concern model. Texts often refer to distributive and integrative models, but some use other terms for the same essential concepts. [NDR: Batra, *Integrative & Distributive*] For example, the distributive model sometimes is called positional, zero-sum, competitive, adversarial, or hard negotiation. The integrative model sometimes is called interest-based, win-win, cooperative, problem-solving, or principled negotiation. In the extreme version of the distributive model, "negotiators exchange offers trying to get the best possible outcome for themselves, assume that one side's gain is necessarily the other side's loss, make legal arguments to gain partisan advantage, act tough, and use hard-bargaining tactics to gain advantage over their adversaries." In the ideal version of the integrative model, "negotiators seek outcomes benefitting both parties, explicitly identify their interests, generate numerous options that might satisfy the parties' interests, consider various factors in negotiation (such as the parties' interests, values, and the law), and seek to build cooperative relationships" (Lande 2015: 68). [NDR: Liao, *Style & Culture*]

Some theorists have proposed hybrids or alternatives to the two common models. For example, Charles B. Craver (2012) describes a "competitive/problem-solving" strategy in which negotiators use problem-solving techniques to advance their interests by maximizing the counterparts' satisfaction as long as the negotiators get favorable results for themselves. Lande (2015) describes an "ordinary legal negotiation" approach in which counterpart lawyers seek agreements satisfying both parties based on typical settlement and trial outcomes. I also argue there that the two negotiation models do not fit many situations very well because they posit false dichotomies, assume that component variables are highly correlated, and assume that all negotiators use the same model in a given situation.

Alternatives to a Negotiated Agreement and Bargaining Zone

Negotiators typically evaluate potential agreements by comparing them to possible alternatives to a negotiated agreement (ATNA). Texts typically suggest that negotiators compare offers with the best alternative to a negotiated agreement (BATNA) (Korobkin 2014). This makes sense when negotiators are certain what the alternative would be. For example, if an employee is satisfied with her job and receives another job offer, her BATNA is her current position. When negotiators are not certain about what would happen without an agreement, as normally happens in disputes, they typically compare offers to estimates of their most likely alternative to a negotiated agreement (MLATNA). When considering the risk of unfavorable results, they may consider their worst alternative to a negotiated agreement (WATNA). Negotiators set "reservation points" (or "bottom lines"), which are the limits to what they are willing to agree to. In setting these limits, in addition to considering the ATNAs, negotiators consider factors such as risk tolerance, transaction costs, and tradeoffs with other goals such as interests in relationships, reputation, privacy, or publicity (Lande 2015).

If the negotiators' reservation points overlap, the space between them is known as the "bargaining zone" or "zone of possible agreement." It represents the "cooperative surplus" created by negotiation, which the negotiators allocate between them (Korobkin 2014). The reservation points may change during negotiation as negotiators learn new information and change their assessments: thus the bargaining zone is not a fixed space. Moreover, even if there is a zone of possible agreement, negotiators may not reach agreement if they cannot agree on how to divide the cooperative surplus (Lande 2015).

Criteria of Success

Marc Galanter (1988) identifies three general categories of potential benefits for evaluating the quality of settlements in the legal context, though many of the factors can be adapted in other contexts. The first category involves satisfying parties' preferences in that they choose negotiated agreement over alternatives. The second set of criteria involves saving of time and expense by the parties and the courts. The third set of benefits involves the quality of the outcomes, including that (1) agreements represent intermediate resolutions between parties' initial positions, (2) parties have more knowledge of the facts and their interests than the courts, (3) settlements reflect the parties' norms, which are much broader than legal norms used by courts, (4) parties can invent solutions that courts could not order, (5) parties are more likely to comply with their own agreements than court decisions, and (6) agreements have general effects "radiating" to non-parties. Of course, these do not result in every negotiation, and may be considered in evaluating the success of particular negotiations.

Stages of Negotiation

Many theorists identify specific stages of negotiation, though there is no consensus about the number or content of the stages. Pamela S. Chasek (2001) analyzes stage theories of seven analysts, finding theories ranging from three to eight stages. She places those stages into four categories: diagnosis, formula-building, negotiation of details, and implementation, and proposes a six-stage framework including precipitants to negotiation, issue definition, statements of initial position, drafting or formula building, bargaining over details, and ratification and implementation. Donald G. Gifford (2007) argues that social scientists and legal scholars have found a general pattern of the following four stages: orientation and positioning, exploration of issues, bargaining, and final stage of agreement or termination of negotiation. Instead of defining stages, some theorists focus on "tasks" including assessing the situation, taking positions, making concessions, and closing the deal (Lewicki, Saunders, and Barry 2015). Some writers caution that negotiations often do not follow a regular sequence of stages (Chasek 2001; Gifford 2007).

Negotiation Strategy and Planning

Theorists often analyze strategy in terms of whether to use an integrative or distributive model (Rau, Sherman and Peppet 2006; Gifford 2007). Robert H. Mnookin, Scott R. Peppet, and Andrew S. Tulumello (2000: 227-248) provide a variation of this approach, suggesting that negotiators may choose "net-expected-outcome" and "interest-based" approaches in the same legal negotiation. The net-expected-outcome approach involves increasing the value to the parties, saving transaction costs, taking advantage of differences in parties' interests, and using legal norms and values. The interest-based approach focuses on identifying parties' interests (including some not directly related to the dispute) and relying on non-legal norms.

Roy J. Lewicki, David M. Saunders, and Bruce Barry (2015) define strategy as the overall plan to achieve negotiators' goals. The strategy ideally leads to a planning process, which may include (1) defining the negotiation goals, (2) identifying issues related to the goals, (3) ranking the priority of the issues, (4) defining one's own interests, (5) understanding the alternatives to reaching agreement, (6) understanding the resistance points to further negotiation, (7) analyzing the counterparty's goals and resistance points, (8) setting targets and initial offers, (9) assessing the context of the negotiation, and (10) presenting the issues to the counterparty.

Information Bargaining

Information is needed to understand the subject of the negotiation as well as parties' interests, strategies, priorities, and openness to particular arrangements. Negotiators have varying degrees of "epistemic motivation," i.e., a desire to get an accurate understanding of the situation. Negotiators may especially want information when they feel personally invested in the matter, are in competitive situations, feel weaker than their counterparts, feel uncertain about their knowledge, and will be held accountable (Koning and van Dijk 2013).

Negotiators receive, disclose, and sometimes conceal information. Their approach generally varies depending on whether they are using a competitive or cooperative strategy. When competing, they are likely to gain advantage by learning their counterparts' interests and bottom line, disclosing information that casts doubt about the attractiveness of the counterparts' alternatives to a negotiated agreement, and concealing information that casts doubt on the attractiveness of their own alternatives. When cooperating, negotiators generally are more open about seeking and disclosing information because this enables the negotiators to identify options that create value by trading on differences in interests and priorities (Gifford 2007).

Escalation, Impasse, and Failure to Agree

Negotiators encounter emotional, cognitive, and behavioral barriers to agreement that can lead to escalation of conflict, impasses, and ultimate failure to reach agreement. Specific barriers include negative feelings based on parties' history due to violation of expectations, misunderstandings, distrust, desire for retaliation, conflicting values, unrealistic expectations, lack of negotiation skill, zero-sum assumptions, influence of others, unsatisfied interests, and not feeling "in sync" (Spangle and Isenhart 2003; Druckman and Olekalns 2013).

Daniel Bar-Tal, Eran Halperin, and Ruthie Pliskin (2015) describe dynamics of intractable international conflicts, which sometimes occur in other contexts. When parties suffer through prolonged struggle, they may develop an ideology of conflict reflecting their version of history. This ideology provides an ethos of conflict based on beliefs about victimization, delegitimization of their counterparts, positive self-image, need for security, and the justice of their cause. Parties develop a "culture of conflict" including extensive sharing of the conflict narrative woven into their lives, which may satisfy psychological needs for such things as predictability, safety, identity, mastery, and positive self-esteem, and may be related to strong negative emotions such as fear, hatred, and anger. This configuration of beliefs and emotions contributes to freezing of beliefs, which helps negotiators resist inconsistent information and counter-arguments. In international conflicts, membership in a community of protagonists reinforces the ideology and culture of conflict.

Conflict can escalate though negative perceptions of the counterparts' actions and intentions, perceptions of harm, accusations, distrust of counterparts' statements and ideas, hardening of positions, threats, harassment, attacks, counterattacks, and withdrawal (Spangle and Isenhart 2003).

Negotiators may fail to reach agreement because of differences in definition of the problem, uncertainty, inaccurate information, secrecy, deception, cultural or other misunderstandings, mistrust, overconfidence, demonization of counterparts, inflammatory communication, negative interpersonal "chemistry," hostile negotiation tactics, fear of being perceived as weak, cognitive biases, lack of preparation, ineffective or counterproductive strategies, inability to react effectively to changing situations, power imbalances, dominance of "hard-liners," internal disorganization or conflict within one or more parties, lack of risk-taking spirit, problems arising from principal-agent relationships, lack of hope, unrealistic goals or expectations, lack of mutually acceptable options, insistence on unnecessary demands, high transaction costs, differences in interests regarding timing, lack of sense of urgency or of the historical moment in the conflict, reputational concerns, pressure from others, media coverage (or lack thereof), lack of effective external control mechanisms, failure to use mediators, and ineffectiveness of mediators (Faure 2012; Faure and Zartman 2012).

Overcoming Barriers to Agreement

When negotiators are at an actual or anticipated impasse, they sometimes reach a turning point where they reconceptualize the situation (Druckman and Olekalns 2013). This may not occur until they experience a "hurting stalemate" where negotiation is the only or best "way out." [NDR: Zartman, *Stages*] This requires a credible new idea leading to an "unfreezing" of their perspectives and consideration of alternatives to the status quo. Negotiators' acceptance of the new idea may be facilitated by the counterpart's confidence-building measures, recognition of the costs of continued stalemate, and/or third-party intervention (Bar-Tal, Halperin and Pliskin 2015).

Tactics for overcoming barriers include analyzing outcomes resulting from the failure to agree; understanding the counterparts' background, perspectives, and interests; resisting impulses to react negatively to counterparts' statements and actions; de-escalating emotional interactions; making conciliatory gestures; acknowledging understanding of counterparts' perspectives; giving apologies; building a climate of trust; developing an effective negotiation strategy; identifying benefits from reaching agreement; inviting counterparts to make suggestions; "splitting the difference" and trading concessions ("logrolling"); combining elements into a "package" deal; reaching agreements contingent on specified conditions; making credible threats to withdraw from negotiation; developing suitable mechanisms and incentives promoting performance of agreements; and engaging mediators (Spangle and Isenhart 2003; Folberg and Golann 2011; Cede 2012)

Legal and Ethical Constraints

Laws may affect negotiators' behavior. When legal processes are the alternatives to negotiated agreements, negotiators "bargain in the shadow of the law," influencing what they are willing to accept in negotiation (Mnookin and Kornhauser 1979). The law regulates the ability of agents to enter agreements binding on their principals. In collective bargaining labor negotiations under US law, for example, parties have a legal duty to bargain. Some laws create incentives for negotiation by limiting admissibility in court of statements in negotiation and by allocating litigation expenses following failures to settle. Contract law governs interpretation and enforceability of agreements. In some cases, such as those involving minor children and class action settlements, agreements are enforceable only with judicial approval (Menkel-Meadow, Schneider and Love 2014).

Professional regulation may create additional constraints. Lawyers in the US, for example, are subject to rules establishing duties of diligence and loyalty, requiring lawyers to protect confidentiality of communications with clients, avoiding impermissible conflicts of interest, allocating decision-making responsibility between lawyers and clients, and being truthful with counterparts (Lande 2015). These rules often are referred to as "legal ethics," which are distinct from ethics generally, referring to social standards about right and wrong. Negotiators may seek to comply with ethical duties, community norms, and/or their own consciences (Lewicki, Saunders and Barry 2015). [NDR: Hinshaw, *Ethics*]

Individual Negotiators

Individual Qualities and Skills

Negotiators may use default approaches such as to compete, accommodate, avoid, compromise, or collaborate in negotiation. They may have general dispositions to be more or less "prosocial," trusting, confident, attentive to interpersonal cues, sensitive to threats to their public image, or "Machiavellian" (i.e., cynical about others' motives, selfish, and unwilling to change positions under pressure). Psychologists have identified the "big five" personality factors, which also may affect negotiation: extraversion, agreeableness, conscientiousness, emotional stability, and openness (Lewicki, Saunders and Barry 2015).

General skills that can affect negotiation include cognitive abilities, use of emotional intelligence, perspective-taking ability, and ability to function well in different cultural settings (Lewicki, Saunders and Barry 2015). More specific skills include developing a helpful reputation, preparation, eliciting trust, questioning, listening, managing emotion, displaying integrity, acting courageously, building relationships, using creativity, giving apologies, and exercising power (Spangle and Isenhart 2003; Menkel-Meadow, Schneider and Love 2014). Important skills for professional negotiators include learning clients' needs, interviewing, counseling, and developing good relationships with counterparts (Menkel-Meadow, Schneider and Love 2014; Lande 2015).

Identity

Negotiation may be affected by people's identities defined in terms of demographic characteristics such as gender, race, ethnicity, national origin, religion, and culture. More broadly, people's identities may reflect a wide range of elements in how they think of themselves and how others perceive them, such as age, political identification, sexual orientation, socio-economic level, and educational level. This may be particularly relevant as negotiators identify others as being similar to or different from themselves based on particular characteristics. Some analyses of culture focus on general worldviews and values, such as preferences for individualism or collectivism, egalitarianism or hierarchy, and direct or indirect modes of communication. Perceptions of negotiators may affect factors such as trust, listening, and reciprocity (Folberg and Golann 2011; Menkel-Meadow, Schneider and Love 2014). Professional cultures of professional negotiators may serve as a bridge or cause rifts in negotiation, depending on the perceptions and actions of the counterparts (Sjöstedt 2003).

Perception, Cognition, and Emotion

Negotiators' perceptions of others and the negotiation context affect what issues are negotiated, how they are discussed, and the outcomes reached. Negotiators perceive things through "frames" defining the subject of the negotiation, desired outcomes, process to be used, identity in negotiation, characterization of others, and risks and rewards of various options. Negotiators may conflict because of differences in how they frame the situation such as whether they perceive a conflict in terms of parties' interests, rights, or power. Conflict can aggravate problems in properly processing information. Negotiators make systematic errors due to irrational escalation, failure to consider possible mutual-gain options, "anchoring" their assessments on irrelevant facts, framing of issues positively or negatively, availability of information, perception of the ease or difficulty of negotiation, overconfidence, extrapolation based on limited information, self-serving biases, overvaluation of things negotiators feel that they own, failure to consider others' perspectives, and reactive devaluation of counterparts' ideas (Lewicki, Saunders and Barry 2015).

People's emotions affect negotiation dynamics which, in turn, can affect their emotions. Positive feelings may lead to a positive attitude about counterparts, persistence, use of an integrative approach, and successful negotiation. Conversely, negative feelings may lead to reduction in negotiators' analytical abilities, definition of situations as competitive, retaliation, escalation of conflict, distributive tactics, and unfavorable outcomes. Negotiators are likely to have positive emotions when they believe that negotiation involves fair procedures and when they think that they received favorable outcomes compared with others in their situation. Negotiators are likely to have negative emotions when they feel uncertain, have a competitive mindset, and experience impasse in negotiation (Lewicki, Saunders and Barry 2015).

Negotiation Relationships

In General

Negotiations occur in the context of relationships which may be a major source of conflict in themselves. Before negotiation, parties may or may not have been in a relationship with each other. During negotiation, one or more parties may wish to have (or continue) a relationship in the future. Even when there has been no prior relationship and there is no expectation or desire for a future relationship, the parties are in a relationship during negotiation. Interactions in negotiation may affect the relationship, prompting parties to seek a closer relationship, a cautious relationship, or no continuing relationship.

Relationships can be categorized into four major types (or some combination). Communal relationships, such as in families and tribes, are based on group membership, common identity, and feelings of belonging. Authority relationships involve asymmetric ranking based on status, power, and deference. Equality relationships, such as in teams, involve reciprocity and equality of contributions and distribution. Market relationships involve calculated exchanges of commodities based on cost-benefit analyses. The distinctions between types of relationships reflect differences in parties' motivations and illustrates that many negotiators do not focus solely on market exchanges, as commonly assumed (Lewicki, Saunders and Barry 2015).

Reputations

Negotiators' reputations are "lenses" focusing people's perceptions and expectations of others, which can affect people's emotional reactions and negotiation behaviors. One's reputation is a reflection of others' perceptions of characteristics, behaviors, and accomplishments over time, which may be based on direct experience and/or communications from others. [NDR: Tinsley et al., *Reputation*] Once reputations are set, they can be hard to change, especially negative reputations. Although a person may have a particular reputation with some people, he or she may have a different reputation with others (Lewicki, Saunders and Barry 2015).

Agents, Teams, and Leadership

Principals regularly employ agents, such as lawyers, real estate agents, and government officials, to represent them in negotiation. Agents can provide benefits due to their skills, knowledge, relationships, emotional detachment, and ability to use tactics like good cop-bad cop gambits. Agents and their principals often have somewhat different interests, which can affect negotiation. [NDR: Nolan-Haley, *Agents*] At least in theory, agents have an interest in "shirking," i.e., not working as hard as possible to achieve the principals' goals. Because principals often are aware of this risk, they may incur "agency costs" to monitor and control agents to behave as desired. There is no foolproof way for principals to control their agents, and this dynamic can affect the negotiation process and the net outcome for principals (i.e., the benefits for principals after deducting any agency costs). (Lewicki, Saunders and Barry 2015).

Negotiations sometimes involve teams of individuals representing one or more parties. Typically, there are negotiations within teams ("behind the table"), which may affect the negotiation with other parties ("across the table"). [NDR: Sally et al., *Teams*] Teams use more or less formal methods for reaching decisions, such as voting or processes designed to reach consensus. Group dynamics within teams may affect decisions based on emergent norms and roles. Teams may assign negotiation tasks based on the formal position of team members and/or skills related to particular tasks. Given these phenomena, negotiators may have more uncertainty and challenges when negotiating with a team than with an individual (Goldman and Rojot 2003).

Team leaders may have the authority to make unilateral decisions for their teams but even in those situations, they may seek guidance or support from their teams (Goldman and Rojot 2003). Leaders' effectiveness may depend on their personality, motivation, and ability to rally relevant constituencies to cooperate, as well as the ripeness of situations for negotiation (Rubin 2002).

Multiple Parties and Coalitions

Multi-party negotiations are more complex than two-party negotiations. Increasing the number of parties increases the range of information, perspectives, and interests to be accommodated and decreases the average proportion of time that parties can express themselves. Larger negotiation configurations can make it more difficult to reach agreement in some situations but also can lead to "groupthink" in other situations. An increased number of parties may require additional procedural negotiation to manage the process, and may create additional logistical challenges in convening parties. An increased number of parties complicates the strategic dynamics as parties consider more counterparts' interests and the interaction of parties' strategies. [NDR: Kaufman et al., *Multiparty*] Parties may form coalitions to gain advantage through coordinated action. Coalitions may focus on a specific issue for a limited time and/or focus on a range of issues over an extended time (Lewicki, Saunders and Barry 2015).

Negotiation Audiences

Negotiators' actions may be observed by various audiences who may or may not physically attend negotiations or be directly involved, or give feedback of approval or disapproval. Negotiators' awareness of audiences may affect their behavior, for example by prompting them to seek audience approval by working hard or demonstrating "toughness" (Lewicki, Saunders and Barry 2015).

Negotiation Interactions

Communication Modes

Negotiators communicate through face-to-face communication, postal letters, telephone, conference calls, videoconferences, email, text messages, and software applications. [NDR: Schneider & McCarthy, *Communication Choices*] Face-to-face interaction permits real-time non-verbal communication, including offstage encounters during breaks. Telephonic communication includes audible cues such as tone of voice, inflection, volume, and pauses. Written communication generally lacks non-verbal communication and thus is prone to misunderstandings about sensitive matters and attempted humor. Online communication generally does not lend itself to "small talk" to build rapport, though negotiators who build rapport in advance may promote respect, trust, information-sharing, cooperation, reciprocity, and agreement. Because of the rapid proliferation of multiple communication modes, the choice of mode itself may be a source of difficulty, especially considering that various age cohorts may be more or less comfortable using particular modes (Folberg and Golann 2011).

Communication Units and Sequences

Units of verbal communication can be categorized as substantive, strategic, persuasive, task-related, affective, procedural, attacking, defending, integrating, creating value, claiming value, pushing for closure, managing the process, providing or seeking information, substantiating claims, making offers, reacting, expressing mutuality, clarifying, relating to others, asserting interests, asserting rights, and asserting power, among others. Non-verbal communication can be distinguished in terms of vocal pitch, expressiveness, volume, fluency, engagement, mirroring, and emphasis, as well as body language involving posture, head movement, hand movement, eye gaze, and facial expression. Communication tactics can be combined into reciprocal, complementary, or structural sequences. Reciprocal sequences involve direct matches of counterparts' tactics. Complementary sequences are consistent with their counterparts' moves, but are not exact matches. Structural sequences reflect a shift from the counterparts' moves. More broadly, communication sequences can be analyzed in terms of more or less routine scripts rather than intentional combinations of tactics or sequences (Adair and Loewenstein 2013).

Trust

The level and nature of trust between negotiators can have a major impact on the process and outcome of negotiation. Trust is associated with information sharing, cooperative behavior, good communication, and greater understanding. Integrative negotiation processes are likely to engender more trust than distributive negotiation (Lewicki, Saunders and Barry 2015).

Trust and distrust are distinct and somewhat independent, so it is possible for negotiators to both trust and distrust each other in various ways. [NDR: Lewicki, *Trust*] Trust is confident positive expectations about another's conduct and distrust is confident negative expectations. They may be calculus-based (i.e., based on calculations about likely costs and benefits) or identification-based (i.e., based on compatibility of values, goals, and emotional attachment). The levels of trust and distrust in negotiation may depend on negotiators' general dispositions in trusting others, the history of their relationship, and situational factors. Negotiators may use strategies to manage trust and distrust based on whether they are calculus-based or identification-based. Over time, as negotiators' relationships develop, their orientation of trust (and/or distrust) as calculus-based or identification-based may shift from one to the other (Lewicki, Saunders and Barry 2015).

When trust has been broken between negotiators, they may repair the breach through apologies, reparations, and arrangements to prevent recurrence. Apologies include some or all of the following elements: expression of regret, explanation of the incident, acknowledgment of responsibility, expression of repentance, offer to repair the problem, and request for forgiveness. The effectiveness of apologies in regaining trust may be related to promptness, sincerity, acceptance of responsibility, whether the incident was an isolated event or part of a pattern, and whether the problem was caused by deceptive behavior (Lewicki, Saunders and Barry 2015) [NDR: Brown & Robbenolt, Apology].

Fairness and Justice

Negotiators feel that they are treated fairly when they believe that their counterparts: treat them sincerely and respectfully (interactional justice), provide factually-supported explanations (informational justice), use unbiased and ethical criteria for their demands (procedural justice), and do not make demands that exceed their needs or impose hardships (substantive justice). Negotiators may increase their counterparts' perceptions of being treated fairly by justifying their demands using credible standards of comparison, providing generous offers, listening carefully, using fair procedures, treating them with respect, behaving in trustworthy ways, and offering timely, credible, and sincere accounts. When negotiators feel that their counterparts have treated them unfairly, they may feel distrustful and seek vindication. They may be less likely to negotiate at all, and if they do negotiate, they may be less likely to make concessions, reach agreement, or comply with their agreements (Conlon and Ross 2012) [NDR: Welsh, *Fairness*].

Power and Influence

Negotiators sometimes use power to influence their counterparts to reach a desired agreement. Power is the *potential* to alter counterparts' attitudes and behavior and influence is the *actual effort* to do so. Both concepts are complex and have been conceptualized in multiple ways. Negotiators may have power to coerce counterparts ("power over") and/ or cooperate ("power with"). Actors derive power from information, expertise, ability to dispense rewards and punishments, legitimacy derived from official positions and affiliations, and their personal characteristics. People targeted for influence are likely to act based on their perceptions of the actors' power rather than the actual power. When negotiators have comparable levels of power, they may negotiate more cooperatively than when there are significant disparities. Nonetheless, more powerful parties may limit their use of power so that counterparts will engage in the process, be more satisfied, maintain good relationships, and implement agreements without constant monitoring (Lewicki, Saunders and Barry 2015).

Actors may use a "central route" to influence counterparts or a "peripheral route" to do so less explicitly. The central route involves explicit messages designed to elicit agreement by making attractive offers, framing messages favorably, appealing to accepted norms, and suggesting agreements in principle. [NDR: Shestowsky, *Psychology & Persuasion*] These messages may include rebuttal of counterarguments, "fractionating" arguments into understandable pieces, repetition, vivid language, threats, and encouragement of participation. The peripheral route to influence may be affected by factors such as whether key points are at the beginning or end of statements (rather than the middle), messages are conveyed in an appropriate communication mode, and the presence of distractions. Actors are more likely to influence counterparts if they have credibility because of their qualifications, expertise, reputation for integrity, confident presentation, status, apparent motivations, positive affiliations with others, and persistence. Actors' "attractiveness" can also affect persuasion due to their friendliness, ingratiation, likeability, assistance, perceived similarity, and positive emotional expression. (Or just their good looks, and a perceived rise in one's social status by associating with such good-looking people.) [NDR: O'Connor & Ormiston, *Faces*] Contextual factors may also affect persuasion, such as reciprocity between the negotiators, use of commitment techniques, social validation, perceived scarcity, and rewards and punishments (Lewicki, Saunders and Barry 2015).

Conclusion

Although there is some overlap in coverage and perspectives about negotiation theory between disciplines and individual theorists, there is little overall coherence. Indeed, theorists are even far from a consensus on the definition of negotiation.

This chapter synthesizes a general framework of issues in negotiation theory by stitching together work from multiple disciplines. It provides only brief summaries of key issues, omitting deep analysis of those issues and any discussion of some important issues. (As noted above, however, many of the topics thus lightly treated are the subjects of more detailed analyses elsewhere in this book.) Nonetheless, it provides a general framework that could help provide greater coherence in negotiation theory across disciplines, thus helping the different academic "tribes" to manage problems of the blind men and the elephant and develop more useful theory.

Notes

With the usual disclaimers, I thank Noam Ebner and Rafael Gely for comments on an earlier draft of this chapter.

[1] Many of these categories or topics, as well as others noted briefly throughout this chapter, are the subject of detailed treatment by other contributors—so many, however, that I will not cite all possible references internal to this book, lest the chapter become unreadable. A quick review of the table of contents will alert the reader to many such resources, however.

References

Adair, W. L. and J. Lowenstein. 2013. Talking it Through: Communication Sequences in Negotiation. In *Handbook of Research on Negotiation*, edited by M. Olekalns and W. L. Adair. Cheltenham, UK; Northampton, MA: Edward Elgar.

Bar-Tal, D., E. Halperin and R. Pliskin. 2015. Why Is It So Difficult to Resolve Intractable Conflicts Peacefully? A Sociopsychological Explanation. In *Handbook of International Negotiation: Interpersonal, Intercultural, and Diplomatic Perspectives*, edited by M. Galluccio. Cham: Springer.

Carnevale, P. J. and C. K. W. De Dreu. 2006. Motive: The Negotiator's Raison d'Être. In *Negotiation Theory and Research*, edited by L. L. Thompson. New York: Psychology Press.

Carrell, M. R. and C. Heavrin. 2008. *Negotiating Essentials: Theory, Skills and Practices*. Upper Saddle River, New Jersey: Pearson.

Cede, F. 2012. Failures: Lessons for Practice. In *Unfinished Business: Why International Negotiations Fail*, edited by G. O. Faure, with the assistance of F. Cede. Athens: University of Georgia Press.

Chasek, P. S. 2001. *Earth Negotiations: Analyzing Thirty Years of Environmental Diplomacy*. Tokyo; New York: United Nations University Press.

Conlon, D. E. and W. H. Ross. 2012. The Effect of Perceived / Felt (In)Justice on Cooperativeness: Implications for Negotiators as "Justice-Enhancing Communicators" in an Era of Social Networking. In *The Psychology of Negotiations in the 21st Century Workplace: New Challenges and New Solutions*, edited by B. M. Goldman and D. L. Shapiro. New York: Routledge.

Craver, C. B. 2012. *Effective Legal Negotiation and Settlement*, 7th edn. Newark, NJ: LexisNexis/Matthew Bender.

Druckman, D. and M. Olekalns. 2013. Punctuated Negotiations: Transitions, Interruptions, and Turning Points. In *Handbook of Research on Negotiation*, edited by M. Olekalns and W. L. Adair. Northampton, MA: Edward Elgar.

Faure, G. O. 2012. Failures: Lessons for Theory. In *Unfinished Business: Why International Negotiations Fail*, edited by G. O. Faure, with the assistance of F. Cede. Athens: University of Georgia Press.

Faure, G. O. and I. W. Zartman. 2012. Introduction. In *Unfinished Business: Why International Negotiations Fail*, edited by G. O. Faure, with the assistance of F. Cede. Athens: University of Georgia Press.

Folberg, J. and D. Golann. 2011. *Lawyer Negotiation: Theory, Practice, and Law*, 2d edn. New York: Aspen Publishers.

Galanter, M. 1988. The Quality of Settlements. *Journal of Dispute Resolution* 1988: 55-84.

Gifford, D. G. 2007. *Legal Negotiation: Theory and Practice*, 2nd ed. St. Paul, MN: Thomson/West.

Goldman, A. L. and J. Rojot. 2003. *Negotiation: Theory and Practice*. New York: Kluwer Law International.

Koning, L. and E. van Dijk. 2013. Motivated Cognition in Negotiation. In *Handbook of Research on Negotiation*, edited by M. Olekalns and W. L. Adair. Northampton, MA: Edward Elgar.

Korobkin, R. 2014. *Negotiation Theory and Strategy*, 3rd edn. New York: Wolters Kluwer Law & Business.

Lande, J. 2015. *Lawyering with Planned Early Negotiation: How You Can Get Good Results for Clients and Make Money*. 2d edn. Chicago, Illinois: American Bar Association.

Lewicki, R. J., D. M. Saunders and B. Barry. 2015. *Negotiation*, 7th edn. New York, NY: McGraw-Hill/Irwin.

Menkel-Meadow, C. J., A. K. Schneider and L. P. Love. 2006. *Negotiation: Processes for Problem Solving*. New York, NY: Aspen Publishers.

Mnookin, R. H. and L. Kornhauser. 1979. Bargaining in the Shadow of the Law: The Case of Divorce. *Yale Law Journal* 88: 950-997.

Mnookin, R. H., S. R. Peppet and A. S. Tulumello. 2000. *Beyond Winning: Negotiating to Create Value in Deals and Disputes*. Cambridge, MA: Harvard University Press.

Olekalns, Mara and W. L. Adair. 2013. The Complexity of Negotiating: From the Individual to the Context, and What Lies In Between. In *Handbook of Research on Negotiation*, edited by M. Olekalns and W. L. Adair. Northampton, MA: Edward Elgar.

Rau, A. Scott, E. F. Sherman and S. Peppet. 2006. *Negotiation*, 2d edn. New York: Foundation Press/Thomson West.

Rubin, J. Z. 2002. The Actors in Negotiation. In *International Negotiation: Analysis, Approaches, Issues*, 2nd edn. edited by V. A. Kremenyuk. San Francisco: Jossey-Bass.

Sjöstedt, G. 2003. Lessons for Research and Practice. In *Professional Cultures in International Negotiation: Bridge or Rift?*, edited by G. Sjöstedt. Lanham, MD: Lexington Books.

Spangle, M. L. and M. W. Isenhart. 2003. *Negotiation: Communication for Diverse Settings*. Thousand Oaks, CA: Sage.

Section XI: It's a Bit Technical

Section XI addresses the postmodern era of communication, in which hardly anyone with a negotiating proposal to make puts it in a "letter". It begins with a chapter that surveys the confusing panoply of options now available as media and technologies, and outlines a way of making sense of them. Next we move to what has probably become the baseline method of ordinary, day-to-day communication, particularly of components of a negotiation that has yet to be framed in complete documents—i.e., e-mail. Yet texting has now become so routine that even people who don't believe they negotiate by text are likely to, at least as to some procedural issues or fragmentary data or component ideas; this is analyzed in the next chapter. From there, it's a short hop to recognizing that you actually negotiate, or will soon negotiate, through still other technologies; the next two chapters respectively address videoconferencing—by now, almost routine, for many—and an array of less common additional technologies, many of them proprietary.

Two very different groups have particular needs and uses for technology in their negotiations: lawyers, and the young. The final two chapters of this section analyze first lawyers' needs, and how technology is changing their practice, and then, the youngest adult generation—who are such avid users of technology that it is barely possible to reclaim their attention from it.

❧ 59 ❧

Choosing Among Modes of Communication

Andrea Kupfer Schneider & Sean A. McCarthy

Editors' Note: This chapter serves as the overview to all of the chapters on the use of different media and technology as part of negotiation. How do we make sense of all our options? The authors argue that knowing your own "default", while understanding your counterpart and the context, is crucial. Being able to choose wisely among the different modes requires careful consideration of the advantages and disadvantages that go along with each of these.

This chapter can usefully be read in conjunction with Thompson, Ebner, and Giddings on Nonverbal Communication, as well as with the technology chapters—particularly, Ebner's chapters on Email, Texting, and Videoconferencing.

Differences in Modes of Communication

It is helpful to outline the differences between the modes of communication, and then to think about how they operate in a negotiation. First, different modes permit varying levels of social intuition [NDR: Schneider & Ebner, *Social Intuition*] as well as perception of nonverbal language. [NDR: Thompson et al., *Nonverbal*] Face to face conversations are considered media "rich" because they allow tracking of multiple social cues (Barsness and Bhappu 2004; Bhappu and Barsness 2006). In face to face conversations (in person and online via video), you can interpret body

Andrea Kupfer Schneider is a Professor of Law at Marquette University Law School, where she teaches Dispute Resolution, Negotiation, Ethics, and International Conflict Resolution and is the director of Marquette's nationally-ranked dispute resolution program. Professor Schneider is the co-author or editor of more than 10 textbooks in dispute resolution and negotiation. She has also written numerous articles on negotiation skills and styles, dispute system design, international conflict, and gender and negotiation. Professor Schneider received her A.B. cum laude from the Woodrow Wilson School of International Affairs and Public Policy at Princeton University and her J.D. cum laude from Harvard Law School.

Sean McCarthy is an athletic compliance monitoring coordinator at Texas Tech University and a graduate of the University of Minnesota and Marquette University Law School. He is a lifelong fan of the Minnesota Vikings and football guy Mike Zimmer.

language, tone, eye contact, and facial expressions in addition to hearing the content of the conversation. Phone conversations provide some of this; through the tone, pauses, and inflections of even a verbal conversation, we can learn a lot about how the other party is feeling, in addition to the content. Email (or texting), on the other hand, does not incorporate those contextual elements. We will discuss below how to add "e-empathy" to your communication to try to bring that media richness into all of your communications.

The difference between modes of communication is also reflected in the content that comes across. In face to face conversations, the conversation often rapidly switches between the personal and the professional, the mundane (think the weather) and the more on point. In email communications, the content tends to be more task oriented. What do we need to get done? What is the answer to X? This is less personal, unless we take the time in the email (often at the beginning or end, or both) to add the personal touches. We are more trained (at least in U.S. culture) to schmooze automatically at the beginning of a face to face negotiation; this same impulse does not necessarily occur online.

Another noticeable difference is the timing of conversations. Face to face conversations are, by their very nature, synchronous conversations. In other words, both parties are engaged at the same time. Even when one side is talking, the other person is interacting through their body language and responses. Online communication may occur simultaneously, particularly with texting, but only if both parties happen to be on their devices at the same time and choose to engage that way. Often, our emails are sent without direct knowledge of whether the other party is available to read one at that time (or even within a short period of time.) In face to face conversations, also, we often take turns—question, response, follow-up question, response, etc. Via email, particularly when one of the parties is at meetings or otherwise unavailable, the communication can stack up. We've all been in this situation—10 emails waiting for us about a topic where others might already have chimed in. Or the situation has evolved over the course of time, and you are reading the fifth email about a particular issue that arose several hours ago. Notably, many of us also tend to read emails from most recent to least recent—meaning that we read them in the opposite order in which they were generated.

Finally, the asynchronicity of email also means that while our "work" hours might be over for the day, our work communication via email or text can continue (for better and worse) throughout our waking hours. And this flexibility impacts the level of distraction as well as on what device we typically read. We might be reading email about important subjects over dinner in the evening, while watching television, or in the midst of putting kids to sleep. We might be reading over a small phone versus a full size computer screen. Not surprisingly, this opportunity to read email or texts into the night can also affect the quality of our reading.

Why the Differences in Modes Matter for Negotiation

Negotiation experts regularly discuss the importance of building trust [NDR: Lewicki, *Trust*] and a relationship [NDR: Hollander-Blumoff, *Relationships*] in a negotiation. Much of your ability to create rapport comes from the ability to see or at least hear the other party. Our mirroring skills in body language, the level of eye contact, even nodding, are all impossible via email. And so when we send and receive email messages, there is much less context for the content of the email. Is the other party joking when they say that they are crushed not to receive a draft of the report today? How about their disappointment at our missing a meeting? In face to face communication, we would immediately know if someone was sad or happy, joking or snarky. Over email, we have to make guesses. In work situations, in more formal contexts, or when dealing with superiors, we are more likely to assume bad intentions or worry that something is wrong. Our reading of the emails is more analytical and literal, since that is the only information in front of us (Ebner 2014).

The content of the information exchange is also different. Without the ability to explain in real time, ask questions, and clarify ambiguities, we often make assumptions about the content of the email. Even when we ask questions, these might not be answered directly. Or we ask several questions and the response might only cover one or two of the questions.

Finally, developing relationships and trust over email is more challenging. Several studies have shown that parties are more adversarial with each other via email (and even over the phone) compared to face to face negotiations (Ebner et al. 2009). Parties tend to share less information and cooperate less in the process of negotiation via email, resulting in lower levels of trust and higher potential for deceptive practices. And without the facial and verbal cues of face to face communication, we have higher levels of negative attribution. In other words, we assume the worst and are more likely to attribute poor motives to our counterpart.

How Differences Matter in Negotiation (or, the Pros and Cons of Different Modes)

Given these differences in communication, it is useful to think about how these differences might play out in a negotiation. [NDR: Ebner, *Email* and NDR: Ebner, *Texting*] On the one hand, email communication is often more contentious than face to face because, as described above, we misread cues. On the other hand, in an antagonistic relationship or with a topic that might be difficult to raise, the distance of email might help the conversation move forward without that emotion. Similarly, cooperation could become problematic on email. But email could also be better in reducing unconscious bias and in permitting more participation by "lower status" people. In a group setting, senior leaders typically dominate the conversation and less experienced members tend to go along once that person has expressed a preference. On email, however, where a free flowing conversation has already started, lower status people participate more (Bhappu, Griffith and Northcraft 1997). Once one person expresses doubts, others feel freer to chime in with their concerns. Finally, in some email negotiations, we might worry about less integrative solutions when there is less rapport between the parties. On the other hand, a longer information exchange, where parties have outlined their thoughts more fully in writing, might demonstrate opportunities for log-rolling and trade-offs. As the above examples demonstrate, there is no one "right" way to communicate during negotiation. Furthermore, many negotiations will consist of more than one mode. We need to think carefully about the pros and cons of each mode throughout the communication. The question is which mode of communication, in what context, and when.

Understanding Your Defaults

As you contemplate how to choose among modes of communication, it is important to examine yourself and your counterpart in terms of default modes. Ask yourself a simple question. When you pull out your phone, what is the first app that you examine? Do you check your voicemail? Your text messages? Your email? Or your Facebook (or other social media)? This is your default—at least with your personal communications—and the mode of communication with which you are most comfortable. Perhaps equally important to your comfort level is your skill level at each of these modes. Examine all the modes to think about your strengths and weaknesses. Do you prefer to make requests in person or via email? When you have a question for a colleague, do you email him or her, or pick up the phone? One approach is to communicate through your most comfortable mode, as long as that mode seems acceptable to the other party, because it will help you ask for what you want.

Understanding Their Defaults

At the same time, of course, it is crucial to learn about the modes of communication in which your counterpart prefers to negotiate. This does not mean that you always choose that particular mode—rather that you have thought about this choice consciously. So, first, think about their habits when communicating with you. Do they show a preference for email or phone or videoconference or face to face? And how technologically savvy is your counterpart? Some of us will deal with colleagues who are first adopters—they were tweeting at you before you even heard of Twitter and have already been wearing their Apple watch from the day it came out. (Readers after 2017 are invited to substitute technologies that are up-to-the-minute, since these are so only as of the time of this writing.) Other colleagues are more traditional—and phone calls will be necessary to draw their attention to the email that you sent. The issue is not to judge. Rather we need to understand what is going to be most persuasive to *them*. Sometimes this is contextual—someone might regularly text their children, but tend toward email for professional communications. And sometimes this is generational, depending on what technology was created when, be that phone, email, or texting. In a professional context, the initial communication may be the most formal—letter attached to an email, for example. But that may or may not reflect the actual best way to negotiate with them.

As the relationship evolves, like many work relationships, a continuing awareness of modes of communication is useful to keep in mind. The formality of the relationship might relax so that the tone of your emails is more casual, or perhaps you are texting short notes. Your counterpart may start to adopt newer technology and develop more of a comfort level with that. And the technology or social media itself may change, allowing different modes of communication as well—think about the onset of Skype or FaceTime and how phone calls can now include that face to face component in order to build rapport. [NDR: Ebner, *Videoconferencing*]

Thinking Strategically about How to Communicate

Having now thought about both your defaults and your counterpart's, there are a few more elements to consider. Obviously, you will want to consider the promptness of your communication and the reply. For example, if you can get someone on the phone or in their office, your communication will be immediate. And so that might be worth trying if you need a quick answer. On the other hand, phone messages are sometimes returned slower than email or texts (one reason why you want to think about your counterpart's defaults). When time is of the essence, which mode will get the response most promptly?

And this could also be part of a sequence of communications. You might, for example, stop by someone's office and then follow up with an email if they are not there. Or you might send a long email explaining a complicated issue but leave a quick voicemail (or text) letting them know that a more detailed email is awaiting their response.

Other times, the sequence of your modes of communication should shift if your purpose of communication is different. You might use different modes of communication for record-keeping versus getting a response. After meeting in person, it could be very helpful to write the details in an email confirming both of your understandings of the conversation. Or you might use certain modes, like face to face, Skype, or phone calls, for schmoozing in advance of a longer email request. (Studies show that even a short phone call in advance of a longer email will help break the ice and build rapport; e.g. see Morris et al. 2002.)

Finally, you should always be thinking about the importance of the communication. A short text or phone call letting someone know you are running late is perfectly appropriate. Asking someone for a raise via text message, however, would likely be viewed as unprofessional (at least for now). And for significant interactions, professional exchanges will still be via letter—even if that "letter" is scanned to PDF and sent via email.

Skills in Modes of Communication—Particularly Online

Often, negotiation advice assumes that the interaction is in person. Key skills—of assertiveness, empathy, flexibility, and social intuition—should not be lost in other modes of communication (Schneider 2012). Rather, attention must be paid to them differently. To close this chapter, here are a few considerations as you are implementing your e-negotiation skills.

For assertiveness via email, your writing ability needs to be good. If you are lousy at grammar and proofreading, carefully review your emails to double-check your language. It is hard to be taken seriously, and you will undercut your own requests, if your emails are full of mistakes. Additionally, make sure your language is clear—and use the subject line of the email to help your counterpart keep your messages straight. Be sure to outline and frame your requests as persuasively as you would in person. And beware of putting too much in an email—often the latter part of long emails do not get read, particularly if your counterpart is reading your email on her phone. It might make more sense to write a longer letter and attach it (with the hope that they will print the attachment) or to send separate emails with separate requests.

Creativity and flexibility can sometimes even be easier in email exchanges, as we have noted above. Using an email to clearly outline options—I could work on this project, or I could research another avenue—might in fact get a better response from the other party since email inherently allows them some time to reflect on your question. [Note, though, that contrary to popular usage, in the brain, creativity and flexibility are *not* two sides of the same coin. [NDR: Jendresen, *Creativity*] Similarly, reading emails to understand *their* priorities—and having the ability to reread and reflect—might help *you* generate options as well. On the other hand, if talking something out is your way of thinking something through, then video conferencing or meeting face to face makes more sense.

Creating and demonstrating empathy on emails is a recognized challenge. Emojis, smiley faces, and exclamation points can help...and can also be annoying and perceived as juvenile. Instead, create empathy through words rather than symbols. Start an email—particularly if it is a new exchange—with the same schmoozing that you would start a conversation. "Hi. Hope you are well. How's the summer going?" Perhaps you can refer back to your last interaction ("It was great to meet you last May at the conference") or the last communication ("Thank you for your letter last week"). Think of the first paragraph of an email as an opportunity to introduce yourself before getting to business. Again, this empathy creation is stronger if you have met face to face, or on Skype, or had a phone call. So we should consider starting with that mode. As you close the email, consider this an additional opportunity to create empathy with words—share about yourself, or sign off with more than your name.

This links to social intuition [NDR: Schneider & Ebner, *Social Intuition*], in which you need to stay attuned to how the communication is occurring. The choice of communication mode should be highly influenced by your attention to the emotional tenor of the negotiation. Email negotiations—and the fact that we don't know when someone received the email, when they are going to respond, or what they are thinking—can be fraught with miscommunication. Part of social intuition is managing your own anxiety as well as theirs. What are the expectations for responding to emails? Do others in your workplace seem to respond within twenty-four hours, or is a more leisurely rate acceptable? Different assumptions operate in different environments. When, for example, you need a quick response (as noted above) you might want to signal that importance through more than one mode, so that your messaging to your counterpart is clear. If, on the other hand, you know you cannot get back to someone right away, it might be helpful to let them know that—much as we set "out of office" functions. "I've received your email and need to talk to my boss before getting back to you. I'll be in touch soon. Thanks much."

One final note on social intuition—when you are worried about the tone of an email or text that you are going to send, re-read it as if you were an angry or suspicious recipient. Could your counterpart misinterpret your tone? And when reading an email that you have received (and have started that negative attribution described earlier in the chapter), try rereading that email assuming that your counterpart is happy with you. Before starting down the spiral of angry exchanges, it is important to make sure you *want* to engage in that way. Sometimes, stepping away from the computer for a few hours, or sending your preferred (obnoxious, witty, awesome comeback) email response only to yourself, will help you find the equilibrium you need.

Conclusion

Thinking about the mode of communication is as important as any particular skill in your negotiation. Each mode can play to your strengths (or weaknesses); can help be more persuasive (or less); and can build relationships (or tear them down). Thinking carefully about this element of negotiation will add to your effectiveness and your ability to get what you want.

References

Barsness, Z. I. and A. D. Bhappu. 2004. At the Crossroads of Technology and Culture: Social Influence, Information Sharing, and Sense-Making Processes During Negotiations. In *The Handbook of Negotiation & Culture*, edited by M. J. Gelfand and J. M. Brett. Palo Alto, CA: Stanford University Press.

Bhappu, A. D. and Z. I. Barsness. 2006. Risks of Email. In *The Negotiator's Fieldbook: The Desk Reference for the Experienced Negotiator*, edited by A. K. Schneider and C. Honeyman. Washington DC: American Bar Association.

Bhappu, A.D., T. L. Griffith and G. B. Northcraft. 1997. Media Effects and Communication Bias in Diverse Groups. *Organizational Behavior and Human Decision Processes* 70(3): 199-205.

Ebner, N. 2014. Negotiation Via (the New) Email. In *Negotiation Excellence: Successful Deal Making*, 2nd ed. edited by M. Benoliel. World Scientific Publishing: Singapore.

Ebner, N., A. Bhappu, J. G. Brown, K. K. Kovach and A. K. Schneider. 2009. You've Got Agreement: Negoti@ing Via Email. In *Rethinking Negotiation Teaching: Innovations for Context and Culture*, edited by C. Honeyman, J. Coben, and G. De Palo. St Paul, MN: DRI Press.

Morris, M., J. Nadler, T. R. Kurtzberg and L. Thompson. 2002. Schmooze or Lose: Social Friction and Lubrication in E-mail Negotiations. *Group Dynamics* 6(1): 89-100.

Schneider, A. K. 2012. Teaching a New Negotiation Skills Paradigm. *Washington University Journal of Law & Policy* 39: 13-38.

∝ 60 ∝

Negotiating via Email

Noam Ebner

Editors' Note: Email is typically the first technology people think of when they start to imagine negotiating using a computer. By now, this is a common practice, at least for parts and phases of a typical negotiation. Yet few practitioners or students pause to consider how the technology affects what is said, how it is said, and when and how it is heard. Reviewing what is now a substantial body of research, the author finds seven major challenges in negotiating via e-mail, most of which are as yet poorly understood. He goes on to provide practical advice on each one.

Introduction

Negotiation interactions are increasingly taking place through channels other than face-to-face encounters. Negotiators find themselves communicating with each other online, using a variety of e-communication channels. This chapter will deal with one particular medium that, given its ubiquitous use across professional as well as personal contexts, warrants special attention: negotiation via email. Once a seemingly static mode of communication, email has, of late, become a moving target, with changes in its software, hardware, and modes of use. This chapter aims to provide a roadmap for negotiating via email. [Other applications of technology to support negotiation are discussed in NDR: Ebner, *Texting*, NDR: Ebner, *Videoconferencing* and NDR: Ebner, *Other Technologies*. Ethical issues raised in these processes are discussed in NDR: Rule, *Online Ethics*]

Noam Ebner is a professor in the Negotiation and Conflict Resolution program, at Creighton University's Department of Interdisciplinary Studies. Previously an attorney and a mediator, he has taught mediation and negotiation in a dozen countries around the world. He was among the first teachers to engage in online teaching of negotiation and conflict studies, and to explore the potential for Massive Open Online Courses in these fields. Noam's research interests include online negotiation and dispute resolution, trust and its role in dispute resolution, negotiation pedagogy and online learning. Noam can be contacted at NoamEbner@creighton.edu; his work can be found at ssrn.com/author=4251-53.

Negotiation—All Around, and Online Too

Given the broad definition granted to the term "negotiation" in this field's literature, and the many types of interactions and relationships we now conduct online, many of us are often engaged in online negotiation. This is especially true in the business world. Two lawyers email offers and counteroffers late into the night as they attempt to settle a case before a court hearing; a purchaser in New York emails her Australian supplier, requesting a discount; a landlady informs her tenant of a rent increase, should he be interested in extending his lease; a team leader sends out a group message asking his team to work longer hours. All are engaging in negotiating via email. Does this choice of medium matter?

Email Negotiation is Unavoidable—and Very Different

As opposed to several years ago, when students and clients would regularly inform me that they would never negotiate anything important by email, today this statement is rarely voiced, and with good reason. In today's world, we cannot avoid finding negotiation messages in our inbox even if we wanted to—so we need to understand this mode of negotiation, and learn how to conduct it well. That, in a nutshell, is the purpose of this chapter. [Further thoughts on when to *prefer* email for negotiation, or on how to fit email communication in amongst an array of channels used in a negotiation can be found in NDR: Schneider & McCarthy, *Communication Choices*.]

Before we delve into the nuts and bolts of email negotiation, though, we need to lay two pieces of groundwork. The first is an understanding of the effects that different communication media have on the content and dynamics of communication conducted through them, known as "media effects". The second is an investigation into just what type of communication medium email is, in order to put those effects into context.

The Medium Affects the Message: A Theoretical Model

The communication channel through which negotiations are conducted is neither passive nor neutral; it affects what information negotiators share, and how that information is conveyed, received and interpreted (Carnevale and Probst 1997; Friedman and Currall 2003).

Intuitively, we know that some information is easier to communicate face-to-face, whereas other messages might be hampered by a face-to-face setting and would be better off written in an email. Similarly, we might respond to a message one way in a face-to-face setting—and completely differently when reading it in an email. What underlies these differences? Zoe Barsness and Anita Bhappu (2004) ascribe them to the effects of two dimensions of communication media:

Media richness: A communication medium's capacity to convey "contextual cues". Body language, facial expressions, tone, etc., account for a significant proportion of a message's meaning. Supporting all of these, face-to-face communication is a "rich" medium. By contrast, email is a "lean" medium: it transmits neither visual nor audio cues. We cannot see the other's gestures or facial expressions, or hear their tone of voice.

Denied these contextual cues, negotiators both transmit and receive information differently. On the transmitting side, this affects both presentation style and content. Email negotiators rely more heavily on logical argumentation and the presentation of facts, rather than on emotional or personal appeals (Barsness and Bhappu 2004). They are more task-oriented and depersonalized than those engaged in face-to-face interactions (Kemp and Rutter 1982). The ability to transmit visual, audio and verbal cues face-to-face, meanwhile, provides for more immediate feedback, which facilitates communication of information of a personal nature (Daft and Lengel 1984).

Message receiving is also affected by media richness. Information exchanged in email tends to be less nuanced than information exchanged face-to-face (Friedman and Currall 2003; Valley et al. 1998). Communicating through lean media, negotiators focus on the actual *content* of messages (Ocker and Yaverbaum 1999; see also Sokolova and Lapalme 2012), lending much more salience to the words that are chosen, and their interpretation.

Interactivity: The potential of the medium to sustain a seamless flow of information between two or more negotiators (Kraut et al. 1992). Interactivity has two dimensions. The first is the *synchronicity* of interactions. Face-to-face communication is synchronous. Each party receives an utterance just as it is produced; speaking "turns" tend to occur sequentially. Email is typically *asynchronous*: negotiators can read and respond to others' messages whenever they desire—and not necessarily sequentially. Minutes, hours, or even weeks can pass between the time a negotiator sends a message and the time their counterpart reads it, and reading messages out of order is a common cause of misunderstandings.

The second dimension of interactivity involves *parallel processing* —a medium's capacity for simultaneous message transmission. Face-to-face communication includes overt parallel processing; in the heat of an argument, or in a rush of creativity, both negotiators might speak at the same time. Email also permits the simultaneous exchange of messages—but negotiators might not *know* that this is occurring, giving rise to the common phenomenon of "crossing messages," and the confusion this entails.

These two characteristics of email—asynchronicity and allowing for parallel processing—have been found to have significant effects on the way messages are transmitted and the way they are received. On the transmission side, the use of asynchronous media may accentuate analytical-rational expression of information by negotiators, as opposed to an intuitive-experiential mode (Epstein et al. 1996). This favors individuals who tend to rely more heavily on logic and deductive thinking, and to engage in developing positions and reservation points, logical argumentation, and fact-presentation. By contrast, individuals tending towards appealing to emotion and sharing personal stories (Gelfand and Dyer 2000) may be put at a disadvantage. On the receiving side, email imposes high "understanding costs" on negotiators. Negotiators' understanding is challenged by the lack of contextual cues. The timing and sequencing of information exchange further hamper negotiators' efforts to accurately decode messages they receive (Clark and Brennan 1991). In addition, the tendency of email negotiators to "bundle" multiple arguments and issues together in one email message (Adair, Okumura and Brett 2001; Friedman and Currall 2003) can place high demands on the receiver's information-processing capabilities.

In summary, these two elements, media richness and interactivity, account for important differences across media in the structure, style, and content of information exchanged (for more detail, see Bhappu and Barsness 2006; Ebner et al. 2009). However, before we go on to explore how these elements significantly alter negotiation dynamics—and what we can do about it—we must take into account the sands shifting under our feet: Email is changing, and these changes will affect any insights or suggestions we might offer regarding its use for negotiation.

Using Email: A Moving Target

Only a few years ago, the notion of communicating via email conjured up a more-or-less uniform picture of a person seated at a desk or in her home office, typing on a computer, or perhaps seated at a café table working on her laptop. Indeed, the research literature reinforced this image by discussing it as a monolithic, defined, communication tool or medium, used in certain ways in defined contexts to mediate communication between users sitting behind their computer screens. However, email has already known many variations, in terms of the software used for accessing it, of the hardware upon which it is read and composed, and of the culture or policies within which its use is embedded (for discussion of all these, see Ebner 2014).

The most significant shift affecting negotiation via email over the past few years has been an upheaval in the realm of hardware: the advent of the smartphone. In the age of the smartphone, we are "unleashed"—no longer bound by a physical connection to a static modem. Most emails are now read on mobile devices, not on computers. Emails are now read and written on buses and trains; while watching the kids at the playground; during classes, rock concerts and movies; and even (though most of us would never admit to this) while driving. And, lest this not be clear, we can replace the words "Emails are now read and written" with the words "We now negotiate..."

This revolution has significantly affected our negotiation habits. The smartphone has introduced new elements of accessibility, distraction, environment, timing and technical limitations to email communication. Some of these will be discussed below, presented as particular challenges or advantages related to email negotiation. One overarching shift, though, relates to the interactivity aspect of email's nature as a communication channel. Previously, email has always been considered a form of asynchronous communication. With the current degree of smartphone saturation, most people now walk around carrying their inboxes in their pocket, hyper-alert to notifications of incoming messages (so much so, in fact, that most people now experience phantom phone vibrations leading them to constantly check for incoming calls and messages; see Rosenberger 2015). As a result, email has become a "semi-synchronous" communication medium (Ebner 2014). Specific exchanges or rounds of conversation might be categorized as synchronous or asynchronous, but our perceptions and expectations of the medium must be more complex than any such dichotomy would allow.

Just so we don't get too comfortable, we will end this section by noting that future disruption to our currently evolving negotiation habits is already in the works, as smartwatches, and other wearable technology giving access to email, reach the market. This reinforces the importance of remaining mindful of change, and of shifting media effects, as we consider email negotiation.

Negotiating Through Email: Seven Major Challenges

We now move on to delineate seven areas in which interacting via e-mail affects elements or dynamics of negotiation. A discussion of the challenges posed by the medium in each area will be followed by a set of practical recommendations for negotiators with regards to that area (with the usual caveats regarding "tips" and "recommendations" in negotiation, of course). These areas are:

1) More contentious, and less cooperative, process
2) Fewer, or less, integrative outcomes
3) Diminished trust
4) Increased attribution and increased misinterpretation
5) Diminished privacy
6) Diminished negotiator focus
7) Diminished negotiator commitment and investment

1. More Contentious, and Less Cooperative, Process:

In online communication, parties tend to be even less inhibited than in face-to-face communication, due to physical distance, reduced social presence, reduced accountability, and a sense of anonymity (Griffith and Northcraft 1994; Weisband and Atwater 1999; Thompson 2004). The lack of social cues causes people to act more contentiously than they do in face-to-face encounters, resulting in more frequent occurrences of swearing, name calling, insults, and hostile behavior (Kiesler and Sproull 1992). E-negotiators are more likely to threaten and issue ultimata (Morris et al. 2002); to lie or deceive (Naquin, Kurtzberg and Belkin 2010); to confront each other negatively; and to engage in flaming (Thompson and Nadler 2002).

Another media effect, deriving from email negotiation's lack of synchronicity, involves what Anne Marie Bülow has dubbed a "double monologue" style of interaction: Parties cherry-pick pieces of the conversation that they wish to relate to, ignoring others; they relate to these issues in long, argumentative statements. One result is that communicating through email, negotiators tend to *work simultaneously to persuade each other that they are right*, rather than *explore ways to work together*. This precludes questioning, so less information is shared. It also precludes uptake—I'm too busy rejecting your stance to relate to the information itself—so information the other has shared might not be discussed, clarified and expanded. Finally, to the extent that queries are used, they tend to be short and specific—extracting specific information but not opening the door to other information. As a result, one might extract a factual detail from one's counterpart, but not the interest underlying it (Bülow 2011).

All the above can easily result in a lack of process cooperation, as parties focus on the person rather than on the problem, and as they do so, the potential for effective information-sharing decreases. Parties may not elicit, or may ignore, important information the other has conveyed, as well as relational cues. The use of email may, therefore, accentuate competitive behavior in negotiations (Barsness and Bhappu 2004). Not only do parties to email negotiation act uncooperatively—they feel *justified* in choosing this pattern of behavior (Naquin, Kurtzberg and Belquin 2008). Couple email's high tendency for contentious behavior and its low tendency for information sharing with the comparative ease of walking away from an email negotiation process (see below), and we are faced with a recipe for overall diminished process cooperation.[1]

In practice:
1) Context: Take advantage of email's "lean" nature: Use email, when you feel that transmission of visual and verbal cues might set people off (see, e.g., Bhappu and Crews 2005) rather than facilitate constructive conversation. Similarly, consider preferring email's use over richer media for exchanges in which you think your voice, or the voice of someone else in the conversation, might go unheard, or if you think you are at risk of suffering from the impact of conflict-triggering unconscious biases, such as gender, race, accent, national origin, etc. (Greenwald, McGhee and Schwartz 1998). Email reduces the salience of social group differences, providing a conducive medium in which

more people can, and do, participate (Bhappu, Griffith and Northcraft 1997). Over email, parties cannot shout each other down or interrupt.

2) Unmask yourself: The mutual invisibility inherent in email negotiation facilitates adversarial, contentious behavior. It is easier to cause damage to a faceless other—particularly when one feels protected by a shield of anonymity and physical distance. This can cause people to assume that they can get away with this behavior, and lower any moral inhibitions they might have against doing so (Nadler and Shestowsky 2006). By adopting a proactive agenda of unmasking ourselves—making ourselves human, present, and real in the other's eyes—we can protect ourselves from these dynamics. Share personal information, build rapport, and reduce the perception of distance through shared language, or shared geographical or cultural references. Or, even, have a phone call once in a while—or a meeting! (See below.)

3) Unmask the other: Remember, there is a person behind the other screen as well, whether they have had the foresight to engage in unmasking themselves or not. They are not computers or inboxes; rather, human beings who will respond to your messages on emotional, cognitive and behavioral levels which you must deal with (see Mayer 2000).

4) Interaction pace: Use email's semi-synchronicity to your advantage; vary the interaction pace, always answering at the pace that works best for you. This will allow you to avoid getting "emotionally hijacked" into conflict escalation (see Goleman 1995), or otherwise suffer the consequences of a knee-jerk response (see Bhappu and Crews 2005). Read a received message twice instead of banging out an angry reply—and delay sending what you've written, to read it again a little later. Be particularly mindful on this front while communicating via smartphone; the fact that you *can* now answer instantly in more cases than ever before doesn't mean that you should!

5) Use interest-related language intentionally, and often, when discussing your own position and inquiring about theirs. Use process-cooperative language overtly, and try to set the tone for others to do so. This might give process-cooperation a much-needed boost.

6) If your counterparty relates to some of the issues you raised in a letter, but not to other issues raised, do not always assume that this is a deliberate, contentious omission—it may simply be information overload, or inadvertent cherry-picking. Consider calling their attention to this as an oversight, before assuming there is some underlying meaning in the omission.

7) Some people may find writing long, well thought-out messages on the small screen and keyboard or touchpad provided by a smartphone to be a daunting task; cooperative, information-sharing messages may sometimes fall into this category. Rather than discard such opportunities, you might give more careful thought to the question of which machine you would best type your message on. Choose to wait to write a longer message from home, versus typing out three words on your smartphone and considering the response complete.

2. Fewer, or Less, Integrative Outcomes

The potential for email negotiation to result in lower rates of integrative outcomes is partially connected to the previous challenge of reduced process cooperation. As process cooperation diminishes, so too does information exchange. We've noted how information shared in email negotiations is likely to be constrained, analytical, and contentious. Even if process cooperation devolves no further, this information is hard to work with, which might explain an email negotiator's reduced accuracy in judging the other party's interests (Arunachalam and Dilla 1995). Such reduced accuracy would reduce negotiators' ability to accurately assess differential preferences and identify potential joint gains. In turn, this might reduce their motivation to engage in cooperative information sharing; yet another vicious cycle reveals itself.

Indeed, many experiments measuring these two elements—process cooperation and integrative outcomes—illustrate significant challenges. First, e-negotiation appears to entail lower rates of process cooperation, and lower rates of integrative outcomes, when compared to face-to-face negotiation (Arunachalam and Dilla 1995; Valley et al. 1998; see also Nadler and Shestowsky 2006. For contrasting research, see Galin, Gross and Gosalker 2007; Nadler and Shestowsky 2006; Naquin and Paulson 2003). Second, in email negotiation the potential for impasse appears to be greater than in face-to-face negotiation (Croson 1999; Bülow 2010).

These findings, though, don't clearly explain just *why* email negotiation results may be less integrative. Is it an outcome of reduced process cooperation? Of increased contentiousness? Of diminished rapport? Of reduced trust? Or, perhaps, of a combination of some or all of these elements? This crucial issue—which determines if email negotiation might be, inherently, a value-*diminishing* playing field—continues to intrigue researchers. Recent writing on this issue has suggested that negotiator orientation towards cooperation or competition determines whether the outcome will be integrative far more than the communication channel affects this issue. People with cooperative orientations will generally be able to convey and implement this despite any challenges that constraining communication channels pose to them (Swaab et al. 2012). Parties mindful of this should take care to demonstrate and pursue this orientation through value-creating behaviors and a tendency toward more, rather than less, communication overall—behavior which has been shown to increase joint gain in email negotiation (Parlamis and Geiger 2015).

In practice:
Most of the suggestions made above (regarding process cooperation) apply here as well. In addition:

1) Choose wisely: The research indicating that email is not as good a playing field for reaching integrative agreements is not conclusive—but it is not dismissable. If you face a negotiation in which an integrative outcome is not only beneficial, but absolutely *crucial*, consider picking up the phone, or getting on a plane.

2) Paint a picture: Consider using the multimedia potential now available in e-mail in order to portray integrative offers or ideas. Charts, graphs, presentations—all easily attached to an email —are powerful tools for overcoming the challenges of lean media.

3) Bundle: Email negotiators tend to bundle multiple issues together in one letter. Use this in order to create relationships between issues, through logrolling and prioritization; this might well result in integrative agreements, in a manner that separate discussion of each issue might not.

4) Frame: In email negotiation, every message is an opportunity to set a new frame around the interaction, much more so than rapid-fire statements and reactions in face-to-face processes. Intentional and repeated integrative framing might have an effect on the outcome.

5) Talk more, talk cooperatively: If you are worried about whether you might not be communicating enough, you probably are not; more communication often translates into higher joint gain. Email's lack of synchronicity allows for reflection and for careful, overt use of cooperative language, which may increase the odds of reaching an integrative outcome.

3. Diminished Degree of Inter-Party Trust

Trust has been identified as playing a key role in enabling cooperation, problem solving, integrative solutions, negotiator effectiveness and dispute resolution (for a review of the literature on the topic of trust in negotiation and how it is affected by the online environment, see Ebner 2012). [See also NDR: Lewicki, *Trust* and NDR: Lewicki, *Trust Repair*]

Communicating via email, negotiators must cope with threats to trust that are inherent in the medium and in its use (Ebner 2007). Email negotiators trust their counterparts less than negotiators in similar face-to-face interactions, at all stages of the process. Before the process's inception, e-negotiators report a comparatively low level of trust in their opposite. This low trust-level persists throughout the course of the negotiation, resulting in diminished process cooperation and information sharing (Naquin and Paulson 2003). Even after reaching deals with their opposites, e-negotiators trust their opposites less than participants in face-to-face negotiations, manifesting in lower degrees of desire for future interaction with them (Naquin and Paulson 2003). Why do people distrust each other online—or, more to the point, what is it they are worried about? It may be that they are specifically concerned about intentional deception. There is little research available on lying in e-negotiation, although it has been suggested that people may have more tendency to act deceptively when communicating through lean media (Zhou et al. 2004). This gives cause for concern, given that we are considerably less skilled in intuitively detecting deception online than we are in face-to-face settings; while more deliberate methods for picking up on textual cues are being developed, a great deal of technical sophistication is required to successfully conduct such analysis in the course of a real-life e-negotiation (see Farkas 2012). To compound the issue further, research has shown that e-negotiators are more likely to *suspect* their opposite of lying, even when no actual deception has taken place (Thompson and Nadler 2002). As negotiators, then, we are suspicious of our counterpart's honesty—but our suspicions rarely target the true liars out there. Given that in lean media we tend to react strongly in retaliation to perceived lying, we may damage a relationship irreparably over an erroneous judgment—or our counterpart may do so, over their judgment of our own veracity.

In practice:
The following practices are helpful for building trust in email interactions (for more on these and other methods, see Ebner 2007):

1) Build rapport: Bonding—building an ad hoc relationship with your opposite—is always important in negotiation, for building rapport and trust. Light, social conversation does not come as naturally by email as it does face-to-face, but that does not render it superfluous. Even minimal pre-negotiation, socially-oriented contact, such as preliminary email introductory messages, can build trust, improve mutual impressions, and facilitate integrative outcomes (Morris et al. 2002; Nadler and Shestowsky 2006).

2) Mix media, when possible: In situations where interparty trust does not exist, consider whether the negotiation, or even just the first part of it, might be conducted by other methods. This is even more relevant in cases where parties actually distrust each other. Holding a preliminary face-to-face meeting can assist in setting the stage for a trust-filled e-negotiation. (Rocco 1998;

Zheng et al. 2002) Meeting face-to-face in the middle of the process, or using the smartphone you are reading an email on to call the other party in response, may also positively affect trust.

3) Show e-empathy: Displaying empathy for a counterpart serves multiple purposes in negotiation, including trust-building. E-negotiators who show empathy are trusted by their negotiation opposites more than those who do not (Feng, Lazar and Preece 2004). Don't neglect this just because the medium seems to be cold, formal or impersonal. Email allows you to use language thoughtfully to intentionally show empathy (see Ebner 2007).

4. Increased Attribution and Increased Misinterpretation

Communicating through lean media increases the tendency toward the fundamental attribution error: parties perceive negative actions or statements on their opposite's part, and interpret these as outgrowth of the other's negative intentions and character—rather than as unintended results of circumstance. Reduced social presence and few contextual cues lend a sense of distance and vagueness to the interaction. People tend to overestimate the degree to which they communicate clearly over email. Subtle elements of communication, such as sarcasm or humor, are particularly vulnerable to such overconfidence (Kruger et al. 2005). The media richness element of interactivity compounds this: E-negotiators ask fewer clarifying questions than face-to-face negotiators—leaving more room for assumptions to form and take root (Thompson and Nadler 2002). Attribution dynamics will cause these assumptions to tend toward the negative. Analysis of failed email negotiations shows that they tend to include unclear messages, irrelevant points, and long general statements (Thompson 2004), each of which provides ample breeding ground for attribution.

In practice:
1) Increase your social presence: constantly remind the other of the real person opposite them. Use physical imagery in your writing, to reinforce this issue—for example, mention the city you are in, your surroundings at the time of writing (your office, hotel), a place you went to, a physical sensation, etc.
2) Write clearly, taking into account negative interpretations. Clarify *much* more than you would face-to-face. Here are several rules of thumb for enhancing email clarity:
   a) Avoid unnecessary length—don't overload your opposite.
   b) Use "In summary" sentences to highlight your main points.
   c) Use the subject field intentionally. This introduces your letter (preparing your opposite for the content), provides a frame through which it will be read (diminishing negative

      interpretation), allows your opposite to find it when they want to review it for clarity before responding, and helps organize messages bundling multiple issues.

d) Avoid use of emoticons—particularly in early message exchanges. Later, when you have a better sense of their capacity to successfully convey shared meaning between you and your counterpart, you can consider their appropriateness.

e) If you are writing your message on a smartphone, be alert to the changes this causes in your writing style. If it causes you to respond in short messages, or constrains the way your email is laid out, consider how that might look through the eyes of your negotiation opposite. You might hold off and respond on a different machine, or simply let them know that you are responding to them via smartphone, which will explain issues of style and help stave off negative attribution.

3) Even as you mind your own writing style and framing, try not to read too much into stylistic issues in your counterpart's email. They may not be mindful, or skilled with the medium. The length or brevity of their writing should not be overanalyzed either. Many factors affect the length of your counterpart's emails that have absolutely nothing to do with you or with the negotiation itself—including age, gender, the device they open the email on, the day of the week, the time of day and their email traffic volume (Kooti et al. 2015).

4) Waiting and perceived delay cause anxiety, which is conducive to negative attribution. Manage both sides of this cycle: Don't expect immediate answers to your own emails, while doing your best to provide prompt responses to your counterpart's (see Thompson and Nadler 2002). Many of the same factors that affect email length affect email response time as well; don't read too much into what seems to you to be a slow or quick answer. Consider how smartphone use may have affected your expectations (as well as your counterpart's) on this issue. Remember that you and your opposite might use multiple machines for email, each with its own nature with regards to message reading, message writing and other timing issues.

5) Be careful with the jokes: Humor has been shown to be a valuable tool in online negotiation, leading to increased trust and satisfaction levels, higher joint gains and higher individual gains for the party who initiated the humorous event (Kurtzberg, Naquin and Belkin 2009). However, humor is often misunderstood, misinterpreted and misattributed—and can easily backfire. This is particularly true when your counterpart comes from a different culture.

6) If you are concerned that all this mindfulness and caution might not suffice, learn to recognize situations in which you need call your counterpart or meet with them in person. As said above, think about the medium being used to communicate.

5. Diminished Privacy

Maintaining privacy in a negotiation process is never an easy task. In face-to-face negotiation, parties can, and do, share information about the negotiation with their friends, families and colleagues, and occasionally with wider circles. However, parties can, at least, meet in a private setting, close a door on the world, or lower their voices—eliminating real-time "sharing." In email negotiation, by contrast, you never know who is "in the room" with you. Your opposite may have showed your email to their boss, their colleagues or your competition, before responding to you. The messages you transmit are forever archived somewhere beyond your control. The information you share might reach people with whom you had no wish to share it. Your counterpart doesn't have to be malevolent in order for this to happen. It might be you who unintentionally clicks "reply all" instead of "reply," sending your private message into a public domain!

In practice:
1) Consider each address field carefully. To whom should a message be sent? Should anyone appear in the "cc" field? Do you want anyone invisibly lurking in the corner of the conversation, from the "bcc" field?
2) Use the lack of privacy to your advantage: Archive the interactions, return to them when things become unclear, and relate to them when it seems the other party is being inconsistent. Share messages with anybody you feel you need to share them with, and consult—often—about the process. Consulting with others is an excellent way to reduce many of the challenging media effects of email noted in this chapter. Email provides recorded messages—allowing us to consult optimally. Receiving email on our smartphone makes this easier than ever, as we can show someone the original message on the spot—"Here, look at this"—without forwarding it to them, lugging a laptop around, or calling them into our office.
3) As individuals' online activities are increasingly becoming public, widespread, sought out by future opponents and admissible in court, be very cautious of what you write in an email, particularly before significant trust is established.

6. Diminished Party Focus

Communicating via email, negotiators are likely to suffer media-related effects including confusion, low cognitive retention of previous messages, and diminished concentration. This is due to several factors, including time passage between information exchanges, the tendency to answer emails in spurts and sections rather than finding the time to write full messages, and the tendency to answer emails in less-than-optimal surroundings and circumstances. In addition, email is often not something we train our full attention on, but rather something we do as part of our media multitasking. We check our email as we surf the web, and we surf the web as we read or reply to our email—perhaps holding in-person or phone conversations at the same time.

In general, research suggests that in the digital age, human attention span is decreasing. The explanation that we are now "multitasking" provides no relief, given the research indicating that we are not as good at multitasking as some of us like to think we are. Heavy multitaskers suffer a range of shortcomings as opposed to "focusers," many of which are pertinent to negotiation: They are not good at filtering out irrelevant information, and are easily distracted. They tend to have low detail recall, and despite their tendency to switch between tasks rapidly, they are not skilled at this, as their brain is always somewhat focused on the task they are *not* doing (See Ofir, Nass and Wagner 2009; Microsoft 2015). Negotiators suffering from any of these, due to their multitasking tendency, work surroundings, or email-management habits, might be confused and unfocused. So, too, might be negotiators communicating via smartphone in noisy or crowded environments without taking care to consider the effects their surroundings may have on their capacity to focus. In particular, the multi-screen environment presented by many home, work and entertainment venues primes our brains to latch onto new stimuli (Microsoft 2015). Negotiators who multitask while they are negotiating, in the form of reading messages on a smartphone while negotiating face-to-face, have been found to achieve lower outcomes (Krishnan, Kurtzberg and Nauqin 2014). Without social norms holding us back from reading that message that just came in, we are much more likely to allow ourselves to let attention slip in this way. [For more on attention and negotiation in the digital age, see NDR: Newell, *Digital Generation*]

In practice:
1) Stay focused: The greater the importance of the negotiation to you, the more it pays to concentrate on it. Read and write messages in an environment that allows you to concentrate. One simple rule of thumb to follow would be to close your internet browser while reading and writing email. Another is to finish your response to one email before moving on to reading another.

2) Don't trust your memory: Mindful of the distraction we all suffer from, make a point to read all of the email you are responding to, and carefully, before you reply. Did you take a break in the middle of your answer, to deal with other urgent multitasking such as checking your other email or social media? Read the email again, *and* the written part of your own response, before continuing to write.

3) The costs of distraction: Negotiating via email on your smart-phone might seem like a good way to make the most of your train ride into the office in the morning—but you may be setting yourself up for poor negotiation performance. Align email tasks suitably to the environment. For example, clearing your junk email in noisy places is probably fine; thinking carefully about a response might not work as well.

7. Diminished Party Commitment and Investment

Parties to e-mail negotiation might be less motivated than face-to-face negotiators. They have not displayed the minimum commitment of get-ting up, getting dressed and coming to the table; indeed, they might not have any sunk costs at all. Smartphones have compounded this issue by reducing even the value of the time invested in writing the email; people can now do this during low-value time—while commuting, waiting for someone to show up, during lunch, etc. Email allows people to easily initiate low-investment "shot in the dark" approaches. This might par-tially explain reports of higher impasse rates in email negotiation (see above), as well as the phenomenon of email negotiations evaporating, with one party simply dropping out of the conversation.

In practice:

1) Stay on top of things: Provide regular contact, keeping your counterpart engaged—without getting pushy (see Shipley and Schwalbe 2007, for some guidance on this balance).

2) Bridge time gaps: Try to create the experience of an ongoing, flowing conversation. For example, write "As I wrote you...," and then copy and paste a quote from your previous letter. Use time-markers, such as "Last week, we discussed."

3) It could happen to you: The implications of this section are not only about roping in and maintaining contact with your oppo-site. You, yourself, might be prone to underinvestment and a low level of commitment. Email negotiation tends to confuse us in this regard; keep a constant eye on your motivation level, and make sure to match it to your commitment and the resources you invest. In low-motivation situations, the temptation to "ghost" your counterpart (i.e., to disappear without notifying the other you are shutting them out) can be strong, particularly for

conflict-averse people. Beyond manners and etiquette, you might consider whether you might *need* this relationship, in some way, in the future, as well as how this might affect your reputation.

Conclusion

Already a challenging medium to negotiate through, email has recently developed into a semi-synchronous communication channel, and continues to evolve rapidly. Communicating by email, negotiators face a rougher playing field, a likely more contentious opposite, and numerous process challenges. The good news is that, armed with some knowledge and a healthy dose of awareness, negotiators can navigate these challenges, and even turn the medium to their advantage.

Notes

[1] It would be interesting to see some of the research recounted in this section replicated today and at different points in the future. It may be that our acclimatization to the online environment in general, in addition to individuals' accumulated body of experience with any particular medium, might cause some of these negative effects to diminish.

References

Adair, W. L., T. Okumura and J. M. Brett. 2001. Negotiation Behavior When Cultures Collide. *Journal of Applied Psychology* 86(3): 372-385.

Arunachalam, V. and W. N. Dilla. 1995. Judgment Accuracy and Outcomes in Negotiation: A Causal Modeling Analysis of Decision-Aiding Effects. *Organizational Behavior and Human Decision Processes* 61(3): 289-304.

Barsness, Z. I. and A. D. Bhappu. 2004. At the Crossroads of Technology and Culture: Social influence, Information-Sharing Processes During Negotiation. In *The Handbook of Negotiation and Culture*, edited by M. J. Gelfand and J. M. Brett. Palo Alto, CA: Stanford University Press.

Bhappu, A. D., T. L. Griffith and G. B. Northcraft. 1997. Media Effects and Communication Bias in Diverse Groups. *Organizational Behavior and Human Decision Processes* 70(3): 199-205.

Bhappu, A. D. and J. M. Crews. 2005. The Effects of Communication Media Conflict on Team Identification in Diverse Groups. *Proceedings of the 38th Hawaii International Conference on System Sciences.* Los Alamitos, California.

Bhappu, A. D. and Z. I. Barsness. 2006. Risks of Email. In *The Negotiator's Fieldbook: The Desk Reference for the Experienced Negotiator*, edited by A. K. Schneider and C. Honeyman. Washington DC: American Bar Association.

Bülow, A. M. 2010. Argument, Cognition and Deadlock in Email Negotiation. Working Paper, Copenhagen Business School. Available online at http://openarchive.cbs.dk/bitstream/handle/10398/8239/Email%20working%20paper.pdf?sequence=1 (last accessed January 13, 2016).

Bülow, A. M. 2011. The Double Monologue Principle: Argumentation in Email Negotiation. Working Paper, Copenhagen Business School Press. Available online at http://papers.ssrn.com/sol3/papers.cfm?abstract_id=1899225 (last accessed January 13 2016).

Carnevale, P. J. and T. M. Probst. 1997. Conflict on the Internet. In *Culture of the Internet*, edited by S. Kiesler. Mahwah, NJ: Lawrence Erlbaum Associates.

Clark, H. H. and S. E. Brennan. 1991. Grounding in Communication. In *Perspectives on Socially Shared Cognition*, edited by L. B. Resnick, J. M. Levine and S. D. Teasley. Washington, DC: American Psychological Association.

Croson, R. T. A. 1999. Look at Me When You Say That: An Electronic Negotiation Simulation. *Simulation & Gaming* 30(1): 23-27.

Daft, R. L. and R. H. Lengel. 1984. Information Richness: A New Approach to Managerial Behavior and Organizational Design. *Research in Organizational Behavior 6*:
191-233.
Ebner, N. 2007. Trust-building in E-negotiation. In *Computer-Mediated Relationships
and Trust: Managerial and Organizational Effects*, edited by L. Brennan and V.
Johnson. Hershey, PA: Information Science Publishing.
Ebner, N. 2012. Online Dispute Resolution and Interpersonal Trust. In *Online Dispute
Resolution: Theory and Practice – A Treatise on Technology and Dispute Resolu-
tion*, edited by M. S. Abdel Wahab, E. Katsh and D. Rainey. The Hague: Eleven
International Publishing.
Ebner, N. 2014. Negotiation Via (The New) Email. In *Negotiation Excellence: Successful
Deal Making*, 2nd edn. edited by M. Benoliel. World Scientific Publishing: Singa-
pore.
Ebner, N., A. D. Bhappu, J. G. Brown, K. K. Kovach and A. K. Schneider. 2009. You've
Got Agreement: Negoti@ing via Email. In *Rethinking Negotiation Teaching: Inno-
vations for Context and Culture*, edited by C. Honeyman, J. Coben and G. De
Palo. St Paul, MN: DRI Press.
Epstein, S., R. Pacini, V. Denes-Raj and H. Heier. 1996. Individual Differences in Intu-
itive-Experimental and Analytical-Rational Thinking Styles. *Journal of Personality
and Social Psychology* 71(2): 390-405.
Farkas, B. 2012. Old Problem, New Medium: Deception in Computer-Facilitated Negoti-
ation and Dispute Resolution. *Cardozo Journal of Conflict Resolution* 14(1):
161-193.
Feng, J., J. Lazar and J. Preece. 2004. Empathy and Online Interpersonal Trust: A
Fragile Relationship. *Behavior & Information Technology* 23(2): 97-106.
Friedman, R. A. and S. C. Currall. 2003. Conflict Escalation: Dispute Exacerbating Ele-
ments of E-Mail Communication. *Human Relations* 56(11): 1325-1357.
Galin, A., M. Gross and G. Gosalker. 2007. E-Negotiation Versus Face-to-Face Negotia-
tion: What Has Changed—If Anything? *Computers in Human Behavior* 23(1):
787-797.
Gelfand, M. and N. Dyer. 2000. A Cultural Perspective on Negotiation: Progress, Pit-
falls, and Prospects. *Applied Psychology: An International Review* 49(1): 62-69.
Goleman, D. 1995. *Emotional Intelligence: Why it Can Matter More Than IQ*. New York:
Bantam Books.
Greenwald, A. G., D. E. McGhee and J. L. K. Schwartz. 1998. Measuring Individual Dif-
ferences in Implicit Cognition: The Implicit Association Test. *Journal of Personal-
ity and Social Psychology* 74(6): 1464-1480.
Griffith, T. L. and G. B. Northcraft. 1994. Distinguishing Between the Forest and the
Trees: Media, Features, and Methodology in Electronic Communication Research.
Organization Science 5(2): 272-285.
Kemp, N. J. and D. R. Rutter. 1982. Cuelessness and the Content and Style of Conver-
sation. British Journal of Social Psychology 21: 43-9.
Kiesler, S. and L. Sproull. 1992. Group Decision Making and Communication Technol-
ogy. *Organizational Behavior and Human Decision Processes* 52(1): 96-123.
Kooti, F., L. M. Aiello, M. Grbovic, K. Lerman and A. Mantrach. 2015. Evolution of Con-
versations in the Age of Email Overload. Proceedings of the 24th International
World Wide Web Conference (WWW'15), Florence, Italy, May 2015. Available on-
line at http://arxiv.org/pdf/1504.00704v1.pdf (last accessed January 12, 2016).
Kraut, R., J. Galegher, R. Fish and B. Chalfonte. 1992. Task Requirements and Media
Choice in Collaborative Writing. *Human-Computer Interaction* 7(4): 375-407.
Kruger, J., N. Epley, J. Parker and Z. W. Ng. 2005. Egocentrism Over E-Mail: Can We
Communicate as Well as We Think? *Journal of Personality and Social Psychology*
89(6): 925-936.
Krishnan, A., T. R. Kurtzberg and C. E. Naquin. 2014. The Curse of the Smartphone:
Electronic Multitasking in Negotiations. *Negotiation Journal* 30(2): 191-208.
Kurtzberg, T. R., C. E. Naquin and L. Y. Belkin. 2009. Humor as a Relationship-Building
Tool in Online Negotiations. *International Journal of Conflict Management* 20(4):
377-397.
Mayer, B. 2000. *The Dynamics of Conflict Resolution: A Guide to Engagement and In-
tervention*. San Francisco: Jossey-Bass.
Microsoft. 2015. Attention Spans: Consumer Insights. Microsoft Canada, Winter 2015.
Available online at https://advertising.microsoft.com/en/WWDocs/User/display/
cl/researchreport/31966/en/microsoft-attention-spans-research-report.pdf ac-
cessed July 16th, 2016).
Morris, M., J. Nadler, T. Kurtzberg and L. Thompson. 2002. Schmooze or Lose: Social
Friction and Lubrication in E-mail Negotiations. *Group Dynamics* 6(1): 89-100.

Nadler, J. and D. Shestowsky. 2006. Negotiation, Information Technology and the Problem of the Faceless Other. In *Negotiation Theory and Research*, edited by L. L. Thompson. New York, NY: Psychology Press.

Naquin, C. E. and G. D. Paulson. 2003. Online Bargaining and Interpersonal Trust. *Journal of Applied Psychology* 88(1): 113-120.

Naquin, C. E., T. R. Kurtzberg and L. Y. Belkin. 2008. E-Mail Communication and Group Cooperation in Mixed Motive Contexts. *Social Justice Research* 21(4): 470-489.

Naquin, C. E., T. R. Kurtzberg and L. Y. Belkin. 2010. The Finer Points of Lying Online: E-mail Versus Pen and Paper. This article is not included in your organization's subscription. However, you may be able to access this article under your organization's agreement with Elsevier. *Journal of Applied Psychology* 95(2): 387-394.

Ocker, R. J. and G. J. Yaverbaum. 1999. Asynchronous Computer-Mediated Communication Versus Face-to-Face Collaboration: Results on Student Learning, Quality and Satisfaction. *Group Decision and Negotiations* 8(5): 427-440.

Ofir, E., C. Nass and A. D. Wagner. 2009. Cognitive Control in Media Multitaskers. *Proceedings of the National Academy of Sciences* 106(37): 15583-15587.

Parlamis, J. D. and I. Geiger. 2015. Mind the Medium: A Qualitative Analysis of Email Negotiation. *Group Decision and Negotiation* 24(2): 359-381.

Rocco, E. 1998. Trust Breaks Down in Electronic Contexts but can be Repaired by Some Initial Face-to-Face Contact. In *Proceedings of the 1998 SIGCHI Conference on Human Factors in Computing Systems*. Los Angeles, CA: ACM Press.

Rosenberger, R. 2015. An Experiential Account of Phantom Vibration Syndrome. *Computers in Human Behavior* 52: 124-131.

Shipley, D. and W. Schwalbe. 2007. *Send: The Essential Guide to Email for Office and Home*. New York: Alfred A. Knopf.

Sokolova, M. and G. Lapalme. 2012. How Much Do We Say? Using Informativeness of Negotiation Text Records for Early Prediction of Negotiation Outcomes. *Group Decision and Negotiation* 21(3): 363-379.

Swaab, R. I., A. D. Galinsky, V. Medvec and D. A. Diermeier. 2012. The Communication Orientation Model: Explaining the Diverse Effects of Sight, Sound, and Synchronicity on Negotiation and Group Decision-Making Outcomes. *Personality and Social Psychology Review* 16(1): 25-53.

Thompson, L. (2004). *The Mind and Heart of the Negotiator*, (3rd ed.). Upper Saddle River, NJ: Prentice Hall.

Thompson, L. and J. Nadler. 2002. Negotiating via Information Technology: Theory and Application. *Journal of Social Issues* 58(1): 109-24.

Valley, K. L., J. Moag and M. H. Bazerman. 'A Matter of Trust' Effects of Communication on the Efficiency and Distribution of Outcomes. *Journal of Economic Behavior & Organization* 34: 211-238.

Weisband, S. and L. Atwater. 1999. Evaluating Self and Others in Electronic and Face-to-Face Groups. *Journal of Applied Psychology* 84(4): 632-639.

Zheng, J., E. Veinott, N. Bos, J. S. Olson and G. M. Olson. 2002. Trust Without Touch: Jumpstarting Long-Distance Trust with Initial Social Activities. In *Proceedings of the SIGCHI 2002 Conference on Human Factors in Computing Systems*. New York, NY: ACM Press.

Zhou, L., J. K. Burgoon, D. Twitchell, T. Qin and J. F. Nunamaker. 2004. A Comparison of Classification Methods for Predicting Deception in Computer-Mediated Communication. *Journal of Management Information Systems* 20(4): 139-165.

੭ **61** ੩

Negotiation via Text Messaging

Noam Ebner

Editors' Note: "Never!" That's the typical reply, says the author, when he queries a negotiator about negotiating through text messages. Not so fast, Ebner says—look closely at how your day goes and how your various forms of communication fit together, and you may well find yourself already handling part of that traffic via text. Furthermore, he says, in the future you can expect to use this medium more, as more and more of your counterparts depend on it. Yet negotiating via text is significantly different even from email negotiation. Ebner walks you through the assets, and the liabilities.

Negotiation via Text—Who, Me?

Many professionals I speak with regarding negotiation via text messaging are surprised, saying they would *never* commit negotiation processes to this medium. I don't press the point. But if I did, I'd recall hearing the same responses ten years ago, with regards to negotiating via email, and that they petered out quickly as use of this medium spread [see NDR: Ebner, *Email*]. With young professionals and students, on the other hand, any surprise is limited to "Hey, that's right—I never thought of it that way!" If any of the three conversations captured below is familiar to you, you already negotiate via text messaging. If not, I'd suggest, you will in the future—and soon.

Noam Ebner is a professor in the Negotiation and Conflict Resolution program, at Creighton University's Department of Interdisciplinary Studies. Previously an attorney and a mediator, he has taught mediation and negotiation in a dozen countries around the world. He was among the first teachers to engage in online teaching of negotiation and conflict studies, and to explore the potential for Massive Open Online Courses in these fields. Noam's research interests include online negotiation and dispute resolution, trust and its role in dispute resolution, negotiation pedagogy and online learning. Noam can be contacted at NoamEbner@creighton.edu; his work can be found at ssrn.com/author=4251-53.

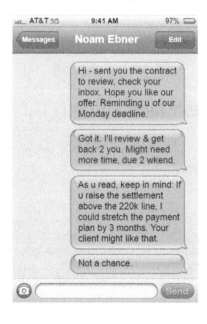

Entire Negotiations, or Elements of Negotiation

In saying that many of us already negotiate via text messaging, I take into account that in many cases, multiple media are used over the course of a negotiation—and that text often plays a role even when it is not the primary negotiation medium. While negotiation is sometimes entirely conducted through text messaging, in many other cases, this medium *supports* negotiation processes being held through other media. The nature of this support varies from case to case. A text message might call attention to the primary communication medium (e.g. "I tried to call you, but you weren't in; please call me back so I can respond to your offer"). It might be the channel for a sub-negotiation that the negotiation process involves (e.g. "I can't meet you at six as you requested; come by my office at seven?"). It might provide a channel to bring another figure into a face-to-face negotiation (e.g., a prosecutor texting his boss to ask her authorization to a plea bargain being cut on the courthouse steps). [Suggestions for when text messaging should be the medium of choice for different purposes can be found in NDR: Schneider & McCarthy, *Communication Choices*]

Such use of text messaging for supporting all, most, or some of the negotiation process can be illustrated by the following two demonstrations of how text messaging is woven into the professional practices of two attorney colleagues of mine—with quite different approaches to its role in their negotiation activities with clients.

One attorney, specializing in expunging criminal records, generally conducts her initial client intake over the phone. After a short conversation, she asks them to obtain a copy of their record (from the police, or the courts, depending on the case), take a picture of it using their mobile phone (this document is generally 2-4 pages long), and send it to her via WhatsApp, the most common messaging app in her area. Having received and reviewed the records, she responds through WhatsApp to coordinate another call, in which she and her client discuss the situation and decide what services are necessary. Her fee is discussed and agreed to on the phone, and a fee contract is delivered via fax or email. As text messaging has already become a normal part of their interaction, most future interactions are initiated with WhatsApp—setting meetings, clarifying timetables, etc. Many of these interactions involve negotiation, and while she does her best to avoid negotiating the fee itself via text, other financial issues (payment schedule, payment method and more) are often negotiated through this medium.

Another attorney, specializing in immigration law, prefers to hear the client's full story on the phone, rather than review documents early on. Having heard the case, he promises the client to be in touch with a fee proposal. He does this via text messaging—a brief message along the lines of "I'll handle the case for $X". He prefers this method as it gives him time to consider the amount of effort the case might require, and a more relaxed space in which to organize his thoughts. A conflict-averse person, he feels this also allows him to request higher fees than he could comfortably request in a face-to-face setting. Clients sometimes text him back with agreement; other times, with a request for a discount; still other times, they request a phone conversation for this purpose. Once a client agrees to the fee in principle, they receive a full, detailed, fee and services agreement by email.

What might best practices be for negotiating via text messaging? The negotiation literature's cupboard is fairly bare, at this point in time. This chapter will delve deeper into the wide variety of uses we have for this medium, noting how these uses are expanding. Applying communication theory, it will explore how people's capacity for text messaging is expanding together with their perception of its richness and effectiveness. Exploring all this through a negotiation perspective will generate suggestions for how to become an effective text messaging communicator in negotiation contexts.

We Do Text a Lot, Don't We?

Negotiation activity is only one area in which text messaging plays a much more significant role today than it did just a few years ago; we have woven it into the very fabric of our interactions. Research now shows that *everybody* texts. While text messaging *frequency* is inversely related to age (causing generational differences, which will be discussed below), we all use this medium to some extent (Forgays, Hyman and Schreiber 2014). The more our use of this medium increases, the more likely we are to use it for increasingly significant interactions, including negotiation interactions. To understand just what types of interaction are intended by the term "text messaging," let's review a bit of our recent interactional history.

Casting a Wide Net for Text Messaging

While text messaging of sorts has been around since humans etched characters on rocks, this chapter discusses messaging taking place via information technology. The past twenty years have offered different methods to conduct such interaction, each enjoying its moment in the spotlight. Peer-to-peer interaction via "instant messaging" programs became popular in the mid-1990s with the spread of AOL Instant Messenger, ICQ, and other platforms. While some programs allowed for more robust interactions beyond conveying text (such as transferring files), their primary use, in practice, was allowing text-based conversations, supported by a limited range of emoticons. In that same period, chat rooms allowed multiple users to discuss, through text conversations, specific topics or shared interests. Somewhat in parallel, Short Message Service (SMS) text messaging debuted on mobile phones in the mid-1990s and proliferated in the early 2000s. Further boosts to text messaging were provided by instant messaging—like functions offered by Facebook, Twitter, and other social networks. Text messaging-related divides between mobile phones, smartphones, mobile devices and computers then diminished (e.g., many mobile providers now allow subscribers to send SMS messages from their computers; a single Facebook account can be used to message on multiple devices connected to the internet). For the purposes of this chapter, all such interactions are bundled together under the term "text messaging".

Writing in 2017, the current chapter in text messaging's evolution incorporates two branches: the spread of mobile-based messaging systems combining elements of social networks and SMS, and the devolution of some email platforms into media resembling text messaging more than they do traditional email.

With the spread of the smartphone, typical phone-based text messaging—once primarily in the form of SMS text messages, limited to 140 characters—has evolved into a much richer medium, with much wider capacity for communication. Messaging apps (e.g., WhatsApp, Viber, and Telegram) are displacing SMS as the primary means for quick communication. These apps allow for much richer communication than text messaging—longer messages, embedded pictures, video clips and other multimedia, and more. They facilitate group discussions, with ease. As they work over the internet rather than over phone systems, they allow access even when cellular service is not available (or comes at high cost).

In many contexts, messaging systems which cast aside the formalities of email are on the rise. The distinctions in functionality and capacity between these and other messaging systems embedded in social networking platforms (e.g., Facebook's messaging system) as well as in other online platforms (such as online learning management systems) are increasingly blurred. More stylized and somewhat more versatile and formal systems are making quick advances in the business world; corporations are adopting and branding internal platforms for intra-organizational communication (see Baldwin 2014).

As some email systems devolve into messaging systems on the one hand, and text messaging gains richness and flexibility on the other, we face an emerging array of primarily text-based communication systems perceived to be less formal than email—yet still supporting substantial interaction. Negotiation interactions certainly already take place over intra-organizational email-like systems. They also take place over phone-based text messaging, as discussed above.

My decision to include all these types of messaging systems under "text messaging," for the purposes of understanding this medium's uses for negotiation, does not intend to imply that differences don't exist. Indeed, I look forward to research delineating between such tools, based on meaningful distinctions. For the purposes of this chapter—a first attempt to apply a negotiation lens to text messaging—I will settle for acknowledging this, and continue painting with a broad brush. Casting this wide net will allow drawing in a larger body of research on text-focused interactions, and applying it to a wider range of text-focused negotiation interactions. Generally speaking, very little is known about negotiation through such systems; what limited research there is has focused on computer-based instant messaging in contrived and controlled settings. So much has changed since then—in terms of the hardware typically used, the functionality of the messaging platforms, environmental factors (most of your text messaging no longer takes place as you sit at your desk, and you don't often set an agreed and dedicated time to engage in a text messaging exchange), and more—that such research needs to be applied with caution. In order to expand the available base of knowledge, I will foray beyond the negotiation literature and couch negotiation via text messaging against a background of communication theory.

Text Messaging Surprises Communication Theorists

Text messaging's specific applications and challenges as a tool for negotiation relate to its nature as a communication medium in a more general sense. What are its major attributes, and in what areas is it significantly different from other media? These attributes create unique "media effects"—elements altering the communication loop on either end, resulting in messages being sent, and understood, differently, owing to the medium through which they were conveyed. As I've noted elsewhere, a large body of research shows that:

> The communication channel through which negotiations are conducted is neither passive nor neutral; it affects what information negotiators share, and how that information is conveyed, received and interpreted [NDR: Ebner, *Email*].

To explain the media effects of text messaging, I will first apply a model of communication theory called Media Richness Theory. Media is "rich" to the extent that people using it as a communication channel can convey "understanding-changing" information within a limited time period; it is "lean," to the degree that they cannot. The more conducive the medium is to a mutual learning process developing for parties using it for communication, the richer it is.

Richer media offer more channels for cues to pass through (sight, sound, smell, hearing, and taste) and more types of communicative cues (verbal, non-verbal, visual). It primes and allows users to employ more types of language (e.g., natural, formal, or technical) and allows them to personalize their messages. It allows higher degrees of interactivity, i.e., it supports providing instant feedback between communicators (Daft and Lengel 1984). This notion of instant feedback involves the nature of the medium's interactivity: Is interaction synchronous or asynchronous? Is it sequential, involving parties taking turns? It also incorporates the notion of parallel processing—does the medium support both parties transmitting and receiving simultaneously? (see Bhappu and Barsness 2006)

Media Richness Theory suggests that the richer the medium, the more conducive it is to clear, unequivocal communication, reducing uncertainty and ambiguity. Richer media are therefore more suited to complex tasks requiring and precise comprehension. They are more conducive to tasks requiring relationship-building based on mutual understanding, in order to avoid conflict and its escalation. Negotiation is an excellent example of such a task.

Looking at text messaging through a media richness lens, it would seem to fall into a category of somewhat lean media, most closely compared to email. Text messaging seems to fall below email on some indicia of richness, whereas it enjoys advantages over email on others. Communicating through text messaging, parties are denied some of the non-verbal cues common in emails—e.g. bolding, underlining or italicizing text, using different fonts or font sizes, utilizing bullets, numbering or paragraph-separation to convey intent and facilitate proper interpretation. Parties are left with straight text, augmented only by the ability to write in capital letters, and emoticons. In some forms of text messaging, messages are limited to 160 characters, further diminishing richness. This tends to guide many into using informal language; indeed, adding any formality, even into text messages unfettered by character-count, requires some effort. On the other hand, text messaging is conducive to short, snappy, responsive interactions, with a high degree of interactivity which sometimes involves some degree of parallel processing. However, this is not always the case. While messaging can be used in this way, it can also often be asynchronous, with long time-lags between interactions. Elsewhere, I've discussed how the spread of smartphones has put our email inbox in our pockets, changing the nature of email synchronicity; I suggested that email has now become a semi-synchronous medium [NDR: Ebner, Email]. I suggest that text messaging is also a semi-synchronous medium. The difference between them on the synchronicity front might be a matter of perceptions and expectations; text messaging communicators may have higher *expectations* of synchronicity than they do with email.

Given this application of media richness theory to text messaging, one might easily reach the conclusion that text messaging is a fairly lean medium, with low capacity for clear communication, open conversation, explicit and detailed interchanges, relationship-formation and trust-building. Or, in short, not a very suitable medium for negotiation.

Surprisingly, some of the research conducted on text messaging as a communication and a negotiation medium runs counter to this conclusion. This research has found that text messages tend to be linguistically simpler, more personal and more affective than phone calls, a seemingly richer medium (Holtgraves and Paul 2013). People have reported they feel more able to honestly express their feelings through texts, than through other media (Crosswhite, Rice and Asay 2014). Much of the research on text messaging has focused on students and young adults. Indeed, for all the confusion this may cause an older generation, text messaging of one form or another has increasingly been a primary mode of communication for younger people for well over a decade now. It is not just a coordination tool, or something to pass time with (under the table) in boring meetings—it is a communication channel through which people connect, interact, fight and make up—or break up (Forgays, Hyman and Schreiber 2014). They use it to maintain family relationships (Crosswhite, Rice and Asay 2014), form and support romantic relationships, and engage in sexual activity (see e.g. Drouin and Landgraff 2012; Luo and Tuney 2015). It is such an integrated element of daily living that restraint from texting causes people to suffer anxiety (see e.g. Skierkowski and Wood 2012). For many adolescents, texting is the last thing they do before falling asleep (Troxel, Hunter and Scharf 2015).

In short, many people, particularly younger people, use text messaging for a wide variety of purposes, and see it as suitable for affect-related tasks and tasks requiring cognitive effort as well as creativity. What might explain the discrepancy between the suggestions of Media Richness Theory and these findings of actual practice?

Texting: A Rich Medium, Especially if You Are Under 30

Two suggestions might explain the divergence of these findings from what would be expected based on a media richness analysis: Either text messaging is a richer medium than initially thought, or it is *perceived* by some to be a richer medium, and is therefore being *used* as one. As it turns out, both of these are probably true.

Text messaging—particularly for those who began using it on pre-smartphone phones—was originally heavily text oriented. Character-based emoticons, e.g., ;-) were the only cues that could be added —and their use was often discouraged. However, as computer and smartphone-based messaging developed, text messaging evolved in terms of the cues it afforded. Many phones and services now accommodate sending SMS with unlimited characters. Messaging apps such as WhatsApp also have no character limitations, allowing users to send text messages as detailed as emails, should they choose to. Twitter, the last holdout in this regard (its character limit had become part of its brand) has recently foregone character limitations in its direct messaging. Ambiguous, character-based emoticons have given way to a wide range of colorful and even animated emoji. Even basic phone-based text messages can include attachments—pictures, audio files, documents and more, which will be conveyed either as an SMS or as an MMS (multimedia messaging service). Messaging apps allow for sending multimedia-heavy files, incorporated into the flow of the message rather than as a separately-accessed attachment. This paints a new picture—of a cue-rich medium, allowing multiple types of language usage.

In addition to the medium becoming richer, I suggest that text messaging, in particular, brings to light a strong *subjective* element of media richness. It seems to be one particular mode of communication in which there is a *very* tangible generational divide. I've noted above that research has found an inverse correlation between age and texting: The older you are, the less you text. However, I suggest that numbers do not truly capture the generational divide. Adolescents and young adults use text messaging for different purposes, and in different ways, than older people do, and this is all related to a generational divide regarding how text messaging is perceived. Findings on text messaging could be reconciled with Media Richness Theory, if our understanding of richness would involve a *subjective* measure: If someone *sees* text messaging as a rich medium, they will *use* it as one, and do so effectively.

To understand the effects of such a subjective measure, I will introduce another communication model, Channel Expansion Theory, which contributes a subjective expansion to Media Richness Theory. This theory suggests that media should not be measured in the abstract, focusing on specific richness characteristics. Instead, richness has a subjective element; it is not dependent on inherent characteristics of the channel—but on how a particular user *perceives* the channel's capacity for reducing equivocality and diminishing uncertainty. These perceptions are based on each user's experiences; the greater the user's experience, the richer the medium will be perceived to be (Carlson and Zmud 1999). Experience is important, as it allows individual communicators to "develop associated knowledge bases that may be used to more effectively both encode and decode rich messages on a channel" (Carlson and Zmud 1999:155). Specifically, four types of experience build up such knowledge bases: experience with the medium, partner, topic and context. The more you are experienced with a medium, the more you will understand about using it skillfully. This will enhance your perception of its richness. The more experienced you are with the topic under discussion, with the organizational context in which the discussion is being held, and with your counterpart, the more adept you will become with the tasks of coding and decoding the cues that are the building blocks of richer use, and of greater apparent richness, of the medium you are using. A loop forms: You grow more skilled with using any medium as a rich medium with experience, and you perceive higher media richness as you grow more skilled with it.

Channel Expansion Theory, therefore, suggests that media richness is not static—it is dynamic, it is subjective, and it increases over time. The more you use a medium, the more things you will be able to use it for, and the better you will be able to identify and decode rich elements that less experienced users might be blind to.

This would explain why teens and young adults (as well as some less-young adults) are able to communicate *very* explicitly through emoji, understanding the differences in nuance between a dozen different smiley faces and having a vocabulary of emoji to demonstrate a variety of emotions or to call to mind a wide range of situations and places. People less experienced with texting might easily dismiss this as frivolous or ambiguous—which it sometimes is—without appreciating the rich package of intent and meaning it conveys, and conveys *well*—provided that the coder and decoder are both experienced with the medium as a rich medium.[1]

Channel Expansion Theory has been tested through a number of empirical studies, holding true across a range of media, including instant messaging (D'Urso and Rains 2008).

A final theoretical model contributing to understanding of text messaging is that of Use Richness. Whereas Channel Expansion Theory explores perceived media richness, capturing users' *perceptions* about a medium's capabilities, Use Richness Theory reflects users' *behaviors* regarding the medium's capability. It suggests that communicators are more likely to *utilize* the communication medium features when these are perceived to be capable of supporting their communicative tasks (Anandarajan et al. 2010). Use richness is not limited to measuring how often a user employs the communication medium in general, but also explores the extent to which a sender utilizes any and all of the capabilities of a given communication medium to broaden communication bandwidth in ways that eliminate ambiguity and reduce uncertainty. These include utilizing any features allowing instant feedback, conveyance of nonverbal cues, personalization of messages and alternation between language types.

This theory provides additional closure to the loop described above: Media richness is determined subjectively by users' experience with it; users gather such experience through accumulating instances of actual use; actual use of a medium increases with increased perception of the medium as rich enough to facilitate mutual understanding.

In the emoji-related example given above, Media Richness Theory and Channel Expansion Theory explained why some people are so skilled at conveying and decoding meaning through emoji; Use Richness Theory explains why they continue to get better at this, and why they are likely to use emoji across an ever-widening span of interactions.

This also explains why, even if you think that text messaging is largely frivolous, or only to be used for short notifications or to send an address and a phone number, others see it as a rich, multifunctional, high-capacity tool to be used across a wide range of contexts. The subjective nature of media richness and adoption therefore explains why text messaging's spread to business and formal contexts, including widespread negotiation activity, is inevitable and unpreventable—your assumptions about appropriateness notwithstanding.

Appropriate? Depends Who You Ask

As this chapter begins to segue into the latter half of the theory-to-practice flow, I'd like to acknowledge, and assuage, a feeling I know some readers may experience—both in reading about users' behavior when communicating via text-messaging, and while experiencing those behaviors in real life.

The material discussed above suggests that there are several divides with regards to text messaging: Generational, experiential and contextual. When someone uses a communication medium in a way we are not accustomed to, we might cognitively categorize this to be inappropriate behavior. Beyond this, we might emotionally experience a jolt of annoyance or feel affronted. With regards to text messaging, I experienced this myself, the first time a student texted me to ask for an extension on a paper's deadline, and included a ";-)" as part of her explanation. I felt it again the first time a counterparty texted me his counterproposal for the sum of child support his client would pay. Others have shared experiencing this same type of reaction with me, across a number of divides. For example, when others text them on formal business issues, text them late at night, or text them on a private line, as opposed to a work phone, they are annoyed. Or, for another category of examples—when others use abbreviated spelling (common to texting, but uncommon in formal settings), adopt informal language, or incorporate emoji.

I am not recommending that anyone adopt any of these behaviors, as a necessary element or form of text communication. However, my first piece of practical advice is, should you find yourself on the receiving end of any such behaviors, and, as a result, you experience annoyance or feel disrespected: get over it.

By "get over it" I don't intend that this must become a new norm you allow. If you think such communication is unsuitable, inappropriate, or lowers effectiveness, deal with it through setting organizational norms, or by direct or indirect channeling of communication. For example, when negotiation counterparts contact me via Facebook Messenger, I respond by asking them to send me an email so that I'll remember to deal with it when I'm at work. However, I recommend recognizing the real causes for your annoyance, and abandoning a direct effort to educate the offender on why they are offensive. Our assumptions about what is appropriate and what is not are rooted in our own culture and experience, and augmented by the false consensus bias which, generally speaking, leads us to assume that our opinions, views, and judgements are more or less shared by everyone else (Ross, Greene and House 1977). We may have grown up in a world in which bad news was delivered in person and not by email; birthday wishes were sent by a card in the mail and not by three words on a Facebook wall; and people in a hierarchal system needing information from their boss sent them an internal memo and received a response three days later. We may have read a corporate memo a decade ago, informing us that emoticons are unsuitable for business communication—and find it hard to understand why people are ignoring that memo. Remember, however, that these assumptions—and their resulting delineation of appropriateness—are all in our minds. If you desire others to conform to them, clarify your view of the boundaries of appropriateness; don't expect others to guess them, or take for granted their inherent sharing of those boundaries. Unless you have clarified those boundaries explicitly, do not infer disrespect, inappropriateness, unprofessional communication or uncouth behavior.

Best Practices—And the Path to Improvement

Whatever your views on its appropriateness, you are likely to find yourself negotiating via text messaging, in one form or another, soon—and increasingly often. Sometimes, this will be of your own choosing [on how to conduct such media choice when you have the luxury of doing so, see NDR: Schneider & McCarthy, *Communication Choices*]; in others, it will just be the way things play out.

Elsewhere, [NDR: Ebner, *Email*] I've made recommendations for best practices in negotiation via email, some of which are very likely to be pertinent to text messaging as well, given their shared characteristics as somewhat lean media with semi-synchronous interactivity.

Below, I will list a number of recommendations for good practices relating to text communication specifically, based on the discussion above, specific research, and experience (my way of inviting readers to learn from my own mistakes).

Fast typist? Play to your strengths: Research exploring computer-based instant messaging and chat—near-synchronous communication channels—has shown that messaging is a conducive medium for negotiators who are "fast-talkers." They are able to utilize pre-planned arguments to dominate the conversation and to elicit concessions. In email exchanges, the slowed-down pace allows people to protect themselves against competitive fast-talkers; in messaging exchanges, their counterparts are left at a loss to respond, and therefore make concessions (Lowenstein et al. 2005). While, of course, counterparts may choose to slow down the interaction and not respond to your message immediately, they might be drawn into a synchronous, rapid-pace exchange anyway.

Punctuation matters, period. In lean media, we strain to infer meaning from any cues we can. One recent piece of research shows that text messages ending with a period tend to be judged, by their recipients, as less sincere (Gunraj et al. 2016). Unless you are intentionally adopting a very formal style, forgo periods. Always

Use synchronicity for rapport-building: The lack of visual cues, and the text-focused medium, affect the way your counterparty perceives you. Social distance forms, leading to suspicion and sinister attribution. This all has the potential to challenge rapport-forming, the precursor of interparty trust. [See NDR: Ebner, *Email*] Near-synchronous interactions can go a long way towards reducing this sense of distance. You don't always need to respond to a text message the moment it is received; often, you will want to consider it, or wait for an opportune moment to respond. However, even one protracted near-instant back-and-forth session, which has you both waiting "on the line" to see what the other is typing (on some platforms, you are even notified that the other is typing a response, even if you cannot yet see it) can create a powerful sense of social presence—and facilitate rapport.

Double-check the spell-checker: While employing spell-checkers is generally a good idea when communicating via text, spell-checkers —particularly those installed on mobile phones—are notoriously prone to do the wrong thing at the wrong moment. Making an offer to your counterpart, you would not want the autocorrect feature to add another zero on to your offer! Spell-checkers are often programmed to recognize your own language and its usage and add it to its dictionary—which might result in it preferring words that are unsuitable, inappropriate, or downright offensive—and inserting them even when you typed the intended word in correctly. The internet is full of horror stories of spellchecker mishaps; my own first negotiation-via-text spellchecker incident occurred when I once suggested to a counterpart that "I think this would be a good time to share our BATNA's with each other." My autocorrect changed the acronym BATNAs (Best Alternatives to Negotiated Agreement) to BANTHAS (a woolly, horned, elephant-sized creature native to the sunny planet of Tatooine); my suggestion that we share these with each other received the electronic equivalent of a raised eyebrow.

Text more than you currently do: Negotiators would be wise to increase their own texting activity. The more experience you have using text messaging apps on your smartphone to communicate with your family and friends, the better an edge you will have when it comes to negotiating though this medium. This has been borne out directly with regards to negotiating via email: Negotiators with higher rates of email affinity (including email preference, email comfort and email clarity, or their ease of understanding and conveying thoughts using email) directly increased individual and joint gains, and were able to affect the way issues are subjectively valued in negotiation (Geiger and Parlamis 2014). Channel Expansion Theory suggests that this would hold true for other media as well.

Learn the characteristics of the platform: Different messaging platforms give you different types of capacities and information. For example, WhatsApp lets you know when the last time your counterpart opened the application was—allowing you to keep tabs on their activity. Phone-based SMS messaging does not provide this information. WhatsApp, Facebook Messenger and other messaging services indicate whether your counterpart has read a message you have sent them. SMS services do not. Not only should you familiarize yourself with what you might be able to learn from the system about your counterpart's actions; think about this through a defensive frame as well, in order to not to accidentally let the system divulge information about you which you would prefer not to share. At the very least, in addition to the characteristics of your own preferred messaging platform, learn the nature of your phone's basic SMS delivery system. SMS currently remains the default text-messaging option for two people who do not tend to use the same messaging platform, or who are not able to connect with each other through one they do share.

Use the system beyond-the-basics: Don't settle for using the medium the same way, multiple times. Use Richness Theory suggests that actual use of the different capabilities of the medium will enhance your overall effectiveness with it, more than repetitive use of the basic features. Even if you don't find it suitable to use emoticons or emoji, practice browsing through the icons your phone offers, and consider which emoji you would insert if you *did* use them. This will give you a better understanding of your counterpart's intentions, when they text you "Have you considered my offer? Don't take too long ;-)".

Consider using the dark side: If it suits your style of negotiation, you might consider using expressions of anger, strategically. Research has shown that expressions of anger may have unique effects via text messaging; responding with an expression of anger to a counterpart's behavior and offers might lead them to make a larger ending concession (Johnson and Cooper 2015; also see Johnson, Cooper and Holowczak 2016). Examples might be "I can't believe you're asking for another discount—we've been over this before and I've told you I can't!!! How many times do I need to tell you no???" or "First you disappear on me for a month, and then you show up with that insulting offer!!! This is going nowhere!!!"

Maybe we think too much for our own good: Using lean media, our strain to infer meaning can carry us away. For example, if we see our counterpart has read our message, we might wonder why they have not yet responded. As time goes by, we may feel anxious, and infer that they are up to something. In reality, of course, they may not have noticed our message, they may prefer to respond when they have cleared quiet time to concentrate, or they may have read it while *driving*, and are still sane enough to put off responding until they have parked. Another example might be us noticing that the other party is responding in 1-2 word messages, and inferring that they are curt, rude, or annoyed with us. In reality, they might be using a phone on which it is less convenient to type than on your own; they might be prioritizing providing us quick answers over later ones, or they might be typing under the table at a meeting, and are keeping it short to avoid getting caught. A good rule to remember, in text messaging, is that *we infer more than they intend.*

They infer more than we intend: Help your counterpart avoid such overthinking, too. If you receive a text and know you can't fully respond right now, "touch base" with a text saying "Got your offer, will sit down with it tonight" in order to keep the other's mind in the right zone. If you are in the middle of a near-synchronous back-and-forth exchange and need to leave, don't disappear; explain your leaving, such as by writing "Called into meeting with boss now; I'll ask her about your proposal and we can continue this later."

Teachers? Encourage In-Class Texting

One final recommendation aims at negotiation educators: Incorporate negotiation via text messaging into your course. If you have not yet been convinced of its importance, ask your students what *they* think—and they will likely tell you that they do it all the time. All it would take, to introduce the topic and connect it to the rest of the material in a negotiation course, is an out-of-class negotiation simulation conducted via text-messaging—and follow-on in-class discussion of it. Use a simulation reflecting real-life, everyday text messaging use—in some locales, a typical car sales/purchase bargaining negotiation would be suitable. You can ask students for a topic they have experienced negotiating via text—and you may be surprised by the variety of their answers. Choose one, and write a simulation-game contextually suitable for text messaging (for the importance of such context/medium matching, and general suggestions for conducting simulations at-a-distance, see Matz and Ebner 2011).

Another way to generate exercise ideas, or actual simulations, even as students engage in a learning activity, is to have students choose a situation that they view as suitable for text messaging, and design role information for a simulation-game centering on it (see Druckman and Ebner 2008; Druckman and Ebner 2013). Finally, students could also conduct a longer-term negotiation in which they are allowed full discretion as to media choice, and instructed to communicate as they would in real life—with the debrief specifically exploring the multiple ways in which parties communicated—including texting, email, *and* face-to-face meetings.

Notes

[1] Perhaps the richness of this medium to those viewing it as rich might be demonstrated by the National Young Writers Festival soliciting submissions of stories written solely in emoji-form (see http://theconversation.com/storytelling-with-a-wink-and-a-smile-the-arrival-of-the-emoji-pocalypse-48308. Emoji are developing as a

language in their own right, displaying signs of syntax, order, preferred usages and more (see e.g., Robb 2014)

References

Anandarajan, M., M. Zaman, Q. Dai and B. Arinze. 2010. Generation Y Adoption of Instant Messaging: An Examination of the Impact of Social Usefulness and Media Richness on Use Richness. *IEEE Transactions on Professional Communication* 53 (2): 132-143.

Baldwin, H. 2014. Instant Messaging is Going Corporate. *Forbes*, February 17, 2014. Available online at http://www.forbes.com/sites/howardbaldwin/ 2014/02/17/instant-messaging-is-going-corporate/#2715e4857a0b621bd3e26541 (last accessed January 16, 2016).

Bhappu, A. D. and Z. I. Barsness. 2006. Risks of email. In *The Negotiator's Fieldbook: The Desk Reference for the Experienced Negotiatior*, edited by A. K. Schneider and C. Honeyman. Washington, DC: American Bar Association.

Carlson, J. R. and R. W. Zmud. 1999. Channel Expansion and the Experiential Nature of Media Richness Perceptions. *The Academy of Management Journal* 42(2): 153-170.

Collister, L. 2015. Storytelling with a Wink and a Smile: The Arrival of the Emoji-pocalypse. *The Conversation*. Available online at http://theconversation.com/ storytelling-with-a-wink-and-a-smile-the-arrival-of-the-emoji-pocalypse-48308 (last accessed June 20, 2016).

Crosswhite, J. M., D. Rice and S. M. Asay. 2014. Texting Among United States Young Adults: An Exploratory Study on Texting and its use Within Families. *The Social Science Journal* 51(1): 70-78.

D'Urso, S. C. and S. A. Rains. 2008. Examining the Scope of Channel Expansion: A Test of Channel Expansion Theory with New and Traditional Communication Media. *Management Communication Quarterly* 21(4): 486-507.

Daft, R. L. and R. H. Lengel. 1984. Information Richness: A New Approach to Manage-rial Behavior and Organizational Design. *Research in Organizational Behavior* 6: 191-233.

Drouin, M. and C. Landgraff. 2012. Texting, Sexting, and Attachment in College Stu-dents' Romantic Relationships. *Computers in Human Behavior* 28(2): 444-449.

Druckman, D. and N. Ebner. 2013. Games, Claims, and New Frames: Rethinking the Use of Simulation in Negotiation Education. *Negotiation Journal* 29(1): 61-93.

Druckman, D. and N. Ebner. 2008. Onstage or Behind the Scenes? Relative Learning Benefits of Simulation Role-play and Design. *Simulation & Gaming* 39(4): 465-497.

Forgays, D. K., I. Hyman and J. Schreiber. 2014. Texting Everywhere for Everything: Gender and Age Differences in Cell Phone Etiquette and Use. *Computers in Hu-man Behavior* 31: 314-321.

Geiger, I. and J. Parlamis. 2014. Is There More to Email Negotiation than Email? The Role of Email Affinity. *Computers in Human Behavior* 32: 67-78.

Gunraj, D. N., A. M. Drumm-Hewitt, E. M. Dashow, S. S. N. Upadhyay and C. M. Klin. 2016. Texting Insincerely: The Role of the Period in Text Messaging. *Computers in Human Behavior* 55(B): 1067-1075.

Holtgraves, T. and K. Paul. 2013. Texting Versus Talking: An Exploration in Telecom-munication Language. *Telematics and Informatics* 30(4): 289-295.

Johnson, N. A. and R. B. Cooper. 2015. Understanding the Influence of Instant Messag-ing on Ending Concessions During Negotiations. *Journal of Management Informa-tion Systems* 31(4): 311-342.

Johnson, N. A., R. B. Cooper and R. D. Holowczak. 2016. The Impact of Media on How Positive, Negative, and Neutral Communicated Affect Influence Unilateral Conces-sions During Negotiations. *European Journal of Information Systems*. Available online at http://dx.doi.org/10.1057/ejis.2016.4 (last accessed June 20, 2016).

Luo, S. and S. Tuney. 2015. Can Texting be Used to Improve Romantic Relationships? The Effects of Sending Positive Text Messages on Relationship Satisfaction. *Com-puters in Human Behavior* 49: 670-678.

Matz, D. and N. Ebner. 2011. Using Role-play in Online Negotiation Teaching. In *Ven-turing Beyond the Classroom* edited by C. Honeyman, J. Coben, and G. De Palo. St Paul: DRI Press.

Robb, A. 2014. How Using Emoji makes us Less Emotional: And What Linguists Say it Means if Your Smiley Face Has a Nose. *New Republic.* Available online at https://newrepublic.com/article/118562/emoticons-effect-way-we-communicate-linguists-study-effects (last accessed June 20, 2016).

Ross, L., D. Greene and P. House. 1977. The "False Consensus Effect": An Egocentric Bias in Social Perception and Attribution Processes. *Journal of Experimental Social Psychology* 13(3): 279-301.

Skierkowski, D. and R. M. Wood. 2012. To Text or Not to Text? The Importance of Text Messaging Among College-aged Youth. *Computers in Human Behavior* 28(2): 744-756.

Troxel, W. M., G. Hunter and D. Scharf. 2015. Say "GDNT": Frequency of Adolescent Texting at Night. *Sleep Health* 1(4): 300-303.

෬ 62 ෨

Negotiation via Videoconferencing

Noam Ebner

Editors' Note: Here, Ebner addresses a tool which has crept up on nego-tiators. Videoconferencing for negotiation was first hailed long ago with certain expectations: high quality video at high cost, to be used for negotiation between business teams in expensively equipped conference rooms. But now, these conditions are largely supplanted by widespread use of lower-resolution videoconferencing tools such as Skype and other low-to-no-cost programs, of varying quality and reliability. As one result, people now find themselves, routinely, in face-to-face negotia-tions with people whose faces cannot be seen very clearly. The social effects go far beyond this, too—concerns about who might be listening out of camera view, and other privacy and confidentiality issues, com-bine with widely varying levels of comfort with this technology to cre-ate a significant likelihood of a mismatch between parties who do not trust, or cannot manage, the technology or the setting equally. Ebner provides a matrix of considerations that apply to nonverbal communi-cation in video conferencing, and another to help a negotiator under-stand features and risks of using video.

Introduction

In the 1989 movie *Back to the Future II*, Marty McFly's character re-ceived a video call on a widescreen in his den. A colleague persuades McFly to join an illegal business operation, against his better judgment. A moment later, another call comes in, from his employer. Having moni-tored the previous conversation, McFly's boss fires him on the spot. His remonstrations are to no avail, and his boss reiterates that he is termi-nated; the words "You're fired" flash in bold letters on the screen, as

Noam Ebner is a professor in the Negotiation and Conflict Resolution program, at Creighton University's Department of Interdisciplinary Studies. Previously an attorney and a mediator, he has taught mediation and negotiation in a dozen countries around the world. He was among the first teachers to engage in online teaching of negotiation and conflict studies, and to explore the potential for Massive Open Online Courses in these fields. Noam's research interests include online negotiation and dispute resolution, trust and its role in dispute resolution, negotiation pedagogy and online learning. Noam can be contacted at NoamEbner@creighton.edu; his work can be found at ssrn.com/author=4251-53.

three other machines in McFly's house spit out faxes bearing the same message.

In the movie's timeline, this scene takes place in late 2015—or, loosely, today—projecting that today, interactions via videoconferencing would be the norm: people would engage in it naturally, all houses would be equipped for such interactions, and significant conversations—including negotiations—would occur through this medium.

While this projection is not as far off the mark as other projections made in that film, communication through videoconferencing is only just beginning to approach the ubiquity anticipated in the movie, whilst people's comfort level with the medium—particularly for significant negotiation interactions—has yet to match the movie's projection. Also interesting is that this communication channel—portrayed as futuristic, next-millennia technology—already existed, and indeed, was already *old*, when the film was made.

In order to understand the capacity of videoconferencing for supporting negotiation interactions, this chapter will briefly describe the developmental history of this medium. It will couch interactions via video in two models of communication theory, explaining implications of this media for human interactions. Zooming in on negotiation interactions, specifically, the chapter will detail areas in which negotiation via videoconferencing poses negotiators challenges and opportunities. Throughout, the chapter will explore the research pertaining to utilizing videoconferencing for negotiation, and provide negotiators with practical advice.

To note, communication over video has many names: Videophone, videotelephony, videochat, videoconferencing, and more. Distinctions have been suggested, but there is no commonly-accepted terminology. With both the Oxford and Cambridge dictionaries now recognizing "Skype" as a *verb*, we can expect terminology to become even more confusing. The term *videoconferencing* will serve for the interactions described in this chapter. As a working definition using that term, in the context of negotiation: Negotiation via videoconferencing is negotiation between two or more people, who are not in the same place, communicating with each other through a medium in which they see real-time motion images of each other whilst concurrently hearing each other in real-time audio. This captures familiar interactions such as Skype or FaceTime conversations, as well as more immersive interactions such as multi-screen telepresence, screenless holographic co-presence, and others.

History of Videoconferencing: It's Longer than You Thought

The 21st century is clearly characterized by lighting-paced adoption of technology and innovation. The smartphone, for example, has already been hailed as the fastest-spreading technology in human history. Conversely, videoconferencing might be one of the *slowest* developing, and *slowest* spreading, technologies of the current era. Envisioned over a century ago, and technologically feasible since the 1920s (essentially, since the invention of long-distance TV broadcasting), slow development, poor product development choice, and surprisingly slow consumer adoption resulted in videoconferencing effectively coming of age only towards the end of the 2000s. By the end of that decade, over 1/5 of Americans had engaged in videoconference over one platform or another, and multiple software channels were available to support even the least savvy of users.[1]

While precise data on the percentage of people engaging in videoconferencing today is surprisingly hard to pin down—only scattered numbers, rather than hard statistics, are available—the answer is, clearly, "many" (for example, Skype has over 300 million subscribers, and Apple reports about 15-20 million FaceTime calls, daily.) Perhaps users today even include 'most' people, at least in certain contexts, in certain parts of the world.

Throughout most of its developmental history, videoconferencing's use for negotiation was probably marginal. While the technology for international and transatlantic videoconferencing existed, it played no role in the historically high-stakes negotiations of its time. Chamberlain flew to Berlin in 1938. Roosevelt, Stalin and Churchill traveled to Teheran in 1943, and to Yalta in 1945, despite the danger of their travel and other difficulties. Sadat flew to Jerusalem in 1977. Even the Moscow-Washington D.C. hotline, intended for use in situations that might certainly require person-to-person conversations between the leaders of the US and the USSR/Russia, has never included video communication.[2]

With regard to more day-to-day negotiations, pinning down a timeline for the spread of videoconferencing's acceptance is challenging. Other than a handful of early-adopting corporate and government contexts, in which implementing videoconferencing was institutionalized into organizational operations, negotiation via videoconferencing is probably spreading at the same pace that communication via videoconferencing is spreading in general—with a few years' lag. Personal acceptance has been key to professional acceptance; people initially resisting negotiating via videoconferencing might accept it once they utilize videoconferencing for private matters—managing relationships at-a-distance, speaking with distant grandchildren, and the like. Readers might reflect on their own path to considering use of videoconferencing for negotiation, to understand how those dynamics play out. Resulting advice would be to never assume that your intended counterparts share your degree of comfort or experience with videoconferencing; differences are at least as likely as similarities.

Videoconferencing as a Communication Medium

To fully understand videoconferencing's applications and challenges as a tool for negotiation, we must explore its nature as a communications medium in a more general sense. What are its major attributes, and how do these diverge from those of other media? These attributes create "media effects"—specific ways in which messages are transmitted, received and interpreted differently, owing to the medium they were channeled through. Media effects influence negotiation conducted via the medium. As I've written elsewhere, a large body of research shows that:

> The communication channel through which negotiations are conducted is neither passive nor neutral; it affects what information negotiators share, and how that information is conveyed, received and interpreted. [NDR: Ebner, *Email*]

To understand videoconferencing's media effects, we will apply two models of communication theory—Media Richness Theory and Social Presence Theory—to videoconferencing, and examine their ramifications for negotiation.

Media Richness Theory

Media richness is the degree to which a communication channel can convey information that can change understanding within a limited time period. In other words, the more a medium is conducive to a mutual learning process occurring via information exchanges it supports, the "richer" it is.

Richness is measured by the number of channels for cues to pass through (sight, sound, smell, hearing, taste) and the cues that are involved in communicating through it (verbal, nonverbal, audial, and sensory). It is also measured by the types and number of languages it primes, and allows, users to employ (e.g., natural, formal or technical) and by the degree to which it is personalized. Finally, it is measured by the degree of interactivity—the medium's capacity for instant feedback between communicators (Daft and Lengel 1986). This notion of instant feedback can be further broken down into a medium's degree of interactivity (is the interaction synchronous or asynchronous? Is it sequential, involving parties taking turns?) and its allowing for parallel processing (both parties transmitting and receiving at the same time) (Bhappu and Barsness 2006). Media Richness Theory suggests that the richer the medium, the more conducive it is to clear, unequivocal communication, reducing uncertainty.

A related theory of human interaction is known as Social Presence Theory. This theory classifies communication media along a spectrum, based on the degree to which one party to the communication interaction is *aware* of the other party. If a medium can support an amount of awareness sufficient for the level of interpersonal co-involvement necessary for the task at hand, communication can be effective (Short, Williams and Christie 1976). There are different approaches to measuring this awareness, in terms of what its object is. Some researchers stress the potential of a medium to support interpersonal emotional connection; others stress its potential to convey the sense that the party is "real" and "there" (Lowenthal 2009).[3]

Media with a high degree of social presence are seen as sociable, personal and warm, suitable for supporting negotiation—a complex interaction involving relational and affect-based elements in addition to cognitive information-processing and communication. The richer the medium, the more signs of social presence it conveys, enhancing perceived social presence and reducing perceived social distance.

Social distance affects negotiation by diminishing awareness of the other's personal situation and emotional state. Negotiators show less interest in the other's words, reducing information sharing as well as identification of key elements of that which is shared, such as a counterpart's underlying interests. The more distant parties perceive themselves to be from one another, the more they focus on self-interest rather than collective gain, and the more they may exhibit self-interested behaviors on the contentious side of the behavioral spectrum.

Videoconferencing seems to score high on nearly all of the measures these theories provide. It allows for visual and aural channels, and a rich variety of verbal and nonverbal cues. Some platforms allow parties to share screens, whiteboards or slides, expanding the number of channels, the types of information that can be shared through them, and the multiple types of languages accommodated by the medium. Clarification can be an instantaneous process, and all communication can be personalized. Parties are not only visible to one another, but their instinctive reactions to one another—a laugh, a nod of the head, a "Yes, exactly" or even a "Never!" all give the sense of parties being present, "there," and "real". While the medium does not provide one significant channel for interpersonal emotional connection—the tactile level—it provides multiple channels for conveying and receiving expressions of empathy, understanding, dissatisfaction and anger, all common ingredients in the mix constituting the interpersonal emotional connection between negotiating parties.

An additional caveat pertains at this point: While applying these models to videoconferencing, it is important to regard them as general principles about a general category of activity—and not precise descriptions of a specific interaction. Videoconferencing is *not* a uniform activity. It takes place across a wide number of hardware platforms (e.g., smartphones, desktops), and (concurrently) a variety of software platforms (e.g., Skype, WebEx, Zoom). These might be intended for generic use, or may be systems running proprietary software, tailored to a particular conference room or a particular format of interaction. Geographical location impacts available bandwidth (and therefore, call quality) and its cost (and therefore, availability and duration of conversations). Screen size—often an outcome of each party's choice of laptop or smartphone—impacts the user's sense of spatial presence in the interaction, thereby affecting their sense of social presence. A user's choice to wear a headset or utilize the phone's speaker might relate to their phone's quality or the noise level of their surroundings—yet affect the degree of their sensation of immersion in the interaction (Bracken et al. 2010).

However, one can speak generally, if cautiously, about shared characteristics of videoconferencing, and the theoretical background provided above should help in forming important differentiations and helpful guidelines. Two overall principles that might derive from applying the models to videoconferencing would be:

1) Make use of the richness afforded by the medium. Be intentional in using different channels, languages, and cues in order to make the most out of the medium.

2) Don't assume that the medium creates sufficient social presence for you, as a passive player. Be proactive: Use verbal and non-verbal cues to lessen perceived distance between you and your counterpart.

What Do We Know about Negotiation via Video-conferencing? Very Little.

Little research activity has explored negotiation via videoconferencing. Such research seems particularly scarce, when compared to the expansive research conducted on negotiation via email [NDR: Ebner, *Email*]. It may be that email, posing a medium very different from face-to-face interactions, with clearly presenting media effects, has been more enticing and perhaps simpler to study than videoconferencing. Videoconferencing, researchers may have felt, was just one or two steps down the media richness, interactivity and social presence spectrums from face-to-face interaction—far less worthy of focused attention. As explained below, this sense that people generally expect things in videoconferencing negotiation to be identical or very similar to face-to-face interactions is an academic blind spot, as well as a practitioner pitfall.

In fact, much of the existing research on negotiating via videoconferencing has been conducted outside of the negotiation field, by investigators exploring computer-mediated communication, management, or technology-related issues; the fact that the interaction measured in experiments was a negotiation was often incidental, rather than fueled by desire to understand negotiation issues in particular.

Beyond its paucity, three other question marks overshadow the current validity of existing research. First, it did not involve negotiation experts, but rather lay people negotiating for the purposes of the experiment; often, college students. Second, videoconferencing was relatively rare before 2010; research predating this point may very well have added medium inexperience to task inexperience, through involving participants undergoing their first videoconferencing session. This is one reason to suggest that, in general, the older this research is, the less likely it is to fully apply to the current day. A third, related, question mark relates to technology: Research on videoconferencing in the 1980s and the 1990s was conducted using technological platforms different from those in use today—with regards to software, hardware, screen size, refresh rate, resolution, color, screen freezes, audio quality, audio/video synchronization and a host of other issues that all affect the media effects under examination. As a result, even well laid-out and comprehensive comparisons of videoconferencing and other media (for a good example of one such study, see Purdy, Nye and Balakrishnan 2000) are unlikely to reflect current-day reality. It would be good to see researchers replicating such studies.

Negotiating Successfully via Videoconferencing: Three Starting Points

In the next section, I will discuss three areas that are particularly important for negotiators to consider with regards to videoconferencing. While the medium affects many areas of negotiation interaction, these pose particularly new challenges and opportunities to negotiators, as compared to face-to-face interactions or other forms of negotiation. I will share research findings pertaining to each, reminding readers to consider these cautiously; I will also engage in practice-based conjecture beyond these findings, supported by findings in other fields as well as by application of the communication models discussed above.

These areas are:
1) Nonverbal communication
2) Trust
3) Security, privacy, and confidentiality

The Return of Nonverbal Communication

While many negotiators are familiar with the interpretation of Albert Mehrabian's (1972) findings, according to which 93% of all communication occurs on the nonverbal plain, writing and teaching in the negotiation field rarely dealt with nonverbal communication in negotiation in a specific and prescriptive manner [NDR: Thompson et al., *Nonverbal*]. Only when text-based negotiation spread with the advent of email—a medium with little capacity for conveying nonverbal micro elements and cues—did the negotiation field begin to comment on the effects of these elements' absence, decrying email as a lean medium, unconducive to collaboration and complex interactions; negotiators were warned to beware its effects or avoid it altogether [see NDR: Ebner, *Email*]. However, lamenting the loss of nonverbal cues in text-based communication did not increase focus on the benefits of effective nonverbal communication in face-to-face interactions.

Jeff Thompson's groundbreaking work on nonverbal communication in mediation (Thompson 2015) led to his development of the METTA model for mapping out, understanding and improving nonverbal communication. This model has been adapted to the online environment (see Ebner and Thompson 2014), as well as to enhancing negotiators' effectiveness in the nonverbal realm [NDR: Thompson et al., *Nonverbal*].

Table 1 introduces the METTA model demonstrating the issues clustered under each dimension of nonverbal communication.

Movement	Gestures, posture, body orientation, eye movement and contact, facial expressions, head nodding, shaking and angling
Environment	Location, distance between people, layout of the room, and background
Touch	Handshaking, adaptors (touching self, such as twirling hair; touching objects, such as clicking a pen or playing with a drinking straw)
Tone	Clarity, pauses, 'ums' and 'ahs', volume, rises and falls, music
Appearance	Clothing, accessories, and adornments

Table 1. METTA

The reintroduction of nonverbal cues into negotiation, as video-based negotiation spreads, may have some experts sighing with relief. At last, communication-at-a-distance has shed its text shackles, and the visual cues provided in videoconferencing bring negotiation 'back to normal'.

However, viewing nonverbal communication in face-to-face settings and in videoconferencing as identical, or as close enough to make no difference, is illusory. Many differences distinguish between these two modes of encounter, with regards to nonverbal communication. These range from absolute differences (we do not fully know how the senses of smell and taste serve us in in-person negotiation, so we can only note their absolute absence in video-based conversations) to much more nuanced, micro-level, elements of nonverbal communication. Focusing on this zoomed-in level, Table 2 notes particular characteristics of videoconferencing communication that are significantly different than in face-to-face communication, with regards to each dimension of METTA.

Movement	Motion is less fluid, and sometimes choppy. Owing to camera/screen resolution, we notice fewer facial expressions, eye movements, and nods. Eye contact is illusory, artificial and confusing. We only see movement in the area captured by the camera. Behavior is constrained, as people do not get up and move about.
Environment	Some sense of distance between you and other negotiator exists in your mind—you feel a few feet, and a million miles away, at the same time. Negotiators see only some of their counterparts' environment. Camera placement and settings affect what the other sees. Negotiators notice counterparts looking at off-camera things: Is she looking at a clock? At someone else? Checking email? Lighting is a much more important factor than it is in face-to-face settings. A noisy background can cause disturbance; a busy background can cause distraction.
Touch	There is no physical touch between negotiators. We cannot view off-camera adaptors (e.g., a counterpart playing nervously with a paper clip outside of the area captured by the video camera)—thus losing information regarding anxiety, stress, confidence, etc.
Tone	Our ability to learn from tone depends on audio quality. Technology can degrade tone, making things seem different than they are.
Appearance	Negotiators see less, due to screen/camera resolution, and only what is on camera. Negotiators might be affected by wearing or viewing artificial accoutrements (microphones and headsets)

Table 2. Elements of nonverbal communication specific to videoconferencing

Awareness of these nonverbal effects of videoconferencing will allow you, while negotiating, to be mindful of your own actions and of how these may be interpreted by your counterpart, and improve the chances that your nonverbal communication will be congruent with your verbal communication.

Table 3 lists suggestions for proactive application of METTA for effective nonverbal communication while negotiating via videoconferencing.

Movement	Be mindful of perceived eye contact and gaze. Intentionally keep hand gestures in the video box.
Environment	Use the entire box provided by the webcam mindfully, to complement body-related with environment-related nonverbal elements. Review your background before initiating the call. Is anything unsuitable, or distracting, captured on-screen?
Touch	Don't fiddle with things off-screen. Provide verbal surrogates for physical touch, such as "It's good to meet you, I wish we could shake hands".
Tone	Try to be more mindful of enunciation and tone. Be careful not to misidentify your counterpart's pauses and talk over them.
Appearance	Dress in a contextually suitably manner—taking into account the nature of the interaction while remaining congruent with your background environment. Complimenting, or asking to see up-close, a piece of jewelry or an object can reduce social distance.

Table 3. Applying METTA proactively in negotiation via videoconferencing

Two nonverbal issues stand out as being particularly and practically important:

Eye contact: One challenge to creating a sense of social presence as well as rapport in videoconference communication is the issue of eye contact. If you look directly into your counterpart's eyes on the screen, your camera will show you looking elsewhere. In laptops, for instance, the camera is usually placed at the top center of the screen; as a result, anyone looking directly at the screen will appear to others to be looking downwards. While there are ongoing efforts to create technological solutions to this challenge through "gaze correction" and enhancing "eye contact perception"—including hardware adaptations that would place devices' cameras behind and in the middle of the screen, and software that would "correct" the image actually captured by the camera and artificially transmit to the other party video in which you are looking directly at them—this issue remains unresolved. One way to alleviate it, is to gaze directly into the camera, as if you were looking into your counterpart's eyes. However, this requires you forgo viewing your counterpart and harvesting visual elements of their nonverbal communication. Another way around this issue is through redesigning your screen layout, which some platforms allow you to rearrange. Reposition your counterpart's videostream-box to be as close as possible to the webcam lens, and you will appear to be looking into their eyes as you watch them on-screen (see Ebner and Thompson 2014).

Webcam positioning: One experiment found that positioning your webcam low, pointing up at you, will give your counterpart the sense that you are taller than they are—leading, in turn, to some degree of dominance (Thomas and Pemstein 2015). Clearly, more exploration of positioning is required. Another positioning issue relates to the optimal distance between you and your webcam—affecting the portion of your body that is visible, its resolution and the natural-ness of the interaction. A Goldilocks approach is recommended here: Not so close that the other is presented with a close-up of your face only, and not so far away that it is hard to make out your expressions and body language, with your surroundings receiving more onscreen salience than you yourself do. Rather, choose a distance allowing the camera to capture your face as well as enough of your upper body to include hand gestures, posture, and body orientation; leave some background visible for providing pre-considered cues while not drawing attention away from yourself (Ebner and Thompson 2014). Most videoconferencing platforms show you concurrently with your counterpart as two live videostreams, allowing you to monitor your own positioning in real-time; additionally, most platforms allow you to operate your camera for testing purposes before the call is initiated, allowing you to preposition your webcam, and yourself, optimally.

This section has demonstrated how nonverbal communication in videoconference-based interactions is significantly different than in face-to-face settings. One particularly challenging, counterintuitive, issue is that the better video gets, and the more true-to-life the interactional experience is, the more likely one is to ignore or dismiss any differences between video and face-to-face settings. Being mindful of the nuances of nonverbal communication, a challenging enough issue in face-to-face negotiation, is even more challenging in videoconferencing-based negotiation—and requires special attention.

Trust

Trust, considered essential for any success in negotiation, is at the core of everything deemed desirable in negotiation processes: cooperation, information sharing, generosity, empathy, integrative solutions, and more (for a detailed discussion of the literature on trust see Ebner 2012).

Trust, however, is a tricky thing to conceptualize, measure, manipulate, and apply in negotiation. Some approaches to negotiation therefore attempt to downplay, or sidestep altogether, the role of trust (e.g., Fisher, Ury and Patton 2011) [see also NDR: Cristal, *No Trust*]. However, for the most part, this challenge has led to increased field-wide focus on trust. [NDR: Lewicki, *Trust* and NDR: Lewicki, *Trust Repair*]

Trust is a challenge to create and maintain under the best of circumstances; the online environment offers new challenges, posing obstacles to a variety of types of trust (See Ebner 2012; Ebner and Zeleznikow

2015). Focusing on interpersonal trust, in previous work I've listed eleven areas in which trust in online negotiation is challenged:

1) Lack of contextual cues: E-negotiators are denied many of the nonverbal cues that we rely on in interpersonal communication for assessing another person's trustworthiness.

2) Increased attribution and increased misinterpretation: The tendency to put the worst possible face on another's intentions and meanings increases in e-communication. As a result, e-negotiators will perceive the other's intentions through the most distrusting lens possible.

3) Increased contentiousness—a vicious cycle: We've already noted how people are more apt to lash out at each other online. It is difficult to trust someone treating you this way—or to gain someone's trust, after doing this yourself.

4) Low expectations of trust: E-negotiators have low expectations regarding the other's trustworthiness walking into the process, and this becomes a self-fulfilling prophecy.

5) I'm anonymous, the other is faceless: The mutual invisibility inherent in e-negotiation facilitates trust-breaking behavior. It is easier to cause damage to a faceless other, particularly when we feel protected by a shield of anonymity and physical distance.

6) Physical distance and interpersonal "otherness": The sense of separation inherent to e-negotiation results in reduced identification with the other, challenging identity-based trust.

7) Empathy, online? Building trust by showing empathy for a negotiating opposite is a challenge even in a rich communication channel; in e-negotiation, the need for empathy is often ignored.

8) Privacy: In ODR processes, parties can never know who is "in the room" with you. Messages transmitted, or real-time conferences can be recorded and are beyond a party's control. This might lead to reduced information-sharing and risk-taking, associated with trust.

9) Human expectations and asynchronous communication: The internet incorporates two clashing characteristics: instant access to anything and anyone, and asynchronous communication. This duality gives rise to unmatchable expectations between negotiators, breeding distrust.

10) Diminished party commitment, investment and focus: Parties to e-mail negotiation might be less motivated than face-to-face negotiators. The low entry costs associated with online processes means that a party's mere agreeing to participate does not have a trust-inducing effect on the other. A lack of constant, active participation might be interpreted by a negotiation opposite as untrustworthiness.

11) Negotiating the new dispute resolution environment: The Internet, still a novelty to many, is distrusted even by its most

fervent advocates. Additionally, even professional negotiators are inexperienced at e-negotiation, and lack skill at trust-building through online media. (Ebner 2012: 217-218)

Which of these pertain to videoconferencing-based negotiation? Applying the discussion of media richness and media effects, prefaced above, would suggest that a number of those challenges derive from media effects specific to text-based communication such as email (e.g., challenges posed by asynchronous communication, or by the other being a faceless, dehumanized e-mail inbox entity rather than a visible human being). Others, however, are not as clear-cut (e.g., the effects of physical distance, challenges to displaying empathy, and trust expectations peculiar to the medium) and might persist even when parties view each other via videoconferencing. Some challenges people might intuitively expect to disappear may do so—only to resurface in novel forms (as has been suggested above with regards to the contextual cues provided by the nonverbal elements of communication; many of these have trust-effects). Still others (such as those related to distrust of the online environment in general, and to trust effects of media novelty and inexperience) would seem likely to continue to challenge trust-building efforts in online negotiation, even in the rich medium offered by videoconferencing. Given the limited research on the media effects of video on negotiation, I've included the entire list here so negotiators can be on the lookout for old pitfalls even if they take new shapes.

Why is the persistence of these challenges so difficult to pin down? Once again, this relates to the meager research on negotiation via videoconferencing discussed above. In a paper focusing on the role of trust in videoconference-based mediation, co-author Jeff Thompson and I noted that in the literature on online negotiation and dispute resolution processes there was very little trust-related material discussing video interactions—a gap thrown into sharp relief by the wealth of material on trust in text-based interactions. We suggested that

> There seems to be an assumption, voiced or not, that in video-based communication the challenges to trust would diminish to their proportions in face-to-face communication. Indeed, while research has found video interactions to be generally more conducive to trust emergence than other media other than face-to-face interactions (Bos et al. 2002), it does not follow that video communication does not pose its own, unique, challenges to trust. (Ebner and Thompson 2014: 105)

What new trust-related challenges might videoconferencing, in particular, pose to the negotiator? I will list four, intending them only as examples:

Trust effects of the new nonverbal communication: Identification-based trust is facilitated, amongst other issues, by rapport, immediacy, and empathy demonstration. Knowledge-based trust develops as your counterpart feels that he or she knows the way you usually act, the patterns you have previously demonstrated, the degree to which you have kept your word in the past; all of these are often predicated on your counterpart's clear understanding of the communication between you [NDR: Lewicki, *Trust*]. As noted above, the introduction of a new set of nonverbal cues and constraints—particularly, when this set is viewed through a filter not aiming to differentiate them from face-to-face communication, but rather assigning the same patterns of inference—can result in new forms of miscommunication, which may have substantial effects on both these types of trust.

Beyond mindfulness to elements of nonverbal communication discussed above, coping with these effects on trust might be done by priming the other party to recognize media effects, rather than attributing negative intentions to you. You might say something along the lines of "Isn't it great that we can meet on this platform? It's almost like meeting face-to-face, even though I know there must be some differences."

Video restores "otherness": Video reintroduces issues into the negotiation process, whose effects were diminished by text-based communication: race, gender, stereotypes and more (see Ebner 2007). The salience of these elements is heightened once again by parties' visual availability to one another. Some of their effects include challenges to trust—ranging from the challenge of creating quick identification-based trust with a counterpart who is very different from you in appearance to the bigger-picture dynamics of in-group/out-group stereotyping. In videoconferencing, these issues may turn out to be even more salient than in face-to-face settings! The side-by-side portrayal of both participants' videostreams in videoconferencing settings results in both of them being highly visible to each other concurrently, whereas in face-to-face settings, you see the other—but, for the most part, you do not look at yourself. This may serve to bring differences to the forefront of the subconscious identification process.

If you are concerned about such issues coming between you and your counterpart, use the medium as an excuse to embrace diversity. "Isn't it great, the way technology allows people who come from such different places, to get together and do business with each other? In this new world, we are all next-door neighbors."

Technology and trust: At the time of writing, technological mishaps remain fairly common in videoconferencing. Screens freeze, video or audio sometimes cut out, audio/video lag occurs, and more. Technological mishaps often have trust-related effects. Try to remember, nostalgically perhaps, the era in which talking by phone was the communicational norm. Picture yourself sitting in an office, speaking with someone else on the phone, when you suddenly hear static, or buzzing on the line. Your counterpart asks you to repeat what you've said, but can't hear you the second time, either. You check that your phone is plugged in well, or take a look to make sure you have good cell reception on your phone—but all appears as it should be. You start to feel frustrated. Your counterpart, raising their voice now, asks you to repeat what you said, only enunciating more clearly this time. At this point, you might begin to feel annoyed by the other. After all, your equipment and surroundings are all fine; there's something going on, on your counterpart's side. Why can't your counterpart buy a better phone? Why can't they stay put in a place with good cell reception, instead of moving around all the time? Are they showing you a lack of respect, by doing other things as you converse? Might they be doing this on purpose, to throw you off your game? Either way, they are being unprofessional and perhaps contentious. Should you really roll the dice on reaching a deal and working with them?

This situation easily and often replicates itself in videoconferencing interactions. When this occurs, judgmental biases such as the false attribution error are quick to kick in—and these can easily undermine trust.

While there is no sure-fire way around these challenges, you can preempt technical mishaps proactively; in fact, take leadership in this area. In a study on online mediators, mediators' expertise with the medium, and ability to troubleshoot, were found to be trust-generating in parties (Hammond 2003); a similarly positive effect might occur in negotiation. Take the time to familiarize yourself with the ins-and-outs of a platform, so you can guide others experiencing trouble. Another way to demonstrate leadership and savvy as well as pre-empting some of the attribution effects discussed above, is by recommending that you decide ahead of time on a backup communication channel—a different videoconferencing platform, or a phone call conversation.

I trust you as far as I can see you: In videoconferencing-based negotiation, we can see our counterpart; however, our view is limited to a very particular box, and from a single perspective. Quite naturally, we wonder what is going on *outside* of that box. Is something else attracting our counterpart's attention? Is the entire setting congruent with what we see, or might our counterpart be putting on a show? Is there anyone else in the room, listening in, without our counterpart letting us know?

These lines of thought are often triggered by other issues discussed in this chapter—such as technical limitations and misinterpretation of body language. Their cause notwithstanding, these thoughts often take on the flavor of *suspicion*, an initial level of distrust. Suspicion presents a fertile breeding ground for false attribution error—with its detrimental effects on trust.

To alleviate such issues, do your best to keep the other's focus inside the box—and that begins with keeping your *own* focus inside the box. Don't play with objects outside of your counterpart's field of vision, don't type on your computer as you speak, and don't look at (or, relate to) people outside of the camera's field. If you need to do any of these, provide your counterpart a word of explanation. You might relate, more proactively, to your surroundings, even showing them to your counterpart (e.g., the view from your window, the weather outside, etc.) if it is contextually suitable, in order to dispel curiosity, or suspicion, regarding your off-screen surroundings.

Security

People considering negotiating via videoconferencing might be concerned by issues of security. While technologically minded people might be concerned about specific issues (e.g., the encryption system of a communication platform), negotiation professionals might be concerned about several things that often congregate, in the context of negotiation and dispute resolution processes conducted online, under the term "security". A previous paper (see Ebner and Zeleznikow 2015) has suggested a framework for discussing these different realms of "security"; adapting this framework to videoconferencing-based negotiation specifically, these realms might include issues of:

1) Information Security: The security of the negotiation process in terms of protecting parties' information from being shared with outsiders as a result of human activity. In this realm are included parties' contracting with each other to keep a process confidential, and, in some contexts, the legal notion of privilege.

2) Data security: The protections set in place around the communication channel: the software, the servers and the hardware used for videoconferencing. A system is secure, in this context, to the extent that it is protected from external people seeking to hack into it and obtain non-public information, whether this involves a front-row seat from which to observe your video recording, or more tangential information (e.g., the names of the contacts in your Skype account, or the length of your calls).

3) Personal security: The provision of safe and clearly defined processes to protect users from actual harm, whether physical or emotional.

4) System security: The degree to which users feel confident that the videoconferencing service they are using—the technological platform or its human operators—is not misusing their information, participation, behavior or data in any way.

Generally speaking, third party "interception" of videoconferencing has not been a significant security issue thus far. Videoconferencing software either encrypts the video, or routes it in ways that cannot be spied upon, in order to protect it. The question of whether a 3rd party such as the videoconferencing service provider itself, perhaps acquiescing to requests from government agencies, may have back doors into these transmissions remains unsettled, but on the whole, videoconferencing appears to have thus far been safe from external interception by intent or by chance. All videoconferencing platforms describe their security capacities in detail. If you are concerned about your conversations being intercepted, choose the software that seems most secure, and make sure to configure your security options according to their advice.

Another type of security breach involves, rather than external interception, the video being accessed via eavesdropping on your own computer. Certain malware can take over your computer, including your video camera, and alter the way it works. Theoretically, such malware could also record your conversations. Preventing malware from gaining control and stealing video data from your machine may require protections beyond basic antivirus software; numerous sources evaluate and rate competing products that offer more comprehensive coverage (often under a rubric such as "complete internet security" or something similar).

Another worrying form of data leakage is the possibility that the other party is recording your data by creating a screen recording of *their own* computer, which can easily be done entirely on their end of things. There is, simply, no way around this—it is a valid concern. It may be that many users do not know how to do this—but many do, or their IT departments can explain it to them. Some videoconferencing software even includes built-in options for creating recordings of the conversations. This might involve the software notifying all parties that recording is taking place, or not. Perhaps in an effort to instill confidence in their users, neither Skype nor Google Hangouts currently support recording of calls natively; however, third-party plugins allowing recordings are available for both. If the other party wishes to record your conversation, they can do so; it is worth keeping this in mind—perhaps as a default assumption—as you interact. A not unrelated concern is that there may be someone in the room, off-camera, hearing and viewing the interaction without you being aware.

When dealing with counterparts who you sense might be hesitant about using videoconferencing for a negotiation for security-related reasons, you might preemptively offer that the interaction take place over their own platform, or invite them to choose a platform through which to conduct it. As for you, it may be that, especially prior to trust being established, a good rule of thumb would be: Don't say anything in a videoconference that you would not want shown on the news.

Considerations for Media Choice

The theoretical models discussed above, and the discussion of challenges unique to videoconferencing-based negotiation, suggest some considerations for negotiators to keep in mind, as they consider whether videoconferencing is a suitable platform for a particular negotiation. [also see NDR: Schneider & McCarthy, *Communication Choices*]

Synchronicity: Do I think better on my feet, or does the slower pace of email serve me better?

Availability: Will a conversation via videoconferencing be challenging to set up, given the time-zones involved? Is it likely to entail my participation at an inconvenient hour for me, or one at which I will not do my best?

Technology: Do we both have access to suitable equipment and bandwidth for good quality videoconferencing? Am I satisfied with the data security and privacy provided by the platform?

Savvy: Am I skilled enough with the medium to perform well? Do I think the other has experience with the medium?

Beyond these considerations, you might find videoconferencing to be particularly helpful for effective negotiation in specific situations:

- When you need to pin down the answer to a question your counterpart has not responded to through email—and perhaps is trying to avoid.

- When email conversations have been fruitful—but are moving along slowly, with long lags during which you wait for the other's responses.

- When you feel issues of language and meaning continually rein in your email communication—and you want to be able to ask and answer questions, or request clarifications, in real-time, rather than conduct multiple email exchanges to clarify small points. One good session can provide clarity, allowing you to return to email exchanges, now working off the same page.

Back to the Future

One must be cautious predicting, in writing, the development of technology—or risk looking very silly in a few years' time. Still, I think it is safe to say that the near future will see videoconference-based negotiation continue to spread. While it is unlikely to sweep through negotiation practice like wildfire, videoconferencing use will increase as people become increasingly familiar and comfortable using it for other purposes. The range of readily accessible videoconferencing platforms will expand, as will their capabilities. Hardware—including cameras, microphones and speakers—will also improve. Fixed and mobile broadband will continue to expand and improve, supporting better sound and video quality as well as newer technologies. Indeed, we can expect to see advances in communication via holograms, immersive telepresence systems, and—perhaps sooner than we expect—virtual reality technology interfacing with traditional videoconferencing technology, engendering the sense of co-presence at the same physical location. The information provided in this chapter will speak to these technologies, but its application will require adaptation depending on the unique qualities and media effects of each technological development.

To cope well in the present, and to prepare ourselves for future innovations, I will end with two recommendations.

First, to negotiators: Get used to it. Practice communication via videoconferencing in personal interactions—and gradually incorporate it into professional situations. The notion that the more you use a medium, the more effective you will be negotiating through it, has been borne out in research on email negotiation (Geiger and Parlamis 2014); this might hold true for other communication media. You might practice by conducting a negotiation simulation with a friend via videoconferencing, recording the screen, and reviewing the recording.[4]

Second, to negotiation educators: Teach it. Negotiators will definitely find themselves interacting via videoconferencing, at some point in their future. Understanding the differences between this modality and the face-to-face default taught in our negotiation courses will be critical for their success. Negotiation via videoconferencing needs to enter our curriculum, including reading material and simulation, much as email negotiation required similar incorporation only a few years ago (see Ebner et al. 2009). Some guidance for teachers already exists (for suggestions on conducting simulations at-a-distance, including videoconferencing, see Matz and Ebner 2010; Smolinski and Kesting 2012; such videos might also provide a helpful assessment tool—see Manwaring and Kovach 2012). By preparing negotiators for the current state-of-the-art with regards to technology, we will facilitate their later adapting to other technologies.

Notes

[1] A watershed event may have been the release of the iPhone4 in June 2010. Featuring a front-facing camera, required for videoconferencing, as well as Apple's FaceTime videoconferencing software, this model put everything users needed at their finger-tips—wrapped up in a popular device.

[2] It has never been a telephone connection either, for that matter; all depictions of 'the red phone' are fictitious. In its current form, the hotline is a dedicated email-like connection.

[3] I'd suggest that the former stress "social", and the latter stress "presence," and there may be differences between these two with regards to negotiation via videoconferencing.

[4] For one available simulation, contextually suitable for negotiating via video-conferencing, see *Live8.org* (Ebner 2009).

References

Bhappu, A. D. and Barsness. 2006. Risks of Email. In *The Negotiator's Fieldbook*, edited by A. K. Schneider and C. Honeyman. Washington, DC: American Bar Association.

Bos, N., J. Olson and D. Gergle, G. Olson and Z. Wright. 2002. Effects of Four Computer-Mediated Communications Channels on Trust Development. In *Proceedings of SIGCHI Conference on Human Factors in Computing Systems*. ACM Press: New York.

Bracken, C. C., G. Pettey, T. Guha and B. Rubenking. 2010. Sounding Out Small Screens and Telepresence: The Impact of Audio, Screen Size, and Pace. *Journal of Media Psychology Theories Methods and Applications* 22(3): 125-137.

Daft, R. L. and R. H. Lengel. 1986. Organizational Information Requirements, Media Richness and Structural Design. *Management Science* 32(5): 554-571.

Ebner, N. 2012. Online Dispute Resolution and Interpersonal Trust. In *ODR: Theory & Practice*, edited by M. S. Abdel Wahab, E. Katsh, and D. Rainey. The Hague: Eleven International Publishing.

Ebner, N. 2009. E-mail Negotiation Simulation: Live8. In *Negotiation: Readings, Exercises & Cases* 6th ed, edited by R. Lewicki, D. Saunders, and B. Barry. Burr Ridge, IL: McGraw-Hill/Irwin.

Ebner, N. 2007. Trust-Building in E-Negotiation. In *Computer-Mediated Relationships and Trust: Managerial and Organizational Effects*, edited by L. Brennan and V. Johnson. Hershey, PA: Information Science Publishing.

Ebner, N., A. Bhappu, J. G. Brown, K. K. Kovach and A. K. Schneider. 2009. You've Got Agreement: Negoti@ing Via Email. In *Rethinking Negotiation Teaching: Innovations for Context and Culture*, edited by C. Honeyman. J. Coben, and G. De Palo. St. Paul, MN: DRI Press.

Ebner, N. and J. Thompson. 2014. @Face Value? Nonverbal Communication & Trust Development in Online Video-Based Mediation. *International Journal of Online Dispute Resolution, Forthcoming.*

Ebner, N. and J. Zeleznikow. 2015. Fairness, Trust and Security in Online Dispute Resolution. *Hamline Journal of Public Law and Policy* 36(2): 143-160.

Geiger, I. and J. D. Parlamis. 2014. Is There More to Email Negotiation Than Email? The Role of Email Affinity. *Computers in Human Behavior* 32: 67-78.

Lowenthal, P. R. 2009. The Evolution and Influence of Social Presence Theory on Online Learning. In *Online Education and Adult Learning: New Frontiers for Teaching Practices*, edited by T. T. Kidd. Hershey, PA: IGI Global.

Manwaring, M. and K. Kovach. 2012. Using Video Recordings: A Mirror and a Window on Student Negotiation. In *Assessing our Students, Assessing Ourselves: Vol. 3 in the Rethinking Negotiation Teaching Series*, edited by N. Ebner, J. Coben and C. Honeyman. St. Paul: DRI Press.

Matz, D. and N. Ebner. 2010. Using Role-Play in Online Negotiation Teaching. In *Venturing Beyond the Classroom: Vol. 2 in the Rethinking Negotiation Teaching Series*, edited by C. Honeyman, J. Coben, and G. De Palo. St. Paul: DRI Press.

Mehrabian, A. *1972. Nonverbal Communication.* Chicago: Aldine-Atherton.

Purdy, J. M., P. Nye and P. V. Balakrishnan. 2000. The Impact of Communication Media on Negotiation Outcomes. *International Journal of Conflict Management* 11(2): 162-187.

Short, J., E. Williams and B. Christie. 1976. *The Social Psychology of Telecommunications.* London: John Wiley & Sons.

Smolinski, R. and P. Kesting. 2012. Transcending the Classroom: A Practical Guide to Remote Role Plays in Teaching International Negotiation. *Negotiation Journal* 28(4): 489-502.

Thomas, L. E. and D. Pemstein. 2015. What You See is What You Get: Webcam Placement Influences Perception and Social Coordination. *Frontiers in Psychology* 6: 1-7.

Thompson, J. 2015. *Nonverbal Communication and the Skills of Effective Mediators: Developing Rapport, Building Trust, and Displaying Professionalism.* Thesis, PhD Doctorate, Griffith University, Brisbane.

⊰ 63 ⊱

The Technology of Negotiation

Noam Ebner

Editors' Note: Here, the author follows up on his Email and Text negotiating chapters, both of which discuss technology which by now have become quite generic. This chapter is different: Ebner here describes representative examples of a burgeoning class of proprietary programs, which individually address one or another situation or problem a negotiator may have. Together, they form an expanding array of electronic helpers—and merely hint at what may be available not far into the future. It is increasingly evident, as a result, that keeping up with the field is no longer simply a matter of reading; learning new programs as they come along is virtually guaranteed to become more and more essential.

Introduction: Information Technology and Negotiation

The technological upheavals of the past generation have affected all forms of human action and interaction. They have changed the way we do everything—from shopping to dating, and from worshipping to banking. They have also changed who we interact with, and how we interact with them.

The activity of negotiation is no exception to this shift. Technology, and the social, behavioral, psychological, and emotional changes it has brought about, affect the negotiation process, and, indeed, negotiators themselves. (Ebner, 2017)

Noam Ebner is a professor in the Negotiation and Conflict Resolution program, at Creighton University's Department of Interdisciplinary Studies. Previously an attorney and a mediator, he has taught mediation and negotiation in a dozen countries around the world. He was among the first teachers to engage in online teaching of negotiation and conflict studies, and to explore the potential for Massive Open Online Courses in these fields. Noam's research interests include online negotiation and dispute resolution, trust and its role in dispute resolution, negotiation pedagogy and online learning. Noam can be contacted at NoamEbner@creighton.edu; his work can be found at ssrn.com/author=4251-53.

With few exceptions [see, e.g., NDR: Newell, *Digital Generation*] the discussion regarding technology in the literature of the negotiation field focuses on technology providing negotiators with new communication tools—and how to best navigate this new interactional landscape. Many studies have focused on individual communication channels, detailing challenges and disadvantages and best practices for their advantageous use [see NDR: Ebner, chapters on *Email*, *Videoconferencing* and *Texting*, for examples and literature reviews regarding each medium]. Other studies have compared a number of widespread communication channels, for understanding their relative benefits and improving negotiators media choice (see, e.g., Purdy, Nye and Balakrishnan 2000; Mor and Suppes 2014). [NDR: Schneider & McCarthy, *Communication Choices*] Combined, these lines of inquiry seek to inform negotiators of how to best continue to play their familiar roles, through different communication technologies.

However, media effects and media choice are not the only areas of negotiation affected by technological developments. This piece sets these aside, and applies a different prism to the technology-negotiation interface, oriented towards more direct application of technology to negotiation.

Such direct application involves technology playing an active role; it not only constitutes a medium, it *contributes* to the negotiation process. It may contribute to one party only, or to both parties concurrently. It may also assist a third party working with both parties (although, as noted below, this is beyond the scope of this chapter).

In this chapter, I will discuss software applications designed specifically for supporting negotiation processes, or for assisting individual negotiators. Compared to the literature on negotiating through different communication media, the body of literature regarding negotiation-tailored software is slim, mainly detailing individual experiments on this front. Only a few of these developments have been reported on in the negotiation literature; others have appeared in a somewhat separate body of literature focusing on the field of Online Dispute Resolution (ODR). Still others may have flown beneath the radar of both of these fields.

This is not a piece on ODR in general.[1] It is specifically aimed at negotiators interested in using technology in their negotiation endeavors—whether settling disputes, or making deals. Much of the focus on negotiation in the ODR field is on the dispute resolution, rather than the deal making, side of negotiation. This chapter focuses on both types of negotiation, but will not go beyond negotiation to discuss applications of technology to 3rd party-assisted processes. As Orna Rabinovich-Einy and Ethan Katsh explain, one of the first recognized benefits of applying technology to dispute resolution was the ability to automate negotiation processes, leading to interest and experimentation in this area. [NDR: Rabinovich-Einy & Katsh, *ODR*]

Technology at Three Points

Seeking a helpful way to categorize different applications of technology to negotiation, I discarded two early technology-focused candidates. One differentiated between computer-installed programs and web-based platforms; another separated computer applications from mobile applications. Each was abandoned, as these distinctions are rapidly fading and losing their salience.[2] Instead, I adopted a negotiation-focused differentiation between software applications, based on the *phase of the negotiator's experience* they are intended to assist with.

Without addressing the debate of whether the negotiation process involves distinct and sequential stages, as opposed to a mix of non-sequential elements concurrently at play (see Ebner and Kamp 2010), I suggest that negotiators certainly go through a cyclic process which includes learning about negotiation in general, preparing for a specific negotiation, and conducting that negotiation. [NDR: Zartman, *Stages*] Reflection on this negotiation experience adds to the negotiator's general stockpile of knowledge, and the negotiator's cycle continues. Each of these phases, as this chapter will show, can be enhanced by technology.

Figure 1. The Negotiator's Cycle

An Invitation, Not a List

While this piece surveys a variety of possibilities for such enhancement, and particular pieces of software designed to do so, I do not intend to fully survey all of the software currently available, or provide a comprehensive list of possibilities for technology's contribution to negotiation. On the contrary—the next piece of helpful software is out there, waiting to happen; one intention of this piece is to bring readers into the circle of potential developers. The next piece of software may tweak an existing piece of software and improve on it; it may identify an uncharted point in the negotiator's cycle supportable by technology; or, it might apply a new approach to negotiation to a temporal point addressed by another program. Another purpose of this chapter is to familiarize negotiators with software that is readily available out there, right now, and to encourage them to consider how these might be adopted to improve their own practice. While this piece discusses specific apps or software products for that purpose, these are only examples, and not endorsements of any particular product or service. There are likely to be several different pieces of software out there for negotiators to choose from, for each phase in the cycle, and the variety is likely to grow; I recommend negotiators explore, and experiment with, more than one tool. In fact, by the time this chapter is published, there will likely be new apps created that did not exist at the time of writing.

Technology Helping Negotiators Prepare for Specific Negotiation Processes

How might technology be able to help negotiators in preparing for negotiation? One might envision a wide range of software applications preparing negotiators for different elements of the relational and economical aspects of an upcoming negotiation.

As examples of existing software, I'll discuss three such applications, each with a different focus.

Situation Assessment:

The *Making Conflict Work* app (https://play.google.com/store/apps/details?id=com.makingconflictwork.makingconflictwork&hl) was developed by Peter Coleman and Robert Ferguson of Columbia University, based on their book of the same name (2014). While not strictly a negotiation app (given that it adopts a wider conflict focus), it is easily applicable to many negotiation situations, and gives a sense of what a somewhat similar tool for negotiation situation assessment might look like. A negotiator using this tool is first asked a series of questions about the situation (e.g., is it personal, or professional? How important is the goal to you?). The app then helps to map out the negotiator's relative power, names the negotiator's situation, and gives recommendations for how to proceed. As not a great deal of *specific* detail regarding the situation is input into the software, the recommendations are at the level of strategic choice (e.g., elaborations on "engage," "avoid," or "cooperate") rather than a detailed list of tactical actions to take (e.g., "Do X, and then do Y."). Receiving such strategic guidance could be a first good step in preparing to handle an important negotiation situation.

Preparation-by-Model:

ExpertNegotiator (http://www.negotiationinstitute.com/content/software) is software designed by Marty Latz around his book *Gain the Edge* (2005). The program takes into account that you might only have a limited amount of time to prepare, and allows you to choose the depth of the preparation, and the number of variables you need to input. It also allows users to create special preparation templates for themselves or their company. In organizational settings, managers can check in and make sure their team is actually preparing for negotiation processes according to predetermined company best practices. [NDR: Borbely & Caputo, *Organizations*]

Another interesting feature of this software is the "Counterpart Intelligence Bank" in which you input and store information about your counterpart, on an ongoing basis. This can be shared between multiple colleagues negotiating with the same person, enhancing institutional knowledge about counterparts, and preserving it against the event of team members leaving the organization. Once enough input has been provided, patterns will begin to emerge, and you will be able to notice whether your counterpart often implements certain tactics—especially contentious tactics, such as ultimata or walkouts—at particular points during the process.

Learning to Prepare, Preparing by Learning:

The Negotiation Planner app (https://play.google.com/store/apps/details?id=com.valgui.NegotiationPlanner&hl=en), developed by George Seidel of the University of Michigan, provides a detailed checklist for negotiators to use ahead of an upcoming negotiation. It also provides a set of supplementary checklists and questionnaires for addressing specific issues likely to come up in the negotiation, such as ethics and power.

The app combines planning with learning, thereby closing the loop on the cycle portrayed above. Learning elements built into this app include links to instructional videos on negotiation, and a "performance review" questionnaire aimed at helping negotiators conduct a post-negotiation self-debrief, in which they reflect on the negotiation experience and consider ways to improve.

Technology Supporting Parties in Conducting Actual Negotiation Processes

Creating systems supporting both negotiating parties in their thinking and their interaction patterns has long captured the attention of researchers (see, e.g., Lodder and Thiessen 2003; Druckman, Druckman and Arai 2004; InterNeg E-Negotiations Research Project[3]). Some have focused on the incorporation of artificial intelligence, and others explored game theory. Researchers have named these types of software Negotiation Support Systems (NSS).

In practice, some NSS relying on these sophisticated theoretical underpinnings have found their way into software applications available to negotiators. Other software, built on less complex—but perhaps no less effective—underpinnings has also been developed. In this section, I will introduce four different applications of technology for supporting the conduct of the negotiation process itself.

Automated and Assisted Negotiation:

The software implemented at eBay (and, later, at PayPal) focuses on automation. Designed for dispute resolution in a given commercial environment (rather than deal making, or dispute resolution in a wide variety of settings), it categorizes disputes into a limited number of categories. Parties are then sent pre-scripted, category-suitable, forms to fill out, in the hope that the exchange of information will lead them to agreement. In addition to providing automation, the system channels communication towards constructive exchanges; parties are primed by the forms they fill out as to what information to share. If parties are unable to reach agreement, there are other layers of the system to assist them, but these are outside the realm of negotiation (for more on the eBay system and its development, see NDR: Rabinovich-Einy & Katsh, *ODR*; for extra-negotiation potentialities of such systems, see Modria.com's diverse, ongoing, applications of the eBay platform).

Optimizing Outcomes:

Another type of system focuses on individual cases rather than multiple claims—and engages with each process in great depth. *Smartsettle Infinity* (http://www.smartsettle.com/home/products/smartsettle-infinity/) requires parties to examine their interests in depth—and prioritize them, through assigning them relative value. After both parties have done so, each party is shown different system-suggested solutions, visually represented so that they understand the degree to which their prioritized interests are being met. They are able to tweak these solutions, and communicate the reasons for this with their counterparty. After parties have agreed on a solution, *Smartsettle Infinity* introduces a semi-automated advice phase: The software asks parties if they would like to receive an "optimized" solution to consider—even as their current agreement serves as the default outcome. If they refuse this option, their agreement stands and the process is at an end. If they choose to see the system's optimized solution, the software presents a package that strives towards a pareto-optimal result, based on the values parties have input. Parties can either accept this expanded-pie solution as their new agreement, or remain bound by their independently-reached agreement.

Smartsettle Infinity, then, supports negotiators by nudging them to detail and prioritize their interests, providing visualizations and dynamic representations of offers and preferences, suggesting multiple solutions, providing a communication channel, and optimizing final solutions (Thiessen, Miniato and Hiebert 2012). Another level of support that such software provides parties is that in assisting them to manage cognitively complex issues, it lessens their tendency to ruminate counterfactual thoughts about better outcomes they might have reached—increasing overall party satisfaction (Ow, O'Neil and Naquin 2014).

Smartsettle Infinity represents the type of software offering not only the most types of support, but also the highest level of technological sophistication. Other programs have been developed utilizing algorithms, artificial intelligence, and mapping tools for approaching complex issues and preferences. However, these have remained largely at the experimental level, never crossing over into commercial use. One example is *Family Winner*, developed by John Zeleznikow and Emelia Belluci (2003) of Victoria University. This software was framed as providing decision support, using game theory to identify optimal solutions based on information provided by parties. Parties were free to accept or reject the advice; they can also repeatedly choose to revise the information given to the system, allowing it to generate new advice.

Blind-Bidding:

Other systems aim far lower in terms of the type and range of support they provide, yet succeed in filling a real need. Blind-bidding systems, such as *Cybersettle* and *Smartsettle One* (http://www.smartsettle.com/home/products/smartsettle-one/), accommodate negotiations that boil down to deciding a single number, with regard to a single issue (e.g., agreeing the amount of a settlement, or agreeing the price of a car).

Blind-bidding is roughly equivalent to two parties each writing down their bottom-line offer on a piece of paper and handing them to a third party, who looks at them and announces whether there was overlap, and thus agreement—or not, in which case, impasse results without parties knowing their counterparty's bottom line. Such systems need not be very sophisticated. They primarily support negotiators by eliminating the postures of the bargaining dance, by keeping their bottom line figures private, and by significantly reducing the time required to reach agreement or impasse.

Cybersettle's system had negotiators conduct three rounds of entering numbers; if, in one of these, parties' offers overlapped, the system announced agreement, splitting the overlapping value evenly between parties. If three rounds ended with no overlap, the system declared impasse. [For further discussion of *Cybersettle*, see NDR: Rabinovich-Einy & Katsh, *ODR*]

Smartsettle One works largely on the same principles, with three tweaks worth mentioning: First, parties can make an unlimited number of proposals to each another. Second, overlap-created surplus is not divided up evenly; rather, a greater portion is awarded to the party who has been more generous with concessions—thus, creating incentive for such generosity. Third, the system allows parties to submit the issue at hand to a form of binding arbitration in the event of negotiation impasse—offering parties the certainty of a final outcome, through agreement or arbitration, at the end of the process.

Determining a Yesable Zone:

Another NSS that lies somewhere between these two extremes of pareto-optimal seeking and blind-bidding simplicity is *Adroit*[3] (http://www.adroit3.com/). This software can only handle bargaining over a single numeric sum. Parties enter their demands (e.g., a claimant seeking compensation types in $20,000, and her insurance company types in $0). Parties then spend 45 minutes responding to system-generated questions, asking each of them (privately) whether they would settle for different sums in-between the extremes. Parties provide the system with responses to each such hypothetical offer, on a four-item scale ranging from "Under no circumstances" to "I would give this sum a fair amount of consideration". After both parties have responded to the eighteen sums the system generated, the software has ostensibly learned enough about both parties' flexibility, determination and positions in order to conduct a numerical analysis and generate a sum that might be agreeable to both of them. Parties then have ten minutes in which to decide to accept, or reject, the system-offered sum. If they do not, the session ends with impasse.

Support for One Party:

To give a sense for the different types of support to an ongoing negotiation process that technology can provide negotiators, I'll note one final application that differs sharply from the previous three. Rather than providing a platform for supporting both parties, *NegotiateIt* (https://itunes.apple.com/us/app/negotiate-it-save-money-phone/ id545864961?mt=8), a mobile app, supports only one party as she engages her counterparty over the phone. Designed by Ramit Sethi, based on his book *I Will Teach You to be Rich* (2009), the app contains detailed information about the best way to negotiate with those service providers we all come in contact with, at one point or another: banks, credit card companies, cellular providers, cable companies, and more. This information is not in the form of tutorials or lessons; the app doesn't *educate* you on how to negotiate with these entities *in general*—rather, it scripts out *exactly* what you need to say, in a wide variety of interactions, with a wide variety of specific entities. Missed a credit card payment on your

American Express card, and want to ask the company to waive the fee incurred? The app provides you with a precise script to follow, based on the creator's knowledge of the patterns these entities' service representatives (who are, essentially, repeat player negotiators) follow. Once you've identified whom you need to talk to and the issue at hand, the app will provide you with the relevant telephone number, and even make the call for you, while the screen of your device displays a script for you to follow.[4] This type of software also introduces the possibility of an even playing field with the mass-repeat-player/script-using companies described by Menkel-Meadow and Dingwall. [NDR: Dingwall & Menkel-Meadow: *Scripts*]

Technology for Learning and Tracking Improvement

The third type of software to be discussed is educational in nature. Before discussing the different types of programs available, however, I'll stress one distinction between educational material and educational software.

There is a huge amount of negotiation information freely available on the internet—books, articles, educational videos and more. Some of these take the form of individual items; others might be robust collections (such as the Social Science Research Network's searchable database, which includes thousands of articles related to negotiation[5]) or structured compilations (such as the dozens of video lectures prepared for NegMOOC, a Massive Open Online Course on negotiation offered by the author at Creighton University[6]).

However, most of this material is not educational *software*. The central feature of a software program is that it does something *operationally*, going beyond passive accessibility. Thus, software with a primary focus on negotiation education goes far beyond a YouTube video or a screen full of text, and draws users into an experience in which they *interact* with the program, which is *responsive* to them. This might take all or any of the following forms: The software might assess users' learning needs; teach according to their preferences; react to their choices; record their information and provide input on it; or provide feedback on their actions. There are many ways to envision this, at varying levels of sophistication, and with varying types of interaction. The software discussed below encompasses a variety of design and interaction approaches.

Close My Deal (https://itunes.apple.com/us/app/close-my-deal/id398492625?mt=8) is a mobile app, in which users go through a diagnostic process analyzing their negotiation style—and learn about their style's strengths and challenges, including comparing it to other styles. Through learning material including text, graphics and videos, users can learn about various issues in negotiation. Some of the features are fairly passive; others are exercises involving user interaction. The app allows users to create their own collation of the tips and ideas they see as most valuable, for quick reference.

Another mobile app with a primary educational focus is *Learn to Negotiate by Negotiating with "Friends"* (https://itunes.apple.com/us/app/learn-to-negotiate-by-negotiating/id716831054?mt=8), designed by Ravnit Singh. This app leads users through a series of "lessons", which include both reading material and simulations. The unique feature of this app is the way the simulations are conducted; users are paired up with other users of the app, and negotiate with people they are unfamiliar with. After the simulation is concluded, the software provides feedback, including portrayals of how the pie was divided and what value was left on the table—as well as advice for what users might have done better.

Another app combining educational material with a simulation experience is *Negotiate!*, which is designed by Rational Games (http://www.rationalgames.com). This app currently offers one simulation-game, in which users (negotiating with the software, rather than with live counterparts) can choose to play either role.

These apps demonstrate how the primacy given to simulations in negotiation education (see Druckman and Ebner 2013) is carrying over to technological educational applications. As negotiation education engages with online communication, and with online teaching of negotiation, teachers and learners face the challenges of conducting simulations at-a-distance (Ebner et al. 2009; Matz and Ebner 2010). The apps described in this section demonstrate new ways to address these challenges.[7]

A web-based program designed to teach negotiation is *Strategy Shaper*, designed by Andrea Schneider of Marquette University and educational software company 3C (www.strategyshaper.com). This software—designed particularly for researchers and academic scientists—takes users through several self-awareness tests including the DYNAD (Schneider and Brown 2014) as well as assertiveness, empathy, flexibility and social intuition scales. In the framework of a self-paced course, the user plays a series of games practicing negotiation skills in job and promotion negotiations as well as in co-authorship and mentorship discussions.

Finally, one app focuses not on *teaching* negotiation principles, but rather on enhancing users' ability to implement them, and to *improve* over time, through reflection, debriefing and growth. *Negotiation 360* (https://itunes.apple.com/us/app/negotiation-360/id949271941), developed by Michael Wheeler of Harvard Business School, applies a diagnostic tool exploring a number of attributes and skills people have. Users only have a given number of points to allot to all of the attributes, so they need to carefully consider which areas they consider themselves to be least proficient in. Based on their answers, users are categorized into five categories, such as "Assertive Value Claimer," or "Empathetic Value Creator." Next, users begin to keep a scorecard; for each ensuing negotiation process they examine their work on different measures, score their performance, and note lessons learned. By filling out the scorecard over several processes, users begin to see patterns in their own behavior, which they can attempt to adjust the next time around. The app also offers a number of videos on negotiation, with short lectures by the creator.

Looking Ahead

As highlighted at the beginning of this piece, the software introduced in this chapter is intended as a set of examples of applying technology to negotiation, beyond using common communication platforms for conducting it. Once familiar with the types of software available, negotiators can consider applying them in their work—or consider what other applications of technology might improve the art or science of negotiation.

As an increasing number of negotiation experts contemplate that last question, what might the future hold? Whether you attribute the original complaint to baseball legend Yogi Berra or quantum physicist Niels Bohr, it really *is* difficult to make predictions, particularly about the future. This may be particularly true with regards to predicting future *technological* developments. At the risk of sounding silly in a year or three, though, I will note some current trends that might develop further, and suggest some open spaces that technology could fill.

Several of the programs discussed in this chapter were developed by academics, based on their own model of negotiation, often espoused in a book. The model provides theoretical underpinnings, and the software facilitates their application to negotiators' real-life situations. This approach could be adopted for other books and models, and indeed might set the tone for future publications. Most books are currently accompanied by a dedicated website; a software application might turn out to be the next trend in bringing theory to practice, or the next requirement by publishers.

Another trend seems to be the movement from developing computer and web-based software, to apps designed for mobile devices. The shift towards mobile—a global trend, extending far beyond the world of negotiation—is likely to increase. One might consider whether certain points of the negotiator's cycle are particularly suitable for mobile support.

Clearly, there is so much more yet to come; any number of software applications could be imagined. For the sake of demonstrating how a process of deliberation and brainstorming could easily lead to a range of suggestions, I will provide three examples:

Picture an app (called *Contract Negotiator*, if only in my mind) that keeps track of the service contracts you are a party to (mobile phone, cable or satellite TV, Internet service provider, and more). As an administrative self-organizing tool, the app not only keeps the price and terms readily accessible, but also sends notifications reminding you of contract milestones such as expiration dates, price changes, etc. More substantively, if the app design was approached through a negotiation perspective as opposed to a more general consumer perspective, the app could provide important negotiation information. In the realm of alternatives, it could regularly scan for better deals on comparable services, calculate when terminating one contract and replacing it with another might be a good idea, and notify the user. On a more tactical level, it could draw in not only users' general ratings of the service provider, but also users' negotiation-specific experiences and insights about them: How they reacted to particular negotiation moves, what discounts were given and under what circumstances. Users could also share information regarding deals or arrangements they were offered that are not advertised by the service provider. These could be used as precedents providing standards or objective criteria for users to refer to in their own negotiation with the service provider. They could also inform the creation of a wider variety of options that users can raise for consideration as they negotiate with the service provider.

Picture a program for car purchasers, which allows them to collect, and keep track of, their alternatives. The program (called *BATNA Buddy*, if only in my mind) might identify dozens of vehicles, offered for sale online, answering to user-input criteria. The program would store all of these away, and constantly monitor them—updating price changes, deleting sold vehicles, and adding new vehicles through repeating the original search periodically. When the negotiator actually walks into a dealership or used car lot, he or she is provided an up-to-date list of alternatives to the car being offered, and at the touch of a screen can identify the current, top of the list, alternative—in real-time. Another feature *BATNA Buddy* might easily incorporate would present the average time-to-sale for similar vehicles, based on previous online offerings and transactions, thus allowing the user a realistic, if statistical, picture of the seller's alternatives. This might help to counter the classic "someone was in here, wanting to buy it, just this morning" tactic. Such software would fall under the "conducting actual negotiation" phase of the negotiator's cycle.

Another example, falling under the "preparing for actual negotiation" phase of the cycle, would be an app assisting negotiators to prepare themselves emotionally for a negotiation. This app (dubbed, perhaps, *NegEmo*) would run a series of diagnostics mapping out the negotiator's particular emotional strengths, challenges, triggers, best times of day, reactions to different counterparts and any number of emotional aspects of negotiation. Once your basic information has been input to the system, you could then access the app an hour or two before an upcoming negotiation, input some information about the anticipated encounter, and receive guidance on how to prepare for it, emotionally speaking. Based on the variables, preparation might include breathing exercises, walking, speaking with a friend, nourishment, caffeine intake and more. The app would then walk you through implementation of that advice: guiding you through breathing exercises, mapping out a walk of suitable length, offering to dial a friend's number, suggesting types of food that would provide the blend of nourishment you require, or directing you to the Starbucks nearest to the negotiation venue.

Finally, I'll suggest that exploring other fields can be helpful for conceiving of new ways to enhance learning and understanding, task preparation, and task conduct in general. Negotiators might be familiar with software applications in any other field, and consider whether the way they support the activities of that field might be adaptable for negotiation. For example, I am familiar with different applications of technology for running. In this field, technology's initial foothold was in the form of hardware—running tracks used as a replacement for outdoor running. Hardware/software hybrids were developed, in the form of heart-rate monitors and other wearable technology (mainly, but not all, in watch form) that could count steps (pedometers), estimate calorie burn, measure time and distance, etc. As technology advanced, many of these and other functions found their way into mobile apps. A wide range of these exist for planning, conducting and tracking runners' activities. GPS technology allows runners to plan or to chart their run on a map. There are apps that not only know what kind of music a runner likes, but choose to play particular songs when her pace lags or the incline increases, and she seems to need a lift. Some apps are socially-oriented—runners can run routes previously charted by other runners, or share their running activity through social media for motivation or support. Other apps have competition or gamification elements built in, allowing runners to compete against others running the same route or a similar route on the other side of the world. Some take gamification to the extreme, plunging the runner into a virtual storyline transforming their innocent run into a simulated escape through a post-apocalyptic, zombie-infested landscape.

To demonstrate how reviewing technological application in other fields might lead to innovation in applying technology to negotiation, I'll suggest that considering the field of running might highlight two developmental lines for negotiation: addition of gamification elements, and incorporation of hardware.

Gamification—the adding of game or game-like elements to serious activities—has been shown to have significant effects on learning, motivation and achievement (see McGonigal 2011). Applying gamification to learning environments is a rapidly growing area of research and practice (for previous discussion of gamification as a tool supporting negotiation education, see Blanchot et al. 2013), and one could easily see this applied to software focused on the "learning to negotiate" part of the negotiator's cycle. Applying elements of gamification to real-life negotiation activity would require more sophisticated thinking, but might have powerful effect. For example, envision an app such as *Negotiation 360*, discussed above, with gamification elements added in: As users' improvement is tracked, they receive rewards for charting more negotiations, for different types of improvement, or for achieving milestones. What might be the motivational effect of such gamification elements? In *Strategy Shaper*, for example, users receive stars at the end of playing each game for poor, fair, good, or excellent results and then can replay the games until they have received all the possible stars. Experience in other fields suggests it could be extremely powerful.

Currently, negotiation-related technology is all in software form. One can imagine, however, that combining hardware and software elements might produce new capacities. For example, picture a negotiator wearing a pulse monitoring watch. Should her heartbeat rise past a certain point, it would send a message to her smartphone suggesting she take a break. The negotiator would appear to have received a disturbing message (which she has), which might certainly be an understandable reason for her to ask to take a break. With her emotional equilibrium restored, she can return to the meeting with enhanced capacity. For another example: consider a negotiator equipped with a wearable camera aimed at her counterpart, combined with software for tracking and interpreting facial expressions. A certain sequence of microexpressions might trigger the software to send the negotiator a text telling her "He is extremely nervous" or even (assuming expression analysis software ever gets this sophisticated) "He is lying.[8]"

I will end this piece as I began it: All of the software described in this chapter—real, and imagined—is only the tip of the iceberg of possibilities afforded by applying technology to negotiation. It is certainly easy to predict that the future of this aspect of negotiation is going to be very exciting—whether you are just following along, involved in innovating, or actively utilizing the possibilities that technology has unlocked for negotiators.

Notes

[1] For more on ODR in general, see NDR: Rabinovitch-Einy and Katsh, *ODR*; for in-depth exploration of different areas of this field, see Abdel-Wahab, Katsh, and Rainey 2012.

[2] As a result, in this chapter, the terms "software," "program," "platform," and "application" are used interchangeably, intending to lend flavor to the item under discussion but not to technically differentiate it from anything else.

[3] Available at http://interneg.concordia.ca/index.php?id=paper

[4] This detailed account of the app's developmental process may be of interest to negotiators considering app-development of their own; see Sethi (undated blog post), at http://www.iwillteachyoutoberich.com/blog/announcing-negotiate-it-ramits-iphone-app-and-bonus-gifts last viewed March 10th 2016.

[5] See www.ssrn.com

[6] See this material at the author's YouTube channel at https://www.youtube.com/channel/UCgk5FU8Xr2JADtt8ZRNYKmg/videos or google "YouTube Noam Ebner". For more on this course and its material, see Ebner 2016.

[7] These apps are not the only educational software involving a strong focus on simulation. There are a number of platforms offering educators and trainers the ability to

conduct simulations online. Some examples are *Sea Change Simulation* (http://www.seachangesimulations.com/), which provides educators a platform for creating and conducting online simulations; *Negotiation Expert* (http://www.negotiationinstitute.com/content/software), discussed above under "Technology helping negotiators prepare," offers software supporting negotiation teachers in setting up, managing, and conducting their classroom simulations; the Danish company *Outcome* (https://negotiationtrainers.com/about/) is developing a simulation platform aimed towards HR managers and trainers, in beta stage at the time of writing. These simulation platforms have different features and foci: Some offer system-generated analysis and feedback; others are primarily a communication platform tailored for simulation management on the educator's side, and conduct on the students' side. Note, however, that these are all platforms supporting *educators*; they do *not* offer an educational experience that the general internet public can click on and enter, or download and interact with, as the other educational applications described in this section do. In this sense, the software described in this section aims to engage users/students directly, circumventing the teacher and the classroom.

[8] Such software could be based on the facial-micro-expressions focused system of lie-detecting developed by Paul Ekman (2002); this system has been specifically adapted for, and applied to, negotiation contexts by Clark Freshman (2011).

References

Abdel-Wahab, M. S., E. Katsh and D. Rainey. 2012. *Online Dispute Resolution: Theory and Practice*. The Hague: Eleven International Publishing.

Blanchot, E., N. Ebner, C. Honeyman, S. Kaufman and R. Parish. 2013. The Education of Non-Students. In *Educating Negotiators for a Connected World: Vol. 4 in the Rethinking Negotiation Teaching Series*, edited by C. Honeyman, J. Coben and A. Wei-Min Lee. St Paul: DRI Press.

Coleman, P. and R. Ferguson. 2014. *Making Conflict Work: Harnessing the Power of Disagreement*. New York: Houghton Mifflin Harcourt.

Druckman, D., J. N. Druckman and T. Arai. 2004. e-Mediation: Evaluating the Impacts of an Electronic Mediator on Negotiating Behavior. *Group Decision and Negotiation* 13(6): 481-511.

Druckman, D. and N. Ebner. 2013. Games, Claims, and New Frames: Rethinking the Use of Simulation in Negotiation Education. *Negotiation Journal* 29(1): 61-93.

Ebner, N. 2016. Negotiation Education in the Age of the MOOC. *Negotiation Journal* 32(3): 231-260.

Ebner, N. 2017. Negotiation is Changing. *Journal of Dispute Resolution* 2017(1): 99-143. Available at SSRN: http://ssrn.com/abstract=2915204.

Ebner, N and A. Kamp. 2010. Relationship 2.0: Not Setting Students Up for Failure (This Time). In *Venturing Beyond the Classroom: Vol. 2 in the Rethinking Negotiation Teaching Series* edited by C. Honeyman, J. Coben and G. De Palo. St Paul: DRI Press.

Ebner, N., A. Bhappu, J. G. Brown, K. K. Kovach and A. K. Schneider. 2009. You've Got Agreement: Negoti@ing via Email. In *Rethinking Negotiation Teaching: Innovations for Context and Culture*, edited by C. Honeyman, J. Coben and G. De Palo. St Paul, MN: DRI Press.

Ekman, P. 2002. *Telling Lies: Clues to Deceit in the Marketplace, Politics and Marriage*, 3rd edn. New York: W. W. Norton.

Freshman, C. 2011. Lie Detection and The Negotiation Within. *Harvard Negotiation Law Review* 16: 263-296.

Katsh, E. and J. Rifkin. 2001. *Online Dispute Resolution*. San Francisco, Jossey-Bass.

Latz, M. 2005. *Gain the Edge! Negotiating to Get What you Want*. New York: St. Martin's Press.

Lodder, A. R. and E. M. Thiessen. 2003. The Role of Artificial Intelligence in Online Dispute Resolution. Proceedings of the UNECE Forum on ODR 2003.

Matz, D. and N. Ebner. 2010. Using Role-Play in Online Negotiation Teaching. *In Venturing Beyond the Classroom: Vol. 2 in the Rethinking Negotiation Teaching Series*, edited by C. Honeyman, J. Coben and G. De Palo. St Paul: DRI Press.

McGonigal, J. 2011. *Reality is Broken: Why Games Make Us Better and How They Can Change the World*. New York: Penguin.

Mor, S. and A. Suppes. 2014. The Role of Communication Media in Negotiation. In *Negotiation Excellence: Successful Deal Making*, 2nd edn., edited by M. Benoliel. Singapore: World Scientific Publishing

Ow, T.T., B. S. O'Neill and C. E. Naquin. 2014. Computer-Aided Tools in Negotiation: Negotiable Issues, Counterfactual Thinking, and Satisfaction. *Journal of Organizational Computing and Electronic Commerce* 24(4): 297-311.

Purdy, J., P. Nye and P. V. Balakrishnan. 2000. The Impact of Communication Media on Negotiation Outcomes. *International Journal of Conflict Management* 11(2): 162-187.

Schneider, A. K. and J. G. Brown. 2014. Dynamic Negotiating Approach Diagnostic (DYNAD). *Marquette Law School Legal Studies Paper No. 13-11*.

Sethi, R. 2009. *I Will Teach You to be Rich*. New York: Workman Publishing Co.

Thiessen, E. M., P. Miniato and B. Hiebert. 2012. ODR and eNegotiation. In *ODR: Theory & Practice*, edited by M. S. Abdel Wahab, E. Katsh and D. Rainey. The Hague: Eleven International Publishing.

Zeleznikow, J. and E. Belluci. 2003. Family Winner: Integrating Game Theory and Heuristics to Provide Negotiation Support. *Proceedings of Sixteenth International Conference on Legal Knowledge Based System*. Amsterdam, Netherlands: IOS Publications, 21-30.

❧ 64 ❧

Lawyers and Online Negotiation

Orna Rabinovich-Einy & Ethan Katsh

Editors' Note: In the next decade, lawyers' roles will change dramatically because of the expansion of online dispute resolution (ODR). As technology increasingly pervades professional life, demand for efficient negotiation tools and software-supported dispute resolution processes can also be expected to grow. The authors discuss how lawyers' practice is changing as a result of the advent of high technology specific to their field, and outline both the uses and risks for lawyers that are associated with a whole series of specific platforms and programs that are increasingly being used to transact or settle cases online and offline, including in courts. Finding the technologies to be constantly evolving and disruptive of existing practice, the authors nevertheless conclude that lawyers have little option but to learn, use and advise their clients about these platforms. They point out that some of the new technologies promise to obviate a great deal of unrewarding work, to speed up possible resolution and, if designed appropriately, to enhance fairness and access to justice, reinforcing the negotiation field's strong interest in "process pluralism".

Orna Rabinovich-Einy is an associate professor at the Haifa Law Faculty. Her areas of expertise are online dispute resolution, alternative dispute resolution, and civil procedure. She has published widely on the impact of technology on dispute resolution, the relationship between formal and informal justice systems, and dispute systems design. Most recently she has co-authored a book with Ethan Katsh entitled *Digital Justice*: *Technology and the Internet of Disputes*. Rabinovich-Einy holds a J.S.D. from Columbia University. She was admitted to the Bar in Israel (1998) and in N.Y. (2001), and was certified as a mediator in N.Y. (2003).
Ethan Katsh is Professor Emeritus of Legal Studies at the University of Massachusetts and Director of the National Center of Technology and Dispute Resolution (www.odr.info). He is widely recognized as one of the founders of the field of online dispute resolution (ODR). With Janet Rifkin, he conducted the eBay Pilot Project in 1999, which led to eBay's current system that handles over sixty million disputes each year. He has published widely about law and technology and, most recently, is co-author *of Digital Justice: Technology and the Internet of Disputes* (Oxford University Press 2017.)

Introduction

Technology and the online environment increasingly influence the work of lawyers. Lawyers today commonly communicate with clients through email. Their expertise, experience and contact information are easy to locate online. In addition to using Web sites, lawyers are often active users of social media platforms. Online tools dominate legal research, document drafting and assembly, and filings. However, when lawyers have a court hearing or an ADR session, they are usually required to attend in person. This will change in the future as the field of online dispute resolution ("ODR") matures and expands.

ODR tools and systems allow disputing parties to conduct a variety of dispute resolution processes online. Among the most advanced ODR mechanisms currently used are those that facilitate negotiation. These developments are significant for lawyers on several levels. First, lawyers, like other internet users, are likely to encounter disputes that arose on-line, where parties are in different locations and for which ODR may be the only redress option. Second, as use of ODR expands, lawyers will have to advise their clients as to circumstances where they should use such processes, and in some instances may need to take part in these processes on behalf of their clients. Finally, lawyers can also play a sig-nificant role in advising their clients on dispute systems design: How to best prepare for future disputes when setting up their business, structur-ing a transaction, or thinking of how to manage workplace conflict. In many of these contexts, an understanding of the role of technology in dispute systems design can help lawyers provide valuable advice on how to structure better dispute resolution systems, which both resolve dis-putes in a fair and effective manner and prevent disputes from arising, thereby bringing value to their clients even before disputes arise.

In Part I below, we provide some background on the rise of ODR. We then expand on the significance of online negotiation, a dominant form of ODR, to the lives and work of lawyers—as internet users (Part II), as counselors to clients in an age in which ODR expands to courts (Part III), and as dispute system designers in an age in which clients need to pre-pare for future conflict, on- and offline (Part IV). We conclude with a list of key issues for lawyers in the area of online negotiation specifically and ODR more generally.

Part I: What is Online Negotiation?

The Rise of ODR

In the 1990s, as use of the internet began to expand, some scholars be-lieved that the internet was a separate space to which legal norms did not (and should not) apply. This view was highly contested and, to a large extent, disproved over time. Courts and legislatures have made various modifications to existing legal doctrines and statutes in an attempt to catch up with the changing reality. Nevertheless, adapting law to the challenges posed by internet communication and enforcing legal norms in the online context continued to be difficult, as the costs associated with litigation remained prohibitive and the global nature of online activity often rendered such attempts futile. The history of file sharing and the challenges it has posed for the legal departments of record labels and movie studios presents a potent example.

Even though the need for law online was contested, norm elaboration and enforcement online were essential components of online engagement from the early days of the internet. Disputes became more common as the scope, frequency and pace of online communication grew. A major contributor to the growing number of disputes arising online was the lifting of the ban on commercial activity on the internet, in the early-1990s (Katsh and Wing 2006). Much of the interaction online took place among strangers, often across borders, making it necessary to overcome linguistic and cultural barriers and adjust expectations to differing legal regimes. The novelty of online activities coupled with the growing level of complexity of various online interactions increased the likelihood that problems, and hence disputes, would emerge.

While conflict as a "growth industry" (Fisher and Ury 1981: xvii) became true for online conflicts, avenues for addressing such conflicts remained a scarce resource. For many online disputes, litigation was not a viable option, as the value of the disputes was often low, particularly compared to the costs of conducting a face-to-face process in the context of global cross-border interaction. An American eBay purchaser, for example, would not sue in court for the harm caused as a result of an unsuccessful $50 transaction with a merchant residing in Europe. In other cases, conducting a formal legal process was not an option because the dispute did not constitute a legal wrong. So, for Wikipedia editors arguing over a description of the "Arab Spring," litigation would not present a viable dispute resolution avenue. In both cases, however, it soon became clear that absent mechanisms for addressing wrongs, participation in such online endeavors would be limited. Therefore, over time, online mechanisms for addressing online disputes were introduced, later termed "online dispute resolution" or ODR (Katsh and Rifkin 2001).

ODR vs. ADR

Initially, ODR processes were meant to provide an online equivalent to familiar ADR processes, such as negotiation, mediation and arbitration, with the necessary adjustments that resulted from the shift to the new medium. In that vein, early ODR providers offered mediation through email, and arbitration processes that relied on the delivery and sharing of written documents, and occasionally video-conferencing. These latter technologies only became widely available in acceptable quality in recent years as bandwidth expanded, devices shifted from PC to mobile and better, more advanced software applications were developed.

Over time, designers of ODR systems and processes have moved beyond trying to mimic familiar, offline processes and have come to appreciate the new opportunities created by the shift from face-to-face dispute resolution to an online medium. This translated into the design of completely new processes for which there was no offline equivalent, the primary example being the various forms of online automated negotiation that were created. Some of these processes matched complainants' description of the problem and desired remedy with solutions that were acceptable to respondents (the early eBay dispute resolution system), while in others the software was able to uncover an acceptable middle-ground sum that was in the range of both parties' "bottom line" (the Cybersettle blind bidding tool). A more complex software application called Smartsettle evaluated the interests of disputing parties and suggested creative solutions. In both the Cybersettle and Smartsettle cases, a new process emerged that lay in between direct negotiation and mediation, with the software playing the role of an intermediary of sorts. In other cases, familiar processes were associated with nontraditional traits in light of the nature of online media. One example is Wikipedia's ODR system which offers a form of open, non-confidential mediation. That system also allows for new tools such as conducting an online survey regarding a dispute with other Wikipedians, thus taking advantage of online capabilities and the power and appeal of crowdsourcing.

Over time, the significance of ODR for online and offline disputes grew. Online, eBay became the ODR poster child, handling a staggering 60 million disputes a year primarily through automated negotiation systems. Offline, the use of ODR has been increasingly introduced into the small claim, low dollar value dispute zone, in light of such processes' accessibility, efficiency and low cost. Several courts are in various stages of adopting ODR schemes, realizing that such processes' potential expands beyond small claims, and are experimenting with application to the family and neighbor dispute arenas (as explained in part II).

As use of ODR grows and is being applied to offline disputes as well, it is tempting to view ODR as being no different from traditional dispute resolution, with merely a change in medium. In fact, however, ODR processes are distinct from traditional formal and informal dispute resolution avenues in three important ways: (1) they are delivered online, (2) they rely on the intelligence of the machine, and (3) most communications exchanged online are automatically recorded, leaving a "digital trail." These characteristics have meant that masses of disputes could be handled at very low cost, relieving the problems of capacity and cost associated with a human third party decision-maker or facilitator. This has also meant that large amounts of data on disputing patterns and dispute resolution are becoming available, and can be analyzed effortlessly and at low cost. These characteristics allow for better quality control over the functioning of dispute resolution processes, as well as the uncovering of the sources of various disputes, shifting efforts from *ex-post* dispute resolution to *ex-ante* conflict prevention. At the same time, documentation has meant far less privacy in ODR processes, a dramatic development for an activity in which confidentiality has occupied a central role.

Online Negotiation Processes

Automated negotiation first emerged in the SquareTrade negotiation tool developed for eBay. Buyers and sellers who had a dispute with one another could file a dispute through SquareTrade's online form and conduct a fully automated negotiation process with their counterpart. The forms employed by SquareTrade were based on a typology of common problems and solutions while leaving room for free text, which was later analyzed and incorporated into the structure of the process. Surprisingly, perhaps, the automated system successfully resolved 80% of the complaints filed. The system was highly popular, handling over 2 million disputes by 2003.

But the SquareTrade system was impressive not only in terms of capacity. It was the first time that the characteristics of online communication were embraced and celebrated as the ODR process did not mimic its offline equivalents. When using SquareTrade, parties did not merely exchange views online, but engaged with one another through structured dialogue processed via software. The software program therefore reframed some of their language, geared them towards accepted resolutions and toned down some of the emotions. A similar process was later employed by the European Union in an early pilot using automated negotiation for cross-border inter-European e-commerce disputes.

Over the years, additional automated negotiation software programs were designed, each with its own qualities and goals. In 2003, as eBay decided to administer its dispute resolution process in-house, Colin Rule designed an elaborate dispute resolution center. Like the SquareTrade system, software design made automated negotiation a hybrid of negotiation and mediation. By auto-composing the first message from the buyer to the seller, eBay's system would eliminate potential threats and insults, engender constructive communication and gear the parties towards resolution. eBay's internal dispute resolution system sought to address problems at an earlier stage than the SquareTrade process, which came into play once the problem had matured into a full-fledged conflict, matching problem descriptions with agreed-upon solutions. The in-house eBay dispute resolution center, by contrast, sought to identify, for various dispute types, the points in which miscommunication occurred and the type of information that was missing, and could help the parties clarify misunderstandings and resume a collaborative mode.

Over time these systems were also implemented in the PayPal context, when PayPal was purchased by eBay. This served as a conflict *prevention* mechanism, resolving some of the earlier problems that arose between buyers and sellers over payments. (PayPal also required its own set of automated processes, to address disputes peculiar to its structure on a mass scale through ODR.)

Two particularly interesting automated negotiation tools, referred to earlier, were those offered by Cybersettle and SmartSettle. The developers of these two software applications found particular points in the offline negotiation process where the use of information was ineffective or inefficient. Cybersettle developed a fairly simple application that facilitated *"blind bidding"* online. Originally aimed at malpractice claims but usable in any negotiation involving money, one party to a dispute instructed a computer as to how much it was willing to pay, and the other party instructed the computer as to the minimum it was willing to accept. The parties agreed that if the offer and demand were within some percentage of each other, they would split the difference and settle. If they were not within range, however, there would be no settlement and the offer and demand would not be revealed to the other party (Kirgis 2010).

Blind bidding was a simple but creative way of doing something online that was possible but relatively inefficient (and risky) when done offline. It took advantage of the computer's capability for calculation and communication and for following a programmed rule to decide whether there would be a settlement or not. This allowed parties to overcome strategic and cognitive barriers that prevented them from reaching an agreement despite the existence of a "zone of possible agreement" (Ayres and Nalebuff 1997; Mnookin, Peppet and Tulumello 2004). In later years, use of Cybersettle's software expanded beyond malpractice cases to include monetary claims against the City of New York, but more recently the company went out of business due to a combination of factors which resulted in low profitability.

Smartsettle was developed by a computer scientist, Ernest Thiessen, who found that the introduction of technology into interest-based negotiation increased the likelihood for parties to reach *pareto-optimal* resolutions. Building on the insights provided by game theory, the Smartsettle software is a *negotiation support system*, which asks parties to list their interests and to assign numerical values to them, thereby creating a spectrum along which the parties can negotiate. Based on the parties' input, the software generates various "packages" for the parties' consideration. The software allows for a visual display of the level of satisfaction each package represents for the parties in light of their own initial ranking of the interests. Furthermore, the software offers a unique optimization feature, offering parties an option to improve their negotiated deal if it is not *pareto-optimal* (Thiessen and McMahon 2000).

The tools and systems described above are prominent examples of ODR mechanisms based on online negotiation. In addition to these ODR systems and tools that can be plugged into web sites, most internet sites now offer some method for complaining online and negotiating a complaint with a fellow user. This means, as we explain in the following section, that most of us will inevitably use some form of ODR as we engage with others online, and will do so with some frequency in the not too distant future.

Part II: Lawyers as Internet Users

Lawyers, like most other people today, are active internet users, and, as such, can be expected to use some form of online negotiation or complaint processing. Anyone communicating online is bound, at some point, to experience problems and require online avenues of redress. A Facebook user whose picture was uploaded without prior approval, a copyright owner asking to remove an infringing song on YouTube, an editor on Wikipedia whose edits were reverted by others, and a person requesting Google to delete search results based on their "right to be forgotten" will use online avenues to raise and resolve their problem. Frequently, these avenues will be automated and will rely on some form of negotiation.

In terms of commercial transactions, many of us, lawyers included, purchase certain goods online on eBay, Amazon and other e-commerce sites, and book various services through the on-demand economy, ranging from a place to stay abroad to cleaning and delivery services back home. Health services have also become entangled in the online arena, as electronic health records, online doctor appointments, and online prescriptions have become more widespread. Also, as professionals perform work from afar, much of it on a freelance basis, the door has opened for online legal services. Lawyers are now being recruited to draft legal documents and perform discrete legal services in various parts of the globe through such sites as Upwork. In addition, lawyers, like many others, use social networks for professional, as well as personal ends. A recent ABA survey found that lawyers' use of social networks has increased and in 2013 was at 59%, with a significant percentage reporting that such presence attracts new business (Ambrogi 2013).

In all of the contexts mentioned above, as online activities increase, so do opportunities for misunderstandings, problems and conflicts. Indeed, in many of these domains we are already witnessing "conflict as a growth industry," (Fisher and Ury 1981) with new types of disputes arising at a scale vastly different from the offline context. The nature and quantity of digital disputes have made traditional face-to-face processes inaccessible in many instances and have made it necessary to institute new avenues of redress online. In addition to the eBay example above, Facebook and Twitter offer automated notice and take-down procedures for addressing content that allegedly infringes on copyright. Facebook also instituted a process allowing users to interact regarding content uploaded that one of the users finds offensive. Twitter has instituted a variety of measures for complaining about harassment. Following a European Court of Justice ruling, Google has instituted a process for removing search results that conflict with the "right to be forgotten." Upwork has a system for handling disputes between clients and freelancers over work hours and quality of work delivered. Airbnb offers a dispute resolution system for refunds and additional payments that need to be transferred between the host and guest. These are only a few examples of new online complaint and dispute resolution systems that are now available to internet users on some of the more prominent sites, the majority of which are premised on online negotiation.

What important lessons can we draw from the experience with these systems for lawyers as users of online negotiation? The most important lesson seems to be that users' reputations are becoming a more significant force than the "shadow of the law" (Katsh, Rifkin and Gaitenby 2000) [See also NDR: Tinsley et al., *Reputation*]. Often, both sides to a transaction or relationship seek to maintain a positive reputation. In some areas, such reputation is translated into financial incentives and gains, in other instances it is a guarantee against "outing" and "shaming" campaigns.

Another important lesson is that while ODR processes are available for addressing certain problems, they are unavailable or ineffective for a wide range of other problems. Indeed, the availability of redress avenues is the product of legal and other incentives and is often reflective of societal power structures, making redress available for the "haves." In that respect, it is not surprising to find that there are many more effective redress avenues for online consumers and copyright owners than for online freelancers.

Significantly, lawyers as internet users may have an advantage over users with no legal training in that they are better able to assess their "procedural BATNA"—to what extent traditional mechanisms are available to address their problem and what costs and benefits are associated with following each route. Also, as members of an empowered group fully aware of their rights, lawyers could prove to be important voices in the demand for the adoption of effective avenues of redress online.

Part III: Lawyers Counseling Clients Who Are Active Online

Initially, automated negotiation was perceived either as a threat to lawyers, because it removed the need for their services (as intermediaries and dispute resolvers), or as irrelevant to their practice, because it dealt with small scale disputes for which lawyers were not required. This is changing as ODR processes have begun to spread from the online-commercial setting to the public-offline arena, most notably courts, presenting new professional opportunities for lawyers. After some early experiments with ODR in courts in such places as Australia and Singapore, some courts are in the process of instituting mature ODR systems that include online negotiation, facilitation and adjudication. Legislation introducing such a system has already been adopted in British Columbia, a pilot program is being launched in the Netherlands, and ODR has been recommended for the British court system in formal reports prepared by the Civil Justice Council Advisory Group on ODR in 2015 and the Lord Justice Briggs in July 2016.

These developments were preceded by experiments with ODR by American regulatory agencies, an ongoing attempt by the United Nations to develop an international ODR system for cross-border disputes, and the adoption of ODR in a formal regulation by the EU for cross-border disputes within Europe.

Most of these systems currently intend to use ODR for small-scale disputes in which legal representation is typically rare. Some, however, apply to areas such as family law, where representation is more common, and could create new opportunities for lawyers. Under the ODR system developed for the Netherlands, for example, lawyers review agreements reached by divorcing parties through automated negotiation (without legal representation) to ensure that they comply with the law. Also, given the changes we have witnessed in the habits and preferences of users in the areas discussed above—online shopping, working and socializing—it seems that a broader scope for ODR in courts and government agencies, as well as in more complex disputes, is only a matter of time.

Given these developments, successful lawyers will need to play an active role in counseling clients as to the desirability of ODR and the choice of ODR processes, advising clients on strategies for ODR participation, and representing clients in certain ODR proceedings. In fulfilling these roles, lawyers should be aware of the many ways in which online negotiation differs from face-to-face negotiation.

For one, ODR enhances access to justice by lowering direct and indirect costs associated with dispute resolution, due to the ability to conduct the process asynchronously, 24 hours a day 7 days a week, from the comfort of one's home. These processes are quicker than face-to-face ones: the availability of a structured process relying on preexisting choices and forms, as well as automated prompts and reminders, speeds up the process and time to resolution. Also, as noted above, the algorithms used in online negotiation can overcome strategic and cognitive barriers as evidenced in the design of such systems as eBay's ODR center, as well as Cybersettle's and Smartsettle's negotiation tools. At the same time, it is important to bear in mind that algorithms can be biased and unpredictable, and online negotiation is inherently less private than meeting face-to-face, potentially exposing online negotiators.

Part IV: Lawyers Helping Design Better Online Negotiation Processes

A final and important capacity in which lawyers need to be familiar with online negotiation and ODR in general is their role as dispute resolution experts and ongoing advisors to their clients. In such capacity, they can help ensure that the design of ODR mechanisms is not only effective, but also fair, and meets expectations of due process. Often lawyers are not only being called upon after a dispute has arisen, but are involved in the structuring of a transaction which includes a dispute resolution clause, or advising their clients on the adoption of dispute resolution systems for conflicts that arise within their workforce or vis-à-vis their clients. In all of these contexts, ODR is another important option that should be considered as a sole option, a parallel option, or as part of a hybrid system which includes both face-to-face and online elements. Technology has become an essential (albeit somewhat neglected) part of the field of "dispute systems design" (Rabinovich-Einy and Katsh 2012).

The role of technology in dispute systems has been described through the metaphor of the "fourth party" (Katsh and Rifkin 2001). Originally, the fourth party emphasized the network's novel communications capabilities and tools that enable a human third party to interact with parties at a distance. The fourth party may, in less complex disputes (such as many e-commerce disputes) replace the human third party by helping the parties identify common interests and mutually acceptable outcomes. Templates and structured forms can be employed that allow users to choose from various options and, by comparing the choices made by the parties, can highlight potential areas of agreement. More commonly, the "fourth party" assists, enhances or complements the mediator or arbitrator. For example, consider the specific informational tasks performed by third party neutrals. These might include brainstorming, evaluating, explaining, discussing, identifying, defining, organizing, clarifying, listing, caucusing, collecting, aggregating, assigning meaning, simulating, measuring, calculating, linking, proposing, arranging, creating, publishing, circulating and exchanging, charting, reminding, scheduling, monitoring, etc. Some of these are simple or clerical, but some involve making decisions at appropriate times and in appropriate ways. Technology can assist with all of these efforts. In Katsh and Rifkin's early book on ODR, they point out that a successful ODR system can be represented by a triangle which has sides representing *convenience, expertise* and trust (Katsh and Rifkin 2001). Any ODR system should include all three elements, albeit not necessarily to the same degree. All three are needed if the system is to attract users; but the shape of the triangle can change and, by doing so, emphasize that more of one element is present than another. The role of the fourth party in a given ODR process will be a key factor in determining the shape of the triangle.

The benefits of early ODR systems were mostly in the area of convenience, in the sense that the network allowed communication to occur at a distance and asynchronous communication allowed participation at any time. In so doing, the technology removed many physical constraints or boundaries of time and space. On the other hand, expertise, in the sense of taking advantage of the computer's processing capabilities, was exploited much less. eBay and SquareTrade used structured forms to collect data and to manage the conversation between buyers and sellers. Cybersettle had a simple algorithm and Smartsettle a fairly complex one, but the fourth party, until fairly recently, largely rested on the convenience side of the triangle.

Applications such as Youstice (www.Youstice.com), Modria (www.Modria.com) or Picture it Settled (www.Pictureitsettled.com) now use the computer to substitute in part or in whole for the *expertise* of a mediator. In the future, we shall see increasingly intelligent machines enabling or suggesting solutions to parties. The manner in which the machine manages information or communication may be different from the manner in which the neutral human would, but the outcome provided by many of these applications is likely to be similar, if not the same. This is not to say, however, that human expertise is no longer required where ODR mechanisms are employed; but in some contexts their expertise will migrate to the design and programming of the machine (Barendrecht and Honeyman 2014).

Another perspective on the evolution of ODR concerns replacing ODR tools with ODR *systems*. [See NDR: Rule, *Online Ethics* for more on the ethical dilemmas of this.] With a few notable exceptions, most contributions of technology to ODR thus far have involved the development of tools. These tools usually focus on a narrow task that could help a neutral to resolve either online or offline disputes. A National Science Foundation project at the University of Massachusetts, for example, developed a highly detailed model of the brainstorming process, and designed software that could assist parties who wished to brainstorm at a distance. This replaced the use of flipcharts, the most common brainstorming tool employed in face to face negotiations. For many in the ADR field, the future of ODR has been assumed to lie in an expanding array of tools that will open up new options for third parties to help reach agreement.

A more dramatic impact of ODR may lie in the area of systems, such as eBay's dispute resolution system. Here, technology and ongoing data analysis could substantially improve dispute systems' capabilities for preventing disputes *ex ante*, not only resolving them *ex post*, through ongoing learning of patterns of data use and implementation of the lessons and improvement of the dispute resolution system, as well as the operations of the company which it is serving. Indeed, this is the flip side of the preservation of data and reduction of privacy in ODR: data can be used to study patterns of conflicts, prevent disputes, and study the fairness and effectiveness of the dispute resolution system. [NDR: Amsler, System Design] At the same time, access to data is power, and power can be abused. Lawyers can have a key role in ensuring that such data is used responsibly, while protecting the rights of the users of ODR mechanisms.

Conclusion

Online negotiation and ODR more generally are fast becoming part of the legal landscape. When ODR was first introduced in the mid-late 90s, it was viewed as an avenue for addressing low-dollar value disputes that arose online and for which there was no alternative avenue of redress. Over the years, the potential of ODR has expanded, together with the growth in online activities and the application of ODR to offline settings. In light of these developments, lawyers must become familiar with ODR processes, feel comfortable in using them, and be able to anticipate when and how they should be employed by their clients. Therefore, we offer below several broad **themes** that should guide lawyers in thinking about online negotiation.

1) **The online-offline distinction is constantly shifting:** This means that the line between what can and cannot be done online and offline is moving, undermining the distinction itself. Ultimately, these changes translate into a broader mandate for ODR as more and more activities take place online and related problems will need to be addressed online, and as online tools become increasingly common in face-to-face settings, such as courts and administrative hearings.

2) **The impact of technology is disruptive:** (Bower and Christensen 1995) This has meant that it may require a rethinking and rejecting of accepted practice at the same time that it brings new ways and new ideas about how to achieve goals. New technologies change what is possible to do and, in the process, raise a range of questions about the value and need for doing either what was difficult before or not possible at all. By opening new capabilities, new technologies can lead to a reassessment of goals, priorities, assumptions and expectations. Lawyers are already understanding that easy and inexpensive access to information that had been difficult to find, and costly to use, threatens the legal profession. ODR presents lawyers with new opportunities to employ technology in supporting new kinds of relationships and complex transactions.

3) **ODR is enhancing process pluralism:** (Menkel-Meadow 2006) Technology has broadened the range of processes available to parties, with such options as automated negotiation, crowdsourced juries, and online surveys. Also, some traditional processes have adopted non-traditional characteristics when designed in the online environment, such as the loss of privacy

in certain online mediation processes. This fine-grained design, with a broader array of process types within which characteristics vary, can allow for a more tailored fit between the "fuss" and the "forum" than we have been accustomed to in the face-to-face ADR arena (Sander and Goldberg 1994).

4) **Technology is not neutral:** Behind the technology used in ODR there are human beings who design the systems and can determine the extent to which such systems are accessible, fair, efficient and accountable. Digital technology can, however, structure discretion through the process that is embedded in the software and lends itself to ex-post quality control measures, because of the digital trail that is left automatically when communicating online. While these features do not guarantee that ODR processes will function effectively, when used appropriately they can support the operation of a fair ODR mechanism, engendering trust and legitimacy.

For lawyers, the combined effect of the above themes will be dramatic. As Richard Susskind aptly states in his thought-provoking book *Tomorrow's Lawyers*: "The future of legal service is neither Grisham nor Rumpole. Nor is it wigs, wood-panelled courtrooms, leather-bound tomes, or arcane legal jargon. It will not even be the now dominant model of lawyering, which is face-to-face, consultative professional service by advisers who meet clients in their offices, whether glitzy or dusty, and dispense tailored counsel. To meet the needs of clients, we will need instead to dispense with much of our current cottage industry and re-invent the way in which legal services are delivered" (Susskind 2013: xv). We predict that in that future world of legal services, online negotiation will come to play an increasingly important role.

References

Ambrogi, R. 2013. Lawyers' Social Media Use Grows Modestly, ABA Annual Tech Survey Shows. *LawSites*. Available online at http://www.lawsitesblog.com/2013/08/lawyers-social-media-use-continues-to-grow-aba-annual-tech-survey-shows.html (last accessed August 29, 2015).

Ayres, I. and B. Nalebuff. 1997. Common Knowledge as a Barrier to Negotiation. *UCLA Law Review* 44: 1631-1659.

Barendrecht, M. and C. Honeyman. 2014. Dispute Resolution: Existing Business Models and Looming Disruptions. *Dispute Resolution Magazine*. Available online at http://www.americanbar.org/publications/dispute_resolution_magazine/2014/spring/dispute-resolution--existing-business-models-and-looming-disrupt.html (last accessed June 5, 2015).

Bower, J. L. and C. M. Christensen. 1995. Disruptive Technologies: Catching the Wave. *Harvard Business Review* 73(1): 43-53.

Fisher, R. and W. Ury. 1981. *Getting to Yes*. New York: Houghton Mifflin Co.

Katsh, E., J. Rifkin and A. Gaitenby. 2000. E-Commerce, E-Disputes, and E-Dispute Resolution: In the Shadow of "eBay Law". *Ohio State Journal on Dispute Resolution* 15: 705-734. Available online at www.umass.edu/cyber/katsh.pdf (last accessed October 22, 2015). Katsh E. and J. Rifkin. 2001. *Online Dispute Resolution: Resolving Conflicts in Cyberspace*. San Francisco, CA: Jossey-Bass.

Katsh, E. and L. Wing. 2006. 10 Years of Online Dispute Resolution (ODR): Looking at the Past and Constructing the Future. *University of Toledo Law Review* 38: 19-46.

Kirgis, P. 2010. Cybersettle and the Value of Online Dispute Resolution. *Indisputably July 7, 2010.* Available online at http://www.indisputably.org/?p=1456 (last accessed August 29, 2015).

Menkel-Meadow, C. 2006. Peace and Justice: Notes on the Evolution and Purposes of Legal Processes. *Georgetown Law Journal* 94: 553-580.

Mnookin, R. H., S. R. Peppet and A. S. Tulumello. 2004. *Beyond Winning: Negotiating to Create Value in Deals and Disputes.* Cambridge, MA: Belknap Press.

Rabinovich-Einy, O. and E. Katsh. 2012. Technology and Dispute Systems Design. *Harvard Negotiation Law Review* 17: 151-199.

Sander, F. and S. Goldberg. 1994. Fitting the Forum to the Fuss: A User-Friendly Guide to Selecting an ADR Procedure. *Negotiation Journal* 10(1): 49-68.

Susskind, R. 2013. *Tomorrow's Lawyers: An Introduction to Your Future.* Oxford: Oxford University Press.

Thiessen, E. M. and J. P. McMahon. 2000. Beyond Win-Win in Cyberspace. *Ohio State Journal on Dispute Resolution* 15: 643-668.

෴ 65 ෴

Reclaiming Attention in the Digital Generation Negotiator

Lauren A. Newell

Editors' Note: So many successive generations of people have remarked on how they don't understand the next generation that it's now become a cliché. Yet the "digital generation" does represent a departure from years of assumptions of how people will typically get and process information, how they understand the world, and how many different things they ought to expect to do at the same time. Newell reviews the research on the digital generation's ability to maintain sustained attention over time, and finds that, yes, there is a difference. Multitasking—defended by many as an efficient way to process multiple concurrent streams of information—has been exposed as something of a myth. And there are other prices paid for assuming that one can handle multiple digital forms of communication, from cognitive overload to neurological changes. Yet communication technology is here to stay, Newell says: we have to learn how to handle it. She offers a succession of techniques for reclaiming and holding attention.

Introduction

Complaining about youth is a time-honored tradition. The basis for complaint changes—whether it is dancing the waltz, playing chess, or writing with ballpoint pens[1]—but the underlying sentiment does not: There is something wrong with "kids today," and the future will suffer because of it.

Complaints about today's youth—a group I refer to as the Digital Generation[2]—stem largely from the Digital Generation's affinity for technology. The ubiquity of cell phones, computers, tablets, mp3 players, and other forms of information and communication technologies ("ICTs")[3] in

Lauren A. Newell is an associate professor of law at the Ohio Northern University Pettit College of Law, where she teaches courses on negotiation, business organizations, and securities regulation. Her research focuses on the psychological aspects of negotiation and lawyering, including the emotional dimension of negotiation and the impact of new technology on negotiation and lawyering. She received her J.D. from Harvard Law School and her B.A. from Georgetown University.

the Digital Generation's lives has given rise to many accusations. Perhaps the most popular of these is that the Digital Generation's constant ICT usage renders them unable to pay sustained attention to anything. Concerns about the upcoming generation's attentional capacity are especially salient for those in disciplines that demand strong powers of attention, such as negotiation.

This chapter considers the relationship between ICTs and attention and the consequences of this relationship for the Digital Generation negotiators of the future. It proceeds in three parts. The first part explores the mechanics of attention and the importance of attention in negotiation. The second part, directed to elder generations of negotiators, aims to help these negotiators understand how ICTs affect the Digital Generation's attentional capacity.[4] The third part, directed to Digital Generation negotiators, offers practical suggestions for improving their focused attention.

Understanding Attention and Its Role in Negotiation

Defining Attention

It is difficult to provide a precise definition of attention because attention is not a unitary concept. Rather, it is a property of multiple different perceptual and cognitive operations that are in extensive communication with each other. In fact, attention has become "a catch-all term for how the brain controls its own information processing" (Chun, Golomb and Turk-Browne 2011: 74). While recognizing that attention means different things to different people, this chapter adopts a narrower, more functional definition, namely "the ability to attend to desired or necessary stimuli and to exclude unwanted or unnecessary stimuli" (Jacobson 2010: 421). This section describes the anatomical bases of attention and the mechanisms of attentional control.

Where Does Attention Come From?

One influential theory of the source of attention envisions attention as an organ system composed of at least three constituent networks. Dr. Michael I. Posner, a leading researcher in the field of attention, refers to these networks as the alerting, orienting, and executive networks (Petersen and Posner 2012; Posner 2012). All of these networks work in concert together in our everyday lives.

The alerting network makes us sensitive to our surroundings and ready to take in information from the environment. It is akin to vigilance. For instance, when a loud noise startles us, our alerting network heightens our alertness as we try to determine what the sound was, where it came from, and whether it is significant.

The orienting network helps us to allocate attention to a particular sense or location in order to prioritize what our senses take in from the environment. In other words, it helps us to pick what information we absorb from all the information available to our senses. We can align our attention with a source of sensory signals either overtly (our eyes move as our attention moves) or covertly (no eye movements). As we pay attention to one stimulus in the environment, the other stimuli competing for our attention lose their influence; we stop paying attention to them. For example, as we try to read a book while sitting in a bustling café, our orienting network overtly orients our attention toward the book (i.e., we look at its pages), and away from the sounds of the conversations happening around us.

The executive network monitors and resolves conflicts among thoughts, feelings, and responses occurring simultaneously in different brain areas. In this way, it helps us to make sense of the world. Activity in different parts of the brain creates competition for control of our behavior; the executive network permits expression of activity from one area and represses expression of competing activity in other areas. For instance, if we are sipping a cup of coffee and a bee flies straight at our face, our executive network resolves the conflict between the part of our brain that wants to keep holding onto the cup and the part that wants to drop the cup and wave away the bee.

The Types of Attentional Control

Posner's attentional networks model explains the anatomical mechanisms involved in paying attention, but it does not fully explain how it is determined what we pay attention *to*. For example, as we sit in the café, how does the orienting system decide whether to orient to the book or to the conversations? Researchers have discovered that we have both automatic and voluntary attentional control mechanisms. The automatic form of attentional control is widely referred to as "bottom-up" or "stimulus-driven" or "exogenous" attentional control, and the voluntary form is known as "top-down" or "goal-directed" or "endogenous" attentional control (e.g., Roda and Thomas 2006: 560; Jacobson 2010: 429; Chun et al. 2011: 77; Baker and Brown 2014: 348-49).

Bottom-up attentional control refers to the mechanisms by which external events capture our attention involuntarily. Factors external to us, such as the salience of stimuli (e.g., the brightness of a sudden flash of light), determine what we attend to (Awh, Belopolsky and Theeuwes 2012). Bottom-up control is largely instinctual and automatic; our brains constantly review the environment for disturbances and we are pre-programmed to attend to novel or sudden changes. At one time, these reflexive shifts in attention were an important survival mechanism to avoid having predators take us by surprise. Though times have changed, our brains have not—we still attend automatically to novel stimuli thanks to our bottom-up control mechanisms.

In contrast, top-down attentional control refers to the voluntary attention we pay to processing information and regulating our internal mental lives. This control is goal-directed and driven by internal factors (e.g., we voluntarily allocate attention toward the goal of finding our favorite toothpaste among the thirty different types available on the shelf). Top-down attentional control draws upon the executive attention mechanisms to select between alternatives competing for attention, and allocates attention to the effortful mental activities that require it. Our exercise of top-down control can help us achieve conscious, high-level concentration.

Our top-down attentional processes are in a constant battle with our more powerful bottom-up attentional processes, which makes it hard to pay attention without getting distracted. While the top-down system fights to keep our attentional resources directed toward a particular activity (such as writing a memo), the bottom-up system continually determines whether other sensory information in the environment (like a knock at the door) deserves our attention at any given moment. It takes significant cognitive effort for the top-down system to maintain focus without interruption or interference from the bottom-up system. Often, top-down attentional control succumbs to bottom-up control and results in distraction (so we automatically look up from our memo when we hear the knock at the door). This distractedness is problematic because our success in performing tasks that involve reasoning and other higher-order cognitive operations is determined by our ability to control our attention. Simply put, we will have trouble finishing our memo if we keep getting distracted by people knocking on the door.

Why Attention Is Necessary During Negotiation

Knowing what attention is, negotiators might next wonder why they need it. Negotiators need strong powers of attention for two reasons. The first is that attention is crucial for everyone. Because our processing capacity is limited, we need our attentional mechanisms to focus our capacity efficiently on the information that is most important for our goals and behaviors at any given time. Every aspect of our basic daily functioning—from performing simple motor movements, such as reaching and grasping, to engaging in higher-order cognitive operations, such as planning, learning, and remembering things—requires attention.

The second reason is that negotiation is a highly complex endeavor. In any given negotiation, a negotiator may need to listen carefully, evaluate offers, propose options, respond to positions, calculate figures, plan strategies, read contracts, write emails, remember agreements, wait for replies, exercise patience, and soothe tempers, among countless other things. Negotiation makes demands upon negotiators' cognitive abilities, emotional competencies, and impulse control capabilities—all of which rely upon the negotiators' powers of attention, particularly their executive attention mechanisms. It stands to reason that a negotiator who cannot pay attention effectively is unlikely to be an effective negotiator.

How ICTs Interfere with the Digital Generation's Attention

Given attention's importance in negotiation, anything that prevents Digital Generation negotiators from paying attention is cause for concern for their elder counterparts. With this in mind, this second part explains to elder negotiators the various ways in which ICTs can interfere with the Digital Generation's attention.[5]

The Costs of Multitasking

It is frequently claimed that the Digital Generation love to "multitask." They do not just watch television—they watch television while surfing the Internet on their phones. They do not just type an essay on their computers—they type an essay while sending instant messages to friends on Facebook and listening to music. The Digital Generation use ICTs a lot—more than seven and one-half hours per day, according to a recent Kaiser Family Foundation survey, not even counting the time they spend using media for school-related purposes, talking on a cell phone, or texting (Rideout, Foehr and Roberts 2010: 11).[6] And almost a third of the time that youngsters are using digital media, they are using multiple media at once, which means they are exposed to more than ten and one-half hours of media per day (Rideout, Foehr and Roberts 2010: 11, 33).[7] The Digital Generation find unitasking (doing only one thing at a time) utterly boring. What's more, they believe themselves to be good at juggling multiple tasks. They see nothing wrong with using their ICTs to multitask.

There is only one problem with this: Multitasking—defined as doing two or more things simultaneously—is something of a myth. Researchers generally agree that, rather than doing multiple tasks simultaneously, the Digital Generation are actually rapidly shifting their attention back and forth between tasks (Rosen 2012). Their inability to engage in true multitasking is due in large part to the fact that attention is a limited resource. Human brains have severe limitations in the amount of information they can process, the number of choices they can make, the number of tasks they can execute, and the number of responses they can generate.

Because of these limitations, the Digital Generation suffer three primary efficiency costs when they try to combine tasks (using ICTs or otherwise). First, they experience "switch costs" when they shift attention from one task to another. These switch costs are the time it takes for their brains to change their goals, remember the rules needed for the new task, and block interference from the prior task. Switch costs make shifting between tasks take about twenty percent longer than doing tasks sequentially (Jacobson 2010: 438). Second, they experience "resumption lags"—lag time, sometimes up to several minutes, between when they finish the interrupting task and go back to the original task. Third, their performance slows down after an interruption even if they do not change tasks, exacting a "restart cost" before they resume what they were doing. Added to these efficiency costs are other performance costs from attempts to multitask, including decreases in accuracy (sometimes by as much as twenty to forty percent (Jacobson 2010: 440), impairments to memory, and increased feelings of stress and anxiety.

A simple example can illustrate these various costs. Jorge is doing his calculus homework. He is working through a complex proof when he receives a text message from Sara. He puts down his pencil, picks up his phone (three-second switch cost), types a response, puts down his phone, picks up his pencil, turns back to his proof, and tries to remember where he was and what the next step is (twenty-second resumption lag). The phone dings again, signaling another text. Jorge pauses again and looks at his phone, then decides to answer the message after finishing the proof (two-second restart cost). This twenty-five-second delay is hardly the end of the world; Jorge's homework will get done. But now imagine that Sara sends Jorge forty texts and he answers all of them—his homework will take significantly longer, and the chance that he will make mistakes is greater. And now imagine that Jorge is a neurosurgeon who gets interrupted by an observer's beeping pager in the middle of surgery—even a brief delay or lapse in concentration could make an appreciable difference to his patient.

Interference with Attentional Control

Neurological Changes

ICTs have other implications for the Digital Generation's attention beyond their facilitation of multitasking. One issue that has received a lot of press coverage (and has played into a lot of the elder generations' fears) is the possibility that ICT exposure may be causing neurological changes in the Digital Generation's brains that in turn change how—and how well—the Digital Generation pay attention. The brain is a changeable, or plastic, organ and is capable of change throughout the lifespan. Though the research is still in its early stages, there is evidence to support the claim that ICT exposure is changing the Digital Generation's brains in certain ways. Some believe the changes are primarily positive, suggesting that the Digital Generation may process, categorize, and absorb information more quickly, may have faster reflexes and greater ability to respond to visual cues, may be superior multitaskers, and may even have higher intelligence levels than their predecessors do. Others believe that the changes are primarily negative, accusing the Digital Generation of being socially awkward, impatient, incapable of sustained concentration, narcissistic, and unable to empathize. Still others believe that the Digital Generation's brains are neither better nor worse, but merely different, than those of their elders. Adding to the confusion, it is not clear whether these brain changes should be understood as "permanent," or whether they are temporary and can be undone by virtue of the brain's plasticity if the Digital Generation take a sufficient digital hiatus.

What has received greater scientific consensus—and is of greater immediate relevance to elder generations of negotiators—is the notion that ICT exposure is contributing to the erosion of the Digital Generation's attentional control. Three significant factors linking ICT exposure to this erosion are (1) stimulus-driven distractions, (2) cognitive overload, and (3) stress and anxiety.

Stimulus-Driven Distractions

The first of these is the most intuitive: ICTs are designed to alert their users when something of interest is happening—to ding or ring or flash or buzz or pop up (or sometimes all of these) when a new call or message comes in, or when it is time for an appointment, or when a friend has just posted pictures on Instagram. These message indicators undermine the Digital Generation's top-down attentional control mechanisms because they are designed to trigger their bottom-up processes. The flashes and dings and pop-up messages are novel or sudden changes in the Digital Generation's environment—the very things their bottom-up attentional control systems are primed to be alert to. When the Digital Generation are engaged in a task and their ICTs produce an auditory or visual notification (the equivalent of the knock on the door), the battle between their top-down and bottom-up control systems ensues. This is not to say the bottom-up systems always win, but they frequently do.

As a result, the Digital Generation shift focus from their original task to the interrupting stimulus as they consult their ICTs to determine the reason for the notification. In other words, they try to multitask. For all the reasons explained above, this impairs their performance on both tasks. The more complex the original activity is, the more impairment the distraction causes. This is not to overstate the gravity of hearing a message indicator—compared to, say, a blaring fire alarm, a text message is a pretty mild stimulus. But neither does this mean an ICT disruption is a harmless one. Anything that engages the Digital Generation's bottom-up mechanisms imposes an extra burden on their top-down mechanisms and makes it harder for them to exercise top-down attentional control. And anything that invites attempts to multitask brings with it the related performance costs.

Cognitive Overload

The second way in which ICTs interfere with attentional control is by contributing to cognitive overload. Cognitive load refers to the information that enters our working memory at any given time. When the amount of information being taken in exceeds working memory's capacity to process it, we experience cognitive overload. In the grip of cognitive overload, we are more likely to become distracted and lose focus, we are unable to transfer new information from working memory to long-term memory or to make connections between the new information and what is already in our long-term memory, we struggle to filter out irrelevant information, we become restless, and our attention span is reduced.

ICTs contribute to the Digital Generation's cognitive overload in two ways. First, ICTs add extraneous problem-solving to the primary task, meaning they force the brain to do something that is mentally demanding but superfluous to the primary task. For example, when the Digital Generation read an online newspaper article, they are exposed to hypertext—text containing hyperlinks to related information located elsewhere. As they try to read the story, their brains have to make numerous decisions about whether each individual hyperlink is worth clicking on. This is an extraneous problem-solving task (Carr 2010); evaluating the relevance of a hyperlink is both cognitively demanding and yet not crucial to the primary task of reading the article.

Second, ICTs contribute to cognitive overload by dividing attention. In addition to bombarding the Digital Generation with distracting message indicators, ICTs also deliver information through "hypermedia"—the Internet's combination of hypertext and multimedia (Carr 2010: 129). For instance, not only is that online newspaper article full of hypertext, but it also has embedded videos in it that play—sometimes automatically—as the Digital Generation are trying to read the article. Now their attention is divided between reading the text, evaluating the relevance of hyperlinks, and watching the videos. It was once thought that hypermedia would deepen comprehension and strengthen learning because it presents information in multiple forms (audio, video, text, etc.), but instead it appears to divide attention in a way that strains cognitive abilities, decreases learning, and weakens understanding.

Stress and Anxiety

The third way that ICTs diminish the Digital Generation's attentional control is by contributing to their stress and anxiety, which have adverse effects on attention and the capacity to control it. ICTs first contribute to stress and anxiety because, as noted previously, their message indicators are designed to be interruptive. Interruptions are a type of stressor, and frequent interruptions make us tense and anxious. Interruptions engage the body's autonomic nervous system (the "ANS"), which controls certain vital functions, such as the beating of our hearts. Arousal of the ANS sends a signal throughout the body that something is happening and something needs to be done about it. It also signals our attentional networks to seek out information about the interruption, which diverts our cognitive resources from whatever we were doing before the interruption. Coping with the interruption requires conscious effort and monopolizes our attentional resources, reducing our capacity for pursuing thought processes and cognitive activities unrelated to the interruption. Our other cognitive functions suffer in the face of this stress.

It is easy to see the problems ICTs pose. According to one estimate, ICTs produce alerts—i.e., interruptions—at least twelve times per hour (Carr 2010: 132).[8] Under the cumulative stress of all these alerts, the Digital Generations' brains ultimately begin to panic,[9] and their bottom-up processes start to overwhelm their top-down processes. When the brain is in this "survival mode, the frontal lobes lose their sophistication, intelligence dims, and the brain is unable to think clearly" (Jacobson 2010: 433). In this way, ICTs cause the Digital Generation to lose not only cognitive efficiency and effectiveness, but also attentional control.

The second way that ICTs contribute to the Digital Generation's stress and anxiety is by dividing their attention, putting them in a state known as "continuous partial attention," a condition in which the Digital Generation's brains are "continually staying busy—keeping tabs on everything while never truly focusing on anything" (Small and Vorgan 2008: 18). Continuous partial attention is a state of inherently stressful hyper-alertness. The Digital Generation's brains never get to rest when they are on alert for new information and new contact at all times. As the Digital Generation become used to being constantly on alert, continuous partial attention starts to feel normal, even desirable, to them. This condition can be acculturating and potentially even addictive.[10] But because human brains are not meant to maintain this heightened monitoring state for extended periods of time, trying to do so can cause a form of stress that in the long term can impair cognition, lead to depression and irritability, and diminish the capacity to pay full attention to anything.

The third way in which ICTs contribute to stress and anxiety is by creating a culture that makes possible—and demands—instantaneous communication and constant connectivity. Long gone are the days in which a letter sent to a friend might not receive a reply for weeks. Now, thanks to ICTs, the Digital Generation can be reached practically any time, anywhere, no matter what they are doing or how far they are physically from the people trying to reach them. While this is wonderful progress from a communications standpoint, this technological capability is also problematic insofar as it has led to societal expectations of instant responses. Modern message senders expect that the recipients will answer immediately and may grow anxious, frustrated, or angry in the face of unresponsiveness. In turn, message receivers feel the pressure of these expectations and may feel overwhelmed by the demands of keeping up with their digital lives. As a result, those on both sides of the screen may experience heightened arousal, feelings of stress and anxiety, and the associated cognitive and attentional decrements.

How Digital Generation Negotiators Can Improve Their Attention

Given the obstacles ICTs present to focused attention, it is tempting to recommend to Digital Generation negotiators a blunt solution: simply turning the ICTs off. But the Digital Generation's near obsession with ICTs makes this advice unlikely to work for Digital Generation negotiators.[11] This third part offers Digital Generation negotiators[12] two alternative solutions with greater potential.

Take Technology Breaks

The first is to take "technology breaks"—designated times during the day that are reserved for checking messages and otherwise interacting with ICTs. Some authors have suggested checking messages as infrequently as once a day, while others have advocated taking one- to two-minute technology breaks as frequently as every fifteen minutes, with intense periods of focus in between each break. The latter formulation has more promise for Digital Generation negotiators, since research shows they feel genuine anxiety when they are separated from their ICTs for long stretches of time (Tapscott 2009).

Implementing the technology break advice might look like this: During preparation for a negotiation, Digital Generation negotiators might set a countdown timer to alert them every fifteen minutes that it is time for a technology break, and a second countdown timer to alert them when the break is over.[13] Otherwise, their ICTs would remain silenced, with visual alerts disabled, during the fifteen-minute work period. The process would be similar during the negotiation itself. The frequency of technology breaks could be negotiated at the beginning of the negotiation session with the other agenda items, such as meal breaks or breakout sessions.

The technology break suggestion neatly balances the benefits of minimizing distractions and the challenges posed by turning off ICTs altogether. Limiting ICT usage to specified break times should reduce external distractions similarly to turning the ICTs off. In addition, technology breaks may help to minimize the Digital Generation's internal distractions. Knowing that a break is coming makes it easier to focus on the current task for the specified amount of time, so their attention should improve during the time in between breaks. Moreover, having all parties take a technology break simultaneously during the negotiation should reduce the number of times that one or more negotiators is distracted by an ICT while another is talking.

Despite these benefits, a technology break is not a perfect solution. Designating specific times for technology breaks by no means prevents negotiators from checking their ICTs between scheduled break times. The technology break solution still requires some modicum of discipline and practice. And if Digital Generation negotiators become accustomed to taking breaks with a certain frequency when they are on their own, it may be difficult for them to focus for longer intervals if the parties have agreed to less frequent breaks—much as it may be challenging for negotiators to wait until 1 p.m. for lunch if they are accustomed to eating at noon.

Further, technology breaks are inherently disruptive. Taking a technology break may mean cutting short a productive conversation, and taking frequent breaks may unnecessarily protract a negotiation, since it will surely take time to bring the parties back to attention after a scheduled break. The breaks may be worthwhile if there is a marked improvement in the parties' attention in between breaks, but they may be a waste of time if the parties remain distracted throughout the negotiation. Finally (perhaps obviously), technology breaks are best suited to negotiations conducted face-to-face; they are likely impractical for negotiations held via telephone or videoconference.

Practice Meditation

The second promising solution for improving Digital Generation negotiators' attention is one that, admittedly, requires some up-front investment: practicing meditation. The benefits of regular meditation practice are numerous and well-documented, including enhancing clarity of thought and focus, improving sensory data processing, reducing stress, and—most relevant here—strengthening various facets of attention. Pioneering educators have introduced the dispute resolution community to the benefits of including meditation practice as part of dispute resolution training,[14] and incorporation of meditation training in dispute resolution classes is becoming more mainstream. If this training is offered in their classes, Digital Generation negotiators should embrace it.

But if Digital Generation negotiators are not taught to meditate as part of their dispute resolution education, they should develop a practice on their own. (Though some negotiators may find formal meditation instruction helpful, it is certainly not a prerequisite to learning how to meditate; any negotiator can become a meditator on his or her own and enjoy the benefits.) Meditation training is widely accessible through informal meditation groups, books and audio programs obtainable from bookstores and libraries, smartphone and tablet apps, and podcasts, many of which are free and available to everyone. These informal channels can help Digital Generation negotiators overcome any cost or access barriers to learning to meditate so they can reap the attentional benefits of regular meditation practice.

There are two obstacles to improving attention through meditation: time and effort—both as an initial matter, in learning to meditate, and on an ongoing basis, to maintain a meditation practice. Changing the brain through meditation requires at least twenty minutes of regular practice, preferably daily (Horstman 2010: 31). The Digital Generation may have trouble resisting the siren song of their ICTs for long enough to establish a regular meditation practice, especially if they do not view themselves as suffering from attentional problems. They may also find it challenging to carve out blocks of time from their busy schedules to sit quietly and meditate. Or they may view meditation as unrelated to negotiation and deem it not worth their time. Admittedly, improving attentional powers through meditation is a solution in which Digital Generation negotiators must actively invest themselves. But if they do, they may find it to be a powerful one.

Conclusion: ICTs Are Inevitable

It is easy to complain about a younger generation and, given the research about ICT exposure's effects on attention, it is easy to feel justified in complaining about the Digital Generation's rampant ICT usage. The elder generations are correct in believing that attention is important, both generally and particularly in negotiation. But the solution cannot be to shun ICTs entirely. ICTs are a fact of our current society, the same as sewing machines, cars, microwaves, and all the other forms of technology that were once seen as radical and destructive by those who lived before they were invented. ICTs are tools—only as "good" or "bad" as the ways we employ them. We must learn to live with ICTs, not simply run from them. To this end, negotiators—both current and future—should embrace techniques that help improve their attention but still permit them to enjoy all that ICTs have to offer.

Notes

[1] The waltz, introduced to the English court in 1816, was seen as a "contagion" that threatened respectable society, an "indecent foreign dance" involving "voluptuous intertwining of the limbs and close compressure of the bodies" (Knowles 2009: 32). In 1859, *Scientific American* railed against the "pernicious excitement to learn and play chess" then sweeping the nation, calling chess "a mere amusement of a very inferior character, which robs the mind of valuable time that might be devoted to nobler acquirements . . . ." (Munn, Wales and Beach 1859: 9). And in 1950, ballpoint pens were decried as "'the ruin of education in our country'" (Collins and Halverson 2009: 31).
[2] The eldest of the Digital Generation are currently in their early thirties, while the youngest are just being born. Others have divided this broad span of years into at least two different generations, but the dividing lines seem rather arbitrary and are not consistent from researcher to researcher. I consider the entire group to be the Digital Generation. However, because most of the research on this group focuses on today's "tweens," teens, and college-age youth—i.e., young people roughly ages eleven to twenty-two—I use "Digital Generation" primarily in reference to American youth in this age group. For a more expansive discussion of the Digital Generation and many of the topics addressed in this chapter, see Newell (2015).
[3] I refer to ICTs in the broadest, most inclusive sense, including both the devices we use (e.g., tablets, smartphones) and the websites and programs we run on those devices (e.g., email, social media websites). The broad generalizations I make about "us" and "the Digital Generation" are intended to reflect the average experience of adults and youths in the United States, with the caveat that these generalizations are likely not applicable to adults or youths in every country worldwide, or even in every socio-economic group within the United States.

[4] Newell (2015) provides a more in-depth discussion of the science of attention and the effects of ICT exposure on attention, including citations to the research mentioned in this chapter.

[5] As this chapter's focus is the impact of ICT exposure on the Digital Generation, the neurological effects and attentional impediments outlined here are described as if they apply only to the Digital Generation. Despite this choice of language, all ICT users—regardless of their generation—likely experience these effects and suffer from these impediments.

[6] This figure includes the average amount of time that American children between eight and eighteen years old spend watching TV and movies, playing video games, listening to music, using computers, and—for just a small part of this time—reading print media (Rideout, Foehr and Roberts 2010). These findings come from a nationally representative survey conducted in 2008 and 2009 of 2,002 third through twelfth grade public, private, and parochial school students aged eight to eighteen, including 702 volunteers who completed seven-day media use diaries, with a plus or minus 3.9 percent margin of error (Rideout, Foehr and Roberts 2010: 6).

[7] Media exposure refers to the amount of media content young people consume in a day, without taking multitasking into account (e.g., if a teenager listens to music for the entire hour he spends using a computer, the report accounts for two hours of media use) (Rideout, Foehr and Roberts 2010).

[8] Carr (2010: 132) estimates that the Internet interrupts an average person with at least twelve alerts per hour, and possibly many more.

[9] Dr. Edward M. Hallowell (2005: 58), a psychiatrist and leading expert in the field of attention deficit hyperactivity disorder, describes this "panic":

> Beneath the frontal lobes lie the parts of the brain devoted to survival. These deep centers govern basic functions like sleep, hunger, sexual desire, breathing, and heart rate, as well as crudely positive and negative emotions. When you are doing well and operating at peak level, the deep centers send up messages of excitement, satisfaction, and joy. They pump up your motivation, help you maintain attention, and don't interfere with working memory, the number of data points you can keep track of at once. But when you are confronted with the sixth decision after the fifth interruption in the midst of a search for the ninth missing piece of information on the day that the third deal has collapsed and the 12th impossible request has blipped unbidden across your computer screen, your brain begins to panic, reacting just as if that sixth decision were a bloodthirsty, man-eating tiger.

[10] Though many authors (e.g., Palfrey and Gasser 2008; Small and Vorgan 2008; Jacobson 2010; Rosen 2012) refer to Internet "addiction," the most recent version of the *Diagnostic and Statistical Manual of Mental Disorders (DSM-5)* published by the American Psychiatric Association does not include Internet usage as a disorder. *DSM-5* lists "Internet Gaming Disorder" as a condition warranting more research, though "the criteria for this condition are limited to Internet gaming and do not include general use of the Internet, online gambling, or social media" (American Psychiatric Association 2013).

[11] Newell (2015) discusses this solution's shortcomings in detail.

[12] Though offered to the Digital Generation, these suggestions likely also have value for negotiators of other generations, particularly insofar as they have begun adopting the Digital Generation's habits.

[13] This sounds somewhat cumbersome, but a quick Google search reveals countless free online programs that do all the heavy lifting. http://www.online-stopwatch.com/ is just one example.

[14] Professor Leonard L. Riskin of the University of Florida Levin College of Law is one such pioneer. Riskin (2004) provides an overview of the value of meditation (particularly mindfulness meditation) to dispute resolution and some of the ways in which meditation has been incorporated into dispute resolution training.

References

American Psychiatric Association. 2013. "Internet Gaming Disorder Fact Sheet." Accessed August 17, 2015. http://www.dsm5.org/Documents/Internet%20Gaming%20Disorder%20Fact%20Sheet.pdf.

Awh, E., A. V. Belopolsky and J. Theeuwes. 2012. Top-Down Versus Bottom-Up Attentional Control: A Failed Theoretical Dichotomy. *Trends in Cognitive Science* 16: 437–443.

Baker, R. L. and D. P. Brown. 2014. On Engagement: Learning to Pay Attention. *University of Arkansas at Little Rock Law Review* 36: 337–385.

Carr, N. 2010. *The Shallows: What the Internet Is Doing to Our Brains.* New York: W. W. Norton.

Chun, M. M., J. D. Golomb and N. B. Turk-Browne. 2011. A Taxonomy of External and Internal Attention. *Annual Review of Psychology* 62: 73–101.

Collins, A. and R. Halverson. 2009. *Rethinking Education in the Age of Technology: The Digital Revolution and Schooling in America.* New York: Teachers College Press.

Hallowell, E. M. 2005. Overloaded Circuits: Why Smart People Underperform. *Harvard Business Review* January: 55–62.

Horstman, J. 2010. *The Scientific American Brave New Brain.* San Francisco: Jossey-Bass.

Jacobson, M. H. S. 2010. Paying Attention or Fatally Distracted? Concentration, Memory and Multi-tasking in a Multi-media World. *Journal of the Legal Writing Institute* 16: 419–462.

Knowles, M. 2009. *The Wicked Waltz and Other Scandalous Dances: Outrage at Couple Dancing in the 19th and Early 20th Centuries.* Jefferson, NC: McFarland.

Munn, O. D., B. H. Wales and A. E. Beach. Chess-Playing Excitement. *Scientific American*, July, 2: 1859.

Newell, L. A. 2015. Redefining Attention (and Revamping the Legal Profession?) for the Digital Generation. *Nevada Law Journal* 15: 754–825.

Palfrey, J. and U. Gasser. 2008. *Born Digital: Understanding the First Generation of Digital Natives.* New York: Basic Books.

Petersen, S. E. and M. I. Posner. 2012. The Attention System of the Human Brain: 20 Years After. *Annual Review of Neuroscience* 35: 73–89.

Posner, M. I. 2012. *Attention in a Social World.* New York: Oxford University Press.

Rideout, V. J., U. G. Foehr and D. F. Roberts. 2010. Generation M2: Media in the Lives of 8- to 18-Year Olds. *The Henry J. Kaiser Family Foundation.* Available at http://kff.org/other/event/generation-m2-media-in-the-lives-of/ (last accessed February 15, 2017).

Riskin, L. L. 2004. Mindfulness: Foundational Training for Dispute Resolution. *Journal of Legal Education* 54: 79–90.

Roda, C. and J. Thomas. 2006. Attention Aware Systems: Theories, Applications, and Research Agenda. *Computers in Human Behavior* 22: 557–587.

Rosen, L. D. 2012. *iDisorder: Understanding Our Obsession with Technology and Overcoming Its Hold on Us.* New York: Palgrave Macmillan.

Small, G. and G. Vorgan. 2008. *iBrain: Surviving the Technological Alteration of the Modern Mind.* New York: Collins Living.

Tapscott, D. 2009. *Grown Up Digital: How the Net Generation Is Changing Your World.* New York: McGraw-Hill.

Section XII: Organizations and Teams

This section turns our attention to Organizations and Teams. Following a chapter analyzing how some real, live—and even famous—teams actually work in their internal and external dealings, the second chapter argues that organizations that hope to be truly successful in their negotiations should learn from those which foster a consistent, company- or organization-wide approach.

Next is a chapter, by contrast, on the productive uses of disagreement within a team or organization; this is followed by one on the negotiator's role—which includes a moral role—within a whole framework for participating in as well as designing disputing systems. And finally, there is a chapter that reviews the history, in one major industry and two other domains, of parties actually and productively thinking ahead about inevitable conflict, so as to avert it. The chapter goes on to propose that other industries and organizations learn to do likewise.

❦ 66 ❧

Two Heads Are Better than One: Team Negotiations in Research and in Professional Soccer

David F. Sally, Kathleen M. O'Connor & Ian Lynam

Editors' Note: This chapter analyzes the research on what individuals accomplish, when compared to teams in which the members have differentiated functions. Not surprisingly, the teams turn out to be able to handle more information more accurately more of the time. But of course, that's not the whole story. The authors, who include two advisors to professional sports teams, use examples from professional sports to show where you might want a team to negotiate, and where it makes sense to use an individual.

Introduction

From a supplier negotiating terms with a national retailer to pairs of spouses bargaining with sellers over house prices, teams very often turn up to negotiate. And research finds that, whether this decision is deliber-

David Sally has a PhD in Economics from the University of Chicago and is co-author of *The Numbers Game: Why Everything You Know About Football Is Wrong*, published by Penguin UK, translated into a dozen languages, and praised by *The Times* as "the book that could change football forever." He co-founded Anderson Sally LLC and has consulted with clients around the globe about football tactics, personnel moves, organizational change, and acquisitions.

Kathleen O'Connor is an Associate Professor at the Samuel Curtis Johnson Graduate School of Management at Cornell University and a visiting faculty member at London Business School. She has studied questions related to negotiators' reputations, the influence of past negotiation experience on subsequent negotiations, the negative impact of negotiator stress, and, more recently, how negotiators' physical features are interpreted by partners in ways that either improve or undercut deal quality.

Ian Lynam is a Founding Partner in the specialist sports law firm Northridge Law LLP. He advises clubs, athletes, brands, governing bodies and agents on the negotiation of sports contracts. He writes chapters in the leading textbooks *Sport: Law & Practice* and *The Sports Law Review* and is ranked as one of the nine "Most Highly Regarded Individuals" for sports law globally by *Who's Who Legal*.

ate or arrived at by default, sending a team can pay off. In fact, studies show that negotiating teams enjoy clear advantages when compared to solo negotiators (Thompson, Peterson and Brodt 1996; O'Connor 1997). When at least one party at the table is a team, for instance, both sides reach better quality deals than are reached between solos. A deeper dive into process reveals why this is the case. Teams of negotiators exchange relatively more information across the table compared to solos, and this may explain why teams are relatively better at identifying mutually beneficial tradeoffs across issues. Significantly, too, teams are relatively more likely to recognize poor deals and walk away from the negotiation rather than accept them (Cohen, Leonardelli and Thompson 2014). On a range of dimensions, then, negotiations are better left to teams than to solo bargainers.

As beneficial as it can be to negotiate in this mode, teams too often fall short of their potential. For a host of reasons—from inability to exploit their numerical advantage to a lack of coordination—some teams miss the mark. In this chapter we take real-world examples of negotiating teams, draw on the scientific literature to explain why the team was effective or not, and then make recommendations for practitioners who are looking to improve their team performance. Given the expertise of our author team, we focus our examples on sports negotiations, and in particular, football negotiation (soccer, to our American readers). When one considers that the global market for sports—including revenues from tickets, media rights, sponsorships, equipment and fitness spending, for example—was estimated to reach $700 billion annually, or 1% of global GDP, in 2014 (A.T. Kearney 2014: sports industry growing faster than GDP), these negotiations are important in the global economy.

What we have not yet said is that sending a team rather than a solo to conduct the negotiation is more expensive, as multiple people are being paid to do what one person could conceivably handle. In any decision to employ a negotiating team instead of a single bargainer, these costs must be weighed against the possible benefits. In this chapter we hope to make a persuasive case for bearing the cost of sending in a team, and we provide a bit of assistance to those looking to optimize team performance. To do that, we review two advantages that teams have over solos, and we also describe two rather common problems that can interfere with the performance of negotiating teams. For the latter, we offer practical advice for overcoming these obstacles.

Negotiating in Teams: What to Do

Divide and Conquer

While a young player's agent and a club's CEO are at an impasse over the player's value, the legendary and long-serving club manager travels to meet the young prospect and his parents at their home. Walking into the living room, he immediately takes notice of the photos of their son the parents have scattered around the room. The manager, careful to communicate that the CEO is a very good businessman, but not a football guy, speaks to the parents about how he sees the young player, what his potential is like and how much work will need to be done to turn him into a top-level player. Feeling comfortable with the manager, believing they can trust him, the family concede their salary demands for a chance for their son to play in the manager's club.

Speaking with one voice is critical for a negotiation team, so as to avoid miscommunication and to keep the talks on track. Done right, however, there can be advantages in having more than one person working on the team's behalf, perhaps with each wearing a different hat to bring the deal to a successful close. The good cop/bad cop tactic (Hilty and Carnevale 1993) is likely the best known of the team tactics. It depends on having two different people perform each role in the proper order (bad cop, then good cop) (Brodt and Tuchinsky 2000). In the story above, the manager is able to play the good cop, building trust with the player and his family. He is able to shore up his good cop persona by gently noting how the CEO really is not one of them, and in this way, he casts the CEO as the (relatively) bad cop. The manager then uses his increasingly warm and trusting relationship with the player and his family to encourage them to reduce their aspirations and agree to the deal the CEO had tried to get the agent to take. What this tactic requires, of course, is tight coordination among the two players.[1] Each has a role to play, and must stick to it if this tactic can be effective. But effective it can be.

Build and Exploit Two-Way Trust

One summer, a foreign player's agent was negotiating with a number of clubs in a country's top league. The outlines of a deal were agreed with one club and a meeting was set up to finalize matters. Both sides sent teams to the meeting: the player's agent was accompanied by two other agents, and the club's CEO, secretary and lawyer represented the club. The meeting ran for three hours with little progress on a couple of key outstanding points. The club's manager showed up a bit late to join his team. After a few minutes, he took the lead agent aside, and spoke with him for 15 minutes in their shared

native tongue. Upon return, they hugged and explained
to the others that the final points had been agreed.

To the extent that trust between parties encourages them to exchange
critical and sensitive information (O'Connor 1997; Butler 1999), building
trust is an important precursor to reaching mutually-beneficial deals.
Some studies go even further and show that the more one side has as its
goal building a good and trusting relationship with the other, the more
likely she is to make concessions to her counterpart, showing how far
trust and liking can go at the table (O'Connor and Arnold 2011).

Negotiations between solos have one dyadic pathway available for
building and capitalizing on trust. With more people at the table, teams
have multiple opportunities either to rely on established dyadic relationships or to forge new pairwise relationships. In this way, teams improve
the statistical odds that two people at the table will generate enough trust
between them as individuals to enable them to exchange critical information to reach higher quality deals or to encourage the other party to concede. That this is more than a theoretical possibility has been confirmed
in a field study of labor negotiations (Friedman and Podolny 1992).

Negotiation in Teams: What Not to Do

Decades of research show that the losses suffered by teams through
uneven participation, overconfident members, and problems coordinating can make teams far less effective than they should be. Below we
review two common problems faced by teams, and offer empirically-based advice for overcoming them.

Who's in Charge?

A dazzling 19 year old striker has just had an unbeliev-
ably successful season on the pitch. The timing could
not be better as his agent renegotiates his contract with
his club—a storied team that has had a solid, though not
stellar, season with this player, who has made a difference to its fortunes. Unlike other teams, this club uses
data analytics to assess their players. Knowing this, the
player's agent, too, relied on expert football analysts to
create sound arguments for why the young star should
see a doubling of his salary and incentives. When the
time came to negotiate, the agent met with the club's
CEO (of course) and (unusually) the head of analytics
for the club, who was there to provide support. To make
his point about the player's worth, the agent emailed his
team's analysis to the CEO and the analytics lead. As the
expert, the analytics lead reviewed the agent's work and

sent his rather negative response to the CEO, challenging the agent's conclusions and methods. An expert in running a business, the CEO had no understanding of analytics and thus was unable to incorporate the analyst's input into his negotiation approach. Rather than work together to fashion a response, informed by the analyst's input, the CEO simply forwarded the analyst's response to the agent. From there, the negotiation foundered, and in the end, the player failed to agree to terms with the club, a loss for both the player and the club.

Like our CEO and analyst team, teams have an advantage over solos in that they can span areas of functional diversity, giving them greater breadth of expertise from which to draw. Assembling a team that includes both process and content experts, strategic as well as tactical thinkers, number crunchers and smooth talkers allows for a range of knowledge, skills, and abilities that is likely to outmatch those of any single team member. In theory, teams allow for both a division of labor and a combining of skill that means that N + 1 heads are better than one (Hill 1982).

As our story highlights, what theory predicts and what practice reveals can be very different. The challenge to groups whose members have distinct sets of expertise is to *integrate* these, in ways that allow the team to behave as a cohesive unit. Rather than the team speaking with one voice, by forwarding the analyst's response—a response that may have been drafted for intrateam communication only, without any softening of tone or positioning toward the counterparty—the CEO in our story in effect stepped back and allowed the analyst to direct the negotiation. Their negotiation approach became an uncoordinated, unplanned, flip-flopped good cop-bad cop routine, causing bad feelings and confusion on the player's side.

A few process interventions could have helped. Experts routinely advise teammates to spend time together to develop what scholars call psychological safety (Edmonson 1999; Nembhard and Edmondson 2006). When teammates feel psychologically safe, they feel comfortable enough with each other to raise questions and objections without a fear of being embarrassed or appearing foolish (Edmondson 1999). A stronger relationship between the CEO and analyst could have helped create the safety necessary for the CEO to reveal what he did not know and press the analyst to explain his position. Armed with greater understanding of the analyst's objections, the CEO might have been able to incorporate them into his response. Not only would he have maintained his leadership of the team, but also he would have presented a response that was more compelling than the analyst's narrow dismissal of the arguments. This may have avoided the confusion and offense felt by the other side.

It may have been that the CEO and the analyst had spent sufficient time together, but perhaps they misspent their time. It is not unusual for team members to focus their internal discussions around facts and opinions they hold in common, leaving unique pieces of expertise or bits of data out of the conversation (Gigone and Hastie 1992: Lu, Yuan and McLeod 2012). When this expertise and specific knowledge is critical to the decision, the cost is a low quality outcome (Stasser and Stewart 1992). To be effective as a team, negotiators may need to sacrifice short-term time efficiencies. Spending backstage time to understand one another's points of view and to work collaboratively to hammer out a single statement that integrates these viewpoints could be time consuming, but also is likely to pay off, both by eliminating confusion and by building cross-table trust. And if this same team continues to work together, its earlier investment in developing a shared understanding of expertise will continue to make a positive difference to their future negotiations.

Are We on the Same Team?

In December, a desperate manager identified an (expensive) defensive mid-fielder he believed the team needed to finish the season near the top of the league table. Without him, the manager argued to his "teammate" the CEO, the team's chances of ending the season with great success would be out of reach. For the good of the club, the manager argued, it was imperative that the CEO do everything possible—including paying a very high fee—to bring the player to the team in January. And while the player could very well be good for the team, a strong finish to the season was especially important to the manager, who wanted to maximize his annual performance bonus. Though the CEO had similar aspirations for the club, he needed to weigh a wider set of interests, including the balance sheet. Worried that the CEO would not "do the right thing," the manager secretly contacted the player's agent to provide a bit of background, as he called it, on the team's position, making it clear just how much he valued the player. When talks with the CEO opened, the agent believed his player was essential to the manager's plans for the second half of the season and was able to extract a much higher fee for the player than the CEO had hoped to offer. Thus by opening up a twin track, the manager undermined the position of the club's official negotiator.

Social psychologists distinguish between purely cooperative teams and purely competitive ones (McGrath 1984). Cooperative teams have members who share the same motives and incentives and are focused on reaching a common goal. Members of competitive teams, including those involved in social dilemmas, are motivated to maximize their own gains irrespective of others' outcomes. Negotiating teams face a more complicated set of constraints. They have incentives to cooperate to speak with one voice, but members may represent conflicting interests or have very different incentives. When this is the case, members have reason to act in ways that may be costly for the team.

Studies show that conflict within the negotiation team can significantly undermine the team's ability to craft good deals with the other side (Keenan and Carnevale 1989; Halevy 2008). Examining cross-table dynamics, work shows that teams that experience internal disagreements are slower to make concessions, make fewer mutually beneficial offers to the other side, and present more demanding final offers relative to teams that were not marked by conflict (Keenan and Carnevale 1989). None of these is good for deals.

As scholars would advise any team, clarifying the team's goals to the members and getting their commitment to those goals is critical to the team's success. As the story above highlights, crafting appropriate member incentives that align with what the larger group is trying to achieve is also important.

Lack of coordination can cause teams to fracture, a risk not faced by individual negotiators. [See, however, NDR: Deutsch, *Internal Conflict*] As the size of the team grows or as team members become more heterogeneous, the potential for intrateam conflict similarly increases. The intrateam negotiation might end in an impasse as a team struggles to integrate the interests, positions, opinions, and outside options of all its members. It is essential to recognize that this struggle is not all bad: in fact, many intrateam disputes do not block performance (Amason 1996). Conflicts that are focused on the task at hand, disagreements over the best strategy, or hashing out whether one set of issues deserves more or less consideration, can help the team sort out its priorities and come to a better outcome than would have been possible had the team avoided the conflict. However, when the conflict becomes personal, the performance of the team is likely to suffer. Teams need to make sure that their conflicts remain task focused (Jehn 1994). This work also implies that teamwork will require time above what solos will need, especially during the critical preparation stage where teammates are getting to know each other and are working to pull together a plan for their negotiation.

The risks from intrateam division also can be mitigated if teams agree to internal decision making rules before the negotiation begins. Without this, even if the immediate conflicts among teammates over priorities were resolved originally, the team is likely to face considerable difficulties in deciding whether to accept a particular offer, risking impasses in the process. Anticipating difficulties when it comes to making decisions about finalizing deals, it would be helpful to teams to agree on a decision rule. Although unanimity is ideal for satisfying each teammate, the team may be best served by a majority decision rule that ensures that most parties get what they need from the deal—or a consensus principle that ensures that no decision is reached without everyone at least agreeing that they have been heard.

Conclusion

When deciding between sending a team or a solo to hammer out a deal, there is little doubt that teams are the way to go. Before the team leaves, however, it needs to prepare so it can make the most of its advantage. As is true for all teams, performance is better if the team has created the psychological safety that is necessary for the members to freely share and challenge opinions, perspectives and assumptions. During their pre-negotiation time together, it would be helpful, too, for the team to clarify its goals as well as the roles each member should play at the table. Coordinating in this way can head off the process losses that too often undermine team performance.

After the team has put in the time to plan, there is still work to be done at the table to help it capitalize on its potential. Team members would be wise to work independently to build as much cross-table trust as possible, and to work hard to stick to the goals and roles the team had put in place before the negotiation got under way. Small suggestions, to be sure; but these can go a long way toward helping the negotiating team convert its potential into a profitable deal.

Notes

[1] Note that this tactic depends on a bit of intrateam division on the player's side, as the agent was not present—a problem we will get to a little later in this chapter.

References

Amason, A. C. 1996. Distinguishing the Effects of Functional and Dysfunctional Conflict on Strategic Decision Making: Resolving a Paradox for Top Management Teams. *Academy of Management Journal* 39: 123-148.

Brodt, S. E. and L. Thompson. 2001. Negotiating Teams: A Levels of Analysis Approach. *Group Dynamics: Theory, Research, and Practice* 5: 208-219.

Brodt, S. E. and M. Tuchinsky. 2000. Working Together but in Opposition: An Examination of the 'Good-Cop/Bad-Cop' Negotiating Team Tactic. *Organizational Behavior and Human Decision Processes* 81: 155-177.

Butler, J. 1999. Trust Expectations, Information Sharing, Climate of Trust, and Negotiation Effectiveness and Efficiency. *Group and Organization Management* 24: 217-238.

Cohen, T. R., G. J. Leonardelli and L. Thompson. 2014. Avoiding the Agreement Trap: Teams Facilitate Impasse in Negotiations with Negative Bargaining Zones. *Negotiation and Conflict Management Research* 7: 232-242.

Edmondson, A. 1999. Psychological Safety and Learning Behavior in Work Teams. *Administrative Science Quarterly* 44: 350-383.

Friedman, R. and J. Podolny. 1992. Differentiation of Boundary Spanning Roles: Labor Negotiations and Implications for Role Conflict. *Administrative Sciences Quarterly* 37: 28-47.

Gigone, D. and R. Hastie. 1993. The Common Knowledge Effect: Information Sharing and Group Judgment. *Journal of Personality and Social Psychology* 65: 959-974.

Halevy, N. 2008. Team Negotiation: Social, Epistemic, Economic, and Psychological Consequences of Subgroup Conflict. *Personality and Social Psychology Bulletin* 34: 1687-1702.

Hill, G. 1982. Group Versus Individual Performance: Are N+1 Heads Better than One?. *Psychological Bulletin* 91: 517-539.

Hilty, J. and P. J. D. Carnevale. 1993. Black-Hat/White-Hat Strategy in Bilateral Negotiation. *Organizational Behavior and Human Decision Processes* 55: 444-469.

Jehn, K. A. 1994. Enhancing Effectiveness: An Investigation of Advantages and Disadvantages of Value-Based Intragroup Conflict. *International Journal of Conflict Management* 5: 223-238.

Keenan, P. A. and P. J. D. Carnevale. 1989. Positive Effects of Within-Group Cooperation on Between-Group Negotiation. *Journal of Applied Social Psychology* 19: 977-992.

Lu, L., Y. C. Yuan and P. L. McLeod. 2012. Twenty-Five Years of Hidden Profiles in Group Decision Making: A Meta-Analysis. *Personality and Social Psychology Review* 16: 54-75.

McGrath, J. E. 1984. *Groups: Interaction and Performance*. Prentice-Hall, Inc.: Englewood Cliffs, NJ.

Nembhard, I. M. and A. C. Edmondson. 2006. Making it Safe. The Effects of Leader Inclusiveness and Professional Status on Psychological Safety and Improvement Efforts in Health Care Teams. *Journal of Organizational Behavior* 27: 941-966.

O'Connor, K. M. 1997. Groups and Solos in Context: The Effects of Accountability on Team Negotiation. *Organizational Behavior and Human Decision Processes* 72: 384-407.

O'Connor, K. M. and J. A. Arnold. (2011). Sabotaging the Deal: The Way Relational Concerns Undermine Negotiations. *Journal of Experimental Social Psychology*, 47, 1167-1172.

Stasser, G. and D. D. Stewart. 1992. Discovery of Hidden Profiles by Decision-Making Groups: Solving a Problem Versus Making a Judgment. *Journal of Personality and Social Psychology* 63: 426-434.

Thompson, L. L. 2013. *Making the Team: A Guide for Managers*. Prentice-Hall, Inc.: Englewood Cliffs, NJ.

Thompson, L., E. Peterson and S. E. Brodt. 1996. Team Negotiation: An Examination of Integrative and Distributive Bargaining. *Journal of Personality and Social Psychology* 70: 66-78.

ଓଃ 67 ଧ୍ୟ

The Organization as Negotiator

Adrian Borbély and Andrea Caputo

Editors' Note: The authors discuss the surprising shortage of research on how organizations negotiate or plan to negotiate, when the work is considered on a broader than individual level. They contrast this with evidence that certain organizations have profited enormously, and even become dominant players in their markets, largely by adopting and enforcing one consistent style and approach to negotiation, one which supports in every detail the organization's overall strategy. They argue that building on this evidence represents a potentially huge strategic opportunity for organizations which have not yet tackled consistency of purpose and of execution across all of their relationships with suppliers, employees and other stakeholders. They note, however, that the results of such consistency are not always attractive to the outside observer.

Most of the literature on business negotiation (and the largest part of this volume) focuses on how individuals negotiate, how they prepare, whether they negotiate individually or in teams, and how they act and interact at the negotiating table. A deep understanding of those human behavior processes is indeed crucial for a sound comprehension of negotiation. However, the larger picture of negotiations taking place within and around an organization can be lost if we focus too much attention on

Adrian Borbély is an Assistant Professor of International Negotiation at IESEG School of Management in France. A litigation lawyer by training, he also holds a Master's degree in Public Affairs from Indiana University and a PhD in Management from ESSEC Business School. He is also a trained mediator. His research interests cover the promotion of negotiated dispute resolution within organizations, lawyer-client relationships and the interplay between negotiation, management and corporate strategy. He is also much interested in the development of innovative teaching tools, such as real-life negotiation cases and a problem-based approach of negotiation teaching.

Andrea Caputo is a Reader in Entrepeneurship at the Lincoln International Business School in the United Kingdom. After his PhD in Management at the Tor Vergata School of Economics in Rome, Italy, he served as Assistant Professor of Business Administration at Princess Sumaya University of Technology in Amman, Jordan. His research relates to negotiation, decision-making, entrepreneurship and strategic management. He is currently coordinating the Italian chapter of an EU-funded project on New European Industrial Relations, analyzing the practice and effect of collective mediation in labor disputes across Europe. He is also an active management consultant and negotiator.

fine detail. We attempt to provide an overview of that picture in this chapter.

Quite often, during negotiation courses and trainings, top executives ask, "How do I make my *business* better at negotiating?" Accordingly, we hope with this chapter to construct a coherent response to this kind of question, which arises from the "real" world and which the academic literature has not yet answered. Indeed, we will question the motto that "organizations do not negotiate but individuals do," instead arguing that negotiation can and should be considered as a capability at the organizational level.

The usual response to that question is given as: "train your key personnel, those people directly involved with negotiation." Since negotiation training and continuing negotiation practice offer a nearly unlimited learning curve to mindful individuals, further coaching may be suggested, in order to translate classroom skills into the field. However, the initial question calls for a more insightful answer, which requires an integrated perspective that would fill the disciplinary gap between negotiation and management as we know it.

Acknowledging Different Perspectives on Negotiation

We opt for a wide definition of negotiation that encompasses all forms of joint human decisions (Zartman 1977), which include the obvious, visible negotiations (sales and purchasing, collective and individual employment relations, etc.) as well as the more ordinary, everyday negotiations that occupy most of every manager's time in every organization.

Broadly speaking, research has taken two main approaches to the study of negotiation (Stimec 2014). Currently, the most widely-used one is the micro-level, or behavioral one, which looks, usually through the prism of organizational psychology, at the human interactions at and around the negotiation table, with little concern for *what* is being negotiated. A second approach, the contextual one, focuses on particular types of negotiations and their specific contingencies. The problem, however, is that the specifics of the behavioral approach are taken as a given, a sort of black box, for the contextual approach—and vice versa. This has led to a plea for a third approach, which would cover both the behavioral and the contextual aspects of negotiation. Such an "integrated" approach has been suggested by William Zartman (1988) and combines behaviors and processes in the context of specific negotiations; to serve its promises, this approach relies mostly on case studies from the geopolitical arena. Although its characteristics would easily allow for an application to business contexts, this has not yet happened; Zartman's approach has received limited attention from those studying organizational or business negotiations.

Our contribution aims to look, from a theoretical and methodological standpoint, at what such an integrated approach in organizational settings would look like, and how it would enhance our understanding of negotiation as it is actually experienced by practitioners. We begin by describing three possible macro perspectives on negotiation, each of which will take a wider perspective than the last. First is the study of negotiation linkages, i.e. "the way in which one discrete negotiation influences or determines the process or outcome of another" (Crump 2010: 3). Grounding his work in international relations cases, Larry Crump isolates different linkage mechanisms and makes the case that such a wider, more strategic approach to negotiation may offer a better perspective on complex situations and allow us to better understand the players' full interests and available strategies.

A second, wider lens is offered by Arnaud Stimec, a French researcher on negotiation and mediation at *Sciences Po Rennes*. He suggests an infrastructure approach to negotiation within the organization, which would require researchers to bridge the micro and contextual approaches outlined above. In terms of methodology, this means observing behaviors in real-life, instead of laboratory settings. By mixing negotiation theory with organizational theories, the objective would be to draft guidelines for action through an understanding of negotiation's systems effects and reflectiveness in negotiation steering and results. That is: looking at how the organization manages its different negotiations (including its informal ones), pools them together and tries to derive performance from this whole. In doing so, Stimec sets an agenda for research that "deals not only with the characterization of the observed negotiations and the level of regulation at play but looks deep into the system's ability to articulate the different negotiations within an infrastructure that could be in part thought and formalized, in part tacit or empirical." (Translated from Stimec 2014: 210)

Following this line of thought, more work is being done which focuses on whether organizations develop their own signature way of negotiating. A pattern in the organizations' behavior is shown across different studies, in particular with reference to contract negotiations (Lee et al. 1998; Luo 1999; Luo and Shenkar 2002). Recent works on institutional practices help us understand the dimensions of organizations' behavior in negotiations (Helms et al. 2012; Helfen and Sydow 2013). If we think about unions, public agencies or NGOs, their negotiation strategies are broadly consistent despite changes in negotiating teams, showing some form of institutional movement behind individual practices. In addition to converging interests, there appears to be an imprinting of the organizational culture on negotiating (Sydow, Schreyögg and Koch 2009). Certain patterns may create coherence among organizational negotiation practices; however, this remains to be formally documented in research. Nonetheless, as for example with the U.S. Government's well-known statement that "we do not negotiate with terrorists," we can often identify a sort of negotiating culture in organizations.

The third level takes an even wider perspective, by treating negotiations from a systematic viewpoint. This requires acknowledging the reciprocal relationship between an organization's strategy and its negotiation practices. In what follows, we will suggest ways to examine the different processes through which (1) strategy may impact negotiation practices and (2) negotiations may influence the way strategy is defined and implemented. Here, regrettably, research is scarce in both directions.

Certain key variables in strategy formation may impact conflict-proneness and negotiated relationships between headquarters and foreign subsidiaries; for example, if subsidiaries are given increased autonomy to adapt to their local context, this creates avenues for internal negotiations and decreases the level of conflict with headquarters (Pahl and Roth 1993). Similarly, some strategic decisions taken at the centralized level (e.g. recourse to complex outsourcing contracts) give the organization structured and clearly identifiable ways to negotiate with their external stakeholders (Quélin and Duhamel 2003). Also similarly, the strategic positioning of the company (e.g. as a leader in its market) dictates the behavior of its agents at different negotiation tables; for example, when a leading company opts for a cost-killing strategy, this necessarily translates at diverse negotiation tables into hard-bargaining tactics on the financials (Borbély 2014).

Conversely, negotiation also plays an influential role in strategy formation. If we examine this process through the top-down model of strategy making, several studies have clearly shown the relationship (e.g. Amason and Schweiger 1997; Elbanna, Ali and Dayan 2011; Parayitam and Dooley 2011). Such a stream of research considers strategy as a top-down phenomenon, with leaders defining strategy in formal settings, often behind closed doors. In these settings, when conflict arises, it may affect the strategic decision making process. If, however, we use the emergent model of strategy, which posits that strategy emerges from practices and human interactions at all levels of the organization (Mintzberg 1978), this suggests that social dialogue, employee participation, and negotiation culture within an organization will all strongly impact strategy formulation and implementation. In any case, very little research has looked beyond certain negotiations of strategic importance to study how negotiation can and should be nurtured from a strategic point of view.

Negotiation as Organizational Capability

To justify efforts towards a negotiation infrastructure within an organization, one first needs to recognize that negotiations taken as a whole may provide a comparative advantage to the organization and, consequently, that negotiation should be approached, at the organizational level, as a capability.

Our discussion thus far suggests that organizations *should* look at negotiation from a systemic perspective, in order to reap its full benefits. Consider several organizations supplying similar products (goods or services) to the same market: the one that negotiates best with internal and external stakeholders will undoubtedly take the lead. All other things being equal, negotiation, especially when considered at the organizational level, needs to be perceived as a source of performance and growth, supporting competitive advantage. Negotiation is therefore linked with performance, an idea congruent with the strategy literature, in particular the Resource-Based View of the firm (RBV).

As one of the dominant theories in business, RBV seeks to understand how competitive advantage is created and sustained over time, by focusing on the internal organization of firms, rather than placing the focus on the firm's positioning in its market. Competitive advantage can be achieved and sustained if the firm possesses, through development or acquisition, resources that are valuable, inimitable, rare, and non-substitutable (e.g. Wernerfelt 1984). RBV therefore posits that organizations own a unique set of resources and capabilities, the latter being defined as their ability to deploy the former in the most productive way[1].

The RBV literature stresses the notion of human capital (Schultz 1961), which, in negotiation terms, leads to the idea of "relational capital", defined as "the set of all relationships—market relationships, power relationships and cooperation—established between firms, institutions and people that stem from a strong sense of belonging and a highly developed capacity of cooperation typical of culturally similar people and institutions" (Welbourne and Pardo-del-Val 2009: 486, citing Capello and Faggian 2005). Following this reasoning, the fruit of successful negotiations is defined as *part of the firm's capital*, thereby stressing negotiation's potential impact on the organization's performance. This applies to commercial negotiations (sales and purchasing) but also to the organization's ability to regulate its internal relationships through negotiation, from the work floor (unions) to the board's table (strategy). Well-managed ongoing negotiated relationships, such as an innovative collective agreement with the workforce or an influential lobbying relationship with the regulator, are therefore assets for an organization.

Recognizing negotiation as a capability does not seem to conflict with the literature, which, in particular, provides cases in which organizations' negotiation and conflict management abilities protect them from adverse aspects of their environment. As an example, doing business in fragile, war-torn areas of the world requires specific skills, in order to be accepted by the local communities and shielded from the consequences of local conflicts (Ganson 2014). Similarly, contexts of intractable labor conflict may prevent organizations from efficiently doing business, or even making key decisions. A recent example may be found in the deadlock at Air France, the French national air carrier, in September 2014: the board's plan to develop a Europe-wide low cost airline, described as the only way to address competition, was stalemated because of failed negotiations with the pilot unions (Clark 2014).

Few companies exemplify the recourse to negotiation to further their competitive advantage better than Ryanair, the Irish low cost airline (Borbély 2014). For the first decade and a half of our century, Ryanair has managed to leverage its ultra-low fare positioning in the highly competitive European air travel market with spectacular financial results. To achieve this, it relies on a thorough cost-killing approach, which goes beyond its operations to negotiation with its key stakeholders. By leveraging its market domination, the company has proven able to capture much value in its negotiations with customers, employees, aircraft manufacturers and regional airport operators. As an example of their success in negotiation, some airports pay Ryanair a "marketing fee" to serve them, rather than the more common agreement in which the airport *collects* a landing fee from each airline. Such arrangements alone are said to generate more revenue every year than the airline's published yearly profits (Borbély 2014). If this proves true, it means that Ryanair actually loses money on their air operations, making the results of their negotiations all the more central to the company's performance. Ryanair has built its business success on an ultra-hard-bargaining stance, often equated to a "take-it-or-leave-it" approach, which it applies to all its stakeholders: customers and staff are explicitly told to go to the competition if they are not satisfied. It uses a similar approach toward the all-powerful airplane manufacturers, Airbus and Boeing: the case study shows how, facing extreme demands regarding discount prices, Airbus has decided not to deal with Ryanair despite well-engaged discussions in 2003, while Boeing has. Ryanair got cheap deals on its fleet, in part because they placed their two last giant orders for 737s in times of hardship for Boeing, i.e. when Boeing had a poor BATNA (in the midst of the moribund, post 9/11 aircraft market in 2003, and during the 787 Dreamliner "teething troubles" in 2013) (Borbély 2014). We can therefore identify idiosyncratic processes of negotiation within this airline which stand at the root of its financial performance. The example of Ryanair shows that an organization may negotiate in a consistent manner, regardless of the agent sent to the table, the counterpart, the stakes, or the context of the different negotiations. Thereby, organizations' larger strategies have an imprint on daily negotiation practices on the ground.

Daily negotiation behavior in a company is difficult to observe with either of the classical methodological lenses used in negotiation research (behavioral or contextual), requiring instead an integrated approach, which unveils the ways that coherence is created, maintained and exploited within an organization. Furthermore, organizational studies may help us understand how organizations nurture good practices into a true capability.

We were only able to locate two works in the literature that explicitly claim that negotiation is an organization-wide capability. The first to argue in that direction was Danny Ertel (1999); Hal Movius and Lawrence Susskind (2009: 5) followed ten years later, providing support for the idea in the bluntest possible terms: "organizations that look past negotiation as a core capability do so at their own peril." From a negotiation perspective, the idea that successful negotiations create value is thereby transposed from the level of individual exchanges to the organizational level. The central question then becomes: how can an organization drive the entirety of its negotiation practices so as to secure competitive advantage? Research in organizational negotiations, and in management as a whole, is surprisingly quiet on this point.

Growing Negotiation as an Organizational Capability

How can managers reap maximum value from the organization's negotiation practices? We believe that this requires some conscious, visible change efforts. Some contextual aspects also play a role, as the way people negotiate depends on the organization they serve; one explanation may therefore have to do with organizational culture. Apart from the classical agency theory incentives argument (e.g. Pratt and Zeckhauser 1985), we do not know how a specific negotiation culture naturally spreads within an organization. A possible alternative explanation may have to do with strategy: as the Ryanair case exemplifies (Borbély 2014), people negotiate based on their leaders' strategic impulse and the resources and positioning of the organization they work for (e.g., Bazerman, Magliozzi and Neale 1985; Appelt and Higgins 2010). For example, a purchaser for Walmart does not negotiate in the same way as his equivalent at the local food co-op; among other factors, it is easier (at least in theory) to negotiate for a powerful company than for a small start-up. Comparing Ryanair with other successful negotiating companies may lead to the emergence of a set of strategic features associated with better negotiating practices.

Beyond these contextual elements, we suggest that business managers take steps to cohesively structure their organization's negotiation streams. By this, we mean a broad management change and organizational structuring effort, designed to lead the company to view negotiation from a systematic perspective, rather than, or in addition to, individual negotiations taken individually. These steps must be grounded in reflections about the negotiation performance of the organization, perhaps starting from one set of issues in particular (sales, purchasing, employment relations, employee participation and quality of life at work, etc.), [NDR: Abramowitz, *Learning from Sales*] or possibly taken from a global perspective. Following are some ideas provided by the few existing sources on this issue.

In their 2009 book, Movius and Susskind offer a consulting approach, which follows up on negotiation training and attempts to give trainees the tools to apply the mutual gains method in their work. Their step-by-step method, which can either emanate from the leadership (top-down) or individual negotiators (bottom-up), begins with a diagnosis of current negotiation practices. Change efforts then focus on innovation diffusion (tailor-made training programs, experiments, exchange of good practices, etc.); adaptation of processes (especially negotiation preparation); and changes in the incentive structure. The final step in their method is the traditional ex-post assessment of the change effort, in order to tackle persistent barriers.

Although published somewhat earlier than Movius and Susskind's book, consultant Danny Ertel's 1999 *Harvard Business Review* article offers a more detailed picture. (Ertl 1999) He lists different mechanisms through which negotiations may be influenced from an organizational perspective, in addition to the hiring, training, and retaining of individual negotiators. He first explicitly invites managers to move away from a situational to a more strategic and systematic approach to negotiation— i.e. they should look at all negotiations simultaneously, instead of each negotiation individually. He advocates coordinating all negotiations, rather than creating stricter rules and regulations, or setting stricter mandates to negotiators. His advice may be categorized along the following two lines.

First, Ertel suggests creating a negotiation infrastructure, which not only enables people to share information, brainstorm, and exchange good practices, but motivates people toward such coordination efforts. Setting aside the idea that each negotiation is unique, such an infrastructure aims to provide negotiators with organizational support, by standardizing processes, imposing some form of management control over negotiators, and changing the way employees approach negotiation. This can lead to the creation of a central database of all negotiations, to be used as a reference in one's individual negotiation efforts.

Second, Ertel offers reflections about how to better incentivize negotiators to make the organization's negotiation efforts more efficient overall. This requires modernizing negotiators' key performance indicators to better align their remuneration scheme with the objectives of the company. For example, instead of quantitative successes (turnover, clients, etc.), negotiators may be evaluated on the quality of the relationships they create, or the innovative character of their deals. When correctly incentivized, negotiators may become less concerned with their immediate gain and work harder toward long-standing business relationships; this may in particular help them quit responding to relationship issues with concessions on the substance (e.g. discounts). Furthermore, negotiators need to be reassured that it is fine for them to walk away when a proposed deal does not fit with the organization's interests. Finally, for coherence purposes, Ertel insists that such efforts need to transcend organizational boundaries, be applied by management, and be aligned with the company's public relations efforts.

All of these consultants offer cases where successful management changes were applied at the departmental or company level to align negotiation practices to better serve the organization's strategic objectives. Such structuring changes are directed by management and aim to increase overall negotiation outcomes on a company-wide basis, rather than individual negotiations, so that negotiation best serves the organization's strategic objectives.

At this point, three remarks appear necessary. First, neither source claims to be comprehensive. They provide examples and methods to increase efficiency, without aiming to cover the entire field. Second, their methodology is experiential. They do not provide empirical support for their central argument that a negotiation infrastructure makes the organization more efficient overall. Finally, neither source was able to observe more than a handful of organizations that had actually implemented the methods that they recommend. Their contribution is therefore a basis upon which to begin to build a global understanding of the diffusion of negotiation within organizations; but this work remains to be done.

Taking Negotiation to the Organizational Level

So how do we go from training better negotiators to ensuring that the organization as a whole negotiates more efficiently? In other words, how do we ensure that negotiation serves its role in fulfilling the organization's strategy and reaching its objectives? Approaching the question from this angle can permit us to merge fundamental negotiation theories (as discussed in other sections of this volume) with research on sales management, dispute resolution systems design, social dialogue, happiness at work (which largely deals with "invisible" everyday negotiations), and corporate strategy.

We recommend that these efforts begin with an attempt to determine whether various companies consider negotiation as anything more than an individual skill to nurture among their employees. We need to know how companies structure their negotiation efforts, whether along the lines suggested by Ertel (1999) and Movius and Susskind (2009), or through other methods. We should also carefully define "efficient negotiation processes" by identifying and mapping the different processes and settings of negotiation throughout the organization, in a systematic way, such that inter-organizational and cross-cultural comparative studies are made possible. This also mandates the establishment of efficiency indicators, either on a longitudinal basis, or as rigorous, cross-sectional dependent variables.

Whether we follow Henry Mintzberg (1978) with his idea of "emerging strategy," or we approach strategy formulation as a top-down phenomenon, strategy needs to be diffused within and around the organization, in part through negotiation among different actors and stakeholders. One may therefore hypothesize that, across the board, the efficiency of such negotiations will positively impact the success of the strategy, and therefore the organization's performance. If we postulate that organizations that negotiate better perform better, can we justify this with empirical data? This will require us to use the existing performance indicators for strategy (or create new ones) and build the appropriate key performance indicators for negotiation. It will also mandate a careful look for (possibly numerous) exogenous factors that may mediate the relationship between negotiation and strategy.

The way people negotiate within an organization may impact its strategy in terms of how well that strategy is implemented, but also in other ways. For example, one may also hypothesize whether efficient negotiation practices, consistently applied throughout the organization, lead to less conservative, more entrepreneurial strategy formulation, with more risk-taking and innovative potential. The Ryanair example seems to suggest this: companies that perform persistently well in negotiation may be able to set, and reach, more ambitious objectives. A structured approach to negotiation at all levels of the organization may profoundly impact its culture, for example through employee participation processes and collective feedback on negotiation practices, which may in turn lead to more creative strategy ideas.

A systematic map of different organizational practices regarding negotiation may enable us to isolate best practices. Some structuring efforts may work, others may not, and some may only work in certain circumstances. Ertel suggests giving more freedom to negotiators and incentivizing them to search for creative deals. This may work for some functions of the firm or in certain industries, and prove non-productive in others.

A structured approach to negotiation practices does not have to follow the organization chart. Often, the cases showcased by the different sources talk about purchasing, sales, human resources, or strategy formulation. Beyond helping specific functions of the firm negotiate better, can a structured approach to negotiation help all functions of the firm to achieve better results? We conclude that the coherence of negotiation practices across the various functions of the firm (one is tempted to use here the word "negotiation culture") may have a significant impact on overall performance.

Notes

[1]It is worth noting that the strategy literature hosts numerous conceptual debates around the notion of capability, which is often characterized by an adjective such as "dynamic", "strategic", "competitive" or simply "corporate" or "firm". We do not wish to enter the debate about what type of capability best suits negotiation, as it is highly technical and beyond the point we are making here. For a deeper understanding please see Hine, Parker, Pregelj and Verreynne (2014).

References

Amason, A. C. and D. M. Schweiger. 1997. The Effects of Conflict on Strategic Decision Making Effectiveness and Organizational. In *Using Conflicts in Organizations*, edited by C. K. W. de Dreu and E. Van de Vliert. Thousand Oaks, CA: Sage.

Appelt, K. C. and E. T. Higgins. 2010. My Way: How Strategic Preferences Vary by Negotiator Role and Regulatory Focus. *Journal of Experimental Social Psychology* 46: 1138-1142.

Bazerman, M. H., T. Magliozzi and M. A. Neale. 1985. Integrative Bargaining in a Competitive Market. *Organizational Behavior and Human Decision Processes* 35: 294-313.

Borbély, A. 2014. *Negotiations, Ryanair-Style*. Case available at the Case Center (www.thecasecenter.org), ref. 314-293-1.

Capello, R. and A. Faggian. 2005. Collective Learning and Relational Capital in Local Innovation Processes. *Regional Studies* 39: 75-87.

Clark, N. 2014 (29/09/2014). "Air France, After Strikes, Faces New Uncertainty" *New York Times*, September 29, 2014,

Crump, L. 2010. Strategically Managing Negotiation Linkage Dynamics. *Negotiation and Conflict Management Research* 3: 3-27.

Elbanna, S., A. J. Ali and M. Dayan. 2011. Conflict in Strategic Decision Making: Do the Setting and Environment Matter? *International Journal of Conflict Management* 22: 278-299.

Ertel, D. 1999. Turning Negotiation into a Corporate Capability. *Harvard Business Review* 77: 55-71.

Ganson, B. 2014. Business in Fragile Environments: Capabilities for Conflict Prevention. *Negotiation and Conflict Management Research* 7: 121-139.

Helfen, M. and J. Sydow. 2013. Negotiating as Institutional Work: The Case of Labour Standards and International Framework Agreements. *Organization Studies* 34: 1073-1098.

Helms, W., C. Oliver and K. Webb. 2012. Antecedents of Settlement on a New Institutional Practice: Negotiation of the ISO 26000 Standard on Social Responsibility. *Academy of Management Journal* 55: 1120-1145.

Hine, D., R. Parker, L. Pregelj and M. L. Verreynne. 2014. Deconstructing and Reconstructing the Capability Hierarchy. *Industrial and Corporate Change* 23: 1299-1325.

Lee, J. R., W. R. Chen and C. Kao. 1998. Bargaining Power and the Trade-Off Between the Ownership and Control of International Joint Ventures in China. *Journal of International Management* 4: 353-385.

Luo, Y. 1999. Toward a Conceptual Framework of International Joint Venture Negotiations. *Journal of International Management* 5: 141-165.

Luo, Y. and O. Shenkar. 2002. An Empirical Inquiry of Negotiation Effects in Cross-Cultural Joint Ventures. *Journal of International Management* 8: 141-162.

Mintzberg, H. 1978. Patterns in Strategy Formation. *Management Science* 24: 934-948.

Movius, H. and L. Susskind. 2009. *Built to Win: Creating a World-Class Negotiating Organization*. Boston: Harvard Business Press.

Pahl, J. M. and K. Roth. 1993. Managing the Headquarters-Foreign Subsidiary Relationship: the Roles of Strategy, Conflict, and Integration. *International Journal of Conflict Management* 4: 139-165.

Parayitam, S. and R. S. Dooley. 2011. Is Too Much Cognitive Conflict in Strategic Decision-Making Teams Too Bad? *International Journal of Conflict Management* 22: 342-357.

Pratt, J. W. and R. Zeckhauser. 1985. *Principals and Agents: The Structure of Business*. Boston: Harvard Business School Press.

Quélin, B. and F. Duhamel. 2003. Bringing Together Strategic Outsourcing and Corporate Strategy: Outsourcing Motives and Risks. *European Management Journal* 21: 647-661.

Schultz, T. W. 1961. Investment in Human Capital. *The American Economic Review* 51: 1-17.

Stimec, A. 2014. Vers une Ingénierie des Négociations dans les Organisations. *Recherches en Sciences de Gestion* 102: 95-212.

Sydow, J., G. Schreyögg and J. Koch. 2009. Organizational Path Dependence: Opening the Black Box. *Academy of Management Review* 34: 689-709.

Welbourne, T. M. and M. Pardo-del-Val. 2009. Relational Capital: Strategic Advantage for Small and Medium-Size Enterprises (SMEs) Through Negotiation and Collaboration. *Group Decision and Negotiation* 18: 483-497.

Wernerfelt, B. 1984. A Resource-Based View of the Firm. *Strategic Management Journal* 5: 171-180.

Zartman, I. W. 1977. Negotiation as a Joint Decision-Making Process. *Journal of Conflict Resolution* 21: 619-638.

Zartman, I. W. 1988. Common Elements in the Analysis of the Negotiation Process. *Negotiation Journal* 4: 31-43.

⚘ 68 ⚘

Productive Disagreement

Howard Gadlin

Editors' Note: The author earned his living for many years mediating between 20,000 scientists and working with interdisciplinary research teams. Reflecting on his career, Gadlin finds himself valuing disagreement (at least sometimes) more than agreement. Especially among scientists or other people who must think and work in teams, disagreement can spur new thinking. Developing this theme, Gadlin finds that the maintenance of productive disagreement has its own principles, and is at the heart of professional practice in an increasing number of occupations and settings which depend on developing new intellectual property.

The idea first came to me on the tennis court. I was in the midst of an exciting match marked by extended rallies in which my opponent and I were pushing each other to our limits. As the match progressed and each of us did what we could to win each point, I suddenly understood why in tennis one's opponent is often called one's partner. As the set went on I felt a growing connection to, and appreciation of, the person on the other side of the net. That feeling continued whether I won or lost the points. There was pleasure in the competition itself, independent of outcome, and in many ways playing well almost mattered more than winning.

Driving back to NIH from that match I was reviewing in my mind a presentation about conflict resolution I had given to a team of scientists. Although the talk was well received and seemed to address concerns such as how to deal with problematic post-docs and students, I still felt I hadn't directly touched the matters that affect them the most. It felt as if the

Howard Gadlin retired after serving for 18 years as Ombudsman at the U. S. National Institutes of Health. Before that he was University Ombudsperson and director of the UCLA Conflict Mediation Program and co-director of the Center for the Study and Resolution of Interethnic/Interracial Conflict. Earlier he was Ombudsperson and Professor of Psychology at the University of Massachusetts, Amherst. Currently he is studying the dynamics of scientific collaborations and developing approaches to address conflicts among scientists. He is co-author of *Collaboration and Team Science: A Field Guide* and author, among other writings, of *Bargaining in the Shadow of Management; Conflict, Cultural Differences, and the Culture of Racism*; and *Mediating Sexual Harassment*.

whole sensibility of conflict resolution was not quite right for people engaged in scientific research. That's when the connection to tennis kicked in. Tennis is a competition, but one cannot aim to address the underlying interests of both parties because their interests (winning) are antithetical; there are no compromise solutions and the competition is the only way to get to the end of the match. In many ways, science is similar.

Scientists thrive on, and science depends upon, disagreement—productive disagreement. Previously accepted ideas get challenged and discarded; research results are questioned; facts lose their credibility and are reformulated [NDR: Adler, *Negotiating Facts*]; theories are updated and eventually replaced by more powerful or more elegant theories. While the conflict resolution approach I was presenting might be helpful for addressing interpersonal issues that were interfering with the scientific work in the lab, it wasn't quite relevant to the scientific work itself. In some ways, in the field of science, the conflict is more interesting than the resolution. To be really helpful to scientists I needed to shift the focus of my presentations from techniques for resolving conflicts to approaches for creating the conditions for *productive* conflicts—conflicts grounded in substantive and methodological disagreements.

Getting Past Resolution

As a mediator I've always leaned toward a facilitative style; I pride myself on being very attentive to the dynamics of communication and power, and working to enhance disputants' appreciation of each other's interests and understanding of each other's stories. Still, lurking in the background, and informing what I say and how I intervene, is watchfulness for possible solutions to the obstacles or problems that are keeping the parties from resolution. But as I worked more with scientists, especially with scientists working in complex collaborations or large scientific teams, I noticed that increasingly I was paying less attention to potential paths to resolution, because resolution no longer seemed central to our work. Instead I was focusing on how they handled and communicated about differences; differences in discipline, theoretical framework, methodology, preferred forms of data and statistical analysis, and a host of other differentiating factors. It seemed that helping to ensure that the scientists were having the same conversation was more important than where that conversation ended.

It doesn't make sense to think about resolution if the "disputants" are not having the same conversation. This is a pivotal point. Many work disputes revolve around differences in interests and preferred outcomes. The mediator's work often involves helping people to move beyond a narrow win-lose sensibility toward a joint problem-solving framework. However in many of the science situations with which I work, the initial framework *is* a problem-solving framework: they have common interests such as to develop a vaccine for a particular disease, or to identify the underlying mechanism for a particular biomedical problem or phenomenon. The various parties *are* collaborators, not opponents. They are partners in the project on which they collaborate. Also, collaboration seems to raise different challenges with respect to differences among parties than conflict does. In conflict, differences are often at least part of the cause of the conflict; in collaboration differences are essential, as they are meant to be the basis of cooperative efforts. Within conflict, differences introduce a divisive tension; in collaboration differences provide, or at least should provide, a creative tension.

Recent work in team science supports the value of differentiating between the task and social dimensions of collaborative efforts (Fiore, Carter and Asencio 2015). Successful scientific collaborations manage and contain relationship conflicts while supporting the creative exploration of differences among team members regarding ideas, methodologies and conceptual frameworks regarding the scientific tasks to be accomplished. At the same time, I began to wonder if perhaps the difference between collaboration and conflict is not as clear-cut as it seems. Inevitably, once I began to pay more attention to the conversations scientists were having than to the outcomes of those conversations, my work with non-scientists shifted in the same direction. More deeply than before, I began to appreciate how many of the workplace disputes that came to me involved parties who were not really talking about the same thing. For example, one person focused on meeting a deadline, while her work partner was worried about accuracy and quality. Their conflict was not merely a reflection of different underlying interests; more centrally, it concerned broader differences in their understanding of the problematic situation. Helping disputants recognize that they were concerned with different issues, or different dimensions of the shared problem, was often the first step in guiding them into the same conversation, one in which both aspects of the work situation (and therefore, both their concerns) were addressed. Many workplace disputes, even those involving people with different status or power, are essentially problems in cooperation and collaboration. For example, a supervisor might be concerned with the productivity of the employee, whereas the employee was bothered about how the supervisor delivered criticism.

The Value of Disagreement

There are many reasons why we have to be careful not to treat cooperation and conflict as opposites. Keeping conflict alive requires cooperation between disputants, though not in the same way as collaboration does. By collaboration I am referring to an intentional and self-conscious working together to solve a problem or address an issue. The sort of cooperation I observe among people in conflict is typically not self-consciously intentional, but rather an exchange of provocations and responses to provocations. Most mediators have witnessed the way people in conflict "cooperate" to keep their conflict alive even while believing or even asserting that they want to resolve it. These disputants keep giving each other reasons to keep the conflict going. It is almost as if the conflict creates a negative bond between disputants. Typically, the mediator's job is to help the parties find a way to resolve rather than sustain the conflict, when the parties are unable to do this on their own. One of the great satisfactions in mediating is witnessing the shift to problem solving, and then seeing the disputants resolve their dispute. However, careful observations of how disputing parties cooperate in *sustaining* their conflict often provide hints about how they might cooperate to resolve the conflict.

For me, this observation now sometimes serves a different purpose. My experience mediating disputes among scientists and working with scientific collaborations and interdisciplinary research teams has moved me even further away from focusing on possible paths toward settlement. Instead, I have increasingly been attending, and in much greater detail, to helping to create conditions in which conflict can flourish and disagreement can be fully expressed. Early in my involvement with scientific disputes I believed that in collaborative efforts one does not want every kind of conflict to flourish, but just those conflicts which, when engaged, help to advance the scientific work. Those conflicts tend to revolve around *substantive* disagreements—differences with respect to theoretical formulations, methodological approaches, preferred modes of data analysis, etc. Such disagreements should be differentiated from conflicts grounded in interpersonal differences, tensions, rivalries and enmity. The goal in establishing collaboration was to contain interpersonal conflict while inviting and supporting the exchange of perspectives and the expression of disagreement.

However, I now think that even the understanding of collaboration as focusing on substantive matters, separated from interpersonal factors, can be a simplification. Of course conceptually it is easy to differentiate between conflicts built around scientific differences and those that are based on personal dislike or enmity. But in real life the two forms of conflict are not so easily separated; when working with disputing scientists, one cannot simply address the substantive issues and put personal differences to the side. The primary reason is that for many scientists, and others engaged in intellectual professions, their work is very personal, and they are deeply identified with their ideas and methodologies and even their research findings. No matter how committed they may be to intellectual dialogue, it is difficult to remain completely impassive when discussing ideas in which one is invested. And since scientists are very much like other people in this regard, they too can take offense when someone, even a friend, disagrees with them.

Of course, how one reacts to someone voicing an opinion or perspective different from their own is shaped by their relationship with or perception of the other. In general, if you trust or respect someone, you are more likely to give their ideas credibility, and to consider seriously the evidence or arguments that support those ideas. At the same time—and here we are close to the circumstances of the ideal tennis match described in the opening paragraphs—if your relationship is solid, you both might be free to engage in a very spirited debate, pulling no intellectual punches and pushing each other to your intellectual limits. In such circumstances there can even be pleasure in disagreement, which sometimes can be experienced as just another form of play, and as a reflection of intimacy. I've encountered many such relationships among scientists who have worked together for many years, and they are almost always described with great warmth. Still, even with strong friendships, an intellectual disagreement can spill over into personal territory and tap into the tensions and competitive feelings that are part of all close relationships.

Certainly, the interaction between substantive disagreement and interpersonal relationships is equally complicated when the basic interpersonal relationship is one of distrust and/or enmity. In this case, receptivity to an opinion or a finding presented by someone who is disliked or distrusted is most likely to be extremely limited. Their ideas and the evidence or arguments for them will be seen skeptically and the desire to reject them may well be motivated more by a need to defeat them and see them look bad than by any interest in determining the "truth." And while in my work I sometimes see a previously good relationship strained because of substantive disagreements, it is less common to find situations where coming to an agreement on a substantive matter leads to improvement in a relationship. But it does happen, in part, I believe, because finding or coming to agreement can lead previously antagonistic people to see each other in a better light. For example "if we can agree upon these facts about climate change, perhaps there are ways we could collaborate in efforts to address the problem." The recent collaboration on criminal justice system reform between groups like the ACLU and groups supported by the Koch brothers is a surprising and fascinating example of enmity being set aside by a shared understanding of a problem and a mutual interest in addressing it, even when underlying interests diverge.

Finally, as anyone who has ever been in a relationship that lasted longer than one week knows, there are times when a disagreement about an idea (or a scientific or political position) can be the beginning of a personal conflict, sometimes with ramifications that outlast the resolution, or putting aside, of the substantive disagreement. And at other times, a substantive disagreement can emerge on the heels of other interpersonal tensions or differences, thereby exacerbating those tensions and providing "reasons" for further interpersonal strain. But in my experience working with scientists, when there is a strong interpersonal relationship, or strong trust based on a history of successful collaboration, substantive disagreements do not automatically threaten the working relationship.

There is yet another factor that complicates the task of separating substantive and interpersonal matters in conflicts among scientists: the mediator cannot always tell what the disputants are arguing about merely by listening to what they say. Sometimes a scientist will use the substantive disagreement as a vehicle for expressing interpersonal anger. At other times the interpersonal issues are the grounds on which a scientist hopes to strengthen his or her scientific position. For example, a brilliant but aggressively assertive scientist may dominate discussions about the direction of a research project both by his/her style of arguing and the strength of their scientific argument. Unable to counter that person's science, his/her potential scientific partner may focus on criticizing the partner's overbearing style as a way of creating space for his/her perspective to at least be considered in the discussions of the project. In the reverse situation, a scientist might use a critique of a colleague's methodology as a means of expressing personal anger because of the colleague's intimidating style of interacting. I should note that I do not believe this sort of mixing of messages and modes is peculiar to scientists, although I do think it is more common among those who live and work in the land of ideas than in others. (See *Thanks for the Feedback* by Stone and Heen (2014) for an extended discussion of the complications associated with mixing messages of a personal and work nature.) As with many other types of relationship conflicts, what the disputants are saying is not always a direct indicator of what the conflict is about. As Friedman and Himmelstein (2008: Preface at xxix) state so succinctly "...conflicts are best resolved by uncovering what lies under the level at which the parties experience the problem." This holds even if we shift our focus from resolving conflicts to managing them and making them productive. We need to develop a full understanding of both the substance of a conflict and its dynamics.

Moreover, most negotiators know that not only is separating the personal from the substantive not as easy as it sounds; in some cases it might not even be desirable, let alone possible. First of all, in science, as in tennis, (and many other activities) the activity itself is often deeply personal. The scientist's work is not simply her or his job; it is intimately connected to her or his identity. In that case, a criticism of the scientist's theory, or research results, or methodology is in many ways a criticism of the scientist herself, and therefore can be experienced as much more than a mere disagreement about ideas. When certain kinds of adversarial or competitive activities occur over time, the relationship between the competitors becomes a rivalry—a collaboration where the intent is not necessarily to resolve differences, but one where each partner is sustained by those differences and is energized by the disagreements. And we all know that rivalries can be friendly or they can be bitter. Indeed there are many indicators that enmity is something that, at least for some people in some circumstances, fulfills a deep personal need. Sigmund Freud (1953) once commented, "My emotional life has always insisted that I should have an intimate friend and a hated enemy. I have always been able to provide myself afresh with both, and it has not infrequently happened that the ideal situation of childhood has been so completely reproduced that friend and enemy have come together in a single individual—though not, of course, both at once or with constant oscillations, as may have been the case in my early childhood."

However, not everyone succumbs to the pleasures of that need. In some of his research endeavors the behavioral scientist and Nobel Prize winner Daniel Kahneman introduced the idea of "adversarial collabora-tion" (Kahneman and Klein 2009). Dismayed at the common practice in academia whereby proponents of opposing interpretations of a particular phenomenon would publish a succession of articles criticizing the other's work, he approached his opponents with an offer to collaboratively develop, conduct and publish research designed to empirically test their competing hypotheses. Essentially, they created a framework within which they could conduct a productive conflict. The resolution, as it were, is not the result of a negotiation but rather of the research that was designed through a negotiation between the previously disputing scien-tists. The articles that resulted from these studies include both jointly and separately written discussions of the studies' outcomes and identify both emerging points of agreement as well as areas of continuing or newly refined disagreement. [For an analogous situation with additional possible approaches, see NDR: Wade, *Dueling Experts*] In addition, the collaborative effort provides the opportunity to identify possible future research that could enable the researchers to further refine their under-standing of the phenomenon in question. The important lesson for me in Kahneman's work is that, at least in science and probably in other disputes as well, opponents can be collaborators and even seemingly divisive tensions might be transformed into creative tension.

Even more dramatic instances of transforming potential enmity into successful collaborations are described by Susan Podziba (2012) in her book *Civic Fusion: Mediating Polarized Public Disputes*. Podziba de-scribes three projects that involved bringing together people divided by "passionate differences" to address a shared public problem. Arguably the most dramatic instance was her work in the aftermath of fatal shootings at two women's health clinics in Massachusetts in 1994. She and Laura Chasin, founder of the Public Conversations Project, cofacilitated secret talks among leaders on both sides of the abortion conflict: those who support legal abortion and call themselves "pro-choice" and those who oppose legal abortion and call themselves "pro-life." The end result of this extended 6-year process was not a resolution. If anything, the partici-pants' views were more strongly held at the end of the talks; but their stance toward and understanding of each other were drastically altered. Podziba (2012: 96) quotes an article written by the participants for the Boston Globe:

> We hope this account of our experience will encourage
> people everywhere to consider engaging in dialogues

about abortion and other protracted disputes. In this world of polarizing conflicts, we have glimpsed a new possibility: a way in which people can disagree frankly and passionately become clearer in heart and mind about their activism, and, at the same time, contribute to a more civil and passionate society.

While the disciplinary and personal differences among collaborating scientists are rarely, if ever, as emotionally charged and value-laden as those in the abortion discussions described above, there is one important similarity in that parties are sincerely engaged in the conflict. What is most interesting to me about the world of interdisciplinary scientific collaboration is that difference and disagreement have to become the *strength* of the working relationship. If the differences among collaborating partners are minimized or overlooked, then the research endeavor is less likely to be successful. The whole idea of the collaboration is to engage the problem—identify the gene underlying a specific disorder, or discover a cure for a disease—by combining the strengths associated with the different disciplines, even though it is not known at the outset whether or how the disciplines can be effectively integrated.

But the fact that scientific collaborators must find ways to work together cooperatively if they are to achieve their individual and mutual goals does not mean that they are not also competitors. Almost always, collaborating scientists are pursuing individual careers. Advancement depends, in most universities and research centers, on *individual* achievements. This requirement of independent achievement holds even within institutions that encourage their faculty to be engaged in collaborative research. In science the primary indicators of success are related to accomplishments that highlight the importance of one's singular contributions, despite work that is essentially collaborative in nature. Scientific collaborators who are close personal friends might be competing for an endowed chair at a prestigious university, or a deanship or other high status or high salary position.

It is one of the ironies of scientific collaboration that each partner places herself or himself in a situation where their personal success is no longer in her or his own hands, but rather is dependent on the contributions of one's collaborators—even while the larger scientific community will try to identify each partner's individual contribution to the collective endeavor. Of course, most of us will recognize this dilemma as a variant of the fundamental challenge in any ongoing or long-term relationship— how to maintain some degree of personal autonomy and independence while also being part of a collectivity—a couple or a family or a team or a partnership or a friendship. And in any of these collaborative arrangements, managing difference and dealing with disagreement are essential to individual satisfaction and collective functioning. For this reason I would argue that the major contribution that the field we call conflict resolution can offer is not bringing disputes to an end, but rather creating the conditions in which disagreement can flourish and conflict can strengthen relationships.

My conclusion here parallels, and is indebted to, the theme of Bernie Mayer's (2009: 272) book *Staying With Conflict*: "Our ability to engage in conflict for which there is no easy solution, and to do so with energy, élan, optimism, and realism, is essential to our capacity to work effectively on the big issues of our lives and times." The fields of negotiation and dispute resolution need to move beyond their current conflict-phobic stance toward embracing conflict—and taking it away from those who wish only to fight.

References

Fiore, S., D. Carter and R. Asencio. 2015. Conflict, Trust, and Cohesion: Examining Affective and Attitudinal Factors in Team Science. In *Team Cohesion: Advances in Psychological Theory, Methods and Practice*. Research on Managing Groups and Teams, edited by E. Salas, W. B. Vessey and A. X. Estrada 17: 271-301. UK: Emerald Group Publishing.

Friedman, G. and J. Himmelstein. 2008. *Challenging Conflict: Mediation Through Understanding*. American Bar Association.

Freud, S. 1953. *The Interpretation of Dreams*. Hogarth Press and the Institute of Psychoanalysis.

Kahneman, D. and G. Klein. 2009. Conditions for Intuitive Expertise: A Failure to Disagree. *American Psychologist* 64(6): 515-526.

Meyer, B. 2009. *Staying with Conflict*. San Francisco: Jossey-Bass.

Podziba, S. 2012. *Civic Fusion*. American Bar Association.

Stone, D. and S. Heen. 2014. *Thanks for the Feedback*. New York: Penguin.

☙ 69 ❧

The Negotiator's Role within a Dispute System Design: Justice and Accountability

Lisa Blomgren Amsler

Editors' Note: To many who are frustrated with ill-organized, expensive, catch-as-catch-can approaches to handling entirely predictable conflict, dispute system design has seemed a logical, socially productive way of planning to reduce the costs of conflict, and effectuating justice on a larger scale. Amsler shows how this is not always the case, beginning with an analysis of how Boston lawyers on all sides effectively conspired to keep the pattern and practice of abuse of children in the Roman Catholic Church quiet for decades. This was a system at work—there is no denying it. Thus questions of justice and accountability rise at the outset when analyzing or, even more important, planning any dispute resolution system. Amsler lays out the criteria and makes proposals for how to design and effectuate a system that is not only systematic, but requires justice.

Negotiators need to understand the institutional context within which they work. These institutions will vary widely; analyzing them involves the field of dispute system design (DSD). Negotiators have an opportunity to take a system apart, critique it, and make the system accountable. In fact, their failure to do this was the subject of a recent movie, "Spotlight," about the *Boston Globe* team of journalists whose reporting took apart the system the Roman Catholic Archdiocese put in place to protect priests who engaged in sexual abuse of children in their parish. The *Globe* reporters described a DSD in the shadow of the formal justice

Lisa Blomgren Amsler (formerly Bingham) is Keller-Runden Professor of Public Service at Indiana University's School of Public and Environmental Affairs, Bloomington, and Saltman Senior Scholar at the William S. Boyd School of Law, University of Nevada-Las Vegas. An elected fellow of the National Academy of Public Administration, Amsler received awards for empirical and doctrinal legal research from the American Bar Association Section of Dispute Resolution, Association for Conflict Resolution, International Association for Conflict Management, American Society for Public Administration, and Labor and Employment Relations Association. Her research addresses dispute resolution, collaborative governance, public engagement, and dispute system design.

system, in which lawyers on both sides negotiated settlements to hide all evidence of the abuse and ensure there were no public court records that would demonstrate the pattern and practice of transferring priests repeatedly from one parish to another. As negotiators, lawyers for both sides knowingly participated in this system, rationalized their participation through lawyer codes of ethics that require attorney-client confidentiality, and got paid for doing it.

How can negotiators play a role in making systems accountable? How do we define and measure accountability for DSD? This chapter will encourage the use of lateral thinking by crossing several different silos of scholarly work in law, political science, public administration, psychology, and philosophy. It discusses how negotiators should approach DSD, both for public institutions in governance and private sector institutions in the shadow of the law. It introduces DSD, its history, and a related research area, Institutional Analysis and Development (IAD). It introduces accountability and performance measurement from public administration. It explores how we might apply concepts of justice from psychology, philosophy, and jurisprudence to measure accountability.

It will then examine the negotiator's role in accountability in three different DSDs, involving forced or mandatory arbitration, systematic suppression of evidence of sexual abuse by priests of minors in "Spotlight," and Ferguson, Missouri's systemically racist DSD in the local criminal justice system of police and courts. As negotiators, we need transparency in how DSDs promote justice; we need to build accountability and performance measurement into DSD; and we need to take responsibility for helping to ensure that these systems are accountable to the people who use them and to the public.

DSD Applied to Governance: Voice Across the Policy Continuum

Negotiators can use DSD in a much broader array of settings than originally conceived; they can use it at different points for "voice" from stakeholders or the public across the entire policy process. The policy process is like a stream, running from headwaters upstream in legislation downstream to adjudication of conflicts. DSD applies across this policy continuum (Bingham 2009a) whenever institutions design and provide opportunities for voice (Bingham, Nabatchi and O'Leary 2005; Bingham 2010). For example, DSD applies *upstream* in the legislative or quasi-legislative process for making policy when sponsors design opportunities for public engagement, dialogue, and deliberation. It applies *midstream* in the executive branch when administrative agencies implement policy through collaborative or network public management (e.g. disaster management) and forms of dispute resolution (e.g. environmental mediation). This view of DSD's range is broader than the traditional *downstream* use of DSD to manage conflict through alternative or appropriate dispute resolution (ADR) in quasi-judicial (e.g. EEOC hearings), judicial (e.g. courts), or adjudicatory systems (e.g. grievance arbitration).

During the final third of the twentieth century, the way that we talk about both government and conflict evolved. Certain problems cannot be solved or solved easily by one entity acting alone (Agranoff and McGuire 2003) because they cross state, national, regional, or global jurisdictional boundaries. "Wicked problems" like environmental health and climate change challenged the capacity of a single governmental unit operating in hierarchy using command and control management strategies. Scholars shifted their emphasis to the concept of governance, rather than government (Bevir 2011). Governance suggests steering rather than top-down directing.

Negotiators need to understand their context, whether they are working toward a particular policy through a city council's draft ordinance on which there is public engagement, or helping agencies, churches, and NGOs negotiate their relative roles and jurisdictions in emergency management after a hurricane, or collaborating with local, state, and federal actors in negotiation over a terrorist hostage situation. [NDR: Volpe et al., *The Unknown*] Negotiators operate across the policy continuum, whether they are representing a client as a lobbyist or are inside an organization and acting as its agent in a network of other organizations. [NDR: Nolan-Haley, *Agents*]

Dispute System Design

While humans have developed evolving systems for managing conflict in social groups for millennia, the modern field of negotiation and dispute resolution gave rise to DSD about thirty years ago (for a more comprehensive history, see Menkel-Meadow 2000; this discussion is adapted from Amsler, Martinez and Smith 2017). In 1918, Mary Parker Follett proposed integrative negotiation as a way for people to resolve conflict, one that involved a deeper examination of what disputants truly need and want (Follett 1998). While other scholars built on her work in labor negotiation (Walton and McKersie 1965), Roger Fisher and William Ury's groundbreaking book *Getting to Yes* (1981) introduced integrative bargaining to the broader public as negotiation based on interests (basic human needs like security, economic well-being, belonging, recognition, and autonomy). They termed it principled or interest-based negotiation (Fisher, Ury and Patton 2011). Building on this work, William Ury, Jeanne Brett and Stephen Goldberg (1988) introduced DSD by examining how systems for managing conflict in labor relations address disputants' interests, contractual and legal rights, or respective power. Historically, disputants in collective bargaining primarily used rights or power to manage conflict. Ury, Brett and

Goldberg (1988) proposed that a healthy DSD should primarily rely on addressing the parties' interests through negotiation and mediation, with rights-based approaches like grievance arbitration as a fallback. They advocated against using power (e.g. strikes or lockouts).

Since this birth of DSD as a field, other scholars have broadened its reach outside labor relations. Using their wide experience in the public, private, and international sectors and building on the organizational development literature, Costantino and Merchant (1996) advocated DSD for all organizations based on values of openness, tolerance of diversity, learning, involvement, appreciation, and management of differences. DSDs should be open systems that generate valid data and use mechanisms for feedback. They viewed DSDs as arrangements of dynamically interrelated parts influenced by their environment. Lipsky, Seeber and Fincher (2003) used their longitudinal research on DSD in large businesses like the Fortune 1000 to provide a taxonomy of organizational conflict management styles; they provided a deeper dive into the building blocks and elements of conflict management systems for employees and employers. Lawyers have effectively been doing DSD, for example, by drafting forced, mandatory, or adhesive arbitration clauses, but without the express training they need (Bingham 2009b). Recently, Nancy Rogers, Robert Bordone, Frank Sander and Craig McEwen (2013) provided a casebook on DSD in law and courts in both domestic and international settings.

DSD now applies outside courts and organizations; it applies to all kinds of human institutions, and in public, private, and nonprofit contexts (Amsler, Martinez and Smith 2016 forthcoming).

Accountability in Public Administration

The "Spotlight" story illustrates a failure of accountability in the DSD in the shadow of the civil justice system. Public administration is a field of scholarship focused on systems of governance and the role of people in them. Public servants are accountable to the public. Accountability means the obligation or willingness to be responsible for one's actions; it means being called to account for one's actions to carry out the public will and the values it embodies. It is an instrument for a higher authority to exert control. There are three key elements: 1) information provided by the accountable party, 2) discussion between the accountable party and the oversight body, and 3) the consequences for the accountable party (Brandsma and Schillemans 2013).

Scholars in public administration have provided a frame for analyzing accountability which can be applied to DSD. Dubnick (2005), Dubnick and Frederickson (2010), and Dubnick and Yang (2011) propose and discuss six promises implicit in a public servant's accountability. Dubnick suggests that these six accountability promises include three instrumental promises that are means or mechanisms for accountability and three intrinsic promises that are ends or virtues of accountability. The means or mechanisms include control (inputs), ethical behavior/choices (processes), and performance (outcomes). The ends or virtues include integrity (inputs), legitimacy (processes), and *justice (outcomes)* [emphasis added]. Dubnick and Frederickson (2010: i145) describe the six promises, abbreviated and paraphrased below:

1) The promise of *control* assumes standardized procedures will provide greater accountability.
2) The promise of *ethical behavior* assumes agencies can prevent corruption through procedural accountability.
3) The promise of *performance* assumes performance measurements will hold people to account so they will perform better.
4) The promise of *integrity* assumes people want to be part of an accountable culture.
5) The promise of *democracy* assumes accountability procedures will produce democratic outcomes.
6) The promise of *justice* (or equity) assumes there will be fair or just outcomes when people seek justice due to some act.

The three instrumental promises of control (inputs), ethical behavior/choices (processes), and performance (outcomes) imply performance measurement. Public agencies need to use performance information to assess past action and plan future action as a means to ensure accountability.[1] We will return to this structure later when we apply it in DSD.

Institutional Analysis and Development, Collaborative Governance, and DSD

DSD is a relatively new frame for examining conflict management systems in industrial relations and law. As DSD scales up to encompass systems for managing conflict and collaboration in governance, it connects with other well established scholarly literatures. The late Elinor Ostrom, Nobel Laureate in Economics and political economy scholar, contributed the Institutional Analysis and Development (IAD) framework, a disciplined methodology for understanding the diversity of institutions that humans use to govern their behavior (Ostrom 1990, 2005, 2011). It provides a language and syntax to analyze human institutions. Ostrom suggested seven (7) categories within an "action arena" that is at work in any institution, including DSDs for managing conflict:

1) participants (individual or corporate)
2) their positions or roles
3) potential outcomes
4) allowable actions and the outcome function
5) individual control over this function

6) information available to participants about actions and outcomes, and

7) costs and benefits (incentives, deterrents)

(Ostrom 2005: 14). Ostrom examines rules that shape human behavior in institutions, both rules on the books and rules that emerge from practice. She also places the action arena in the context of the biophysical or material conditions and attributes of community (Ostrom 2005: 15). Ostrom sees institutions as nested. There is a large body of empirical literature using Ostrom's work and the IAD framework to examine how stable collaborative governance structures can arise in communities managing common pool resources like forests or fisheries (Ostrom 1990, 2005). As negotiators focus on the specific DSD within which they find themselves negotiating, IAD can help them think about how it is nested in the bigger picture.

Zooming in Using a DSD Analytic Framework

Smith and Martinez (2009) proposed an Analytic Framework for Dispute System Design to help negotiators and dispute resolvers more closely analyze the specific DSD context in which they find themselves practicing. A revised version of this framework appears below (adding context and culture, Amsler, Martinez and Smith 2015: 12-13, quoting Amsler, Martinez and Smith 2017 forthcoming):

---

1) Goals
   a.   What do the system's decision maker(s) seek to accomplish?
   b.   Which types of conflicts does the system seek to address?
2) Stakeholders
   a.   Who are the stakeholders?
   b.   What is their relative power?
   c.   What are their interests and how are their interests represented in the system?
3) Context and Culture
   a.   How does the context of the DSD affect its viability and success?
   b.   What aspects of culture (organizational, social, national, or other) affect the workings of the system?
   c.   What are the norms for communication and conflict management?
4) Processes and Structure
   a.   Which processes are used to prevent, manage, and resolve disputes?
   b.   If there is more than one process, are they linked or integrated?
   c.   What are the incentives and disincentives for using the system?
   d.   What is the system's interaction with the formal legal system?
5) Resources
   a.   What financial resources support the system?
   b.   What human resources support the system?
6) Success, Accountability, and Learning
   a.   How transparent is the system?
   b.   Does the system include monitoring, learning, and evaluation components?
   c.   Is the system successful?

Figure 1: An Analytic Framework for Dispute Systems Design

Can We Measure Accountability in DSD through Varieties of Justice?

People who design and manage DSDs should be accountable to the people who are participants in these conflict management systems. Courts and government agencies are accountable to the public. How do we hold those implementing private justice systems accountable? [NDR: Gross: *Arbitration's Shadow*] There are many ways to measure a system's performance. In the field of dispute resolution, researchers and program evaluators have used win-loss rates, outcome as a proportion of demand, satisfaction with process and outcome, time to disposition, interpersonal transformation, or willingness to use a system again or recommend it to others. While there are useful and practical performance measures, one might question whether they represent sufficient accountability to those who participate in the system.

The Analytic Framework for DSD emphasizes transparency, accountability, and measuring success as key components for systems. Dubnick's sixth and final intrinsic promise for accountability is justice (Dubnick and Frederickson 2010). Might we use some concept of justice as a means to measure a DSD's performance and ensure accountability? There are many definitions of justice, both in terms of process and outcome or means and ends. An over-simplified grouping of definitions includes justice related to outcomes, procedures, organizations, and communities (for a longer yet still partial list, see Bingham 2009b). [See also NDR: Wagner & Druckman, *Achieving Justice*]

Justice related to outcomes includes distributive, substantive, utilitarian, and social justice. The field of dispute resolution has considered distributive justice in its dialogue about whether ADR is "second class justice." Distributive justice looks at who gets what as the outcome of a system. Differing distributive justice theories might contrast equal shares with equitable shares of a good such as wealth. Distributive justice might provide ways to examine the pattern of outcomes or ends a DSD produces. For example, the U.S. Department of Justice's ADR program collected data on the use of ADR in litigation conducted by the Assistant U.S. Attorneys (AUSA) in their representation of federal agencies. One ongoing debate is whether ADR provides second-class justice. Since the AUSAs represent the public and taxpayers, this raises a question of accountability. Often, researchers use outcomes of litigation, defined as the proportion of the claim awarded, as a measure of success. This is a form of distributive justice downstream in the judicial arena on the policy continuum. One study found no statistically significant difference in outcomes between samples of cases matched on claim, subject matter, and district in which AUSAs use ADR compared to those using traditional litigation without ADR (Bingham et al. 2009a).

Justice related to voice and control over processes includes procedural justice, reflected by one's ability to participate, respectful and dignified treatment, and information. [NDR: Welsh, *Fairness*] Procedural justice provides a way to examine the process a DSD uses to produce its ends or outcomes. For example, the U.S. Occupational Safety and Health Review Commission (OSHRC) had outside evaluators assess its Settlement Part Program, in which its pool of administrative law judges (ALJ) served either as mediators or as adjudicators (Bingham, et al. 2013). OSHRC is the appellate body for Occupational Safety and Health Administration (OSHA) cases citing employers for violating the law. This program is within an administrative agency and midstream in the quasi-judicial arena of the policy continuum. A survey of lawyers representing employers and OSHA used procedural justice to measure perceptions of fairness in the program. Researchers found the majority (over 73%) were satisfied with the fairness of the mediation process and that repeat players (lawyers who had multiple cases before OSHRC) preferred mediation to adjudication with an ALJ.

Within organizations, procedural justice becomes organizational justice, which includes components of interactional, informational, and interpersonal justice. These forms of justice specifically relate to the way employees, supervisors, and managers interact in a grievance procedure or other process for managing conflict within the organization. In the U.S.P.S. REDRESS Program, outside evaluators used procedural and organizational justice measures to assess participants' perceptions of a mediation program for complaints of discrimination based on race, sex, age, disability, or other civil rights laws (Nabatchi, Bingham and Good 2007; Nesbit, Nabatchi and Bingham 2012). This program was also in the quasi-judicial arena, but within an organization and therefore upstream relative to litigation. For twelve years, evaluators reported exit survey data on employee and supervisor perceptions of and satisfaction with the mediation process by zip code region every six months as a measure of accountability (Bingham et al. 2009b). Researchers found the great majority of both employees and supervisors either satisfied or highly satisfied with the mediation process, mediators, and outcomes of mediation. Employees voluntarily participated in the program at the rate of 75% or higher; participants reached settlements in mediation or closed the case at the rate of 70% or higher. Researchers regularly reported program results to the public. Transparency in data made the program more accountable to both stakeholders and the public.

Justice for a community may include corrective, retributive, deterrent, restorative, and transitional justice. DSDs use these forms of justice to address an individual's violation of norms, for example by committing a crime. Community mediation and victim-offender mediation programs use performance data to assess both process and outcomes, for example, recidivism (Jones 2004). Recidivism can help assess deterrence as a form of justice. These are just a few examples of how various forms of justice are used as performance measures in public programs.

All of these forms of justice may provide measures of a system's impact on public policy and/or its impact on people who experience or participate in the system. In relation to Dubnick's six promises of accountability, they provide performance measures relevant to each program's legitimacy and justice. In this way, varieties of justice provide a lens to make systems accountable.

Responsibility of Individual Negotiators as Actors

Negotiators shape DSDs and participate in them. The following examples illustrate how negotiators should take a critical perspective on various DSDs in which they practice as drafters of arbitration clauses, as negotiators settling civil cases, and as administrators of a community's civil and criminal justice system.

Negotiators as Drafters and Designers in DSD: Arbitration Clauses

Companies are adopting forced arbitration clauses in personnel handbooks and consumer product warranties. Forced arbitration, also called mandatory arbitration, entails an adhesive clause in employment or consumer contracts or transactions that mandates arbitration in lieu of resort to court for a dispute. [NDR: Gross, *Arbitration's Shadow*] These arbitration clauses represent DSDs for conflicts between the company and employees over discipline or between the company and consumers over defective products. As a DSD, an arbitration clause is itself nested in the justice system. The justice system must apply exogenous rules as Ostrom considers them: laws enacted by Congress such as the Federal Arbitration Act (FAA, 9 U.S.C. § 1 et seq.). At present, the U.S. Supreme Court has interpreted the FAA to permit forced arbitration clauses for employment and consumer disputes; it has also authorized arbitration clauses to ban class actions entirely, whether in court or in arbitration. Many critics observe that this case law means forced arbitration DSDs may effectively deprive employees and consumers of meaningful recourse to the public justice system (Sternlight 2015). Moreover, because arbitration is generally confidential and there is no transparency, there is insufficient accountability for the system (for a more detailed analysis, see Amsler 2014).

In other words, forced arbitration as a DSD may gut public law on discrimination in employment and consumer protection. If a consumer may not join a class action to vindicate a small claim, and if the cost of an individual arbitration exceeds by far the claim's value, most consumers will abandon the claim. The forced arbitration DSD has effectively deprived the consumer of economic rights enacted by our democracy through a public law on consumer protection. This represents a failure of distributive justice. Moreover, the FAA dramatically restricts judicial review; an arbitrator's error of law is not grounds to overturn the award. This too is a failure of accountability.

Negotiators Participating in an Unjust DSD: Spotlight and the Church

The Analytic Framework for DSD empowers negotiators to get clarity on the forces that are shaping the negotiation. For example, let's return to the Roman Catholic Archdiocese in Boston as portrayed in the movie "Spotlight." The Archdiocese designed a system that operated in the shadow of the courts. Its goals were to preserve the reputation of the Church as an institution, minimize exposure to liability for sexual assault of children by priests through prompt confidential settlements, transfer priests from the relevant parish, and provide leave and/or treatment. However, parents and children as parishioners were also stakeholders in the system. Their interests were not effectively represented in this system. The context and culture of the Catholic Church both affected the system and fostered its effectiveness; that culture is hierarchical and patriarchal. Many of those injured as children spoke of priests as respected authority figures whom they did not question. In Boston, the formal legal system, starting with the police, helped the Church manage these disputes by providing an early alert and opportunity for the Church to negotiate with victims before formal charges were filed. Many members of the police force in Boston were Catholics and members of the same church culture. The Church had tremendous economic resources and specialized legal counsel to handle these disputes, contrasted with low income parishioners, most of whom lacked resources. The system was entirely private and publicity about cases was effectively suppressed through collaboration between the Church, courts, police, and news media.

As portrayed in the film, it took an outsider, Martin Baron, as the new editor for the Boston Globe who was not a member of the Catholic Church but instead raised in a different faith, Judaism, to urge the Spotlight team to question the system in its totality rather than focus on an individual case of sexual abuse. Lawyers operating as negotiators within the system had grown to accept it, rationalizing that the Church does much good in communities. It took reporters months to study the only public records, directories of priests put on leave and being transferred from parish to parish around Boston, before they saw the scope of the systemic impacts of this DSD.

Negotiators and Oversight: Ferguson's Police and Courts

The events in Ferguson, Missouri in 2014 provide a dramatic example of systemic failure of accountability in a local government DSD. Michael Brown, a young, unarmed African American man, was shot to death in the street by a police officer after an alleged shop lifting incident. Witnesses claimed Brown had his empty hands up when shot. Mainstream media, smartphone video, and social media gave rise to "Hands Up Don't Shoot" and massive protests in Ferguson. The USDOJ Civil Rights Division conducted a year-long investigation into Ferguson police, local government, and municipal courts in response to protests and the grand jury's failure to indict the police officer. It found systemic racism in the police force, city government policies, and municipal court procedures (U.S. Department of Justice 2015).

Ferguson had a DSD for addressing allegations of civil and criminal conduct and violations of law. That system included the police department, the finance department, and the municipal court, nested within local government and state government. When we look at what happened in Ferguson, Missouri in light of the U.S. Department of Justice's report on civil rights violations there, we see a systemic failure of accountability (U.S. Department of Justice 2015). Table 1 illustrates each of the six promises as applied to Ferguson's Police Department in its institutional and DSD context in 2014.

The Nightmare Scenario: Ferguson Police and Courts		
	Means: Mechanisms	Ends: Virtues
Inputs	Control: Police control violations of law, minor infractions of codes	Integrity: Police act within their technical authority but biased enforcement
Processes	Ethical Behavior: Arrests by police and contempt enforcement by municipal court	Democracy: Under-representation by race in elected officials and police hiring; convictions disenfranchise voters
Outcomes	Performance: Collection of revenue to support Govt. with performance of police measured by city	Justice/Equity: Systemic pervasive violation of civil rights and racism; discrimination by class and race

Table 1

Ferguson illustrates a public administration theory, called "the New Public Management," run amok. In the New Public Management, government agencies should behave more like private sector companies; they should find ways to become more economically efficient and generate revenue from organizations or people who make use of their services. Ferguson's DSD succeeded in generating substantial revenue. In terms of means or mechanisms, police kept their promise of control by issuing tickets for various violations of law, including traffic and housing code infractions. The police in concert with the municipal court kept their promise of ethical behavior by submitting infractions to the municipal court for adjudication; this was not vigilante justice. When defendants failed to show up or pay fees, they were held in contempt of court and subject to additional fees. Ferguson met the promise of performance by collecting revenues in this DSD and measuring police productivity based on numbers of citations for infractions.

However, this system failed in regard to ends or virtues. While police acted within their technical authority, there was racially selective bias in enforcement and hence the system failed to demonstrate integrity. The system did not produce democratic outcomes in that racialized policing produces a disproportionately high proportion of African American voters who are disenfranchised by a felony conviction, which in turn may lead to underrepresentation by race in local elected office and in the hiring of police (Amsler 2016). Finally, the system failed to produce justice; instead, the U.S. Department of Justice found it guilty of pervasive and systemic violations of civil rights and discrimination by class and race, in violation of the Fourteenth Amendment.

Notably, no internal system held this DSD accountable. It was only rendered accountable to the public by virtue of an external investigation by the federal government and extensive interviews and data collection. Where were the negotiators in this system? Police had an opportunity to negotiate before they write a ticket or arrest someone. Prosecutors were negotiating plea bargains. Judges had discretion in finding people in contempt of court. Ferguson municipal courts only recently adopted a system for working with people who owe fines instead of jailing them. Individual negotiators at any point could have stepped back and looked at what the system was producing. They could have gone to the press or sought a public hearing. They could have sought data under the public records laws. We do not know what they did or did not do when they found themselves in this system. So what should we be teaching the next generation of negotiators to do?

Implications of an Accountability Frame for Research on DSD

Elinor Ostrom (2005) observed that we need to use institutional design to build shared meaning. If we do not, we will end up with empirical studies that talk past each other because they do not use the same frame for analysis. She called this a babbling equilibrium, where we compare apples and oranges. The field of dispute resolution has experienced this in our efforts to evaluate the effectiveness of mediation and arbitration programs in courts, employment, the environment, education, communities, families, and criminal justice (see e.g. an effort to review empirical research using DSD as a frame for analysis, in Jones 2004). We do not control for differences in DSD in various systems; the controversial "Rand Report" on ADR in federal courts purported to find no beneficial outcomes, while other researchers found significant impacts. The American Bar Association Section of Dispute Resolution adopted recommendations that all courts collect ten top performance indicators so that the field could systematically compare DSDs in various state and federal courts (see ABA DR Section website).

We need to incorporate performance measurement into DSD to provide accountability. Specifically, we need to build in measures that will allow us to determine whether a system delivers some form of justice to those who participate in it. We also need transparency in how a design promotes the relevant concept of justice. The USDOJ Ferguson Report revealed how the interrelationship of police, municipal finance, and courts created unconstitutional racist practices in a system the ostensible goals of which were the rule of law and due process. Without the report shedding light on the system in Ferguson, injustice would have continued indefinitely. Now similar investigations are underway in other cities.

By measuring the impacts and nature of justice a system produces, the USDOJ promoted accountability to the residents of Ferguson and the public nationally. By revealing how the church, lawyers, press, police, and courts functioned together to enable priests to sexually abuse children, the Boston Globe's Spotlight team made the system accountable to the victims, their parents, and the public. By making sure we understand all the DSD elements of a system within which we find ourselves working as negotiators, and by providing the information and transparency that justice demands, we can play a role in ensuring that these systems are accountable.

Notes

This chapter draws significantly from the author's article "The Dispute Resolver's Role within a Dispute System Design: Justice, Accountability, and Impact", published in the University of St. Thomas Law Journal, vol 13(2): 168-191, 2016.

[1] Congress enacted the Government Reporting and Results Act of 1993 (GPRA, 5 U.S.C. Sec. 306, et seq.) to provide a mechanism for ensuring that administrative agencies in the federal government engage in systematic and strategic performance measurement to provide data to assess the effectiveness of public policy and programs. GPRA requires strategic planning, annual performance plans, and annual performance reports. These all require using performance measures. GPRA requires that indicators be quantitative, objective, and measurable. Measurement types include inputs (resources consumed), outputs (quantities produced), and outcomes (results). The Government Performance and Results Modernization Act of 2010 moved from emphasizing the production of agency performance plans and reports to focusing on goals and measures to improve the effectiveness and efficiency of Federal action. It emphasized using performance information to plan future action.

References

Agranoff, R. and M. McGuire. 2003. *Collaborative Public Management: New Strategies for Local Governments*. Washington, DC: Georgetown University Press.

Amsler, L. B. 2014. The Evolution of Social Norms in Conflict Resolution. *Journal of Natural Resources Policy Research* 6(4): 285-290.

Amsler, L. B. 2016. Covenant VI: Claiming Our Democracy Ten Years Later. In *The Covenant with Black America: Ten Years Later*, edited by T. Smiley. Carlsbad, CA: SmileyBooks, Hay House, Inc.

Amsler, L. B., J. K. Martinez and S. E. Smith. 2015. Christina Merchant and the State of Dispute System Design. *Conflict Resolution Quarterly* 33 (S1): S7-S26. doi: 10.1002/crq.21149.

Amsler, L. B., J. K. Martinez and S. E. Smith. 2017 forthcoming. *Dispute System Design*. Menlo Park, CA: Stanford University Press (under contract).

Bevir, M. (ed). 2011. *The Sage Handbook of Governance*. Thousand Oaks, CA: SAGE Publications Ltd.

Bingham, L. B. 2009a. Collaborative Governance: Emerging Practices and the Incomplete Legal Framework for Public and Stakeholder Voice." *Journal of Dispute Resolution* 2009(2): 269-326.

Bingham, L. B. 2009b. Designing Justice: Legal Institutions and Other Systems for Managing Conflict. *Ohio State Journal on Dispute Resolution* 23(1): 1-50.

Bingham, L. B. 2010. The Next Generation of Administrative Law: Building the Legal Infrastructure for Collaborative Governance. *Wisconsin Law Review* 10(2): 297-356.

Bingham, L. B., C. J. Hallberlin, D. A. Walker and W. T. Chung. 2009a. Dispute System Design and Justice in Employment Dispute Resolution: Mediation at the Workplace. *Harvard Negotiation Law Review* 14(1): 1-50.

Bingham, L. B., D. Malatesta, S. L. Foxworthy and T. Reuter. 2013. *Dispute Resolution in the Administrative Process: Evaluation of the Occupational Safety and Health Review Commission Settlement Part Program*. Washington, DC: Occupational Safety and Health Review Commission. Available online at http://www.oshrc.gov/publications/IU_Final_Report.pdf (last accessed May 28, 2016).

Bingham, L.B., T. Nabatchi and R. O'Leary. 2005. The New Governance: Practices and Processes for Stakeholder and Citizen Participation in the Work of Government. *Public Administration Review* 65(5): 547-558.

Bingham, L. B., T. Nabatchi, J. M. Senger and M. S. Jackman. 2009b. Dispute Resolution and the Vanishing Trial: Comparing Federal Government Litigation and ADR Outcomes. *Ohio State Journal on Dispute Resolution* 24(2): 225-262.

Brandsma, G. J. and T. Schillemans. 2013. The Accountability Cube: Measuring Accountability. *Journal of Public Administration Research and Theory* 23(4): 953-975. doi: 10.1093/jopart/mus034.

Costantino, C. A. and C. S. Merchant. 1996. *Designing Conflict Management Systems: A Guide to Creating Productive and Healthy Organizations*. San Francisco, CA: Jossey-Bass.

Dubnick, M. 2005. Accountability and the Promise of Performance: In Search of the Mechanisms. *Public Performance & Management Review* 28(3): 376-417.

Dubnick, M. J. and H. G. Frederickson. 2010. Accountable Agents: Federal Performance Measurement and Third-Party Government. *Journal of Public Administration Research and Theory* 20: i143-i159.

Dubnick, M. J. and K. Yang. 2011. The Pursuit of Accountability: Promise, Problems, and Prospects. In *The State of Public Administration: Issues, Challenges, and Opportunities*, edited by D. C. Menzel and H. L. White. Armonk, NY: M. E. Sharpe.

Fisher, R, W. Ury and B. Patton. 2011. *Getting to Yes: Negotiating Agreement without Giving In*. New York: Penguin Books.

Follett, M. P. 1998. *The New State: Group Organization the Solution of Popular Government*. University Park, PA: The Pennsylvania State University Press.

Jones, T. S. (ed). 2004. Special Issue: Conflict Resolution in the Field: Accessing the Past, Charting the Future. *Conflict Resolution Quarterly* 22 (1): 1-320.

Lipsky, D. B., R. L. Seeber and R. D. Fincher. 2003. *Emerging Systems for Managing Workplace Conflict: Lessons from American Corporations for Mangers and Dispute Resolution Professionals.* San Francisco, CA: Jossey-Bass.

Menkel-Meadow, C. 2000. Mothers and Fathers of Invention: The Intellectual Founders of ADR. *Ohio State Journal on Dispute Resolution* 16: 1-37.

Nabatchi, T., L. B. Bingham and D. H. Good. 2007. Organizational Justice and Workplace Mediation: A Six Factor Model. *International Journal of Conflict Management* 18(2): 148-176.

Nesbit, R., T. Nabatchi and L. B. Bingham. 2012. Employees, Supervisors, and Workplace Mediation: Experiences of Justice and Settlement. *Review of Public Personnel Administration* 32(3): 260-287.

Ostrom, E. 1990. *Governing the Commons: The Evolution of Institutions for Collective Action.* Cambridge, MA: Cambridge University Press.

Ostrom, E. 2005. *Understanding Institutional Diversity.* Princeton, NJ: Princeton University Press.

Ostrom, E. 2011. Background on the Institutional Analysis and Development Framework. *Policy Studies Journal* 39(1): 7-27.

Rogers, N. H., R. C. Bordone, F. E. A. Sander and C. A. McEwen. 2013. *Designing Systems and Processes for Managing Disputes.* New York, NY: Wolters Kluwer.

Smith, S. and J. Martinez. 2009. An Analytic Framework for Dispute System Design. *Harvard Negotiation Law Review* 14: 123-169.

Sternlight, J. R. 2015. Disarming Employees: How American Employers Are Using Mandatory Arbitration to Deprive Workers of Legal Protection. *Brooklyn Law Review* 80(4): 1309-1356.

U.S. Department of Justice Civil Rights Division. 2015. *Investigation of the Ferguson Police Department.* Washington, DC: U.S. Department of Justice. Available online at http://www.justice.gov/sites/default/files/opa/press-releases/attachments /2015/03/04/ferguson_police_department_report.pdf (last accessed May 29, 2016).

Ury, W. L., J. M. Brett and S. B. Goldberg. 1988. *Getting Disputes Resolved: Designing Systems to Cut the Cost of Conflict.* San Francisco, CA: Jossey-Bass.

Walton, R. E. and R. B. McKersie. *1965. A Behavioral Theory of Labor Negotiations: An Analysis of a Social Interaction System.* New York, NY: McGraw Hill.

⌘ 70 ⌘

Thinking Ahead

James P. Groton, Chris Honeyman & Andrea Kupfer Schneider

Editors' Note: In several distinct domains of conflict—heavy construction, international relations and U.S. labor relations—there are by now highly sophisticated and widely-adopted techniques for anticipating future conflict. If not ensuring outright that there will be only minimal such conflicts, these techniques at least encourage the conflicts which inevitably follow the formation of a new relationship to be handled with a minimum of time, cost and stress to all involved. For the most part, the evidence is that these systems work. Surprisingly, however, most other industries and domains have yet to adopt anything comparable. The authors analyze the history and the sources of resistance, and offer a new strategy toward wider adoption and adaptation of these proven tools.

In 2007, two of the authors of this chapter, with three other colleagues, wrote an article that attempted to analyze a puzzling phenomenon: a pattern of large organizations, with predictable conflict in the offing,

James P. Groton is a retired partner in the Atlanta law firm of Sutherland, Asbill and Brennan (since 2016, part of Eversheds Sutherland), where he headed its Construction and Dispute Prevention and Resolution practice groups. Groton has conducted research and written extensively on processes used in the construction industry and other relationship-based businesses to prevent and de-escalate disputes (see www.jimgroton.com). In his work for the Global Pound Conference he advocates for broader use of these processes. He holds degrees from Princeton University and the University of Virginia Law School.
Chris Honeyman is managing partner of Convenor Conflict Management, a consulting firm based in Washington, DC. He is co-editor of *The Negotiator's Desk Reference* and five other books, and author of over 90 published articles, book chapters and monographs. He has directed a 25-year series of research-and-development programs, advised many academic and practice organizations, and served as a mediator, arbitrator and in other neutral capacities in more than 2,000 disputes.
Andrea Kupfer Schneider is a Professor of Law at Marquette University Law School and is the director of Marquette's nationally-ranked dispute resolution program. Professor Schneider has written numerous books, book chapters and articles on negotiation skills and styles, dispute system design, international conflict, and gender and negotiation. She was named the Outstanding Scholar by the ABA Section of Dispute Resolution for 2017.

nevertheless routinely—or even deliberately—failing to think ahead. (Honeyman et al. 2007) That article reviewed the consequences of recent failures to anticipate or prepare for events, analyzed causes and explanations of these failures, reviewed the resources that make it possible to do strategic anticipatory planning, and outlined possible ways in which appropriate skills can be brought to bear to advance the field of conflict anticipation and management. The article also argued that it was time that our field developed a new professional specialty, of assistance to companies and other organizations to encourage them to take the proactive steps necessary in their organization's medium-and longer-term interest.

Even at that time there were already in existence some well-established examples of parties doing exactly what we were suggesting: successful uses of proactive steps to anticipate and manage conflict. A prime example was the construction industry, which had, during the past 40 years, developed a sophisticated suite of tools for preventing, solving, de-escalating, and achieving almost instantaneous resolution of problems and potential disputes. (CPR 1991; CII 1995) Other examples of similar tools existed in the fields of labor relations and international relations. And use of these tools had spread to many segments of business. (Groton and Haapio 2007)

The value of such tools should have been widely appreciated, for they exemplify time-honored "best practices" that have become legend: "An ounce of prevention is worth a pound of cure." "A stitch in time saves nine." "Fortune favors the prepared mind." "Blessed are the peacemakers."

Yet it must be admitted that in the decade since that original article, there has been less to show as new development in this area than we would have liked. There has also been recent evidence, particularly in the financial industry in its conduct before and since the 2008 financial crisis, that some elements in business and government—and even in the dispute resolution professions—see it as antithetical to their interests for conflict to be handled, as we might put it simply, better and less expensively. [NDR: Nolan-Haley, *Agents*]

We believe the time is now ripe for industrial, commercial and other relationships to benefit from demonstrated successful experience with these tools. This chapter will illustrate how existing tools for conflict anticipation and management can be used in a wider variety of business and public service contexts, and then advocate how dispute professionals can adjust their thinking and practices to advance a new "anticipation and prevention movement."

There are three principal classes of tools that are being used to anticipate and prevent conflict: tools for Problem Prevention, Problem Solving, and Dispute De-escalation and "Real Time" Resolution. They are most effective if they are mutually agreed upon by contracting parties *before* any conflicts or disputes have arisen.

Problem Prevention Tools

Problem Prevention Tools are implemented during the planning stages of a business relationship, and structure the relationship in ways that avoid many problems that are otherwise almost inevitable. Some specific practices and techniques follow.

Good, Open Communications

The best business relationships are maintained through good communications between participants in the relationship or transaction, so that any incipient problems can be identified, brought out into the open, discussed, and solved before they can become serious problems. Channels need to be developed to open up dialogue between all participants. The "red" phone that directly linked the U.S. and the Soviet Union, even at the height of the Cold War, is one international example.

Realistic Allocation of Risks

One of the most powerful ways to prevent and control disputes between contracting parties is to allocate risks rationally, by assigning each potential risk of the business relationship to the party that is best able to manage, control or insure against the particular risk. Conversely, if a party with superior bargaining power forces a misallocation of risks, the result is usually retaliatory behavior that ends up in conflict. (Groton and Smith 2010)

Unfortunately, this fundamental principle of good business management and dispute prevention is not widely recognized or understood. In particular, if lawyers involved in contract negotiations for their clients seek zealously to obtain the "best possible deal" by shifting all possible risks to the other party, they can sometimes create problems of a far greater magnitude than any temporary benefit or satisfaction gained by "winning" the "battle" of the contract negotiations. Indeed, one early proponent of the field of preventive law urged that lawyers focus more attention on legal audits and legal autopsies, to both prevent disputes and learn from disputes. (Brown 1965)

Risks that cannot be effectively handled or even insured against by *either* party, however, have to be dealt with through bargaining. The results of that bargaining will likely be reflected in the economic terms of the deal—at least approximating some kind of fairness.

Joint Initial Analysis

At the inception of any business relationship it is helpful for both parties to conduct a joint analysis of the potential for disputes in the relationship, to use this analysis to anticipate potential future problems, and to design systems that will be suited to resolve the kinds of problems that are likely to occur.

The Construction Industry Institute (CCI), as the result of a study into the causes of construction disputes and whether certain characteristics of construction projects are more likely than others to generate disputes, developed for construction projects a predictive tool (called the "Disputes Potential Index" or DPI)—a test that identifies the presence of dispute-prone characteristics on a project, evaluates them, and reports the results to project team members so they can take action to correct them *before* they actually generate problems. (Diekmann, Girard and Abdul-Hade 1994; CII 1995; CII 1996) If the DPI is administered at the beginning of the project, the test results enable project leaders to take action in any weak areas to minimize the risk of project disputes. The DPI in effect is a "cholesterol test" of the health of a construction project. Similar tools could be developed for other types of business relationships and transactions.

Providing Incentives to Parties to Encourage Cooperation

Where a business is contracting with a number of different organizations which have diverse interests, and where the cooperation of these organizations with each other and with the business is important to the success of a transaction or business objective, it is often helpful to structure a system of incentives to encourage such cooperation. Well-conceived positive incentive programs can be an effective means of aligning the goals of all of the participants, can encourage superior performance, and can discourage conflict. Such incentives can take many forms.

One example is the leader of the enterprise creating a bonus pool which, upon attainment of specific goals, will be shared among all of the organizations with whom the leader contracts. Under such a system, the bonus is payable only if *all* of these participants meet the assigned goals; the bonus is paid either to every organization, or to none. This provides a powerful incentive to the participants to work cooperatively with each other, and reduces conflicts which can occur in a common enterprise when every participant might otherwise be motivated solely by its limited perception of its own short-term interests, rather than the success of the enterprise as a whole.[1] On construction projects such "bonus pool" arrangements have been used successfully to convince subcontractors to work together cooperatively as a project team. (CPR 2010)

And in international relations, those incentives exist as well. The willingness to abide by the rulings of the World Trade Organization is with the understanding that countries will realize increased trade benefits over time. Even when it might be in a nation's short-term interest to ignore a court ruling, the long term's incentives of compliance generally result in adherence to any particular ruling.

Establishing a Partnering Relationship

Partnering is a team-building effort in which the parties establish cooperative working relationships through a mutually-developed, extra-contractual strategy of commitment and communication. It is typically an aspirational, good faith process. But it can be contractually reinforced by a mutual commitment of fair dealing and good faith.

In any common business enterprise, if individual parties are left to their own devices in trying to achieve their own goals, they are likely to be guided primarily by narrow self-interest, which is likely at some point to conflict with the narrow self-interests of other participants. This conflict can be a breeding ground for disputes. In partnering, the parties develop and share mutual goals to the extent possible. Sharing mutual goals encourages the formation of synergistic relationships, leveraging the whole process to the advantage of all.

Partnering can be initiated on an *ad hoc* basis, or by language in the contract. It can be used for long-term relationships, or on a transaction-specific basis. Long term partnering is typically a mutual commitment between two business organizations which are in a long-term relationship or which engage in repeated transactions, for the purpose of achieving specific business objectives through a strategic alliance which maximizes the effectiveness of each participant's resources.

When used on a transaction-specific basis, partnering is usually instituted at the beginning of the relationship by holding a retreat among all personnel involved in the transaction who have leadership and management responsibilities. In that format the participants, assisted by an independent facilitator, become acquainted with each other's objectives and expectations, recognize common aims, develop a teamwork approach, initiate open communications, and establish nonadversarial processes for resolving potential problems, such as a mutual agreement that it is more important to "fix the problem" than to "fix the blame." (CII 1996; Carr 2010)

A good example of these provisions in action on the international level is in Peru, regarding how it handles international investment disputes. Because international investment requirements are decided at the federal or national level, but then often implemented (and violated) at the local level, inter-agency partnering is crucial for dispute prevention. Peru has created a system to inform sub-local, local, and municipal entities about any requirements taken on at the federal level regarding international investment and trade. And as disputes arise, there is a lead coordinator among government entities to respond to the investor early and with full information. (UNCTAD 2010)

Partnering is now gaining increasing acceptance by groups of businesses or organizations that can benefit from teamwork with each other. One example: A large company had several different divisions which were operating independently, unwilling to give up power, and behaving like a dysfunctional family. A partnering facilitator was brought in, the leaders and key employees in all of the divisions participated in partnering exercises, and the result was an alignment of interests between all divisions, for the overall good of the company. Similar partnering has been used in mergers and acquisitions, where the leaders and key employees of previously independent entities, with different cultures and histories, have been brought together.

Another example began when the United Auto Workers and the Big Three auto companies, starting in the 1980s, established a pattern of labor-management cooperation, which involved a radical rethinking of the historical animosity between these parties. Conflict by no means ended; but the demonstration that it was actually possible for labor and management teams to work together constructively *most* of the time spread well beyond its industry of origin, and may have been instrumental indirectly in still other industrial arrangements that were less formalized.

Problem-Solving Tools

Problem-Solving Tools involve the use of various contract and negotiation techniques to deal constructively with problems that can actually arise.

Notice and Cure Agreements

A useful provision to include in any agreement is a requirement that each party who experiences a problem must immediately give notice to the other party and propose a good faith solution, in writing; and that the other party must reciprocate with a good faith written response. The concept of "notice and cure" clauses, meanwhile, is analogous to typical wording in the early stages of a labor contract's grievance procedure, in which a clear and prompt (and usually, expressly time-limited) opportunity to raise a problem triggers a clear (and often time-limited) obligation to make an explicit response. Ducking the issue is thus not permitted on either side. Similarly again, open sharing of basic information is a requirement built into many grievance procedures, as well as the underlying labor law. As noted above, Peru's international investment "alert" system also tries to do this.

Covenant of Good Faith and Fair Dealing

Although many legal systems already require this, it is useful for any business agreement to contain an explicit covenant that each party will act in good faith and engage in fair dealing.

Agreements that Encourage Rational Behavior

When drafting contracts that deal with future economic conditions, consider using devices such as a "buy/sell" agreement (where one party establishes a price and gives the other party the option to buy or sell), or a "baseball" arbitration agreement (which requires the arbitrator to make a binary choice of alternatives proposed by the parties), to encourage rational behavior. It is also possible to outline damages for breaches in advance. (Hardaway 1997: 175)

In-House Problem Solving Tools

There are a number of steps which an organization can take to "keep the peace" within the organization and encourage good prevention practices:

- Appoint an Ombuds to deal confidentially with employee and internal problems. An Ombuds can clear up communication problems or misperceptions of an employee's relationships with the organization or fellow employees.
- Charge the transaction costs of a dispute to the budget of the department that generated the dispute, so that managers are made aware of the true costs of the dispute.
- Institute sensible document-preparation and retention policies that can be useful in case disputes occur or escalate. For example: Preserve evidence that you acted reasonably. If an employee writes a "bad memo" which could be interpreted as injurious to the company, it is good preventive practice to write other memos that put the earlier memo in perspective, and correct the errors in the bad memo.
- Consider and organize in advance how the organization would handle various possible crises.
- Conduct a corporate legal audit regularly to help foresee where problems might occur. (Brown 1965)

Dispute De-Escalation and "Real Time" Resolution Tools

Dispute de-escalation and "real time" resolution tools that level the playing field provide transparency, defuse conflict, or provide prompt resolution of pending disputes. These measures can also prevent disputes that do arise from becoming intractable.

Encourage the Open Sharing of Basic Information

Create a level playing field and provide transparency for all participants by establishing a common web site or other system for full sharing of important information about the business enterprise or transaction. ICANN (Internet Corporation for Assigned Names and Numbers; the governing body of the Internet) is an example of this on the international stage, where the allocation of web addresses and other important functions have been handled through a common web site with clear policies and procedures posted. Comments and blog posts have been collected and publicized. ICANN's use of social media has also tried to provide transparency.

Negotiation

Negotiation is of course the time-honored method by which parties try to resolve disputes through discussions and mutual agreement. There are many different techniques of negotiation, as discussed throughout this book; what deserves emphasis here is simply that negotiation is not only a stand-alone process, but also a useful adjunct to every other dispute resolution technique.

Step Negotiations

A variant of negotiation is the "step negotiation" procedure, a multi-tiered process that can often be used to break a deadlock. If the individuals at the lowest level in each organization who are involved in the dispute are not able to resolve a problem at their level promptly, their immediate superiors, who are not as closely identified with the problem, are asked to confer and try to resolve the problem; if *they* fail, the problem is then passed on to higher management in both organizations. Because of an intermediate manager's interest in keeping messy problems from bothering higher management, and in demonstrating to higher management the manager's ability to solve problems, there is a built-in incentive to resolve disputes before they ever have to go to the highest management level.

Stepped negotiations are in fact a hallmark of collective bargaining, dating back long before the technique's introduction into the construction industry (and, perhaps, the inspiration for its use there, given the prevalence of unionization in large construction.) Typically, grievances under labor contracts in the U.S. are first raised either by the individual employee with an individual supervisor, or by (or in the presence of) a first-level shop steward. The progressive rise in the level of successive steps, as unsettled grievances become the province of higher level union and management officials, operates for precisely the same reasons articulated above in the section on construction, and the effects have also been similar. The vast majority of grievances are resolved at low levels in most such procedures, with little time lost, relatively little acrimony, and little transaction/economic cost.

One difference from the construction pattern, however, is that the most typical final step in these contracts is binding arbitration, usually before an arbitrator selected via an independent public or private agency such as the Federal Mediation and Conciliation Service or the American Arbitration Association. This does not offer the advantage, enjoyed by the construction industry's standing neutrals (see below), of deep familiarity with the problems of the job site on the part of the neutral. On the other hand, it offers in exchange the possibility of a fresh face, with no necessary prior or continuing relationship with either party. In a setting which has had more than its share of meta-conflict on a class, political and social level, this has its advantages.

Use of a "Standing Neutral"

Because the Standing Neutral is probably the least widely understood but potentially most useful dispute prevention and resolution tool of all those that have been developed, we will give it more space here. One of the most innovative and promising developments in controlling disputes between parties who are involved in any type of continuing or long-term relationship (such as a joint venture, construction project or outsourcing arrangement) is the concept of having a highly qualified and respected pre-selected or "standing" neutral to serve as a monitor or dispute re-solver *throughout the course of the relationship*. A single neutral or a board of three neutrals (designated variously as a "standing neutral," "mutual friend," "referee," "dispute resolver," or "dispute review board") is selected mutually by the parties early in the relationship; is briefed on the nature of the relationship; is furnished with the basic documents describing the relationship; routinely receives periodic progress reports as the relationship progresses; and is invited to meet occasionally with the parties in the absence of any immediate dispute, simply to maintain a feel for the dynamics and progress of the relationship.

The standing neutral is expected to be available on relatively short notice to make an expert recommendation to the parties to assist them in resolving any disputes that the parties are not able to resolve promptly themselves. It is important to the effective working of this process that the parties be mutually involved in the selection of the neutral, and that they have confidence in the neutral's integrity and expertise. Typically the neutral's role, if called in to help resolve a dispute, is to render an impartial but *nonbinding* decision (not a compromise proposal) on the dispute. (Vorster 1993; Groton 2009; Hafer 2010; Groton and Dettman 2011)

Although the standing neutral's decisions are typically not binding, experience has shown that on those relatively rare occasions where a dispute is referred to the neutral, the neutral's decisions have generally been accepted by both parties, without any attempt to seek relief from any other tribunal. This result is enhanced where there is a contract stipulation that in the event of any subsequent arbitration or litigation, the decisions of the standing neutral will be admissible in evidence. When used in accordance with the guidelines advocated by the Dispute Resolution Board Foundation and carried forward in the AAA Dispute Review Board Procedures, this technique has been remarkably success-ful; in practice, 95% of all disputes actually referred to a DRB are re-solved without arbitration or litigation. (DRBF 2007)

It bears repeating that three critical elements are essential to the success of the standing neutral technique: (DRBF 2007)

- Early mutual selection and confidence in the neutral;
- Continuous involvement by the neutral;
- Prompt action on any submitted disputes.

This is because the existence of a pre-selected neutral, already familiar with the business relationship between the parties and its progress, avoids many of the initial problems and delays that are involved in selecting and appointing neutrals after a controversy has arisen. Similarly, the ready availability of the neutral, the speed with which he or she can render decisions, and particularly the fact that this neutral will hear every dispute which occurs during the history of the relationship, all provide powerful incentives to the parties to deal with each other and the neutral in a timely and frank manner. The combination discourages game-playing, dilatory tactics, and the taking of extreme and insupportable positions. And the evaluative but non-binding nature of the standing neutral, available if necessary to provide a "dose of reality" to the parties, encourages them to be more objective in their dealings with each other. At the same time, by giving the parties an opportunity to construct their own solutions to problems, it tends to strengthen the relationship between the parties and create trust and confidence between them.

In practice, the nature of this process is such that the mere existence of the neutral generally results in minimizing—and often totally eliminating—the number of disputes that have to be presented to the neutral. In effect the standing neutral serves not only as a standby dispute *resolution* technique but also as a remarkably successful dispute *prevention* device.[2] Even though some expense is involved in the process of selecting, appointing, initially orienting, and periodically reporting to the neutral, the costs are relatively minimal, even when the neutral is called on to resolve disputes.

There can be many variations of the standing neutral process. For example, in the case of a closely-held corporation where there might be deadlocks between equal owners, there are techniques that can be employed in drafting the corporate charter and by-laws that can avoid the later paralysis of a deadlock, by using one or more outside directors as standing neutrals:

1) One technique is for the stockholders who have evenly-divided interests to elect as a director a neutral outsider who is knowledgeable about the business and has a reputation for integrity. (An example of such a person could be the dean of a local business school.) This outside director is paid a significant director's fee, is furnished the key management reports that are provided to other directors, and is expected to attend all board meetings, ask questions, participate in discussions, and get a good perspective on the affairs of the company. However, this outside director has a vote only in the case of a disagreement among the

"inside" directors, in which case the outside director has the deciding vote.

2) Another technique where there are two stockholders with equal ownership, and a concern about possible deadlock, is to establish a five-person board of directors, two of whom represent the evenly-matched "insiders" and three of whom are highly-respected independent "outside" directors. They all function as a real board, and each director has a vote. The advantage of the arrangement is that in any case where the two inside directors disagree, it takes the votes of at least two of the three outside directors to carry the vote.

3) In a business where there are two stockholders with a great disparity in ownership interests, and a concern that the majority stockholder will ride roughshod over the minority stockholder to the detriment of the company, the by-laws could provide for a five-person board of directors, two of whom are appointed by the majority stockholder, one of whom is appointed by the minority stockholder, with two more highly-respected independent "outside" directors appointed jointly by both stockholders together. Under this system, the majority needs the vote of only one independent director, while the minority needs the vote of both independent directors. But in a case where the majority is acting abusively, the independent directors are likely to perceive the potential for abuse, and both are likely to vote with the minority stockholder.

In all of these situations, because the independent outside director(s) can control the outcome, there is an incentive for all directors to exercise good judgment and act reasonably for the best interests of the company. (For additional elements of prevention practices tailored specifically for corporate governance, see IFC 2011; O'Neal 1978)

Standing Arbitrator

A variant of the standing neutral process is to give the neutral the power to render binding decisions, thus acting as an arbitrator. A certain percentage of labor contracts, particularly in industries such as basic steel, have employed umpires, or continuing arbitrators, known sometimes as "permanent" arbitrators despite the adage that "there's nothing as temporary as a permanent arbitrator." Some of these arrangements have used the arbitrator in the same quasi-judicial capacity as most *ad hoc* arbitrators, few of whom are encouraged to mediate by the parties. Others have accepted and even encouraged a mediating role, sometimes including an expectation that the neutral is to apply a larger view with the object of helping the parties avoid repetitive cases; these arrangements come closest to the construction industry practice with standing neutrals.

Standing Mediator

Another variant of the standing neutral process is the designation by the parties of a mediator, at the commencement of the relationship, to assist the parties in resolving disputes. The concept behind a standing mediator has worked for institutions. The United Nations Secretary General often acts a mediator in international conflicts. Ombuds within government agencies or universities or business also can serve the role of mediator (or funnel the disputes to other mediators) and can move quickly to intervene before the conflict worsens. South Korea, for example, has created an ombuds office in its investment promotion agency, accountable directly to the Prime Minister, in order to help foreign investors navigate any issues that might arise while doing business in Korea.

A New "Anticipation and Prevention" Movement?

Dispute resolution professionals, of all people, should inherently recognize that the essence of ADR is its innate flexibility and adaptability to the needs of the public; that the disputes field is constantly changing; and that invention and creation are part of the lifeblood of ADR. New ideas and innovative processes for anticipation of conflict, and dispute prevention, are essential for the growth and sustainability of the field. (Brown 1965) And it is simply in their own career interest, as noted by Bernard Mayer, for dispute resolvers to think more broadly about the uses of their skills. [NDR: Mayer, *Allies*] (Mayer 2004; see also Barendrecht and Honeyman 2014.)

Skills and specialties in conflict management have been growing in recent decades, and the recognition and uses of these skills have also been growing rapidly. Up until now these skills have been used mainly on conflict that has already happened. But the anticipatory/preventive/ proactive concept provides a philosophical frame for a different way of thinking about conflict in advance, and should become the basis for advancing a new "anticipation and prevention movement" throughout the business and public service communities.

Dispute professionals should be able to adjust their focus and learn that many types of problems which become conflicts could be either averted entirely, or handled at minimum cost, if the necessary skills are applied further "upstream." [See also NDR: Amsler, *System Design*] We believe dispute resolution professionals are well placed, and should be encouraged, to develop their skills further to become dispute anticipation and prevention professionals, specifically adding "problem anticipation and dispute prevention" techniques to their professional credentials. Individual dispute prevention professionals, by studying these new concepts and conducting further research into how they can best be adapted for use in all kinds of business contexts, can use these new skills to broaden the horizons of their prevention and resolution repertoires. These repetoires can be expanded to teach parties, when beginning a new relationship, to focus on implementing a relationship that works in practice rather than just getting to a deal. (Ertel 2004)

Yet the core elements of any new prevention movement must come from the affected companies and other organizations themselves. In-house corporate counsel, and far-sighted members of top management, have long talked a good game about the need to move toward just such proactive methods and systems. Perhaps the availability of cross-comparisons between such dissimilar yet successful existing users of "thinking ahead about conflict" as construction, international relations and labor relations will encourage them to actually commit their organizations to move forward.

There has very recently emerged one promising development in the field of anticipating and managing conflict: The delegates at the first seven Global Pound Conferences (so far, in the year 2016) have heavily favored, as tools that should be *prioritized* to improve the future of dispute resolution, "pre-dispute or pre-escalation processes to prevent disputes." It will be interesting to see whether the delegates to the approximately 33 further Global Pound Conferences will follow this promising trend, and whether the Final Report of the GPC (to be issued in 2018) will encourage greater participation in the anticipation and prevention movement.

We will close with a tool beloved of many in corporate management, a flowchart. This one is a hard-headed effort to compare the type of system we propose with the typical conflict-handling system which, whether admitted or not, obtains in most relationships. The left column of the flowchart illustrates typical existing conflict-handling practices; the right column illustrates the kinds of advanced practices that are consistent with the new anticipation and prevention movement. (See Ertel 2004 for more on such practices.)

Do you really want *your* organization to live its life in the left column?

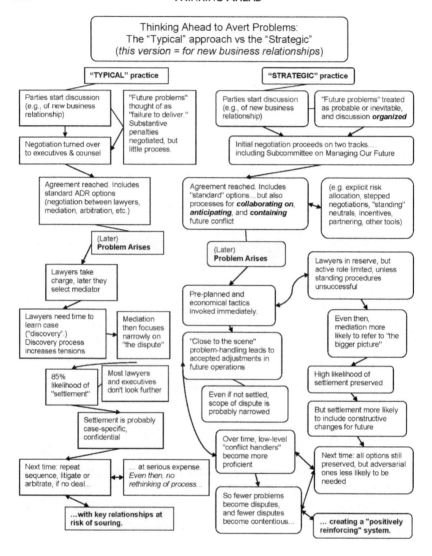

Notes

[1] The bonus pool is, in effect, a commercial adaptation of the traditional reward structure of the collaborative arts. See, e.g., Rachel Parish's description of the process of collaborative theater (Honeyman and Parish 2013). In these settings, a failure to collaborate—among artists with typically very strong individual will—has publicly conspicuous and financially painful consequences to all concerned. This area of conflict research is in its infancy; further study of the collaborative arts may yet reveal other parallels—and perhaps some not-so-obvious techniques which could be adapted for other domains.

[2] The same is true for the very process of sitting down to resolve the details of the preventive techniques that will be employed. Perhaps in the end the single most effective technique shared between labor relations and the construction industry is employed long before any specific agreement. It is virtually universal, at least in U.S. labor relations practice, for there to be a substantive and sometimes lengthy discussion, in the course of hammering out the first collective bargaining agreement between an employer and a new labor organization, of how to handle disputes that arise

under that agreement. The fact that stepped negotiations are the typical result obscures the tailored process by which that result is reached, which include a myriad of considerations of how many steps, who is to be involved at each stage, how long should be allowed for each category of response or higher-level claim, what recourse should be made to third parties, etc. These discussions have relationship-building as well as procedural and substantive content and effects.

A (non-labor) experience of one of the authors may help explain one of the effects of "hammering out" an agreement: In the late 1990s this author was retained as an advisor to a consortium of electric power companies establishing for the first time a mediation and arbitration system to handle disputes over power distribution issues on the grid. This advisor was charged with recruiting a particularly high-level group of professionals for two panels, of mediators and arbitrators, to deal with high-pressure and high-dollar cases among parties who traditionally had fought these issues with zeal before a Federal regulator (with a characteristic disregard of transaction costs and time wasted.) This advisor proceeded to round up many famous names in the field. The entire slate passed review and was empaneled.

Several years later, our author one day encountered one of the most famous panelists in person, who complained that he had never been asked to serve on a case. The author also noted that he himself, though listed on one of the two panels, had never gotten a case either. The author then inquired of the panel administrator what had happened with the elaborate dispute resolution system that had been set up. The panel administrator replied "Oh, there haven't been any cases." It developed that the utilities, in the course of the knock-down, drag-out discussions that produced the agreement to create the panel, had come to understand each other's corporate traditions, expectations, cultures and needs so much better than they had in the past that the preliminary stages leading up to a request for a hearing or mediation had been sufficient to resolve every single case that had arisen.

(Another observation: Perhaps the parties' awareness that their behavior in any intractable dispute would immediately become known to a trusted and expert mediator or arbitrator may have helped persuade them to behave rationally—similar to "The Hawthorne Effect", which applies in the Standing Neutral context: Parties who know they are being—or might soon be—observed, generally behave more constructively.)

References

Barendrecht, M. and C. Honeyman. 2014. Dispute Resolution: Existing Business Models and Looming Disruptions. *Dispute Resolution Magazine* 20(3): 17-21.

Brown, L. M. 1965. Legal Audit. *Southern California Law Review* 38: 431-445.

Carr, F. 2010. Partnering: Aligning Interests, Collaboration, and Achieving Common Goals. *CPR Dispute Prevention Briefing: Construction.* Available online at https://www.cpradr.org/resource-center/toolkits/construction-briefing-partnering/_res/id=Attachments/index=0/CPR-Construction-Partnering-Briefing.pdf (last visited January 26, 2017).

CII. 1996. Partnering Toolkit. Construction Industry Institute Research Tool 102. Available online at https://kb.construction-institute.org/Knowledge-Areas/Project-Organization-Communication/Topics/RT-102/pubs/IR102-2 (last visited January 26, 2017).

CII. 1995. Dispute Prevention and Resolution Techniques in the Construction Industry. Construction Industry Institute Research Summary 23-1. Available online at https://kb.construction-institute.org/knowledge-areas/risk-management/topics/rt-023/pubs/rs23-1 (last visited January 26, 2017).

CPR. 1991. Preventing and Resolving Construction Disputes, Special Supplement by Center for Public Resources. *Alternatives to the High Cost of Litigation* 9(12): 182-187.

CPR. 2010. *Dispute Prevention Initiative, and Practice Manual for Reducing Disputes Through Wise Prevention Practices.* New York: International Institute for Conflict Prevention & Resolution. Available online at https://www.cpradr.org/news-publications/articles/2010-11-23-cpr-prevention-practice-materials (last visited January 27, 2017)

Diekmann, J. E., M. Girard and N. Abdul-Hade. 1994. DPI – Disputes Potential Index: A Study into the Predictability of Contract Disputes. *CII Source Document 101*. Available online at https://kb.construction-institute.org/More-Filter-Options/result/Topics/RT-023/pubs/SD-101 (last visited January 26, 2017).

Dispute Resolution Board Foundation (DRBF). 2007. Dispute Review Board Manual. Available online at http://www.drb.org/manual_access.htm (last visited January 26, 2017).

Global Corporate Governance Forum, International Finance Corporation, World Bank Group (IFC). 2011. *Toolkit 4: Resolving Corporate Governance Disputes*. Available at http://www.ifc.org/wps/wcm/connect/topics_ext_content/ifc_external_corporate_site/ifc+cg/resources/toolkits+and+manuals/adr_toolkit (last visited January 26, 2017).

Groton, J. P. 2009. The Standing Neutral: A 'Real Time' Resolution Procedure that also Can Prevent Disputes. *Alternatives to the High Cost of Litigation* 27(11): 177-185.

Groton, J. and H. Haapio. 2007. From Reaction to Positive Action: Dispute Prevention Processes in Business Agreements. In *Proceedings of the International Association for Contract and Commercial Management*, London.

Groton, J. P. and K. L. Dettman. 2011. How and Why the Standing Neutral Dispute Prevention and Resolution Technique Can Be Applied. *Alternatives to the High Cost of Litigation* 29(10) : 177-192.

Groton, J. and R. J. Smith. 2010. Realistic Risk Allocation: Allocating Each Risk to the Party Best Able to Handle the Risk. *CPR Dispute Prevention Briefing: Construction*. Available online at https://www.cpradr.org/resource-center/toolkits/construction-briefing-risk-allocation/_res/id=Attachments/index=0/CPR%20Construction%20Realistic%20Risk%20Allocation%20Briefing.pdf (last visited January 26, 2017).

Hafer, R. 2010. Dispute Review Boards and Other Standing Neutrals: Achieving 'Real Time' Resolution and Prevention Disputes. *CPR Dispute Prevention Briefing: Construction*. Available online at https://www.cpradr.org/resource-center/toolkits/construction-briefing-dispute-resolution-boards-other/_res/id=Attachments/index=0/CPR-Dispute-Review-Boards-and-Other-Standing-Neutrals-Construction title.pdf (last visited January 26, 2017).

Honeyman, C., J. Macfarlane, B. Mayer, A. K. Schneider and J. Seul. 2007. The Next Frontier is Anticipation: Thinking Ahead about Conflict to Help Clients Find Constructive Ways to Engage Issues in Advance. *Alternatives to the High Cost of Litigation* 25(6): 99-103.

Honeyman, C. and R. Parish. 2013. Choreography of Negotiation: Movement in Three Acts. In *Choreography of Resolution: Conflict, Movement and Neuroscience*, edited by M. LeBaron, C. MacLeod and A. F. Acland. Washington, DC: ABA Books.

Mayer, B. 2004. *Beyond Neutrality: Confronting the Crisis in Conflict Resolution*. San Francisco, CA: Jossey-Bass.

O'Neal, F. H. 1978. Preventive Law: Tailoring the Corporate Form of Business to Ensure Fair Treatment of All. *Mississippi Law Journal* 49(3): 529-590.

United Nations Conference on Trade and Development (UNCTAD). 2010. Investor-State Disputes: Prevention and Alternative to Arbitration. *UNCTAD Series on International Investment Policies for Development*, March 2010. Geneva. Available online at http://unctad.org/en/docs/diaeia200911_en.pdf (last visited January 26, 2017).

Vorster, M. 1993. Alternative Dispute Resolution in Construction With Emphasis on Dispute Review Boards. *CII Source Document 95*. Available online at https://kb.construction-institute.org/More-Filter-Options/result/Topics/RT-023/pubs/SD-95 (last visited January 26, 2017).

Section XIII: Negotiation Everywhere

"Everybody negotiates" is a trite phrase, but often even its users don't realize how true it is. Section XIII analyzes a series of settings that take the concept to its logical extreme and, yes, find negotiation operating in the professional boxing ring; between police and hostage takers; between businesses that act like hostage takers, and their counterparts; in the military; and in martial arts.

The last two chapters in this section explore what happens when a party who should be negotiating refuses to admit that there is anything to discuss, and how to negotiate implementation of a new program—using the example of peer mediation programs for children.

Negotiations and Professional Boxing:
The Ringside Physician

Habib Chamoun-Nicolas, Randy D. Hazlett,
Joe Estwanik MD, Russell Mora, & Gilberto Mendoza

Editors' Note: The authors, who include unimpeachable experts on boxing, review what actually happens in the ring and in the frequently unspoken dialogue between the boxers, the referee, and the fight doctor. They find negotiation behavior routinely taking place in this most unlikely of environments. They explain why, and also show the price that is paid in injury, and sometimes a life, when the referee or the doctor gets the subtle signals wrong.

It is round 10 in what *Ring Magazine* dubs as the 2005 Fight of the Year. Both fighters are battered, wearing the evidence, especially around the eyes. Diego "Chico" Corrales exits his corner with one eye virtually shut

Habib Chamoun-Nicolas is an Adjunct Professor and executive board member at the Cameron School of Business, University of St Thomas in Houston; Lecturer at the Red McCombs School of Business, University of Texas at Austin; and Honorary Professor at the Faculty of Entrepreneurial Specialties at the Catholic University of Santiago de Guayaquil. Over the past 25 years, Dr. Chamoun-Nicolas has conducted negotiation and business development activities in diversified sectors, oil and gas, petroleum, petrochemical, chemical, industrial, commercial, pharmaceutical, institutional, and government.
Randy Hazlett is an Associate Professor in the McDougall School of Petroleum Engineering at the University of Tulsa. He obtained a PhD in Chemical Engineering from the University of Texas at Austin. Dr. Hazlett's research spans a broad range of topics in reservoir engineering and asset management. He is a long-time business associate of Dr. Chamoun and co-author on a number of negotiation and business related projects.
Joseph Estwanik MD trained in Orthopedic Surgery at Wake Forest University and The Cleveland Clinic. He is a Fellow of the American College of Sports Medicine, author of Sports Medicine for the Combat Arts (Boxergenic Press 1996) and Past President of the Association of Ringside Physicians.
Russell Mora is living his dream as a Professional Boxing Referee in Las Vegas. He was born into a boxing family and completely fell in love with boxing as a child. He currently arbitrates sanctioned world title fights not only in Las Vegas, Nevada but also around the world. Russell has been a two time Golden Gloves regional champion.
Gilberto Jesus Mendoza is the elected President of the World Boxing Association.

and a small cut under the other. Jose Luis Castillo enters the round more intact, but sporting clear evidence of attempts to control the bleeding from multiple abrasions above his left eye. Twenty-five seconds into the round, Castillo lands a crushing left hook, sending Corrales to the mat. Referee Tony Weeks promptly orders Castillo to a neutral corner and gathers a visual cue from the timekeeper before starting the count at 3. Corrales appears to be ready to rise to his feet, but waits until the count of eight to do so. Referee Weeks urges Corrales twice, "Come to me". He asks the fighter if he is alright, then if he wants to continue, to which Corrales clearly replies in the affirmative. Referee Weeks promptly calls time before action is allowed to commence, for Corrales is without his mouthpiece. Corrales is clearly clocked again within 10 seconds of re-sumed action, and following a few more unabated blows, Corrales goes down for the second time. This time Corrales labors to a ready position but is to his feet at the count of nine. Referee Weeks again beckons the fighter and asks twice if he is alright while physically wiping the gloves checking for signs of weakness. He promptly calls timeout again, since the mouthpiece is not in place. Referee Weeks invokes a one point pen-alty for intentionally spitting out the mouthpiece, sometimes used by fighters as a delaying tactic.

The deduction and time required to secure another mouthpiece from his corner gives Corrales some much needed clarity. Corrales' corner tells him, using graphic language, that he had better get inside now. The fighters stand toe-to-toe exchanging blows in what seems to be a test of how much punishment Corrales can endure before the fight is stopped. Corrales is hurt again but fails to go down. Castillo steps back after a right hand attempt by Corrales. Corrales takes this as a positive sign and follows with a series of blows that backs Castillo to the ropes. Referee Weeks repositions himself to get a good look at the action. His eyes are locked onto Castillo's. Castillo fights his way back off the ropes only to return. While against the ropes, Castillo appears helpless to defend him-self. Castillo's head pops backward after a series of hits. Referee Weeks promptly steps in to cover Castillo with his body and ends the fight. In a fight seemingly ripe for prior intervention, Corrales is astoundingly declared WBC World Champion.

Professional boxing is a combative sport in which contestants oper-ate by a set of rules with a referee to ensure safety of the fighters and fair play during the competition. A full set of rules and responsibilities is available from the Association of Boxing Commissions (ABC). The ABC requires referees to attend clinics and know all the rules. The referee is the sole arbitrator of the fight; however, at any time he may consult with the ringside physician. The ringside physician and the referee arrive with two completely different backgrounds. The referee must be expert in the combat sport and must understand the rules of boxing, while the doctor is an expert in the medical field and understands the human body. Working together as a team they complement each other as they care for the fighters. While the referee also enforces fairness, the physician's sole objective is the safety of the competitors.

In combative sports, and professional boxing in particular, it is not clear that parties negotiate. But using Christopher Honeyman and Rachel Parish's (2013) terms, we might label portions of what goes on in the ring as kinetic intelligence in a choreography of negotiation. Indeed, it takes two to tango in boxing. Each fighter looks for opportunity using knowledge, experience, physics, and intuition. The fighters, managers, fans, referee, and fight doctor all look for nonverbal clues, knowing each combatant will go to great lengths to mask any sign of weakness or injury that could signal his opponent or someone in authority to usher the bout to a rapid close. This forces the referee and fight doctor, also invited to the dance, to heighten their perception of unintended nonverbal clues. Habib Chamoun and coauthors (2013) examined this violent sport more closely and concluded that negotiations proceed on multiple levels and to different degrees between boxers, management, fans, and referees. However, they concluded that the standard negotiation styles should be renamed for descriptive clarity in this arena. [For more on styles, NDR: Abramson, *Effective Style*] The traditional conflict management style labels of competing, collaborating, compromising, avoiding, and accommodating, introduced by Robert Blake and Jane Mouton (1964) and popularized through the tool developed by Kenneth Thomas and Ralph Kilmann (1974), were replaced with *Fight Like a Spartan, Facilitate Like a Phoenician, Judge Like Solomon, Avoid Like a Politician,* and *Delegate Like a Diplomat*, respectively. A new tool was introduced to classify the negotiation style of boxing referees in terms of preference and the style adopted when exposed to a particular situation.

Herein, we present the results of a follow-up study, using a variant of the previously developed tool, designed for fight doctors. The intent of these studies is to assist boxers, referees, promoters, doctors, and managers in decision-making by recognition of styles and ramifications in this high-octane sport of split-second judgments.

Returning to the opening case study, some compelling questions in this "fan favorite" fight beg for clarification. In particular, "Where was the fight doctor, and why did we not see any examination or intervention by anyone other than the third man in the ring?" The referee did not utilize all resources, as he did not seek opinion or request the doctor in a timely manner to evaluate the boxer on multiple scenarios as earlier enumerated. Usually, the doctor must be requested by the referee to perform an up close evaluation. Though Castillo never went down in Round 10, Referee Tony Weeks saw in the final exchange a vulnerability he had not witnessed in the prior Corrales knockdowns. Surprisingly, our developed instrument, a questionnaire constructed specifically for fight doctors to identify negotiating style, revealed the dynamics of this fight are characteristic of the dominant response of fight doctors sampled—to avoid influencing the outcome rather than proactively intervene. Consequently, Diego "Chico" Corrales was crowned champion on the ruling of the referee, not the ringside physician. By many state laws, the doctors are not legally provided the option to initiate action, but only provide services upon the referee's request.

While nearly everyone in boxing would categorize a fight as maximum assertiveness without cooperation, Habib Chamoun and coauthors (2013) argued that fighters "cooperate to a significant degree to ensure a fair outcome with significant value for themselves, their business partners, and the fans that ultimately finance the sport. In addition, they cooperate by agreeing to abide by the rules of boxing." They must additionally abide by the instructions of the referee and fight doctor as caretakers of their safety.

Dr. Robert Gambrell (2007) summarizes the role of the fight doctor:

> The role of the ringside physician is to protect and care for each boxer before, during, and after competition. Unlike in many sports, in boxing, the ringside physician is an official and has the authority to intervene whenever necessary. This authority comes with a responsibility to act prudently and not interfere with the normal conduct of the bout. The ringside physician acts in conjunction with the referee to ensure that each competitor is able to effectively defend him or herself throughout the course of a bout.

Dr. Gambrell additionally points out that the physician may be asked by the referee to examine a fighter, or proactively make an examination request either during or between rounds based on professional commission or amateur rules. According to Dr. Joseph Estwanik, the ringside physician is present to ensure the safety of the boxers and is constantly watching every movement of the boxers for signs of danger, and is ready to intervene in an instant, while avoiding interference. The fight doctor does not work independently, but in cooperation with the referee. In the balance of this chapter, we focus on conflict management styles from the perspective of the ringside doctor.

With regard to conflict management styles of ringside physicians serving within the Combat Arts, Estwanik reminds us that many doctors serving in this capacity were trained within specialties where life and death or limb-saving decisions require end-of-line decision making. There is no format for the delay of decisions or process for delegation of responses to in-the-ring decisions. Many installed rules are the result of previous decision-making or the failure to make a timely decision, resulting in serious injury or death. As boxing or martial arts competition exists within customary 3- or 5-minute, continuous-action rounds, there exists no opportunity to delay time-compressed medical safety opinion. Most state commissions or organizations only allow the referee (and/or physician) to end a professional boxing match based on medical/injury conditions. According to the Unified ABC rules the referee is the sole arbitrator and the only one authorized to stop the fight. If the doctor wants the fight stopped he must inform the referee and, based on the advice of the doctor, the referee must stop the fight. As between-round timeouts are only of one minute's duration, there are no avenues for procrastinators nor decision-by-committee. In addition to these tight parameters and rules, group decisions or group projects—often present by design within MBA curricula—are not often found within traditional medical school grading systems. Thus, whether by training or conflict management "personality gravitation" toward medical education, ringside physicians tend to possess a narrow range of responses and decision-making approaches to their demanding role as "Doc" when they sit in the "hot seat" immediately adjacent to the ring. Their attitudes are, however, responsive to a situation where they must influence the outcome of an event defined by seconds rather than minutes.

Five Styles

We developed a tool to assess conflict management styles for ringside physicians, and we will disclose some results at the end of this chapter. First, let's review the five styles according to Chamoun and coauthors (2013), and illustrate each ringside physician style with an actual historical example.

Fight Like a Spartan

The Spartans were ancient Greece's most formidable warriors, with a "win at any cost" attitude, solidified with viable, time-proven battle strategies and an unswerving sense of honor. Boxers will rapidly associate with this style, and exhibit it most often, in pre-fight rhetoric and assertion of fight control in the ring. It will be most often conferred on the aggressor and is most visible between boxers content to go "toe-to-toe." The doctor also must use this style in situations of life or death in order to safeguard the life of a boxer in peril. Overuse of this style, however, is not appreciated by fans who want the fighters to control the outcome. The best doctor will judiciously exercise his competitive style (in recognition of the gender "skew" in this field, we will use the male gender here, while acknowledging that women can increasingly be expected to serve as "Doc" in the future), choosing to exhibit enough authority to ensure safety and fairness without being the center of attention.

In the middleweight fight of Fernando Guerrero and Michael Walker (2010), Guerrero dominated the match from beginning to end. Walker was against the ropes unable to answer, while Guerrero flailed unabatedly with a barrage of punches. A series of connecting uppercuts was observed patiently by the referee. The commentators repeatedly commented that the fight should be stopped. Finally, the bout comes to an end in the second round only when the doctor physically enters the ring, asserting his prerogative. Walker expressed dissatisfaction that the fight was stopped, even while the doctor was conducting a post-bout examination in the ring.

Facilitate Like a Phoenician

The style high in cooperation and assertiveness we re-label as *Facilitate Like a Phoenician*. The Phoenicians were an ancient Mediterranean people known for their negotiation skills (Chamoun and Hazlett 2008). In a prolonged period of regional conquest, the Phoenicians made themselves more valuable as business partners to the political and military powers in play than as a subjugated people. Thus, we associate conflict management styles that involve a high degree of cooperation and concern for effectiveness with these highly skilled negotiators of the past.

While physical domination is a fighter's goal, a fighter who is unable to defend himself/herself or bleeding uncontrollably is in peril. Boxers and their corner representation make appeals throughout a match. The degree to which this information is processed into decision making is up to the referee. While this may on the surface resemble arbitration rather than negotiation, the ringside physician operating with this style is open to input from participants and is actively engaged with the fighters. The doctor working in this style could also be interpreted as negotiating with himself for the benefit of the fighters and the sport. An example of this style can also be seen when the fight doctor requests to conduct an examination between rounds or allows the cutman to make every attempt to keep a fighter eligible.

Judge Like Solomon

This style is perhaps the one most in need of alternate imagery from the original language of Thomas and Kilmann. Compromising means making concessions to the other in order to gain ground on those terms most important to you. Sportsmen do not typically envision compromise as a useful style. However, if we examine the motivating forces (the axes in the style chart), we find this style as a balance in both cooperation and assertiveness. This style can easily move into any of the other styles with small shifts in motivation. We choose to rename this style *Judge Like Solomon* to capture the keen sense of fairness exhibited by Solomon, as recorded in Hebrew scripture.

While combatants may not claim to operate in the arena of compromise, the appropriate strategy strikes a balance between offense and defense, aggression and caution. The skilled fighter can operate with such a balance, reserving opportunity to both seize advantage and protect against disadvantage. Sometimes the best "cooperative" strategy is to simply wait to prolong the window of opportunity. Meanwhile, the ringside physician seeks to use this conflict management strategy for preference, working with the referee and combatants, but ever ready to interject himself between referees and the fighters as the authority figure in the ring. We envision this style not as one of compromise, but rather as one of judicious and decisive balance.

Avoid Like a Politician

We can easily identify the avoidance tactic with politicians who place reputation and votes over positions and policies. The avoiding strategy is often portrayed in boxing as both an offensive and defensive tool. Against a slower opponent, a boxer may choose to maintain advantage through constant motion. It can also be used to great advantage if there is a marked difference in reach. While the jab seldom results in a knockout, it scores points nevertheless. Avoidance could likewise be a tactic to counter an obvious advantage in power. A boxer knowing he cannot effectively trade blows toe-to-toe can exercise avoidance. From a conflict management style, *Avoiding Like a Politician* is low on both the cooperation and assertiveness scales. A clear case in boxing when the fight doctor literally did nothing was the 12th Round of the match between Benny (The Kid) Paret and Emile Griffith. The fight ended with Paret being carried out on a stretcher with a subdural hematoma—bleeding in the brain; in this case, a fatal injury. In pre-bout antics, Paret had resorted to a sexual slur, which seemed to spur Griffith to deliver a relentless beating. According to Sports Illustrated writer Gilbert Rogin (1962), "Benny was helpless, bleeding from his nose and a cut on his right cheek; his puffed eyes were closed. Still Griffith punched him, with mounting and maniacal rage, as though determined, literally, to wipe out both Paret and the memory of his taunt. There were, in all, about 15 uppercuts, followed by several hooks. Then Referee Goldstein was tugging at Griffith from behind, pulling him off. As Emile, berserk, struggling passionately in Goldstein's embrace was dragged away, Paret, now obviously senseless, crumpled slowly and collapsed. The doctors fluttered into the ring and crouched about him like "ravens.""

In his defense, Referee Goldstein commented on Paret's history of surviving intense punishment. Rogin makes no commentary whatsoever concerning the fight doctor who unmistakably avoided intervention—resulting in Paret's death.

Delegate Like a Diplomat

The accommodating style is quick to please, surrendering leadership or control; but while this type of behavior is exhibited in sports, it is seldom seen in boxing referees. Thus, we have labeled this conflict management style as *Delegate Like a Diplomat*. A diplomat goes to great lengths not to offend and always errs on the side of relationship. This style is seldom effectively used by boxers, though there is historical precedent in Ali's rope-a-dope strategy deployed against a younger, stronger, but less durable Foreman. In general, to surrender to the opponent is almost always a defensive strategy by a hurt fighter trying to protect themselves just long enough to regain faculties. A ringside physician using the *Delegate Like a Diplomat* strategy for decision making in conflict management relinquishes his power and position to the referee, which is a risky strategy depending upon the medical astuteness of the referee. In such fights, the ringside physician may never draw attention to himself or his role, or as in the case of Humberto Soto versus Francisco Lorenzo, seek a decision from others.

According to one of our authors, the Soto vs Lorenzo (boxrec.com 2008) case was so bizarre that even the doctors were dumbfounded and avoided the conflict. According to BoxRec.com, "In round four, Soto dropped Lorenzo twice, however after the second knockdown, Soto intentionally hit Lorenzo after he took a knee. With blood streaming from his face, Lorenzo remained on the deck. The referee spent several minutes consulting with other officials before deciding to disqualify Soto". Humberto Soto was winning the bout by a landslide when Lorenzo uncharacteristically dropped to his knee. Soto delivered an intentional foul to the back of Lorenzo's head while Lorenzo was in the prone position. Had Lorenzo not been bleeding so profusely, it may have gone unnoticed, but the blood already pooling on Lorenzo's face splattered on the canvas. The Unified ABC rules state; if an intentional foul causes an injury, and the injury is severe enough to terminate the bout immediately, the boxer causing the injury shall lose by disqualification. The referee and doctors are required to follow the rules.

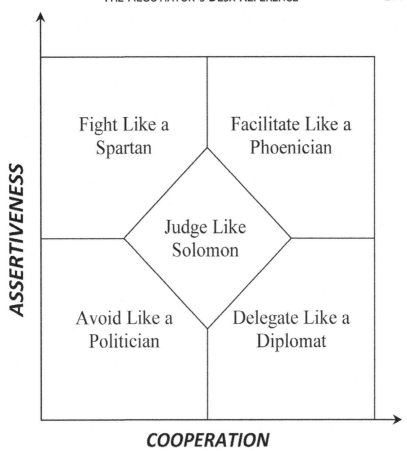

Figure 1. Proposed Thomas-Kilmann conflict management styles reinterpreted for application in combative adjudicated sports.

Identifying Dominant Conflict Management Styles

A modified TK instrument was developed to assess the conflict management style of fight doctors with designed redundancy and the ability to identify style preference and situational choice, because when the safety of competitors is at stake, different doctors manage the tension differently. This model allows the physician to "mirror" in order to analyze and understand his personality and personal approach to his mission. Selected sample questions from this tool are:

    1)   During a fight I am aware of the fans' negative responses when I enter the ring:
        a. Always
        b. Usually
        c. Sometimes
        d. Seldom
        e. Never

2) I watch for fighter or corner glances in my direction:
   a. Always
   b. Usually
   c. Sometimes
   d. Seldom
   e. Never

3) I ignore arguments for fighters or corners to let the bout continue:
   a. Always
   b. Usually
   c. Sometimes
   d. Seldom
   e. Never

4) During a fight if there is an unusually messy nosebleed, I would:
   a. Stop the action, assess, and give the corner time for intervention
   b. Stop the action, and tell the corner to apply intervention
   c. Request examination for broken bones or septum issues between rounds
   d. Let the fight continue
   e. Stop the fight due to amount of blood lost

5) If a downed fighter fails to respond appropriately to 1 of 4 questions posed, I would:
   a. Determine a course of action based upon the physician exam
   b. Ask the fighter again
   c. Use thorough neurological and physical exam to determine fitness to continue
   d. Ignore it, since 3 out of 4 is okay
   e. Terminate the bout

6) If I became aware during a pre-bout exam of an undocumented significant sparring injury, I would:
   a. Follow the action in the ring more closely
   b. Document any sustained impairment in a post-bout exam
   c. Request a between-round exam if showing impairment
   d. Treat the fight as any other
   e. Stop the fight at first sign of medical disadvantage

The tool was administered to a group of 80 fight doctors. We note that the dominant physician style can change with referees, combatants, time, and experience. In particular, we found 40% of the fight doctors evaluated were Spartans and 50% were avoiders. The results are summarized in Table 1.

Style	Primary	Situational
Avoid Like a Politician	50%	0%
Fight Like a Spartan	40%	12%
Facilitate Like a Phoenician	2.5%	0%
Judge Like Solomon	7.5%	75%
Delegate Like a Diplomat	0%	13%

Table 1. Results of the style identification tool as applied to 80 ringside physicians indicating both the preferential conflict management style, as indicated in responses to questions similar to samples 1-3, and that adopted when placed in particular situations, such as those outlined in questionnaire samples 4-6.

Thus, we found avoiding is a very typical conflict management style for the ringside physicians. In an interview, our collaborator Dr. Estwanik mentioned that especially if a round or match is about to end, it is less time sensitive to stop a fight unless a significant danger to the fighter exists. Thus, the physician is unlikely to intervene when the clock will imminently do so. Our results are coherent with Dr. Estwanik's comments. However, it should be noted that when faced with a described set of circumstances, as in the second half of the questionnaire, style migrated toward strict adherence to the rules using the *Judge like Solomon* style.

Role of the Ringside Physician Outside of the Ring
We would be remiss if we relegated the role of the ringside physician solely to the actual fight. The original American Association of Professional Ringside Physicians (AAPRP) was established in 1997 to develop medical protocols and guidelines to ensure the safety and protection of professional boxers. The reorganized Association of Ringside Physicians (http://www.ringsidearp.org 2012) has developed position statements on medical recommendations on safety improvement, ethics, clearance of older fighters, use of headgear in amateur competition, mouth guard standards, the use of hormonal supplements, weight management, and screening for blood-borne infectious diseases. All of these could be seen as aspects of a meta-negotiation within the sport, though they do not map neatly onto the ringside style chart.

Research continues to make the sport safer. Clausen and fellow researchers (2005) documented encouraging trends regarding chronic traumatic brain injury (CTBI). Assuming exposure to repetitive head trauma is a major contributing factor in CTBI, these authors found a historical trend toward less rounds in the ring and fewer fights in a typical boxing career. They cite, "The incidence of boxing related CTBI will diminish in the current era of professional boxing because of the reduction in exposure to repetitive head trauma and increasing medical monitoring of boxers, with pre-participation medical and neuroimaging assessments resulting in the detection of early and potentially pre-symptomatic cases of CTBI." Evidence of brain injury has historically been sufficient to exclude boxers from further participation. However, with a spectrum of possible degrees of injury and the increased ability to medically detect less obvious anomalies, we have ethical questions regarding when enough is enough. These situations also trigger what in effect are negotiations, over both policy issues and individual bouts.

Miele and coworkers (2006) attempt to address this through case studies. They state that subdural hematomas in sports are more common than epidural hematomas. Both represent traumatic brain injury as pooling of blood applies pressure to brain tissue, but each presents different symptoms and time before symptoms are evidenced. The differing degrees of injury and the wide range of participant symptoms and impairment make blanket conclusions difficult. Some recover fully and can be cleared to participate further, while others sustain life-altering, progressive deterioration. While the Muhammad Ali Boxing Reform Act mandates that all U. S. states honor the suspensions and bans by another state, nothing prohibits a boxer from pursuing post-injury fights outside of the United States.

Although significant concern exists regarding the potential risks of boxing, Robert Gambrell (2007) reported that injury rates in amateur and female professional boxing compare favorably with other contact sports when placed on an hourly participation basis. He further stated that the most common reasons for disqualification during a bout are uncontrolled bleeding, laceration, or head injury, and experienced ringside physicians appreciate the role and duties of cutmen and allow them an opportunity to control or stop bleeding before disqualifying the boxer.

We find the role of ringside physician, a vital one to the sport of boxing, to be rich in negotiations and conflict management styles. The public sees the role of the fight doctor as a dichotomy—those who took an oath to do no harm hold a job that calls many to act only in dire circumstance. Indeed, 50% of the fight doctors tested with our instrument would prefer to avoid making a decision to end a bout, and instead, let the referee control the interaction and the combatants decide the outcome. (Note that State laws and Commission rules do dictate the protocol for physician involvement. Thus, some delays by ringside physicians are not voluntary.) When each individual physician perceives it is indicated,[1] ringside physicians do indeed actively intervene. In other words, the style differences between ringside physicians clearly imply that some will intervene when others will not ... a telling indicator that even in the most combative of sports, some doctors negotiate to close cases in one way and some in another.

Notes

[1] The similarity here to observations of other medical personnel faced with a possibly-disclosable adverse medical event—is worth pointing out. [See Morash, *Non-Events*, in this volume.]

References

Association of Ringside Physicians, accessed 08/06/2015,
    http://www.ringsidearp.org/.
Blake, R. R. and J. S. Mouton. 1964. *The Managerial Grid: Key Orientations For Achieving Production Through People*. Houston: Gulf Publishing.
BoxRec.com. 2008. Accessed 08/06/2015, http://boxrec.com/media/index.php/ Humberto_Soto_vs._Francisco_Lorenzo.
Chamoun-Nicolas, H., R. D. Hazlett, R. Mora, G. Mendoza and M. L. Welsh. 2014. Negotiation and Professional Boxing. *In Educating Negotiators for a Connected World: Volume 4 in the Rethinking Negotiation Teaching Series*, edited by C. Honeyman, J. Coben, and A. Wei-Min Lee. St. Paul, MN: DRI Press.
Chamoun-Nicolas, H. and R. D. Hazlett. 2008. *Negotiate Like a Phoenician*. Kingwood, TX: KeyNegotiations.
Clausen, H., P. McCrory and V. Anderson. 2005. The Risk of Chronic Traumatic Brain Injury in Professional Boxing: Change in Exposure Variables Over the Past Century. *British Journal Sports Medicine* 39: 661-664.
Estwanik, J. 2015. *personal communication*.
Fernando Guerrero vs. Michael Walker 2/2. 2010. Retrieved 08/06/2015, https://www.youtube.com/watch?v=W3kpZzgEHSE.
Gambrell, Robert C. 2007. Boxing: Medical Care In and Out of the Ring. *Current Sports Medicine Reports* 6: 317-321.
Honeyman, C. and R. Parish. 2013. Choreography of Negotiation: Movement in Three Acts. Chapter 6 in *Choreography of Resolution: Conflict, Movement and Neuroscience*, edited by M. LeBaron, C. MacLeod and A. F. Acland. Chicago: ABA Books.
Humberto Soto vs. Francisco Lorenzo. 2008. accessed 08/06/2015, BoxRec.com, http://boxrec.com/media/index.php/Humberto_Soto_vs._Francisco_Lorenzo.
Miele, Vincent J., J. E. Bailes, R. C. Cantu and C. H. Rabb. 2006. Subdural Hematomas in Boxing: The Spectrum of Consequences. *Neurosurg*. Focus 21, October, 1-6.
Rogin, G. 1962. The Deadly Insult. *Sports Illustrated*, April 2, retrieved 08/06/2015, http://www.si.com/vault/1962/04/02/593537/the-deadly-insult.
Thomas, K. W. and R. H. Kilmann. 1974. *The Thomas-Kilmann Conflict Mode Instrument*. Tuxedo Park, NY: Xicom, Inc.

ℭ 72 ℬ

Negotiating with the Unknown

Maria Volpe, Jack J. Cambria,
Hugh McGowan & Chris Honeyman

Editors' Note: What happens when all of the classic negotiation advice about preparation goes out the window? Negotiations "on the street" teach us how extensive preparation for the process itself—for teamwork, roles, communication patterns, and trust—is crucial for success when everything you might ordinarily want to know to prepare for a specific case is impossible to find out in time.

In order to understand the ordinary or near-ordinary, sometimes it pays to study the extreme. This chapter will use the extremely high-tension experiences of hostage negotiators to discuss a few facets of negotiation that are rarely taught to others, but that increasingly seem relevant far

Maria R. Volpe, Ph.D. is Professor of Sociology, Director of the Dispute Resolution Program, and Director of the CUNY Dispute Resolution Center at John Jay College of Criminal Justice, City University of New York. An internationally known scholar, she has lectured, researched, and written extensively about dispute resolution processes, particularly mediation, and has been widely recognized for her distinguished career in the field of dispute resolution.

Jack Cambria retired from the New York City Police Department in 2015 after nearly thirty-four years of dedicated service. For over sixteen years he served in the Emergency Service Unit (ESU), whose primary focus is to provide rescue, SWAT, and counterterrorism services to the City of New York. He ended his NYPD career as the longest-standing commander of the Hostage Negotiation Team, serving in that capacity for over fourteen years.

Hugh McGowan retired in 2001 from the NYPD after 35 years of service, serving for his last 13 years as Commanding Officer and Chief Negotiator of the Hostage Negotiation Team (HNT). He has personally responded to and coordinated negotiations at over 1,500 hostage, barricade and suicide incidents, and has instructed crisis negotiators for the NYPD and many other agencies. McGowan has a Ph.D. in Criminal Justice from the CUNY Graduate School.

Chris Honeyman is managing partner of Convenor Conflict Management, a consulting firm based in Washington, DC. He is co-editor of *The Negotiator's Desk Reference* and five other books, and author of over 90 published articles, book chapters and monographs. He has directed a 25-year series of research-and-development programs, advised many academic and practice organizations, and served as a mediator, arbitrator and in other neutral capacities in more than 2,000 disputes.

beyond their original setting.[1] [For more on teaching this see NDR: Kirschner & Cambria, *Captive Audience*]

Imagine having to negotiate with an unknown entity where, more often than not, the parties have no way of anticipating who they will interact with, or what questions or issues to expect. The parties meet for the first time at a tense scene, with each side typically separated from the other by a closed door. Interested parties tend to be numerous and insistent. Some of these interested parties may be closely associated with the hostages or the hostage taker, such as family, friends, colleagues, neighbors. Some are closely associated with the hostage negotiators, including supervisors and other law enforcement experts. Many others may be strangers to both parties, such as observers, media representatives and politicians. This potentially vast gathering of "significant others" creates what a former commander of the New York Police Department's hostage negotiation team refers to as "negotiations within the negotiation." And, to add to the tension, it is not unusual for weapons to be omnipresent on both sides.

Variations on these circumstances describe the "normal" context of the work of police hostage negotiators. They conduct their negotiations wherever and whenever there are highly stressful situations involving individuals being held against their will (or barricading themselves in) and where the ongoing communications with the hostage takers are high-stakes, involving potential loss of life. In these encounters, hostage negotiators have one distinct advantage over hostage takers: experience in dealing with such individuals in different situations. Hostage takers have typically never taken hostages before. Hostage negotiators, however, have collectively acquired a wide range of coping skills. These skills, we now believe, are needed in many other settings—settings that do not provide comparable training opportunities. In this chapter, we will discuss several of the most salient.

The reality of police hostage negotiations clashes with conventional wisdom about good negotiation strategy, which emphasizes the need to be prepared. Such preparation normally includes learning as much as one can, not only about one's own position, interests and needs, but as much as one can about the other side, before any meeting takes place. But when a call comes in that triggers a hostage negotiation, this kind of preparation is impossible. On the surface, this inability to prepare for a specific negotiation is unique to hostage situations. But closer examination calls this into question. [NDR: Taylor & Donohue, *Business and Hostages*] In many ways, hostage negotiation work mirrors the work of a variety of other professions which experience "dealing with the unknown" during the course of their workday. Obvious examples include emergency room doctors [See NDR: O'Shea, *Compassion*], train conductors, and television reporters (each role, of course, has existing training in dealing with forms of "the unknown" other than the ones discussed here), but many others find themselves in situations where at least some aspects are unknown enough to fit our premise. The core of our argument here is that it is possible to approach even the unknown as an informed negotiator, albeit in a different sense from the normal usage of that term.

Background: The Emergence of Hostage Negotiations

The deliberate use of police hostage negotiators began in 1973 with the formation of a hostage negotiation team by the New York City Police Department. Created in response to concerns that grew out of the Munich Olympics of 1972, the Attica Prison Riots, the "Dog Day" Brooklyn Bank Robbery and the Williamsburg Sporting Goods Store Robbery, the NYPD Hostage Negotiation Team (HNT), which now has 100 officers, is trained to respond to a variety of situations. As the nation's oldest and largest hostage negotiation team in one of the most diverse and vibrant urban areas in the world, the practice of negotiating with hostage takers has evolved significantly. Central to the NYPD Hostage Negotiation Team's ethos is its motto, "Talk to Me," which is actually more than a motto—it is a working heuristic, guiding the work of the officers. That catchphrase serves as a constant reminder of the need for officers to be good listeners, patient communicators, and articulate team members. Since hostage situations may go on for many hours, both listening to what the hostage takers are really saying and keeping them engaged in dialogue are extremely important. A basic rule of thumb for the hostage negotiator is 90% listening and 10% talking. Encouraging subjects to speak at great length lowers their emotional intensity. One analogy is a pressure cooker, which if not allowed to let off its built up steam, will surely explode. The dissipation of emotional levels gives countering rational levels an opportunity to rise to a point where subjects may be in a more receptive state to consider alternative options.

But it is also important to recognize that when NYPD hostage team officers respond to hostage situations, they are part of a large, complex operation. They are always backed up by the Emergency Service Unit (ESU) officers, commonly known as the tactical team and equipped with shields, shotguns and other weaponry, as well as the Technical Assistance Response Unit (TARU) officers, who provide investigative technical equipment and tactical support. Each of these units has specialized training, and together they function to achieve two common goals: getting the hostages out safely, and getting the hostage taker to "come out"—if possible, safely and voluntarily. Every hostage taker comes out in the end, one way or another, and all of the discussion that follows regarding the need to recognize the hostage takers' humanity is in the context of that fact.

The Elusive Qualifications

Preparation of officers to become members of the hostage negotiation team begins long before an officer is selected. In New York City, hostage negotiators must be sworn police officers who have achieved the rank of Detective with at least 12 years of experience in the Department. Virtually all hostage negotiators are nearly 35 years old when first chosen for the team. This rigorous experience requirement answers the need for officers who will be knowledgeable about police procedures, have achieved stature within the Department as detectives, and are also, simply, old enough to have personally encountered some of life's knocks—love, hurt, disappointment, success, rejection, and most important, failure. Thus when a hostage taker complains about one or another vicissitude of his life, the negotiator can say with credibility "You know what, I know about that too, and we can talk about it." Training in the martial arts is also viewed as an asset, because of its stress on compassion, benevolence, courtesy, sincerity and loyalty—qualities that may seem counterintuitive to those who have no familiarity with martial arts. [NDR: Lee & Shanahan, *Martial Arts*] The real-world criteria for consideration for this team may also be a hint as to the requirements for a successful negotiator in other "no direct preparation possible" environments (See e.g. Crampton and Tsur 2013).

Furthermore, to make meaningful selections from among the nearly 40,000 officers of the NYPD, the hostage negotiation team has developed informal networks of trusted people, often current or former members of the team themselves, who are asked to keep their eyes open for new talent. The team regards with some amusement other organizations' tendency to rely heavily on brief interviews with potential new colleagues, joking that each such candidate tends to show up wearing a "chameleon suit." The better recommendation comes when a known-reliable coworker says, "This is just the way this person is. S/he talks to everybody that way; s/he is not putting on an act."

The officers' life experiences and substantive knowledge of police work are supplemented with an intensive two-week training program. Since the hostage team members all have permanent day-to-day assignments unrelated to the team, and are dispersed across many precincts of the sprawling city (in order to ensure that there are always trained negotiators available 24/7 within a reasonable distance of wherever an emergency may take place), they do not necessarily know each other. New HNT officers come together for the first time during the special hostage negotiation training. This training program provides the officers with highly specialized substantive knowledge and process skills, some of which would be familiar to readers of this book from many other fields. The first week consists of selected negotiation theory and practice; the second week consists of Emergency Psychological Training (EPT),[2] [NDR: Jeglic & Jeglic, *Mental Health*] where officers are introduced to psychological, mental illness, and drug-related conditions that they will experience during the course of the "jobs." (In HNT usage, a "job" is an individual hostage negotiation case). Proper selection and training of negotiators are vital to future success of the team; improper selection of the negotiator ensures failure. It is essential to have the right person in a role that often holds life in the balance.

Establishing Respect and Trust

When you cannot prepare for a specific negotiation, the next best thing is to figure out what substitutes may be available. To establish communication with an unknown entity, what needs to be done? The HNT officers need to communicate that they are not going to operate solely from a position of authority and power, with a gun and a badge. Simultaneously they need immediately to demonstrate respect for the person they are talking to, as the beginning of establishing trust. [NDR: Lewicki, *Trust*] It is important to emphasize that some of the people they are encountering may never have been treated with respect before, by almost anyone they have known. (Hostage takers, naturally, are not a random sample of the population; many have been in trouble at some other point in their lives). There is a duality to this process, however, which must be acknowledged. On one level, the hostage negotiator must "respect people whom no one else may care to respect." On another level, both the respect and the development of trust are limited in scope and serve the overall goal of getting everyone out alive, which must be kept in sight at all times. Treating the other party with respect becomes a very powerful tool toward that goal.

Respect is demonstrated in several ways: greetings, taking the time to make small talk (i.e. schmoozing), articulating ground rules, and clarifying assumptions. Collectively, these techniques "warm up" hostage takers, make them feel more comfortable with continued discussion, and build trust. The specific functions of these techniques are discussed below. [See NDR: Cristal, *No Trust*]

Greetings

At the outset, the officer who is the designated negotiator (i.e. the speaking role in a team that almost always has more than one qualified negotiator) has to figure out how to address the hostage taker. For example, the officer may ask, "Mr. Carson, can I call you Mr. Carson?" If the hostage taker responds, "No, I want you to call me Superman" (and this has actually occurred), an acknowledgment that the individual has a right to name himself can defuse the tension created by a grandiose claim. Later on, the hostage taker may say, "Don't call me Superman, my name is Jack"—to which the trained hostage negotiator responds, "Can I call you Jack?"

Politeness, here, is more than "just politeness." It gives the hostage taker a dignity that he may never have experienced before, or not in a long time—particularly from the police. The politeness takes them back a little bit, and the emotional level comes down, when that exchange is just the whole dialogue. It is not about getting to the gun or getting the person out, but it is really almost like getting to first base. If the HNT cannot get to first base, it can never get home. Cambria relates a rather involved negotiation with a suicidal man threatening to jump off his fire escape. After some hours of discussing the reasons why he felt he needed to die that day, and when the situation had stabilized itself, Cambria told the man that it looked like he could use a hug. With much skepticism and a long stare, the man finally extended his hand to him, whereupon he was assisted back into the apartment. Probably this man had not received a hug, or for that matter, any human contact for years, and so he welcomed the opportunity. Cambria notes that he did give the man a hug; but only after first closing the window so he wouldn't change his mind and jump out again.

Schmoozing

A subtle and subjective indicator of suitability for the hostage team is an ability to schmooze. In the particular sense in which this term is used within the hostage negotiation team, this is neither a waste of time, nor a phony gambit just to get close to someone or to buy time for setting up some other kind of action. It is, instead, recognition that the other person, regardless of what they have done, is a human being, and needs some human interaction. (Of course, it also does serve to buy time.)

Ground Rules

The hostage negotiator begins the negotiation itself by establishing boundaries for the ensuing exchanges. Hostage negotiators are trained to explain what they are going to do, and explain again when they are doing it. It is a slow process, but a key part of preparing the other party to deal with the officers constructively. If this is skipped, in the interest of "saving time," the hostage taker is likely to get a wrong impression about what the officers intend—starting a slippery slope toward a true disaster.

Clarifying Assumptions

It is easy for hostage negotiators to think that everybody else understands what they are doing. But experience shows that assumptions are dangerous, and can backfire on the hostage negotiators in almost unimaginable ways, leaving the hostage negotiator standing with his/her jaw dropping asking "but didn't you understand what I was trying to do?" The challenge in negotiating with the unknown is to avoid assuming that what you are doing is understood, taking the time to explain your actions even in the midst of a tremendous amount of activity and potential danger. As a result, hostage negotiators always talk about the "drill." This means that the hostage negotiators explain to all of the people involved what the hostage team's role is and what will be done.

Part of the drill is to get the onsite negotiation team together in a football-like huddle, so that when others inevitably try to rush them in the negotiation process, the negotiators are ready to respond—by saying, for instance, "here's what we're going to do: we're not going to talk about the gun, we're not going to talk about the fact that that the kids got slapped around. Here's what we're going to do: we're going to—." The negotiator will attempt to relay a premise that it's not so important how we got here, but rather how we can get out of this together. The hostage taker is thus given a theme. The theme is like a working paper; it is not etched in stone, and it certainly can change. But it has a continuing function; it helps the hostage taker understand that no sudden action, such as a surprise attack, is contemplated, and that also demonstrates to others that the negotiation team has a plan and has the situation under control. This proves beneficial when the negotiator is able to deliver on that plan. *"Men, when they receive good from whence they expect evil, feel the more indebted to their benefactor."* (Machiavelli 1532).

Assumptions are routine and heuristics are not entirely avoidable by anyone who must act in the real world. One purpose of the 12-year minimum of prior experience is to try to ensure that an officer has encountered enough situations in other settings where his or her assumptions turned out to be wrong that the lesson would not have to be learned under life-threatening circumstances.

McGowan has an example from his early career. He was riding with an older officer when they received a stolen-car call, and were dispatched to make out the complaint report. The more experienced officer went up to the person who had called about the car, and was waiting on his porch. The senior officer began by introducing himself, taking his hat off, and starting a general conversation about what kind of car it was. When the man told both officers "It was a '57 Chevy with nice trim on it" the senior officer did not immediately pull out a report pad, but instead recognized that that model was particularly valued by many people, and asked "did it have—(some option or other)?" The owner replied yes, it did have that feature, "it even has an AM/FM radio" (not common on that model.) The two strolled off the porch, out to the front of the house, where there was an empty spot—where the car was supposed to be. They stood in that spot, and simply chatted for a while about the car. After a bit, the senior officer asked the owner "Now, do you have your registration with you?" The man had it—in a piece of plastic, so it didn't get dirty. The officer said "Why don't you give it to this young fellow here and he can start the paperwork?" The man took it out, and gave it to McGowan—who was treated, to his befuddlement, as if he were an assistant. The senior officer and the car owner continued to talk while McGowan recorded all the information.

When McGowan and the senior officer got back in the police car and headed toward the station house, the senior officer realized that McGowan did not understand what he had been doing. The senior officer noted that this car owner had devoted a lot of his time and effort to his car, which was probably one of the most valuable possessions he had. It was obvious that he really took pride in it. The senior officer pointed out that if a police officer had come along and said, "Just give me your registration," the rudeness of that interaction would have stayed in the owner's mind as an example of disrespect by the police. What the owner needed from them, the senior officer felt, was a little bit of compassion. The car was still stolen, and given the statistics, the officers probably would not be able to get it back; but at least after the officers left, the taste in the owner's mouth would be a good one as to the attitude of the police toward his loss. McGowan reflects now that working with this partner taught him that a lot of decent police work had to do with the way people are treated—and the story is now used as a reminder to new negotiators about how one makes an entry into a situation. In the negotiation process, the showing of respect comes first; only then can you get to the heart of the matter.

Stories as Context

The use of such stories to teach "negotiating with the unknown" is deliberate. These are not merely stories about how the officers "won out over the other guy;" they are presented to demonstrate how the officers are able to break down resistance by dealing with the emotions in a way that works. The emotions being experienced by the hostage taker may even be the same emotions experienced by the hostage negotiator—a little fear, a little anxiety, and a little concern over saying and doing the right thing can be expected on both sides.

One of the key functions of the stories is to help officers get past their official status, because their working experience up to that point has been that official status often functions to ensure compliance. By authorizing officers to give a little bit of themselves, a little bit of their authority to the hostage taker, such as giving the hostage taker the authority to say "No, I want you to call me by my full first name and full last name" or "You got to call me Superman," officers are giving the hostage taker not only respect, but in a small way, power, which may never have been given to them before. This, the team has found, always seems to work to the hostage negotiator's advantage in the end. Since it is counterintuitive to do this, and since officers cannot be taught how to handle every specific situation, the storytelling, which draws on real experiences, validates the use of techniques that often depart radically from standard police training.

The Team's Structure on Site

The use of a team is central to hostage negotiation work. It is designed to help the negotiators concentrate on the process. [NDR: Sally et al., *Teams*] The "speaking" hostage negotiator is not out there alone; there is a structure. This consists of a primary negotiator; at least one backup coach; a "scribe;" and a coordinator. The role of the coordinator (usually the senior hostage negotiator present) is to bring corporate memory to the situation, provide insights to external police commanders and to the tactical team, and to run interference on behalf of the other negotiators. In this last, critically important function, the coordinator buffers the negotiators from the Chiefs—the term is used here as shorthand for all levels of supervision, described in more detail below—so that the other officers can do their job. Hostage negotiation is far from the only circumstance in which the person responsible for a negotiation must somehow report to difficult supervisors, who may try to micromanage a job and too often do not appreciate the intricacies, the need for patience and the time inevitably involved in making talk work. But in a police department, the hierarchy is overt and often insistent. There could easily be a district commander in the wings, saying, "I don't have any time for this, this guy is blocking traffic," or resenting the fact that the case happened on their watch, because there is a meeting to go to, or theater tickets to be considered. Hostage takers, however, cannot be told to come back tomorrow. The role of the coordinator is therefore to handle all of the *external* negotiations that threaten to disrupt the all-important negotiation "at the door." When McGowan was promoted to chief negotiator, he was informed that that did not mean that he got to negotiate any time he wanted. It meant he got to negotiate with the Chief—a significantly less desirable and more challenging honor.

But the other roles played by hostage negotiators such as scribe, coach, etc., are also near-essential in a complex and often fast-moving environment (though it must be admitted that sometimes, despite the desirability of clear role differentiation, shortages of trained personnel on-site mean that someone has to "wear more than one hat"). The team structure is more than just an administrative arrangement; its purpose is to ensure that the negotiator who is doing the talking is not overwhelmed by all of the other tasks that have to be done. This helps both their ability to focus and their ability to keep from rushing into any given phase of the negotiation, unless there is an immediate "Man is holding child out the window" exigency.

Training of Other Officers

It is important to emphasize that "ordinary" police training is now stressing some of the material developed for hostage negotiators, as police commanders begin to realize that it would be valuable for every police officer to learn much of it as early as possible in a career. [See NDR:

Kirschner & Cambria, *Captive Audience*] Patrol officers are the first responders to all types of calls made to the police; basic communication and perception skills are central to hostage negotiation work, but perception and communication are also at the heart of any police officer's role. To further shift the mindset of the first responding officer in managing incidents involving the mentally ill, the NYPD recently changed the vernacular that has been ingrained in the officers' corporate memory. More specifically, for several decades, the acronym EDP was widely used to refer to Emotionally Disturbed Persons. As part of the transition to more suitable responses, EDP now refers to Emotionally Distressed Persons. This simple change can help to make a difference in the officer's response approach, away from urgency toward one demonstrating more understanding. [See NDR: Morash, *Non-Events* for other examples of the importance of such an ostensibly "simple" shift in language] The reference to "distressed" suggests a more temporary condition experienced by subjects, thereby helping the responding officer to better relate to and better demonstrate empathy. It stands in contrast to the more rigid prior reference to "disturbed", a term which for the officer might be more likely to elicit fear of an unknown entity. The jury is still out on the effectiveness of this new language and its impact on better police interventions involving the mentally ill. But it is certainly a positive move away from the NYPD's earliest description, when EDP in practice was taken to mean "psychos". (Of particular note, to the hostage negotiator, EDP still means Every Day People.)

This shift in language and concepts is not the only new development, though getting sufficient training time built in for "softer" skills continues to be a significant challenge, in police departments as for other organizations where comparable skills are arguably required in order to do the actual job properly. Competing demands for "floor time" in training are a fact of life in large organizations of all kinds. Despite this, the NYPD recently tasked Cambria to produce a short video, to be incorporated into a new three-day training curriculum entitled "Smart Policing." The video addresses basic negotiation concepts and active listening skills for patrol officers, and is designed to quickly develop rapport in difficult street encounters.

Still, particularly in terms of police departments' need for constant communication with and the general trust of the public, it is clearly important to reduce the number of rookie mistakes. For example, not telling a citizen precisely what is happening, because it is far too minor, is a thrown-away opportunity when a police officer (usually, one who has little experience, for reasons discussed below) is asked, by a citizen whose stroll has been interrupted by a police barrier, "What's going on?" Often, such an officer will not realize that the citizen is not merely curious, but is concerned about whether there is a problem in his/her neighborhood, whether his/her family is all right, and so on—but has not formulated the question in such a way that this is obvious. An officer who responds with just "Move along!" is throwing away some degree of future potential cooperation of that citizen. An officer who responds with a human level of detail, though, such as "We have a man who is acting a little strange down the block, and has a gun, and we just want to make sure that everything is OK"—which is certainly less detail than the same officer would supply if it was the Mayor's motorcade that was interrupted—is improving the likelihood of some other officer, someday, getting critically important information from that citizen or someone in his/her family.

We believe the operational value of training people in basic human understanding, not just in police departments but in many jobs in society, is under-recognized. But to stick with police departments for now, officers are currently given relatively thorough training in key elements of law. Not yet fully integrated into basic training in police departments, however, are ways to get across the explicit message: "Your career will have more to do with communication than it will have to do with the law. Your career will have more to do with talking to people than with shooting people. Your career is going to have more to do with how you present yourself, so that you are seen by everybody you deal with as recognizing that you represent the entire Department, and that you know they will be dealing with the Department again." We believe the consequences are both serious, and potentially something of which a police department can become convinced: it is part of the folklore of police work that officers who have relatively little time on the job are more vulnerable to civilian complaints. What that means, in a nutshell, is that a key function of training has been deferred, from an organized short training period in a "no harm, no foul" police academy environment into what might be years of errant practice, till wisdom catches up with the rookie. How many other kinds of organizations fall prey to this temptation to false economy on basic training is unknown, but we believe the number may be large.

The Limitations of Training

Yet in some ways, we must accept that training is unlikely to carry the emotional learning effectiveness of actual work experience. Common sense and compassion [NDR: O'Shea, *Compassion*] are two virtues that cannot be easily taught at the police academy; they are something that one may or may not possess. Individuals who are adept at expressing compassion whenever they encounter others' suffering are able to ease the emotional anguish being experienced. When someone is hurting, expressing compassion will assist in establishing rapport in what may begin as a difficult encounter. Cambria relates a formative moment in his own career, which would be difficult to replicate in formal training. As a young police officer, one day he was coming back from court on the subway. As he got off the train in Brooklyn, the station clerk called over:

"Officer, there's a guy who just went under the turnstile, a homeless guy, just went down toward that end of the platform." Cambria did not know what to do with such a minor problem, i.e. whether to issue a summons or not. On balance, he decided the best way to handle it without undue expenditure of time would be simply to tell the homeless man to go out to the street, because obviously people cannot use the subway without paying. Cambria walked all the way down to the end of a long platform, where he saw the homeless man, disheveled, about 50 years old—although he looked older—and with a satchel under his arm. Cambria told him "You didn't pay the fare. You have to leave the subway." Having issued a firm statement, Cambria anticipated some degree of argument, but the man merely said, "Okay Officer, I understand." Cambria and the homeless man began walking together back down to the exit, at the other end of the platform. As they were walking, Cambria asked, "What do you have in the bag?" The homeless man replied, "Oh, in my bag, Officer, is a screenplay, it's a play I wrote." Cambria was taken aback. Curious, he asked what the play was about.

The homeless man replied that the play was titled Crabs in a Basket. "If you've ever seen a basketful of crabs, they're all trying to get out. When one finally gets almost to the top of that basket to get out, another crab grabs it and brings it back down, grabs it back down. It's kind of like my life ... it's autobiographical, it's about my life ... every time I get to the top of that basket, some force comes along and grabs me back down." Cambria describes himself as "blown away." As they approached the exit, he looked again at the homeless man and said "This ride's on me. Have a good day." Cambria told the man he hoped to see the play performed someday. At the cost of irritating the station clerk, Cambria felt he owed the homeless man something, for teaching him an important lesson: he had approached the homeless man with a preconceived notion, and had learned that just because the man was homeless didn't mean he was ignorant, or dangerous. This homeless man was down on his luck, yet he was a human being, with a sense of himself and of his circumstances, and an ability to explain them with eloquence—if given the opportunity. The sense of every individual as a person of worth, deserving of individual and not rule bound responses, is not easy for a new police officer—or lawyer, or doctor, or other new professional with sudden "status"—to learn. What price do we pay, in our unexpected negotiations, for our failure to incorporate such learning into the training of every such new professional?

In an attempt to make the knowledge and skills of hostage negotiators available to others, together with theater director Rachel Parish, we recently designed a pilot project to provide newer police officers and trainees with the basics of the skill set crucial for hostage negotiators to cope with their own emotions. (See Parish and Cambria 2018) Drawing from civically engaged arts practice used by theater professionals, a mixed group of students, conflict resolution professionals and police officers participated in a series of six workshops to learn new ways of being open to others' perspectives and emotions, by observing and engaging with a variety of everyday situations using techniques they had not previously experienced. While the participants felt that they had gained new information and insights about showing empathy and compassion, we were not able to measure any significant changes in their inherent emotional competence or resiliency. More encouragingly, there was some evidence that even this short workshop series may have helped raise each participant's *awareness* of his or her respective ability in this area, and thus made it more likely that it will be employed more in the future. There was also evidence that the series created a shared sense of the purpose and value of such engagement—potentially, a factor that might help offset what Cambria has called the "locker-room atmosphere" of a typical police station. It is still very much "early days" for this kind of experiment, and we hope that it will be possible to develop further and more sophisticated efforts along this line.

The Broader Implications: Other Occupations

We believe there is a variety of other occupations where the skills of a hostage negotiator could be useful to "best practice"—or arguably, essential to avoid malpractice. Emergency room staff [NDR: Morash, *Non-Events*; NDR: O'Shea, *Compassion*], hospital administrators, utility workers, transit workers, airport employees [NDR: Dingwall & Menkel-Meadow, *Scripts*], urban teachers, even the military [NDR: Lira, *Military*]: the list goes on and on. Hostage negotiators have frequently encountered social situations in which someone in one of these jobs will ask what they do for a living. When they answer "hostage negotiation," the inquirer replies, "Oh, I couldn't do what you do." But in fact, people in these kinds of jobs are involved in unexpected negotiations on a daily basis. These jobs are simply *unrecognized* as involving significant levels of "negotiations with the unknown" except by the more perceptive of their current incumbents. At least one of the critical elements of hostage negotiation training—the officers' need to treat a person who has probably committed a grave offense as a human being—should be, if anything, easier to apply in settings where a violation of criminal law is probably *not* the presenting issue. Teaching those who must deal with stressed members of the public that treating the person as a human being is the first need, if not the foremost in the end, should not be impossible. Teaching all professionals to be prepared, at a moment's notice, at least to explain honestly and respectfully what they are doing should not be all that difficult.

Seen this way, the training of police hostage negotiators is no longer so specialized or so mysterious that others cannot expect to make use of it. Instead, it is surprisingly close to the core of the new conception of a larger context of negotiation and conflict management, i.e. the broader notion of negotiation partly as a force for social good and partly as the essential lubricant in the increasingly complex machinery of a postmodern society (discussed in the Introduction to this book). This societal change demands matching changes in ways of relating to other people, as part of basic training in a whole range of professions. The training of hostage negotiators, and their success in practice, shows that it can be done.

Notes

[1] For a primer on the life and times of the NYPD's Hostage Negotiation Team, see Cambria et al. 2002.

[2] The EPT component grew out of the 1984 Eleanor Bumpers case, in which an elderly African-American grandmother was killed by police, when she lunged at them with a knife while they were attempting to follow through on an order to evict her from her Bronx apartment. Although the officer who fired the shotgun was acquitted of criminal wrongdoing, the case led to significant soul-searching as to the level of police understanding of mental illness, and the resulting EPT training was made available to ESU officers, and subsequently, to HNT officers.

References

Cambria, J., R. J. DeFilippo, R. J. Louden and H. McGowan. 2002. Negotiation Under Extreme Pressure: The "Mouth Marines" and the Hostage Takers. *Negotiation Journal* 18(4): 331-343.

Crampton, A. and M. Tsur. 2013. Negotiation Stands Alone. In *Educating Negotiators for a Connected World*, edited by C. Honeyman, J. Coben and A. W-M. Lee. St. Paul: DRI Press.

Machiavelli, N. 1532. *The Prince*.

Parish, R. and J. J. Cambria. 2018 (in press). *The Other Side of the Door: Arts in the Future of Policing*. St Paul: DRI Press.

✑ 73 ✐

Lessons from the Extreme:
What Business Negotiators Can Learn from
Hostage Negotiations

Paul J. Taylor & William Donohue

Editors' Note: The high-stakes world of the hostage negotiator draws instinctive respect from other negotiators. But if you operate in another domain, you could be excused for thinking that hostage negotiation has nothing to do with you. That impression, it turns out, is quite often wrong. Here, two researchers draw parallels to several kinds of business and other disputes in which it often seems that one of the parties acts similarly to a hostage taker.

Understanding what hostage negotiators have learned to do in response can be a real asset to a negotiator faced with one of these situations. Read this in conjunction with Tinsley, Cambria and Schneider on Reputations, and Volpe et al. on with Negotiating with the Unknown, and you may find yourself formulating a new idea you can use tomorrow.

In a typical hostage negotiation situation, a hostage taker threatens to harm himself or another person as a means toward an end. The hostage

Paul Taylor is Professor of Psychology at Lancaster University, UK, and Professor of Human Interaction at Twente University, NL. Supported by over £10m in funding, Paul's research combines experimental, archival and field methods to understand the nature of human cooperation and, more practically, the kinds of verbal and nonverbal behaviors that promote peaceful resolutions. On October 1, 2015, Paul became Director of the UK Centre for Research and Evidence on Security Threats (www.crestresearch.ac.uk), which was commissioned by the ESRC with funding from the UK security and intelligence agencies. **William A. Donohue** is a Distinguished Professor of Communication at Michigan State University. He received his Ph.D. from The Ohio State University in 1976. Dr. Donohue has published extensively in conflict, communication, negotiation and mediation while also conducting workshops and other intervention activities focusing on communication, leadership development, and conflict management. His co-authored book *Framing Matters: Perspectives on Negotiation Research and Practice in Communication* provides a broad understanding of the role of framing in negotiation research. Dr. Donohue is a past president of the International Association for Conflict Management and is on the editorial board of several major journals. Dr. Donohue is also a Fellow of the International Communication Association.

taker may have been caught robbing a convenience store and taken the hostage as leverage to improve his (nearly all hostage takers are male) situation. Or he may have some religious, political, or psychological motivation that he hopes to draw attention to by threatening to commit suicide.[1] In hostage scenarios such as these, the police work to end the incident without any loss of life. This is typically achieved by a trained response team that works quickly to contain the scene and create an environment in which the incident commander can employ a number of different strategies. Because of its success as a non-lethal approach, the most common strategy is negotiation.

What makes hostage negotiation unique as a communicative event is the high stakes and heightened ambiguity that underlies the interaction. The hostage taker is negotiating for his life, and the police are negotiating for the lives of the hostages. Such a negotiation is not embedded in the traditional dynamics of normative thinking and good faith, but in the extreme dynamics of emotional arousal and anxiety. The negotiators must listen carefully, resist the temptation to react defensively, and work to build trust and cooperation. The stakes are high, the stress is extreme, and the demands on the negotiators are fierce. [NDR: Volpe et al., *The Unknown*] When the communication context is stretched in this manner, it opens an important window into the complex dynamics of mixed-motive negotiation.

By the end of this chapter, we hope to give the reader not only an understanding of the dynamics that are important to hostage negotiation, but also some "food for thought" about how best to approach more normative bargaining challenges. While often perceived as unique interactions, hostage negotiations are shaped by a set of dynamics and rules that can inform other negotiation contexts. For example, sales agents are often faced with very hostile buyers who negotiate by giving ultimatums. This form of aggressive, highly distributive bargaining is common in early stages of hostage negotiation, and sales agents can learn many lessons about how to defuse these kinds of aggressive strategies. Indeed, many critical features of negotiated interaction have been easier to identify in the hostage context than in its normative counterparts, due to the saliency of interpersonal actions within a high-pressured, crisis context (Donohue et al. 1991).[2]

The way police negotiators interact with hostage takers may therefore have important lessons for negotiators outside of the hostage context. In this chapter, we explore six aspects of hostage negotiation that are critical to reaching a successful resolution. As it turns out, these aspects contain lessons that are important for negotiators who want success in a wide range of contexts.

Containment First

Experience has taught police teams that it is necessary to contain the hostage takers before engaging in dialogue. Almost without exception, a police team will delay interaction until they are satisfied that they have eliminated routes into and away from the scene, and minimized (as much as possible given current communication options) the ability of the hostage takers to contact third parties. The dangers of not containing a scene are made transparent by incidents in which well-intentioned members of the public are harmed (McMains and Mullins 2001). Equally problematic, and unfortunately more common, are incidents in which information from a third party (e.g., TV coverage, social media) undermines the police negotiator's position.

The availability of information from third parties can dramatically shift the balance of power and undermine a well-crafted persuasive position in many bargaining contexts. Yet negotiators and scholars outside of the hostage context continue to focus on events at the negotiation table, with only cursory recognition of the "negotiations" that occur away from the table. Away from the table, negotiators will often work to manipulate the perceived value of issues, try to gain influence and power, and work to develop and protect their personal identity (Donohue and Hoobler 2002; Donohue and Taylor 2003).

Containment also serves purposes more subtle than minimizing the interference of outside players. For example, the elimination of other opportunities and exit routes is known to have a positive effect on individuals' cooperation within an interaction. Negotiators without alternatives typically show more interdependence, they are more likely to reciprocate concessions, and they achieve higher joint outcomes than negotiators who have alternative options (Donohue and Taylor 2003; Giebels, De Dreu and Van de Evert 2000). Police negotiators often refer to this as creating a "we-are-in-it-together" environment, whose rationale centers on the fact that it is more difficult for an individual to withdraw from the negotiating process when they perceive themselves as having a stake in its success.

Containment also plays an important role in police negotiator efforts to present information persuasively. It not only allows negotiators to limit a hostage taker's knowledge of the available options, but it also allows them to distort the value of the alternatives. For example, police negotiators will often remonstrate at length about the difficulty of providing something to the hostage taker, even when its actual provision is relatively trivial. This approach draws on people's typical reaction to scarcity, [NDR: Guthrie, *Getting Your Way*] which is to view a resulting offer or concession as considerably more attractive than would otherwise be the case (Cialdini 2001: 203). Similarly, police negotiators will always try to break down any substantive considerations into their constituent parts. Rather than talk about a pizza, they will talk about where the pizza should be bought, what toppings it should have (and whether the police negotiator and hostage taker have common preferences in toppings), what the base should be (and the problems with cold "stuffed crust"), what drink should be included, whether or not there should be any side orders, and so on. A dialogue along these lines might occur as:

> "You know Chris, we're trying to help you out. We got you the pizza. We got you the base you wanted, you know that thin crust because I know you hate deep crust. We got you the toppings, what was it? Ham, mushroom and extra pineapple? I'm not sure I could stomach the extra pineapple personally but that's your choice and we got you that. And, we got the pizza from Store A. My boss reckoned we should just go to Store B because it's closer. But I said that's not what Chris wants, he wants a pizza from Store A. So I pulled you in a bit of a favor there by getting the pizza from Store A."

The result is an interaction in which negotiators are able to share a joke over topping preferences, demonstrate concern that the hostage taker also have a drink, concede on providing the desired side order and pizza toppings (which is a concession that deserves reciprocation), and provide the hostage taker with needed food. By controlling the presentation, the police negotiator expands the topics of discussion and simultaneously verbally contains the hostage taker by keeping him occupied over the details of the pizza order. They make clear that they are conciliating on far more than a pizza and by doing so find areas of "agreement" between themselves and the hostage taker.

In summary, police negotiators rely on containment to limit the influence of unpredictable outside factors and to allow for some control of how information is fed to the other party. The impact of *not* containing these factors is very apparent in the high-stakes, uncertain environment of hostage taking, where a mismatch between what negotiators say and what others do or say can critically reshape the conflict, as the end of the Branch Davidian siege at Waco unfortunately testifies (Wright 2003). The lesson here, then, is to remember that negotiations are often shaped away from the table, and that individuals' perceptions and beliefs while at the table may be crafted to be very different from the reality away from the table, but only if the negotiation is successfully contained.

Sweating the Small Stuff

It is often said that negotiators should not "sweat the small stuff" and should focus their efforts on the issues that matter. In hostage crises, however, paying attention to little details is instrumental to whether a negotiation succeeds or fails. As a number of authors have argued, little details emerge as important in the initial few minutes of an encounter as the hostage taker forms a first impression (Wells, Taylor and Giebels 2013). As a result, negotiators are careful to not imply a familiarity with the hostage taker's position, and they avoid making assumptions (Arkowitz et al. 2008). For example, Fowler and DeVivo caution against the use of "why" questions within the first five minutes of a negotiation, because it may be perceived as a challenge to the perpetrator's legitimacy (Fowler and DeVivo 2001).

One approach that emphasizes the importance of small details, and which is used extensively by hostage negotiators and other law enforcement officers keen to build rapport, is active listening (Abbe and Brandon 2013; Wells, Taylor and Giebels 2013). An active listener pays careful attention to what his or her interlocutor says and how they say it (known as focused listening), while resisting the urge to interrupt or otherwise shape the dialogue (responsive listening) and while providing minimal encouragement (e.g., positive backfeeds). They then begin a response to the other party with a paraphrased summary of what they have heard.

Although this may sound like it will lead to a laborious interaction, active listening has important advantages. [NDR: Itzchakov & Kluger, *Listening & Understanding*] The summary response serves to demonstrate respect for the hostage taker's position and opinion (Nugent 1992), something that has been found to be particularly effective for parties who do not feel listened to or understood (Ufkes et al. 2012). It also provides the opportunity for the hostage taker to correct errors in what a negotiator understands about the situation. Such corrections may not only address instrumental facts but they may also relay non-tangible details, such as the hostage taker's motivations or feelings. Finally, active listening can help dissipate the emotion and conflict within an incident via the use of emotional labeling (Kennett 2009). By observing the hostage taker's affect, as displayed through intonation, word use, and body language, and then commenting on them, the negotiator is able to address underpinning issues in the hostage taker's own words.

At the heart of active listening, and of the general focus on attending to the small stuff, is recognition that language choice and "localized behavior" are the building blocks of negotiator positions (Taylor and Donald 2003). A number of authors have demonstrated that matching the language style of a hostage taker—that is, their lexical choices with respect to factors such as pronoun use, formality, and so on—is related to negotiation outcome (Taylor and Thomas 2008; Richardson et al. 2014). Over time, in an iterative fashion, the synchrony in language engenders a common view of how to understand and frame the conflict, which ultimately leads to cooperation (Taylor 2002). What is particularly impressive is how successful negotiators achieve this. Successful negotiators appear to recognize when they are out of sync with the presentation style of the hostage taker (presumably as a result of good active listening, among other things), and they temporarily reduce the amount they talk by approximately 40% (Ormerod, Barrett and Taylor 2008). They stop, listen, and re-engage the hostage taker in an appropriate way.

As researchers have begun to better understand the small stuff, so they have been able to make more and more detailed recommendations for how best to act in a particular situation. One area where this is particular true is with respect to cross-cultural negotiations. For example, the use of rationale persuasion as a means to elicit concessions is less effective when used with hostage takers from collectivist cultures (e.g. Morocco, Russia) compared to individualistic cultures (e.g. the US, UK) because such messages can be construed as too direct and not respectful of the relational priorities of dialogue (Giebels and Taylor 2009).

Another area where emerging research suggests that sweating the small stuff matters is in relation to error recovery. Errors are an inevitable part of negotiation, particularly in the high-stakes and pressurized context of a hostage incident, and they can have a significant negative impact on rapport and cooperation (Oostinga et al. 2016). In their studies of suspect interactions, Miriam Oostinga and colleagues[2] have shown that both fact related errors and errors of judgment (e.g. misconceiving the hostage taker's feelings or identity) negatively impact the aggrieved party's trust, willingness to cooperate, and belief in the other's competence (Oostinga et al. 2015). However, of the two forms of errors, an error of judgment has a more negative impact. Importantly, however, the impact of both can be ameliorated to some extent by an apology and, to a greater extent, by an "acceptance" message, which acknowledges the error, notes how it occurred, and seeks to ensure that it does not happen again (e.g. "I've written your sister's correct name down on our record sheet so we won't make that error again"). Thus, just as good listening requires careful attention to language, so does good error recovery. [NDR: Brown & Robbennolt, *Apology*]

Expanding the Emotional Pie

Most negotiation research recognizes the importance of "expanding the pie" and searching for optimal solutions. However, negotiators and negotiation theory have traditionally viewed this integrative strategy as relating to substantive issues. For police negotiators, however, issue exploration comes second to emotional exploration. Recent estimates suggest that nearly 80% of all hostage situations are emotion or relationship driven (Van Hasselt et al. 2005). For this reason, police negotiators have learned to work quickly to understand and negotiate around expressive aspects of the situation. They seek to reduce the tensions and perceived threats of the context, and they focus early efforts on developing trust and identifying face-saving strategies (Donohue et al. 1991; Taylor 2002).

What is unique about this perspective is not the recognition that emotive factors play a role in negotiation, since this is now recognized across many disciplines (Barry 1999). The unique aspect of this perspective is the way in which emotive concerns are viewed. In many traditional negotiation contexts, relational and identity dynamics continue to be viewed as mediating factors that help or hinder efforts to work towards a substantive agreement. The traditional view is to conceptualize emotion as something that needs to be dealt with before considering instrumental issues (Hammer and Rogan 1997), or as something that informs understanding of instrumental positions (Van Kleef, De Dreu and Manstead 2004). In contrast, for the police negotiator, it is as important, if not more important, to search the emotional pie and address emotions as negotiation issues in their own right.

To illustrate this shift in perspective, consider a hypothetical organizational take-over and efforts by the potential buyer to identify what is likely to persuade the organization's board. In all likelihood, a traditional buyer would seek to determine the board's perception of the organization's value by gleaning information about costs and overheads, the value of subsidiary assets, whether money can be saved in staffing, and so on. A police negotiator, however, would seek to determine whether members of the board are concerned for the well-being of their employees, are worried about their personal reputation after the take-over, have a desire to retain influence on the board, and so on. By answering these kinds of emotive questions, a negotiator begins to uncover what might persuade the board members to accept less attractive offers than would rationally be the case when dealing with instrumental factors.

So how do police negotiators expand the emotional pie? There are at least two dimensions to the answer. The first is that police negotiators work proactively to manage a hostage taker's anxieties (Miron and Goldstein 1979; Noesner and Webster 1997). Rather than rush to deal with instrumental aspects of the negotiation, police negotiators use techniques such as mirroring, self-disclosure, and paraphrasing to show their interest in the hostage taker's emotive concerns (Hammer and Rogan 1997; Noesner and Webster 1997; Vecchi, Van Hasselt and Romano 2005). By coupling this with supportive feedback and non-assumptive questions (e.g., "I've not been in your position, but I guess you must be feeling very lonely"), the negotiator's efforts to show interest encourage the hostage taker to express their concerns while simultaneously venting their emotions. Police negotiators do not try to counter emotionality with rational debate, which is generally ineffective in high-pressure scenarios (Vecchi, Van Hasselt and Romano 2005). Instead, they accept that emotion itself is an important issue of the negotiation, which must be continuously monitored, explored, and addressed. [NDR: Heen & Stone, *Perceptions & Stories*]

The second is that police negotiators work to identify the hostage taker's main underlying problem or driver. At any one time, a hostage taker will communicate about one particular concern or issue, ranging from concerns about personal identity, to concerns about relational issues such as trust and power, through to concerns about substantive issues (Taylor 2002; Taylor and Donald 2004). Police negotiators listen carefully to the hostage taker's dialogue, and seek to identify this prevailing issue. They then address it by matching the framing of their own message to the hostage taker's framing. For example, it is not useful to make substantive offers when the hostage taker's real concern is for his personal identity and the shame the incident will bring to his family. By focusing on an inappropriate frame, a negotiator is in danger of making the hostage taker feel misunderstood or unvalued, which may lead to further conflict and heightened emotions. By interpreting the focus of dialogue, negotiators may also act proactively to identify under-explored issues that will expand the emotional pie. For example, by keeping track of changes in dialogue it is possible to gauge how much time has been spent discussing various identity, relational, and substantive issues. If negotiations come to a standstill, negotiators are able to review the motivational focus of previous dialogue and move to an issue that has yet to be covered.

Much of police negotiators' effort to resolve hostage crises relies on their ability to explore and understand the emotional drivers of the hostage taker. Far from being hindrances or mediating issues in the interaction, emotions are defining points of bargaining that often determine how the interaction unfolds. The lesson for traditional contexts here, then, is that one can never overestimate how beneficial it will be to spend some time exploring aspects of the emotional pie.

Primacy of Relationship

Hostage negotiation revolves around the interplay between demands and issues that both sides must manage. Hostage takers are usually able to articulate their demands. They may want specific, concrete items like money or freedom, or they may make more nebulous demands for revenge. However, they often have difficulty articulating the underlying issues that brought them to this precipice. This negotiation problem, of course, is not unique to hostage takers. Similarly, police negotiators' demands clearly center on freeing the hostages and ending the incident peacefully. But the process of executing this goal is often driven by various issues that can be difficult to sort through, such as staff fatigue, overtime costs for maintaining the scene, and police jurisdictional and publicity issues.

These demands and issues interact, and the ability of both sides to craft a resolution rests on their ability to transform their relationship into one that can manage the two features. The key transformation involves moving from a highly distributive, competitive relationship to a more collaborative orientation. The route to this transformation begins by providing some time for people to emotionally disengage, after which it becomes possible to slowly exchange relatively low-risk information (e.g., small talk). [NDR: Hollander-Blumoff, *Relationships*] This helps to build trust, which provides a basis for negotiators to develop a working relationship that can focus on problem-solving. Such problem-solving centers on simple issues such as food and electricity in the beginning, but ultimately the negotiators need to move toward a more engaged collaborative relationship that focuses on underlying issues. When collaborating, the fundamental, underlying basis of the conflict becomes exposed, and personal needs (tied to self-concept) emerge, allowing mutually fulfilling outcomes to emerge in turn.

A factor driving the extent to which the parties are able to build a relationship is the configuration of biases that the parties bring to the interactions. In his literature review of cognitive biases that impact negotiation, Andrea Caputo (2013) reveals that the five biases studied relating to decision making in negotiation are anchoring, overconfidence, framing, status quo, relationship, and the toughness bias. However, he argues that these additional biases deserve more research: the fixed-pie error, the incompatibility error, and the intergroup bias. The cumulative effect of these various biases might be to overweight, or underweight the value of the relationship in influencing outcomes. For example, police negotiators who are overconfident, approach with a negative frame, and are too tough at the wrong time might undervalue the relationship and risk failing to establish a rapport with the hostage taker. The key is for negotiators to reflect on their biases and understand their influence.

An example might serve to illustrate these points. In an airline hijacking in the early 1970s, a passenger hijacked an airplane bound for Atlanta by packing dynamite under his coat. When negotiations began, the hostage taker shared demands for many items that included money and fuel to get to Cuba. As the interactions unfolded, the police negotiator learned that the hostage taker hijacked the plane to demonstrate his manhood to his partner, with whom he had fought the night before. This personal issue became a turning point from cooperation (sharing demands and information) to collaboration, in which underlying issues were explored. The resolution called for the hijacker to release the passengers in exchange for a phone to call his partner. The passengers were released, and the phone call was made. Unfortunately, in this instance, the hijacker committed suicide while on the phone. Yet if the hostage negotiator had not taken the time to overcome potential biases and develop a relationship with the hostage taker enabling that person to reveal his true motives, the negotiations might have ended with additional loss of life.

As negotiators manage their issues and demands, both their competitive and collaborative orientations present paradoxical relational challenges. A collaborative relationship is paradoxical because parties like and trust one another, but resist the kind of engagement that would expose them extensively. They are pushing the other away while also pulling them closer. Similarly, a competitive relationship is also paradoxical, since parties do not like and trust one another, but they are highly engaged. They are pulling the other closer in order to defeat or in other ways harm them.

In the opening movements of a hostage negotiation, very competitive relationships tend to dominate. The police negotiator tries to slowly, but deliberately shift away from this approach into more of a time out period characterized by exchanging preliminary information, and moving hostage takers away from demands and threats. Parties explore roles and engage in a great deal of small talk. The goal of the police negotiator is to build sufficient trust to move toward a more cooperative relationship, but without compromising personal credibility. These preliminary discussions often center on such substantive issues as food, heat, light, and logistics as a means of moving the hostage taker into a more cooperative orientation. Once a collaborative orientation starts to emerge, then more substantive issues and demands can be explored. Collaboration is marked by cautious but positive problem-solving for both parties (Cambria et al. 2002).

The key to moving through these relational frames is to avoid compromising trust [NDR: Lewicki, *Trust*] and moving in the wrong direction, away from cooperation and back to coexistence. If trust can be established through relatively minor exchanges of food for hostages, then more important demands can follow—but not too rapidly. Thus, police negotiators are keenly aware of how to manage the relational perspectives of hostage takers to build the foundation that allows certain issues and demands to emerge. Without this foundation, executing the substantive goals becomes quite difficult.

The implications of managing relationships effectively are profound. For example, consider the sales agents referred to above. Often they are confronted with hostile buyers who, in a sense, treat these agents like police negotiators, while themselves taking on characteristics of hostage takers. Even if the buyers "must" buy from the sales agent, they often begin by making outrageous demands using the "take-it-or-leave-it" tactic. Thus, the first goal of the agent is to shift the relational frame from competition to coexistence, then to cooperation, and if possible, to collaboration. But the critical shift is the first one, to coexistence or a relational state in which people disengage from the task and simply try to get to know one another. That shift requires at least superficial information sharing, to build trust and affiliation. For example, the agent might ask the buyer to elaborate on his or her demands to uncover a rationale. [NDR: Abramowitz, *Learning from Sales*] Then, once the conversation gets rolling, personal topics and affiliative language can be used to move toward more cooperation and greater information exchange.

Going Beyond Yes and Closing the Deal

Generally, once the parties enter at least a moderately collaborative mode, with key issues being exposed and substantive problem-solving holding its course, the parties craft the outline of a deal. At some point, as in the hijacking incident, a deal is struck and both parties say yes. However, one of the most difficult times within hostage taking comes at the end, once an agreement has been reached. At the point of surrender, the hostage taker has lost his leverage, and is very sensitive to any suggestion that he has been tricked, duped, or generally led into a deal that appears different from what he envisaged. To deal with this problem, police negotiators stress the need to move slowly through the surrender sequence, in a very deliberate fashion. Each detail must be carefully orchestrated so that everyone's safety can be maximized.

The lesson for other contexts here is a simple but important one. Aftercare is a big business in negotiation. The goal is not simply to "get to yes," but to close the deal after "yes" has been heard. This closing requires meticulous attention to detail about how the process will unfold, and specific markers of success. [NDR: Wade & Honeyman, *Lasting Agreement*]

For example, once the buyer has said yes to the agent about the money part of the deal, then all the process issues kick in. How will the deal be consummated? Steps 1 through N must be laid out and clearly documented, leading toward the final delivery of the product. The post-yes steps might even include follow-up to ensure customer satisfaction. The key point is that clear steps make the deal work, just as they do in hostage negotiation.

Keeping Up with the Changing Nature of the Other

As with any negotiation context, the last decade has brought significant changes to who "sits across the table" in hostage crises. This has led researchers and negotiators to spend increasing time trying to understand, *a priori*, the characteristics and motivations of the hostage takers that law enforcement officers are likely to confront. For example, Dolnik and Fitzgerald point out that the Jihadi hostage-taking manuals and the tactics of other cause-based hostage takers are likely to change the nature of future barricade hostage sieges (Dolnik and Fitzgerald 2011). These hostage incidents, focused more on ideology and religion, are being conducted by "new terrorists" who present new challenges to law enforcement because these individuals have read the crisis negotiation manuals and studied past incidents; use religious rhetoric that may be unfamiliar to law enforcement; are more willing to execute hostages to enforce deadlines; are more ready to die for their cause; have direct lines of communication to colleagues beyond the incident; and are tactically savvy, well-armed, and well-prepared.

The implication associated with this more radicalized threat is that law enforcement must begin to rethink how it approaches hostage negotiations, for several reasons. First, these new challenges alter the power dynamics in the situation (Donohue and Taylor 2003). Dolnik and Fitzgerald argue that hard bargaining is less likely to be effective with the more radicalized, well-informed and prepared hostage takers, since limiting resources is likely to be anticipated and may result in more escalation. Second, hostage negotiators might need to rethink what constitutes a "successful" outcome. While any loss of life is certainly repugnant to law enforcement, and often triggers a shift from negotiation to a "tactical" resolution, it may be the case that negotiation options should remain open even after hostages have been harmed. If the hostage takers are prepared for typical law-enforcement responses, curtailing negotiations too soon might be counter-productive.

Third, it is apparent that these new hostage takers communicate differently, both before the incidents and during the incidents. Gabriel Weimann (2014) notes that terrorist organizations have turned to social media for propaganda, psychological warfare, and weapons tutorials. They recruit and radicalize and return to social media, even in the course of a hostage event. This suggests that law enforcement is faced with a particularly challenging set of communication issues when dealing with a hostage event. In a planned, multi-site hostage situation, the hostage takers might be transmitting the event on social media knowing that it will get picked up and transmitted through traditional media. In this new environment, the communication challenges officers face are no longer confined to the incident location or traditional media of interaction. Confinement ceases to be a realistic first step.

Given that (some) hostage takers are now likely to be more experienced, trained, well-informed and willing to sacrifice their lives, how should law enforcement respond? In such scenarios there is a difficult balance to be struck between acting quickly to ensure the safety of potential victims, and not being seen to act aggressively in a way that may prompt reciprocal escalation (Donohue and Taylor 2003). If bargaining does occur, it may be brief, given that the hostage takers may *want to* sacrifice their own lives for a more visible political statement. Thus, there may be two different approaches to negotiation—one that is briefer, which is aimed at acquiring tactical information, and one that is more traditional, and is aimed at using prolonged negotiation exchanges to achieve a settlement. How to distinguish between the two remains an unanswered question.

Lessons from Hostage Negotiations

Several lessons about the normative negotiation context can be derived from the crisis context. First, and perhaps most important, the crisis approach to negotiation is very proactive and deliberative. One police negotiator termed it "dynamic inactivity." He meant that hostage negotiation is all about working aggressively behind the scenes to develop strategies and tactics aimed at solving the problem while slowing down a process that might naturally turn frenetic. The goal is to move by "known successful" steps to achieve a successful resolution. For example, police need to contain before negotiating to ensure bargaining in good faith. That rule cannot be compromised except in extreme circumstances. After containment, it is considered critical to explore feelings and emotions while developing the relationship between the hostage taker and negotiator. Negotiators in more normative contexts, such as business, often underestimate the importance and value of being deliberate and thorough and not shortcutting the process. [NDR: Borbély & Ohana, *Mindset*]

The second lesson focuses on the need to understand the foundational issues in conflict. Police negotiators cannot deal with superficial treatment of issues because they may not be able to save lives until the hostage taker's deeper issues are at least acknowledged, and probably addressed overtly. The crisis orientation is always focused on uncovering the hostage taker's key drivers. Business negotiators face a similar challenge. In this context, negotiators can get lost in such superficial issues as price and delivery dates, and ignore the larger issues that are really driving the deal. Again, the need to be expedient and take shortcuts often compromises the outcome.

The third lesson is that hostage negotiators need to understand how their own biases about hostage takers, negotiation and conflict impact their ability to work constructively with hostage takers. While it is difficult to understand the full range of cognitive biases that any given negotiator might face, it would be useful for any negotiator to explore one or two fundamental biases that are well understood, like framing, for example. Certainly negotiators don't want to handicap themselves with cognitive constraints that might hinder their ability to see settlement opportunities. Thus, gaining feedback about these biases would be important.

A final lesson that emerges from this analysis is the need to look at a negotiation comprehensively. Crisis negotiation is not a process that is reducible to focusing only on gain or loss frames, or negotiator style, or power differentials. A crisis negotiator has to understand the entire context including constituent relations, events happening external to the scene, and certainly the process of interaction. Of course, the effective business negotiator must take this same broad view. They must also feel their way through a complex web of issues and relationships. Thus we can gain many important insights by exploring the interplay between the normative and crisis negotiation contexts.

Notes

[1] Despite the absence of a true hostage, current practice treats these cases similarly, as both the underlying causes and the teams and techniques found useful are similar to those that are effective in a classical hostage scenario.

[2] Note that in cases of suicide intervention, the police negotiator's primary goal remains the same; it is to contain the threat by eliminating the hostage taker's ability to take the alternative option of taking their life (Donohue and Taylor 2003; Giebels, De Dreu and Van de Evert 2000).

References

Abbe, A. and S. E. Brandon. 2013. The Role of Rapport in Investigative Interviewing: A Review. *Journal of Investigative Psychology and Offender Profiling* 10(3): 237-249.

Arkowitz, H., H. A. Westra, W. R. Miller and S. Rollnick (eds). 2008. *Motivational Interviewing in the Treatment of Psychological Problems*. New York: Guilford Press.

Barry, B. 1999. The Tactical Use of Emotion in Negotiation. In *Research on Negotiation in Organizations*, edited by R. J. Bies, R. J. Lewicki and B. H. Sheppard. Bingley, UK: Emerald Group Publishing.

Cambria, J., R. J. DeFilippo, R. J. Louden and H. McGowan. 2002. Negotiation Under Extreme Pressure: The "Mouth Marines" and the Hostage Takers. *Negotiation Journal* 18(4): 331-343.

Caputo, A. (2013). A Literature Review of Cognitive Biases in Negotiation Processes. *International Journal of Conflict Management* 24 (4): 374-398.

Cialdini, R. B. 2001. *Influence: Science and Practice*. Needham Heights, MA: Allyn & Bacon. P. 203

Dolnik, A. and K. M. Fitzgerald. 2011. Negotiating Hostage Crises with the New Terrorist. *Studies in Conflict and Terrorism* 34(4): 267-294.

Donohue, W. A. and G. D. Hoobler. 2002. Relational Frames and Their Ethical Implications in International Negotiation: An Analysis Based on the Oslo II Negotiations. *International Negotiation* 7(2): 143-167.

Donohue, W. A. and P. J. Taylor. 2003. Testing the Role Effect in Terrorist Negotiations. *International Negotiation* 8: 527-547.

Donohue, W. A., G. Kaufmann, C. Ramesh and R. Smith. 1991. Crisis Bargaining in Intense Conflict Situations. *International Journal of Group Tensions* 21: 133-154.

Fowler, R. and P. P. DeVivo. 2001. Analyzing Police Hostage Negotiations with the Verbal Interactional Analysis Technique. *Journal of Police Crises Negotiations* 1(1): 83-97.

Giebels, E., M. S. D. Oostinga and P. J. Taylor. 2016. The Cultural Dimension of Uncertainty Avoidance Impacts Police-Civilian Interaction. Working paper.

Giebels, E. and P. J. Taylor. 2009. Interaction Patterns in Crisis Negotiations: Persuasive Arguments and Cultural Differences. *Journal of Applied Psychology* 94(1): 5-19.

Giebels, E., C. K. W. De Dreu and V. Van de Evert. 2000. Interdependence in Negotiation: Effects of Exit Options and Social Motive on Distributive and Integrative Negotiation. *European Journal of Social Psychology* 30(2): 255-272.

Hammer, M. R. and R. G. Rogan. 1997. Negotiation Models in Crisis Situations: The Value of a Communication-Based Approach. In *Dynamic Processes of Crisis Negotiations: Theory, Research, and Practice*, edited by R. G. Rogan, M. R. Hammer and C. R. Van Zandt. Westport, CT: Praeger Publishers.

Kennett, R. 2009. *Crisis Negotiation*. Unpublished PhD Thesis, University of Kent, Canterbury UK.

McMains, M. J. and W. C. Mullins. 2001. *Crisis Negotiations: Managing Critical Incidents and Hostage Situations in Law Enforcement and Corrections*. Cincinnati: Anderson Publishing Company.

Miron, M. S. and A. P. Goldstein. 1979. *Hostage*. New York: Pergamon Press.

Noesner, G. W. and M. Webster. 1997. Crisis Intervention: Using Active Listening Skills in Negotiations. *FBI Law Enforcement Bulletin* 66: 13-18.

Nugent, W. R. 1992. The Affective Impact of a Clinical Social Worker's Interviewing Style: A Series of Single-case Experiments. *Research on Social Work Practice* 2(1): 6-27.

Oostinga, M. S., E. Giebels and P. J. Taylor. 2015. The Effect of Error Making and Error Recovery in Conflict Interactions. Presentation at the 2015 IACM conference. Clearwater, USA.

Oostinga, M. S. D., E. Giebels and P. J. Taylor. 2016. Error Orientation as a Determinant of Communication Error Repair in Crisis Negotiations. Presentation at the European Association of Psychology and Law. Toulouse, France.

Ormerod, T. C., E. C. Barrett and P. J. Taylor. 2008. Investigative Sensemaking in Criminal Contexts. In *Naturalistic Decision Making and Macrocognition*, edited by J. M. Schraagen, L. G. Militello, T. Ormerod and R. Lipshitz. Aldershot, UK: Ashgate Publishing Limited.

Richardson, B. H., P. J. Taylor, B. Snook, S. M. Conchie and C. Bennell. 2014. Language Style Matching and Confessions in Police Interrogations. *Law and Human Behavior* 38: 357-366.

Taylor, P. J. 2002. A Cylindrical Model of Communication Behavior in Crisis Negotiations. *Human Communication Research* 28(1): 7-48.

Taylor, P. J. and I. Donald. 2003. Foundations and Evidence for an Interaction-based Approach to Conflict Negotiation. *International Journal of Conflict Management* 14(3/4): 213-232.

Taylor, P. J. and I. Donald. 2004. The Structure of Communication Behavior in Simulated and Actual Crisis Negotiations. *Human Communication Research* 30(4): 443-478.

Taylor, P. J. and S. Thomas. 2008. Linguistic Style Matching and Negotiation Outcome. *Negotiation and Conflict Management Research* 1(3): 263-281.

Ufkes, E. G., E. Giebels, S. Otten and K. I. van der Zee. 2012. The Effectiveness of a Mediation Program in Symmetrical Versus Asymmetrical Neighbor-to-neighbor Conflicts. *International Journal of Conflict Management* 23(4): 440-457.

Van Hasselt, V. B., J. J. Flood, S. J. Romano, G. M. Vecchi, N. de Fabrique and V. A. Dalfonzo. 2005. Hostage-taking in the Context of Domestic Violence: Some Case Examples. *Journal of Family Violence* 20(1): 21-27.

Van Kleef, G. A., C. K. W. De Dreu and A. S. R. Manstead. 2004. The Interpersonal Effects of Emotions in Negotiations: A motivated Information Processing Approach. *Journal of Personality and Social Psychology* 87(4): 510-528.

Vecchi, G. M., V. B. Van Hasselt and S. J. Romano. 2005. Crisis (Hostage) Negotiation: Current Strategies and Issues in High-Risk Conflict Resolution. *Aggression and Violent Behavior* 10(5): 533-551.

Weimann, G. 2014. *New Terrorism and New Media*. Washington, DC: Commons Lab of the Woodrow Wilson International Center for Scholars.

Wells, S., P. J. Taylor and E. Giebels. 2013. Crisis Negotiation: From Suicide to Terrorism Intervention. In *Handbook of Research on Negotiation*, edited by M. Olekalns and W. L. Adair. Gloucestershire, UK: Edward Elgar Publishing Limited.

Wright, S. A. 2003. A Decade After Waco: Reassessing Crisis Negotiations at Mount Carmel in Light of New Government Disclosures. *Nova Religio: The Journal of Alternative and Emergent Religions* 7(2): 101-110.

☙ 74 ❧

Negotiation in the Military

Leonard L. Lira

Editors' Note: Since as long as anyone can remember, negotiators have used war metaphors as a way to frame what they were thinking, and as an analogy to what might happen if no deal is reached. But the warriors themselves have wised up. In this chapter, U.S. Army Colonel Leonard Lira shows how the military has learned some hard lessons. Now, the military is well on the road toward sophistication about its own needs and practices in negotiation.

After fifteen years of continual conflict, conventional wisdom in the U.S. can no longer hold that the military is employed when negotiations have failed. In the modern era of conflict, as witnessed by state intervention enacted out of fear or in conquest, and in the regional internecine fighting in Afghanistan, Iraq, Syria and Northern Africa during the first part of this century, war is not only the last option when diplomacy fails, but as a point of fact, has often been used as the first option. Nonetheless, if there is one thing that the U.S. military has learned in the last decade-plus of conflict, it is that force alone is insufficient to win the peace.

While the Army still views its core mission as war fighting to fulfill its Congressional mandate of "Preserving the peace and security and providing for the defense of the United States," the predominant professional view no longer holds that the Army's core function is to destroy the enemy state's combat forces. In fact, the Army's capstone statement of doctrine, "ADP-1 The Army", acknowledges that the environment has adapted, and that it must "recognize and fully embrace the changes in the environment that offer us new avenues to maintain our preeminence"

Leonard (Len) L. Lira is a Colonel (ret. 2016) in the U.S. Army. His final posting was as the Director of the Center for Teaching and Learning Excellence in the Army University. He has a PhD in Public Administration from the University of Kansas and teaches Public Administration at San Jose State University. He served in two combat tours in Iraq during Operation Iraqi Freedom and also served in Afghanistan, as Director of the Combined Joint Operations Center for the NATO HQs in Kabul. The views presented in this chapter are the author's alone and do not necessarily represent the views of the U.S. Government or the U.S. Army, or San Jose State University.

(CADD 2013: 1). So while the Army still embraces its utility to compel the nation's adversaries in military campaigns, the focus is on "deliver[ing] lasting strategic results." As such, the military profession has accepted the changing nature of its professional ethic, and has begun to acknowledge that it must use negotiation skills as one of the tools at its disposal to accomplish the overall strategic goals of the nation during conflicts.

This chapter supersedes my chapter "The Military Learns to Negotiate", published in 2006. (Lira 2006) I will review here not only how the Army *has* learned to negotiate, but what it has learned from its need to negotiate. This chapter updates the evaluation of this phenomenon, previously conducted at the three levels of analysis according to military science—strategic, operational, and tactical—to include the organizational levels of analysis, from institutional, organizational, and individual perspectives.

A Changing Military and the Need for Negotiation

The recognition of the need for negotiation as a tool in military operations arose from the early 1990 deployments to peace operations. Primarily due to this role as peacekeepers, the military found itself interacting with a multitude of organizations and individuals in operations that necessitated a safe resolution to volatile situations. These situations dictated that military personnel need to be able to negotiate responsibility and effectively (Goodwin 2004).

This requirement did not go away with the onset of the violent campaigns in Afghanistan and Iraq after 2001. If anything, the military learned that negotiation was more important than ever, given that it now found itself operating in the "3-block" war. This metaphor is meant to depict that the military is engaged in a full-on firefight on the first block. On a second block, they are negotiating with locals to either stop them from fighting or to help re-build stability, and on the third block, they are negotiating with other government and non-government organizations to gain the resources and humanitarian support needed to bring a peaceful resolution to the conflict (Krulak 1999).

This construct of the 3-block conflict confirmed my assertion from the 2006 chapter that the goal of military operations in all phases of conflict (on any block it is on) is conflict *transformation*. That is, that one of the military's main goals is nothing less than changing the environment from war to peace, from violent dissonance to prosperous economic and political competition indicative of social consonance. This goal emanates from the U.S. military's need for legitimacy in the eyes of its main stakeholder, the American people.

Recently, however, American society has become more reluctant to confer its endorsement for continued military operations beyond the existence of perceived direct threats. This lack of endorsement has caused a reevaluation of the professional military ethic (Pfaff 2005). For example, in the most recent conflicts, non-combatant casualties and the abuse of prisoners in both Iraq and Afghanistan during post-combat military operations threatened to undermine citizen support for continued military operations in these countries (Pew Research Center 2004; Pfaff 2005).

The professional military ethic, which once would have been more accepting of non-combatant casualties—even without hesitation, due to the primacy of mission accomplishment—is now forced to recognize the moral and legal limitations that shape American society's opinion regarding the application of military force. These constraints impress upon modern military professionals the need to adopt a "police" model of ethical standards during all operations in the conflict environment (Pfaff 2005). Both the military and police ethical standards revolve around the question of the amount of force to be used in any given situation. Where the military model focuses on the *most force permissible* in any particular conflict scenario, the police model concentrates on the *least force possible* (Pfaff 2005).

The recent combat operations worldwide have required Army professionals at all levels, from General to Sergeant, to consider negotiations as one of their preferred tools to resolve conflicts. These professionals have served as U.S representatives in meetings and negotiations with coalition partners, other U.S. government agencies and non-government organizations, local leaders, and the local populace (Department of Defense 1997; Heidecker and Sowards 2004). The exigencies of war, such as the lack of time, the crisis of impending physical violence, and rationing of resources (manpower, technology, and money) for the primary military objective already make the operating environment constraining. The additional complication of political, organizational, and functional constraints in the modern conflict environment make it doubly so. One can observe examples of these limitations at multiple levels of analysis, and one can also observe the lessons that have moved the military profession forward as it hones its skills at negotiating through conflict.

Varying Levels to Analyze Negotiations in Military Operations[1]

It is important at this point to define the levels of analysis applied in this chapter. As used in the 2006 chapter, we can view the analysis of the military's application of negotiations through three traditional levels of analysis from military science theory: strategic, operational, and tactical. New to this chapter is the analysis of lessons learned from this application of negotiation via the traditional levels of analysis from the social sciences: the institutional, organizational, and individual.

The Strategic & Institutional Levels of Analysis

In the military sciences, the strategic level is where the nation determines national or multinational strategic security objectives. Actions at the tactical level may have strategic implications, as in the notion of the strategic corporal, but only the highest political and military levels decide the shaping of the strategy and why the military is doing a particular operation, or not. For example, the President of the United States, through the national security decision-making process, develops guidance as to how to use national resources (military, diplomatic, economic, informational, and legal) to accomplish these objectives. Military strategy, thus derived from policy, provides a framework for conducting operations.

The negotiation field utilizes the concept of strategy in both similar and different ways. It is similar in that both fields see strategy as goal-oriented. Developing a strategy in the military is about the selection and definition of goals, and then aligning goals, or ends, with ways, or actions, and means, or resources, in a way that will lead to the achievement of the goals. The negotiation field defines strategy as "the overall plan to accomplish one's goals in a negotiation and the action sequences that will lead to the accomplishment of those goals" (Lewicki, Saunders and Barry 2005). Strategy differs in the military field from the negotiation field in that, for the most part, the negotiation field focuses on the individual level of analysis. It describes strategy as individual decisions to achieve goals through either a distributive or integrative approach. The military takes a more institutional approach, in describing strategy from a hierarchical perspective where decisions are made to shape or modify either goals, ways, or means to produce a viable strategy. In the negotiation field, strategy quickly transitions to the tactical level, in that the tactics then describe the individual decision of the negotiator on how to employ the selected strategy. [See, however, NDR: Borbély & Caputo, *Organizations*, for their argument that civilian organizations such as companies would profit from adopting a more institutional view of negotiation.] For example, if the strategy is an integrative one, the tactics are based on how the individuals decide to describe their interests while deciding how to learn the interests of the other parties, to span the gap between the strategy selected and the tactics employed.

To analyze the lessons learned at the institutional level, the discussion in this chapter follows Richard Scott's (2008) articulation of institutions as the combination of rules, norms, and cognitive-cultural identity. In this construct, rules are the written, or doctrinal enshrinement of prescribed behavior expected of members of the institution. Once members of institutions agree to a behavior expected of its members, those expectations can be codified as rules. Norms are similar to rules, with the exception that they are not necessarily written. Norms are similar to customs; they are the unwritten rules of expected behavior. Cognitive-cultural identity is how the members of the institution see themselves in relation to their rules, norms, and interaction with their environment. For example, in the changing military ethic, do the members of the military see themselves more from the maximize-as-much-force-as-permissible perspective, or from the minimum-force-as-necessary perspective? Thus, this section of this chapter will describe how lessons from the employment of negotiation at the strategic level have shaped the military as an institution in terms of its revised rules, norms, and cognitive-cultural identity.

The Operational & Organizational Levels of Analysis

The second set of analysis are the operational and organizational levels. For scholars of military science, the complexity of the military structure and its political requirements necessitates a level of analysis that details how the military develops the implementation processes to align people, money, and other resources to allow the tactical actions to accomplish the strategic goals (Naveh 1997; Olsen and Creveld 2010). In military science theory, this level is called the operational level, and often referred to as operational art. The operational level links the tactical employment of forces to strategic objectives by focusing on the use of military resources to achieve strategic goals through the design, organization, integration, and conduct of strategies, campaigns, major operations, and battles. It is at this level of analysis that the operational constraints on time, manpower, technology, and money become observable for complex organizations like the military. Since the military engages a volatile, uncertain, complex, and ambiguous environment, making decisions on the above is less a science than it is an art.

Despite the lack of description of an operational level of analysis in the negotiation or other social science fields, the lessons learned by military professionals employing negotiations at this level can be assessed at the organizational level of analysis. In particular, we can study the evolution of organizational decision-making processes of military organizations as they adopt new strategies and synchronize the resources necessary to allow tactical actions to implement those strategies.

The Tactical & Individual Levels of Analysis

The last two levels of analysis are the tactical level and the individual level. Current military doctrine defines the tactical level as the employment of units in combat. The individual level of analysis describes the individual decisions, skills, competencies, and behaviors that Army professionals have adopted as a result of their involvement in negotiation activities in the conflict environments they have operated in the last decade-plus. The tactical level of analysis includes how individual leaders have decided the ordered arrangement of their organizations in relation to their adversaries and other friendly organizations, with a view to gaining a tactical advantage. However, as recent peace and post-combat operational histories indicate and this chapter will show, tactical units conduct far more activities than just combat in conflict environments, especially as related to their negotiation activities. Therefore, while this chapter will use the tactical level of analysis to update observations of the functional negotiations of the small unit and the individual military professional in negotiation situations, it will use the individual level of analysis to assess the lessons learned at this level of operations.

Strategic Level Negotiations and Institutional Lessons Learned

In *The Future of the Army Profession*, Snider and colleagues document two types of political negotiations that military professions encounter at the strategic level (Snider 2005). The first is political negotiation in the form of a dialogue between civilian and military leaders, as military leaders offer their professional advice of what they believe is militarily feasible, and as the civilian leaders make the final strategic decisions based on what is politically acceptable. The second form is the negotiations that the military profession engages with other stakeholders that have an impact on the strategic direction of any military policy.

A primary example of the first type of negotiation occurred during the U.S. war with the Saddam regime in Iraq. The top military officer charged with executing that operation, General Tommy Franks, engaged in this very type of negotiation with civilian leaders. In particular, he negotiated with then Secretary of Defense Donald Rumsfeld over the build-up, execution, and post-combat operations to remove the Saddam regime and replace it. As Franks describes it, it was "a long deliberate process" (Franks 2009: 329). What was being deliberated in the planning for the Iraq campaign was not whether the U.S. should do it, but the how of it. This was a back-and-forth process between Commander and Secretary over what was politically expected, what was militarily feasible, and then based on that, what was politically suitable. This discussion revolved around the level of troops the U.S. would use. The military planning called for forces in the 500,000 range, but eventually, the number was reduced down to about 292,000 personnel. According to other accounts of the planning for Iraq, Franks was on the losing side of the negotiations over the troop levels with his civilian overseers, whom he did not trust and who were always pushing him to do more with less (Ricks 2006). Furthermore, in this back-and-forth, senior military planning staff officers knew that Rumsfeld intended to keep the troop numbers low and to make the military "fight for every incremental size increase" (Ricks 2006).

Analysis of the second type of strategic level negotiation draws largely from sociologist Andrew Abbot's (1998) study of the System of Professions. Abbot indicates that the three military professions (maritime, aeronautical, and land) are continuously engaged in fierce bureaucratic competitions with peers, outside agencies, and foreign governments/militaries for control over the situations in which they apply their expertise, i.e. the content of their organizational jurisdiction. This competition manifests itself in ongoing formal negotiations over the effective integration of service capabilities under the combatant and coalition commanders, also known as "roles and missions" debates (Snider 2005).

One particular example of this second type of strategic application of negotiation by military professionals is in the forming and maintaining of military coalitions and alliances. Scott Wolford points out that the negotiation and maintenance of military coalitions and alliances create new theoretical models that combine transactional theory with "coalition formation, crisis bargaining, and alignment of decisions, as well as a unique empirical strategy introducing new levels of analysis" (Wolford 2015: 7). Examples of this come from World War II, which birthed the North Atlantic Treaty Organization, or small-scale contingency operations such as the recent Ebola crisis in Africa. This requirement further drives the need for military professionals to negotiate at a level that helps facilitate such strategic level cooperation—and which the military never previously viewed as part of their professional domain. The recognition of that need led the researchers of *The Future of the Army Profession* to conclude that "As part of this process, or even separate from it, strategic [military] leaders will find that they need to understand the art of negotiation" (Wong and Snider 2005: 616). The central lesson that the U.S. military learned over the last fifteen years of conflict is that these types of military operations *will* require cooperation with other military, government, and non-government organizations.

Institutional Analysis of Change

Given this strategic imperative to negotiate the political and social context that the military operates in, the logical question that follows is: What institutional effect has this had on the military? In observing the evolution of the military as an institution over the last fifteen years, one can see that its rules, in the form of its doctrine; its norms, in the shape of its operating procedures; and its cultural identity, in the form of how its professionals see themselves, have all evolved.

One of the first tangible examples of institutional change that indicate the need for this new skill requirement was the publication of the Army doctrinal manual of counterinsurgency operations, "FM 3-24." According to this doctrinal manual, the fact that the military would find itself in conflict with extremist groups whose worldview would prevent negotiations necessitates finding other groups and organizations "with goals flexible enough to allow productive negotiations to determine how to eliminate the power of extremists without alienating the populace" (CADD 2009: 3-24). Over the years, additional doctrinal manuals were published by the U.S. Army highlighting the significance and impact that negotiation can have in conflict environments toward achieving military goals (CADD 2013: 4; CADD 2013: 3-07), and further, how to conduct negotiations (CADD 2013: 6-22). The institutional evolution that these doctrinal developments display is the change from the prescriptive nature of military doctrine to a more descriptive nature, which provides more latitude to the military professionals as to how to conduct their business.

This descriptive latitude presents itself not only in the Army's doctrine but also in how it operates. The need to overcome the ambiguous and complex situations that military professionals increasingly find themselves in dictates that the decision-making authority move toward the lowest levels, or at least to where the Army as an organization comes into contact with its environment—a concept known in the Army as "Mission Command." This decentralized mode of operation is not typical of an organization that is culturally reliant on hierarchy. However, the conflicts over the last fifteen years have taught Army leaders that one of the central imperatives to success on the modern battlefield is the need for its formations to be learning organizations. Army leaders have recognized that if they maintained a prescriptive top-down hierarchical means of operating, in environments that consist of overwhelming complexity, they would inhibit success. This change in leadership style has had institutional effects on the cultural identity of military professionals themselves.

We can observe this change in cultural identity in the most seasoned leaders and also down to the lowest ranks. For example, Tom Ricks describes this cognitive-cultural identity transformation in some of the most senior leaders who served in Iraq. His main example is General Raymond Odierno, the former top commander in Iraq and later, the 38th Chief of Staff of the Army. In Ricks' first volume on the Iraq adventure, *Fiasco*, he paints a picture of Odierno as conveying a belligerent leadership style that was adopted pervasively throughout his unit in Iraq. When Odierno's unit replaced the Marines in Tikrit, the forceful (and strikingly different) tactics that Odierno's unit employed led to the Marine after-action report indicating a "dichotomy between two different peacekeeping strategies" employed by the Marines versus Odierno's forces (Ricks 2006).

However, in Ricks' follow-up volume *The Gamble*, he paints an entirely different picture of Odierno. When Odierno returned to Iraq as the top commander, he was transformed. The heavy-handedness he employed during his early tour was completely absent. Essentially, his perspective changed from one of looking at conflict from an enemy-centric paradigm to one of looking at it from a holistic perspective (Ricks 2009).

Odierno's transformation was so dramatic that the famed British Pacifist Emma Sky would agree to be his political advisor for conflict resolution in Iraq. Over the course of her tour with the U.S. military in

Iraq under Odierno, Sky's assessment was that the U.S. military, as a whole, became a learning organization. In her evaluation, "the Brits came in with more experience in this sort of operations, but over the years, I think the Americans have learned a lot more" (Ricks 2009: 143). The institutional adaptations of the Army discussed above have filtered to the operational and organizational levels as well.

Operational Level Negotiations and Organizational Lessons Learned

At the operational level, the application of operational art by military professionals requires decisions on how to use the given tools and resources at the tactical level to meet the strategic goals. When the environment calls for less violent measures to achieve mission success, such as in the low-intensity level of conflict found in peace or post-combat operations, operational leaders have the opportunity to make decisions and issue guidance that requires their subordinate leaders to utilize negotiation skills that achieve success. However, the most prominent constraint at this level is the ability to apply resources to match the required course of action. Military organizations, primarily organized for combat operations, have resources and training to conduct one form of conflict management: combat. Operational logistics, subordinate training and equipment are all resourced to focus on that one end. Resourcing for situations that require less violent forms of conflict management is usually an afterthought.

Nonetheless, the operational level is also where a lack of guidance, from both strategic leaders and the norms of the professional practice for how military forces should conduct operations, provides the greatest opportunity for operational leaders to exercise initiative in deciding the best course to accomplish their mission. Initiatives for alternative courses of action have their best chance for success because the operational leader has the knowledge of the strategic goals and controls the tools to develop actions toward achieving them. The operational leader is also in a position to observe the interests of the population and then to determine the local tribal or community leaders' best alternatives to a negotiated agreement, compared to his or her own organization's alternatives. In a new geopolitical multi-polar world, this means that successful negotiations at the operational level will be highly dependent on the operational leaders' ability to exercise initiative in utilizing the given resources in varying and ambiguous operating environments.

A prominent example, in Operation Iraqi Freedom, was then Major General David H. Petraeus, commander of the U.S. Army 101st Airborne Division during the combat and post-combat phases of Operation Iraqi Freedom. Shortly after major combat operations ended, General Petraeus took the initiative to begin post-combat operations to stabilize his area of responsibility, by reorganizing his division into a stabilization force. A New York Times report indicated that one of his first decisions was to have one of his subordinate units begin negotiations with local sheiks and Iraqi customs officials to restore trade with Syria (Gordon 2003). Additionally, General Petraeus supported agreements negotiated by his subordinate leaders, for instance when he wrote a letter—stamped by the division's notary public—decreeing that the funds be provided to pay government workers, and to negotiate with the strategic leaders of the American forces.

To induce support from the local population, and enhance greater security for his troops, he instituted a policy of "cordon and knock," also called "raid and aid" missions, in which Petraeus stressed with his troops the selective use of force as they conducted operations to capture insurgents.[2] Further, Petraeus negotiated with the Coalition Provisional Authority (CPA) to make a temporary exception to its policy of barring professors of a local university from returning to work because they had been registered Ba'athists under Saddam Hussein. Actions such as these gave General Petraeus enough influence with local leaders that he was able to enter into successful negotiations with the various ethnic groups and tribes to form a local governing council, long before the CPA formed any substantive interim government in Baghdad. The report went on to point out that General Petraeus' willingness to go outside the norm of his profession and embrace the approach of so-called nation-building as a central military mission became a major element of success in the northern region of Iraq following the end of combat operations.

The primary skill used in that approach was negotiation. In his negotiation plan, General Petraeus focused on mutual interests, and he invented options for mutual gain when he directed his forces to negotiate the opening of the trade route between Iraq and Syria. By negotiating with the CPA to make the exception for the professors, he separated the people within his area of responsibility from the problem of the policies of the old totalitarian regime, which were the principal source of contention concerning the CPA. Finally, by using objective criteria for evaluation of where and how to apply limited force, he was able to distinguish between possible insurgents and the non-combatant population of Mosul. From this analysis, two lessons can be drawn. The primary lesson learned from this example is that it is the operational level, the level where leaders make the decisions on how to implement the tools and resources of the organization, which offers the best opportunity for the initiative to use other conflict engagement tools. And to seize that initiative, leaders at this level have to be willing to make the mental leap outside of the norms of their professional practice.

Organizational Analysis of Change

To assess the impact of military professionals' decisions to apply negotiation at the operational level, the perspective of organizational decision-making theory, in particular, intra-organizational decision making, is employed. According to James March and Herbert Simon (1993), the best way to analyze organizations and how they operate in their environment is not through how they are structured, but through the way in which they make decisions. The fact the Army's leadership now recognizes that they need to view the environment through a holistic environmental lens, versus an enemy-centric lens, and that the Army has adopted a decentralized, versus hierarchical, form of decision-making, has led to major changes in how the military actually conducts decision-making. With over fifteen years of experience in the recent conflict, the U.S. Army recognized that the conflicts it finds itself in now and in the future are pervasively complex, ill-structured, and volatile. In a word, these conflicts are inherently "wicked", and thus require a different form of decision-making.[3]

This operating environment has led the Army to adopt the application of "Design" from organizational sciences (Simon 1996). Applying design thinking calls for Army planners, regardless of whether they are planning for lethal activities, such as combat, or non-lethal activities, such as negotiations, first to gain an understanding of the environment, and then to identify the problem, before trying to apply military power to solve that problem. In fact, since most of the conflicts now involving the military are not conducive to purely military solutions, one of the biggest lessons learned by the military is that it sometimes has to collaborate with other organizations (e.g. State Department, NGOs, and local government institutions) in the decision-making process. After identifying the problem, the Army Design Methodology calls for the creative art of design to develop a solution.

The key to this step is the inclusive aspect of the creation of the solution, one that accounts for the environmental factors and the actors in that environment. Part of that accounting may entail the inclusion of relevant environmental actors in the decision-making process—a significant departure from the normal ways of operating, for a security-conscious organization.[4]

Tactical Negotiations and Individual Lessons: Every Soldier is Still a Diplomat

The military uses negotiation most at the tactical level, where foot soldiers previously never had the power to negotiate—nor did they have the need to (Goodwin 2004; Tressler 2007). With the advent of the Afghanistan and Iraq campaigns, soldiers at all levels, including tactical level leaders, have found that for the overall military mission to succeed, they need to take part in negotiations in a variety of situations. The constraints at this level are functional, and stem from the organizational culture of military professionals as well as the operating environment. Nonetheless, the Army has begun training its personnel in negotiation at both its professional military education centers and its national training centers.

In 2005, the faculty of the U.S. Military Academy's Department of Social Science observed the need for this training from surveys they sent to tactical level leaders redeploying back from Iraq. The responses to the inquiry indicated that the number one skill required by tactical leaders in the post-combat phase of operations was negotiation skill. The respondents provided an array of examples requiring negotiating skills, such as construction project contracts, property disputes, pay for former Iraqi government officials, the establishment of local Iraqi governing councils, and the surrender of insurgents surrounded by military forces in cordoned parts of urban areas.

The functional constraint indicative of organizational training and design in the military became more apparent in an online follow-up survey, in which 78% of respondents reported conducting some negotiations in scenarios outside of their training as military professionals. Soldiers are trained from their first days in the military to attack, not to comfort "the enemy". They learn a code of professional conduct that espouses a willingness to close with and destroy an enemy through violent combat. This is the warrior ethos inculcated in every U.S. soldier by their basic combat training. Many in the military profession believe this ethos makes soldiers "ill-equipped for non-combat missions and that assigning them to such missions degrades the ethos and compromises soldiers' safety" (Blackstone 2005: 43). Other military professionals acknowledge that to operate in this confusing environment, negotiating skills are in fact critical to providing force protection.[5]

Many of the respondents to the survey cited above commented that one of the hardest aspects of negotiating with the indigenous population was working through interpreters across cultural divides. [NDR: Kaufman, *Interpreters*] Tactical leaders quickly had to become experts in the local cultures, for example understanding the rituals, such as gift giving, and the chronic lack of awareness of time. [NDR: Goh, *Cultural Errors*] More than one respondent stated that learning such cultural customs would have been easier if they had prior training on using interpreters. Tactical leaders had to work through issues of translation and of interpreters' attempts to tone down or shape the translation to what they thought the tactical leader wanted to hear. In one example, a tactical leader stated that the interpreter kept trying to answer the leader's questions for the local population—without even translating the questions over to the local population for their reply.

The survey discussed above demonstrates that military professionals at the tactical level need to learn and adopt the basics of "principled negotiations" and inter-cultural communications. This adds to the findings of other studies of the use of negotiation at the tactical level. One such study is David Tressler's (2007) examination of the military's application of negotiation at the tactical level, which led him to identify three main elements of negotiation conducted by military professionals. The first element is the unique context military professionals find themselves in when needing to conduct negotiations. It is usually multi-party, involving multiple variables, and the hard-to-accurately-identify interests of all parties, because the dynamics of the political, economic, and social settings cause interests to shift in mid-negotiation. Secondly, Tressler found that while culture is important, its practical significance varies greatly depending on the context. He asserts that culture can significantly affect the conduct and outcome of a negotiation—or more surprisingly, culture may have very little effect. Sometimes, according to his interviews, the nature of transactional negotiations and the exchange of services for work transcended cultural boundaries. Tressler's third finding is that a variety of factors unique to military negotiations in post-combat operations shape the element of power, such as stability and reconstruction operations. In particular, Tressler asserts that how military negotiators value the relationships in negotiations and how military negotiators use their negotiating power make a difference in whether military professionals later view their mission as successful.

Individual Level of Analysis

Post-deployment surveys of individual soldiers conducted by the Army University's Combat Studies Institute captured additional insights on how individual soldiers view negotiation at the tactical level (U.S. Army Command and General Staff College 2013). The Operational Leadership Experiences (OLE) project is a collection of interviews that provide first-hand, multi-service accounts from military personnel who planned, participated in and supported operations in Iraq and Afghanistan. From these interviews, several common characteristics of the individual military professional experience with negotiations at the tactical level can be observed. These characteristics include the importance of preparation for negotiation—both negotiation training and pre-negotiation preparation; the impact of culture on negotiations in conflict environments; the role of power; and the power of relationships.

In analyzing the OLE interviews, two main topics arise that discuss negotiation preparation activities by military professionals. The first is training for negotiations, and the second is the individual pre-negotiation preparation.

Individual Training for Negotiations

As Goodwin notes, "Soldiers are professional combatants, not professional negotiators, who are placed in a chaotic and dangerous working environment. Within this environment, they must ply their trade, diverse as it is, with only a brief pre-operational negotiation training, if they are lucky" (Goodwin 2004: 79). While this training has increased over the years, it remains at the basic level, and reserved for the top leadership.

For example, one Army Major indicated the following about his negotiation training before deployment:

> They had some folks come in [referring to contractors from the Titan Corporation who specialized on culture and negotiations] and we had an entire day dedicated to that, but still, one day dedicated to a thousand years of culture? Come on...we had one full day at the post theater where we went over culture and a few other things. But we probably could have had a few more days in there that could have been better served spending time on negotiations and culture rather than some of the individual tasks we had to go through (Mineni 2008).

As such, the training that military professionals received in the early to middle years may not always have prepared them well for the variety of negotiation scenarios they were called upon to handle. The following quote demonstrates some of the complexities that military negotiators dealt with, and which required skills that fell outside of their core competencies:

> I was in a position where I had to negotiate with the Independent Electoral Commission of Iraq (IECI) on national-level stuff for an entire province of 1.3 million people. Let's register 1.3 million voters. How do you go about negotiating to do that? I had no idea (Mineni 2008).

Other interviews from the OLE project indicate that training should focus on more than bilateral negotiation (i.e. between two parties) for short-term or intermediate transactions. Additionally, the training needs to expand from negotiation 1.0 skills (fundamentals of basic distributive and integrative negotiation) to more advanced skills that include managing multi-party cross-cultural negotiations and facilitation or mediation skills as a third party intermediary. As one Major indicated:

> I would recommend that we focus our attention more on negotiations and mediation training. We didn't have a lot of that, and I found myself doing that every day with my Iraqi counterpart. I would say we needed more cultural awareness training, to include language (Crosbie 2007).

Another Major described the current level of negotiation training as good but not sufficient:

> *The best part was the negotiation training. My company and the other troops in the brigade had a pretty good handle on most of the kinetic stuff because we had been practicing that for the last seven years or so. The hard part was the interpersonal aspects that I really didn't have because you just don't focus on that, especially in 2003. I thought that classes such as working with an interpreter, how to conduct negotiations and how to conduct meetings were by far some of the best classes I've ever had, be it academically or militarily* (Gilmore 2007).

Lastly, this training needs to be allocated not only to top leaders but to all members. One Major indicated that a lack of this particular skills training among all personnel was significant:

> *I don't think my soldiers got any [negotiations training] at all. If that's not a shortfall, I can't tell you what is. At a minimum, everyone should have had one hour of that training. Time would have been better spent working on negotiations and understanding culture and relationships, working those kinds of scenarios with the soldiers who were going to be doing that every day out in the field* (Mineni 2008).

The same Major proposed that the solution lay in education:

> *Either the Army needs to build more civil affairs units, train more people, increase the Department of State's capabilities or train more Regular Army combat arms guys to do the job we're being asked to do. I think leader development and the school system is the way to target that by adding more hours of leadership and relationship training as well as negotiation training to the curriculum because we're not going to get it anywhere else. Units aren't going to go out and do negotiation training. They're going to shoot their weapons, drive their vehicles and do land navigation. They're going to do soldier skills and they very well should. However, they can put these curriculum changes into the noncommissioned officer education system (NCOES) and the officer education system (OES) schools. They can give our leaders more leadership training because it's all about leadership. If you understand relationships, you can pretty much work anywhere. They need*

to target leader development, make it a formal pro-
gram and drive on with it (Mineni 2008).

Individual Preparation for Negotiations

Pre-negotiation preparation requirements match what the literature on negotiation training seems to indicate. Per the negotiation literature, it is vital for military negotiators to do their homework to identify the BATNA and ZOPAs and understand the interests and positions of all parties involved in a negotiation. This is where the planning skills inherent in the military culture provide strength to military professionals. By training, military professionals are expert planners, who have multiple tools to gather information to use as they prepare for their future negotiation actions. Some military professionals are well versed in developing a deep analysis of the different environmental variables they may encounter. These variables may include background information on relevant actors from the political, social, economic, military and religious sectors. Also, they have the tools to analyze the local geographical area, structures, capabilities of the population, organizations, individual people, and historical events. The problem, however, is that these skills are specialized, and the soldiers with the skills to do this analysis are generally found at the higher headquarters. They pull an immense amount of information from the frontline soldier to fill in all the blanks on the variables listed above. While the knowledge they create is necessary for high-level decision-making, it does not always flow back down to the units in the field, or if it does, it does not do so promptly enough to be useful in the tactical decisions that soldiers from lower echelons need to make. This deep analysis needs to be used to help prepare the actual front line negotiators.

As part of the pre-negotiation prep, one skill military negotiators exercise as a matter of professional practice from their primary training is in the realm of rehearsals:

> *We did any rehearsals that had to be done regarding*
> *any bilateral negotiations we were going to conduct.*
> *We rehearsed with the interpreters. We rehearsed*
> *what we were going to bring and how long we were*
> *going to stay. We had to decide what tasks we were*
> *going to train the Iraqi Border Police (IBP) on and*
> *what the task, condition, and standard were for those*
> (Maddaloni 2008).

The term of art that military professionals use for such rehearsals is "war-gaming," which is a form of course of action analysis designed to help planners think through the potential what-ifs of any given scenario. It is only a short mental leap for the military professional to apply this type of analysis to negotiation preparations. For example, if the selected strategy calls for an integrative approach to an upcoming negotiation, military planners have learned to play out potential directions that a negotiation may take, to anticipate how to address whatever new problems or opportunities may transpire in the negotiations.

My experience from multiple deployments is that these rehearsals are key to the success of negotiations done by military professionals. Also, they helped when we conducted after-action-reviews of the negotiation event. Keeping good notes on how we thought the negotiation would go, how it actually went, and what we assessed afterward helped us not only to prepare for future negotiations but also to hone our skills as military negotiators through each iteration where we could practice this valuable skill. What we lacked in training, we made up for in experience.

One issue with the way military professionals conduct their analysis, however, is how they view their environment and present their findings. Culturally, military analysts are trained to present their analysis in an enemy-focused fashion. This perspective is not a suitable format when the type of action the leader or individual soldier may find themselves in is a negotiated interaction with actors who may fall into categories other than the "enemy." While the usual analysis military analysts develop can result in findings that produce information relevant to lethal military actions, it may be irrelevant to the non-lethal activities such as negotiations. Nonetheless, with a proper education in advanced negotiation preparation, military professionals are well suited to conduct a robust preparation for negotiation events.

The Impact of Individual Culture on Negotiations in Wartime Environments

The relationship between planning and pre-negotiation preparation is how the military professional understands the impact of culture on their negotiation activities. In these negotiating settings, it is never lost on any party that the military always has the underlying cultural purpose of using coercive force to achieve its goals. This is an inescapable fact, especially when, due to force protection concerns, soldiers are required to show up to a negotiation with body armor, helmets, and weapons. Nonetheless, this tendency needs to be overcome by soldiers, and military professionals should take steps to balance their need for force protection with their need to work with their negotiation partners on an even playing field. This is particularly true in situations where the military member may find themselves acting more like a third party mediator to a conflict than a party to the conflict itself.

I describe this type of example in my previous writing in 2010. In that book chapter, I discuss how two warring tribes in an area of Iraq where my unit was assigned could not even come to the table to begin negotiations, because their culture of handling blood feuds with revenge prevented them from even thinking about engaging with one another (Lira 2010). This was such a serious issue that when a member of one tribe began to hold meetings with members of the other tribe, members of his own tribe assassinated him, to avoid tearing open old wounds that would require further revenge to maintain honor. What I learned from this experience was that I was not there to negotiate a settlement in that particular incident, so much as to provide a way for the two parties to build the capacity to begin negotiating a cessation to their conflict. So persistence was key, in that we had to keep consistently bringing the opposing tribal members back to the table with each other. Additionally, we had to hold a great many side meetings and behind-the-scenes meetings with the tribes separately, to help them become comfortable with moving forward without fear of creating new blood feuds. Eventually, we got to a point where we were able to meet with members of both tribes together in secret, and then finally we were able to get them to come officially to the table together.

The issue of culture and the example above highlight another major lesson from the last fifteen years of conflict: that military professionals must have an acute awareness, based on a thorough understanding of the culture, of the many contextual variables that will or might influence their negotiations. In response to a question about the impact of culture, one officer observed:

> I saw some of the factionalism or sectarian effects be-
> tween the Sunnis and Shi'a, and the Christians as well.
> We had a sizable Christian population. Now,
> pre-conflict, they had all gotten along pretty well.
> Post-conflict, there was an influx of Shi'ites, mostly
> from Iran. So one of the biggest challenges right off the
> bat was that we had not liberated the country to allow
> Shi'ites to come in and do a land grab—but that was
> the rumor, the accusation. Understanding the nuances,
> the differences between Shi'ites and Sunnis and, of
> course, the Christians—and even within the Christians,
> there were four or five different groups. Understand-
> ing was key—and I still don't understand too well—the
> Arab mind as far as God's will and fatalism (O'Brien
> 2005).

Another officer observed:

> Our base defense was comprised of U.S. Soldiers, Afgh-
> an Air Force, and the U.S. contract with the Afghan
> security guards. That was a challenge in itself because
> the Afghan soldiers from the Air Force didn't always
> get along with the security guards. A big part of my job

> *was negotiations and keeping the three pieces working together. There were even difficulties with the U.S. Soldiers working with the Afghans, and I think it's based on perception. They may be perceived as not doing something that would be common or standard in U.S. culture. From the U.S. perspective it might be perceived as a kind of shirking their responsibility but in their culture, they weren't shirking their responsibility they were just doing it a different way. As being the lead person in charge of that area I spent a lot of time negotiating with those three entities and making sure they were cooperating, working together, and sharing information* (Linton 2007).

While the above excerpts support the importance of culture to military negotiations, Tressler's research uncovered that while culture is important, it is a relative factor. As noted above, Tressler (2007: 10-1) argues that "[Culture] can significantly affect the conduct and outcome of a negotiation, or, more surprisingly, have little effect." This is because the influence of culture is dependent on "the relative influence that other elements in the negotiation's context exert on the parties, including the many different cultures (e.g., national, organizational, ethnic, tribal, political, regional, professional) at play in a negotiation" (Tressler 2007: 25). The negotiators' individual personalities and negotiation tactics also have an impact.

Individual Perceptions of Power

The OLE interviews also capture the relationship of power and the power of relationships in the negotiations that the U.S. military experienced. As discussed in the earlier paragraph about balancing force protection requirements with restraint of that power in negotiations, military professionals have to understand and balance the role of power in all negotiations they conduct. Essentially, military professionals have learned that regardless of the strength of their military power via force in the modern conflict situations, their real strength lies in the power of the relationships they develop. They have learned that military power can be fleeting:

> *They know you're coming in with great combat power and that you'll run the Taliban out of the area but they know you're only going to be there for a day or a week, and as soon as you leave, the bad guys are going to come back* (Threatt 2006).

They also learned that the real power brokers might not be the immediate party they are negotiating with:

> *It went more towards who was the local leader, community watch-wise, the school leader, the business leaders, university officials, the hospital administrators—that's really who the power players were. Now there may have been sheiks, and they just didn't come out. They may have been behind the curtain...The "A" types tend to do that anyway, but sometimes they'll put someone up to it as well, so you have to watch out if someone's being a front man for someone else. There were a lot of retired and inactive officers from the Iraqi military who were more than willing to give us advice. They had their own neighborhood watches, their own paramilitary type of thing, to protect the neighborhood. So we tried to get with the leadership of that and talk to them. School principals, teachers, union leaders. We had to conduct labor negotiations, so we sat down with the union leaders there* (O'Brien 2005).

These interview excerpts about power coincide with another interesting finding from Tressler's research. In particular, Tressler observed that the closer a negotiation occurred to combat operations, the greater the military professionals' perception that they had more power in the negotiation. This view was also more likely held by their host nation counterparts. Tressler found evidence that Iraqis also believed the American military had the most negotiating power the closer they were time-wise to the cessation of combat actions. However, he further found that the later the negotiation event occurred from the kinetic operations side of the conflict spectrum, and the closer to the non-lethal stabilization and peacekeeping side of the spectrum, the more the perception of who had the most negotiating power switched also.

In essence, Tressler asserted that the threat of direct military force has less control in constituting the military negotiator's power in a negotiation with a host nation counterpart. In this situation, the power of the military professional is more likely to be constituted by social, political, and economic factors, rather than pure military power through the potential application of lethal force. Counterintuitively to the military professional's practice and training, the most significant factor in influencing the power balance is the importance of relationships, as operations change from lethal combat to non-lethal stability and reconstruction operations (Tressler 2007). An example of this is seen in the following interview excerpt where a soldier even identified that short-term security gains were achievable through relationship development:

If I'm at a FOB (Forward Operating Base) with 450 Iraqis and there are 10 of us, how do we effectively perform the force protection role? Obviously, they're looking at it in a linear way. "I have 10 guys. I don't have an infantry platoon for security. How do I protect myself?" Well, you do this through your building relationships. The rapport you build with your counterpart is your force protection…They're professionals at what you're trying to learn. If you build a strong relationship with your partner unit, you don't have to worry about force protection. They'll protect you (Threatt 2006).

Interview responses in his own research similar to the one above led Tressler to assert further that when a negotiated outcome is not necessary for the military to achieve their immediate goals, failing to reach a negotiated agreement may be acceptable to military professionals, and they are more likely to rely on brute power. However, when the military needs a long-term solution, and they cannot accomplish their goals without their counterpart's cooperation, or because there is more tactical value to building the relationship or good will with their counterpart, the use of a threat of force to assert negotiating power is short-sighted. Using force in the latter situation may lead to a greater likelihood of new disputes, grudges, and motives for revenge. Thus, failing to account for the other side's interests may in fact cause the conflict to spiral negatively out of control and lead to failure to achieve the medium or long term objectives.

Nonetheless, Tressler (2007) found that even though military commanders recognize this fact, interviews with them indicated that they still may not necessarily use integrative negotiating tactics and techniques effectively. This finding demonstrates a gap between the institutional development of negotiation skills, resulting from experiences gained in conflict situations requiring negotiation, and the tactical development of negotiation tools, among the individual personnel, with their inevitable personal views of the use of negotiations. It leaves open to further research questions about the efficacy of institutionalizing the type of military culture necessary to conduct the integrative negotiations necessary in today's conflicts.

It may be, as Tressler (2007) asserts, unrealistic to think that military professionals can rely solely on negotiations using an exclusively interest-based approach. Nonetheless, this chapter maintains its assertion that only by fully institutionalizing interest-based negotiations into the military culture, to the point where military professionals feel comfortable with using such tools, will the military become effective at achieving the political and military goals their civilian leaders want. This institutionalization requires military professionals to view power as more than just military power. Perhaps, as a step toward this eventual institutionalization process, military professionals may, as Tressler (200-7) predicts, combine the exercise of persuasive power and military might, with a genuine attempt to meet their host nation counterpart's interests through using relationship building as a tactic at the individual level.

It is important to note that the military, in this respect, is far from the only profession to operate in the "negotiation-constrained" environment in which recent thinking has raised the status and visibility of negotiation. In the 2006 predecessor to this chapter, I highlighted the example of the Catholic Church and its move toward peacemaking (Lira 2006; Appleby 2003). However, given the contemporary examples of a breakdown in community relations with police, another related field in which to study the potential applications of lessons learned by military professionals is the police profession, specifically, as negotiations relate to community policing. (See, for instance, Parish and Cambria 2018.)

The recent trend in the evolution of the police appears to be more toward a militarization of its force (Balko 2014). This institutional change creates complications in police departments' current operating environment and may cause them to adopt more of the integrative negotiation lessons learned by the military from their stability operations, versus the military experience from occupation operations.[6]

While at one point, community policing efforts in America appeared to be the growing wave of the future of policing (Fridell and Wycoff 2004), the recent incidents in the media demonstrate that even once poster examples of community policing (e.g. Chicago, Houston, and New York) are not living up to their past standards (Kappeler and Gaines 2015). While much of the problem may lie in the institutional culture of the police (Epp, Maynard-Moody and Haider-Markel 2014), the fix may also be institutional. Imagine that if institutional racism can be systemic, how institutionalizing negotiation and conflict resolution in police departments and communities across America could help turn the tide back toward more stable communities. If the military could learn lessons from community policing to apply to its peacekeeping operations (Grabosky 2009), is it not possible that the police can, in turn, capitalize on the experience gained by the military over the last fifteen years to improve their community policing operations? As departments across the nation hire more and more military veterans, only time will tell if those veteran hires contribute to their police departments becoming more focused on the use of force, or more focused on the use of persuasion.

Conclusion

This chapter illustrates how military professionals, like other professionals, utilize conflict management skills. In particular, they use negotiation skills to accomplish the goals of their mission. This is in part due to the changing ethics of the battlefield, where the military ethos of utilizing belligerent violence is no longer conducive to accomplishing the overall political goals of society. The practicalities of the post-combat phases, now indicative of all military operations conducted by armies from liberal democratic societies, will continue to necessitate the use of negotiation skills.

Military professionals will continue using negotiation skills at the strategic, operational, and tactical levels of their operating environments. The use of these "new" skills will impact the military institutionally, organizationally, and in its individual members. As demonstrated earlier in this chapter, at the strategic level, military professionals use negotiations in two settings where the constraints are political and institutional. In the first setting, they use negotiations in the civil-military relationship with the client society, to negotiate for control over how the military should implement those functions within that jurisdiction. In the second setting, they use negotiations in bureaucratic competition, to maintain operational control over the content of their organizational jurisdiction, i.e. what it is that military professionals can do that other professions may not do.

The impact of learning how to negotiate has led to an evolution of doctrine, as the institutional rules of the military catch up with the practice. It has resulted in a change in the normative hierarchical structure that prescribes from on high how soldiers should operate, toward a more decentralized and descriptive norm that allows for the practitioner closest to the conflict, and with the most situational understanding, to make decisions that will lead to the accomplishment of the strategic goals. Lastly, the need to rely on negotiation skills over the last fifteen years has impacted the cultural-cognitive identity of the military, evidenced by the acceptance of norms of behavior in its senior leaders that were once viewed as the antithesis of the military ethos.

At the operational level, military professionals also use negotiations to accomplish their mission. The constraints at this level are resource-based. Military professionals may allocate resources for one purpose, such as the combat role, but the conditions of the operating environment may require the operational leader to exercise initiative in re-allocating those resources. For instance, operational level leaders may utilize military troops in negotiation settings and/or police-type operations. From an organizational analysis perspective, this change in operational procedures is exemplified in the adoption of new decision-making processes. These processes include design thinking and design methodology, which allow the military to scan their environment for relevant factors that were once overlooked. In turn this enables the military to identify the problem before immediately jumping to a military solution, and then, to develop a solution inclusively, almost democratically, with relevant agents from other governments, non-government organizations, and local populations. In sharing the power to decide, the status and role of lower echelon soldiers at the tactical level has changed, and their perceptions of the use of negotiation and the role of culture, power, and relationships have changed as well.

This re-allocation of the role of the soldier has increased the need for new training in negotiation skills at the tactical level. At this level, obstacles inherent to negotiating within both organizational and cultural environments present functional constraints that tactical leaders must overcome. To compensate, military negotiators have learned what works and what does not in negotiation training for the environments in which they operate. They have also learned how to rely on their planning skills to prepare for the complex negotiations in which they engage. Lastly, they have learned that culture plays a major role in the perception of power, and have also learned how power shapes the relationships necessary to be successful in negotiations on the modern battlefield.

Practitioners of every profession can draw analogies from the examples of military professionals using negotiation skills described in this chapter. This chapter has suggested that an isomorphic opportunity exists for police professionals to learn from the military in the next era of community policing, just as the military learned from the police as they entered the conflicts of the 21st century. A recent commencement speech from Lieutenant General Ricardo Sanchez to the graduates of Texas A&M University captures this point:

> *Every profession has its battlefields—the courtroom, the classroom, the boardroom.... You will immediately find yourself in your chosen profession's battlefield facing challenges that parallel what I faced as a professional warrior—leading units and [individuals] under very tough conditions to accomplish missions critical to the survival of [your] institution under austere, expeditionary, and uncertain conditions* (Dillon 2005).

Those professions that can skillfully apply the negotiation skill set at every level of their operations will do well in their battlefields, no matter what level of conflict happens to transpire before them. Our ability to study that application of negotiation institutionally, organizationally, and at the individual level will contribute to furthering the effectiveness of the professions that use this skill in their daily conflicts.

Notes

[1] For a complete breakdown of size, strength and leadership rank at the strategic, operational and tactical level, see U.S. ARMY ORGANIZATION, at http://www.army.mil/organization.

[2] When the units from the division mounted a raid, soldiers did not just burst in. They surrounded the house and then went to the door, knocked, and negotiated entry or the surrender of suspected insurgents. Soldiers would then return the next day with funds and humanitarian assistance to repair any damage and to improve the neighborhood.

"These operations disrupted the enemy, engendered support among the population, and frequently led to additional intelligence" (Meese and Morgan 2005: 354).
[3] For discussions of "wicked problems" in negotiation, see chapters 24-27 in Honeyman, Coben and De Palo 2010 and chapters 17-21 in Honeyman, Coben and Lee 2013. [See also NDR: Coleman et al., *Intractable 1 and 2* and NDR: Coleman & Ricigliano, *Getting in Sync*], which describe the same phenomena though under a different name.
[4] For a more in-depth description of the Design methodology used in Army decision-making processes, see Ryan and Banach (2009), and see Perez (2011) for a general description of the Army's use of Design. For an in-depth description of design used in negotiation and planning, see Lira's Chapter 27 in Honeyman, Coben and De Palo 2010.)
[5] Quote from a returning U.S. commander from Iraq in an address to the faculty members of the Department of Social Sciences and cadets of USMA, March 30th 2005 and General Anthony Zinni, USMC (Ret.) (Allard 1995: 71).
[6] See Grabosky (2009) for an example of how police operations influence military operations. It would be interesting to observe if the relationship could be inverted.

References

Allard, K. 1995. *Somalia Operations: Lessons Learned*. National Washington, D.C.: Defense University Press.

Appleby, R. S. 2003. Catholic Peacebuilding. *America: The Catholic Weekly Magazine*. September 8. http://www.americamagazine.org/gettext.cfm?articletypeid=1&textID=3145&issueID=449&search=1.

Balko, R. 2014. *Rise of the Warrior Cop: The Militarization of America's Police Forces*. Public Affairs.

Banach, S. J. and A. Ryan. 2009. The Art of Design: A Design Methodology. *Military Review* March-April.

Blackstone, R. 2005. Somalia: Soldiers in SOSO. *Military Review* 85(2): 39.

Brooks, M. G. Ed. 2010. Interview with Major Stephen Boesen: Operational Leaders Experience Project. In *Eyewitness to War, Volume III: U.S. Army Advisors in Afghanistan*. Fort Leavenworth, KS: Combat Studies Institute Press. http://usacac.army.mil/cac2/cgsc/carl/download/csipubs/EyewitnessToWar_VolumeIII_Brooks.pdf.

Combined Arms Doctrine Directorate (CADD), United States Army Combined Arms Center. 2009. 2: Counterinsurgency. *In Field Manual 3-24*. U.S. Department of the Army.

Combined Arms Doctrine Directorate (CADD), United States Army Combined Arms Center. 2013. *Army Doctrine Publication 1: The Army*. U.S. Department of the Army.

Combined Arms Doctrine Directorate (CADD), United States Army Combined Arms Center. 2009. Army Doctrine Publication 3-07: Stability Operations. U.S. Department of the Army.

Combined Arms Doctrine Directorate (CADD), United States Army Combined Arms Center. 2013. *Army Doctrine Publication 4: Sustainment*. U.S. Department of the Army.

Combined Arms Doctrine Directorate (CADD), United States Army Combined Arms Center. 2013. *Army Doctrine Publication 6-22: Army Leadership*. U.S. Department of the Army.

Crosbie, C. 2007. *Operational Leadership Experiences*. http://cgsc.contentdm.oclc.org/cdm/singleitem/collection/p4013coll13/id/855/rec/8.

Department of Defense. 1997. Doctrine for Joint Operations. In *Joint Task Force Commander's Handbook for Peace Operations*. Washington D.C.: GPO.

Dillon, S. 2005. War on Terrorism Dominates Talks Given at Graduations. *New York Times*. June 12, Section 1, 38.

Epp, C. R., S. Maynard-Moody and D. P. Haider-Markel. 2014. *Pulled Over: How Police Stops Define Race and Citizenship*. University of Chicago Press.

Franks, T. R. 2009. *American Soldier*. Harper Collins.

Fridell, L. and M. A. Wycoff. 2004. Community Policing: The Past, Present, and Future. Washington, D.C.: Police Executive Research Forum, The Anne E. Casey Foundation.

Gilmore, C. 2007. *Part I. Operational Leadership Experiences.* http://cgsc.contentdm.oclc.org/cdm/singleitem/collection/p4013coll13/id/802/rec/9

Goodwin, D. 2004. *The Military and Negotiation: The Role of the Soldier-Diplomat.* London: Routledge.

Gordon, M. 2003. The Struggle for Iraq: 101st Airborne Scores Success in Northern Iraq. *New York Times.* September 4, A1.

Grabosky, P. N. 2009. *Community Policing and Peacekeeping.* CRC Press.

Heidecker, S. P. and J. Sowards. 2004. *Army Magazine* 54(7): 50.

Honeyman, C., J. Coben and G. De Palo. Eds. 2010. *Venturing Beyond the Classroom.* St. Paul: DRI Press.

Honeyman, C., J. Coben and A. W-M. Lee. Eds. 2013. *Educating Negotiators for a Connected World.* St. Paul: DRI Press.

Kappeler, V. E and L. K. Gaines. 2015. *Community Policing: A Contemporary Perspective.* Routledge.

Krulak, C. C. 1999. The Strategic Corporal: Leadership in the Three Block War. *The Marine Corps Gazette,* 83(1). http://www.au.af.mil/au/awc/awcgate/usmc/strateg ic_corporal.htm.

Lewicki, R., D. Saunders and B. Barry. 2005. *Negotiation.* McGraw-Hill Education.

Linton, S. 2007. *Operational Leadership Experiences.* http://cgsc.contentdm.oclc.org/cdm/singleitem/collection/p4013coll13/id/823/rec/1.

Lira, L. 2006. The Military Learns to Negotiate. In *The Negotiator's Fieldbook: The Desk Reference for the Experienced Negotiator,* edited by A. K. Schneider and C. Honeyman. Washington D.C.: American Bar Association.

Lira, L. 2010. Design: The U.S. Army's Approach to Negotiating Wicked Problems. In *Venturing Beyond the Classroom: Volume 2 in the Rethinking Negotiation Teaching Series,* edited by C. Honeyman, J. Coben and G. De Palo. Saint Paul: DRI Press.

Maddaloni, J-P. 2008. *Operational Leadership Experiences.* http://cgsc.contentdm.oclc.org/cdm/singleitem/collection/p4013coll13/id/1155/rec/50.

March, J. G. and H. A. Simon. 1993. *Organizations.* Cambridge, MA: Blackwell.

Meese, M. J. and S. M. Morgan. 2005. New Requirements for Army Expert Knowledge: Afghanistan and Iraq. In *Future of the Army Profession,* 2nd edn. edited by D. M. Snider and L. Matthews. McGraw-Hill.

Mineni, M. 2008. *Operational Leadership Experiences.* http://cgsc.contentdm.oclc.org/cdm/singleitem/collection/p4013coll13/id/1397/rec/44.

Naveh, S. 1997. *In Pursuit of Military Excellence: The Evolution of Operational Theory,* 1st edn. Routledge.

O'Brien. 2005. *Operational Leadership Experiences.* http://cgsc.contentdm.oclc.org/cdm/singleitem/collection/p4013coll13/id/90/rec/18.

Olsen, J. A. and M. Creveld. Eds. 2010. *The Evolution of Operational Art: From Napoleon to the Present,* 1st edn. Oxford University Press, USA.

Olsen, H. and J. Davis. 1999. Training U.S. Army Officers Peace Operations: Lessons from Bosnia. *United States Institute of Peace (USIP) Special Report 56.*

Parish, R. and J. J. Cambria. 2018 (in press). *The Other Side of the Door: Arts in the Future of Policing.* St. Paul: DRI Press

Perez, C. 2011. A Practical Guide to Design: A Way to Think About It, and a Way to Do It. *Military Review* 91(2): 41.

Pew Research Center. 2004. Iraq Prison Scandal Hits Home, But Most Reject Pullout. http://www.pewtrusts.com/pdf/pew_research_iraq_prison_051204.pdf.

Pfaff, T. 2005. Military Ethics in Complex Contingencies. In *Future of the Army Profession,* 2nd edn. edited by D. M. Snider and L. Matthews. McGraw-Hill.

Ricks, T. E. 2006. *Fiasco: The American Military Adventure in Iraq*, 2003 to 2005. New York: Penguin, 2006.

Ricks, T. E. 2009. *The Gamble: General David Patraeus and the American Military Adventure in Iraq*, 2006-2008. New York: Penguin.

Scott, W. R. 2008. *Institutions and Organizations: Ideas and Interests*, 3rd edn. Sage Publications, Inc.

Simon, H. A. 1996. *The Science of the Artificial*. Cambridge, MA: MIT Press.

Snider, D. 2005. The U.S. Army as Profession. In *Future of the Army Profession*, 2nd edn. edited by D. M. Snider and L. Matthews. McGraw-Hill.

Treatt, M. 2006. *Part I. Operational Leadership Experiences*. http://cgsc.contentdm.oclc.org/cdm/singleitem/collection/p4013coll13/id/283/rec/1.

Tressler, D. M. 2007. *Negotiation in the New Strategic Environment: Lessons from Iraq*. Carlisle, PA: Strategic Studies Institute, U.S. Army War College.

U.S. Army Command and General Staff College. 2013. *Operational Leadership Experiences Database*. Available at http://cgsc.contentdm.oclc.org/cdm/landingpage/collection/p4013coll13

Wolford, S. 2015. *The Politics of Military Coalitions*. Cambridge University Press.

Wong, L. and D. Snider. 2005. Strategic Leadership of the Army Profession. In *Future of the Army Profession*, 2nd edn. edited by D. M. Snider and L. Matthews. McGraw-Hill.

❦ 75 ❧

Martial Arts and Conflict Resolution

Joel Lee and James Shanahan

Editors' Note: Is there a relationship between skill in negotiation and skill in martial arts? Counterintuitive as this may be, the authors answer—yes there is. Starting from opposite sides of the planet and very different occupations (law teaching in Singapore, and police work in New York City), the authors have two things in common: they teach negotiation, and they teach martial arts. Here, they compare and contrast the worlds in which they must operate, and show how martial arts training has benefited both of them—and their negotiation students.

Introduction

At first blush, readers may be forgiven for thinking that the title of this chapter is an oxymoron. After all, a diet of Hollywood action and Chinese Kung Fu movies certainly gives one the impression that martial arts is all about "kicking ass" and other violent activities. On the other hand, conflict resolution conjures up images of mediators and other types of peacemakers helping others resolve their differences while New Age music plays and bells chime in the background.

As they say, truth is often stranger than fiction. In this chapter, the authors will draw upon their extensive experience in the martial arts, and show how there are uncanny parallels between martial arts and conflict resolution. The authors believe that these parallels can provide

Joel Lee has been training in the martial arts for 30 years and is the Chief Instructor of the Singapore Wing Tsun Training Centre. Apart from being an exponent of Wing Tsun (詠春), he has also experience in Jeet Kune Do, Kali and Aikido. By day, his secret identity is mildmannered Associate Professor at the Faculty of Law, National University of Singapore, where he teaches conflict resolution and furthers the development of mediation in Singapore. Joel has received the National University of Singapore's highest teaching award and an Honorable Mention by the International Institute for Conflict Prevention and Resolution.
James T. Shanahan is a Detective with the Special Investigations Division of the New York Police Department, an active member of the Hostage Negotiation Team, and the Senior Instructor of the Crisis Intervention Team. He has taught on the adjunct faculty of John Jay College of Criminal Justice, CUNY, is a lifelong practitioner of traditional Japanese martial arts, and is an experienced stage, screen and television actor.

learnings and insights that will inform the learning, training and practice of conflict resolution. Admittedly, this is a relatively undeveloped area of inquiry as yet—but our assessment is not unprecedented. In fact, for most of its 40-year history, the Hostage Negotiation Team of the New York Police Department has looked at training and experience in the martial arts as one indicator of potential in a new candidate for appointment to the team. [NDR: Volpe et al., *The Unknown*]

These learnings and insights can be categorized into:

- Definition and Philosophy
- Maintaining Balance
- Training and Development
- Congruence
- De-escalation
- Redirection and Utilization

Martial Arts: Definition and Philosophy

As with many origin myths lost in the mists of history, there is some ambiguity as to the origin of the martial arts. There is a saying which goes "All martial arts originate from Shaolin". This is a reference to the Shaolin Temple in China, known not just for being the seat of Buddhism but also for its warrior monks. There is also a view that the monks at the Shaolin Temple were taught both Buddhism and the martial arts by Bodhidharma[1], who traveled from India to China to spread the teachings of Buddha. Bodhidharma saw that the monks were weak from meditating full-time, and taught them physical movements to strengthen their bodies. These physical movements would evolve to be kung fu or martial arts.

Whichever of these two versions (or some other) of the origin myth one accepts, there is no dispute that there is a significant Chinese input and influence into the field of martial arts.

But what specifically is Kung Fu or Martial Arts? Kung Fu, or more accurately 功夫 (gong [1] fu [2])[2] literally means "skill attained through work". So while the term 功夫 (gongfu) is commonly associated with martial arts, one could have 功夫 (gongfu) in painting, or tea making, or building a house—or resolving conflicts. In this sense, everyone who is an expert in anything is a 功夫 (gongfu) master. Hence, one who is an excellent practitioner of conflict resolution is also a master of 功夫 (gongfu), in its original sense.

The Chinese term for martial arts is 武术 (wu [3] shu [4]). This is literal. 武术 (wushu) literally means martial arts. What is of more interest is the etymology of the word 武 (wu) or martial. Chinese words are ideographic. This means that different ideograms can be combined to make other words. The word 武 (wu) is made up of two ideograms, 戈 (ge [2]) and 止 (zhi [3]). The character 戈 (ge) means spear. The character (zhi) means, in some contexts, "to stop". Therefore, one way to interpret the Chinese character 武 (wu) is for it to mean "to stop a weapon" or "to stop violence" (Wiktionary 2016). Seen this way, 武术 (wushu) or martial arts can be said to be similar to conflict resolution. And in fact this sense of the phrase is embedded in the ethics of martial arts. Contrary to conventional belief, martial arts do not promote the creation or furtherance of violence. Instead, they seek to bring an end to violence or conflict.

Finally, while some readers may already be familiar with the various martial arts that exist, it is useful to provide a framework that allows the lay person to understand how the various martial arts are categorized. One common categorization used is the distinction between arts which specialize in kicks or in using the hands as striking instruments, vs. grappling or trapping. While we will be making reference from time to time to specific arts, this paper will draw more upon the conceptual and philosophical underpinnings of various martial arts. To this end, it is helpful to think of all martial arts as falling on a quite different continuum, between the hard and soft martial arts.

Hard martial arts generally use force to deal with force. For example, two hard martial artists may throw blows at one another, each hoping to overwhelm the other by pure force. A variation on this might be a hard martial artist using force to block his opponent's attack before launching an attack of his own. Examples of hard martial arts would be some families of Karate and the Chinese art of Tiger Fist.[3]

Soft martial arts generally utilize movement and relaxation to dissolve and redirect an incoming attack. The opponents' own force is then used against them. Implicit in this idea is that the destruction of the opponent is not the desired outcome. Instead, harmonizing and flowing with their force and energy is the ideal. The idea of redirection and utilization also means that there is a karmic effect, in that an opponent using a great deal of force will have that force returned to him or her. Examples of martial arts that operate on this basis would be Tai Chi[4], Aikido or Jiu Jitsu.

Translating this to conflict resolution, the hard martial arts can be likened to positional negotiators who are intent on competing. Unsophisticated positional negotiators may end up in a shouting or table-thumping match. More sophisticated ones may utilize various gambits and strategies such as deception and anchoring to "get a hit in."

On the other hand, soft martial arts can be likened to the interests-based model of negotiation, where the true intention is to see how apparently irreconcilable positions of the parties can nonetheless be harmonized at the level of interests. Competition is not the order of the day. Instead, a collaborative relationship is sought. This correlation between soft martial arts and collaborative conflict resolution is not new. Thomas Crum (1987), for example, has long advocated Aikido as a model for conflict resolution.

Maintaining Balance

Many novices begin their study of martial arts with the objective of "winning" against their opponent. The world is seen as an unfriendly place and everyone is a potential opponent. That opponent is the enemy and "winning" can consist of causing damage to, throwing or securing one's opponent. The means to do so is to learn as many techniques as possible to achieve that end. This worldview also dictates the behaviors we manifest as we interact with the world.

This worldview is affected by a trinity of internal factors: how we feel about ourselves, how we see the world and how we feel about the world. Douglas Stone, Bruce Patton and Sheila Heen (1999) refer to these as the identity, perception and feelings conversations. These internal factors are best illustrated by an example.

Let's assume that Billy is a young man who is insecure and lacks confidence about himself (how he feels about himself). Therefore, he goes out into the world to seek external validation, to prove himself and enhance his self-image. Even if he does not initially set out with aggressive intentions, because he sees the world as an unfriendly place he interprets the behavior of others towards him as offensive or aggressive, regardless of whether the other person intends it. Of course, in Billy's worldview, it really does not matter whether the other person intends it. All that matters is that he perceives it as such (how we see the world). Given Billy's insecurities, he is likely to feel fear or anger[5] (how we feel about the world). But because he also feels the need to prove something (whether to others or himself), he will not walk away or de-escalate the interaction. Instead, he is likely to meet that perceived behavior with aggressive behavior of his own—which may in turn cause an escalation on the part of the other person. This can go very quickly from verbal aggression to physical. And as the saying goes, "That's how the fight started".

With some imagination, one can very easily translate this from the martial arts context to that of conflict resolution. In the competitive model of negotiation, the counterpart is referred to as "the opponent" and "winning" is by definition win-lose. One's ability is therefore measured by how many tactics we can bring to bear to persuade, force or trick the other party into agreement while at the same time seeking to avoid that same fate. Our identity issues (how we feel about ourselves) fix our mindset, creating the perceptual filters through we which we perceive (how we see) the world; and our emotions (how we feel about the world) dictate the actions we take. These actions, in a competitive context, will often lead to escalation.

Implicit in both these scenarios is the confirmation bias and the self-fulfilling prophecy. The former refers to our filters deleting, distorting and generalizing behaviors to align with our predetermined views and beliefs about the world. The latter refers to our behaving in a way (consistent with our views and beliefs) that brings about similar behaviors in others, even if they may not have behaved that way initially. And when they behave in a way that we expect them to (and ironically, possibly caused), it feeds back into the confirmation bias by validating our views were "correct" in the first place. Thereby it justifies our escalation of the interaction.

It is clear from this that the most challenging obstacles to overcome are not external ones but internal ones. Martial arts, and we would argue, conflict resolution too, are not (primarily) about mastering others. They are about mastering oneself. Hence, in martial arts, we speak of personal cultivation and self-mastery as things to aspire to.[6]

What then is the way to self-mastery? To be clear, there are already a number of different tools and frameworks that allow us to deal with the trinity of internal factors. For perception, there are the ladder of inference[7] and the Meta Model.[8] For emotions, there are simple acknowledgement, reframing and emotional de-escalation. For identity issues, there are negotiating congruity[9] and the identity complexification process.[10] And this list is by no means exhaustive. It is intended to give the reader some illustrations of tools and frameworks to deal with the trinity of internal factors.

Since these tools and frameworks exist, why do we not simply apply them and live happily ever after? The reality is that, despite our best intentions, when under stress, our biology runs away with us. There is a part of our brain, the amygdala, which when triggered by a perceived threat hijacks the rational brain. It is the amygdala that puts us into the survival responses of fight, flight or freeze (Goleman 1997). [See NDR: Jendresen, *Creativity* and NDR: O'Shea, *Compassion*] When in this state, our responses to external events are often disproportionate, and expecting anyone in this state to be able to use the cognitive tools and frameworks listed earlier is unrealistic.

This is where insights and lessons from martial arts can be helpful. The notion of amygdala hijack is not new to martial arts. It explains why many practitioners of martial arts are not able to execute their training when faced with assailants. In essence, the amygdala hijack causes them to lose their balance, first mental and consequently physical.

How does one maintain and regain this balance? There are three components to doing this: breath, peripheral vision and physical stability. Let us consider each of these in turn.

It is a truism that in times of stress, we hold our breath. What air we have is usually situated in our upper lungs[11] (thereby raising our mental center of gravity) and our sympathetic nervous system[12] is activated as our body prepares to fight, flee or freeze. This stoppage of breathing is easiest to deal with by simply going back to breathing—but in a very specific way. Rapid breaths in the upper part of the chest will lead to hyperventilation and exacerbate the problem. The breath that helps us regain our balance is diaphragmatic or belly breathing. This means breathing using as much of the lungs as possible, by taking a slow, steady and deep breath and sinking that breath to a point just below your navel. This lowers your mental center of gravity and grounds you. Diaphragmatic breathing will be familiar to those who sing or do 气功 (chi [4] gong [1]) or Yoga. What's significant here is that diaphragmatic breathing will invoke what Dr. Herbert Benson (2000) refers to as the relaxation response.

The second component is activating peripheral vision.[13] The human eye is geared towards two types of vision. The first, foveal vision, is a function of the cone cells. This is central vision, which gives you clarity, accuracy and detail of vision. The second, peripheral vision, is a function of rod cells. Peripheral vision detects context and movement. When we are stressed, we tend to concentrate on foveal vision. Going into peripheral vision activates the parasympathetic nervous system which, among other things, lowers blood pressure and relieves stress. Peripheral vision can be activated by first fixing one's attention (foveal vision) on a distant point (though in the context of a stressful event, one is likely to be in foveal vision already), then paying attention to movement in the environment—without moving the eyes. It takes some practice, and can be assisted by having a friend stand to the side and make hand movements.

The final component is physical stability. It is well known that how we physically hold our bodies affects how we feel.[14] If we are physically not stable, this can affect our mental center of gravity.[15] Therefore sitting and standing with both feet firmly on the floor, about shoulder width apart, can help you regain your physical stability, and can contribute to being internally centered.[16]

Done correctly, these components activate one's parasympathetic nervous system (Dilts, DeLozier and Dilts 2010: 193; Wikipedia 2016d). This correlates with the brain entering into an "alpha" state. This internal state is referred to by some as being in the state of mindfulness, which is in turn characterized as being "in the moment", paying attention to the present (both internally and externally), a subjective slowing down of perceptual time, and a sense of calm. Put simply, it allows one to be the eye of the hurricane; to be calm even though there may be a maelstrom around you. William Ury (1991, 2015) refers to this as "going to the balcony". And with this calm, we can respond to what is actually happening, as opposed to what we anticipate, perceive or create in our minds. This then provides us with the ability to select and engage in the tools and frameworks mentioned earlier.

As we close this section, it is important to remember that maintaining and regaining balance is a type of 功夫 (gongfu). It is skill attained through work. One needs to practice it in non-stress situations until it can be automatically manifested in situations of stress.[17]

Training and Development

There are a number of insights that martial arts has for conflict resolution in terms of training and development. In the martial arts, training and development must be more than intellectual, cognitive knowledge. Mastery is measured in the ability to skillfully *execute* what one learns in the appropriate situation. This does not happen overnight. It requires diligent and dedicated practice.

One of the insights martial arts has to share is trusting in the *process* of training. As the adage goes, one has to learn to walk before one can learn to run. However, in many cases, the novice wants to fly from the get-go. Learning skill sets of any kind involves learning one piece at a time, then practicing that piece until it becomes part of one's unconscious competence. That piece is then integrated with other pieces until it becomes part of a systemic whole.

While learning these individual pieces, novices often suffer from the "What If" demon. "What if they throw a hook?" or "What if they are wrestlers?" etc. The reality is that once they learn, master and integrate the correct pieces, they will be able to handle these scenarios. But they must first trust in the *process* of learning and mastery. [Note the similarity to Moty Cristal's conclusions in situations where developing trust is impossible NDR: Cristal, *No Trust*]

The same is true of conflict resolution training, perhaps even more so. Most trainees are deludedly satisfied with having intellectual and cognitive knowledge of the skills without the practice, mastery and integration. The problem is of course systemic. Without the practice, mastery and integration, one cannot hope to manifest the correct skills at the appropriate time. Instead, in times of stress, we tend to revert to our amygdalic responses of fight, flight or freeze. Trainees of conflict resolution also suffer from the "What If" demon. "What if they refuse to share their interests?" or "What if they have more power?" or "What if they get aggressive?" Trainees need to learn to trust in the process, and practice the equivalent of walking or even crawling before seeking to run.

An example is in the long-worked-out team practice of the NYPD Hostage Negotiation Team: when, as is usual, there are several trained negotiators at the scene of a "job" (as the team calls incidents), the work is subdivided, and the junior negotiator is *never* the one assigned to speak with the hostage-taker. What's more, the senior negotiator isn't either—because long experience has taught the team that the most dangerous person around is not the hostage taker (who is, at least, physically contained before the negotiation really begins) but the area police commander, who typically lacks negotiation training but outranks anyone on the team, and may do something that throws the whole case into a tailspin. So the *senior* negotiator needs to be reserved for negotiation with that police commander. [NDR: Volpe et al., *The Unknown*]

The second insight from training is to *use* and *work* what you have been trained in, rather than seeking to be a jack of all trades. This is a current and common issue today for the martial arts world. Students will begin training but few will stay long enough to master the art. Many will doubt their art, either because of impatience, or their expectations of what the art should be, or comparing what they consider to be the deficits of their art as opposed to the benefits of other arts. This will make a bit more sense with a concrete example.

One of the authors practices 詠春 (yong [3] chun [1]). It is a southern Chinese martial art specializing in close range attacks, speed, sensitivity and using softness to overcome a larger and stronger opponent. Many students, influenced by the popularity of Mixed Martial Arts or Brazilian Jiu-Jitsu, often ask "What happens if you meet an MMA/BJJ fighter and the fight goes to the ground?" Their assumption is that since 詠春 (yongchun) does not have grappling techniques, it is somehow inferior to arts which do. This betrays a non-understanding of the martial adage that there is no ultimate martial art and any art is only as good as the practitioner. It is true that 詠春 (yongchun) does not have grappling techniques, and for good reason. The assumption in 詠春 (yongchun) is that our opponent will be larger and stronger.

Since size and weight makes a difference while on the ground, it makes no sense for a 詠春 (yongchun) practitioner to go to the ground and grapple. This is not to say, however, that 詠春 (yongchun) does not have techniques to deal with a MMA/BJJ exponent, and to avoid being taken to the ground. Stated another way, any good art should have methods to deal with *all* martial scenarios, although across the arts the method to deal with any particular scenario will differ. More pithily put, one should play to the strengths of one's art. It would therefore be nonsense to say that someone who has trained in 詠春 (yongchun) for 20 years should switch to Tae Kwon Do when meeting with a Tae Kwon Do exponent (who has been training in Tae Kwon Do for 20 years). It is obvious that at Tae Kwon Do, the 詠春 (yongchun) practitioner will be outclassed and at a disadvantage.

Translating this to conflict resolution, it is equally strange for someone who is trained in the collaborative model of dispute resolution to somehow shift to a competitive style when dealing with someone who has been trained in that style. The collaborator would be outclassed when playing the competitor's game. It makes far more sense to execute the skills one has been trained in and, hopefully, mastered. The match will at least be fair and determined by skill. For example, when faced with a position presented by a competitive negotiator, instead of playing the positional game, a collaborative negotiator can choose to "take the negotiation into the circle" by reframing that position as an interest or option or a measure of legitimacy. By refusing to react to the competitive negotiator's techniques and by proactively engaging that negotiator in a discussion of interests, options and legitimacy, the collaborative negotiator is executing the skills s/he has been trained in. [NDR: Pappas, *Strategic Listening* and NDR: Abramson, *Styles* both discuss methods a collaborative negotiator can use to avoid the equivalent of being "taken to the ground" by a competitive one.]

The third insight relates to the importance of mental and physical rehearsal. This insight is not confined to the field of martial arts. Sports science has known this for a while. In that domain, it will not be surprising that physical rehearsal is key to building skill. What might be surprising to some is that mental rehearsal can be as effective as physical rehearsal.[18] *Imagining* responding appropriately to someone delivering a roundhouse kick, and "editing that movie" till it runs perfectly can effectively ingrain that response and help someone to manifest it at the appropriate moment. This can be done prospectively (imagining it before it happens)[19] or retroactively (imagining an event that has already happened, but editing it to learn from mistakes made).[20] Shanahan recalls meeting, as a young patrolman, veteran officers who had conspicuously been through this process: "they could talk a rabid dog off a meat truck."

This is equally true of conflict resolution. One can use a form of physical rehearsal (actually taking it to words) *or* mental rehearsal to practice a skill set or to prepare for a potentially challenging interaction, or to review/edit a past interaction. Even though one cannot rehearse the myriad ways in which one's counterpart can respond, readers might be surprised how rehearsal can still adequately prime one for that interaction.

Mind-Body Unity / Congruence

In martial arts, the notion of Mind-Body unity or congruence comes from two separate ideas. The first is that of 六合 (liu [4] he [2])[21] or the 6 Harmonies. The idea of 6 Harmonies refers to the 6 main joints; the ankle, knee, hip, shoulder, wrist and fingers, working in tandem to achieve maximum effect for an attack or a defense. This does not mean they move at the same time; it means that they must move at the *right* time. Every part of the body must move in harmony with every other part.

The second idea is that of 形意 (xing [2] yi [4]).[22] 形 (xing) refers to form, whereas 意 (yi) refers to intention. If there is form without intention, one cannot execute a technique effectively. For example, if one punches someone half-heartedly, that punch may not land, or even if it does land, may have very little effect. One would have to punch like they meant it.

The combination of the ideas of 六合 (liuhe) and 形意 (xingyi) allows one to maximize their effectiveness with minimal effort. Just as light can be aligned as a laser to cut through metal, power in the martial arts is generated not just from physical strength but from physical and mental alignment.

Translating this to the field of conflict resolution, it is equally important to have an alignment between our mindset and our techniques. Where alignment or congruence is lacking, effectiveness is hampered. Two examples relating to congruence (or lack thereof) immediately spring to mind. First, many have been trained in the interests-based, problem solving, collaborative method of conflict resolution. However, most people simply go through the *actions* of collaboration without the supporting *mindset* of collaboration. Put bluntly, they speak the language of collaboration while still thinking competitively. They will come across as incongruent. It is therefore important for one's negotiation goals, strategy and moves to be aligned. Secondly, we have all encountered people who, despite engaging in the behaviors of active listening, aren't really listening. In both these examples, they are engaging in form without intention.

There is therefore value in seeking alignment. Only then will one be able to congruently carry out the full skill set, whether in martial arts or conflict resolution.

De-escalation

As mentioned earlier, a key philosophy in the martial arts is the cessation of conflict. The idea here is to be able to *not* engage in a fight, or if that is not possible, then to terminate the fight with speed and finality. On this second limb, there is a difference in approach between the hard and soft martial arts (just as there is between competitive and collaborative models of conflict resolution).

We will deal with this second eventuality in the next section on Redirection and Utilization. Here it is sufficient to say that even practitioners of the hard martial arts will seek to de-escalate conflict rather than engage in it.

What is the nature of de-escalation? Strangely, there is very little difference between this and conflict resolution. Since we are trying to avoid a fight, words, and behaviors supporting those words, come into play. One could simply walk away from a fight. Or give in to what the other person wants (which may be one's wallet or an apology). Readers will recognize this as the avoiding and accommodating modes of conflict resolution.[23]

Some readers may find this hard to swallow; that is the ego speaking. As mentioned, our identity issues will sometimes get in the way of common sense. Why might one give in to an unreasonable demand? Put simply, there will always be consequences from a fight, and the consequences may outweigh the cost of doing as the other demands. The Chinese have a saying, "When two tigers fight, one will be injured".[24] In the movies, the martial arts expert can take on ten assailants and emerge unscathed and victorious. Reality is different. If someone wants your wallet and that is all they want, it is often better to give up something expendable than to suffer possible injury.

Another mode of de-escalation is encapsulated by the statement "The best self-defense technique I know is to make a friend".[25] Sometimes, showing a potential adversary compassion and kindness may itself de-escalate the conflict. This comes closest to what collaborative conflict resolvers do.

When a collaborative negotiator faces an adversarial counterpart, by listening, paraphrasing and showing that their needs and concerns have been understood, this very often dissolves aggressive behavior. It makes the counterpart more willing to listen and to consider solutions other than the win-lose options they had initially come to the table with. This then sets the tone for the rest of the interaction.

Redirection and Utilization

As mentioned earlier, if de-escalation is not possible and a martial artist has to engage, the goal shifts to terminating the fight with speed and finality. We have also mentioned that when engaging at this stage, there will be differences in approach between the hard and soft martial arts. Hard martial arts will seek to end the fight with the destruction of the opponent. On the other hand, soft martial arts operate on the principle of 以柔克刚 (yi [3] rou [2] ke [4] gang [1]) which translates into "Using softness to overcome hardness". Replace the word "softness" with "collaboration" and "hardness" with "competition" and the parallel between the soft martial arts and the collaborative model of conflict resolution becomes clear.

How does this operate in practice? The key idea is not to fight force with force. Imagine two people facing one another with their palms against one another. Suppose one of them starts pushing against the other. It would not be surprising if the other person started pushing back. This pushing may then escalate and after a time, one might actually forget who started pushing, only that the pushing or conflict exists. This is one possible outcome. But only one.

Another possible outcome is for the person being pushed to pivot 180 degrees to the side of the counterpart. The initial force from the push is redirected into nothingness and the person that was being pushed is now standing next to the "aggressor"—essentially, seeing things from his point of view. This physical metaphor expresses the idea of redirection. Instead of meeting the aggressor's force head on, one redirects it safely away. Utilization then involves taking the force that the aggressor has given you and using it against them. In Aikido, for example, after the opponent's force is dissipated, that opponent can then be led in a different direction—usually culminating in a throw.[26]

Translating this to conflict resolution, redirection means never disagreeing directly with the counterpart. If the counterpart says something which is not acceptable, one acknowledges it (turning to their side and seeing their point of view) and then utilizes it by reframing it as a valid concern, possible solution or measurement of fairness. Alternatively, instead of a reframe, one could ask questions to elicit from the counterpart their concerns and views. Some readers may recognize the similarity between this and what William Ury (1991) refers to as negotiation Jiu Jitsu.

The notion of 形意 (xingyi) (Form and Intention) was discussed earlier in the context of congruence. There is a third part to 形意 (xingyi). This would be 卦 (gua [4]) which can be roughly translated to "transformation". 形意卦 (xingyigua) denotes the journey of mastery (Lee, Mitchell and Fox, 2015). One first learns the form, then learns to put intent into the form. The last part of the journey is to go beyond the form, and be able to manifest the appropriate skill at the appropriate time. One can transform from one move to the other seamlessly. Put another way, one goes beyond the formula and the form.

In terms of conflict resolution, 卦 (gua) is what happens when a negotiator is able to seamlessly collaborate with an initially non-collaborative counterpart.

Conclusion

It is said that if one tries hard enough, one can find parallels between two completely unrelated subjects. And some might say that of this chapter. However, as longtime practitioners of both the martial arts and conflict resolution, the authors deeply believe that the insights and learnings from one field can inform and improve the other. This is of course not uni-directional. The authors have used learnings from conflict resolution to inform their training of the martial arts. In particular, listening and reframing skills are particularly useful to martial artists when seeking to de-escalate conflict.

This chapter has sought to surface some of the learnings and insights from martial arts which readers might find helpful in their learning, training and practice of conflict resolution, without actually having to become martial artists. The authors hope that readers have gained some ideas from this exploration. But we remain well aware of the topic's relatively undeveloped status. If a perceptive reader should discover and write about further parallels or synergies (or, indeed, dissimilarities or discontinuities), we would consider that a very good start indeed.

Notes

[1] Also known as Da Mo or Putidamo (菩提达摩) (Wikipedia 2016a).
[2] The words and numbers in parentheses denote how to pronounce the Chinese characters according to the 汉语拼音 (Han [4] Yu [3] Pin [1] Yin [1]) system of phonetic transcription (Wikipedia 2016e).
[3] 洪拳 (hong [3] quan [2]) (Wikipedia 2016c).
[4] 太极 (tai [4] ji [2]) (Wikipedia 2016f).
[5] And all Star Wars fans know where this leads.

[6] It is heartening to note that others in the field of conflict resolution are also coming to this conclusion. See William Ury's more recent offering *Getting to Yes with Yourself* (Ury 2015).

[7] The ladder of inference is a tool created by Chris Argyris (Wikipedia 2016b; System Wiki 2015; Skills You Need 2016).

[8] See entry on the Meta Model in Encyclopedia of Systemic Neuro-Linguistic Programming and NLP New Coding (Dilts and DeLozier 2000: 733-741).

[9] See entries on the 6 Step Reframe and Visual Squash in *Encyclopedia of Systemic Neuro-Linguistic Programming and NLP New Coding* (Dilts and DeLozier 2000: 1215-1219; 1540). Also See *Getting To Yes With Yourself* (Ury 2015).

[10] The Identity Complexification Process is the creation of NLP Master Trainers John Overdurf and Julie Silverthorn (1995) and captured in the tapes *Beyond Words*.

[11] As we grow older, we tend to breathe more shallowly and in the upper part of our lungs. This will consequently lead to increasing disuse of the lower part of the lungs resulting in a loss of lung capacity.

[12] Our autonomic nervous system is made up of the sympathetic and the parasympathetic nervous system. The former is essentially excitatory and is responsible for our survival responses (Dilts, DeLozier, and Dilts 2010: 193).

[13] This idea comes from a NLP Master Practitioner certification training conducted by Tad James which one of the authors attended in 1996.

[14] Best and humorously illustrated by the Charlie Brown cartoon found at http://www.elephantjournal.com/2011/09/if-youre-going-to-get-any-joy-out-of-being-depressed/.

[15] The authors are taking pains to avoid using the term "mental instability" as this has other connotations.

[16] Amy Cuddy's work on the correlation between power poses and confidence is another application of this idea (Cuddy, Wilmuth and Carney 2012).

[17] Readers familiar with NLP can also use the processes of anchoring and future pacing to transfer this state to appropriate situations. See entries on Anchoring and Future Pacing in *Encyclopedia of Systemic Neuro-Linguistic Programming and NLP New Coding* (Dilts and DeLozier 2000: 29-37; 433).

[18] A study in the 60s involved 2 groups of high school basketball players over a 2-week period. One group practiced shooting free-throws each morning and the other engaged in "mental practice", visualizing making shots but not actually doing real practice. Both groups improved their free-throw shooting (Clark 1960).

[19] See entry on Future Pacing in *Encyclopedia of Systemic Neuro-Linguistic Programming and NLP New Coding* (Dilts and DeLozier 2000: 433).

[20] See entry on the Change Personal History Process in *Encyclopedia of Systemic Neuro-Linguistic Programming and NLP New Coding* (Dilts and DeLozier 2000: 155-159).

[21] For clarification, it is important to note that there is a Chinese martial art called 六合拳 (liu [4] he [2]) quan [2] or the Fist of 6 Harmonies. This is not what this chapter is referring to.

[22] Again, there is a Chinese martial art called 形意拳 (xing [2] yi [4] quan [2]) which is not what this chapter is referring to.

[23] The Accommodating and Avoiding modes are two of the five modes of conflict approaches. (see Schneider and Brown 2013; Kilmann and Thomas 1977).

[24] 两虎相争，必有一伤 (Linguee 2016).

[25] Based on an example from *Sacred Journey of the Peaceful Warrior* (Millman 1991).

[26] It is not surprising that the characters for Aikido translate into "The Way of Harmonizing Energy".

References

Benson, H. 2000. *The Relaxation Response*. New York: Harper Torch.

Clark, L. V. 1960. Effect of Mental Practice on the Development of a Certain Motor Skill. *Research Quarterly* 31(4) (Dec): 560-569.

Crum, T. R. 1987. *The Magic of Conflict: Turning a Life of Work into a Work of Art*. New York: Touchstone.

Cuddy, A. J. C., C. A. Wilmuth, CA. and D. R. Carney, DR. 2012. The Benefit of Power Posing Before a High-Stakes Social Evaluation. *Harvard Business School Working Paper*, No. 13-027 (Sep).

Dilts, R. and J. DeLozier, J. 2000. *Encyclopedia of Systemic Neuro-Linguistic Programming and NLP New Coding*. Scotts Valley, CA: NLP University Press.

Dilts, R., J. DeLozier, J. and D. B. Dilts, DB. *2010. NLP II: The Next Generation - Enriching the Study of the Structure of Subjective Experience.* USA, Capitola, CA: Meta Publications.

Elephant Journal. If You're Going to Get Any Joy out of Being Depressed. Available online at http://www.elephantjournal.com/2011/09/if-youre-going-to-get-any-joy-out-of-being-depressed/ (last accessed June 24, 2016).

Goleman, D. 1997. *Emotional Intelligence: Why it Can Matter More Than IQ.* New York. Bantam Books.

Kilmann, R. H. and K. W. Thomas. 1977. Developing a Forced-Choice Measure of Conflict-Handling Behavior: The "Mode" Instrument. *Educational and Psychological Measurement* 37(2): 309-325.

Lee, J., S. Mitchell and K. H. Fox, 2015. Moving Towards Mastery: 形意卦 (Form-Intention-Transformation) in Negotiation Education. *Tan Pan: The Chinese-English Journal on Negotiation.*

Linguee. 2016. Available online at http://www.linguee.com/chinese-english/translation/兩虎相爭，必有一傷.html (last accessed June 24, 2016).

Millman, D.1991. *Sacred Journey of the Peaceful Warrior.* Tiburon, CA: H J Kramer.

Overdurf, J. and J. Silverthorn, J. 1995. *Beyond Words: Language Change Through the Quantum Field.* USA: Neuro Energetics (Audio).

Schneider, A. K. and J. G. Brown. 2013. Negotiation Barometry: A Dynamic Measure of Conflict Management Style. *Ohio State Journal on Dispute Resolution* 28(3): 557.

Skills You Need. 2016. The Ladder of Inference. Available online at http://www.skillsyouneed.com/ips/ladder-of-inference.html (last accessed June 24, 2016).

Stone, D., B. Patton, B. and S. Heen, S. 1999. *Difficult Conversations: How to Discuss What Matters Most.* New York: Viking Penguin Group.

System Wiki. 2015. Ladder of Inference: Short Circuiting Reality. Available online at http://www.systemswiki.org/index.php?title=Ladder_of_Inference:_Short_Circuiting_Reality (last accessed June 24, 2016).

Ury, W. 1991. *Getting Past No: Negotiating in Difficult Situations.* New York: Bantam Books.

Ury, W. 2015. *Getting To Yes With Yourself: And Other Worthy Opponents.* New York: Harper Collins Publishers.

Wikipedia. 2016a. Bodhidharma. Avalable Online at https://en.wikipedia.org/wiki/Bodhidharma (last accessed July 3, 2016).

Wikipedia. 2016b. Chris Argyris. Available Onine at https://en.wikipedia.org/wiki/Chris_Argyris (last accessed July 3, 2016).

Wikipedia. 2016c. Hung Ga. Available Online at https://en.wikipedia.org/wiki/Hung_Ga (last accessed July 3, 2016).

Wikipedia. 2016d. Parasympathetic Nervous System. Available online at https://en.wikipedia.org/wiki/Parasympathetic_nervous_system (last accessed June 24, 2016).

Wikipedia. 2016e. Pinyin. Available Online at https://en.wikipedia.org/wiki/Pinyin (last accessed July 3, 2016).

Wikipedia. 2016f. Tai Chi. Available Online at https://en.wikipedia.org/wiki/Tai_chi (last accessed July 3, 2016).

○3 76 ᘒ

"Non-Events" and Avoiding Reality

Susan K. Morash

Editors' Note: What do you do when you think something should be discussed, but others don't seem to recognize there's an issue? This essay uses specific examples from health care to make a larger point. Only in recent years have health care professionals adopted standard policies against a former pattern, of choosing not to view supposedly-minor errors and "incidents" as triggering a need for a discussion with a patient. By taking the former view, of course, they had often set themselves up for confrontation or even lawsuits later, when and if the patient found out anyway. In reassessing her findings from 10 years ago, Morash finds there has been some progress, but not enough in practice. Furthermore, the intervening decade has presented society with all too many examples of "avoiding reality" and treating suspected harm to a third party as a "nonevent" in other fields, such as global finance. Do similar assumptions limit discussion with your kinds of clients? What are the consequences?

Much of the literature on negotiation, especially outside the spheres of international and race relations disputes, begins with an implicit assumption that the parties know when they are parties, and that the existence of a "negotiable event" is on the table for discussion by then, even if the merits are questioned. But there are situations where the knowledge that might give rise to the negotiation—or if there is no negotiation, perhaps, to a much more contentious dispute later—is in the possession of only the potentially "responding" party or person. How they react to this power, perhaps a very temporary power, has moral and often legal as well as practical implications. Health care practice abounds in these

Susan Morash, RN, BS, MA, BC-NE is a Nurse Director at the Massachusetts General Hospital. As the Nursing Director she actively leads and supports interdisciplinary care and the development of nursing practice both on the unit level and within the Department of Nursing. Susan holds a Bachelor of Science in Nursing from the University of Massachusetts, Amherst, and a Master of Arts from the University of Massachusetts, Boston, where she conducted research in the area of dispute resolution. She is an active member of the Massachusetts Victim and Family Support Team in Mass Disasters and the Organization of Nurse Leaders (OLN).

moments and is an excellent place to study them. This chapter will focus on health care settings, in order to permit a factually rich inquiry; but the reader is invited to assess whether she knows of similar problems and situations in her own field.

Background up to 2006

"Error ... A commission or an omission with potentially negative consequences for the patient that would have been judged wrong by skilled and knowledgeable peers at the time it occurred, independent of whether there were any negative consequences" (Wu et al. 1997: 770).

In the 1990's some highly publicized cases of serious malpractice, including a lethal overdose of chemotherapy to a prominent health reporter of a Boston newspaper, and the amputation of the wrong leg of a patient in a Florida hospital, came to the public's attention. "These, and other sentinel events, were the impetus for the Institute of Medicine [IOM] Report, To Err is Human" (Correia 2002: 16). Data from this 2000 report indicate that the rate of adverse events in a hospital ranges from 2.9% to 3.7% of hospitalizations. The report also estimated that as many as 98,000 people die every year in the U.S. because of mistakes by medical professionals in hospitals (Kohn, Corrigan and Donaldson 2000). These shocking figures called for attention and immediate action concerning the problem of medical errors and adverse events occurring in our hospitals.

Talking about errors in practice is not easy for anyone, especially those who work in health care. Unfortunately, mistakes by health care workers happen with alarming frequency and are a common "shock and awe" event seen on nightly television news broadcasts and news magazine programs. These stories commonly describe extremely serious mistakes or even events that result in a patient's death, and highlight a patient's vulnerability when they are ill and under the care of medical personnel.

It is painful for anyone to admit their own error, especially to those patients who have been harmed by them. "Nevertheless, offering an apology for harming a patient should be considered to be one of the ethical responsibilities of the profession of medicine. Full and honest disclosure of errors is most consistent with the mutual respect and trust patients expect from their doctors" (Kalantri 2003).

New Standards of Care

The IOM's report prompted calls for immediate changes in how mistakes are documented and reported to patients. In July 2001, the Joint Commission on Accreditation of Health Care Organizations (JCAHO) responded by introducing new patient safety standards, including a requirement that all unanticipated outcomes of care be disclosed (JCAHO Standard RI.1.2.2). This standard clearly indicates that in addition to the documentation that an error has occurred, accredited organizations must tell patients when harm occurs to them in the course of their treatment (Lamb et al. 2003).

A 2002 survey of risk managers in a nationally representative sample of hospitals done by Lamb et al. gave the authors some cause for optimism regarding compliance to the new JCAHO standard for the disclosure of medical errors to patients.

> The vast majority [of risk managers] reported that their hospital's practice was to disclose harm at least some of the time, although only one-third of the hospitals actually had board-approved policies in place. More than half of respondents reported that they would always disclose a death or serious injury, but when presented with actual clinical scenarios, respondents were much less likely to disclose preventable harms than to disclose non-preventable harms of comparable severity (Lamb et al. 2003).

A Call for Further Examination

The survey, done by Lamb et al., contains findings that require further analysis. The phrase in the survey results "...their hospital's practice was to disclose harm at least some of the time" is significant. It seems to reveal both a lack of full compliance with the spirit of the JCAHO standard and a suggestion that subjectivity on the part of medical personnel is a big factor when determining what constitutes harm, in the context of a medical mistake.

The intent of this chapter was originally (in 2006) to review briefly the reporting and disclosure of adverse events policies that several academic medical centers have implemented secondary to the JCAHO's standards for accreditation, and through informal interviews of a modest cross-section of nurses (25), examine how nursing practice conforms to these policies. These incidents are commonly referred to in hospital policies as: *reportable incidents, medical accidents, medical errors, or adverse patient events.*

Several hospital policies will describe how these events are expected to be managed by staff, but the focus of this work is mainly on how nurses react to and manage these events. During the interview, two hypothetical adverse patient events were depicted, and nurses were asked to describe how they would manage the event. The nurses' reported actions in connection with these events as well as the rationale for their actions were also explored.

An additional goal of this survey was to explore the possible motives behind practices that in reality often differ from what many in the public desire, that is, full disclosure of medical errors. Between the planned objective to achieve an atmosphere of trust and a culture of openness about accidents and safety, and the actual culture that still exists in many of our hospitals today, lies some considerable distance.

This project mimics to some extent a 2003 study published in the Journal of the American Medical Association (JAMA) that examined patients' and physicians' attitudes about error disclosure (Gallagher et al. 2003). In that study, physicians were given hypothetical situations involving medication errors and were then asked whether, or how the described medical errors should be disclosed to patients. In this study "[p]hysicians agreed in principle that patients should be told about any error that caused harm, and many said that such disclosure was ethically imperative" (Gallagher et al. 2003). However, they also identified situations in which they might not disclose an error, even if it caused harm to a patient. Reasons not to disclose included feelings that the event was too trivial to mention, belief that some patients would prefer not to be told, and worry that informing patients of the event would lead to a diminished trust in their physician.

Defining Adverse Events

The academic medical centers referred to in this project define a reportable event in similar ways, though with subtle differences. They all appear to be consistent with the intent of the JCAHO standard, to identify unanticipated outcomes of care.

In all cases, a sentinel event is a category of medical accidents of an extreme nature (accidental death, suicide, surgery on the wrong body part, etc.). These events are strictly defined, and require immediate notification to the appropriate authorities. It is the less dramatic events, however, that are of particular interest here.

Management of an Adverse Event

The overall management of adverse events should include four components: treat, report, document, and disclose. The practice for the initial management of an adverse event is consistent in all the institutions in this project. All agree that the first concern is for the well-being of the patient and support of their family. This includes care of the patient with immediate diagnosis, stabilization, treatment, and prevention of further injury.

The intended goals for the management of an adverse event, in addition to the ethical necessity to be honest to patient regarding their care, are to:

- Identify, report and investigate all events inconsistent with optimum care of patients or routine operations of the hospital;
- Strengthen institutional efforts to improve patient safety through the identification of system vulnerability to future events;

- Restore patient confidence that systems are in place to prevent future events from affecting other patients;
- Maximize patient safety by reducing patient mortality and morbidity;
- Support staff that has been involved in an adverse event;
- Identify "near miss" incidents caused by system inadequacies;
- Meet all outside regulatory requirements related to reporting defined events to oversight agencies.

The committees that wrote these policies intended them to encourage an environment that empowered staff to identify system issues and follow through with a full review and analysis.

Management of events in all the facilities in this project includes objective documentation in the medical record, avoiding speculation and blame, as well as timely notification of patients. Academic Medical Center #3 also describes the ethical obligation to inform patients about events that caused significant injuries that led to change in course of treatment or outcome of care. The policy also goes on to specify, "if the event is of a serious nature, it should be reported immediately."

Academic Medical Center #1's policy regarding disclosure states that patients or their family representatives must be fully informed of errors that reach patients under the following circumstances: (1) when there is clear or potential clinical significance; (2) when some unintended act or substance reaches the patient resulting in harm. The policy goes on to give examples of errors that need to be disclosed: "errors resulting in the need for additional treatment, increased monitoring, or transfer to an intensive care unit."

The policies of these three academic medical centers all require the completion of a safety report or an incident report to be filed, as well as objective documentation of the event in the patient's medical record. The information in the safety/incident report in these facilities is for the sole purpose of an internal evaluation of these events and is treated as a confidential and privileged process, and protected as peer-reviewed information. The data and the conclusions from these reports are not disclosed to anyone outside of the facility.

There appears to be room for interpretation by an individual practitioner in all of these cited institutions' policies. This carries with it some risk. A 2002 report by Health Care Risk Control (HRC) System warns,

> Any disclosure policy should include an explanation of exactly what is expected to be disclosed. A policy without clear and concise guidance in this regard will allow too much latitude and individual interpretation of whether the occurrence is reportable. Adverse outcomes, unanticipated outcomes, medical misadventure, medical error, and events are all terms that may vary

significantly in meaning to different health care professionals (ECRI 2002).

All of the hospital policies examined in this project
have a goal to achieve a culture of openness regarding
medical errors. However, as stated by Thomas Gallagher
and his co-authors, "An important component of the response to an error is deciding whether and how to tell
the patient what happened. Disclosing medical errors
respects patient autonomy and truth-telling, is desired
by patients, and has been endorsed by multiple ethicists
and professional organizations" (Gallagher et al. 2003).

But, *does this actually happen*?

Perceptions and Practice: Reporting and Disclosing of Adverse Events Survey Results

Twenty-five nurses were informally surveyed about adverse events. They
were given two hypothetical events and asked to comment on how they
would manage these events, their understanding of the hospital's expected reporting practice, and how they believe these situations are
commonly handled on their units. A discussion followed about their
feeling about errors in general and the actions nurses take when adverse
events occur.

Situation #1

You hear a patient call out for help. When you enter the patient's room
they are on the floor. You help them to the chair and ask the patient what
occurred and they state, "I just felt weak so I just slid myself down to the
floor." They report no injuries. What do you do next? How would you
report this incident?

All the nurses reported that they would immediately help the patient
off the floor, place the patient in a secure position, assess vital signs and
look for possible injuries. Their reporting methods are noted below. The
action reports what the nurses would do in this event. [Note: nurses can
take/select more than one action]. Their rationale describes their personal beliefs about why they feel they, or their peers take that action.

ACTION	# Nurses	(Typical) Rationale
File an incident report	22	"It's the policy for slips and falls" "Our nurse manager would kill us if we didn't" "The incident report protects you if the patient later sues the hospital" "Fill one out just to be on the safe side"
Notify the physician	22	"It is expected for a nurse to call the MD in this situation" "Reporting it to the MD covers you [nurse]"
Document in the patient's medical record	6	"It's an event that happened to your patient on your shift"
No documentation in record	19	"I made out an incident report, I think that's enough"
Do nothing	3	"The patient told you that they just sat down and they state they aren't hurt" "The patient says he's OK. If I file an incident report it just leaves me open to someone looking at it and questioning my assessment of the patient for risk for a fall" "The patient isn't hurt, and I'm too busy to make out an incident report if the patient says he's OK" "The incident report tracks the event back to you" "Some patients fall all the time, if you made out an incident report every time you'd go crazy" (If patient is not injured)

Results Situation #1: Patient Found on the Floor

In this scenario, most nurses responded appropriately and identified this as an event requiring an incident report and physician notification. However, most nurses did not identify or understand the need to document the event in the patient record. Those that "did nothing" as a response to this event described fears of retribution by hospital administration, or a lack of time as the major causes for their decision-making. The majority of the nurses felt that slips and falls are fairly common and for the most part an unavoidable event in the hospital, and that management of such an incident is straightforward.

Situation #2

At the start of the shift you check your patient's Heparin infusion.[1] The patient is ordered for Heparin 1000 Units per hour. You note on the infusion pump that the patient is receiving 1200 Units of Heparin per hour. What are your next actions?

ACTION	# Nurses	Rationale
Notify the Physician	15	"Depends if the patient is having symp-toms" "Depends on why your patient was getting Heparin. In some patients even this small discrepancy could be problematic"
File an incident report	12	"If the MD told me to" "If the MD was notified you should" "Depends on your unit culture" "It's a med error" "Only if the MD thinks it's a problem. They'll just tell you to check the blood level, and if it's OK they won't care about the difference"
Document in the patient's medical record	8	"Only the amount the patient received; not the discrepancy" "Write only objective information about the event and place no blame"
No documentation in record	17	"That would get you subpoenaed" "Never document in the record, that's what incident reports are for" "That would put yourself right out there" "Never in the record" "Only document in the chart if there is some type of medical intervention" "We were taught never to document that kind of thing in the record"
Believe the event would be disclosed to patient (By a Physician)	2	"Unless the patient received a massive overdose or was bleeding, they wouldn't be told." "Some people are lawsuit crazy and this would make them look into everything" "This might cause them to say that now they believe they are sick because of the discrepancy" "Would upset some patients to learn this" "The patients wouldn't trust us anymore"

Do nothing (other than to correct the IV rate)	10	"This is a very small discrepancy. I would follow the policy if it were a large overdose or if the patient was having symptoms" "Heparin has a range of being therapeutic, this small amount wouldn't probably matter" "You'd get your peer in trouble""This happens fairly frequently. It's not a big deal. I would tell the MD if it was 5,000 units over, instead of just 200 units over"

Results: Situation # 2 Heparin Error

After giving their comments to this hypothetical scenario, staff were asked what the correct response should be to this error with the Heparin infusion. We discussed one of the hospital policies that stated, *"A report should be completed whenever there is an injury or potential injury to the patient, or any occurrence inconsistent with quality care"* as well as the policy to document adverse events in the patient's medical record. This sparked a lively discussion about what constitutes harm or injury to a patient, as it related to the Heparin error and medication errors in general. The nurses' responses were on a continuum from voicing the opinion that this patient was most certainly harmed, to the belief that there was no harm in this scenario. Nurses that felt that the patient was harmed were adamant that this was a medication error and should be treated as such. They stated that when the physician is notified of such an error, she would minimally want an additional blood sample to be taken from the patient to check the drug level. This action alone was considered by many of the nurses in the survey to be an additional invasive procedure, and thus a source of harm to the patient. Those that felt the patient was unharmed countered this opinion by stating that patients get blood drawn all the time. "It's part of the routine of being in a hospital."

The discussion was expanded to include the question, "What would you tell the patient if they asked why they were having an additional blood sample taken?" The group of nurses that felt this to be a minor incident stated it would be simple to explain to the patient that the MD ordered an additional sample today, and few patients would question it further. The RN's that felt an error had occurred stated that they would disclose the Heparin discrepancy themselves at this point. They would not mislead the patient in any way. The debate then shifted to include the monetary effect this could have on the patient's hospitalization (charge for the added blood work), and did this constitute, "harm"? The nurses that felt that this event was minor responded to that question by stating, "their insurance covers that, and the patient isn't directly charged." Others disagreed with this rationalization.

It is important to understand in this scenario or with other adverse events in the hospital, the practitioner must first identify the event as adverse before they move to the next step: management. In many hospital policies, these definitions are vague enough to allow for interpretation, and thus for management of the event to vary. In fact, two of the academic medical centers' policies state, *"consideration should be given to disclosing errors that reach patients and do not result in harm. The decision to disclose will depend on the circumstances of the event."* The important variable seems to be, what is considered harm to one health care professional may not be to another. The hospital policies may in some way give support to the nurses' rationalizations not to disclose in situation #2, the Heparin scenario.

Reluctance to Report and Disclose

Are nurses and physicians reporting and disclosing adverse events as required by the JCAHO and hospital policy? If they are not, what are the barriers to compliance? The first question is more complex than at first glance. As indicated earlier, the definitions and policies are somewhat ambiguous, and health care professionals may for different reasons choose to interpret the policy in a manner that they believe protects themselves, their colleagues and even the patient. In the case of a near miss (adverse outcome that almost happened), what should the patient be told? Though there "is no legal obligation to disclose negligence that didn't cause an injury, [even] risk managers disagree over what doctors should say in these situations ... and these incidents need to be decided case by case" (Crane 2001).

When the IOM published its blunt assessment of the large numbers of medical errors in today's hospitals it caused the health care industry to take a closer look at both reporting practices and the inadequate information patients often received if they were the victim of a medical mistake. The results of this survey show that some errors are being reported to the safety office through incident reports. This finding coincides with statistics citied in the Boston Globe. The newspaper reports, "in the latest period measured by state researchers, stretching from July 1, 2002 through June 30, 2003 hospitals reported 757 errors that resulted in injury to patients, including 65 deaths. That compares with 574 mistakes in 2000" (Smith 2003: B1). Some believe that this increase in error reports reflects greater vigilance by medical centers in reporting their mistakes, rather than a true spike in errors (Smith 2003).

The barriers to reporting are well known. The greatest barrier to reporting and disclosing events identified in this small survey and other similar surveys of nurses and physicians is fear of litigation. Nurses and physicians fear that increased documentation and reporting will just increase the interest of lawyers in finding these errors and bringing lawsuits. All of the nurses in this survey, even those that felt that the

Heparin discrepancy in the hypothetical situation was a true error and needed to be reported and disclosed, remarked on the fear nurses have of both litigation and reprisal by hospital administration if they are involved in an adverse event. When nurses in the survey commented on the "Patient Fall" scenario, those that responded that they would "do nothing" [action] spoke of fears that nursing administration would be apt to question their assessment skills regarding the patient's risk for falls, and fault them for not preventing the situation in the first place.

Many of the nurses in this survey commented on the infamous "Betsy Lehman Case" at the Dana Farber Institute in Boston and how the fallout from that case still influences nurses' attitudes on reporting errors. Despite the fact that the American Nurses Association (ANA) and the Massachusetts Nurses Association (MNA) supported the nurses involved in the fatal chemotherapy error to Ms. Lehman, citing a hospital system failure (Trossman 1999), the Massachusetts Board of Nursing (BORN) leveled formal reprimands to those nurses and mandated them to participate in both retraining and re-certification. The Dana Farber Institute and the Department of Public Health (DPH) in this case did not hold the nurses accountable for the error, yet the nurses were at the mercy of the BORN for nearly five years until they rendered their decision. MNA member Judith Shindul-Rothchild, PhD, RN, CS told the Boston Globe "...the proposed new regulations [BORN's power to summarily suspend a nurse's license] present grave problems around holding individual nurses accountable for systems failures" (Massachusetts Board Reprimands Dana-Farber Nurses 1999). The ANA has stressed that a non-punitive culture is needed to support and enhance the reporting of adverse events to relevant oversight bodies, both to learn from these errors and to change systems to prevent future events in the future (Gallagher et al. 2003). The nurses in this survey shared the opinion that at this point, they do not trust that they will be supported by hospital administration if they are involved in an adverse event. They worry about losing their jobs and fear loss of their license to practice nursing as well.

Nurses' attitudes toward disclosure are complex. Nurses do not normally disclose an adverse event to the patient. That job normally belongs to the physician responsible for the patient's care, but the nurses in the survey had strong opinions about this practice. Overwhelmingly, the nurses in this survey stated that patients should always be informed when a medical error has caused them serious harm. In the hypothetical Heparin error, even those nurses that would not have reported the error, stated that if the Heparin was overdosed by enough to cause abnormal or obvious bleeding, or underdosed by enough to cause a clot to form, all reporting and disclosure to the patient should take place. The biggest barrier to disclosure they identified, again, was fear of litigation. The second reason they identified not to disclose was the potentially negative reaction by the patient to the event. Some voiced concern that the disclosure of even a small error, or one that caused no harm, would be upsetting to many patients. Some nurses stated that many patients would not understand that the discrepancy in the Heparin amount was quite minor, and could lead them to imagine unrealistic consequences to their condition, causing undue worry. This could ultimately lead to distrust of all their caregivers. The overwhelming majority (23 out of 25 nurses in the survey) unequivocally stated that the Heparin error in Situation #2 would "never be disclosed to a patient."

Ironically, many patients echo the nurses' attitudes in this survey concerning disclosure. In the similar survey of physicians and patients done by Gallagher et al. (2003), "patients wanted disclosure of all harmful errors and sought information about what happened, why the error happened, how the error's consequences will be mitigated and how recurrences will be prevented." In the case of near misses (errors that are discovered before they reach or harm the patient), though, patients had mixed opinions about whether they should be told. Some patients described that hearing about a near miss could potentially alert them to what errors they should look for and would reassure them that the systems in place to prevent errors were working. Other patients thought that hearing about a near miss would be upsetting (Gallagher et al. 2003). In this same survey, the authors ventured an opinion that medical errors are an unfortunate and usually unavoidable part of medical practice. Despite the IOM report, and new JCAHO standards, debate about what or when to disclose continues.

Conclusion—as of 2006

This project raises additional questions and areas for continued discussion about reporting and disclosing adverse events. It must be mentioned that in this survey of nurses, nearly all of the participants were unaware of either the IOM's report on medical errors or the subsequent changes in JCAHO standards. Ignorance of this information appears to be a significant factor for many in their responses to the hypothetical situations in the survey.

The finding that many nurses are not comfortable reporting errors is not surprising. The more perplexing fact revealed was the high number of nurses that could deny that "harm" had occurred in the Heparin error scenario, and then rationalize their opinion whether an error had indeed occurred in this case. At what point do health care workers feel that a patient is owed details of an error? One explanation for this high number of "non-reporters" may be found early on in this chapter. The definitions and policies surrounding the reporting of adverse events appear somewhat ambiguous, and thus open to subjective interpretation to whether an "event" is deemed harmful or not. Another explanation is a desire to hide errors to avoid possible retribution.

When faced with the commission of an error and possible harm to the patient, most nurses describe becoming panicked at the possible repercussions. However, all of the nurses that participated in this small survey expressed the opinion that if there is obvious, or serious harm to a patient, all reporting and documentation must take place, and the patient informed. The major issue, again, seems to be that what is interpreted as harm by one nurse may not be interpreted as harm by another.

The information obtained in the interviews with the nurses suggests that nurses want to do the right thing. Nurses, however, overwhelmingly still feel that reporting and disclosing errors carries with it the risk of retribution by hospital administration, and probable legal consequences. Nurses need to become more comfortable with reporting, and also understand that reporting even relatively minor errors can identify systems' problems and possibly prevent future errors. They need to feel confident that the key to reducing errors is to focus on systems to improve care, not to place blame on individuals.

There are potential health care-specific remedies for most of these issues. But of greater relevance in the context of this book, none of the issues will get addressed as long as the underlying failure to disclose is considered tenable by large numbers of the professionals involved. How many other professional fields, and potential discussion/negotiation settings, could say the same?

The only honest answer is, no one knows. But most of the motives found in this survey have their counterparts in situations far removed from health care. This chapter is thus offered as a modest hint of the possible extent of the problem of unilateral, self-interested and short-sighted decision-making as to what should even be "put on the table" for discussion.

Many hospitals are working hard to create a safer, "blame-free environment." There is a beginning understanding for some in health care of the need to have frank discussions with patients about adverse events, as well an enlightenment among some in the health care field about the potential opportunity that this new environment presents to partner with patients in an honest dialogue when less than optimal care occurs during their hospitalization. Clearly, more education is needed in this area. Today, episodes of harm or potential harm are analyzed in an increasingly open fashion, both to determine how human factors or systems may have contributed to the event, and to assist the evaluation of new technologies to streamline the reporting and the analysis of the adverse event. Health care workers may not yet realize the potential benefits of disclosing these potentially "negotiable events", but they are beginning to understand the need as well as the moral urgency to be forthcoming when these events occur.

2016: What Has Been Learned?

A decade has passed since the publication of the chapter as formulated above, in the *Negotiator's Fieldbook*. The topic as of then focused on nurses' perceptions around what constituted an error during the delivery of patient care, how they would disclose it, and how the error would or would not be disclosed to the patient. All of these were replete with opportunities for discussion, i.e. negotiation; what was alarming was how regularly a whole constellation of factors conspired to ensure that the opportunity was lost. And nursing, of course, largely stood in the context of that book (and the present one) as an available example—thus as a kind of representative—of who-knows-how-many other professions in which similar pressures might apply.

Yet nursing, along with health care in general, has been the focus of intense society-wide interest over the same decade, for lots of reasons of which the advent of broader coverage is just one. If there had been no improvement in my industry on the issues I discussed in the *Fieldbook*, the picture might be bleak indeed in fields which are less in the public eye.

Thus I report with at least a degree of relief that by the time of this writing (2016), the ethical imperative to report and disclose has been recognized for some time. Nurses and physicians now care for an increasingly educated and informed public that demands no less. Yet in reality, do nurses consistently file safety reports when they witness an error or near miss? And when errors do occur, are they now routinely disclosed to patients?

Healthcare workers *are* now receiving—but continue to need—the training, tools, and support to change the hospital from a culture of blame and shame to an environment where all staff believe that reporting and full disclosure of errors is the right thing to do. It is cited in the literature that medical errors still are not sufficiently reported. "Studies in the United States and the United Kingdom illustrate that underreporting of adverse events may be as high as 96%..." (Barach and Small 2002).

One of the areas of discussion ten years ago was a review of how adverse events were or were not disclosed, as well as the policies that were enacted in various academic medical centers secondary to changes in the Joint Commission's standards for accreditation. These standards were specific to the identification of unanticipated outcomes of care, and specifically how nursing conformed to those policies. Since that time, much has been written in the literature about the need to report and document errors or breaches in safety. These incidents (adverse events), as described ten years ago, were referred to at many institutions as *reportable incidents, medical accidents, medical errors, or adverse patient events*". In that era, these situations were also reported by clinicians via a paper system.

Today, many hospitals utilize an electronic system that more effectively tracks safety related events. These reports are now known at the facility at which I work as *Safety Reports*. This shift in nomenclature, from Incident Reports to Safety Reports, will hopefully reduce the emphasis from "blame" or "error" to a focus on issues that could impact patient safety. [See NDR: Volpe et al., *The Unknown*, as to the potential importance of a "mere" shift in such language, in another high-stress profession] Utilizing an electronic safety reporting system now alerts nurse leaders to an event immediately, so they are able make changes to systems or processes and to provide "in the moment" education and feedback to staff. This electronic filing of reports also allows facilities to track trends, and more effectively identify the root cause of the incident.

"Safety culture has been defined as the integration of safety-related thinking and practices into clinical activities (Singer et al. 2003). Unfortunately, despite this intended culture shift, some nurses still report that they are reluctant to report errors—especially when the error involves a peer. We have made progress in this area, but still have a long way to go. Many articles have been published over the past decade describing the need for hospitals to move from a culture of blame to a shame-free or blame-free culture with regard to medical errors or near misses. We also know that the under-reporting of patient safety incidents reduces the healthcare industry's ability to quantify and accurately measure when patients are actually at risk, and how we can prevent or reduce errors and near-misses.

"As we learn more about accidents, the role of the system in which the accident takes place and the imperfect beings that humans are, we are realizing that blaming the person who made the mistake is the biggest mistake" (Kerfoot 2008).

My belief, as described in the original chapter, was that "between the planned objective to achieve an atmosphere of trust and a culture of openness about accidents and safety, and the actual culture that still exists in many of our hospitals today, lies some considerable distance" (Kerfoot 2008). A large focus of the original work was to examine clinicians' feelings around so-called adverse events, and their comfort level around disclosure of these events to the patients who had been the victim of a near miss or actual event. I believe that *all* hospitals are now making a concerted effort to encourage reporting of these events, in an effort to create a culture of safety for our patients. There is now a greater awareness that when clinicians are honest about their own practice and how hospital policies and human error put patients at risk, we have an opportunity to improve patient safety. It is critical in this paradigm shift that this heightened awareness be coupled with the belief that if clinicians honestly report their own and their colleagues' errors and near misses, there will not be punishment, humiliation, or retribution.

Today, many hospitals survey their employees through The Hospital Survey on Patient Safety Culture, which was developed by the Agency for Healthcare Research and Quality (AHRQ). The purpose of the survey is to assess the safety culture at all levels throughout an organization. The survey looks at a hospital's safety culture in regards to teamwork, management support, communication openness, staffing, frequency of events reported, handoffs and non-punitive response to events. This tool has its limitations, as hospital protocols, policies and processes vary throughout the country, but it can be a useful measure of an individual hospital's performance on specific areas that relate to patient safety. Though most hospitals report favorable results in the areas of *Teamwork within Units, Supervisor/Manager Expectation and Actions Promoting Patient Safety and Organizational Learning, the three areas that showed potential for improvement were Non-punitive Response to Error, Handoffs and Transitions of Care, and Staffing Numbers to Handle the Workload* (AHRQ 2006).

In the past "it was apparent that hospital policy was intended to encourage an environment that empowered staff to identify system issues and follow through with a full review and analysis" (Morash 2006). Policy may have been intended to encourage staff to report mistakes; but as the respondents reported at that time, most clinicians still voiced fear of humiliation, and retribution—including loss of their job or license if they complied with the reporting standards and policies. In the situation of a patient fall, some nurses did not file a file a report, stating, *"...if I file an incident report it just leaves me open to someone looking at it and questioning my assessment of the patient for risk for fall", "The incident report tracks the event back to you", "Some patients fall all the time, if you made out an incident report every time you'd go crazy"* (if the patient is not injured).

These quotes indicate a lack of awareness of the rationale around the reason to report falls. Instead, staff voiced a fear of humiliation, that they would be judged as serving patients poorly if their patient fell while under their care, and a fear of retribution if the incident were "tracked" back to them. As nurses, we *know* that documenting when a patient falls is the first step to identifying potential gaps in patient safety. Accurately tracking falls has been extremely valuable and has helped hospitals to recognize staff learning needs around falls. This new awareness has led to more effective strategies and equipment to prevent falls in the first place. Reports of patient falls have also led to better tools to assess a patient's risk for falls, more appropriate signage to alert staff that a particular patient is at risk, and improved equipment to prevent falls for high risk patients. This is an area of safety reporting where I believe we have made steady progress. Today, I believe that reporting falls is the norm for nurses.

But I believe we still have work to do in other situations when staff see breaches in safety. Speaking to staff nurses and leaders, many reveal that although we talk openly about making our hospital a "blame free" environment when it comes to reporting adverse events or errors, some reluctantly admit that there is still a gap in reporting errors that have been attributed to their peers. Many nurses disclose that they feel more comfortable filing Safety Reports when the situation involves a healthcare worker from another department or discipline.

Why is that? Why don't all nurses see the value in reporting issues that impact patient safety when it involves a peer? Nurses who have been in the field for approximately 5 years or more have most likely heard or personally experienced a medication error before hospitals instituted an electronic medication administration record and automated medication delivery systems. Before these innovations in care, nurses relied on a personal "review" when they were administering a medication; often referred to as the 5 Rights (R's): right patient, right medication, right dose, right time, and right route. Today, nurses electronically select the ordered medication, the delivery system dispenses the medicine, the nurse electronically scans the bar code of the medication packaging, and then scans a bracelet that each patient wears that verifies their medical record number. If anything is a mismatch, the nurse gets a vivid prompt not to administer the medication. The system is not foolproof, but a huge number of mistakes that would have been attributed to human error have certainly been eliminated with these electronic systems.

Logically, nurses know that the vast number of safety reports of medication errors that occurred prior to these electronic innovations led to these improvements in the way nurses administer medications today. Why then don't nurses recognize that with greater reporting of errors or near misses comes the opportunity for further improvements or innovations in care? When asked why they don't report, many state that they don't want to "get another nurse in trouble"; others fear retribution in the form of disruptive behavior from the person whom they report. In speaking to a nurse who recently transferred from another facility, she described that at her previous hospital, more novice nurses often did not file safety reports, not wanting to "report" a peer; but at the same time, more experienced nurses filed more often on their novice colleagues. The feeling among staff was that this typified a "nurses eat their young" phenomenon! Some nurses may also fear disciplinary action against their colleague by a nurse manager or supervisor if they file a safety report. More research is needed in this area, to uncover and develop better responses to all the motivations behind the statistics of why some nurses are fearful to file reports in these incidents.

Another reason not to report, unrelated to retribution, was poor feedback to staff when they did report, or lack of leadership prioritization around safety events when they were filed. In other words, nurses often feel that when they take the time to submit safety reports, nothing appears to change. Ironically, it has been posed as well that in hospitals with strong communication skills, staff may "be inclined to fix problems as they learn about them rather than wait and formally report errors" (Richter et al. 2015).

In conclusion, when it comes to medical errors, there is some reason to focus on the positives. There is definitely a push to shift from a culture of blame to a "Just Culture" in the hospital setting. Again, we now commonly refer to errors as safety events. This shift emphasizes the need to look at *the process around the event* to evaluate ways to improve safety, vs. placing blame on an individual. Many hospitals now have an electronic safety reporting system, which streamlines reporting, allows data to be analyzed in "real time", and affords leadership the ability to give feedback and make improvements in a timelier manner. When staff members see a positive outcome from taking the time to report safety concerns, rather than a waste of their time or even risk to themselves, systems issues and processes have more opportunity for improvement or correction.

Our next challenge seems to be a shift on how leadership follows up with staff when an error occurs, or the perception of how leadership follows up. According to the Safety Culture Surveys conducted nationwide, there still is a perception among staff that follow-up from management or supervisors may be punitive, with these events placed in the employee's file for possible retribution, now or in the future. Leadership has the opportunity to view their scores on this survey and evaluate their style and responses to safety events. Hopefully, when leaders see the positive influence that can be established when they use a supportive, vs. punitive atmosphere on their units, they will alter their approach. Lastly, in terms of reporting, more research is needed to fully understand the reluctance of staff to report errors by their peers. There is surely a component that staff wants to "protect" their peers from embarrassment or retribution, but there also seems to be a component of fear of retaliation in some form, when a staff member reports an error that was attributed to a peer. Nursing is spending a great deal of time on conflict management in the workplace, but disruptive behavior and lateral violence are still behaviors that we need to work on.

For purposes of my industry, it seems fair to conclude that in the years since the above chapter was first published, there has been some progress—though clearly more is needed. It is beyond my professional role to discuss other industries, in which such progress may be far short of even the current level in health care. Everyone knows, however, how the finance industry's widespread failure to observe even the most basic forms of care for others' rights and interests almost brought down the world's economies since the original *Fieldbook* was published. Is it too much to hope that now that at least two industries (I include air traffic control, perhaps the originator of the "safety culture" paradigm shift) have made this switch, pressure might grow on others to stop claiming that it can't be done?

Notes

[1] Heparin is an anticoagulant given intravenously to prevent potentially lethal clots from forming and migrating to sites in the body, such as the lungs or brain. The drug level is checked daily to see that the patient is receiving a therapeutic dose of the drug (too much can cause unwanted bleeding, and too little can result in blood clots). This drug is not particularly sensitive to exact dosages, compared to some other drugs—which is the reason it was chosen for this exercise.

References

Agency for Healthcare Research and Quality (AHRQ). 2006. Hospital Survey on Patient Safety Culture. http://www.ahrq.gov/professionals/quality-patient-safety/patientsafetyculture/hospital/index.html.

Barach, P. and S. Small. 2002. Reporting and Preventing Medical Mishaps: Lessons from Non-Medical Near Miss Reporting Systems. *British Medical Journal* 320: 759-763.

Correia, N. G. 2002. Adverse Events: Reducing the Risk of Litigation. *Cleveland Clinic Journal of Medicine* 69(1): 15-24.

Crane, M. 2001. What to Say if You Made a Mistake. *Medical Economics* 8: 26-36.

ECRI Institute (ECRI). 2002. Disclosure of Unanticipated Outcomes. *Healthcare Risk Control (HRC)*. Plymouth Meeting, PA.

Gallagher, T. H., A. D. Waterman, A. G. Ebers, V. J. Fraser and W. Levinson. 2003. Patients' and Physicians' Attitudes Regarding the Disclosure of Medical Errors. *Journal of the American Medical Association* 289(8): 1001-1007.

Joint Commission on Accreditation of Healthcare Organizations (JCAHO). 2001. *Patient Safety and Medical/Health Care Error Reduction Standard (hospital accreditation standard)*.

Kalantri, S. P. 2003. Medical Errors and Ethics. *Indian Journal of Anaesthesia* 47(3): 175.

Kerfoot, K. M. 2008. From Blaming to Proactively Changing the Future: The Leader's Safety Challenge. *Nursing Economics* 26(4): 280-281.

Kohn, L. T., J. M. Corrigan and M. S. Donaldson, eds. 2000. *To Err Is Human: Building a Safer Health System*. National Academies Press.

Lamb, R. M., D. M. Studdert, R. M. Bohmer, D. M. Berwick and T. A. Brennan. 2003. Hospital Disclosure Practices: Results of a National Survey. *Health Affairs* 22(2): 73-83.

Massachusetts Board Reprimands Dana-Farber Nurses. 1999. *American Nurse* 31(5): 6. Accessed March 15, 2006. http:www.nursingworld.org/tan/99sptoct/farber.htm.

Morash, S. K. 2006. Non-events and Avoiding Reality. In *The Negotiator's Fieldbook: The Desk Reference for the Experienced Negotiator*, edited by A. K. Schneider and C. Honeyman. Washington, DC: American Bar Association.

Richter, J. P., A. S. McAlearney and M. L. Pennell. 2015. Evaluating the Effect of Safety Culture on Error Reporting: A Comparison of Managerial and Staff Perspectives. *American Journal of Medical Quality* 30(6): 550-558.

Singer, S. J., D. M. Gaba, J. J. Geppert, A. D. Sinaiko, S. K. Howard and K. C. Park. 2003. The Culture of Safety: Results of an Organization-Wide Survey in 15 California Hospitals. *Quality & Safety in Health Care* 12(2): 112-118.

Smith, S. 2003. Hospitals Reports Increase in Errors Leading Causes: Falls and Surgical Blunders. *Boston Globe*, October 29, 2003, B1.

Trossman, S. 1999. ANA, MNA Support Dana-Farber Nurses Facing Disciplinary Action. *Nursing World*, March/April 1999.

Wu, A. W., T. A. Cavanaugh, S. J. McPhee, B. Lo and G. P. Micco. 1997. To Tell the Truth: Ethical and Practical Issues in Disclosing Medical Mistakes to Patients. *Journal of General Internal Medicine* 12(12): 770-775.

∝ 77 ∾

Peer Mediation

U.S. Ambassador John McDonald (ret.)
with Christel G. McDonald

Editors' Note: On the surface, the authors describe an ingenious and far-reaching effort John McDonald undertook many years ago to foster peer mediation among students in schools. But for those interested in systemic change, the McDonalds' subject leads farther: this chapter stands as a demonstration of what it takes to use the political system to support a societal change that can be far-reaching for our field.

Introduction

The emergence of negotiation as a field over the past forty years owes something to each of a whole array of influences. They span, in turn, many fields of human endeavor and study. A fair cross-section of them is described in other chapters of this book. Yet all of them have one thing in common: they implicitly or explicitly treat the field as the province of adults, or at least of graduate and sometimes college-level students.

Perhaps no one influence among them, however, offers more long-range potential than one initiative that set out, about thirty years ago, to teach negotiation and mediation to *children*. Because its effects have been widely dispersed, accurate numbers are difficult to compile; but it has been some years since it was first reported that a million children in the U.S. alone had been trained as peer mediators in schools, and no doubt the number has grown. Another crude measure is derived by simply typing [peer mediation in schools] into Google. This returned more than 330,000 sites. Even insisting on the phrase *with quotation*

U.S. Ambassador (ret.) **John W. McDonald** is a lawyer, diplomat, former international civil servant, development expert and peacebuilder, with twenty years in Western Europe and the Middle East and sixteen years working on United Nations economic and social affairs. He retired in 2017 as Chairman and CEO of the Institute for Multi-Track Diplomacy; he co-founded IMTD in 1992, and developed its systems approach on national and international peacebuilding.
Christel G. McDonald (M.A. History), former European Civil Servant, and experienced Historical Researcher, is deeply committed to furthering higher education for young people from around the world.

marks returned upwards of 8,000 websites on which that exact phrase apparently appears.

What's more, the forgivable assumption that something about peer mediation is deeply characteristic of American culture, and therefore unlikely to translate well or be adopted elsewhere, is called into question by this work's take-up in, among other places, Russia—described below.

The "how it happened" of peer mediation is a story worth telling for other reasons. It may serve as an object lesson in the value of negotiation's and mediation's developers taking more seriously a practical field much derided these days, namely, politics. And it says something about the potential for further growth, over generations, in people's understanding of peaceful resolution of differences. This matters particularly if one takes a moment to consider that for every peer mediator working on a dispute in a school somewhere, there must logically be a minimum of 2X child *negotiators*—per case—who are also learning something by the encounter. And finally, this story is an example of how we must negotiate even to implement our programs...while it also shows a relationship to other writings in this volume. [e.g. NDR: Reynolds, *Activism*]

A Brief History

In 1982, Ray Shonholtz and Gail Sadalla of the Community Boards Program in San Francisco, California came up with a new idea. They wanted to help young people to learn how to solve their own conflicts. They called this peer mediation.

They put together a 40-hour training course for teachers, in middle school, and later in high school. They advertised their course, saying that they were the chief trainers. Gradually, teachers around the United States came to San Francisco and took their course.

In 1987, they decided to do a survey of graduates to find out how successful they were. They were shocked to learn that 90 percent of their graduates, on return to their school, were rejected by their school administration. Administrators did not like the idea and typically prevented the teachers from actually teaching this material to students or organizing peer mediation programs. While Shonholtz and Sadalla were shocked, they did not know what to do about this. In a potential lesson for would-be developers of conflict management systems everywhere, however, fate intervened, in an unlikely form: a professional from a very different field and in a very different place (me), was on the point of retirement, and looking for a suitable initiative to launch from a new pad.

The Scene Shifts—to Iowa

I was a U.S. career diplomat for 40 years. I had served 20 years overseas, in settings about as far from American school life as it is possible to get: 8 years in postwar Europe, 8 years in the Muslim Middle East, and 4 years as Deputy Director-General of the International Labor Organization (ILO) in Geneva. Before retiring in 1987, I became a law professor at George Washington University, teaching International Negotiation. When two head-hunters approached me from Des Moines, Iowa, they wanted me to apply to become president of a brand new organization, located in Grinnell, Iowa and called the Iowa Peace Institute (IPI). With my wife's agreement, we moved to Grinnell, in December 1988.

I had heard about Ray Shonholtz's and Gail Sadalla's work in San Francisco, and decided that my first project at the Iowa Peace Institute would be to bring peer mediation to Iowa. But my life experiences had been very different from the grass-roots setting and concerns of the San Francisco Community Boards, and it turned out that this had its uses. In particular, I was comfortable with, and I decided to use, the political route.

Lesson One: Using Politics (to Launch Peer Mediation in Iowa)

The first thing I did was to visit the Statewide Department of Education in Des Moines, Iowa (after several meetings to help me launch the project in Iowa.) With the strong support of my board of directors, I then testified before the appropriate committees of the state house and senate. I also met with the governor. These efforts led to an agreement-in-principle to set up a program in peer mediation. I then prepared a short draft law to establish a program. Crucially, this specified "no cost to the State" and required a report back to the legislature and the Administration the following year.

My draft law was passed unanimously and signed by the Governor. I then sent the law to some 500 school Superintendents. I innocently asked each of them if theirs would like to be the *first* school district in the state to launch a peer mediation program in their school.

By three weeks later 32 school superintendents had responded, each stating an interest in being the first. Suddenly, our program was blessed and launched!

A First Training

My board and I were delighted. But now it was time to train some teachers. Within a few weeks, we brought 30 teachers, from across the state, who wanted to take the 40-hour training. We brought Ray Shonholtz and Gail Sadalla to Iowa and they carried out the first training themselves. At the end of the very successful week, we held the typical graduation ceremony and gave each teacher a big certificate, together with one providing continuing-education credit (e.g. towards a master's degree, if they did not have one.) We also named these teachers charter members of the newly created peer mediation program.

A Time of Outreach

I believe it was largely *because* we had taken a "political route" that peer mediation rapidly became accepted across the state. But, of course, the politics neither began nor ended with the Governor and with formal approaches to the Legislature.

Lesson Two: Look for Ways to Engage Key People

We took a number of initiatives to spread the ideas of peer mediation across the state. I made dozens of speeches at local high school, rotary club, and other institutions to spread the ideas across the state.

I even rented a whole passenger train, to bring state legislators from Des Moines to Grinnell, an hour and half away. Politicians like trains just as much as other people; politicians love a day out on a conspicuously non-political jaunt even more, perhaps. We took them to a local school, and to our office in Grinnell to brief them on what we were doing, and returned them to Des Moines the same day. Over 100 politicians took the train. It didn't hurt our cause that they visibly had a great time.

The Children Go to Work

We began to hear stories coming back. Here's one:

> A mother overheard her husband yelling at their 10-year -old son about something, in the next room. Right in the middle of this diatribe the 10 year old said, "Why don't we sit down and talk about this?" The father was so astonished that he did just that. They settled the problem in few minutes.
>
> After the father left the room, the mother went to her son and said "Where did you learn that stuff? You did not learn from me". He said, "I learnt in school". She said, "I don't believe you". He said, "Well, go ask my teacher." The next day, she did.

She learned from the teacher that, in fact, her son had received ten hours of instruction for peer mediation. And each day, he and a fellow trainee classmate went out on the playground, each wearing a big "Mediators" cloth band across their chest. They worked to solve the problems in the playground before they became violent.

Lesson Three: Showcase Your Best Examples

This kind of experience was being replicated in lots of schools. By two years into the program, we held a statewide one-day conference on peer mediation. Over 600 people from across the state gathered in a local gymnasium. But we did not set this up in typical adults-talk fashion: we wanted to demonstrate how much the children were learning. So the three keynote speakers were 8th graders who had all taken peer mediation training. The third speaker was an African-American from a poor section of Des Moines. By the time she finished her story, there was not a dry eye in the house. And at the end of the event, a professor from the University of Northern Iowa, who had taken our very first teacher training program, came down to the stand to congratulate that student—and to offer the child a free 4 year scholarship to her university, when she was ready to attend higher education.

In a typical American story, once one state had broken the ice, peer mediation went on to spread widely across the U.S. Getting any attention to the concept off the ground elsewhere has been more of a challenge. A few initiatives, however, show that this kind of program is not uniquely American—it can travel. One of the places it has traveled may be truly surprising; again, it shows the value of being willing and able to work at multiple levels of society.

I returned to Washington, DC early in 1992, and co-founded the Institute for Multi-Track Diplomacy (of which I am still Chairman and CEO; we are now located in Arlington, Virginia.) Meanwhile word was beginning to spread across the United States about the peer mediation in Iowa. I was unexpectedly invited to make a presentation to the statewide Board of Education of the State of Maryland, in Baltimore. I gave a talk, answered questions for several hours at the Board of Education, and returned to Washington D.C. I learned later that at the end of the day, the Board had allocated half a million dollars to take peer mediation across the state. Maryland has since become a national leader in the field. In a further but smaller-scale example of how such work spreads, in 2011, I was invited by George Mason University's Fairfax campus to meet 30 teachers to talk about peer mediation. I learned then that half of the 240 schools in Fairfax County were teaching peer mediation—but the other half were not. (Of course, I told my stories to the group, and urged them to lobby the school board to bring peer mediation across the rest of the county.) In a related effort, I helped GMU's School of Conflict Analysis and Resolution (SCAR) engineer and staff a three-hour course on peer mediation at the Master's level. This kind of follow-up work never stops; but it is not time-intensive.

Elsewhere in the World

In a development whose significance became evident only much later, a distinguished member of the Iowa Peace Institute also took the training, way back in the late 1980's: Dr. Noa Davenport (Noa Zanolli) was originally from Bern, Switzerland. When she married Mr. Davenport and moved to Iowa, however, she maintained links back home. Years later, she returned to Bern, Switzerland. She went on to spread the word about peer mediation by teaching the course in German—in Switzerland, Austria and Germany. More recently she has also agreed to teach peer mediation in Libya and the Republic of Georgia, under IMTD auspices, once funding becomes available.

But this was not even the first evidence that our supposedly all-American innovation could function in other cultures. In September 1989, John Marks, Ray Shonholtz and I were invited to Moscow to meet with newly elected members of Parliament—the first free parliament in Russia's history. After our presentation we were invited to return in February 1990. This time, we took a US team of six people, and mounted four very different training programs for different groups, with a hundred participants in all. The first such group was of coal miners; the second was of businessmen. The fourth was on conflict resolution and "track two" diplomacy. [For an example, see NDR: McDonald & McDonald, *Kashmir*]

But the third training was on peer mediation. Gail Sadalla did the peer mediation training by herself, and trained 20 teachers from local Moscow schools. They were so excited about the concept of peer mediation that they immediately established their own local foundation to work with Moscow students. And ten years later, I was visited by someone who had just returned from Moscow and did not know this history—and who told me in tones of amazement "They are teaching peer mediation in *Moscow*!"

Conclusion

I offer this chapter as an example of how an innovation in conflict management actually gets off the ground. In conjunction with my more explicitly international chapter. [NDR: McDonald & McDonald, *Kashmir*] I believe it is actually a fair example of what it takes, for a group of people to take a great idea (in this case, peace building for young people) and make it actually happen, and grow.

It takes someone to have the idea in the first place. It takes, perhaps, someone else, who has the background and influence to get the idea heard and paid attention to in the right rooms. But most of all, to get the idea to spread across the world, it takes *perseverance*.

Section XIV: Agents and Tribes

Section XIV turns to the often-present problems created by the fact that frequently a "tribe" has an "agent" of some variety to negotiate for it. First is a chapter analyzing what happens, and what you can still do, when the other side's agent admits that a deal you thought was in the bag now has to undergo ratification by someone outside the room. The next chapter addresses situations in which the agents are numerous and the parties are diffuse—i.e., almost any major public negotiation. This is followed by a trenchant analysis of agents' frequent failure to ensure that their clients have actually given informed consent to the agent's actions.

One type of agent who tends to come in matched pairs is the specialized expert, called in to buttress a particular position—and liable to get into an expensive and unproductive duel with a similar expert hired by the other side. What to do about this is the subject of the next chapter. The section closes with an explanation of how, despite the tendency of parties to claim that "the facts" are immutable (though, of course, disputed), sophisticated negotiations with huge factual disputes have developed techniques for defining which facts are actually, and productively, subject to a negotiated approach to refining them. The result has been the settlement of (for instance) many supposedly-intractable cases that had disputed scientific components.

⚬ 78 ⚭

Shadow of the Tribe

John H. Wade

Editors' Note: The negotiations have gone on for hours or months or years. A deal is at hand. And now, the other side mentions for the first time that the approval of some previously unremarked person is required, or there is no deal. Could you have prepared for this? Do you have options at this point? Are you, perhaps, the negotiator making the dread announcement that you must respond to a higher power before a deal's a deal? Here, Wade meticulously deconstructs the circumstances that lead to "shadow of the tribe" negotiations, and suggests what you can do.

It is rare for an individual present at a negotiation or mediation to have "unlimited" authority to settle or make decisions. Even the most rugged individualist usually has someone looking over his/her shoulder. This may be a spouse, child, business partner, CEO, board of directors, shareholders, head office in Chicago, club or church members. We are all part of some "system" or "network" of influences. These people in the background, sometimes in the shadows, can be described as supporters, influences, bosses, stakeholders, third parties, constituents, outsiders, armchair critics, bush lawyers, sticky beaks, nosey parkers,[1] ratifiers, destabilizers, tribal members, intermeddlers, cheersquads, principals, hawks, doves or moderates.[2] In this chapter, the terminology of "the tribe" will often be used.

The visible negotiator can be labeled an agent, representative, spokesperson, mouth-piece, pawn, victim, channel, or go-between.

John Wade is an emeritus professor of law of Bond University, Queensland, Australia. He practiced as a lawyer in Australia between 1987 and 2012, and also had an active mediation practice in organizational, family and commercial conflicts during those years. He has taught over 300 mediation and negotiation courses in Hong Kong, New Zealand, London, Canada, the U.S. and Australia. John has published over 100 books and articles (see epublications@bond.edu.au). His teaching awards include best law teacher at Sydney University (1989); at Bond University (1990); and in Australia (1998). John now lives in Vancouver, Canada with his growing family, and teaches intensive negotiation courses there.

Christopher Moore characterizes constituent groups as either "bureaucratic" or "horizontal." Bureaucratic constituents are the hierarchy of decision-makers in companies, government agencies, tribes, schools and many other institutions. "Horizontal" constituents are friends, relatives and co-workers whom a disputant feels obliged to consult and listen to (Moore 2003: 438-41). The following case study illustrates the discovery of a powerful horizontal constituent, namely a spouse.

Case Study 1—Ambushed by a Powerful Spouse

A cotton factory owner contracted with an expert factory designer and builder to renovate sections of his mill for $2 million. When the renovations were complete the owner was disappointed as the promised rate of production did not occur until three months thereafter. The new machinery often did not work during the first three months. The factory experienced repetitive "down-time." Accordingly, the factory owner withheld the last payment of $250,000 to the renovator. Incensed, the renovator commenced court action in one state (the state of the contract) to recover the last installment. Predictably, the factory owner cross-claimed, in the state where the factory was actually constructed, for three months of diminished profits, being around $1 million. The entrenched parties and lawyers were required to attend mandatory mediation.

After lengthy and sometimes vitriolic negotiation between the two teams at the table (eleven people in total), the mediator took the two CEOs for a walk down the street. Standing under a tree for an hour with the mediator reframing and asking "what if" questions led to a settlement between the two CEOs. However, the tough renovator CEO suddenly announced, "Of course I will not be able to settle this today. I will have to run this all past my wife".

The mediator reframed, placated the other irate CEO and retreated with the renovator CEO in order to phone his wife. In a carefully orchestrated conversation, the mediator spoke to the wife (with the husband present) and praised the husband, explained what progress had been made, empathized with her suffering and loss, and brainstormed on the risks of other options. The wife spoke to her renovator husband (with the mediator still present), and in a short time confirmed the grateful husband's decision to settle.

Obviously, some negotiators do not disclose that they will need to convince influential outsiders about any outcome (Johnston and Campbell 1988; Wade 2000). They lie, or are embarrassed, or overestimate their own influence over their constituents. At a later stage of preparation, or at the joint negotiation meetings, more direct questions may unearth the outsiders in the shadows, ever-present in spirit, though absent in the flesh:

- "How will Mary, the head of your department, feel about that sort of result?"

- "Your wife appears to have suffered a lot as your business struggled. How does she feel about this meeting?"
- "Most insurers I meet have an authorized range, but then need to make phone calls once the recommended result is outside that range. I assume that is also true for you?"
- "You will go through blood, sweat and tears at the negotiation. That will change your perspectives. Are there any club/church/party members sitting calmly back home ready to criticize your efforts?"

Despite all this tactful investigation, no one may know until the fateful request by one party to make a phone call at the "end" of the negotiation. The other negotiators may meanwhile live with ignorance or suspicions. Any smiles upon reaching consensus soon disappear when the negotiators take the agreement back to waiting hawks, who then ridicule their own negotiators and tear up the agreement.

Case Study 2—Temple Troubles

One example involved a dispute between the "liberals" and "traditionalists" who attended a large temple. The triggers for deeper disputes were (a) disagreements about the need for headgear, and (b) the use of chairs in the temple. Generational disagreements escalated into harsh words, punches, separate services and calling the police to manage "incidents". Subsidiary disputes broke out about eligibility to vote, the validity of a hurried election, the history of donations to the temple building, and plans to spend money on building extensions and car park. An application was made to court for declarations about the validity of elections, the appointment of a temporary administrator, and if necessary for the sale of the temple. Lawyers assisted in appointing the four most influential representatives of each faction, who then met together for weeks and agreed to a detailed plan of use and management of the temple, with separate spheres of influence and finance for the two factions. However, both groups of "authorized" representatives were then pilloried by their constituents for having "betrayed" their own members. A further town hall meeting for all constituents was scheduled in order to explain the range of solutions, and what excellent work had been done by the eight representatives. This meeting was cancelled when bomb threats were phoned in by anonymous callers. The hawks had "won" temporarily. The dispute languished again in court lists.

In the majority of cultures in the world, the representatives at any important negotiation table or tablet, *does not have* authority to agree, no matter what they profess. They must refer any emerging agreement back to the tribe for approval. This reality comes as a shock in encounters with individualistic Western cultures.

Lawyers as Outsiders

If the outsider or tribal member is a professional adviser, such as an accountant or lawyer, it is especially problematic if they are "absent" from a negotiation meeting. Lawyers are sometimes excluded due to expense, busy schedules, or poor diplomacy skills. In the writer's experience, outstanding lawyers sometimes self-identify as being "part of the problem" in escalated or cross cultural disputes, and therefore choose to be absent or silent at the next round of negotiations. However, lawyers have personal interests in clarity of drafting, closing legal loopholes, minimizing post- settlement regrets for clients, and preserving their own professional reputations. Once an absent lawyer or accountant is identified as a key tribal member, then the following range of options becomes important to consider, and from which to choose.

How to Manage Any Influential Outsiders?

If key tribal members are identified (or suspected) during the routine preparation, or at any subsequent time during a mediation or negotiation, how many ways are there for a negotiator to respond to this information? Set out below are standard responses to add to the toolbox (Wade 1996). All have advantages and disadvantages.

- Refuse to negotiate.
- Adjourn until influential figures are "present."
- Carry on regardless.
- Normalize.
- Ask ritualistic "authority" question.
- Insist on written authority within subjective range or objective range of "fairness."
- Agree to use best endeavors to sell the agreement.
- Opinion from an evaluative mediator or expert.
- Consult with the outside authority/influence before negotiation.
- Consult with outside influences before the negotiation and arrange decision-making process.
- Selected "reporting" team members explain settlement and progress to outside authorities before anyone else.
- Warn of dangers of reneging—"What if ...?"
- Throw tantrum.

Refuse to Negotiate

The first response to knowledge or suspicion about influential outsiders is to refuse to negotiate or mediate. "I am not willing to waste time and money talking to some middle manager, lackey, puppet, or person without authority to settle." This refusal to negotiate may lead to further conflicts or litigation, subsequent lying about authority to settle, or the emergence of the influencers from the shadows. In some non-Western cultures, where it is routine for major figures to keep back until a relationship has developed, it is also unrealistic.

Adjourn until Authority Figures are "Present"

The second response follows normally from the first. That is, one or more disputants may refuse to negotiate or mediate on major questions, unless and until key authority figures are "present" in person or are available on the phone or teleconferencing facility during the mediation or negotiation.

In many conflicts, such brinkmanship is futile as those with persuasive or legal power are too many, too distant, too expensive, or too busy to appear. Nevertheless, many mediations and negotiations are organized creatively to enable:

- An auditorium of constituents and families to be present, witness, speak and vote.
- A CEO from overseas to be "present" via teleconferencing, or telephone.
- Travel of key family or board members to an all-day (and sometimes all-night) meeting in a convenient central location.

The presence of numerous influential people creates constant logistical challenges of expense and coordinating calendars. However, once these logistical difficulties are overcome, they provide helpful pressures to "find a solution now that all of us are here." One possible method to manage time is to encourage many people to attend, on the express condition that the number of speakers will be limited to those who are nominated representatives, or to those given the microphone or some other "talking symbol" by a chairperson. This method has been used effectively in large town hall meetings between angry residents and local councils.

Nevertheless, this solution of "adjourn until" will be opposed strongly by middle managers and family members who fear the presence of their own bosses or family during the meeting. These outside authorities may be resentful for the inconvenience of attending; critical of the disputant for "being unable to sort this out by yourself;" and dangerously judgmental of their own tribal representative if too many skeletons come out of the closet during the negotiation.

Additional opposition to this "adjourn until X can be present" option will sometimes come from the *other* disputants. That is, one set of disputants objects to "interference" and "delays" due to the proposed presence of the other disputant's "officious boss," "nosey brother," "pushy husband," "aggressive union member" or "opinionated accountant." These legitimate objections and perceptions can usually be reframed ("So you would like X to work alone/independently?" or "So you are worried about the dynamics if X is present?"). The objector can then be challenged by questions such as: "If Y does not attend, will X ever settle?" "How will you feel if X wants Y to check any deal you reach?" "How can you ensure that the brother/boss/accountant/wife gives an informed opinion, rather than an ignorant reaction?"

The writer as mediator regularly uses similar questions to persuade disputants that they should consent to and welcome the presence of an "appropriate" influential spouse, accountant, or wise friend to "help" another disputant. Despite sometimes initial resistance, the persuasion has always succeeded on the basis that it is "better to have a visible influence, than someone whiteanting³ in the background." This exercise always involves a further task of trying to find "extra helpers" to equalize numbers present for each faction at the mediation/negotiation.

With a few notable exceptions, the presence of the outside influence has been essential, or at least helpful in order to find a resolution.

Children as Powerful "Outside Influencers"

One common group of powerful influencers who are often not "present" at negotiations and mediations are children. Parents have legal power to make decisions about their children, but sometimes have limited persuasive power, particularly over teenagers in industrialized societies.

Various procedures have been devised to "include" children in negotiations, by the symbolism of empty though named chairs; by a mediator interviewing the children alone before the joint negotiations with the parents; by an advocate appearing on behalf of the children; by an expert child psychologist submitting a written report on behalf of the children; or by alternative plans being submitted to the children for approval or suggested modification.

Carry on Regardless

The third response to suspicions or knowledge of key influencers, or absence of "complete authority to settle," is to say nothing and continue the process.

Some negotiators may decide that even opening the questions of "Do you both have authority to settle?" or "How shall we identify and manage influential outsiders?" is so inflammatory, complex and time-consuming that it is better not discussed. Arguably, the topic will remain safely buried, either because no substantive resolution is reached or recommended (so no telephone calls need to be made); or the settlement is within the "agent's" range (again, so no telephone calls need to be made); or it is so routine for certain disputants (e.g. middle managers, some insurers) to make phone calls, that it is not necessary to discuss what is normal. Moreover, if a settlement is reached and approval is then sought from an outsider, and this procedural ambush causes offense to the other party, then in those (statistically few?) cases, the negotiations can be "managed" at that stage. Why clumsily anticipate what may not turn into a problem?

Others have seen many negotiations stumble and fail due to the influence of tribal members. These scarred negotiators may be reluctant to "carry on regardless" or "wait and see what happens" in relation to these hovering armchair critics.

Normalize

The fourth response to the perceived pressure from outsiders is for the negotiator to give one or more "normalizing" speeches. The aim of these speeches is to attempt to convince one of the negotiators that the need for outside ratification is "normal;" is not devious; is not normally part of a good cop-bad cop negotiation tactic (though it could be that!); that competent negotiators do not fuss over this procedural step; and that progress can be made despite the need for outside approval. For example, "Jill, in my experience it is normal for middle managers in large businesses or government to seek approval for the agreement you hope to reach today. They cannot risk their jobs by settling without higher level approval. If you insist on them having full authority to settle, their easiest escape is to leave the decision to a judge; then they will avoid being blamed for the outcome."

These kinds of speeches by a team member may assist a disputant to persist with the negotiation/mediation, rather than prematurely choose option one—namely, refuse to negotiate.

Ask Ritualistic "Authority" Question

The fifth possible response to the knowledge or suspicion that one or more of the disputants will need to consult an outsider before signing any settlement, is for the negotiator to ask ritualistically, "Do you have authority to settle this dispute?" This question can be asked in writing in the preparation documents required to be completed by each negotiator. Alternatively, this question can be asked or re-asked at both private and joint meetings. Presumably, some negotiators are hoping for a confident or mumbled "yes" as an answer.

The mumble or the body language may suggest a lie or more complex motives. A more precise and tactical answer could be: "Yes, I have complete authority to negotiate or to settle so long as the outcome is fair/reasonable/in the range. If it is an unusual settlement, or one out of the normal range, then obviously I will have to consult my superiors/constituents/family. I assume that you would have to do likewise if you were in my position."

Whatever answer is given, it leaves the parties with some unresolved tensions. A confident affirmative answer may well be a lie or a mask to complexity; a mumbled affirmative answer will raise suspicions; a "correct" tactical and qualified affirmative may open a detailed discussion of the meaning of "reasonable"; and a negative answer may lead to option one—a refusal to negotiate.

Insist on Written Authority to Settle within Subjective Range or Objective Range of "Fairness"

The sixth possible response is for a negotiator to insist that some or all of the negotiators produce a written (and irrevocable) authority to settle. This written step may appear to provide more certainty than the ritualistic oral assurances set out in the previous response.

However, in reality, those who draft such written authorities know that they provide little certainty that the alleged agent will act upon the apparent authority. Why?

This is because an authority can be drafted in one of two ways—subjectively or objectively. A subjective written authority gives the agent the power to enter into such agreement as the agent believes is "reasonable," "fair," "appropriate" or "reflecting common commercial practices." All these words leave the agent with such a broad discretion that if he believes that the outcome is anything other than "advantageous," he may want to consult with the influential constituents anyhow (to protect his/her job or reputation or safety). That is, the representative's broad "legal" authority is qualified by his/her certain knowledge that he has limited "persuasive" authority.

An objective written authority supposedly gives the agent more certainty and less discretion. For example, "My lawyer is hereby given irrevocable authority by me to settle this dispute for an amount not less than $400,000."

However, such an objective authority to settle, is no panacea. First, by defining outcomes only in dollars, it restricts creative packaging. Second, the existence of such a key piece of information, namely the "reservation" or "walk-away," creates the risk that it may be leaked to the other side. Third, the authority may specify a false and flexible figure which can be "accidentally leaked" to the other side. Fourth, the authority does not prevent real or theatrical consultation taking place anyhow.

Agree to Use Best Endeavors

The seventh possible response to the negotiator's knowledge or suspicion that one or more of the negotiators will need to consult with influential outsiders before reaching agreement is to negotiate for the agent to use his/her "best endeavors" to sell the outcome to the constituents.

This option may seem weak. However, the writer and other colleagues have used it successfully on a variety of occasions.

This response anticipates a standard type of conversation between the negotiator (N) and his/her constituents (C) after a mediation or negotiation. For example:

C: "How did the mediation/negotiation go last night?"
N: "Well, we reached agreement. It is not all that you hoped for."
C: "What did you agree to?"
N: "Well, there are four basic provisions as follows ......"

C: "That doesn't seem very fair. Why did we get so little? Are you happy with that outcome?"

N: "Well, I am not happy, but in the circumstances ......"

C: "If you are not happy, why did you agree to it?"

N: "Well, it was the best I (we) could do. The mediator put us under some pressure to be realistic."

C: "We will need some time to reconsider this. It is very disappointing. I certainly will not sign/ratify. They must be laughing about ......"

This standard disclose, disappoint, defend and blame language is clearly foreseeable between some agents and tribes. Many representatives at mediations are in an unenviable position of martyrdom by the awaiting tribal hawks (Pruitt and Kim 2003).

This predictable pattern may encourage a wary mediator or negotiator to go through the following steps. First, ask each negotiator (privately and perhaps publicly) "What if you reach an agreement which you believe is satisfactory but which disappoints your constituents/members/family?" Second, the mediator asks "What if the post-settlement conversation with your constituents is as follows..." (mimics the disclose, disappoint, defend and blame language)? In the writer's experience, the representatives tend to nod glumly.

Third, the mediator asks, "Would you (each) be prepared to return to your club/constituents and highly recommend the outcome you reach (tomorrow, next week, next month etc.)? There is no point working hard for an agreement if you then allow that routine and undermining conversation to occur. You might as well abandon the meeting now."

The negotiators can usually be persuaded to agree orally or in writing as follows:

"If we reach an agreement after working hard through a range of possibilities, we will not report back to X in a half-hearted fashion. We will unanimously report back to X about the issues and the options. We will unanimously and enthusiastically recommend the outcome we reach as satisfactory, workable, and the best option available. We will endeavor to 'sell' the outcome to our constituents."

Opinion from an Evaluative Mediator or Expert

Following the previous response, there is an eighth method to help the representative save face, job, and safety; and to create doubt for any angry hawks lurking among the constituents.

This involves hiring an evaluative mediator who is respected in the field in which the disputants are negotiating; and/or bringing to the mediation or negotiation an expert in the field as an observer and commentator. An oral or written statement from an attending expert, such as, "This negotiated outcome is, in my opinion, within the range of predictable results in (court/the marketplace)" usually gives the nervous negotiators some welcome ammunition against the outside critics.

Consult with the Outside Authority/Influence Before Negotiation

The ninth possible response of a negotiator to the real or suspected existence of an influential outsider is to consult with that outsider before the joint sessions begin.

The writer uses this method in the majority of his negotiations and mediations. A negotiator asks his/her own constituents, and then secretly or openly any accessible supporters behind the "opposition," a series of routine diagnostic questions about causes of conflict, interventions, glitches, risks if the conflict continues, and possible substantive outcomes. These questions often produce important benefits including new perspectives and hypotheses for both the negotiators and the outsiders, and a sense of inclusion and respect from those constituents.

Consult with Outside Influences Before the Negotiation and Arrange Decision-Making Process

There is a tenth important response which every mediator and negotiator needs to have in his/her conceptual and linguistic repertoire when outside tribal members are obvious or unearthed. This response is to insist upon and organize a "decision rule" within each group of constituents (Lewicki, Saunders and Barry 2005).

> There is a variety of methods by which groups can decide to make decisions.
>
> In decision-making groups, the dominant view is to assume that majority rules and at some point take a vote of all members, assuming that any settlement option that receives more than 50 percent of the votes will be the one adopted. Obviously, this is not the only option. Groups can make decisions by dictatorship (one person decides), oligarchy (a small but dominant minority coalition decides), simple majority (one more person than half the group), two-thirds majority, broad consensus (most of the group agrees, and those who dissent agree not to protest or raise objections, and true unanimity (everyone agrees). Understanding what decision rule a group will use before deliberations begin will also significantly affect the group process. For example, if a simple majority will make the decision in a five-person group, then only three people need to agree. Thus, any three people can get together and form a coalition—during the meeting or even prior to the meeting. In contrast, if the

rule will be consensus and unanimity, then the group must meet and work hard enough to assure that all parties' interests are raised, discussed, and incorporated into the group decision (Lewicki, Saunders and Barry 2005).

That is, during preparation for negotiation *between* parties, representatives from each group are required to facilitate discussions *within* each of the parties' tribes on the key question—"By what process will the group make a decision?"

For example, a negotiator (or mediator) can typically go through the following steps described below.

Brinkmanship and Doubt Creation

"I am not willing to negotiate unless both groups decide clearly on how they will vote to approve or disapprove their respective representatives' recommendations."

"No group can agree unanimously on what day of the week it is; so don't come back to me with a unanimity rule."

"I am also not willing to accept a 'wait and see' or 'we will work it out later' voting process. That is a recipe for failure and embarrassment for me as your representative. We all know that some of you will be disappointed with the outcome, and some will be able to live with that same outcome."

Facilitate Agreement on Each Group's "Decision Rule"

"If you wish, I can meet with my group to develop an answer to this key question 'How will we make a decision as a group at the end of the negotiation?'"

"If you wish, I can tell you a range of ways other groups like you have made decisions. You can add those to your list of possibilities before deciding."

Write Out and Publicize the "Decision Rule" of Each Group Before the Joint Mediation or Negotiation Begins

This third step is helpful as it reduces the chances of a whole group later reneging on their decision rule; and encourages negotiators who can see that the decision-rules may be a way of controlling hawks on their own team, or on the opposition's team. Without a visible decision rule in place, a skilled hawk can exploit the inevitable post-recommendation or post-settlement regrets within a group, and organize rejection of many negotiated or recommended agreements. [NDR: Wade & Honeyman, *Lasting Agreement*] The following case example illustrates the use of a pre-determined intra-team decision-making process.

Case Study 3—Face Saving Decision Rule

A mediation occurred between two factions of a church. Both wanted to acquire the church property and exclude the other for a host of alleged miscommunications, misdemeanors and personality defects. Vitriolic litigation had commenced to appoint a trustee for sale of the church.

The two factions were represented at the mediation by 7 and 8 elders respectively. One lawyer took the mediator aside and said that his group of seven could never agree to any outcome as two "hawks" of the seven had paid all his legal fees; were deeply hurt; and wanted victory as a "matter of principle."

The grateful mediator sent each faction away to determine "How to make a decision at the end of the mediation?" The seven decided upon 5-to-2 majority decision; the 8 upon a 5-to-3 majority decision. This was publicly announced.

Eight hours later, a group of two from each faction reached a recommended outcome which they agreed to "sell" hard to their colleagues. They succeeded. The faction of 7 predictably voted 5-to-2 in favor of the recommended package with the two hawks dissenting.

The pre-existing decision rule then enabled both hawks to make speeches that they did not like the outcome, but they were men of honor, and would comply with the agreed majority vote by their friends.

Selected "Reporting" Team Members Explain Settlement and Progress to Outside Authorities Before Anyone Else

This is another vital response which every negotiator needs to add to his/her toolbox in order to deal with armchair critics who are eagerly awaiting the outcome of a negotiation.

This practice can helpfully complement the previous two responses, namely consulting with outsiders and organizing a decision-rule *before* the negotiation (or mediation). After each negotiation session, an appointed reporting negotiator strives to report to the influential constituents *before* or at the same time as other team members do so. This can be done by phone, fax or email with copies being given simultaneously to the team members on one or both sides. This enables the team of negotiators to build upon the interpretation and language adopted in the report. It will also reduce the predictable dilemma for the other team members of reporting, disappointing, defending, and blaming.

The aims of this response are to:
- Protect the negotiating team from hostile outsiders.
- Create doubt for the armchair critics.
- Give the negotiating team and the critics a new set of words, metaphors and expressions to describe the historical events at the negotiation. These words can profoundly influence simmering hostile perceptions and emotions.

- Avoid a defensive negotiator too readily "blaming" another team member, a perceived hawk or dove, or the negotiation process for the outcome.
- Develop further trust in the reporting negotiators who ideally model transparency and problem-solving skills.

The writer uses this practice regularly when organizing negotiations which involve influential outsiders. It sometimes requires persuasion to convince all team members of the potential benefits to them, when a diplomatic "reporting negotiator" provides the first feedback to the waiting constituents. Of course, sometimes hawks break the "reporting" agreement by leaking their own loaded versions about negotiation progress to the press or to their own constituents.

Warn of Dangers of Reneging—"What If ...?"

Negotiators usually have a range of phrases to exhort their own team and the other disputants to perform their agreements, despite pressures from outsiders to renege.

These may have the effect of preparing the disputants for such pressures, and giving them a practiced repertoire of language when placed under such pressures to renege. For example:

- "What will you do in the next week when some of our supporters criticize us for reaching this agreement?"
- "How will you respond when some of our fellow committee members say, "You should have obtained a better deal?"
- "Should we practice that speech now so that we gain confidence and consistency?"

This preparation is particularly important in those disputes where there is a necessary gap in time between agreement and ratification of the agreement by constituents or a court. For example, in family, native title, environmental, succession and human rights disputes it is normal for a mediated or negotiated agreement to require court approval before the agreement becomes legally binding. As many lawyers can nervously testify, this pause provides a dangerous gap of days or weeks when one or more parties can be pressured by constituents or self-doubt to renege.

Throw Tantrum

This response involves a mild-mannered negotiator expressing strong and theatrical disapproval when one party suddenly suggests that he needs to consult with an influential outsider. The theatrical negotiator has the goal of pressuring the wavering negotiator into signing immediately, rather than passing responsibility to outsiders.

A negotiator's exhortations might be as follows:

- "I can't believe that at this stage of the meeting, you want to make a phone call! What kind of message will that send to my team? They are likely to walk out angrily and not come back."

- "We have all put in so much work to reach this agreement. And now you want to risk it all with a break so that you can talk to your relatives?"
- "You can't do this Mary! Your reputation as a negotiator will be in tatters. In the future, our firm will insist on negotiating with anyone but you."

The writer has not used the fake tantrum in these circumstances, but has anecdotally heard of others trying this intervention. It obviously has many risks for a negotiator, including allegations of bullying, cultural clumsiness, or ignorance of other more suitable interventions, or a walk-out.

Conclusion

This chapter has identified and systematized thirteen possible responses to influential tribes and outsiders before, during and after negotiations. There are probably other responses or hybrids which could be added from the repertoires of experienced mediators and negotiators. Obviously, each response has advantages and disadvantages.

In the writer's opinion, this is another common hurdle in negotiations where mediators can add value to "unassisted" negotiations (Stanford Center on Conflict Resolution 1995; Hammond, Raiffa and Keeney 1999; Kahneman 2011) [NDR: Wade, *Final Gap*]. First, the mediator can question strategically in order to identify influential outsiders; second, pose a neutral problem-solving question (e.g. "how to respond to influential outsiders?"); and third, be aware of and, if possible practiced in, the thirteen responses to this question. These three steps can be mastered by expert negotiators. However, a master negotiator may often (rightly?) be suspected by the opposition of strategic manipulation of the process. Less suspicion of bias may fall upon a respected mediator who is employed by all parties to manage negotiation dynamics including the unruly behavior of hawks, doves and moderates in the background.

This analysis raises challenges for the systematic training of mediators and negotiators; questions for research on the actual behavior of mediators and negotiators in relation to managing the influence of outsiders; questions about the rate of use of each of these responses in different areas of conflict and culture; and questions about what evidence, if any, can be collected to measure and predict the rate of "success" of each response to ubiquitous outside influences.

Notes

Adapted from John H. Wade, Bargaining in the Shadow of the Tribe and Limited Authority to Settle, 15 *Bond Law Review* 115 (2003).

[1] A "sticky beak" is "an inquisitive, prying person;" and a "nosey parker" is "a person who continually pries; a meddler" per THE MACQUARIE DICTIONARY OF AUSTRALIAN COLLOQUIALISMS 220, 299 (1984).

[2] A "hawk" is a competitive member of a group who has a clear solution as a goal which is perceived as "winning", and who is prepared to engage in contentious tactics, sometimes including violence, in order to "win" in the short term. A "dove" is a person whose major goal is peace and non-violence, achieved by peaceful methods including yielding, even if achieved at short-term costs. A "moderate" is a person whose goal is to find a solution acceptable to all disputants and interest groups, by a combination of mild contentious tactics, negotiation, face-saving and compromise.

[3] A "whiteant" is a termite which eats timber in houses leaving a veneer of strength, which however collapses under the slightest pressure.

References

Hammond, J. S., H. Raiffa and R. L. Keeney. 1999. *Smart Choices: A Practical Guide to Making Better Decisions*. Danvers: The Crown Publishing Group.

Johnston, J. R. and L. E. G. Cambell. 1988. *Impasses to Divorce: The dynamics and resolution of family conflict*. New York: Free Press.

Kahneman, D. 2011. *Thinking, Fast and Slow*. New York: Farrar, Straus and Giroux.

Lewicki, R. J., D. M. Saunders and B. Barry. 2005. *Negotiation*. New York: McGraw-Hill Education.

Moore, C. W. 2003. *The Mediation Process: Practical Strategies for Resolving Conflict*. San Francisco: Jossey-Bass Wiley.

Pruitt, D. G. and S. H. Kim. 2003. *Social Conflict - Escalation, Stalemate, and Settlement*. New York: McGraw-Hill Education.

Stanford Center on Conflict and Negotiation. 1995. *Barriers to Conflict Resolution*, edited by K. J. Arrow, R. H. Mnookin, L. Ross, A. Tversky and R. B. Wilson. New York: W. W. Norton & Company, Inc.

Wade, J. H. 1996. Tools for a Mediator's Toolbox: Reflections on Matrimonial Property Disputes. 7 *Australian Dispute Resolution Journal* 93: 1-9.

Wade, J. H. 2000. *Representing Clients at Mediation and Negotiation*. Queensland: Bond University Dispute Resolution Centre.

ᜣ 79 ᜥ

Multiparty Negotiations in the
Public Sphere

Sanda Kaufman, Connie Ozawa & Deborah Shmueli

Editor's Note: Most negotiation research in the laboratory, and much practical wisdom in the field, concerns the actions of "dyads", i.e. pairs of individuals negotiating with each other. This is far from the real-world environment of major public disputes. And in such disputes, blindly following the typical advice from less complex environments can get the negotiator or mediator and the clients into real trouble. The authors use case studies from three highly dissimilar environments to unpack the negotiating differences that apply when the parties are many, the stakes are high, and the situation is unstable.

Negotiation research, academic textbooks and popular "how-to" books often describe dyadic (two-party) processes for either triumphing over an opponent or crafting coveted "win-win" outcomes together with the opponent. The term "third party" for interveners such as mediators

Sanda Kaufman is Professor of Planning, Public Policy and Administration at Cleveland State University's Levin College of Urban Affairs. Her research spans negotiations and intervention in environmental and other public conflicts; social-environmental systems resilience; decision analysis; program evaluation; and negotiation pedagogy. Her articles have appeared in the *Journal for Conflict Resolution*; the *Negotiation Journal*,; Conflict Resolution Quarterly; *International Journal for Conflict Management*; *Negotiation and Conflict Management Research*; *Revue Négociations*; and others. B. Arch. and M.S. in Planning, Technion; Ph.D. in Public Policy Analysis, Carnegie Mellon University.
Connie P. Ozawa is a professor in the Toulan School of Urban Studies and Planning at Portland State University, is Director of the PSU-China Innovations in Urbanization Program, and works with the National Policy Consensus Center. Her specialty areas are negotiation and conflict resolution, environmental policy and planning and planning education. BA in Environmental Studies, University of California, Berkeley; MA in Geography, University of Hawaii; PhD in Urban Planning, MIT.
Deborah F. Shmueli is a faculty member in the Department of Geography and Environmental Studies and a co-Principal Investigator of the Minerva Center for Law and Extreme Conditions, University of Haifa, Israel. She is a planner specializing in public policy issues and has published widely in these areas. Strong foci are public sector conflict management, community and institutional capacity building. BS and MCP, MIT (1980); DSc, Technion (1992).

reflects the dominance of the dyadic frame, to the near-exclusion of multiparty conflicts that are neither rare nor lacking in impact. The dyadic perspective prevails even when addressing situations where negotiators represent the interests of two broad, internally diverse groups (Harbom, Melander and Wallensteen 2008). Such are international, labor-management and other conflicts pitting against each other two groups within which multiple, divergent interest subgroups (Lax and Sebenius 1991: 154; Raiffa 1982: 166) must develop a shared stance. Despite the dominance of the dyadic research perspective, recognition of the specific characteristics of multiparty conflicts and of the need to tailor to them negotiation prescriptions is not recent (Nyhart 1983; Bacow and Wheeler 1984; Kramer 1989; Keefe et al. 1989: 222-231; Lax and Sebenius 1991; Polzer, Mannix and Neale 1995; Pruitt 1998; Crump and Glendon 2003). However, multiparty negotiations have yet to receive a comparable share of research attention.

In this chapter, we characterize multiparty negotiation processes. We use three public sector examples. They serve our purpose well: they typically involve individuals, public agencies at multiple levels of government, private and nonprofit organizations, and special interest groups. We highlight what is alike and different from dyadic situations. We discuss what these differences mean for the negotiators, for interveners, for stakeholders who are not at the negotiation table, and for negotiation theory prescriptions.

Dyadic vs. Multiparty Negotiations

Negotiation texts define multiparty negotiations as having more than two parties, whether individuals or monolithic groups (Lax and Sebenius 1991: 154). Even when only one person or entity is added to a dyad, differences between bilateral and multilateral negotiation dynamics emerge, ranging from increased cognitive overload to process intricacies and difficulties in reaching integrative agreements. Some challenges are also present in two-party settings but are intensified, while others are specific to multiparty negotiations.

Similar but greatly intensified challenges include logistics and basic negotiation analytics.[1] Relatively straightforward tasks—coordinating calendars and meeting places, setting agendas, structuring, organizing and running the negotiation process—quickly become more cumbersome with each additional party. As in bilateral negotiations, each party should still heed negotiation theory prescriptions: build relationships, explore mutually beneficial tradeoffs, exchange full proposals rather than negotiate each issue separately, help generate creative and implementable options, and write contingent agreements. The presence of those able to make decisions and implement them remains important, but often becomes more difficult to accomplish. Participants need to (and should) prepare thoroughly; however, the number of issues and the interests embedded and reflected in them proliferate dramatically with more parties. The individuals' cognitive overload from having to handle information about complex issues and about each party, and the higher number of bilateral interactions added to plenary multi-party interactions, can be mentally taxing.

However, the differences between dyadic and multiparty negotiation challenges go beyond simply scaling up. Some difficulties specific to multiparty conflicts include:

- interactions between best alternatives to a negotiated agreement (BATNAs) of multiple parties;
- away-from-the table events;
- coalitions to increase leverage (Polzer, Mannix and Neale 1998; Dupont 1996), whether natural or de facto[2] (Lax and Sebenius 1991: 158);
- the need to negotiate and ensure representation of stakeholding interests even before substantive negotiations begin, and
- the need to negotiate a decision rule.

Together, these differences amount to a qualitative change in the negotiation terrain.

Consider the following: Two parties prepare for negotiations by learning about each other, and strategize by thinking of what the other person might say or do in response to various moves. Each can also explore options that serve their own objectives while also being acceptable to the other; they can find times to meet; and when they do not talk with each other no negotiations are going on. The two parties can discuss the need for an intervener.

With even one additional party, the information load for each participant multiplies and the preparation becomes more time-consuming, as negotiators must consider not only their own relationship with each of the other parties, but also the relationships *between* the other parties. Proposed options have to accommodate a greater number of different interests and are more difficult to change, as one of the parties is likely to see itself as losing something already acquired. Three or more calendars have to be scanned to find meeting times. Strategizing now requires imagining BATNAs related to each of the two other parties, and for the two together, contingencies, as well as leveraging one's own shifting BATNA. And two of the three parties can meet or talk separately, and ally against the third. Although two-party negotiations may also benefit from intervention, the added complexity of multiparty negotiations makes facilitator or mediator help almost imperative. Some even advocate negotiation support systems (Swaab et al. 2002).

Given the differences between two- and many-party negotiations, does what we know about dyadic situations apply to multiparty ones? We argue here that many of the distributive and integrative prescriptions do still apply, but that their application has to be tailored to the challenges of multiparty disputes. We further argue that the unique features of multiparty negotiations require additional analytical consideration.

We describe next multiparty negotiations over public decisions. In this realm, conflicts shift quickly from complicated to complex. That is, the unpredictability of negotiation processes and outcomes rises due not only to interactions among parties and with the systems they are trying to alter, but also because the systems within which they are embedded are in constant flux. [See NDR: Coleman et al., *Intractable Conflicts 1 & 2*; and NDR: Coleman & Ricigliano, *Getting in Sync*] This is more seldom the case in dyadic or within-team negotiations (Kangasharju 1996).

Characteristics of Multiparty Public Decisions

We focus on public decisions because many multiparty conflicts include a public agency. Many public disputes are also place-bound, so the cast of characters in various negotiations overlaps, with negotiators bringing to the table a history of relationships and trust, or lack thereof. In the private sector when negotiations may not directly involve government, agencies nonetheless may be brought in as "second table" stakeholders or to help resolve conflict. For example, construction disputes between contractors and sub-contractors often involve public agencies with jurisdiction over land use, transportation or financing.

Public disputes also have some distinctive characteristics worth noting. While private agreements do have consequences in the short, medium and long term, the longer the horizon of consequences, the less likely the public officials present or represented will benefit or suffer from them or be responsible for their decisions to constituencies, and the more room there is for shifting burdens of solving current problems onto future generations absent from the negotiation table [NDR: Wade-Benzoni, *Future Generations*]. An example that illustrates well all these features is that of intra-national and international negotiations surrounding climate change mitigation and adaptation initiatives.

We describe next three public conflicts[3] at three different sites and scales—community, city-wide and regional. We offer these snapshots to convey the complexity, the backward-and-forward time and issue linkages, the changing contexts, the stakeholders' shifting stances and alternatives and other aspects that challenge multiparty negotiations. These very different cases bring out specific instances of the multiparty effects discussed above, and also show patterns that lie beneath these multiparty attributes. One case was a conflict, while the two others were initiatives around which consensus was sought. All three illustrate the increased complexity (Innes and Booher 2010) of multiparty negotiations, whatever the scale and substance of the conflict or the horizon of decision consequences.

Our Stories

The Nofit-Chawaled Dispute, Israel[4]

Non-agricultural forms of community settlements have joined Israel's rural fabric since the mid-1970s. Their residents belong to syndicated cooperatives operating at municipal, social, cultural and partially economic levels. Nofit, in the Lower Galilee, was formed in 1986 as such a community by 180 families. After the Israeli Ministry of Interior expanded Nofit's municipal planning boundaries in 1997, 350 more families built homes using Nofit's infrastructure, and became part of the community, though not of the syndicated cooperative. A single municipal board was formed in 2003 to unite the original and the newer residents.

The Chawaled Bedouin family has lived for decades on 6.5 acres of land they own directly outside the planning boundaries of the original Nofit, on the scenic drive between its original and newer sections. The clan's 57 members form 12 nuclear families. Their very modest houses, some built before 1965, lack electricity and sewage. Their income derives primarily from outside employment in the region. The Chawaled children attend Bedouin schools in the nearby communities.

After Nofit's boundary expanded, the Chawaled land fell within it. Since then, the Chawaleds applied four times to have their lands rezoned from agricultural to residential. In the late 1980s and early 1990s, Nofit's local board of unpaid, elected community leaders supported the Chawaleds' efforts to gain residential building rights. Their last request entailed less than 2.2 of their 6.5 acres, of which, in accordance with Israeli Planning Law, 40% would then be slated for public use. This plan was rejected at the local level. But the family won its appeal to the National Council for Planning and Building (NCPB), which instructed the local zoning board "to advance a planning solution which will meet the needs of the Chawaled residents on their land." NCPB also linked any future Nofit development, where the community envisioned another 200 homes, to the planning of the Chawaled land. It subsequently approved the plan within which the Chawaleds' 2.2 acres were slated for residential development. Many in the Nofit community saw a Bedouin entity in their midst as a threat to their way of life. A heated dispute arose which made national headlines and created divisions between the Chawaleds and Nofit, and within the Nofit community itself.

The community made efforts to find consensus. Through a collaborative process, it developed a non-binding Strategic Plan that only made a passing reference to the Chawaled land. This plan enabled consensus by essentially burying a conflict which, as was clear even at the time, was bound to reignite. In 2010-2011 the Nofit municipal board hired a mediator to facilitate a discussion about the Chawaled land among a subgroup of 20-30 Nofit community activists, including strong opponents and supporters of the Chawaled residential development. The group unanimously recommended developing an expansion plan for Nofit including the Chawaled land.

In 2012, the Nofit community held board elections in which two competing slates both campaigned on the promise of a future Nofit without Bedouin development in its midst. After the elections the Nofit community was torn again. An editorial[5] in the local newsletter—picked up both regionally and nationally—called for "another voice" than the racist discourse evincing fear of the "other," marked by aggressive speech against Chawaled supporters, and permeating all age groups in both the new and original sections of the community. Residents signed a petition calling for the Nofit board to initiate a community process to reconsider its position with respect to the Chawaleds and Nofit's future expansion. While no open meeting was convened, behind the scenes negotiations began.

Originally the conflict appeared dyadic—Nofit versus Chawaled. However, it quickly became apparent that there were multiple, divergent interest sub-groups within Nofit. Some sought residential expansion of the community, and others did not; some supported the Chawaleds historically and currently, some wanted more information, and some were outright opposed to any concessions. There were divisions even among institutional players: the Israel Land Administration (ILA) and the Regional District Planning Committee held different (and changing) positions. Meanwhile, Bedouin unrecognized villages elsewhere in Israel had become the subject of a national conflict on the brink of eruption. Supreme Court decisions were bringing about changes in national policies. The Chawaled opponents were now out of sync with national and district perspectives. The pro-Chawaled coalition enlisted the support of national NGOs who brought to the community supporters from around the country, along with negative publicity for Nofit's "rejectionist" group.

In 2014 the municipal board originally elected to defeat the Chawaled development, even if it meant no expansion for Nofit, decided to proceed with Nofit's expansion, including a plan the Chawaled family proposed for building on its own land. The board presented its plan in an open Nofit community forum. By 2015 the planning bodies, in collaboration with community committees including Nofit residents and members of the Chawaled family, prepared the combined Nofit-Chawaled plan. Still, dissenting voices—now a small minority—are likely to challenge this new plan, more than 25 years in the making, though they are not expected to impede plan implementation.

The West Eugene Collaborative[6]

For more than two decades, the state of Oregon and local jurisdictions had supported construction of a by-pass parkway to connect I-5 through Eugene to the Pacific coast, to relieve traffic congestion. By the early 2000s, the Oregon Department of Transportation (ODOT) earmarked funding to begin project design and construction. However, during the intervening years, the political landscape changed. Environmental issues gained traction as the 1973 Endangered Species Act was broadened to include habitat conservation plans. The 1973 Oregon land use statute required communities to include citizen participation in decision making, to coordinate transportation systems and to draw an "urban growth boundary" to contain urbanization. Planners and advocates were urged to integrate land use planning, and vocal opposition to ODOT's narrowly-focused plan emerged. On the ballot in the 2002 local elections, the project passed but by only a narrow margin. In 2006, two local elected officials withdrew their support, effectively killing the ODOT plan.

In early 2007, a small group of civic leaders, including the mayor, formed the West Eugene Collaborative (WEC). Its 27 members—both proponents and opponents of the parkway project—included political, government and business leaders, community members, and environmental activists (Oregon Consensus 2009). Despite recurrent invitations, ODOT elected not to participate. The WEC sought assistance from Oregon Consensus, whose director suggested professional facilitation. The WEC pooled contributions from the city, the county, the local transit agency, and local business and environmental organizations, and hired a team of Colorado-based mediators.

Although the WEC's initial impetus was the proposed West Eugene Parkway, participants quickly understood that transportation was tied to broader conflicts about how to develop the West Eugene corridor. Additional issues included wetlands that the federal Bureau of Land Management had recently purchased for protection. Growth management and quality of life were also of concern, as transportation alternatives such as public transit and biking grew increasingly popular in this university town. This shift was accompanied by a change in the nature of the intervention, from mediation ostensibly around transportation issues to facilitated consensus building around a more integrated land use and transportation plan. The Colorado mediators had met regularly with the WEC for several months. However, WEC needed more attention and their funds were strained by out-of-state travel costs. With mutual recognition of these constraints, the Colorado team stepped away, to be replaced by two Portland-based facilitators.

The process had some significant milestones. The Colorado mediators had approached the situation as a dispute. The first milestone was the Portland-based team's reframing of the process into an effort to reunite a divided community through collaborative planning.[7] Another milestone was a "design-storm" event. One WEC participant contributed a set of maps to help ground the WEC's discussions. This event effectively surfaced more than 300 issues that were clustered and winnowed down to a manageable set. The third milestone occurred when a participant introduced a pedestrian-oriented or "multi-use boulevard" vision for a major transportation corridor. This vision enabled the group to link their concerns to physical elements. The lack of technical support to WEC from the public agencies lent importance to this participant's technical contributions, but also created some resentment, as he became "first among equals".

In March 2009, the WEC report presented recommendations for achieving short, medium and long-term milestones. Eight broad objectives ranging from the immediate, practical and measurable to the longer run and the intangible undergird the recommendations:

- Improve efficiency of the transportation network
- Increase public transit
- Enhance pedestrian paths and bikeways
- Intensify development appropriately
- Relocate some land uses
- Enhance open space/natural resources
- Enhance the natural watershed
- Enhance appreciation and connections to natural resources

Participants and local government applauded the WEC process. Not only did all members sign the agreement, but a year after the signing, 15 participants who were interviewed (of the 27 total members) all expressed satisfaction over the relationships they had built with each other [See NDR: Hollander-Blumoff, *Relationships*]. Also, after concluding the agreement, WEC members went out in "unlikely pairs" (business and environmental advocates) to share the report and generate community and public agencies' support.

Implementation of the WEC report action items, however, has proven challenging. Despite the WEC members' presentations to state agencies, little has been added to state transportation and land use departments' budgets for specific projects. On the other hand, local agencies, including the district transit authority, have moved forward on the Eugene's city government's request to route its expansion of a bus rapid transit (BRT) line to West 11th Avenue, where the WEC had recommended a "multi-use boulevard," coincidentally providing for minor street improvements consistent with the WEC report. BRT planning had unfolded concurrently with, but separately from the WEC process. Creek restoration projects consistent with WEC recommendations have also been undertaken, again not because of the report but in response to requirements by the state environmental agency. Thus, several changes WEC proposed for the 5-year horizon have been implemented, but as a timely confluence of similar plans by other agencies. Notably, the BRT project continues to elicit visible opposition from local businesses who were not directly represented in the WEC.

The Vibrant NEO 2040 Initiative[8]

The population of Cleveland, Ohio has steadily declined from nearly one million in 1950, to fewer than 300,000 in 2010. "Legacy" cities such as Cleveland suffer from multiple physical and socio-economic problems.

Conflicts about how to respond to the shrinking city and surrounding communities that depend on it have accompanied the decline. Public, private and nonprofit sector leaders have attempted repeatedly to offer metropolitan and regional answers. Past initiatives have run into difficulties due to lack of resources, acute administrative fragmentation, and lack of consensus. In 2010, the Vibrant NEO 2040 project sought again to tackle current problems in the Northeast Ohio region surrounding Cleveland and to forestall future threats such as climate change.

A newly constituted Northeast Ohio Sustainable Communities Consortium (NEOSCC) with a $4.25 million federal grant set out to plan a 5575 square-mile region (13% of Ohio's area) encompassing twelve Northeast Ohio counties, where almost 4 million people—one third of Ohio's population—reside. In 2011, NEOSCC convened elected officials from the twelve counties and four cities, together with directors of several metropolitan planning organizations (MPOs), planning and housing agencies, regional transportation and infrastructure providers, nonprofit organizations, the Metroparks, two universities, and the Natural History Museum. NEOSCC sought to create "conditions for a more VIBRANT, RESILIENT, and SUSTAINABLE Northeast Ohio ... that is full of vitality, a good steward of its built and natural resources, and that is adaptable and responsive to change" (Vibrant NEO 2040 2014b).

Although NEOSCC had no governance mandate, some of its members did, and could recommend to their organizations and agencies decisions consistent with Vibrant NEO 2040. Relationships forged during deliberations and plan development were expected to yield a regional network of leaders who would continue to coordinate their spatial, environmental, economic and social management decisions using a joint information base. NEOSCC aimed high for a participatory planning process. It intended to respect choice for Northeast Ohio residents; to promote informed decision making; eliminate waste of resources in the region; and to "improve quality of life by promoting integrated regional land use and housing, transportation, and capital investment planning to enhance the region's economic competitiveness, increase its resilience, provide its citizens better access to decent, affordable housing, and offer more cost-effective transportation choices" (Vibrant NEO 2040, 2014a).

NEOSCC participants met monthly from 2011 to 2014. Subcommittees met more often to collect data. A relatively small paid staff handled outreach through websites and community events.

In 2011, NEOSCC conducted public participation events throughout the region. It sought input about preferred urban forms, transportation modes, amenities and relationship to the natural environment. In 2012 NEOSCC presented Vibrant NEO to the public electronically, and at meetings in different locations. It completed a regional land use map showing boundary-crossing roads and infrastructure networks[9]—a first for the 12 counties—and a Conditions and Trends Platform for scenario design. The Platform contained data about natural and built regional assets, and threats to them from air and water pollution and from increasing urban sprawl.

During 2012 and 2013 NEOSCC launched a regional "dashboard" of performance indicators. Consultants generated four scenarios for 2040 regional outcomes, based on trend-based forecasts assumed to be accurate reflections of what would happen in the year 2040.[10] Predicted consequences of planning decisions were also assumed reliable at a 25-year horizon. The scenarios differed in population growth patterns, transportation, community character, environment, agriculture and fiscal health. They were to show which development approaches—ranging from "trend" to "grow the same," "grow differently," "do things differently"—would translate expressed public preferences into regional realities, by 2040,that would achieve Vibrant NEO's objectives to:

- Promote investment in established communities
- Promote the environment
- Increase fiscal health
- Develop economically with accessible options (i.e. public transportation and education)
- Enhance the Regional Transit Authority and other public transportation
- Celebrate local assets and public values
- Expand parks and open spaces
- Preserve farm land

The objectives appear universally desirable, lacking specificity to Northeast Ohio, or any prioritization. (In other words, a classic "wish list".) Objectives and scenarios presented at public meetings were to build consensus around one of the development approaches (Feick and Hall 2001). Attendees expressed their 2040 outcome preferences on maps and through polling devices. Public support for the regional governance approach ("do things differently") scenario was interpreted as sanctioning it.

Despite process and information shortcomings, Vibrant NEO 2040 has value, though not quite as NEOSCC expected. One benefit is the electronic information base now available to the region's planning agencies, universities and nonprofit organization. Another beneficial side effect of the process is strengthened relationships and communication lines among leaders of regional decision-making entities, now willing to share information and even collaborate across administrative boundaries. The relationships may endure even without the NEOSCC structure. However, the main goal of crafting an implementable plan based on regional governance has yet to be attained.

Multiparty Negotiations: Insights from Reality

These three cases illustrate several issues and difficulties common in multiparty negotiations.

Complexity: Due to multiple parties and many moving parts; as a result, stakeholders' BATNAs were often changing. For example, the changes over time in the Israeli regulatory environment forced Chawaled opponents to recognize that their litigation BATNA was weaker than they originally thought. Equally, the Nofit community was subject to several layers of administration that changed rules. WEC and NEOSC participants were buffeted by BATNA-altering political and economic winds. Their stakeholders belonged to numerous organizations and agencies, each responsible for geographically diverse areas. Among them, some had traditionally hierarchical power structures while others were more ad hoc, and some even lacked mandates for representing the interests they defended. NEOSCC contended with the administrative structures and issues of 12 counties, several metropolitan planning agencies, county administrators and elected officials, as well as interest groups—each bound by different operating procedures with different timelines.

Issue linkage: The Israeli NCPB's linkage of Nofit's residential expansion with the submission and approval of a Chawaled residential plan was a turning point in the negotiations. Linkage of transportation to general land use strategies including growth management, environmental protection and quality of life issues resulted in a reframing of the WEC goals in Oregon. Vibrant NEO was predicated on the connections between land use and transportation decisions, and between the Ohio region's quality of life and environmental protection.

Long time spans and changing contexts: The Nofit case began in the late 1980s and ripened into an overt conflict in 2011-2014, when Israeli Supreme Court decisions brought about changes in national policies, resulting in the NCPB overturning district decisions to now favor the Chawaleds. Changing national and district positions grew apart from the fears and aims of the Nofit community and local regional council, which had previously enjoyed anti-Chawaled policy backing.

The transportation issue at the heart of Oregon's WEC predated it by at least 30 years. By 2006, when ground breaking was finally imminent, the political landscape rendered it undesirable. This reversal occurred in part because over time, support for alternative transportation modes and attention to environmental issues, backed by changes in federal and state laws, had gained salience.

Regional governance for halting Northeast Ohio's socio-economic and environmental decline had been proposed and repeatedly rejected since the mid-1970s. Since then, participatory decision making has become the norm, and several energy and economic crises combined with climate change concerns to shift public priorities toward sustainability. This shift afforded elected officials space to consider cooperating to solve regional problems, where competition had previously dominated.

Multiple parallel processes: (Diermeier et al. 2008) There was little continuity between the Nofit 2010-2011 mediated consensus-building process under one local municipal board, and the renewed debate with the next board. Parallel processes occurred outside the WEC, including the planned bus rapid transit extension and the responses of the Bureau of Land Management and other local agencies to federal water quality regulations. Although individuals connected to these other processes were also involved in the WEC, their participation was not formally linked, though they could have provided a channel for information exchange and collaboration. There was also no explicit connection between NEOSCC and previous or ongoing efforts to bring about regional governance in Northeast Ohio, though many NEOSCC members also participated in them. While crafting Vibrant NEO, participating administrators continued to respond unilaterally to federal and state mandates, incentives and funding priorities. Note that while engaging in a parallel process might be viewed as "improving one's BATNA," exploration of alternative avenues to achieve desired goals has the potential to create ripple effects on the other parties' BATNAs in a multiparty negotiation.

Representation: Participation in multiparty processes almost always poses challenges in terms of who is included, excluded, under- or over-represented, and who is able to make binding decisions. In Nofit, the 2010-2011 mediated process included only Nofit residents from both sides of the issue. The municipal committee and the mediator believed they could protect minority voices better in a closed consensus-building process. This led to difficulties in updating constituencies. Those opposed to the Chawaleds' demands at the outset of the 2010-2011 mediated process who *were* at the table changed their position and agreed to include the Chawaled development in the Nofit expansion plan. However, they failed to sway their *constituents*, who remained adamantly opposed and ignorant of information uncovered during the closed process [NDR: Wade, *Tribe*]. Between 2012-2014, the need for away-from-the-table negotiations and coalition formation emerged, and subsequently happened. Dealing with the new municipal board's behind-the-tablexi (Sebenius 2012) barriers proved very difficult. It required probing individual and group interests, and the interests and interdependencies of the local, regional and national institutions involved.

In Oregon, WEC representation issues became stumbling blocks in three ways. First, the absence of ODOT from the WEC was likely a missed opportunity for transportation funding and for technical support, which WEC participants might have viewed as more "impartial" than support from citizen participants or even local agencies. Second, local businesses located along West 11th Avenue were not at the table, which may account for their continued opposition to the current BRT project. Third, the mayor and local agency staff participation in the WEC created some ambiguity about the WEC process in relation to other planning activities unfolding at the same time. The public agencies were not instructed to integrate WEC decisions into their plans, despite the overlap in geographic boundaries and the highly germane topics (e.g. transit planning). How these participants wore their "multiple hats" and how the others understood their roles pose added complex dilemmas in understanding participants' interests and BATNAs.

In Ohio, NEOSCC erred by failing to include effectively the views and interests of Northeast Ohio residents. While elected officials with decision authority took part in devising Vibrant NEO 2040, they would ultimately have to be responsive to constituents who have traditionally balked at regional plans, threatening Vibrant NEO's implementation. During NEOSCC's project, few in the region were aware of or got to participate meaningfully[12] in, crafting vision and solutions. Public events reached only a small proportion of the 12-county population. Participants in these events were essentially polled on whether they would prefer the good life[13] or the bad—and then their rather predictable answers were framed as an endorsement of Vibrant NEO 2040. The project's implementation difficulties may stem partly from the failure to engage the public meaningfully.

Alliances and coalitions: The Chawaleds and their supporters coalesced with those in Nofit for whom expansion was critical to growth (a de facto coalition; cf. Lax and Sebenius 1991). This coalition engaged national NGOs lobbying for Bedouin rights, to boost their leverage. WEC members saw the value of teaming up with those from different backgrounds (the "unlikely pairs" of businessmen and environmentalists) to explain the report to various constituencies. NEOSCC had a like-minded core that spearheaded it. Representatives of the large urban counties coalesced, seeing their interdependence and similarity of interests; they drove the process. Representatives of rural or border counties became relatively disengaged, and some adopted an observer stance which diminished their impact on the outcome.

Information: In all three cases there was a measure of failure to convey information to constituencies not at the table, or between processes. In the moment, concealing information or not disclosing and disseminating it effectively may seem to parties at the table an expedient way to avoid opposition. This strategy is risky if excluded stakeholders perceive their interests to be seriously threatened.

During the Nofit 2010-11 mediation, shared information led to consensus around the table to include the Chawaleds along with the Nofit expansion. This transformation, inadequately communicated to the constituents, resulted in a highly emotional election campaign focused on *opposition* to this recommendation. WEC members presenting the report to the public communicated with established organizations, such as the Chamber of Commerce—but not with the less formally organized businesses lining the BRT path, many of whom continue to oppose the BRT. NEOSCC actively *avoided* including in its public events residents whom they viewed as especially opposed to regional plans. This strategy may yet backfire: should Vibrant NEO move toward implementation, the conflicts avoided during the planning process with those who find their interests threatened by regional plans will surface. In all three cases, failure to transfer information from the negotiation table to constituents—whether strategic or inadvertent—is ineffective at eliminating conflict and sets back implementation of agreements.

The WEC and NEOSCC cases also illustrate the difficulties of managing stakeholders' different types and levels of knowledge, and varying access to data and processing ability. In multiparty situations, the differential capacity of the participants means that information and its management can become devices for surreptitious reallocation of influence and even resources. The WEC attempted to co-construct its information base, but faced with no resources to obtain assistance, allowed one of the members to process data and display it, simply because he had the skills. This implied that the others had lesser comprehension and oversight ability. NEOSCC members collected data and then handed it over to consultants for processing, relinquishing control over the translation of data into knowledge and meaning. They did so for a reason—the highly technical modeling required for representing the data. Yet the result showed that as with the WEC, the effort to co-construct the information base for the negotiation process was flawed.

Types of agreements: While the Nofit-Chawaled dispute resulted in a plan, the WEC and NEOSC consensus building processes reached agreements (captured by reports) that consisted of discrete tasks and of general rather than site-specific and strategic undertakings. But both reports' recommendations were of the "mom-and-apple-pie" or "low-hanging fruit" kind. WEC recommended short-, middle- and long-term objectives. The short-range ones were low-hanging fruit—already in the works, and independently implemented by local agencies. The longer-term ones were more general ("mom-and-apple-pie"), with no indication of responsibilities or implementation process. NEOSCC also framed its recommendations in "mom-and-apple-pie" terms—so positive as to be unobjectionable, but also not implementable without more negotiations.

Initiatives such as WEC's or NEOSCC's that aim for consensus among numerous and diverse stakeholders may end up prizing consensus above resolving the problems that led to the dispute or initiative. Negotiators skirt polarizing issues in order to promote consensus. During lengthy, costly processes, reaching agreement acquires a higher priority than its implementation. Therefore, agreements tend to obscure necessary tradeoffs, and reach for the easily-implementable or broadly acceptable—but also impractical—all-good promises. The result is low implementability of the agreements. Disagreements and serious concerns do not simply disappear; they are merely swept under the consensus rug, likely to re-emerge when actions are imminent and parties understand their interests are threatened [NDR: Wade & Honeyman, *Lasting Agreement*]. Dealing openly with conflicted issues during negotiations, by contrast, can prolong the process and even threaten consensus, but may increase the likelihood of implementing agreements.

The exclusion of those known to hold contentious views is also a result of the quest for agreement. This tactic may seem expeditious. However, dissidents rarely go away. They bide their time and act when it matters to prevent implementation of agreements that appeared consensual among those around the incomplete table [NDR: Wade, *Tribe* and NDR: Reynold, *Activism*]. The understandable desire to negotiate only with friends suggests a profound misunderstanding of consensus building that is illustrated by our three cases. Rather than aiming for *full* consensus—which then does provide an incentive for selecting negotiation partners who are "on the same page"—the objective should be to build *sufficient* (not unanimous) consensus. The "sufficient consensus" standard, explored in a different context by Robert Mnookin (2003), might be generally useful to multiparty negotiations, and contribute to implementing change. This decision rule may free participants from making too many concessions for the sake of consensus, and from seeking to negotiate only with those who think alike.

The three cases also show a tight connection between "who" is represented and the sensitive and critical nature of problem formulation. The "what" that is being negotiated is shaped by the concerns and interests of those who are participating, and the more diverse the membership, the more likely it is that the problem definition will be nuanced and will change from its initial formulation. The WEC case illustrates well such a transformation, from a transportation dispute into a much broader discussion of the landscape and interactions between cars, pedestrians, cyclists and the nearby creek. While this may seem counterintuitive, bringing more groups to the negotiation table might actually create greater opportunities for a stable agreement.

Conclusion

Despite the prevalence of multiparty conflicts, their similarities to, and particularly their differences from two-party processes have drawn rather sparse attention. As analysis of these three cases shows, basic negotiation theory developed in the dyadic context remains valid in multiparty contexts. Additional negotiators create difficulties due to the need to track numerous sets of interests, BATNAs, and moves—a quantitative shift. However, multiparty negotiations are not simply more difficult. They are more *complex* in its more rigorous, scientific sense—a qualitative shift. The passage of time, the potential for concurrent parallel processes, the formation of coalitions and alliances among participants, and the likelihood of issue linkage or integration resulting in "problem re-formulation" combine not only to increase cognitive difficulties, but also require different negotiation tools and strategies. More subtle differences occur due to the parties' interdependence and their understanding of their interests and BATNAs. As a result, multiparty negotiations tend to be far more fraught than dyadic encounters.

We have identified six categories of characteristics of multiparty negotiations:

- complexity,
- long time frames and changing contexts,
- multiple and sometimes parallel processes,
- representation/alliances/coalitions,
- information imbalances,
- intervention processes/decision rules/types of agreements.

In one of the few works that has examined qualities specific to multi-party negotiations, Lawrence Susskind, Robert Mnookin, L. Rozdeiczer and Boyd Fuller (2005) concluded that, "(1) coalition formation; (2) problems of process management; and (3) the constantly shifting or kaleidoscopic nature of each party's best alternative to a negotiated agreement were three crucial differences between multiparty and two-party negotiation..." (Susskind et al. 2005: 396). Our three cases, with different issues and at different scales in three vastly different regions of the world, confirm these multiparty-specific traits, and reveal additional characteristics. Both Susskind et al. and the present analysis underscore that multiparty negotiations warrant special attention. The risks of not refining our understanding of the distinctiveness of and honing our skills specifically for multi-party negotiations are considerable. Without appropriate strategies and tools, participants may spin their wheels going down roads that they might have been advised to avoid.

Our three examples illustrate how multiparty negotiations are distinct from dyadic negotiations. Although basic negotiation theory provides an essential foundation, they show how multiparty negotiations are not a multiplier of dyadic negotiation dynamics. Further research in uncovering the many nuances of multiparty negotiations to build theory in this area will enable us to better understand the nature of conflict and disputes—and to efficiently and effectively address them.

Notes

[1] Lawrence Bacow and Michael Wheeler have called this class of problems "coordination" (Bacow and Wheeler 1984: 104).
[2] According to Lax and Sebenius (1991), natural coalitions emerge among parties who share strong interests, while de facto ones bring together parties who only share some interest in the moment and may subsequently part ways.
[3] Each case was documented by one or more of the chapter's authors.
[4] The Nofit case is based on information from one of the authors, who participated in it as a resident, and documented the process.
[5] This editorial was co-written by one of the chapter co-authors.
[6] The authors collected WEC information from contemporaneous documents and interviews, and from surveys of participants and interveners by the United States Institute of Environmental Conflict Resolution.
[7] Asah et al. (2012) discuss this approach, which they call "diagnostic reframing," in the context of environmental conflicts.

[8] The Vibrant NEO 2040 case study is based on NEOSC documents, interviews with participants, and attendance at NEOSC meetings, events and training workshops by one of the co-authors together with Kathryn Hexter, Director, Center for Community Planning and Development, Levin College of Urban Affairs, Cleveland State University. [9] Prior to Vibrant NEO, some of region-spanning systems' maps stopped at administrative (county or metropolitan area) boundary lines.

[10] If this were true, we should be able to use trends from 1900 to 1950 to predict Northeast Ohio's current population. Forecasters account for the gap between predictions and reality by mentioning discontinuities in the data—events at 10- to 15-year intervals that effectively altered the trends. There is no reason to assume that such discontinuities will not occur and current trends will hold over the next 25 years.

[11] *Behind-the-table* refers to the negotiations the representatives at the table have to conduct with their constituents (e.g., Sebenius 2012).

[12] Meaningful participation entails informing the public and framing its choices in transparent terms.

[13] Asking the public to envision its far future tends to yield predictable results: everyone wants everything. There is easy consensus around the "good life." However, this approach obscures any priorities and differences around them, or any necessary trade-offs. The consensus is thus misleading: the road to the "good life" is paved with short-range decisions bound to satisfy some while displeasing others. Therefore, the consensus conceals and postpones conflicts.

References

Asah, S. T., D. N. Bengston, K. Wendt and K. C. Nelson. 2012. Diagnostic Reframing of Intractable Environmental Problems: Case of a Contested Multiparty Public Land-use conflict. *Journal of Environmental Management* 108: 108-119.

Bacow, L. S. and M. Wheeler. *1984. Environmental Dispute Resolution*. New York: Springer Science+Business Media.

Crump, L. and A. I. Glendon. 2003. Towards a Paradigm of Multiparty Negotiation. *International Negotiation* 8(2): 197-234.

Diermeier, D., R. I. Swaab, V. H. Medvec and M. C. Kern. 2008. The Micro-dynamics of Coalition *Formation. Political Research Quarterly* 61(3): 484-501.

Dupont, C. 1996. Negotiation as Coalition Building. *International Negotiation* 1: 47-64.

Feick, R. D. and G. B. Hall. 2001. Balancing Consensus and Conflict with a GIS-based Multi-participant, Multi-criteria Decision Support Tool. *GeoJournal* 53(4): 391-406.

Harbom, L., E. Melander and P. Wallensteen. 2008. Dyadic dimensions of armed conflict, 1946—2007. *Journal of Peace Research* 45(5): 697-710.

Innes, J. E. and D. E. Booher. 2010. *Planning with Complexity: An Introduction to Collaborative Rationality for Public Policy*. New York: Routledge.

Kangasharju, H. 1996. Aligning as a Team in Multiparty Conversation. *Journal of Pragmatics* 26(3): 291-319.

Keefe, T. F., D. J. Thomsen, W. T. Tsai and M. R. Hansch. 1989. Multi-party Conflict: the Problem and its Solutions. In *Computer Security Applications Conference, 1989., Fifth Annual*. Los Alamitos, CA: IEEE Computer Society Press.

Kramer, R. M. 1991. The More the Merrier? Social Psychological Aspects of Multi-party Negotiations in Organizations. In *Research on Negotiation in Organizations* edited by, M. H. Bazerman, R. J. Lewicki and B. H. Seppard. Greenwich, CT: JAI Press.

Lax, D. A. and J. K. Sebenius. 1991. Thinking Coalitionally: Party Arithmetic, Process Opportunism, and Strategic Sequencing. In *Negotiation Analysis*, edited by H. P. Young. Ann Arbor, MI: University of Michigan Press.

Mnookin, R. H. 2003. Strategic Barriers to Dispute Resolution: A Comparison of Bilateral and Multilateral Negotiations. *Journal of Institutional Theoretical Economics* JITE 159(1): 199-222.

Nyhart, J. D. 1983. Negotiating Conflict over Marine Resources: The Use of Multiparty Models. *Environmental Impact Assessment Review* 4(3-4): 557-560.

Oregon Consensus *West Eugene Collaborative* (WEC). http:/oregonconsensus.org/projects/west-eugene-collaborative-wec/.

Polzer, J. T., E. A. Mannix and M.A. Neale. 1995. Multiparty Negotiation in its Social Context. In *Negotiation as a Social Process*, edited by R. M. Kramer and D. M. Messick. Thousand Oaks, CA: SAGE Publications, Inc.

Polzer, J. T., E. A. Mannix and M. A. Neale. 1998. Interest alignment and coalitions in multiparty negotiation. *The Academy of Management Journal* 41(1): 42-54.

Pruitt, D. G. 1998. Social Conflict. In *The Handbook of Social Psychology*, edited by D. T. Gilbert, S. T. Fiske and G. Lindzey. New York: McGraw-Hill.

Raiffa, H. 1982. *The Art and Science of Negotiation: How to Resolve Conflicts and get the Best out of Bargaining*. Cambridge, MA: The President and Fellows of Harvard College.

Sebenius, J. 2012. *Level II Negotiations: Helping the Other Side Meet its 'Behind the Table' Challenges*. HBS Working Paper No: 13-004 (July 2012). Available online at http://www.hbs.edu/faculty/Publication%20Files/13-004_a587fda3-c822-41b0-98 b8-1436cdf2f9a3.pdf (last accessed May 23, 2016).

Susskind, L., R. Mnookin, L. Rozdeiczer and B. Fuller. 2005. What we Have Learned about Teaching Multiparty Negotiation. *Negotiation Journal* 21(3): 395-408.

Swaab, R. I., T. Postmes, P. Neijens, M. H. Kiers and A. C. M. Dumay. 2002. Multiparty Negotiation Support: The Role of Visualization's Influence on the Development of Shared Mental Models. *Journal of Management Information Systems* 19(1): 129-150.

Vibrant NEO 2040. 2014a. *Vibrant NEO 2040*, A Vision and Framework for Our Future: Initiative and Goals. Northeast Ohio Areawide Coordinating Agency Building. Available online at http://vibrantneo.org/vibrantneo-2040/initiative-goals/ (last accessed on December 22, 2015).

Vibrant NEO 2040. 2014b. *VNEO 2040 Final Report*. Northeast Ohio Areawide Coordinating Agency Building, February 2014. Available online http://vibrantneo.org/vibrantneo-2040/vneo-2040-full-report/ (last accessed on December 22, 2015).

03 80 80

Agents and Informed Consent:
After the 2008 Financial Crisis

Jacqueline Nolan-Haley

Editors' Note: How can you-the-negotiator ensure that your client is really on board? Nolan-Haley argues that by paying more attention to "informed consent" not only before, but again at intervals during a negotiation, and taking care to reaffirm this as the process reaches agreement, agents will not only better serve their clients but reach better, more lasting agreements. Yet revisiting the subject, years after the 2008 financial shocks demonstrated the degree to which large institutions were ignoring these principles, she finds strong evidence that lawyers and other professionals with a duty to their clients have badly failed them. As a result, she concludes that if your attorney isn't asking you the hard questions, it's in your interest to ask the attorney why not. This chapter should be read in conjunction with Wade's Bargaining in the Shadow of the Tribe.

In an earlier iteration of this chapter in 2006, I examined the concept of informed consent and its potential to address principal-agent tensions in negotiation, tensions which, if not managed properly, may present a barrier to settlement. Informed consent operates in a multitude of different settings, from participatory democracy to international treaties on hazardous chemicals. In the broad political context, the principle of informed consent holds that legitimate government depends upon the informed consent of the governed. It is a bedrock principle deeply ingrained in the moral interstices of American ethical and legal culture. As a legal doctrine, informed consent requires that individuals who give

Jacqueline Nolan-Haley is a Professor at Fordham Law School, where she directs the ADR & Conflict Resolution Program and teaches courses in ADR, International Dispute Resolution, and Mediation. She is a member of the ABA Standing Committee on Mediator Ethical Guidance, and of the Ethics Committee of the ABA Dispute Resolution Section. Her recent publications include *Mediation and Access to Justice in Africa: Perspectives from Ghana*, 21 Harvard Negotiation L. Rev. 59 (2016); *Mediation: The Best and Worst of Times*, 16 Cardozo J. Dispute Resolution 731 (2015); and *Procedural Justice Beyond Borders: Mediation in Ghana*, Harvard Negotiation Law Review Online, (co-author) http://www.hnlr.org/2014/03/procedural-justice-beyond-borders/.

consent do so as competent individuals, based on relevant information and acting voluntarily. This means that in the agency context, principals need to understand not only the consequences of authorizing agents to negotiate for them but also the consequences of any outcomes that are reached. In representative negotiations, the principle of informed consent is not an end in itself but is a means of achieving the fundamental goal of fairness. This goal requires that principals know what they are doing when they authorize agents to negotiate for them, that they understand the decision-making process, including their right to withdraw consent and discontinue negotiations, and that they understand the outcome reached in negotiation. In short, informed consent advances three primary goals in negotiation: it promotes human dignity, honors party self-determination and helps to achieve the fundamental goal of fairness. From a more pragmatic perspective, informed consent has a beneficial impact on the long-term durability of agreements that agents negotiate on behalf of principals.

I focused specifically on legal negotiations, and sketched a framework for informed consent based on a robust deliberative exchange between lawyers and clients whose relationship is one of agent to principal. The legal profession's conceptual support for informed consent is grounded in its ethical rules. The ABA Model Rules of Professional Conduct describe informed consent as "the agreement by a person to a proposed course of conduct after the lawyer has communicated adequate information and explanation about the material risks of and reasonably available alternatives to the proposed course of conduct" (American Bar Association 1.0(e)). While the rules provide some conceptual support for the principle of informed consent, they offer little practical guidance to lawyers on how informed consent should operate. Lawyers are required to "explain a matter to the extent reasonably necessary to permit the client to make informed decisions regarding the representation." (ABA Rule 1.4(b)) Guidance on the regulation of client consent rights is somewhat murky. Model Rule 1.2(a), which governs the allocation of decision-making power in the attorney-client relationship, establishes an ends/means approach in which the client decides the ends of a given problem, i.e. whether to accept a particular settlement offer, and the attorney decides the means. The inherent complexity of determining what constitutes real ends and means has created challenges in integrating this distinction into practice.

Other legal and ethical norms are more straightforward in this area. As an agent, the attorney must act in accordance with her principal's instructions and is responsible to her principal if she violates this duty, and ABA Model Rule 1.7 establishes the lawyer's duty of loyalty towards her client (Olfe v. Gordon 1980: 577).

In a world of perfect informed consent practice, the transfer of authority from the client-principal to the lawyer-agent would be a relatively straightforward matter. Principals would understand their positions and the underlying interests that support them as well as the opposing principal's positions and underlying interests. They would also understand the range of possible agreements, and their BATNAs. Likewise, agents would understand their own interests and where they might not be aligned with those of the principal. Agents would inform principals of their divergent interests, clarify the extent of their authority, and determine whether there were any non-negotiable issues. Principals and agents would then discuss all of these issues, principals would grant authority to agents, and negotiations would proceed.

But, in the real world of legal practice, the informed consent process is a complicated project. Enter the human factor—emotions, psychological biases, and different behavioral orientations that affect principals and agents and influence agendas. Mere discussion between principals and agents will be unlikely to create an understanding of the principal's and agent's respective divergent interests. Echoing professional responsibility scholars, I bemoaned the reality that oftentimes, rather than listening to their clients, lawyers presume to know their goals (Ellman 1987; Heller 1994). As an alternative lawyering behavior, I recommended a robust regime that called for intense deliberations between lawyers and clients. Such a deliberative process would help to achieve greater understanding of each other's views, and ultimately to assist clients in making informed decisions.

> *In the give and take of argument and debate, lawyers and clients gain a better understanding of each other's views. The deliberative process calls for careful calculation and reasoned dialogue. It is a reflective activity that requires active participation by principal and agent. The heart of the deliberative process is the exchange of ideas and debate between principal and agent about ends and means, goals and strategies.*

Post-2006

Fast forward ten years later. Much has happened in several fora to reinforce the powerful appeal and significance of the consent principle. The Supreme Court's recent decision in *Wellness International Network, Ltd. v. Sharif* (2015) brings consent to the forefront, emphasizing the importance of a litigant's knowing and voluntary consent when agreeing to forego adjudication in an Article III court.[1] On the international front, the United Nations published a guide for effective mediation that emphasizes the importance of consent in protecting the integrity of mediated negotiations. The report notes that "[W]ithout consent it is unlikely that parties will negotiate in good faith or be committed to the mediation process" (U.N. 2012).

The Financial Crisis of 2008

All of this is less arcane and more practical than some might think. The global financial crisis of 2008 provides a sobering and even searing example. What happened to the consent principle in the events leading up to the market's meltdown? In the aftermath of the global financial crisis, it is instructive to ask—what if the lawyers involved with that crisis had paid more attention to the idea of informed consent in counseling and negotiating for their clients?[2] Would the narratives be different today? One of the many challenges posed by representative negotiations is loss of control by the principal. Jeffrey Rubin and Frank Sander's (1988: 400) classic article on the use of agents in negotiation reinforces the point—"once agents have been introduced the chemistry changes...." Well-known examples of this "chemistry change" arise where the incentives of the principal and agent are not aligned or where the risk preferences of an agent differ from those of the principal. The implication for legal negotiations is that once lawyer-agents become involved, client-principals may find themselves less in control. Paradoxically, the converse may have occurred during the financial crisis, with sophisticated client-principals—the banks and investment houses—controlling their lawyer-agents.

The story of the bottom falling out of the financial market begins with the practice of subprime lending. (Center for Public Integrity 2014). Mortgage lenders made loans to buyers at risk who then offered as security the homes that they purchased with the proceeds of the loan. These loans, as described by Professor Steven Schwarcz (2010), "were ... bundled together as collateral to partially support the payment of complex asset backed securities that were sold to banks and other institutional investors..." Home prices began to decline, resulting in delinquency and default on subprime mortgage loans. Thus, institutions that were deeply invested in these securities were required to "write down their value, causing these institutions to appear if not be financially risky..." (Schwarcz 2010). This precipitated what Schwarcz (2010) has referred to as "systemic shocks" in the financial system:

> As counterparty risk increased, financial institutions stopped dealing with each other, reducing the availability of credit. Similarly as securities backed by subprime loans began defaulting, investors stopped investing not only in those securities but also in securities backed by the types of collateral. That too, reduced the availability of credit. And the lack of credit devastated the real economy.

Much ink has been spilled on the question of identifying the villains and assigning blame in the sub-prime crisis (Hill 2010). Who were the likely suspects? Borrowers? Lenders? Investors? (Thoma 2011; Rakoff 2014). Lawyers did not escape notice. A report issued by The Center for Public Integrity (2014), inquired—"Where were all the lawyers as the system was crashing right in front of them?" Others might have inquired—Where were Anthony Kronman's (1993) "lawyer-statesmen" who could have discovered and safeguarded the public good? (Apparently, they were nowhere to be found.) Were zealous advocates hiding behind the dominant conception of the lawyer's role as neutral partisan? ("Neutral partisan" may seem an oxymoron, but is an accepted concept in legal ethics.) (Luban 1988; Pearce and Wald 2012).

No doubt lawyers played a role with their clients in the negotiations and decision-making that contributed in large part to the near collapse of the market. It is a role, however, that is shrouded in secrecy, enveloped in the privacy of lawyers' ethical rules on confidentiality, the hallmark of the attorney-client relationship (Kellogg 2010; American Bar Association 1.6). Thus, we may never know for sure how lawyers negotiated and navigated the system for their clients, despite investigations conducted by activist attorneys general, the Financial Crisis Inquiry Commission (FCIC) and federal officials.

What if Lawyers Had Paid Attention to the Principle of Informed Consent?

The literature following the global financial crisis has addressed a number of important issues, including the appropriate role of lawyers to both their clients and the public (Rapp 2010; Romano 2014). It is not clear about the extent to which lawyers should share blame for the events that led to the financial crisis.[3] For one, they may have been kept in the dark by sophisticated clients who had enough control of the flow of data to entirely exclude awkward information from their attorneys' reach (Markovic 2014). Alternatively, they may have informed their clients of the adverse consequences of their proposed activities, and have then met with total resistance by powerful clients who fit the profile described by Stephen Ellman almost 20 years ago as those "who enjoy economic leverage over their attorneys, clients whose own expertise rivals their lawyers' knowledge, and even, perhaps, clients who are simply so unusually aggressive as to command their lawyers' close attention..." (Ellman 1987). Other lawyers may have followed the rules of professional responsibility, and learning of their client's intent to engage in criminal or fraudulent conduct, withdrew from representation (American Bar Association 1.16(a)(i)). We simply do not know.

What we do know is that attorneys did represent financial institutions engaged in the purchase and sale of financial products that precipitated a near collapse in the global financial system (Markovic 2010: 2). Consider the multiple transactions and negotiations that must have occurred with in-house and outside counsel surrounding the financial

crisis, and the complex and esoteric documents and financial arrangements that lawyers crafted. We can only imagine what might have happened if lawyers had followed an informed consent regime in negotiating
for their clients instead of what one scholar has described as acting as "...
an obliging butler to their clients who believe their function is to serve up
whatever their clients want to hear" (Kellogg 2010).

Imagine what the deliberative process might have looked like in a
pre-negotiation counseling session. Lawyers, sufficiently educated in
principles of economics and finance,[4] would pose several inquiries to
their clients: Who else should be at the table? (Wade 2006). What is
happening away from the negotiating table? (Doherty and Campbell
2006: 475). What work has been done to evaluate the creditworthiness of
mortgages that have been pooled together and sold as collateralized debt
obligations? Have both the loan officers granting the mortgages and the
investment bankers collateralizing them really reviewed the creditworthiness of the borrowers? How does the compensation structure for
these officers and bankers create incentives for them to grant mortgages
and to collateralize them, and does it go so far as to encourage overlooking problems that should be obvious? Have the lawyers working to prepare the collateralized debt obligations reviewed the documents pertaining to the underlying mortgages? What information has been shared
with the credit rating agencies? Have the credit rating agencies, in turn,
reviewed the creditworthiness of the mortgages that have been pooled
together and sold as collateralized debt obligations? How does the compensation structure for the credit rating agencies impact their incentives
in determining the structure of the pool of collateralized debt obligations? To what extent is the sale of collateralized debt obligations driven
by the liquidity needs of the bank? What role do the profits earned from
the sale of these securities play? What risks does this work create for the
bank? Do you understand the risks associated with these investments?[5]
What is the long-term strategy regarding collateralized debt obligations?
As work in this area grows, what safeguards have been put in place to
protect the bank? What is the likely impact of the growing use of collateralized debt obligations on the subprime mortgage market, the debt markets, and the macro-economy?

As lawyers might have engaged with their clients on these questions,
they also might have informed their clients of the legal, ethical and moral
consequences of their proposed course of conduct.[6] This suggestion is
not purely speculative. The foundation for moral counseling is established in the Model Rules of Professional Conduct, Rule 2.1 which provides that "In rendering advice, a lawyer may refer not only to law but to
other considerations such as moral, economic, social and political factors
that may be relevant to the client's situation." Would understanding
these risks and their potentially harmful consequences have prevented
clients from going ahead with their harmful conduct? Quite possibly not.
Constrained by the duty of loyalty and ethical rules giving clients control

of the outcome, lawyers might still have just gone along, as they have done in some other negotiation contexts.[7]

Conclusion

It is worth considering and re-considering the value of informed consent when agents negotiate. I do not claim that if informed consent regimes had been in place in the negotiations connected with the financial crisis of 2008, America and the world would be in a better economic place, or that the crisis would have been averted. My more modest goal is to suggest that informed consent regimes that operate in negotiations with agents challenge us to think about what could be better ways of negotiating for clients. They should also serve as a salutary warning for clients—who, if their attorneys don't seem to be asking them the hard questions, would be well served by asking their attorneys why not.

Notes

I thank Professor Caroline Gentile, a Fordham colleague specializing in corporate law, for her insights on the questions that lawyers should have asked their financial clients.

[1] "Adjudication based on litigant consent has been a consistent feature of the federal court system since its inception" (Wellness International Network, Ltd. v. Sharif 2015: 17).
[2] Thus far, the legal profession has responded to the fallout from the financial crisis with only aspirational changes in professional responsibility rules (Berger 2011).
[3] Some scholars are agnostic on this issue and note that we do not have the same evidence of lawyer complicity that existed with the savings and loan scandal or Enron (Langevoort 2012).
[4] See Berger's (2011: 14) article for a discussion on the merits of requiring lawyers to be trained in finance and economics and (Schwarcz 2010).
[5] It is not clear that lawyers understood the risks (Markovic 2014).
[6] One scholar has argued that lawyers have the right to inform clients of harmful consequences but not the duty—"individual lawyers should not have to decide, at the risk of liability whether client actions are socially harmful where society itself has not made that explicit determination (by making the actions unlawful) (Schwarcz 2010).
[7] In a study of lawyers' ethics conducted by Professor Art Hinshaw, 30% of the lawyers said they would violate the truthfulness standards in ABA Rule 4.1 if their clients wanted them to do so (Henshaw and Alberts 2011).

References

American Bar Association, Model Rules 1.0(e), 1.16(a)(1), 1.4(b) and 1.6.
Berger, B. E. 2011. The Professional Responsibility of Lawyers and the Financial Crisis. *Review of Banking & Financial Law* 31: 3-15.
Center for Public Integrity. Who's Behind the Financial Meltdown: The Top 25 Subprime Lenders and Their Wall Street Backers. Accessed May 16, 2016. http://www.publicintegrity.org/node/5554.
Docherty, J. S. and M. C. Campbell. 2006. Consequences of Principal and Agent. In *The Negotiator's Fieldbook*, edited by A. K. Schneider and C. Honeyman. Washington, DC: American Bar Association.
Ellmann, S. 1987. Lawyers and Clients. *UCLA Law Review* 34: 717-779.
Heller, J. G. 1994. Legal Counseling in the Administrative State: How to Let the Client Decide. *Yale Law Journal* 103: 2503-2530.
Hinshaw, A. and J. K. Alberts. 2011. Doing the Right Thing: An Empirical Study of Attorney Negotiation Ethics. *Harvard Negotiation Law Review* 16: 95-161.

Hill, C. A. 2010. Who Were the Villains in the Subprime Crisis and Why it Matters. *Entrepreneurial Business Law Journal* 4: 323-349.

Kellogg, S. 2010. Financial Crisis: Where Were the Lawyers? *DC Bar*. http://www.dcbar.org/bar-resources/publications/washington-lawyer/articles/january-2010-financial-crisis.cfm.

Langevoort, D. 2012. Getting Too Comfortable: In House Lawyers Enterprise Risk and the Financial Crisis. *Wisconsin Law Review* 2012: 495-519.

Luban, D. 1988. *Lawyers and Justice: An Ethical Study*. New Jersey: Princeton University Press.

Markovic, M. 2014. Subprime Scriveners. *Kentucky Law Journal* 103: 1-44.

Olfe v. Gordon. 286 N.W.2d 573 (1980).

Pearce, R. G. and E. Wald. 2012. Rethinking Lawyer Regulation: How A Relational Approach Would Improve Professional Rules and Roles. *Michigan State Law Review* 2012: 513-526.

Rakoff, J. 2014. The Financial Crisis: Why Have No High Level Executives Been Prosecuted. *The New York Review of Books*. http://www.nybooks.com/articles/archives/2014/jan/09/financial-crisis-why-no-executive-prosecutions/.

Rapp, W. V. 2010. The Lawyers and the Meltdown: The Role of Lawyers in the Current Financial Crisis. *International Financial Review* 11: 135-164.

Romano, R. 2014. Regulating in the Dark and a Postcript Assessment of the Iron Law of Financial Regulation. *Hofstra Law Review* 43: 25-93.

Rubin, J. and F. Sander. 1988. When Should We Use Agents? Direct vs. Representative Negotiation. *Negotiation Journal* 4: 395-401.

Schwarcz, S. L. 2010. The Role of Lawyers in the Global Financial Crisis. *Australian Journal of Corporate Law* 24: 214-226.

Thoma, M. 2011. Economist's View: Lawyers and Accountants Helped to Cause the Financial Crisis? *Economist's View*. http://economistsview.typepad.com/economistsview/2011/06/lawyers-and-accountants-helped-to-cause-the-financial-crisis.html.

United Nations. Guidance for Effective Mediation. Accessed May 16, 2016. http://www.un.org/wcm/webdav/site/undpa/shared/undpa/pdf/UN%20Guidance%20for%20Effective%20Mediation.pdf.

Wade, J. H. 2006. Bargaining In the Shadow of the Tribe. In The Negotiator's Fieldbook, edited by A. K. Schneider and C. Honeyman.

Wellness International Network, Ltd. v. Sharif, 575 U.S. ___ (2015).[SM2]

"Who's Behind the Financial Meltdown: The Top 25 Subprime Lenders and Their Wall Street Backers." *The Center for Public Integrity*. 2014. http://www.publicintegrity.org/node/5554.

☙ 81 ❧

Dueling Experts

John H. Wade

Editors' Note: Your case is complicated; it involves specialized knowledge, and without some help, the judge probably won't understand it and the jury certainly won't. Furthermore, your chances of negotiating a settlement depend on getting some degree of shared understanding with the other side of what the facts are. So you've hired your expert, and the other side has hired its expert—and now the experts themselves are locked in combat. Could you avoid this next time? In the meantime, what do you do now? Wade analyzes your options at every stage, and shows how even when the experts have delivered black-versus-white reports of the facts, you can still salvage the situation. This chapter should be read in conjunction with Adler on Negotiating Facts.

A common cause of conflict is missing information or data perceived to be inaccurate. One response to data conflict involves the employment of two or more alleged experts to support the opinions of the parties to the conflict. One definition of an "expert" is "a person who has special skill or knowledge in some particular field" (The Macquarie Dictionary 1982: 628). These alleged experts may be medical doctors, engineers, lawyers, valuers, builders, accountants or psychologists—to name a few. Experts who are asked to give opinions frequently give diverse opinions on causes, values, and predicted futures.

One positive side of employing experts is that they may be able to reduce data conflicts, such as:

John Wade is an emeritus professor of law of Bond University, Queensland, Australia. He practiced as a lawyer in Australia between 1987 and 2012, and also had an active mediation practice in organizational, family and commercial conflicts during those years. He has taught over 300 mediation and negotiation courses in Hong Kong, New Zealand, London, Canada, the U.S. and Australia. John has published over 100 books and articles (see epublications@bond.edu.au). His teaching awards include best law teacher at Sydney University (1989); at Bond University (1990); and in Australia (1998). John now lives in Vancouver, Canada with his growing family, and teaches intensive negotiation courses there.

- What caused the concrete to crack?
- What degree of pain will the injury cause in the future?
- How much is the corner store worth?
- What is a judge likely to decide in two years' time?
- How much will the repairs cost?
- How much profit will the business lose over the next ten years due to X?

Many data conflicts are settled due to the dispassionate opinions of one or more alleged experts about history, causation or the future.

But disputants are often astounded to find that two experts can be "so far apart" (Crystal Auburn Pty. Ltd. v. I. L. Wollerman Pty. Ltd. 2004). There is also a darker side to the practice of seeking expert opinions in order to settle conflict (Egan 1994). This problematic side often emerges as the conflict escalates. Instead of being part of the solution, the alleged experts become part of the problem for the clients, and for the mediator or facilitators. The writer has labeled this common phenomenon as "dueling 'experts' syndrome" (Wade 2000). Mediators and professional negotiators become voyeuristic observers of the darker sides of expert assistance.

Dueling Experts' Syndrome

This syndrome involves some or all of the following patterns of behavior: each disputant employs a different expert (ours is the best in the field); each disputant hires an expert who has a reputation for favoring that disputant's preferred outcome (reputational partiality *e.g.*, a plaintiff's doctor); tells different stories to their own expert (garbage in, garbage out); expressly or impliedly hints at the advice she wants from the expert (remember who is paying you). The experts initially do not consult with each other (delusionary isolation); the expert, in order to curry favor and ensure future employment from a repeat player, tells the client in writing what he wants to hear (you get what you pay for); the written over-confident report does not set out either a clear list of factual presumptions made, or the details of the terms of the expert's employment instructions (garbage in, garbage out again), or a clear list of alternative interpretations, or a range from best to worst of alternative "legitimate" views in the field (delusionary certainty); the report is long, rambling and sometimes incomprehensible to the average citizen (mysterious complexity); and each expert is instructed not to show draft reports to the other (no early doubts or compromises).

Once the over-confident (versions of the) expert reports are published, each expert defends his/her version with increasing verbal intensity and insult in order to preserve reputation, ego (now it is personal), future employment and maybe even to settle old scores. Then the expert does what is expected as a snarling Doberman (this is our opening offer). The disputants then invest large amounts of time and money to resolve a personal conflict between the two experts as a pre-requisite to resolving their own conflict.

There are other fascinating psychological and economic dynamics to dueling experts' syndrome, particularly when the dueling experts know each other well, enjoy the game, and carry personal baggage from frequent past encounters. More troubling is the repeated pattern whereby many experts, who advocate a particular view, actually begin to both believe in and emotionally support their own view (Festinger 1957).[1] Wayne Brazil (1978-79: 110) has commented:

> It is commonly believed by many litigators that to simply turn over all the relevant data to a consultant expert is to flirt with disaster: namely, the possibility that your expert will reach a negative conclusion about the role of your client. To reduce the chances of such an eventuality, many litigators carefully control the flow of information to their consultants.... Their hope is that the expert will form a positive opinion, will identify with the attorney's client, and will develop an ego investment in the positive conclusion that the attorney wants reached. Thereafter, the attorney may feed the expert some negative data about the client's conduct in order to prepare the expert to withstand cross-examination. By the time the expert receives the bulk of the negative information (at least so goes the litigator's theory of manipulation), he has so heavily identified with the client's position and has invested so much of his own professional ego in his positive opinion that all his impulses are in the direction of defending rather that reevaluating that opinion. Thus the lawyer hopes to capitalize on the expert's relatively predictable reactions to cognitive dissonance.

The Dynamics of Negotiation and Experts

The normal dynamics of negotiation add additional complexity to, and justification for, dueling experts' syndrome. First, dueling experts know consciously or subconsciously that they are part of a predictable process. It is well known in negotiation research, anecdote and mythology that vigorous claims usually achieve better number outcomes than moderate claims. [NDR: Schneider, *Productive Ambition*] Therefore, if an expert report is both over-confident and near to the "insult zone" (the insult zone is the number of dollars, acres, rockets, which on current information has no objective support from the marketplace or from "the going rate"), then it will usually achieve a better outcome for the client than if the report is balanced, qualified and closer to "the truth" or the settlement zone (Lewicki, Saunders and Barry 2006).[2] Where an expert produces a "moderate" report, then this shifts the bargaining range considerably in favor of the other expert who has produced an extreme report (Lewicki, Saunders and Barry 2006).

Second, an enthusiastic dueling expert provides a useful "bad cop" for the ubiquitous good cop—bad cop negotiation routine. "Deal with the pleasant client, or else we will have to hand this dispute over to our rabid (lawyers, valuers, psychologists, doctors, engineers, etc)." As one CEO whispered to me during a mediation, "can we go outside and talk? We will never get anywhere with all those people arguing their theories" (nodding towards a group of entrenched expert engineers and lawyers). Whereupon the two CEOs and the mediator went for a long walk and settled the dispute under a gum tree. In that case, were the dueling experts helpful to the negotiation or not?

Third, well-known experts who produce long reports may be a useful part of a strategy of attrition to wear out the other disputants. Those other disputants then feel obliged to keep spending on opposing, well-known and highly priced experts in order to create doubt by appearing credible, argumentative, persistent and willing to respond with reactive attrition.

Once again, such apparently dysfunctional routines by dueling experts may sometimes become functional. These are important negotiation dynamics for negotiators and mediators to recognize and try to respond to constructively, even if we do not always approve of these sometimes tiresome, expensive, self-serving and inflammatory routines (Australian Law Reform Commission 1999-2000).

How Can Negotiators and Mediators Respond to Dueling Experts?

Let us assume that the "problem" of dueling experts has already arisen. That is, as conflict managers we are not here considering the important question of how to avoid or minimize preemptively the dynamics of dueling experts. That pre-emptive question will continue to be a major item for law reform agencies and for negotiation tacticians in the future. The writer's preference is for the roadblock of dueling experts to be anticipated by smart conflict managers. Anticipation can then lead to a number of preventive tactics.

As the majority of conflicts are settled or abandoned, mediators and lawyers are often left with the "hard cases," or escalated disputes. This residue often has attracted the dynamics of dueling experts, such as doctors, lawyers or accountants, who are "far apart." What can a negotiator, lawyer or mediator do in these cases?

Where a professional negotiator is able to have preparation meetings with individual disputants in person, by email, or over the phone, this provides the ideal time to identify any dueling experts, define the problem of experts in conflict, lower expectations, and begin to foreshadow the "normal" range of responses to dueling experts. Examples of "preparatory" questions by a negotiator might include:

- "So our valuers have come up with preliminary opinions which are miles apart? What can we each do about that?"
- "What will we do at the negotiation when predictably one lawyer says 'I'm right,' followed by the other lawyer saying, 'No, I'm right'? Will they just blah-blah at each other? How much time should be allocated to the 'I'm right, you're wrong' routine?"
- "From what you say, the engineers' initial reports are on different planets? Is that correct? In my experience, we cannot expect one or both to say suddenly 'Oops, I am wrong'."
- "What can you do about the differing medical reports? Flip a coin? Split the difference? I don't want the negotiation meeting to be a waste of time for us all."

More specifically, when confronted with a standard hurdle in negotiations, mediators and negotiators are often taught to go through the following three steps.

Step 1—When in Doubt, Reframe or Summarize

In joint or separate meetings, the first thing that negotiators (and many other skilled helpers) are taught to do is to put a new or old name humbly on what is happening (Boulle 2001).

"Reframing" is the skill of taking an existing feeling or perspective, and putting this into a new set of words, images or metaphors. [NDR: Gadlin et al., *Metaphors*] Reframing has many potential benefits, including giving new vocabulary, creating doubt and providing a new set of spectacles with which to view an old problem. New perspectives may create changed negotiation behavior.

For example, the problem here might be reframed as, "we both believe that our experts are right, and yet they are so far apart;" "how is it that two experts can come to such different conclusions?;" "our experts seem to have left us with a problem;" "expert one says that the grass is blue, and expert two says that the grass is yellow—is that correct?"

Step 2—Convert the Standard Problem into Standard Problem-Solving Questions

Orthodox problem-solving and decision-making literature emphasizes that "the right question is half the answer" (Hammond, Raiffa and Keeney 1999).

The standard hurdle of dueling experts can routinely be converted into standard problem-solving questions in emailed agendas, on flip-charts or whiteboards in words such as:

- How to respond to conflicted expert opinions?
- What do others do when confronted by differing experts?
- How to solve our problem of dueling experts?

- What can be done about differing (legal) opinions?
- How can our two experts be so far apart?

Step 3—Brainstorm Non-Judgmentally the (Standard) Range of Options

In the writer's experience as a negotiator and mediator, it is very helpful to disputants to realize that their conflict or "problem" is normal, that thousands before them have experienced the same situation, and that the same thousands of disputants have brainstormed through a list of optional solutions and found one which is at least "satisfactory" to both.

Ideally, this list of options should be extracted slowly and put on a flip chart arising out of the suggestions of the disputants. Visible charts can promote clarity and ownership. Prompts may be used such as:

- "What do we do when two plumbers suggest opposite solutions to a roof leak?"
- "How have other businesses handled such conflicting advice?"

These prompts can become more directive:

- "I'm not suggesting that you should do this, but I have had clients who asked the conflicted experts to write a joint report explaining how two experts could be so far apart. Should I add that to the list of possibilities?"
- "Would you like me to write up some of the 12 ways I have seen clients respond to this common problem? You may have other ideas also."
- "Of the 12 methods we have recorded on the board, which have we seen used most often? If you wish, I can circle the three that I have seen my clients use most often."

The Range of Responses to Dueling Experts

Here are twelve common responses to the problem of dueling experts. It should be emphasized that, in any dispute, several of these responses can be tried. They are not exclusive. Some of these listed solutions will be so unsatisfactory to one or more of the disputants that the range of options may be narrowed quickly.

- Try to convince—"mine is better than yours" or "I'm right, you're wrong."
- Experts jointly explain why differences exist.
- Each expert answers a written list of questions.
- Experts write a jointly signed explanation of differences.
- Third advisory expert attends the mediation or negotiation.
- Third expert writes a non-binding opinion.
- Third expert writes a binding decision.
- Create doubt by introducing new or hypothetical facts.
- Split the difference.
- Trade chips.

- Toss a coin.
- Refer the decision to a judge.

Each of these possible responses will now be considered in more detail, with the advantages and disadvantages of each. Thereby a negotiator, mediator, lawyer or other skilled helper can "add value" to the decision-making process of clients.

Try to Convince—"Mine Is Better than Yours"

This first predictable response involves the disputants and their respective experts attempting to create doubt for the other side in a joint meeting, perhaps preceded by a written exchange of questions or assertions. Each party orally points out the strengths in their own expert's reports and opinions, and the weaknesses in the others' reports and opinions. The parties can agree upon a structured question and answer time period for each of the experts and/or the disputants. Sometimes the questions can be put in writing by one or more of the parties ahead of the meeting, or asked through the mediator, in order to reduce ambushes and aggressive cross-examination.

This procedure has many potential benefits—clarification, reducing "garbage in, garbage out" decision-making, and witnessing the skills of each expert when questioned. It is a systematic form of creating doubt and new information to assist better decision-making.

However, these debates have the obvious potential to degenerate quickly into attempts to publicly humiliate, and can lead to entrenchment of existing views, hiding information, and expert strutting. Experts, once scarred by such meetings, may be reluctant to face further semi-public batterings unless protected by clear procedures and a strong mediator as chairperson. Some judges, arbitrators and mediators adapt this type of meeting by excluding clients, and just convening a "conference of experts," in the hope of reducing loss of face. Like all interventions, the conference-of-experts has both advantages and disadvantages.

Experts Jointly Explain to the Disputants Why
Differences Exist

This second response is different in emphasis than the first. However, both overlap and may happen simultaneously.

The predominant goal is not for each expert to justify why he is "right," and the other is "wrong." Rather, each expert tries to explain visually, orally and in simple language to everyone present, how each conclusion was formed and why they are so different.

Obviously, this has the same potential benefits and detriments as the first response.

The writer has seen this response used effectively where groups of accountants have sat around the table and attempted to explain to everyone present why their valuations of businesses were so disparate. The clients have appreciated having underlying assumptions of each expert clarified, and hearing that valuation methods involve discretionary factors. In this way, posturing certainty was reduced to create realistic uncertainty. Judges sometimes use such joint conversational meetings of experts, and these are colloquially referred to as "hot-tubbing" of experts.

The predictable traps observed at these meetings have been that the experts slide quickly into professional jargon and other forms of insiders' shorthand, and become defensive during questioning. All of these may be remedied by use of visuals, reframing, strategic ignorance, admonitions and triangulation.[3]

Each Expert Answers a List of Written Questions

The third response is to negotiate a procedural agreement whereby each disputant agrees to send a written list of question to the "opponent's" experts, who are instructed to respond with written answers within an agreed time period. The cost of the written answers is usually borne by whoever asks for them.

There are some obvious benefits to this process, including clarification, creating doubt (for all sides), avoidance of hostile public cross-examination, considered responses and saving face. Some of these benefits may be absent in relation to the first two responses.

Experts Write a Jointly Signed Explanation

This fourth response to dueling experts is potentially one of the most helpful. This usually requires pre-mediation or pre-negotiation meetings at which the parties identify the dueling expert hurdle and engage in soft or hard brinkmanship. A negotiator proposing a meeting for that purpose might use phrases like these:

- "I do not want to waste our time and money by convening a meeting where we listen to experts making speeches."
- "Do you predict that either of our experts will back down at a public meeting? How can we help them to save face gently?"
- "I don't know about you, but I cannot understand these 52 pages of contradictory opinions. Who can decipher that maze for us all in words of one syllable?"
- "What if we both instruct your experts to sit in a room together for two hours and write out no more than two pages in point form explaining why their reports are so different?"

If persuaded, each disputant employs his own expert for a fixed period of time (say 3 hours) to sit in a room with the other expert, and write a "no more than two page document" explaining in simple language why their conclusions are different; most importantly, both experts must sign that single explanation. The temptation is always to create two more documents and two new explanations of "why I am right and he is wrong."

This response to dueling experts is also reflected in rules of court in many jurisdictions. Judges as decision-makers, like disputants as decision-makers, want to reduce the confusing garbage in (Australian Law Reform Commission 1999-2000).

If this response is potentially so helpful during negotiations or mediation, then anecdotally why is it apparently so uncommon? Here are some observed and hypothesized reasons for resistance by various parties to using this response:

- The joint report may divide the unity of a negotiating team. A key member, namely the expert, may create doubt publicly for his own team.
- An expert who admits to complexity and uncertainty will no longer be an effective "bad cop" in an accepted negotiation routine (and may not be hired again).
- The two (or more) experts may not have the skills to write such a short and simple report.
- The two experts may insist on writing two more reports to prove why their first reports were "correct."
- The joint report costs more money.
- Clients must be assertive in order to make experts (particularly lawyers) do what they want. The experts can legitimately respond: "This process may lead to some dangerous concessions, which will undermine the litigation if we need to proceed to court." (This comment reflects an ongoing and legitimate tension between competition and cooperation in any negotiation or conflict management).
- The jointly signed report may lead to a loss of reputation: "Why didn't you make this clear previously?"

Negotiators need to assist experts to overcome any resistance to revise, with standard comments such as: "Of course, we all know that opinions must be revised as new information emerges"; " I want to hear all the possible bad news early, not in eight months' time"; "We all know that there are legitimate differences of opinion in your fields of expertise, as there are in mine"; "We may have misled you both by feeding different information to you both"; "As you know, a joint report will be ordered by a judge, so let's do it now before our sunk costs escalate." Different cultures have fascinating sentences to help the experts save face.

Third Advisory Expert Attends the Negotiation or Mediation

This response to dueling experts involves both disputants agreeing that they need help, selecting a trusted "extra" expert from a list, or based on a recommendation, and agreeing on how to share payment for this person. Additionally, the parties may agree: that neither disputant will talk to the advisory expert privately; what telephone calls and inquiries can be made, and documents read by the advisory expert; how many meetings the advisory expert will attend; what oral comments are sought from the advisor and whether or not she will write a final report.

The writer has seen this response to dueling experts used very successfully in mediations in a variety of disputes, including renovations of a factory, valuation of superannuation and a business, and dealing with a child's response to a parent moving away.

The advisory expert should normally define her role and limit liability carefully in writing. For example, the written contract could restrict his/her role to that of a "commentator" using "limited" information and state that each party is relying on her own expert's advice. Otherwise, both disputants may turn on the advisor later and declare "but at the mediation/negotiation you told us...."

A skilled and gracious oral commentary by an extra expert, particularly if the commentary suggests "ranges" of possible outcomes, may avoid loss of face for the dueling experts. It is important to discuss whether the extra expert should be a friend, an associate, or a dispassionate stranger. This intervention may also allow the experts to resume bad-cop warfare untouched by diplomacy, if that round of negotiation is unsuccessful (Mosten 1997).

Third Expert Writes a Non-Binding Opinion

This sixth response to dueling experts is analogous to the previous option, except that the advisory expert is contracted to write a written report, explaining differences and recommending possible solutions.

The disputants usually record in this agreed process that neither will be bound by the opinion, that both are free to produce the opinion in later litigation, and that both are free to rely on their own experts if they wish.

The downsides of this response include increasing costs for the provision of a written report, wariness of professionals about publicly criticizing work of colleagues in documents, numerous reservations in the written report based on the ubiquitous proposition "I do not have all the facts," and the tendency to split the difference between the existing dueling experts' reports.

Third Expert Writes a Binding Decision

This seventh response to dueling experts involves the disputants agreeing to a specified process whereby a named third expert will decide the issue being debated by the dueling experts.

The disputants can each agree to be bound by the expert's decision (e.g. relating to valuation; cause of injury; extent of damages) and thereby create costs and estoppel risks if either tries to relitigate the decided question. (Many third party experts will prefer a form of arbitration as this substantially reduces any risk of liability for professional negligence while making the binding decision.)

Most mediators and negotiators have been involved in successful referrals to binding decisions by third parties. This process has many advantages, including privacy. Arbitration also provides nervous middle managers, CEOs, and governments with a third party to "blame" for the outcome when they are reluctant to take personal responsibility for a negotiated outcome (Wade 2001).

However, it should be repeated that this arbitral response to dueling experts also has a litany of well documented disadvantages, such as:

- Loss of control of the outcome.
- Risk of detrimental outcome.
- Delay and expense.
- Cloning the disadvantages of litigation.
- Tendency of arbitrators to split the difference (Murray, Rau and Sherman 1996).
- Lengthy negotiation and documentation concerning what is an appropriate arbitral process (Wade 2001).

Create Doubt by Introducing New or Hypothetical Facts

This eighth response is common, and is often combined with other responses to dueling experts.

A mediator or negotiator identifies a number of factual, evidentiary or "rule" assumptions which apparently provide the building blocks for each expert's opinion. These foundations may helpfully emerge if and when each expert "attacks" the other's report as "wrong." A mediator or negotiator can then gently and systematically go through this list of assumed facts and ask each expert in turn, first privately and then after rehearsal again in joint sessions—"What if the following new fact was accepted by a judge, would your existing opinions need any updating or variation?"[4]

This process of suggesting new hypothetical facts, has potential benefits of:

- Allowing one or both experts to change their opinions without openly admitting any mistake.
- Demonstrating that expert opinions will need to be updated regularly as new "facts" emerge (i.e. creates doubt).
- Enabling experts to remain aggressively confident of their initial reports "so long as no new facts emerge."
- Echoing the reality that judicial and historical fact-"finding" or fact-"reconstruction" is a hit-and-miss process. In the words of the legal realists, "facts are guesses" (Frank 1949; Twining 1984).

Therefore, hypothesizing new or even surprising "facts" or inferences is not an unrealistic decision-making routine. [See also NDR: Adler, *Negotiating Facts*]

Split the Difference

A very common method of managing the real or fake war between dueling experts is to split the difference between those experts. Obviously, this downstream negotiation practice encourages the upstream practice of hiring dueling experts! That is, hiring an extreme expert drags a subsequent split-the-difference outcome in your favor. Phrases a negotiator might use to explore this option include:

- "What if, only for the purposes of today's negotiation, we take the middle figure between the two valuers?"
- "What if we assume for the moment that a judge may award some damages rather than the all or nothing damages predicted by the two lawyers?"

For some disputants, this option of splitting the difference is frustrating as it appears to reward the blatant tactic of generating "false" reports. It also appears to punish further the person who has spent time and money to generate what is perceived to be a more balanced expert report. Nevertheless, the anecdotally frequent use or suggestion of splitting the difference suggests that negotiators need to be ready to manage this frustration.

Splitting the difference between experts is a frequent outcome in certain types of disputes. For example, in the writer's experience in matrimonial property disputes, lawyers routinely prepare for mediations and negotiations a single page summarizing the list of assets and alleged values of each asset. It is common for the right hand side of this summary to have three columns—namely "husband's value," "wife's value," and "mean" or "average value." The average value column gently prophesizes a possible or probable outcome of dueling valuations, at least in poor and middle class families.

Trade Chips (Sometimes Called "Logrolling")

This tenth response to dueling experts is the standard negotiation behavior of trading chips: "If I was prepared to accept (or move towards) your expert's opinion, would you be prepared to give me X?"

Sometimes this strategy may produce a similar substantive result to splitting the difference between the experts. Nevertheless, it may be more psychologically satisfying for one or more disputants who has personal priorities about which element of the packaged outcome is most important. The writer has frequently seen this kind of "trade" eventually take place in matrimonial property negotiations and mediations. A spouse who owns a business often wants his/her dueling expert's valuation of a business to prevail in order to placate business partners, to control future possible tax assessments, or because they have personal insights into the history of the business. Accordingly, the owner eventually is persuaded to make an offer to the other spouse as follows: "If I was prepared to move towards your percentage, would you be prepared to move towards my expert's valuation of the business?"

To which eventually comes the predictable response from the other: "As a matter of principle, yes ... but what do you mean by 'move towards'?"

Toss a Coin

Another possible, and more startling, method to resolve dueling experts is for the disputants to use chance. For example, they can toss a coin and the "winner's" expert prevails.

Ironically, this use of chance has a number of benefits:

- Chance symbolically fulfills the lawyer's comments to their clients that litigation is a "lottery," or "brain surgery with an axe."
- It saves face and egos for the dueling experts.
- Chance provides an instant and cheap outcome.
- Chance avoids the battle of wills and tactics over expert reports whereby one of the disputants feels that (s)he has "lost."
- It enables negotiators to return to head office or to constituents with a definite result, for which, in one sense, the coin is responsible.
- Some negotiators are already accustomed to toss a coin on occasion to resolve other deadlocks, such as the last gap in negotiations. [NDR: Wade, *Final Gap*]

Obviously, such an arbitrary and uncontrollable method as coin tossing may be very unattractive to a risk-averse negotiator, or where the experts are far apart. Nevertheless, merely listing "toss a coin" as a possible solution is so shocking to some disputants that they search more diligently for a more acceptable option from the rest of the list.

Refer the Decision to a Judge

The twelfth response to dueling experts is analogous to the previously-mentioned possibility of consensually appointing an arbitrator. However, this twelfth option can be elected consensually or imposed unilaterally when all other options (momentarily) are unacceptable. Additionally, the third person decision-maker is assigned by the state, rather than personally chosen like an arbitrator.

However, judges also may decide to choose one or more of the responses set out above before they accept the buck being passed to them. For example, ordering the experts to confer and submit a single report explaining why they are at odds seems to be an increasingly popular judicial response.

More specifically, there is a large body of rules and policy which judges attempt to balance when deciding which of two or more dueling experts should be given more credibility (Freckelton and Selby 2002).

The vastness of the judicial and legislative rules concerning dueling experts is both cause and effect of the uncertainty, expense, and delay attached to this last option—namely "we'll leave it to the judicial lottery;" or "of course, you can always leave it to a judge to decide which parts of each expert's report are acceptable."

Paralysis by Analysis?

As with all problem-solving exercises, this analysis of possible responses to dueling experts may stun and shock inexperienced negotiators. Where "one-shot" negotiators are common, such as in personal injury, family, workplace, discrimination, estate and environmental conflict, the parties' search for "justice," or their slow progress through grief, or the words or silence of their lawyers may not have emotionally prepared them for such a routine and mechanized list of options.

Nevertheless, in the writer's opinion, disputants should be introduced to these realistic options as early as they or their constituents have ears to hear. If professional advisers are concerned about later client recriminations concerning money and time "wasted" on dueling experts and about uninformed consent, then the options should be expressed in writing (Wade 2001).

If the preferred versions of "justice" are not available in the vast majority of conflicts, then disputants need to know what lies ahead. They need to be prepared gradually to make wise choices from the routine menus available. Such mechanistic rationality, even when conveyed with skill and compassion, may not be heard, at least the first hundred times (Sarat and Felstiner 1995; Hammond, Raiffa and Keeney 1999).

Conclusion

There are a number of "normal" hurdles which are faced by negotiators and mediators. Dueling experts is one of these. Ideally, wise negotiators, lawyers and conflict managers should anticipate dueling experts syndrome and act preventively. However, it is more likely that mediators and negotiators will be required to react to what has already occurred.

This chapter has attempted to give negotiators and mediators confidence by normalizing this hurdle, reframing, and turning the barrier into a standard problem-solving question such as, "what can be done about the current differing views of the experts?" Finally, twelve possible standard responses to this question have been systematized. No doubt, there are hybrid and other responses which need to be added to this list. Disputants can then discuss which of the twelve standard responses, or hybrids, they prefer, or do not prefer, and in what order of priority.

Learning the process and responses can add confidence and tools to the skilled helper's toolbox.

Notes

[1] Festinger identified the tendency of most human beings to attempt to bring behavior, emotions and beliefs into a degree of harmony; conversely, to avoid personal "dissonance" or disharmony in these three areas. Lawyers' letters and expert reports are behaviors which tend to drag the writers' emotions and beliefs into line with the rhetoric.

[2] The tradition of beginning negotiations just inside the "insult zone" is being challenged by a variety of legislation. For example, section 198J of the Legal Profession Act 1987 (NSW)—now Legal Profession Act 2004 (NSW)—imposed a duty upon lawyers not to make a claim or defense of a claim for damages unless these have "reasonable prospects of success."

[3] One meaning of "triangulation" involves asking or insisting that the disputants speak to the mediator/facilitator/chairperson rather than to each other. The mediator can then summarize or reframe what has been said. This may change the speaker's tone, speed and complexity, especially if the mediator strategically or genuinely alleges ignorance.

[4] The words "what if," "assuming that," or "if" are fundamental for any successful negotiator, mediator, decision-maker or communicator. See the remarkable reference to this in WILLIAM SHAKESPEARE, AS YOU LIKE IT act 5, sc. 4 (1623) ("Your If is the only peacemaker; much virtue in If.")

References

Australian Law Reform Commission. 1999. Review of the Federal Civil Justice System. In *Discussion Paper* 62.

Australian Law Reform Commission. 2000. Managing Justice: A Review of the Federal Civil Justice System. In Report No. 89: 418-436.

Beaumont, N. 2002. What are "Reasonable Prospects of Success"? *Law Society Journal* 40: 42.

Boulle, L. 2001. *Mediation: Skills and Techniques.* Chatswood, N.S.W.: Butterworths.

Brazil, W. D. 1978-79. The Attorney as Victim: Toward More Candour About the Psychological Price Tag of Litigation Practice. *Journal of the Legal Profession* 3: 107, 110.

Cooper, R. E. 1998. Federal Court Expert Usage Guidelines. *Australian Bar Review* 16: 203.

Crystal Auburn Pty. Ltd. v. I. L. Wollerman Pty. Ltd., (2004) 821 Federal Court of Australia 821.

Egan, G. 2013. *The Skilled Helper.* 10th ed. Independence: Brooks/Cole.

Festinger, L. 1957. *A Theory of Cognitive Dissonance.* Stanford: Stanford University Press.

Frank, J. 1949. *Courts on Trial: Myth and Reality in American Justice.* Princeton: Princeton University Press.

Freckelton, I. R. and H. Selby. 2002. *Expert Evidence: Law, Practice, Procedure and Advocacy.* 2nd ed. Sydney: Lawbook Company.

Hammond, J. S., H. Raiffa and R. L. Keeney. 1999. *Smart Choices: A Practical Guide to Making Better Decisions.* New York: Crown Publishing.

Keddie & Ors v. Stacks/Goudkamp, (2012) NSWCA 254.

Legal Profession Act (2004). (NSW).

Lewicki, R. J., D. M. Saunders and B. Barry. 2006. *Negotiation: Readings, Exercises, and Cases.* 2nd ed. Boston: McGraw-Hill/Irwin.

Mosten, F. S. 1997. *The Complete Guide to Mediation: The Cutting-Edge Approach to Family Law Practice.* Chicago: American Bar Association.

Murray, J. S., A. S. Rau and E. F. Sherman. 1996. *Arbitration.* 1st ed. St. Paul: Foundation Press.

Sarat, A. and W. Felstiner. 1995. *Divorce Lawyers and Their Clients*. Oxford: Oxford University Press.

The Macquarie Dictionary. 1st ed. 1982. Australia: Doubleday Australia.

Twining, W. 1984. Taking Facts Seriously. *Journal of Legal Education* 34: 22.

Wade, J. H. 2000. *Representing Clients at Mediation and Negotiation*. Queensland: Bond University.

Wade, J. H. 2001. Don't Waste My Time on Negotiation and Mediation; This Dispute Needs a Judge: When is Litigation the Right Solution? *Mediation Quarterly* 18: 259-280 available at www.epublications@bond.edu.au.

Wade, J. H. 2001. Systematic Risk Analysis for Negotiators and Litigators: How to Help Clients Make Better Decisions. *Bond Law Review* 13: 462 available at www.epublications@bond.au.edu.

◌ 82 ◌

Negotiating the Facts

Peter S. Adler

Editors' Note: Many believe that in negotiations as elsewhere, facts are the bedrock, the only things that can be firmly ascertained and then relied on, in a shifting universe of personalities, perceptions and prefer- ences. Adler, steeped in the mediation of scientific disputes, begs to differ. Facts in science are routinely challenged. Factual disagreement is also at the heart of many public policy disputes, and cannot be suc- cessfully papered over by focusing either on interests or positions. Yet after years of experimentation, public policy negotiators and mediators have made considerable progress in developing systems and structures for uncovering the assumptions and data that underlie many difficult disputes. This makes it possible to address fact-driven disputes more productively—and the technology now exists to do this on a wider scale. Adler shows how. This chapter should be read in conjunction with Wade on Dueling Experts.

> As an adolescent I aspired to lasting fame, I craved factual certainty, and I thirsted for a meaningful vision of human life—so I became a scientist. This is like becoming an archbishop so you can meet girls.
> *Matt Cartmill*

Peter S. Adler, PhD is a planner, mediator, facilitator and a principal in Accord 3.0, a professional network of people specializing in foresight, strategy, and cooperative trouble-shooting. Adler has worked in the government, business and the NGO sectors, and teaches advanced negotiation courses in the Department of Urban and Planning at the University of Hawaii. Prior executive experience includes nine years as President and CEO of The Keystone Center (www.keystone.org), Executive Director of the Hawaii Justice Foundation, and founding Director of the Hawaii Supreme Court's Center for Alternative Dispute Resolution. He is the author of three books and numerous articles.

"Are We Being Poisoned?"

Most of us were taught that a "fact" is something that has been proven through scientific, legal, or rules-of-logic reasoning. Once established, facts become incontrovertible and irreversible knowledge until better proofs appear. But are facts really established only through analysis and competing assertions of the truth of a particular matter? Aren't many "facts" actually negotiated? Consider the following.

A dozen people are gathered in a room at a local community center. They are halfway through an expected yearlong odyssey to answer a dozen similar questions. The suspected and feared culprit is hydrogen sulfide (H2S), a chemical compound that is emitted as a colorless gas with the odor of rotten eggs. Everyone has smelled it and the human nose is extremely sensitive to it even at low concentrations. H2S is heavier than air and potentially poisonous, corrosive, and flammable at high levels and acute exposures. But what about chronic low-level exposure: Is that harmful? Are people exposed to this chemical, from common sources like sewers, septic tanks, old buildings or hot springs, slowly being damaged like the proverbial frog in a slow-boiling pot?

The particular emissions in question are a periodic byproduct from a 38-megawatt geothermal energy plan in the Puna District south of Hilo on the Island of Hawaii. The plant is near Kilauea Volcano. Hawaii is committed to clean energy independence and geothermal is an important part of the emerging fuel mix to get away from fossil fuels. Hawai?i Island has the hottest geothermal resources in the state. It is the Iceland of the Pacific. But there are problems.

Neighbors and anti-geothermal advocates claim damages and resent the intrusion of an industrial energy plant in a rural bucolic area. For some, it is a not-in-my-backyard issue, with H2S and other science and health questions merely part of a larger battle strategy. For others, H2S exposure is an open question that needs answering. Plant operators and local and federal regulators see no evidence to substantiate the health harm claims. Local community members think otherwise.

So in the face of escalating and often vitriolic local arguments, the Mayor of Hawai'i County, Billy Kenoi, has commissioned a Joint Fact Finding Study Group that is investigating a number of the science issues that the community has raised. The group is composed of knowledgeable and science-literate community members on both sides of the issue, plus several outside experts who have academic backgrounds in gas chemistry, bio-statistics, epidemiology, and volcanology. The questions: Does the plant emit H2S, is the H2S damaging people's health, how is H2S being monitored, and what studies should be done to ensure the community's long term health and safety?

The Mayor is committed to taking the results forward, finding future funding, and moving ahead with whatever negotiated result the group can offer. He is a rare politician.

"SIPSD"—The Science Intensive, Politically Snarky Dispute

My particular line of work as a mediator and planner focuses on stubborn, irritable and sometimes seemingly "wicked" public policy problems.[1] Many of these involve the regulations and laws that oversee and manage energy, natural resources, public health, and public investment. More often than not, SIPSDs involve the operating plants of industrial corporations, defensive government agencies, and outraged communities that have lost confidence in governmental, corporate, and scientific institutions. There are lots of sharp-elbowed data-fights.

In the context of such conflicts, good process, better communication, and improved relationships—the usual domain of negotiated mutual gains solutions—are essential but insufficient. Coming to grips with the veracity of competing criticisms and defenses is just as essential. This means finding a way to get a plausible set of facts on the table in the midst of highly charged debates. Consider the following SIPSD examples:

> *Genetic Transmogrification.* In half a dozen states, agricultural practices associated with genetically modified organisms (GMOs) are under attack from environment and food safety groups. The battles to establish the truth of each side's claims and counterclaims are being fought out in legislatures and the courts with everyone bringing forward their own science. Critics argue GMOs and associated practices pose a threat to public health. Defenders say the science their critics are using is flawed.
>
> *Forest Stewardship.* Members of a Native American tribe want full stewardship rights in a national forest that is part of their customary home. They assert a long tradition and cultural obligation of good land practices before the federal government was involved, and want to take care of the forest on their own. Federal representatives explain their duty to provide public access. Government agents talk in terms of "acres," "management areas," and "best forestry practices". The tribe talks about culture, history, and the lives of animals and plants.
>
> *Desalination.* California, suffering severe drought, proposes to open a large coastal desalination plant to produce more fresh water for thirsty water users. Environmental skeptics and community opponents argue that the plant's subsurface intake systems will inhale and grind up local marine life. Proponents say: "we desper-

ately need the water and we have mitigation strategies
to ensure no harm to marine life."
Vaccinations. Worried parents contend that mandatory public health vaccinations put their children at a
higher risk of autism and other behavioral disabilities.
Public health officials argue there is no evidence of
harm and debunk recent studies by anti-vaccination
experts as "junk science." And, as a practical matter,
government wants to tighten vaccination policies to
prevent pandemics.

Is there a factual pathway forward that can reduce some of the political
friction on any of these issues? Daniel Patrick Moynihan, a sociologist,
politician and member of the U.S. Senate, famously said: "Everyone is
entitled to his own opinion but not his own facts." Moynihan was wrong.
In the instantaneous world of tweets, Facebook, bloggers and quick
forming memes, on reality television and on front-page editorials about
local and national political dramas, everyone (it seems) actually *is* permitted their own facts. Sometimes, in the give and take of high profile
science fights, the challenging voices are right, on the dangers of lead in
paint or tobacco as a carcinogen, for instance. And sometimes the challenging views are wrong (as in "Alar on apples causes cancer," "Laetrile
cures cancer," and "Vitamin C prevents the common cold.")

Amplified by media coverage and the electronic means for expressing outrage, many such collisions involve major battles in longer running
ideological and philosophical debates in which science is used as a tactical shield or sword. The battles sometimes seem like pitch-perfect examples of Friedrich Glasl's nine-stage model of conflict escalation (Glasl
1997). In a seminal article on conflict, he described how positions stiffen,
differences are amplified, views harden, debates are exaggerated, and
retaliation and revenge become motives in themselves. In the science
and fact-intensive controversies over GMOs or vaccinations, further
stirred by tweets, Facebook posts, and instagrams, the battles often turn
vitriolic, fracture communities of interest, and further fuel right-left
political differences.

In the pursuit of litigation and legislation, scientific and technical
facts and the argumentation under and around them are used as positions, offensively or defensively, and sometimes with great distortion. So
if Moynihan was wrong, what *are* "facts," and can they actually be negotiated? The usual answers from academic experts imply immutability
and a quick response of "no". But in the realm of SIPSDs, facts are negotiated all the time. Even scientists working to recommend new procedures for pollution abatement or mosquito control admit that their sciences aren't bulletproof, and require consensus-seeking discussions
when it comes to applied decision-making (NCBI 2003).

Facts turn out to be strangely mutable. In general parlance, a "fact" is something that is considered to be indisputably the case, verified, backed by empirical proofs, and assumed to correspond to some certain aspect of reality (Wikipedia 2016). But facts also are established differently, through various professional lenses. Facts in science must be proven by repeatable experiments conducted under accepted scientific methods. Facts in law are built on evidence that is subject to cross-examination and then determined by an adjudicator. Facts in philosophy are epistemologically and ontologically "true," meaning they correspond with the way "knowledge" is created and states of "being" are evaluated. And facts in history don't seem to exist. They are usually interpretations written by the "winners" and then repeatedly revised by challengers.

Science isn't devoid of its own politics, nor is it apolitical when it comes to planning and policy making. "Scientists," says political and social critic Virginia Postrel, "have gotten way too fond of invoking their authority to claim that 'science' dictates their preferred policy solutions and claiming that any disagreement constitutes an attack on science. But, even assuming that scientists agree on the facts, science can only tell us something about the state of the world. It cannot tell us what policy is the best to adopt."

In the raucous world of SIPSDs, finding methodological errors, cognitive biases, or conflicts of interest are common ways of deconstructing all facts. But all alleged facts "come with their own shakiness, their own shimmer of uncertainty. When we pull the thread, there's a tangle waiting" (Gopnik 2013). In my domain, the world of negotiation, helping parties move beyond the deadlock of sometimes "fact-free" conversations, nothing can be considered a fact until we agree it is a fact. Until then, we treat alleged facts as opinions, assertions, and beliefs. Facts are negotiated social, cultural, political, and economic constructions. In SIPSDs, as in many other domains, consensus is the coin of the realm.

How Different Groups and Professions Engage

"Culture" has many definitions, but the one I like most is: "Culture is the way we do things around here." Depending on the specifics of where and what the applied here is, this definition sweeps together many possible dimensions, and allows for a less general and more specific analysis of the cultural contexts involved in a negotiation. The unit *here* could be an ethnic group, a neighborhood, a political party, a profession, a church or any group that claims an identity. And it will always involve overlapping cultural views, since all of us are more than one thing. [NDR: Crampton, *Social Brain*]

When negotiators from different constituencies come together to grapple with SIPSD problems, they interact with the communication constraints imposed by the way they do things in their particular *here*. Posturing and extreme positioning is normal and expected, especially if the parties to an issue are using the old and new media to press or defend their points (Adler, Matz and Thompson 2014). There are also organizational cultures in play.

Government agents often speak in a certain "officialese" that keeps them within the safe boundaries of their legal and regulatory mandates. Unless they are operating in assured-confidentiality settings, corporations and industrial groups typically put out only the information that is required of them by law, and withhold information that they view as "business proprietary". Communities and advocacy groups, on the other hand, may come to the table distrustful of both government and industry and express their anger, fear, and arguments with sharp critiques and high emotion.

Scientists, engineers, lawyers, economists, politicians, and community advocates also bring distinctly different and profession-centric ways of engaging. They search for information and screen for facts through their own *"here"*. Consider the following professional lenses and worldviews that come into play when people sit down to try and negotiate remedies to GMOs, H2S, vaccinations, climate adaptations or other SIPSDs (Lang 1993).

Indices	Engineers	Lawyers	Economists	Politicians
Cultural Values				
Believe in and have respect for:	The laws of physics	Statutory laws	The laws of economics	The laws of survival
	Technology, computations, materials, designs	Authority, precedent, the sanctity of contract; rules in general	Theories and statistical data	Patrons, parties, and partisan loyalty
Cultural Perspective				
See themselves as:	Builders and problem solvers	Defenders of justice, partisan advocates	Planners and policy advisors	Defenders of the public interest; mediators, ultimate decision-makers
Express themselves through:	Numbers and works	Technical words and documents	Money	Approvals and directives
Suspicious of:	Timely project "simple-mentation" and worker performance	Parties' good intentions and pledges	Socio-political variables	Rival bureau-crats and ambitious subordinates
Negotiating Style				
Team role(s):	Leader or technical specialist	Leaders, spokes-person, technical adviser, or excluded	Leader or financial adviser	Leader
Negotiating focus:	Technical specifications	Parties' rights and duties	Costs, prices, payments	Satisfying superiors, avoiding criticism
Future concern:	Project implem-entation	Conflict resolution	Cash-flow risks	Project completion
Communica-tion style:	Precise and quantitative	Precise and logical, but perhaps argumenta-tive	Technical and conservative	Cautious and self-protective

Beyond these organizational, professional, and disciplinary differences, SIPSDs have additional characteristics that tend to ignite and amplify conflict. SIPSDs usually braid together political, moral, economic, social, and technical arguments when government, industry and activist groups sit at the same negotiating table. These disputes involve not just stakeholders, but "rights" holders, overlapping governmental jurisdictions with different missions and authorities, other interest groups who are not at the table, high economic and political stakes, and problems that will often have intergenerational consequences. Equally important, they almost always involve incomplete or contested scientific information and technical uncertainty.

Negotiated "Joint Fact Finding"

Joint Fact Finding (JFF) is a specialized negotiation process that leaders can set in motion to help prevent, manage or resolve SIPSDs. At its simplest, JFF is a carefully designed working group that can be composed of stakeholders, rights-holders, and scientific and technical experts that are invited to engage in a rigorous analytical deliberation. More often than not, a mediator or facilitator is used to assist. With or without third-party help, a JFF carves out key technical and scientific questions that may be at the heart of a controversy, and maps areas of factual agreement that all parties can respect. The process illuminates the reasons for disagreement and puts those areas in a proper context, thus helping to build a platform for policy agreement.

Depending on the situation, JFF can be embedded as part of a larger consensus-seeking effort or set up as a "stand alone" process. Because it can easily be tailored to accommodate the circumstances, Joint Fact Finding may be conducted under different names, including: "Independent Review Panels," "Technical Advisory Groups," "Stakeholder Panels," "Study Groups," "Peer Review Meetings," "Policy Dialogues," "Adaptive Management Working Groups," "Science Advisory Roundtables," or "Independent Scientific and Technical Advisory Panels." [NDR: Amsler, *System Design*]

Joint Fact Finding accomplishes three objectives. First, it focuses on the best scientific and technical information available and sorts out key factual signals in the white noise of heated disagreements. Second, it is a cooperative process that creates a small "port in the storm" and reduces some of the unnecessary friction that emerges when factions take sides on a big SIPSD. Third, it helps build sounder public policy by creating an agreed-upon base of knowledge.

JFF doesn't replace legislative, judicial, executive or regulatory decision-making, but it is usually initiated by a political leader in one of the branches of government to help streamline some of the disagreements that are at the root of opposing stances. While no two JFF processes are the same, a group's charter or mission is usually specific and fashioned to bring back practical results.

For example, a JFF could focus on developing an agreed-upon foundation of facts that might be considered for developing a new law, rule, standard or policy. It might take specific aim at narrowing the range of factual disagreements or conducting a specific inventory of pertinent information. Or a JFF could be used to develop an agreement by all parties on the specific research that is needed to advance policy options or make a decision, conduct a balanced review of the facts that sit behind different policy options, or produce specialized work products such as estimates, trends and forecasts, or cause-and-effect analyses.

JFF negotiations are being used in a growing number of circumstances ranging from the development of new regulations, policies and science priorities for children's health to the management of storm water runoff. Several JFF negotiations have focused on the preservation of future agricultural lands and the appropriate metrics to be used for measuring agricultural water use. One JFF negotiation developed new estimates projecting the cost-per-kilowatt hour of electricity using a new generation of nuclear power plants in the U.S. (Keystone Policy Center 2016).

In March 2015, negotiation scholars and practitioners from the U.S. and Japan met in Honolulu to take stock of the theory and practice of applying joint fact finding to SIPSDs (Accord Network 3.0 2016). While procedures varied greatly both within and between the two countries, everyone believed the critical ingredients for success included the following:

1) *A Political Champion.* Someone in elected or appointed office, or a respected leader in the private or civil sectors, who will use their position to help convene a negotiation.

2) *Participation.* Agreement by key stakeholders and rights-holders to constructively engage in a JFF effort.

3) *A Well-Framed Task.* Specific factual questions that will be the focus of the effort.

4) *Substantive and Procedural Rigor.* A structured process for data gathering, information exchange and synthesis at a high level of thoroughness and sophistication.

5) *Sufficient Resources.* The time and funding needed to accomplish a solid effort.

6) *Skillful Project Management and Consultation.* Facilitation and administrative support as needed, and sufficient to the scope and scale of the task.

7) *Diversity of Skills and Talents.* Identification and recruitment of the right mix of local and/or outside expertise needed for successful give-and-take science-centered discussions. "Experts" typically need to be willing and able to engage as collegial partners, investing substantial time in working with other stakeholders to devise research questions, explain their methods, and involve others in the collection and interpretation of data.

8) *A Nexus to Decision Making.* The results need to carry real weight and importance so any given JFF doesn't simply become an academic exercise (Honeyman et al. 2013).[2]

Back to the Island of Hawai'i

As directed and funded by the County of Hawai'i, the specific mandate of the "Geothermal Public Health Assessment" JFF had three objectives: (1) identify key public health questions pertinent to the production of geothermal energy in the Puna region; (2) create a reliable inventory of existing studies pertinent to those issues that can serve as references for decision-makers; and (3) recommend the priorities and preferred methodologies for future scientific and monitoring studies that may be required or that can best assist the making of informed decisions that protect the long term health of the community.

After nine months and very hard negotiating, the JFF study group brought forward a series of findings and recommendations that included undertaking a comprehensive health effects study regarding chronic exposures of low levels of H2S, beginning with a meta-analysis; establishing a much improved air monitoring system to capture exposure data; ensuring that there is no ongoing contamination from an old nearby geothermal energy production test site, and improving real-time communication on incidents at the existing plant.

All of the recommendations were embraced; some are completed, and others are in progress (Accord Network 3.0 2013). As always happens in difficult and politically important negotiations, not everyone involved was perfectly happy; but they were reasonably satisfied. There was a consensus that everyone could "live with." New facts are now on the table and consensus is again the coin of the realm.

Notes

[1] "Wicked" problems in conflict resolution are described in Chapters 24-27 of Honeyman et al. 2010 and Chapters 17-21 of Honeyman et al. 2013. They overlap braodly with concepts of "intractable" conflict as described in the three NDR chapters by Coleman et al.

[2] All of this, of course, can become expensive. For a starting point towards a potentially less costly set of related tools, see (Honeyman et al. 2013).

References

Accord Network 3.0. 2013. "Geothermal Public Health Assessment."http://www.accord3.com/pg68.cfm. (Accessed May 18, 2016)

Accord Network 3.0. "Joint Fact Finding." https://www.keystone.org/component/content/article/103-science-a-public-policy/services/236-nuclear-power-joint-fact-finding-dialogue.html. (Accessed May 18, 2016)

Adler, P., D. Matz, and D. Thompson. "The Limelight Hypothesis." http://www.mediate.com/articles/limelight1.cfm. Last Modified Apr. 2014,

Honeyman, C., J. R. Coben and G. De Palo. 2010. *Venturing Beyond the Classroom*. St. Paul: DRI Press.

Honeyman, C., J. R. Coben and A. W.-M. Lee. 2013. *Educating Negotiators for a Connected World*. St. Paul: DRI Press.

Honeyman, C., P. S. Adler, C. Rule, N. Ebner, R. Strelow and C. Nagarajan. 2013. A Game of Negotiation: The "Deliberation Engine." In *Educating Negotiators for a Connected World*, edited by C. Honeyman, J. Coben and A. W.-M. Lee. St. Paul: DRI Press.

Glasl, F. 1997. *Konfliktmanagement*. Ein Handbuch fuer Fuehrungskraefte, Beraterinnen und Berater, 5., erweiterte Auflage. Bern: Verlag Paul Haupt.

Gopnik, A. "Closer Than That." http://www.newyorker.com/magazine/2013/11/04/closer-than-that. (Last Modified Nov. 4, 2013)

Keystone Policy Center. "About." https://www.keystone.org/component/content/article/103-science-a-public-policy/services/236-nuclear-power-joint-fact-finding-dialogue.html. (Accessed May 18, 2016)

Lang, W. 1993. *A Professional's View. In Culture and Negotiations*, edited by G. O. Faure and J. Z. Rubin. Thousand Oaks, CA: Sage Publications.

NCBI. "NIH Consensus Statement on total knee replacement." http://www.ncbi.nlm.nih.gov/pubmed/17308549. (Accessed May 18, 2016)

Wikipedia. "Fact." Accessed May 18, 2016, https://en.wikipedia.org/wiki/Fact. (Accessed May 18, 2016)

Section XV: Making Conflicts Less Intractable

This section begins with a trilogy of chapters that, first, analyze, first, analyze how a fairly predictable percentage of conflicts in almost any domain can become "intractable", and outline techniques for handling this. The second chapter goes into more detail about what exactly makes a conflict intractable, and how new insights are developing new levers for change; and the third describes the process of using those levers to actually influence a conflict which supposedly cannot be influenced.

One of the tools frequently advocated for serious conflict is training of groups of the participants—but sometimes these are resistant. The next chapter addresses how you might approach an audience when you expect such resistance—or didn't expect it, but encounter it anyway.

The ensuing two chapters address in detail one of the central factors in many major conflicts: religion. A chapter analyzing how religion can help solve as well as cause conflict is followed by one which explicitly argues that religious people and groups are actually capable of more "prosociality" than others, if they are approached in the right way. And the final chapter in this section analyzes how a consummate practitioner, faced with one of the world's most famously intractable conflicts, actually applied many of the findings that are in the other chapters.

Getting in Sync: What to Do When Problem-Solving Fails to Fix the Problem

Peter T. Coleman & Robert Ricigliano

Editors' Note: In the first of a trilogy on complex cases, the authors estimate that far beyond the usual categories people think of as "intractable"—such as international, race relations or major environmental conflicts—about 5% of disputes of virtually all kinds actually fit this pattern. The authors review why this is, and outline a series of techniques developed in recent years for handling conflict of the worst kind, in any domain. This chapter should be read in conjunction with Coleman, Redding & Fisher's "Intractable 1 and 2" chapters.

Peter T. Coleman is Professor of Psychology and Education at Columbia University, where he holds a joint appointment at Teachers College and The Earth Institute. Dr. Coleman directs the Morton Deutsch International Center for Cooperation and Conflict Resolution (MD-ICCCR) and the Institute for Psychological Science and Practice (IPSP) at Teachers College, and is Executive Director of Columbia University's Advanced Consortium on Cooperation, Conflict, and Complexity (AC4). He currently conducts research on conflict intelligence and systemic wisdom as competencies for navigating conflict constructively, including a focus on adaptive negotiation and mediation dynamics, cross-cultural adaptivity, optimality of motivational dynamics in conflict, justice and polarization, multicultural conflict, intractable conflict, and sustainable peace.
Robert Ricigliano is a Systems and Complexity Coach at The Omidyar Group, where he supports and guides teams within organizations and initiatives to better understand and effectively engage with dynamic systems. Prior to joining The Omidyar Group, Robert co-founded the Master of Sustainable Peacebuilding Degree Program at the University of Wisconsin-Milwaukee (UWM), held senior positions at the Conflict Management Group and Harvard Negotiation Project, and consulted on peacebuilding in complex environments. He has worked with government officials, non-governmental organizations, foundations, leaders of armed groups, and political parties in the U.S. and in conflict zones around the world. He is the author of *Making Peace Last* (2012).

> God, grant me the serenity to accept the things I
> cannot change,
> The courage to change the things I can,
> And the wisdom to know the difference.
> *Reinhold Niebuhr* (1940)
>
> (But, just out of curiosity, God, is there
> another way?)

Negotiators, mediators and conflict resolvers of all stripes like to fix things. We much prefer to enter tense, problematic situations and use our conflict resolution tool kit to help mend fences, solve problems, find win-win, get to yes, and leave behind hordes of satisfied stakeholders. This is why we do the job.

But once in a while—in approximately 1-in-20 of our more difficult cases—we fail (Coleman 2011; Diehl and Goertz 2001). Despite our best efforts, and sometimes the best efforts of our most-skilled colleagues, the challenges we face grind on, escalate, become ever more costly, burn us out, and haunt our dreams. At some point we wash our hands of them, refer them out to the courts, psychiatrists, the gods or other resources, and call it quits. This was one that got away.

Faced with this dilemma, what is an industrious, creative, and committed negotiator to do? This paper outlines a third way—some-where between hauling out our wrench, ruler, and saw to fix the problem at hand and running off in the opposite direction to escape it. Rather than "fix" or "flee," negotiators can think and work *in sync with* the "flow" of these more extraordinarily challenging situations to help unlock the potential energy, ideas and actors from *within* the system to change the system. Think of it as the "turning into the skid" advice for a driver's approach to conflict resolution—counterintuitive but correct. This chapter outlines this approach and highlights the importance of an alternative negotiation skill set for guiding constructive change when addressing unfixable problems.

Urban Violence: A Parable of a Fix that Failed

Often, the toughest social problems are made worse by well-intentioned, well-designed, and even well-executed plans (see Dörner 1996). These initiatives generate some initial positive results and raise hopes that a "fix" has been found. However, in the medium to long term, the good plans fizzle and can even make things worse. This is known as a "fix that fails." Take, for example, Operation Impact.

Operation Impact

For decades, chronic patterns of urban violence have plagued the leaders and citizens of cities from New York to Chicago and from Lagos to Medellin, typically affecting inhabitants of poorer neighborhoods disproportionately. Although the types and levels of violence in cities have changed through the years, the intractability of these patterns of aggression has proved to be enduring. Mayors, chiefs of police, and conflict resolvers have tried myriad methods of conflict management and violence reduction with limited or temporary success. Here is a classic example:

In 2003, the Mayor of New York City, Michael Bloomberg, decided to get tough on school violence. He was sick and tired of hearing reports of chronic patterns of gang violence, attacks, intimidation and robberies on school grounds, and felt increasingly frustrated by school officials and administrators who offered more excuses than solutions. He tried to work with school unions to address the issues, but felt stymied by their response. So later that year, he launched *Operation Impact*, a tough, targeted, zero-tolerance response to school violence in New York City, part of his broader strategy of targeting "hot-spots" of crime in NYC.

The centerpiece of Operation Impact in schools was a "bolstering of police resources" in school communities. The initiative began by identifying the 12 most problematic schools with the worst safety records and then permanently assigning police officers and school safety agents to each of the schools. In addition, a 150-member NYPD school safety task force began to convene to focus on problem areas in these schools, monitor their perimeters, and organize truancy sweeps. New school safety intervention teams were formed at each school to evaluate and revise safety conditions and security procedures. Bloomberg then informed principals at these schools that they would be held accountable for reductions in crime and violence in their schools and if they failed, they would be replaced. Disciplinary procedures for "problem students" were intensified, including detention, suspension, zero-tolerance for serious offenses, and relocation of some of these students to "second opportunity schools." Subsequently, additional schools were targeted as individual school records and conditions changed.

Operation Impact resulted in a decrease in serious crimes in NYC schools of 23% over the first two years, following a national trend. However, this approach also suffered from several drawbacks in the longer run. First, it began to discourage accurate reporting of incidents of school violence (if violence wasn't reported, then there were no consequences for school officials). The dis-incentivizing of accurate reporting resulted in an apparent but erroneous decrease in reports of violence in schools. Second, the unilateral nature of the program's design and rollout alienated school officials, further impairing its implementation. Third, the approach oversimplified the problem of violence by focusing only on crime, missing the myriad ways violence and destructive conflict manifests in school communities, such as physical and psychological bullying and intimidation, ineffectual responses from teachers and school officials, the presence of drugs and weapons, crimes and acts of intimidation which occur in transit to and from schools, and high rates of alienation and suicide amongst students, as well as countless other incidents of humiliation and harassment that went unreported. Fourth, Operation Impact offered broad, general solutions to poorly understood local problems, the circumstances of which varied considerably from one school to the next. And fifth, the program sent a clear signal to the student population: by highlighting containment and deterrence while neglecting prevention, support, and care, it inadvertently sent the message to youth that, ultimately, force and coercion prevail.

Operation Impact: Using a Screwdriver to Fix a Cloudy Day

Top-down, unilateral, strong-arm responses to dangerous problems feel right and can make good sense. However, initiatives like Operation Impact often do not even begin to address the systemic causes of violence evident in many urban schools. Heightened surveillance and security measures are therefore a necessary but insufficient response. Too often, we are attracted to such short-term, seemingly efficient, hard-line solutions to complex local problems. The likelihood is that the solutions will show some immediate effect and signal to our constituents that we are in control of a difficult situation. However, such effects are usually not sustainable, and can actually contribute to making the problems worse.

Why do we respond like this? Because as a culture we are conditioned to believe that if it's "broke, fix it." If schools are suffering from high levels of violence, then make them more secure. However, this sensible, direct, and occasionally effective approach makes a critical, though unstated assumption about how the world works. It assumes that problems, even complex and intractable ones like urban school violence, are mechanical in nature—that a set of knowable causes create, in a predictable way, a certain set of impacts. For example, take the belief that safe schools are the result of proper discipline, accountability for administrators, and adequate security personnel. Conversely, if one or more of these causes is missing, then you will have higher levels of school violence. And, if so, then the "fix" for an unsafe school is to add in discipline, accountability, and/or security personnel as needed.

This way of looking at the problem of school violence—as what is known as a "Clock Problem"—is sensible and valid, but is not the only way of thinking about the problems we face and how to address them. Karl Popper, probably the most influential philosopher of science of the last century, offered a key distinction between what he termed clock problems and cloud problems. *Clock problems* are those, like clocks, that are of a more mechanical, knowable, controllable, and predictable nature. Such problems can be readily disassembled and analyzed—broken down to their component parts and systematically studied to reveal the source of the problem. The "mechanism" can then be repaired and reassembled to resume its original functionality. Typically, problems with automobiles, jet engines, computers and even traffic planning can be solved by approaching them as clock problems. Similarly, many problems negotiators and mediators face are relatively clock-like, such as contractual obligations and disputes, legal and procedural matters, and many aspects of interpersonal or community disputes that are responsive to standard forms of problem analysis and problem solving (Popper 1966).

In contrast to these analysis-friendly problems are what Popper termed *cloud problems*. These are problems like chronic patterns of urban violence, which are of a much more complex, murky, uncontrollable, and unpredictable nature. Think of the myriad factors, issues and stakeholders involved in the school violence that Operation Impact targeted (see Figure 1). These are problems of a highly irregular and disorderly nature, which typically prove unresponsive to standard, proven solutions or attempts at problem solving. These are not simply more complicated problems, but are considered *complex* because many aspects of these problems interact over time in unpredictable ways, and therefore evidence erratic behavior and outcomes. As a result, our good faith attempts to address them can have no identifiable effects, can result in problems going away in the short-term but re-emerging in the longer-term, or can even serve to make matters worse (which some suggest was the case with Operation Impact in schools).

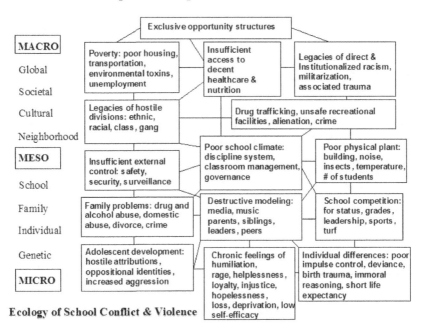

Figure 1: Ecology of Chronic Urban School Violence

In short, if school violence is really a cloud problem and not a clock problem, then thinking we can "fix it" directly by administering one or more mechanical solutions is like thinking we can "use a screwdriver to fix a cloudy day." The "fix" is totally inappropriate for making the change we want to see in the world. But, the insight that "clock tools" are ineffective, or even counterproductive, when dealing with cloud problems, albeit true, is not enough. We are much more familiar and comfortable with "clock tools" like linear planning models and reductionist thinking that give us a feeling of being in control of seemingly uncontrollable problems. On the other hand, we lack the same level of familiarity and comfort with "cloud tools." And, without a sturdy set of cloud tools, we are doomed to the "fix or flee" dilemma described at the opening of this chapter.

In response, we are offering a framework for how to think about and take action in the face of cloud problems like urban school violence. While no set of cloud tools will be as precise as our more familiar clock tools, we hope that this framework will give negotiators new ways of thinking and working that will help us understand and get in sync with the complex realities we face.

Working in Sync: The Approach

Based on years of work with practitioners trying to make change in complex and dynamic environments around the world, we developed the "Sync" framework—named as such because we are proposing that rather than trying to impose solutions, negotiators should learn to work in sync with the people and forces that make up a complex system. This approach is consistent with the discoveries of two cultural anthropologists, Florence Kluckhohn of Harvard University and Fred Strodtbeck of University of Chicago. In 1961, Kluckhohn and Strodtbeck published a groundbreaking and influential book on cross-cultural differences found between groups in the American Southwest. They found that the communities differed on how they viewed the nature of the relationship between humans and the world around them—basically do humans ultimately command and control the world around them, does the world (nature, society, groups, the gods) ultimately control and dictate the fate of humans, or is there some other relationship between the world and us? They found that the communities they studied had developed three very different answers to this question: Mastery, Submission, and Harmony (Kluckhohn and Strodtbeck 1961).

Mastery is the belief that we have the capacity and responsibility to attempt to control nature, society and the world around us. In contrast, *Submission* is based on the belief that the natural (and the supernatural) world is so immensely complex and mysterious that it is ultimately unknowable and unfixable. Somewhere between pure Mastery and pure Submission is *Harmony* or the belief that humans can exercise partial but not total control of nature by living in balance with our surrounding social and environmental forces.

When applied effectively to the right types of clock problems, the Mastery approach can be powerful, effective, responsible, and efficient. In these cases, the role of the problem-solver is that of the expert—like a physician or mechanic—and our job is to apply our expertise to help remedy the problem. However, when Mastery is applied to more complex cloud-like problems, it can lead to a great deal of frustration. This was the result of approaching chronic urban school violence with Operation Impact, clearly a Mastery fix that failed.

Similarly, the Submission approach has the virtue of us not making the situation worse when dealing with complex problems. However, the imperative to *do no harm* can often lead us to prematurely decide that we are powerless. Worse yet, it can breed a strong sense of helplessness, inferiority and bitterness in people and communities, leading to a type of malaise or depression. And as the Holocaust survivor Elie Wiesel famously noted, sometimes inaction is, in fact, collusion with tyranny.

Fortunately, there is a better way. The Harmony response to cloud problems, like urban school violence, is what we call working in Sync—rather than working against or fleeing from complex problems, the Sync framework is intended to help us work with a system to leverage how it is evolving in order to facilitate desired outcomes (e.g. more justice, less violence, better quality of life, etc.). Accordingly, it reorients the basics of conflict resolution significantly (e.g. how we set goals, focus our work and take effective action). The Sync approach is composed of five principles that offer a more effective alternative to Mastery and Submission when dealing with cloud problems:

The Question	Mastery	SYNC	Submission
What is our goal?	Fix the problem	Improve the system dynamics	Do no harm
Where do we focus?	Zoom in on the problem	Understand the evolving problem in context	Zoom out to see the full chaos
How do we engage?	Impose control	Work with the energy in the system	Relinquish control
	Implement solutions	Employ adaptive action	Minimize risk
	Lead change, be the hero	Enable change, be a guide	Avert disaster, be cautious

Table 1: The What, Where and How of Conflict Resolution

Working in Sync: What is Our Goal?

> *Guideline 1: Develop goals for how you want the dy-*
> *namics of the system (family, organization, commu-*
> *nity, etc.) to eventually be qualitatively different—and*
> *produce different outcomes—even if you cannot articu-*
> *late the specific end states you hope to achieve.*

In contrast to the more focused objectives of the Mastery approach (fix the problem, resolve the dispute), or the objectives of Submission (do no harm, avoid making matters worse), the Harmony approach aims more generally to improve the functioning and wellbeing of the broader system (relationship, family, organization, community, environment, etc.) over the long term. This shift in goal is not small or inconsequential: It moves us from problem-centered outcome goals to systemic-process goals.

This guideline most likely contradicts everything you were taught about goal setting (i.e. identify moderately difficult, achievable, measureable goals). These remain true with clocks, but the game changes with clouds. Cloud problems are the products of an ever-changing and inter-connected collection of diverse forces. For example, urban school violence is a product of economics, geography, environmental health, community and family health, cultural norms, public policy, government effectiveness, etc. As such, it is less important to make a short-term dent in the amount of school violence, than to influence the underlying forces that produce the levels of violence that currently exists in our schools. This formulation of the goal will direct us to engage the systemic causes rather than just the symptoms. And because cloud problems inherently take time to affect, a "systemic goal" is better able to support constant adaptation and experimentation than an outcome goal (e.g. a 10% reduction in violence), which we either hit or miss.

This Can Be Achieved By:
- **Identifying your North Star** (a goal that is a navigational tool to help you constantly adapt). What is the broader systemic change we would like to see in the long run? Your ultimate end should be defined in terms of a healthier system (e.g. Urban schools and communities that produce less violence).
- **Defining your Near Star** (5-10 year goal). What is a signifi-cant step toward your North Star that might be achievable in 5 to 10 years? Identify specific outcomes that are likely to emerge as a consequence of affecting the underlying system (e.g. build-ing diverse coalitions of community actors that understand risk and mitigate the drivers of school violence).
- **Asking a Framing Question.** What is the question about how our environment works that would best guide us toward our near/north star? For example, "what forces account for the cur-

rent levels of violence in our urban schools?" Or, even better, "what forces foster safe urban communities and schools?"

- **Increasing your Internal Complexity.** Ideally, what would our team be like in order to maximize our potential to reach our near/north star? Would it be different than today?

Working in Sync: Where Do We Focus?

Guideline 2: Understand the evolving problem in context. Resist the tendency to prematurely oversimplify threatening problems by becoming familiar with the complex forces operating in the context and how they interact over time to create the problem of concern. This "leaning into complexity" will help clarify opportunities for high leverage impact, gateways, and patterns otherwise disguised by the urgency and complexity of the problem.

Orienting our work toward broad, temporally distant goals will necessitate a shift in perspective on where we focus our work as well. A Mastery approach encourages zooming in to analyze, isolate and focus in on the target problem and what we can best change, while a Submission approach emphasizes zooming out to note the overwhelming complexity and unpredictability of the constellation of forces operating in the system. Sync recommends employing both lenses in an iterative sequence. It means developing a holistic understanding the complex and dynamic relationship between the issue we care about (e.g. urban school violence) and the surrounding environment—both physical and social. It requires that we become skilled at *seeing the problem in the context of time and space*: learning to first step back and consider the many complex factors that are operating at different levels (people, groups and institutions) and at different time scales (immediate effects, delayed effects, and trends over time) in the context which drive and constrain the problem—and only then focus in on those aspects of the constellation of forces that are important, high-impact and actionable.

Most of us were educated through the paradigm of the scientific method, which privileges analysis (the process of separating something into its constituent elements) and short-term, linear cause-and-effect relationships between variables. This has taught us a great deal, but it tends to blind us from seeing the whole: noticing how constellations of variables interact in complex ways and form patterns that evolve and stabilize over time. It is like we are trying to make sense of a really long and complicated movie with nothing but still photography as our lens.

Negotiators will benefit from developing new tools that allow them to see how complex dynamics unfold over time to establish, maintain, and transform patterns. Imagine if we could put on a visor and it would reveal how dynamic patterns flow over time in a social system—like time-elapsed photography. This would help us begin to understand the differences between 1) problems, 2) the multiple causes of problems, 3) the relations between these causes, and 4) understanding how these many relationships affect the *dynamics* of a system which results in *patterns* that emerge in the system (chronic violence, chronic poverty, thriving communities, etc.).

This Can Be Achieved by:

- **Complexity Mapping.** We recommend employing the use of complexity mapping to help draw and visualize the constellation of forces affecting particular cases (see Burns 2007, 2015; Coleman 2011; Ricigliano 2012 for illustrations). Developed by Magoroh Maruyama (1963; 1982), mapping is useful for identifying the dynamics that serve to escalate, de-escalate and stabilize destructive patterns of interaction. These maps not only allow us to capture the multiple sources and temporal dynamics of complex problems, they can also help to identify central nodes and patterns that are unrecognizable by other means. Conflict maps can be generated alone as a pre-negotiation exercise, with the help of facilitators or mediators, or in small groups of stakeholders. With conflict-mapping the goal is not necessarily to get it right. The goal at this stage is *to get it different*; to try to reintroduce a sense of nuance and complexity into the stakeholders' understanding of the problem.

- **Identifying Key Levers—the Enabler-Inhibitor Analysis.** Because you can't understand every aspect of a complex environment, you need to focus on what is most important to affecting the issue you care about and answering your framing question. And, because we tend to focus on what is not working (aka "the problem"), it is important that we look at both things that enable the outcomes we want to see as well as those that inhibit them. For example, an enabler-inhibitor analysis based on our framing question about school violence would start with the task of identifying the key things that *enable* safe schools and those that *inhibit* safe schools in the specific content. This analysis is best done in a participatory manner, with diverse perspectives in the room so that participants can understand, challenge, and learn from the perspectives of others and guard against a skewed perspective or one that simply reaffirms people's pre-existing views.

- **Identifying Key Connections—the Upstream-Downstream Analysis.** It is not possible to truly understand a cloud problem by just reducing it to its component parts. Rather, to get a more dynamic and interconnected understanding of a cloud problem, it's necessary to get a holistic understanding of the diverse "causes" of that factor as well as the diverse impacts of that factor on the surrounding environment. One way to do this is simply to take a problem, or any key factor you identified and write it in the middle of a page. Then, above the factor, brainstorm a diverse set of "causes"—things that contributed to the existence of the factor (Upstream)—and below the factor brainstorm a diverse set of impacts—things that the factor contributes to creating (Downstream).

- **Focusing on Patterns, Puzzles, and Potentials, not Problems.** It is almost impossible to predict any specific outcomes in complex, nonlinear systems; there are far too many variables interacting and affecting one another in unpredictable ways. Fortunately, if we are able to observe a problem over the long term, we are usually able to identify patterns in the system. Every ongoing conflict system—be it in a marriage or an ethnically divided community—will evidence some general patterns of interactions between the parties that are more predictable and stable than others. Therefore, we should be less concerned with bringing about specific outcomes in a conflict (generating particular insights, agreements, behavior change), but rather should focus on altering the general patterns of interaction in a more constructive direction.

Once we have identified key factors and developed a preliminary understanding of how they are interconnected, this series of questions can help us identify what can be difficult to identify—opportunities for engaging a system:

- **What trends do you see?** (e.g. things that are getting more or less common; that we are seeing more or less of)
- **What puzzles do you see?** (e.g. things that are hard to explain or raise questions; things that sometimes have positive impacts and other times have negative impacts; things that are "bright spots" (positive deviants); strange connections or counter-intuitive realities)
- **What patterns do you see?** (e.g. behaviors, stories, or outcomes that you see over and over; basic rules that seem to explain how things work)

Working in Sync: How Do We Engage the System?

Guideline 3: Locate and work with the energy for change that resides within the system.

In contrast to a Mastery approach of imposing unilateral control over problematic situations and a Submission approach of relinquishing control, the Sync approach is to start with the assumption that it is the system that is in control. People can't "fix" or control complex systems.

The best we can do is to find those areas in the system where there are people, ideas, or other forces that are creating change in the system and then to work with them to affect the direction of that change so the system produces more of the outcomes we want (e.g. less violence, more peace, more justice, better economic development, etc.).

This Can Be Achieved by:

- **Using Systems Jujitsu** (Harnessing the endogenous sources of energy in the system). Every system has multiple forces that are making things happen, for good or for bad. For example, an analysis of the drivers of quality of life for residents of Hawaii found that the tourist economy was a major driver of change in Hawaii and one that mostly reduced people's quality of life. The tourist economy brought in much needed economic activity to the islands, but it also drove up the costs of living and forced many people into working two or three part-time jobs to make ends meet. Trying to shrink the tourist economy, even if possible, would not necessarily help those in need. Rather, a "systems jujitsu" tactic would be to harness the strength of the tourist economy to seed investment in the non-tourist economy (e.g. through a small tax that would go into a venture fund for non-tourist economic development), which had the potential to produce jobs that supported a higher quality of life for residents.

- **Looking for What's Holding Things Together.** Merely asking stakeholders, "Why doesn't the conflict get worse?" "Why did disputants settle in the past?" or "What provides a sense of hope today?" can orient practitioners towards the more constructive components or dynamics of a system. Or asking, "Where are the islands of agreement (Blum 2007) or the positive social networks today?" Or "What type of taboos exist for destruction and violence here (places of worship, children, hospitals)?" This information—which is too often ignored in standard forms of conflict analysis—can help reveal the autoimmune processes in the system that operates to mitigate the conflict. Our late colleague Laura Chasin of the Public Conversations Project called this tactic, *identifying networks of effective action.* These are the people, agencies and institutions in communities that are already addressing seemingly impossible problems effectively.

- **Shepherding Resonance.** Instead of trying to incentivize or impose a will to change in communities (Mastery), some peacebuilders speak of the value of identifying local areas of resonance when attempting to mobilize change (Burns 2007). *Resonance* is a form of heightened, shared emotional energy that results in people feeling and finding connections with like-minded others, and at times a sense of congruence and purpose (Coleman, et al.)

At a recent workshop on peacebuilding, one speaker noted:

> I was in Kabul, Afghanistan in 2005 observing a partner training of women leaders to help them address domestic violence in their homes and communities. From the back of the room, and without a translator, it was difficult to follow or understand the participants' experiences. However, they began to role play their experience with domestic violence and the room came alive. The energy emerged and there was a palpable sense of 'pushing back' on male relatives and abusers. I experienced resonance when the women looked my way during their role plays—their eyes spoke of intense emotion and commitment to safety and dignity. I believe the women also experienced resonance during their role plays.

Group action can result when this energy crosses a threshold in a group (beyond their resistance to change), and can be constructive or destructive (or both) depending on the valence and direction of the groups shared interests (e.g., a mobilized community addressing abuse in their community versus an angry mob addressing grievances against members of an outgroup).

Working with resonance effectively typically involves identifying, supporting and marshaling waves of motivation and energy in networks of people in service of communal change. It can spring from a variety of sources, including from an increased awareness of unmet basic human needs; from perceptions of wrongdoing or injustice; from the emergence of crises and opportunities; from internal top-down, middle-out or bottom-up leadership, organization and mobilization; or from external actors and events. Resonance is often mercurial; ebbing and flowing and taking different forms at different stages of systemic change. Ultimately, resonance is a vital source of energy useful for driving and sustaining systemic change.

- **Working Upstream.** In the non-linear world of complex systems, working directly on the focal problem—like the Bloomberg administration did originally in attempting to address chronic patterns of violence in NYC—can be largely ineffective or make matters worse. Thus, one strategy recommended when addressing more cloud-like problems is to work upstream away from the primary presenting problem on more peripheral pre-conditions that can, eventually, affect the problem.

This approach has been employed in the work of some social entrepreneurs, such as the Ashoka Fellows, when working in conflict zones (Praszkier, Nowak and Coleman 2010). Typically, they are local people working in innovative ways to help rebuild social capital and provide a sense of efficacy in struggling communities. However, attempts to address these circumstances in the context of a conflict resolution or peace process typically elicit resistance as they are seen as affecting the balance of power in the conflict. Interveners recognizing this will work to address hardship upstream, without making any explicit connection to the conflict or peace processes.

> *Guideline 4: Employ adaptive action: Constantly improve your ability to work effectively for change in your system by pursuing a range of strategies and tactics that will promote effective learning about how the system works and adapting to more effectively engage it.*

The dominant (Mastery) approach to seeking social change in the world of peacebuilding and development is to determine a logical framework which sets out a series of steps that will lead to a desired objective. This plan is usually based on "proven" solutions and success is determined by how well an organization is able to execute the plan. This might work quite well in the "clock world" but less so when dealing with cloud problems. Because cloud problems are difficult or impossible to fully understand, and are constantly changing, the best you can do is try multiple strategies and tactics as long as you are able to minimize the potential costs of failure and maximize your ability to learn effectively and adapt accordingly (also known as "smart fail"—Ricigliano 2012). In the cloud world, you have to learn your way into having impact.

This Can Be Achieved by:

- **Employing Adaptive Action Strategies.** Research has shown that many well-intentioned problem-solvers working in complex systems typically commit a standard set of errors resulting in doing more harm than good (see Dörner 1996). These include acting without sufficient prior analysis of the situation, failing to anticipate the negative side effects or repercussions of their choices, assuming that the absence of immediate negative effects means their measures have worked, and allowing over-involvement in subprojects to blind them to emerging needs and changes on the ground.

However, this research also sheds light on more effective methods of adaptive problem solving within complex systems, which includes:

- **Making More Decisions.** Assessing a situation and setting a course, but then continually *adapting*: staying open to feedback to reconsidering decisions and altering course as needed. Making more, not fewer, decisions as plans unfold. Finding more possibilities for enhancing the system's wellbeing as the situation evolves.

- **Acting in More Diverse Ways.** Taking a wider variety of actions while attempting to achieve one goal ("I'll reduce violence in NYC schools by increasing security, teaching constructive conflict management, better satisfying the students' basic needs, and engaging them more actively in their communities through business opportunities"). This is in contrast to making one decision per goal (increase security).
- **Asking _Why_ More.** Actively investigating the why behind events: the causal links that made up the _networks of causation_ in their community.
- **Staying Focused on their North Star.** Ineffective decision makers get easily distracted and diverted; they shift from problem to problem as each arise. Effective decision makers identify the central issues early on and stay focused on addressing them.
- **But Not on One Near Star.** Effective decision makers do not develop a single-minded preoccupation with one solution. If the feedback informs them that a solution is too costly or ineffective, they alter their approach.

Guideline 5: Enable change: Use your role (your skills, relationships, and knowledge) to create the conditions for the system to change itself, rather than implementing or leading the change directly

Finally, what about us? What role do we, the negotiator, mediator, facilitator or change agent, play in this new, harmonious approach to conflict management? In contrast to the hero role most associated with the fix-it Mastery approach, and the cautionary role most associated with do-no-harm Submission, Sync requires us to create and adopt a new role.

We like to think of the Sync role as a guide or enabler—someone who helps take people on a long journey; who knows the territory well and is good with mapping and navigation; who understands the local terrain, the flora and fauna and the dangers that lurk; who delights in their surroundings—appreciating the interconnectedness and splendor of the natural world and who's joy is contagious; and who is adaptive to sudden changes in the weather or local conditions, but who also knows how to use the stars to navigate successfully. Working in Sync with systems requires that we play the role of enabling the people within the system to make change for themselves and their environment. Our standard conception of leadership defines a good leader as someone who leads others—who knows the better way and helps others get there. The Sync role of an enabler of change is new and foreign to many of us trained as Masters of clocks. It will require a new set of competencies and skills unfamiliar to most of us.

This Can Be Achieved by:

- **Practicing Presence.** Peter Senge and colleagues at MIT have recently developed a theory of change through collective action that highlights the importance of several individual and group competencies central to working in sync with social and physical systems (Senge et al. 2004). The authors suggest that many of our (Mastery) traditions point us away from being present and paying attention to what is organically emerging in social systems. They point out that most leaders are rewarded for making things happen and creating results, not being aware of what is naturally unfolding. They write, It is easy to miss what is emerging when you are busy trying to shape outcomes. A key element of their approach is "Presencing," which requires practicing stillness (not thinking and acting) in order to enhance your capacity to attend to how the system surrounding you is in movement and where it may be heading. As Francois Jullien writes in reference to Chinese wisdom,

  > Rather than set up a model to serve as a norm for his actions, a Chinese sage is inclined to concentrate his attention on the course of things in which he finds himself involved in order to detect their coherence and profit from the way that they evolve. From this difference that we have discovered, we could deduce an alternative way of behaving. Instead of constructing an ideal Form that we then project on to things, we could *try to detect the factors whose configuration is favorable to the task at hand;* instead of setting up a goal for our actions, we could allow ourselves to be carried along by the propensity of things. In short, instead of imposing our plan on the world, we could rely on the potential inherent in the situation (Jullien 2004: 16).

Senge recommends being mindful of your own beliefs, values and proclivities (what we call implicit theories) that might get in the way of attending more accurately to the evolving system, by noting the types of questions you tend to ask and not ask. They suggest asking such questions as "What is the nature of this situation?", "What patterns are present?" and "What is naturally unfolding?"

Working in Sync: A Case Study

The Harlem Children's Zone (HCZ) provides an illustration of the Sync framework in action. Although complex, resource intensive and demanding, and not without its critics, the approach of the HCZ offers a parable of another way to address seemingly impossible problems such as urban violence—by working both informed by and in sync with the contemporary dynamics of the system.

The rate of violent crime in New York City rose exponentially between 1965 and 1990, especially in the Harlem community. Robbery, aggravated assault, and murder were all up and rates of mortality and incarceration for young, black men had skyrocketed. It was in 1990 that the community activist Geoffrey Canada—an African American and native New Yorker (from the South Bronx)—returned to the city to head up the Rheedlen Center for Children and Families in Harlem after attending school at Bowdoin and Harvard University. Canada reports he returned to New York to help "my kids" survive the violence and poverty epidemic in the streets of his hometown. He was particularly focused on helping young, African-American boys avoid premature death and imprisonment.

One of Canada's first initiatives was smart. He established a program for young males in the community, which combined martial arts training (Canada had earned a third-degree black belt in Tae Kwon Do) with conflict resolution training to provide youth with increased discipline, a sense of security, and constructive problem-solving skills. After launching the program and working tirelessly with youth in Harlem for several years, Canada came to realize that the program was a failure. He felt that he had been able to help a few individual boys now and then, but that the vast majority of them got readily pulled back into a life of drugs and gangs and violence (and often early death) in the streets. He felt deeply frustrated and disappointed, but not deterred.

At this point Canada regrouped. Having now spent several years in the community getting to know current conditions on the ground more intimately, he realized that he had failed to see the big picture. He had not quite understood the immense complexity and power of the drop-out/drug/violence/poverty landscape of the Harlem community in the 1990s, and had thought that by providing the youth with enough care, attention and the right non-violent skills, they would thrive. He now realized that his good faith attempts to train the youth could not begin to alter the forcefully destructive dynamics that captured their lives in any significant way. So, he adapted and changed course.

Fed up by now with his own and others' piecemeal approaches to addressing chronic patterns of violence and poverty in poor neighborhoods, Canada launched the HCZ. The HCZ is a revolutionary and evolutionary social experiment that combines educational, social, nutritional and medical services for children from birth through college, meshed into an interlocking web for an entire neighborhood. Recognizing the tightly linked and complex nature of how many different urban problems combine to constitute ecologies of desperation and violence (see Figure 1), he and others in the Zone began to work systemically and comprehensively within a 1-block, then 24-block, then 60-block, and ultimately a 97-block radius of Harlem.

The HCZ approach is both simple and complex. First, they identify the most at-risk children in the Zone by identifying the lowest scorers on public school readiness tests. Then, they attempt to provide these children with everything they need—medical care, good nutrition, safety, tutoring, committed teachers, you name it—to make it from kindergarten through college, and to thrive. The work involves a great deal of perseverance, door knocking, cajoling, adaptation and resourcefulness on the part of the HCZ staff. The theory is if the HCZ can rescue and support the most vulnerable children—the ones that get most easily trapped by the ferocious pull of the streets and fuel the drop-out/drug/violence/poverty syndromes—they will transform the entire community in time. This is a targeted but complex, long-term approach to addressing intractable community problems that is exceptionally promising.

And the data tells the unfolding story. Between 2002 and 2011, 97.3 % of 4-year-olds participating in the Harlem Gems pre-school program scored average or above on the Bracken Basic Concept Scale. The first group of 6th grade students going through HCZ's charter school, Promise Academy, graduated in 2012. Of them, 100% passed the English regents exam, 90% passed the Geometry exam, 96% passed the Algebra 2 and Trig exam, 92% passed the Integrated Algebra exam, and every senior was accepted into and planning on attending a post-secondary school. Between 2011- 2012, Promise Academy I placed in the 99th percentile of city high schools, with the 6th highest score in the city. Not unrelated, crime rates in Harlem have come down markedly to levels not seen since the 1960s, likely due in part to the work of the HCZ (Harlem Children's Zone 2012).

What is the Goal of HCZ? Improve the System

When Geoffrey Canada reoriented his approach in Harlem from Mastery to Sync, he changed the primary aim of the initiative from the specific goal of reducing violence by training young minority youth in martial arts and conflict resolution (Mastery) to the more general objective of enhancing the safety and well-being of the broader Harlem community over time by helping the most vulnerable children thrive (Sync). In other words, his objectives shifted from more precise, shorter-term goals to those of changing qualitatively the complex dynamics of the broader community from impoverished and violent to constructive and thriving.

Where Do We Focus? See the Evolving Problem in Context

When Geoffrey Canada shifted strategies to the HCZ, he changed his focus from the narrower issue of urban male youth violence, to the broader pallet of the multiple determined patterns and trends evident in the Harlem community. This required time and attention to the many different realities present in the community, something most outsiders can't access or afford. But Canada's day-to-day interactions with members of the community provided him with a much more nuanced understanding of the system than he had come in with. However, his aware-ness of the complexity of the problem(s) eventually generated a new sense of clarity, which helped him develop a feasible actionable strategy that he could implement and assess. The immediate crisis and misery associated with destructive problems in Harlem were considerable and demanded attention to the here and now. But it was equally important that Canada broaden his temporal perspective to understand how past and present patterns are likely to shape future outcomes.

How Do We Engage the System? Tap the Energy

While directing the Rheedlen Center for children and Family Services in Harlem, Geoffrey Canada went to school on the dynamics of Harlem in 1990 and learned two critical things. One of the most powerful insights he discovered was that the success of the children and the strength of the community went hand in hand. When kids in the community got lost to drugs and violence and premature death, as so many had, the commu-nity got lost as well. Depression, learned-helplessness and despair were contagious and spread. This was a slippery slope in a neighborhood where rates of poverty, addiction, unemployment, and crime were al-ready very high. However, when young people succeeded—graduated high school or college, became a priest or got a decent job, the families and community members associated with the child brightened and ral-lied.

Due to the complexity of the many forces associated with this child--community dynamic, the HCZ could not begin to control it. However, with an understanding of the vital centrality of it for long-term commu-nity health and wellbeing as a core endogenous driver of change, they began to invest in impacting it positively. This was the primary lever that the tenacious, hardworking staff at the HCZ built on.

Second, given the tightly coupled ecology of poverty and violence in the Harlem community, it became clear that there were no simple solu-tions. Multiple needs and challenges had to be addressed simultaneously to have an impact, but they could never afford to offer every vulnerable child everything they needed. However, Harlem is a community of sub-neighborhoods that change from block to block. So they could achieve some economies of scale by focusing attention on one block at a time, and scaling up from there. This local knowledge helped shape the efficacy of the HCZ strategy. This is but one illustration of how aware-ness of local systems dynamics and tapping into the energy for change from within the system can enable a degree of efficacy, even when facing some of our most daunting problems.

How Do We Engage the System? Adaptive Action

The full story of Canada's involvement with urban school violence in Harlem is, in many ways, a story of trying different strategies, learning from success and failure, and adapting accordingly—even if that adaptation meant wholesale changes in their approach. For example, who thought that by providing sufficient food, safety, healthcare and educational support to a targeted group of at-risk preschoolers in Harlem would eventually lead to significant drops in violent crime in the community? Clearly, the pathways to efficacy of such types of marginal strategies are tricky and often unknown, which makes it all the more important to work with them in highly adaptive ways.

How Do We Engage the System? Enable Change

Canada also shifted his mode of leadership when moving from his initial martial arts based approach to the HCZ concept. At first, Canada did what we all would do—built on a distinct personal competency (martial arts in this case) that would allow him to play a distinctive leadership role in helping people learn a "better way" that he could provide. But, when working on the HCZ, Canada shifted gears in a way that put the community in the lead. Recognizing the good works done in many of the public schools in the Zone in Harlem in helping to address violence and poverty, the HCZ reached out and offered support to each of the schools *in whatever form the school itself deemed necessary*. Thus, instead of imposing one-size-fits-all solutions into schools, the Zone allowed the school principals to determine what they felt would most help them be more effective.

In Harlem, it is interesting to note that Geoffrey Canada worked directly with adolescent African American boys for years achieving little success or drawing little attention to his work. However, when he formally launched the Zone in 2000, which focused on younger pre-school children, the project quickly became more popular and celebrated. This may speak to the relative resonance in the community (and beyond) of serving these two different populations: one mobilized change, the other failed to.

Conclusion

In this chapter we have argued that the dominance of a Western, scientific orientation to problem solving in conflict has severe limitations when facing complex, intractable, cloud-like problems. We offer an introduction to an alternative approach to problem solving, one that works in sync with the situational forces that surround the more difficult challenges we face.

While we believe the Sync approach has a lot to offer those of us dealing with intractable social problems, it also has a lot to offer to people that are skilled in the conflict and peacebuilding skill set. Perhaps the most appealing aspect of the Mastery approach is that it offers the opportunity for one person to make the critical difference—to use their mastery as a decisive ingredient in fixing an important problem. The

Sync approach runs counter to this because it says that while individual action is important, it takes a back seat to collective thinking and acting.

This collective approach requires people of diverse backgrounds, skills, and thinking to work together, challenge each other's thinking with respect and skill, have difficult conversations, and work constructively with their differences. Without the ability to do these things, we may be truly powerless to grapple with the most difficult problems we face.

The good news is that the most likely readers of this chapter are dedicated to building these key skills and can play *the* catalytic role in helping us all work in sync with the world around us.

References

Blum, G. 2007. *Islands of Agreement: Managing Enduring Armed Rivalries*. Cambridge, MA: Harvard University Press.

Burns, D. 2007. *Systemic Action Research: A Strategy for Whole System Change*. Bristol, UK: Policy Press.

Coleman, P. T., K. Mazzaro, N. Redding, R. Ben-Yehuda and J. Rothman. Resonance in Complex Social Systems: A Summary and Synthesis of the Literature. Working Paper.

Coleman, P. T. 2011. *The Five Percent: Finding Solutions to Seemingly Impossible Conflicts*. New York, NY: Public Affairs.

Diehl, P. F. and G. Goertz. 2001. *War and Peace in International Rivalry*. Ann Arbor, MI: University of Michigan Press.

Dörner, D. 1996. *The Logic of Failure: Why Things Go Wrong and What We Can Do to Make Them Right*. Cambridge, MA: Perseus Press.

Jullien, F. 2004. *A Treatise on Efficacy: Between Western and Chinese Thinking*. Honolulu, HI: University of Hawaii Press.

Harlem Children's Zone. *FY 2012 Report* http://hcz.org/wp-content/uploads/2014/04/HCZ-2012-Highlights.pdf (last accessed June 17, 2016).

Kluckhohn, F. R. and F. L. Strodtbeck. 1961. *Variations in Value Orientations*. Evanston: Row, Peterson.

Maruyama, M. 1963. The Second Cybernetics: Deviation-Amplifying Mutual Causal Processes. *American Scientist* (51): 164-179.

Maruyama, M. 1982. Four Different Causal Metatypes in Biological and Social Sciences. In *Self Organization and Dissipative Structures*, edited by W. C. Schieve and P. M. Allen. Austin, TX: University of Texas Press.

Popper, K. R. 1966. *Of Clouds and Clocks: An Approach to the Problem of Rationality and the Freedom of Man*. St. Louis Missouri: Washington University.

Praszkier, R., A. Nowak and P. T. Coleman. 2010. Social entrepreneurs and constructive change: The wisdom of circumventing conflict. *Peace and Conflict: The Journal of Peace Psychology* 16(2): 153-174.

Ricigliano, R. 2012. *Making Peace Last*. Boulder, CO: Paradigm Press.

Senge, P., C. O. Scharmer, J. Jaworski and B. S. Flowers. 2004. *Presence: Human Purpose and the Field of the Future*. New York: Doubleday.

Understanding Intractable Conflicts

Peter T. Coleman, Nicholas Redding & Joshua Fisher

Editors' Note: In the second chapter of our complex-case trilogy, the authors summarize recent findings from complexity science and dynamical systems theory, showing how the new insights provide the possibility of innovative levers for change. Their key findings are presented as a set of five guidelines. This follows the more general explanation in Coleman and Ricigliano on Getting in Sync and is also closely related to the next chapter, Influencing Intractable Conflicts, which also presents a set of five guidelines: this time, for actually working on a conflict which, on the surface, appears impossible to influence.

Scholars report that between five and eight percent of contentious relationships between nations become intractable: they intensify, become locked-in, and persist for an average of thirty-six years (Diehl and Goertz 2001). Similar patterns of entrenched conflict are found in families, organizations and communities. These destructive dynamics wreak

Peter T. Coleman is Professor of Psychology and Education at Columbia University, where he holds a joint appointment at Teachers College and The Earth Institute. Dr. Coleman directs the Morton Deutsch International Center for Cooperation and Conflict Resolution (MD-ICCCR) and the Institute on Psychological Science and Practice (IPSP) at Teachers College, and is Executive Director of Columbia University's Advanced Consortium on Cooperation, Conflict, and Complexity (AC4). He currently conducts research on optimality, adaptivity, and complexity dynamics in conflict contexts.

Nicholas Redding is a research psychologist with the Ulupono Initiative of The Omidyar Group, a social impact investment firm focused on encouraging sustainable energy, food and waste practices in Hawai'i. Prior to joining Ulupono, he was a research program coordinator with the Advanced Consortium on Cooperation, Conflict, and Complexity (AC4) at the Earth Institute, Columbia University. He holds a Ph.D. in Social-Organizational Psychology from Columbia University.

Josh Fisher is the Director of the AC4 consortium at Columbia University. He is also an Adjunct Faculty member in the School of Professional Studies, and an Associate Research Scientist at the Earth Institute, studying conflict management, natural resources, and extractive industry. His current work focuses on natural resource management as a tool for conflict prevention. He works with government, civil society, international organizations, and nonprofit partners to design strategies to constructively manage environmental conflicts. Dr. Fisher received his PhD in Conflict Analysis and Resolution from George Mason University.

havoc and bring considerable suffering, cost and instability to the families, communities, nations and regions involved. For negotiators and conflict resolution practitioners working with parties to resolve these types of conflicts, traditional negotiation tactics are at best insufficient, and at worst can serve to perpetuate or exacerbate existing tensions. This chapter and the next one illustrate how recent findings from complexity science and dynamical systems theory can be applied to these seemingly intractable conflicts, offering new insights into innovative levers for change. The key findings are summarized as a set of guidelines, five in each chapter.

Conflict is about change. It revolves around disputants' needs or desires to address tension from incompatible activities (contrasting interests, beliefs, values or desires) by changing situations, relationships, the balance of power, the other disputants' actions, values, beliefs or bargaining position, or a third party's wish to change a conflict from low-intensity to high (as with some activists), or from high-intensity to low (as with negotiators and mediators). Conflicts often emerge from changing circumstances and relationships and, in turn, change those circumstances and relationships. Therefore, how we think about and approach change—or in the case of intractable conflicts, how we understand social systems that appear to doggedly resist change—is paramount.

There are many theories of change, and disputants as well as conflict resolution practitioners all operate within one or more of these theories, whether implicit or explicit, simple or complex, formal or informal (Coleman 2004). Four hundred years of mostly atomistic, linear, cause and effect approaches to science have left our understanding of conflict and change dynamics largely decontextualized, short term and piecemeal (Coleman 2011). Although many research findings from this paradigm have proven fruitful, and the practices informed by these findings are effective in some contexts, they have infused our theorizing, research and practice with a set of assumptions that severely limit their generalizability and practical utility in our increasingly complex, dynamic world. These include:

- Relating fluid things (conflict dynamics) to fixed things (static attitudes or beliefs).
- Thinking about change *only* in linear, cause-and-effect terms.
- Privileging effects on short-term outcomes over long-term patterns in research and practice.
- Framing complex conflicts in narrow, disciplinary or sectoral ways.
- Focusing primarily on problems and pathologies (violence and war) in lieu of solutions and healthy states (cooperation and peace).
- Marginalizing the role of emotions in our science and practice.
- Over-simplifying or over-complicating our models and methods.

- Missing the invisible or currently unobservable dynamics at play in conflict systems.
- Failing to foresee the unintended consequences of our actions (Coleman 2011; Vallacher et al. 2013).

Although intractable conflicts are often multiply-determined (Coleman 2003), we suggest that it is some combination of 1) their highly complex and dynamic natures, 2) our misbegotten assumptions of how they emerge, evolve and change, and 3) the unintended consequences of our often well-intentioned attempts at changing them, that creates a perfect storm of intractability. Consequently, many conflicts become self-perpetuating and wear on despite multiple good faith attempts at their resolution (Kriesberg 2005: 65-98).

However, complexity science, and in particular dynamical systems theory (DST), a school of thought coming out of applied mathematics, offers new, highly original and practical insights about how systems of all types—from cellular to social to planetary—change and resist change (see Coleman 2011; Vallacher et al. 2010; Vallacher et al. 2013). In this chapter, we outline a new *theory of practice* for addressing long-term conflicts that is emerging from this paradigm.[1]

Guidelines for Understanding Intractable Conflict: A "Dynamical Systems" Theory of Practice

Dynamical systems theory (DST) is a relatively new and increasingly influential paradigm in many areas of science, which offers an innovative set of metaphors, models and methods for conceptualizing and addressing conflict. A dynamical system is defined as a set of interconnected elements (such as beliefs, feelings, and behaviors) that change and evolve in time, where a change in each element depends on influences from other elements. Due to these interacting influences, the system as a whole evolves in time and new elements and dynamics emerge that in turn affect the system's evolution. Thus, changes in any element of a negotiation process (such as levels of trust) depend on influences of various other elements (each disputant's motives, attitudes, actions, etc.), which evolve over time to affect the general pattern of interactions (positive or negative) in the dispute. Likewise, through the negotiation process new dynamics emerge in the relationships between conflict parties that can themselves become grounds for dialogue and new points for negotiation. The implication of this for negotiators and mediators is that they must simultaneously hold space for the original inputs to the negotiation (interests, positions, needs and dynamics), identify emergent issues that occur in-process, and identify appropriate ways to incorporate those into negotiations. The principles defining the evolution of dynamical systems have wide applicability and have been employed to conceptualize and investigate a highly diverse set of conflict-related phenomena (emotion, stereotyping, attitude change, cooperation versus competition in social dilemmas, etc.).

Every theory of practice is based on a particular worldview: a set of images, values and assumptions that are often more implicit than made explicit (Coleman 2004). While there are some basic tenets that underpin most theories of practice, for example "Do No Harm" (Anderson 1999), the DST theory of practice has a few basic tenets that set it apart as a unique approach to practice in complex and intractable situations (for elaboration, see Coleman 2011, 2014; Vallacher et al. 2010; Vallacher et al. 2013). The foundational assumptions of this new approach are:

- **Complexity matters: intractable conflicts operate within a complex network of forces**. This means that there are typically multiple, interrelated causes, actors, perspectives and narratives at play in the conflict system—although some will prove more central to intractability than others. It also means that there are likely multiple entry points, solutions and pathways to peace (Burns 2007).

- **Time matters: both linear and non-linear change dynamics operate in conflict systems.** Focusing on only linear effects (shorter-term cause and effect relations prominent in Western science and logic) often brings unintended consequences and eclipses our understanding of how these linear effects play out over time in complex, nonlinear systems (Dörner 1996). The key is to understand both linear effects and nonlinear dynamics in relation to one another and in terms of different temporal scales.

- **Inclusion matters: given the multiply-determined nature of these conflict systems, more inclusive practices involving a broad and diverse set of stakeholders are likely to be more effective.** More inclusive approaches can provide a more comprehensive view of a system, offer higher probabilities of identifying critical drivers and novel insights, and, if conducted in a manner perceived as legitimate, result in more buy-in and sustainability from a broader set of constituents. However, more inclusive practices can also be more costly and messy, and less efficient, particularly when attempts are made to involve more militant, marginalized groups. There is a thus critical tension in change processes between inclusiveness and efficiency (Coleman and Voronov 2003).

- **Emotion matters: despite their relative neglect in conflict research, emotions often play a vital role in sustaining and transforming intractable conflicts.** The presence or absence of strong reservoirs for positivity and negativity in relational systems in conflict has proven to be among the central parameters for determining enduring conflict and sustainable peace. (Gottman et al. 2014)

- **The system rules: intractable conflict systems have their own exceptionally strong internal propensities.** When you push on a system mired in intractable conflict, it pushes back, and the harder you push, the more it rallies against you. This is why most attempts at intervention fail in these conflicts. Therefore, instead of interjecting new ideas, goals and methods as a means of changing a conflict system, it is best to become intimately familiar with the existing propensities of the system, and then to work *with* the dynamics of the system to affect constructive and destructive probabilities (Jullien 2004; Gal 2013).

The general objectives of the DST approach differ fundamentally from the objectives of more standard models of conflict resolution; they do not aim to identify and satisfy disputants' underlying grievances, interests and needs in order to resolve the presenting conflict. Rather, the DST approach starts with comprehending the dynamics of the system that are maintaining the status quo of the conflict and then exploits these insights by working with the flow of these dynamics to shift the probabilities of destructive conflict and foster sustainable peace processes. Specifically, the objectives are to work with stakeholders to regain a sense of accuracy, agency and possibility in what seems like an otherwise impossible conflict, and then to co-create more sustainable solutions by opening up the system to new information before facilitating a reconfiguration of the patterns of relations—over time—from destructive to constructive. This is accomplished by employing a set of practices aimed at constructively managing the current state of the conflict, while simultaneously working to increase the future probabilities for constructive relations between the parties *and* decreasing the probabilities for destructive future encounters (see Nowak et al. 2010, for access to an online tool for working with these dynamics).

Below is a schematic and set of guidelines for a DST theory of practice. Note that describing these guidelines in a linear, sequential manner only reinforces more traditional linear thinking. Therefore, we organize their presentation around a basic set of change practices on systemic *preparation, comprehension, engagement,* and *learning and adaptation* for working with complex, nonlinear systems (See Figure 1). Rather than adopting these guidelines as a step-by-step approach, readers are instead encouraged to view the guidelines holistically, employing and moving between processes as appropriate during the change process. The first two sets of practices (preparation and comprehension) are covered in the current chapter, while the second two (engagement, and learning and adaptation) will be covered in the following chapter.

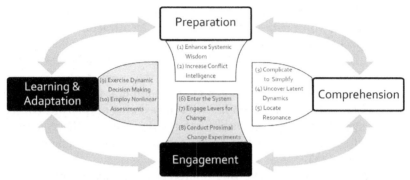

Figure 1 A Dynamical Systems Theory of Practice

We have labeled the first set of guidelines in our model as systemic *preparation*. Working effectively to change complex, dynamic conflict systems is demanding and unfamiliar to most, and requires a set of competencies, skills and approaches to assessment rarely offered in trainings on conflict management. This is not only true for conflict practitioners, but also for leaders, managers, representatives, disputants, third parties and other stakeholders involved in these settings. As such, it is critical for those consulting to parties in these systems, as well as the parties involved, to gain a working familiarity with basic systems concepts. Ideally, practitioners will take this a step further, internalizing these competencies and skills sufficiently to be able to encourage deeper understanding within the parties they are working with. The following guidelines outline two categories of competencies integral for systemic preparation.

Guideline #1: Enhance Individual Competencies for Systemic Wisdom

Because complex conflicts are themselves systems of interrelated factors and dynamics, some of which are obscured by traditional means of understanding conflict, enabling stakeholders to navigate these forces and engage each other more constructively requires that they understand the system as a system. Gregory Bateson (1972: 440) emphasized this when he said, "Lack of systemic wisdom is always punished... Systems are nonetheless punishing of any species unwise enough to quarrel with its ecology. Call the systemic forces God if you will." For Bateson, the first step in creating social wellbeing is enhancing *systemic wisdom*: understanding that we are dependent upon, and participants in, a larger living system.

Previously, we identified a set of basic building blocks that could be considered *core competencies for systemic wisdom* (Coleman 2011). They include:

- Understanding that nonlinear networks of causation are distinct from linear, cause and effect models. Systems are composed of multiple elements interacting and evolving over time, requiring one to identify the multitude of factors that conspire to drive undesirable outcomes, rather than looking for one or two direct causal factors.
- Enhancing complex thinking, feeling, acting, and social identification with decision makers and other key stakeholders.
- Understanding how latent (implicit) processes operate and how they manifest, and the trade-offs of working with both implicit and explicit processes.
- Effectively balancing the tensions between short-term and long-term thinking and action.
- Exercising multilevel thinking: enhancing awareness and acting at different levels (psychological, social, structural, institutional, cultural) simultaneously.

Prior research has suggested that higher levels of five relevant individual competencies are associated with more constructive conflict tendencies: cognitive, behavioral, and emotional complexity, tolerance for ambiguity, and broader temporal scope (i.e. consideration for future consequences.)[2] In a recent study (Redding and Coleman working paper), we investigated the relationships between these competencies and participants' capacities for effectively navigating a complex intractable conflict scenario. After assessing the five competencies through standardized survey measures, participants played a complex computer simulation game, which required them to act as the Prime Minister of Israel working to navigate the complexities of the Israeli-Palestinian conflict to bring about a sustainable long-term resolution.

Preliminary results of the study suggest that these competencies are associated with gaining a more complex understanding of the system, engaging more constructively with the other party, and taking actions more conducive to sustainable outcomes. Participants with higher levels of cognitive complexity took action more quickly at the onset of the conflict in order to begin to better understand how the system operates. They were also, at the conclusion of the simulation, better able to *differentiate* the multiple perspectives relevant to the conflict and to *integrate* those perspectives within a larger context. Additionally, those higher in this trait, along with higher levels of tolerance for ambiguity and consideration for future consequences, were more likely to simultaneously employ multiple approaches to improving the situation—a strategy associated with more efficacy in complex systems (see Dörner 1996)—rather than sticking to one approach. This was demonstrated, for example, by actively engaging with the conflict through political channels, while simultaneously reallocating security forces as needed and advancing infrastructure and economic development projects.

Those higher in emotional complexity tended to identify more of the broader range of actors involved in the conflict, and relied less on drastic measures that would result in long-term negative impacts on their relationships with others in system. In other words, those who were more emotionally complex were less likely to retaliate with violent force to a security violation such as suicide bombing or threats from an extremist group. Lastly, those higher in cognitive complexity, emotional complexity and tolerance for ambiguity employed more constructive actions throughout the simulation as compared to those lower in these competencies. Overall, these individuals focused their actions more on enhancing communication, building trust, coordinating effort and responding to the other party's (i.e. Palestinian) needs.

Research in this area is still nascent but the above findings suggest that there are specific competencies that can be developed for increasing systemic wisdom. In addition to advancing research in this area, our group has developed a three-stage model for coaching those working to ameliorate intractable conflicts (Redding and Coleman working paper), which expands beyond traditional approaches to conflict coaching (see Jones and Brinkert 2007). Essentially, our model proposes that individuals can increase systemic wisdom by avoiding tendencies to over-simplify the narratives they impose on the complex systems they are working with. Instead, it is essential to work consciously toward developing mental models that are sufficiently complex for identifying underlying patterns and dynamics that can be harnessed for positive change. This is accomplished through building systems thinking ability as a competency, and adopting practices that emphasize the identification of all the relevant elements in the system—and the relations between the elements that give rise to the overall dynamics that are observed—before moving to implement change in the system. While engaged in this process, individuals should be aware of tendencies to collapse the complexity of their own emotional experiences when engaged in conflict: experiencing a broad range of emotions can be a valuable source of information when faced with a broad array of decisions. Additionally, it is essential for change makers to build self-awareness around their general level of comfort with ambiguity, as well as their preferences for privileging short-term over long-term thinking. These are difficult tendencies to change. But increased self-awareness can, over time, lead to more adaptive decision making that is essential for fostering long-term sustainable change.

The evidence suggests that higher levels of systemic wisdom enable stakeholders at various levels of power to navigate a conflict system more effectively. Not only this, but stakeholders are thus better equipped to engage the system to encourage more constructive means of action and interaction. Therefore, building or enhancing systemic wisdom among stakeholders is a critical step in enabling them to move from intractable conflict toward constructive engagement. At the individual level, this can be fostered by challenging individual tendencies to oversimplify their understanding of complex situations—including the emotional experience as a participant in the system— instead working within the ambiguity inherent to such challenges. Individual stakeholders can also be encouraged to identify the multiple alternative roles they can occupy as change agents in the system, and to avoid tendencies to reduce ambiguity by engaging in short-term thinking and action.

Another approach to building systemic wisdom among stakeholders in a system is to bring them together. When engaging with multiple stakeholders, groups are typically challenged to consider the broader range of factors and perspectives that are relevant to the conflict. Employing activities such as conflict mapping (see Guideline #3) challenges participants to see the system as a whole rather than through the lens of their individual experience. When these stakeholders begin to see their role in a larger system of influences, their perspectives on the system and understandings of ways to improve the system begin to change.

Guideline #2: Increase Competencies for Conflict Intelligence: Adaptivity, Optimality and Systemic Agency

The capacity to effectively navigate and leverage destructive and constructive conflict dynamics in complex systems also requires enhancing our *conflict intelligence* (Coleman and Ferguson 2014), which entails developing a set of three dynamic, behavioral competencies for conflict adaptivity, optimality and systemic agency.

Exercising Adaptivity

Conflict *adaptivity* is the capacity to employ different strategies in different conflicts, or as the same conflict situation evolves and changes over time, in a manner that achieves goals effectively and is fitting with the demands of the situation (Coleman et al. 2010). It involves a capacity to read situations accurately and then employ distinct strategies (such as Benevolence, Cooperation, Support, Dominance, Competition, Appeasement or Autonomy; see Coleman and Ferguson 2014) where they fit, and in a manner and to a degree that allows for satisfactory progress in achieving one's goals. More adaptive approaches to conflict resolution have been found to be associated with higher levels of efficacy and satisfaction with mediation processes (Beardsley 2010; Beardsley et al. 2006; Jacobs and Aakhus 2002; Kolb 1994; Picard 2004; Riskin 1997) and higher levels of satisfaction with conflict generally. In organizations, conflict adaptivity has been associated with increased work satisfaction, better relationships with co-workers, greater emotional well-being, reduced job stress and fewer intentions to quit (Coleman and Kugler 2014; Coleman, Mitchinson and Kugler 2009). Lastly, at the international level, case-based research on interstate negotiations found parties were more effective in negotiations to the extent that they were able to adjust their strategies to fit the relative (and relevant) power of the other side (Zartman and Rubin 2002).

Seeking Optimality

Optimality is the capacity to combine different approaches to conflict management (such as integrative and distributive tactics with mixed-motive conflicts) optimally to achieve the best possible outcomes (Coleman, Kugler, Kim and Vallacher working paper). Research suggests that effective individuals rarely rely on a single conflict handling style, instead employing more blended or "conglomerated" approaches that utilize the beneficial components of a variety of tactics (Van de Vliert, Euwema and Huismans 1995). For instance, effective attorneys use a pattern of behaviors in negotiations that do not neatly fit any one of the conflict-style categories (Schneider 2012; Williams 1983; 1993). Similarly, recent research in our lab on optimal ratios between more individualistic (self-focused) and more collectivistic (other-focused) behaviors also found more balanced strategies associated with more integrative styles of conflict management, leading to higher levels of satisfaction with conflict outcomes, processes, relationships, goal attainment and job satisfaction (Kim and Coleman working paper).

Fostering Systemic Agency

Finally, *systemic agency* is the capacity to visualize and mobilize networks of collective influence to alter the nature of the context in which a conflict is situated. This is a collective form of efficacy and leverage typically employed when the status quo is unresponsive to more traditional, unilateral methods of constructive conflict resolution. Systemic agency requires systemic wisdom, along with the capacity to comprehend and map the complex networks of causation in which the problem being addressed is situated. But it goes beyond this to include implementing strategies for altering systems dynamics. This perspective is being increasingly adopted in the development sector, with both non-governmental and governmental organizations such as The Omidyar Group, Oxfam, USAID, and the World Bank working to employ systemic mapping and other tools in order to better identify opportunities for change and to mobilize networks of support.

Together, enhancing our own and others' levels of systemic wisdom and conflict intelligence helps to establish a shared language and capacity for working effectively with complex conflict systems. A set of preliminary-assessment questions may be helpful here, especially for determining what skill development and other early-assistance efforts might be needed before any more direct form of intervention can have a chance of success. These include asking whether the stakeholders and facilitators are...

- ...sufficiently comfortable with complexity and ambiguity?
- ...able to avoid reducing the complexity of a situation to simple cause and effect relationships between issues and outcomes?
- ...open to scanning the environment for existing latent processes that could be enhanced to shift the fundamental dynamics of the system?
- ...comfortable with thinking about how the system will change in the short term and in the long term (i.e. over different time scales)?
- ...skilled in *adaptivity*, effectively employing different strategies in different types of conflicts in a manner fitting with the demands of the situations?
- ...comfortable with combining different strategies in complex or evolving conflicts?
- ...skilled at implementing strategies that seek to mobilize networks of individuals that are not directly linked to the conflict but critical to the overall functioning of the system, in order to shift the nature of the context in which a conflict is situated?

Our next set of guidelines focuses on approaches for gaining systemic *comprehension*. In preparation for engaging actively with systems mired in intractable conflict, it is also critical to gain a current sense of the intrinsic propensities of the system in which you are working (Gal 2013; Jullien 2004). Systems' scholar-practitioners offer a variety of methods for conducting such investigations and visualizing systems (see Burns 2007; Eoyang and Holladay 2013; Gal 2013; Liebovitch et al. 2014; Ricigliano 2012). Some methods have been designed for more bottom-up, participatory approaches to community visualization (Burns 2007), others for more top-down, expert approaches (Butland et al. 2007; Ricigliano 2012). While the exact approach for visualizing the complex network of factors and dynamics involved in an intractable conflict will vary based on the context of an intervention, three guidelines seem central to many of these approaches.

Guideline #3: Complicate to Simplify

Because destructive conflicts demand attention to the here and now—to the issues, violence, hostilities, suffering and grievances evident in the immediate context—they often draw attention away from the history, trajectory, and broader context in which the conflict is evolving. Here, we describe two methods for visualizing the broader historical context.

Mapping

First, many peace-practitioners employ the use of complexity feedback-loop mapping to re-contextualize their own and the stakeholders' understandings of the constellation of forces affecting particular conflicts (see Burns 2007; Coleman 2011; Körppen, Ropers and Giessmann 2011;

Ricigliano 2012). Loop analysis (see Maruyama 1963, 1982) is particularly useful for mapping reinforcing and inhibiting feedback processes
that escalate, de-escalate and stabilize destructive conflicts. *Reinforcing
feedback* occurs when one element (such as a hostile act) stimulates
another element (such as negative out-group beliefs) along its current
trajectory. Here, more of A means more of B, or less of A means less of B.
On the other hand, *inhibiting feedback* occurs when one element inhibits
or reverses the direction of another element (such as when guilty or
compassionate feelings mitigate hostilities). Here, more of A means less
of B.

Feedback-loop mapping not only allows us to capture the multiple
sources and temporal dynamics of complex conflicts, but can also help to
identify central nodes and patterns that are unrecognizable by other
means. The mapping process can take different forms, but typically
begins by identifying the *nodal focus of interest*—the central phenomenon we wish to comprehend (violence, stalemate, peace, etc.; see
Vandenbroeck, Goossens and Clemens 2007). Next, the *core dynamics*
are identified, which are those elements and feedback loops most closely
associated with the increase or decrease of the nodal variable. After this,
the maps can be built out further to help visualize *the broader system of
elements and feedback dynamics* that are affecting the core dynamics
upstream. Maps can be generated at the individual level, at the interpersonal level and at the broader group, communal or wider systemic levels.

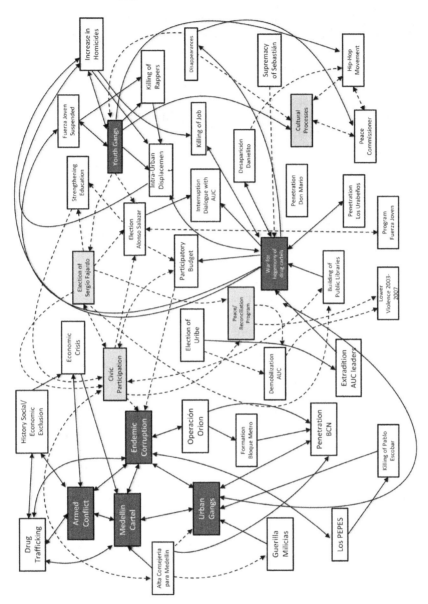

Figure 2: A Visualization of the Feedback Loops Contributing to an Attractor for Violence in Medellin, Columbia

For example, consider the map above in Figure 2. This was generated by our colleague Aldo Civico through a series of interviews he conducted in Medellín, Colombia in 2012. This map captures the dynamics of the system of violence in Medellín over time. It helps to visualize the dynamics that are constantly attracting the system into violence (solid-line loops). But it also shows some of the inhibiting factors that help us understand why the violence doesn't get worse (dashed-line loops; a ceiling effect). It shows hubs that work as major destructive attractors (such as the armed conflict, the Medellín cartel, endemic corruption, the war for hegemony among and within drug cartels, etc.) and the main inhibitors (like civic participation, social and artistic processes in the peripheral areas of the city, the peace and reconciliation program up to 2007, etc.). From this analysis, we can also see that some critical events have strengthened the patterns of violence in Medellín and weakened the effectiveness of inhibitors.

However, feedback loop mapping often results in extremely complex visualizations of a conflict's dynamics, so it is critical to be able offer strategies for subsequently focusing and simplifying. For instance, Eric Berlow (2010) recommends focusing in on *more local elements and loops that are actionable*; in other words, those that can feasibly be addressed. Feasible actions, informed by the complexity of events, can affect the probabilities of constructive change in a conflict system, but they should only be targeted after a fuller mapping of the system has provided a sense of the context in which these elements are operating. Another strategy is to look at each of the elements in the system, and take stock of how many other elements are influencing the element upstream and how many elements are influenced by the element downstream. Elements that receive fewer inputs may be easier to change, while those that influence many other elements in this system may have more impact on the system (Coleman 2011; Ricigliano 2012).

Conflict maps can be generated alone as a pre-negotiation exercise, with the help of facilitators or mediators, or in small groups of stakeholders. With conflict-mapping the goal is not necessarily to get it right. The goal at this stage is *to get it different*; to try to reintroduce a sense of nuance and complexity into the stakeholders' understanding of the conflict. As described above, when individuals engage in the process of mapping—especially in a diverse group of stakeholders—they are challenged to look beyond the factors that are most relevant to them and to their understanding of the system. A broader picture begins to emerge as each individual contributes to a process that leads to a *shared understanding of the system*, which in turn, opens up new avenues for change (Burns 2007).

Inventories

A second method for visualizing the context of disputes is through structured inventories. Recently, we developed an institutional-level inventory for conducting complex conflict assessments in organizations (Coleman, Redding, Ng, Straw & Burke, working paper). It offers a holistic conceptual framework for assessing the reinforcing/inhibiting conditions for constructive and destructive conflict dynamics (and therefore increasing/decreasing probabilities), and provides an inventory for leaders to conduct organization-level assessments and to explore relevant outcomes in their organizations (e.g., conflict climate, innovation, morale, organization-commitment, and procedural justice).

To develop this framework, we surveyed the conflict literature for empirical research identifying factors associated with organizational conflict. We then identified a set of existing metrics and measurement instruments for each of these variables, which when combined provides a systemic inventory of drivers and mitigators of conflict processes. The result is an inventory and a large-scale survey assessment tool. The inventory provides a framework for collecting data through, for example, organization records, environmental analysis, interviews and direct observations. The survey instruments can be used to assess conflict climate perceptions of organization members across levels. Such assessments are useful for identifying potential conflict "hot spots" as well as more subtle or counter-intuitive contributors to destructive conflict. This information may also prove useful in identifying positive organizational dynamics to build on, as well as latent attractors (see below) that could be activated to shift destructive organizational conflict processes in a more constructive direction.

If there is sufficient time, negotiators and key stakeholders can work to develop inventories such as the one we developed for organizational conflict, to fit the context of the conflict scenario. This can serve as an initial step in the comprehension process, allowing for a broader understanding of the factors that are most relevant to understanding the system, a clearer sense of the nodal focus of interest, and identification of the stakeholders and actors that are critical to convene for further mapping and planning activities.

Guideline #4: Uncover Latent (Invisible) Dynamics and Attractors

Although our experiences in protracted conflicts tend to be overwhelmingly negative in relation to the other disputants, we benefit from learning to pay attention to anomalies that occur; in other words, to the actions and events that surprise us. Intractable conflicts are so difficult to change because of *attractors*—emergent structures that stabilize systems, making them highly resistant to change—that ensure that any tendencies towards resolution are fleeting at best. However, these cracks in the foundation of our understanding of the conflict and our sense of the other parties are often important sources of information: evidence that there may be alternative patterns operating below our radar. These *latent attractors* may prove to be our best avenues for escaping or otherwise addressing the conflict—if we can identify them.

For example, a surprising finding from a study we conducted with Palestinians and Israelis in 2002 was the impact on participants of early, positive, serendipitous encounters with members of their out-groups (Coleman and Lowe 2007). Just as early traumatic losses were etched powerfully into the minds of individuals, these positive spontaneous encounters described by participants tended to have an equally powerful effect, long mitigating against their sense of certainty and vilification of the outgroup. The spontaneous nature of these encounters seemed to capture individuals when their psychological defenses were low, thereby allowing the experiences to impact them both emotionally and cognitively.

The potential of latent attractors suggests that any actions in a conflict can have very different effects on three distinct aspects of a conflict landscape: on the current situation (the level of hostility in the conflict right now), on the longer-term potential for positive interactions (latent positive attractors), and on the longer-term potential for negative interactions (negative attractors). For instance, sending riot police into a neighborhood in Baltimore to quell unrest from community grievances over perceived injustices may 1) temporarily reduce violence, 2) increase community resentment and alienation, and therefore the probability of future unrest, and 3) decrease the community's trust and respect for the authorities, also fostering future unrest.

Guideline #5: Identify Resonance

When working with groups and communities, some peacebuilders speak of the value of identifying local areas of *resonance* when attempting to mobilize change (Burns 2007). We define *resonance* in social systems as a form of heightened, shared emotional, cognitive, physical or social energy that results in people feeling and finding connections with like-minded others, and ultimately a sense of congruence and purpose (Coleman, Mazzaro, Redding and Rothman working paper). In other words, resonance is a form of shared energy that gives way in some groups to a sense of unity and shared interests and, sometimes, joint action. Directed group action results when this energy crosses some threshold in a group (beyond their resistance to change). It can be constructive or destructive (or both) depending on the valence and direction of the group's shared interests (e.g., a mobilized community addressing joblessness or sanitation problems in their community, versus an angry mob addressing grievances against members of an outgroup). Ultimately, resonance is the energy necessary to drive and sustain systemic change.

Working with systemic resonance typically involves identifying, supporting and marshalling waves of motivation and energy in networks of people in service of communal change. There are a variety of ways of identifying resonance, beyond relying on one's intuition. According to research rooted in transpersonal psychology, resonance can be fostered by empathically attuned clinicians who are trained to better understand and intervene in the context of changing emotional landscapes, with some advocating for trainings that strengthen somatic experiences of empathy, including how to better communicate at the visual, auditory, interoceptive, proprioceptive, and kinesthetic levels (Lovkvist 2013). In systemic action research, Danny Burns (2011) proposes a framework where facilitators engage through multiple streams and narratives informed by a basic understanding of energy patterns in a system. Burns advocates for an approach where action is seen as important as dialogue, and the act of doing collectively can lead to changes in the landscape and the creation of new "entry points".

Perhaps the most common form of assessment of group-level resonance is through survey administration. At the most basic level, group members have been measured and compared on perceptions of cohesiveness (Stinson and Hellebrandt 1972), coordination (Faraj and Sproull 2000; Lewis 2003), and energy and pleasantness (Barsade 2002). Analysis involves both assessing whether group members identify similar experiences while participating in the group, and the extent to which the experiences are consistent across group members.

To summarize, enhancing systemic comprehension can be facilitated by asking the following questions:

- What are the intrinsic propensities of the system in which you are working?
- Do the stakeholders and facilitator have a sufficient understanding of the constellation of current and historical forces affecting the conflict?
- Have you been able to focus in on aspects of the system that may lend themselves to feasible actions?
- Are there obvious and less obvious (latent) attractor dynamics at play in the broader system?
- Where is there currently resonant energy in the system? Can this energy be marshaled for constructive change?

Up to this point, our discussion has focused primarily on *understanding* intractable conflict. We have proposed that enhancing systemic wisdom and working to build conflict intelligence are critical activities for preparing oneself and others to begin to work in these systems. Additionally, we have described less conventional approaches for comprehending these conflict systems through practices such as conducting feedback loop mapping, identifying latent attractors for positive change, and working with resonance at multiple levels. In the next chapter, we shift to a primary focus on *engaging* with intractable conflicts, in terms of the initial steps for encouraging positive change, and methods for learning and adapting from feedback throughout the change process.

Notes

[1] This chapter was derived from a more comprehensive project to develop a Field Book on applying dynamical systems theory and methods to complex problems associated with conflict and sustainable peace.

[2] For studies on cognitive, behavioral, and emotional complexity see Bledow et al. 2011; Huy 2002; Nicotera, Smilowitz and Pearson 1990; Pruitt and Lewis 1975; Suedfeld

and Rank 1976; Suedfeld, Tetlock and Ramirez 1977; Wallace and Suedfeld 1988; Zaccaro 2001. For relevant findings on tolerance for ambiguity and consideration for future consequences see Cohen and Insko 2008; Joireman, Strathman and Balliet 2006; Nicotera, Smilowitz and Pearson 1990; Teger 1970; Van Lange, Klapwijk and Van Munster 2011; Wolf et al. 2009.

References

Anderson, M. 1999. *Do No Harm: How Aid Can Support Peace—Or War*. Boulder, CO and London, UK: Lynne Rienner Publishers.

Barsade, S. G. 2002. The Ripple Effect: Emotional Contagion and Its Influence on Group Behavior. *Administrative Science Quarterly* 47(4): 644-675.

Bateson, G. 1972. *Steps to an Ecology of Mind: Collected Essays in Anthropology, Psychiatry, Evolution, and Epistemology*. Chicago, IL: University of Chicago Press.

Beardsley, K. C. 2010. Pain, Pressure and Political Cover: Explaining Mediation Incidence. *Journal of Peace Research* 47(4): 395-406.

Beardsley, K. C., D. M. Quinn, B. Biswas and J. Wilkenfeld. 2006. Mediation Style and Crisis Outcomes. *Journal of Conflict Resolution* 50(1): 58-86.

Berlow, R. 2010. How Complexity Leads to Simplicity. *TED Live Conference, TEDGlobal 2010*. Retrieved from http://www.ted.com/ talks/eric_berlow_how_complexity_leads_to_simplicity.html.

Bledow, R., A. Schmitt, M. Frese and J. Kühnel. 2011. The Affective Shift Model of Work Engagement. *Journal of Applied Psychology* 96(6): 1246-1257.

Burns, D. 2007. *Systemic Action Research: A Strategy for Whole System Change*. Bristol, UK: Policy Press.

Burns, D. 2011. Facilitating Systemic Conflict Transformation through Systemic Action Research. In *The Non-Linearity of Peace Processes-Theory and Practice of Systemic Conflict Transformation*, edited by D. Korppen, N. Ropers, and H. J. Giessmann. Farmington Hills, MI: Barbara Budrich Publisher.

Butland, B., S. Jebb, P. Kopelman, K. McPherson, S. Thomas, J. Mardell and V. Parry. 2007. *Foresight. Tackling Obesities: Future Choices. Project Report*. London: Government Office for Science.

Cohen, T. R. and C. A. Insko. 2008. War and Peace: Possible Approaches to Reducing Intergroup Conflict. *Perspectives on Psychological Science* 3(2): 87-93.

Coleman, P. T. 2003. Characteristics of Protracted, Intractable Conflict: Toward the Development of a Metaframework - I. *Peace and Conflict: Journal of Peace Psychology* 9(1): 1-37.

Coleman, P. T. 2004. Paradigmatic Framing of Protracted, Intractable Conflict. *Peace and Conflict: Journal of Peace Psychology* 10(3): 197-235.

Coleman, P. T. and M. Voronov. 2003. Power in Groups and Organizations. In *The International Handbook of Organizational Teamwork and Cooperative Working*, edited by M. West, D. Tjosvold and K. G. Smith. New York, NY: John Wiley & Sons.

Coleman, P. T. and R. Ferguson. 2014. *Making Conflict Work: Navigating Disagreement Up and Down Your Organization*. New York, NY: Houghton Mifflin Harcourt.

Coleman, P. T. and K. G. Kugler. 2014. Tracking Managerial Conflict Adaptivity: Introducing a Dynamic Measure of Adaptive Conflict Management in Organizations. *Journal of Organizational Behavior* 35(7): 945-968.

Coleman, P. T. and J. K. Lowe. 2007. Conflict, Identity, and Resilience: Negotiating Collective Identities within the Israeli and Palestinian Diasporas. *Conflict Resolution Quarterly* 24(4): 377-412.

Coleman, P. T., K. G. Kugler, R. Kim and R. Vallacher. Hoping for the Best, Preparing for the Worst: Regulatory Focus Optimality in Social Conflict. MD-ICCCR Working Paper.

Coleman, P. T., K. Mazzaro, N. Redding, R. Ben-Yehuda, D. Burns and J. Rothman. 2015. Resonance in Complex Social Systems. MD-ICCCR Working Paper.

Coleman, P. T., N. Redding, N., L. Ng, C. Straw and W. W. Burke. Systemic-Level Influences on Organizational Conflict Processes: An Empirical Review, Inventory and New Directions. MD-ICCCR Working Paper.

Coleman, P. T., A. Mitchinson and K. G. Kugler. 2009. Adaptation, Integration, and Learning: The Three Legs of the Steady Stool of Conflict Resolution in Asymmetrical Power Relations. Poster presented at the 22nd Conference of the International Association for Conflict Management. Kyoto, Japan.

Coleman, P. T. 2011. *The Five Percent: Finding Solutions to Seemingly Impossible Conflicts*. New York, NY: Public Affairs.

Coleman, P. T., K. Kugler, A. Mitchinson, C. Chung and N. Musallam. 2010. The View from Above and Below: The Effects of Power and Interdependence Asymmetries on Conflict Dynamics and Outcomes in Organizations. *Negotiation and Conflict Management Research* 3(4): 283-311.

Diehl, P. F. and G. Goertz. 2001. *War and Peace in International Rivalry.* Ann Arbor, MI: University of Michigan Press.

Dörner, D. 1996. *The Logic of Failure: Why Things Go Wrong and What We Can Do to Make Them Right.* Cambridge, MA: Perseus Press.

Eoyang, G. and R. Holladay. 2013. *Adaptive Action: Leveraging Uncertainty in Your Organization.* Stanford, CA: Stanford University Press.

Faraj, S. and L. Sproull. 2000. Coordinating Expertise in Software Development Teams. *Management Science* 46(12): 1554-1568.

Gal, O. 2013. Acupuncture Approaches to Conflict Transformation. *Concept Paper Series, DST Innovation Lab 2013.* Retrieved from http://conflictinnovationlab.org/lab-2013/lab-resources-2013/concept-papers/

Gottman, J. M., J. Gottman, A. Greendorfer and M. Wahbe. 2014. An Empirically-Based Approach to Couples' Conflict. In *The Handbook of Conflict Resolution: Theory and Practice,* edited by P. T. Coleman, M. Deutsch, and E. Marcus. San Francisco, CA: Jossey-Bass.

Huy, Q. N. 2002. Emotional Balancing of Organizational Continuity and Radical Change: The Contribution of Middle Managers. *Administrative Science Quarterly* 47(1): 31-69.

Jacobs, S. and M. Aakhus. 2002. What Mediators Do with Words: Implementing Three Models of Rational Discussion in Dispute Mediation. *Conflict Resolution Quarterly* 20(2): 177-203.

Joireman, J., A. Strathman and D. P. Balliet. 2006. Considering Future Consequences: An Integrative Model. In *Judgments Over Time: The Interplay of Thoughts, Feelings, and Behaviors,* edited by L. Sanna and E. Chang. Oxford, UK: Oxford University Press.

Jones, T. S. and R. Brinkert. 2007. *Conflict Coaching: Conflict Management Strategies and Skills for the Individual.* Thousand Oaks, CA: Sage Publications.

Jullien, F. 2004. *A Treatise on Efficacy: Between Western and Chinese Thinking.* Honolulu, HI: University of Hawaii Press.

Kim R. and P. T. Coleman. 2015. The Combined Effect of Individualism—Collectivism on Conflict Styles and Satisfaction: An Analysis at the Individual Level. *Peace and Conflict Studies* 22(2): 137-159.

Kolb, D. M. and Associates. 1994. *When Talk Works: Profiles of Mediators.* San Francisco, CA: Jossey-Bass.

Körppen, D., N. Ropers and H. J. Giessmann (eds). 2011. *The Non-Linearity of Peace Processes: Theory and Practice of Systemic Conflict Transformation.* Farmington Hills: Barbara Budrich Publishers.

Kriesberg, L. 2005. Nature, Dynamics, and Phases of Intractability. In *Grasping the Nettle: Analyzing Cases of Intractable Conflict,* edited by C. A. Crocker and F. O. Hampson. Washington, DC: United States Institute of Peace.

Lewis, K. 2003. Measuring Transactive Memory Systems in the Field: Scale Development and Validation. *Journal of Applied Psychology* 88(4): 587-604.

Liebovitch, L., J. Fisher, H. Burgess, C. Cohen, T. Feroah, A. Fischer, O. Gal, A. Geller, M. Mohr, J. Roos and C. Straw. 2014. Complexity Mapping in Practice and Research: Methods, Trends, And Future Directions. *Paper Series, Dynamical Systems Innovation Lab 2014.* Retrieved from https://conflictinnovationlab.files.wordpress.com/2014/06/dst_visualization_23june2014.pdf.

Lovkvist, M. 2013. *Somatic Empathic Resonance: Subjective and Intersubjective Experiences of the Psychotherapeutic Dyad* (Doctoral dissertation). Available at ProQuest Dissertations and Theses Database. (UMI No. 3590023)

Maruyama, M. 1963. The Second Cybernetics: Deviation-Amplifying Mutual Causal Processes. *American Scientist* 51: 164-179.

Maruyama, M. 1982. Four Different Causal Metatypes in Biological and Social Sciences. In *Self Organization and Dissipative Structures: Applications in the physical and social sciences,* edited by W. C. Schieve and P. M. Allen. Austin, TX: University of Texas Press.

Nicotera, A. M., M. Smilowitz and J. C. Pearson. 1990. Ambiguity, Tolerance, Conflict, Management Style, and Argumentativeness as Predictors of Innovativeness. *Communication Research Reports* 7(2): 125-131.

Nowak, A., L. Bui-Wrzosinska, P. T. Coleman, R. Vallacher, L. Jochemczyk and W. Bartkowski. 2010. Seeking Sustainable Solutions: Using an Attractor Simulation Platform for Teaching Multi-Stakeholder Negotiation. *Negotiation Journal* 26(1): 49-68.

Picard, C. A. 2004. Exploring an Integrative Framework for Understanding Mediation. *Conflict Resolution Quarterly* 21(3): 295-311.

Pruitt, D. G. and S. A. Lewis. 1975. Development of Integrative Solutions in Bilateral Negotiation. *Journal of Personality and Social Psychology* 31(4): 621-633.

Redding, N. and P. T. Coleman. Assessing Leadership Competencies for Navigating Complex Systems: An Empirical Study. MD-ICCCR Working Paper.

Redding, N. and P. T. Coleman. Coaching to the Complexity of Conflict: Supporting Leaders Navigating Complex Conflict Dynamics in Organizations. MD-ICCCR Working Paper.

Ricigliano, R. 2012. *Making Peace Last*. Boulder, CO: Paradigm Press.

Riskin, L. L. 1997. Understanding Mediators' Orientations, Strategies, and Techniques: A Grid for the *Perplexed*. *Harvard Negotiation Law Review* 1(7): 7-51.

Schneider, A. K. 2012. Teaching a New Negotiation Skills Paradigm. *Washington University Journal of Law and Policy* 39: 13-38.

Stinson, J. E. and E. T. Hellebrandt. 1972. Group Cohesiveness, Productivity, and Strength of Formal *Leadership. The Journal of Social Psychology* 87(1): 99-105.

Suedfeld, P. and A. D. Rank. 1976. Revolutionary Leaders: Long-Term Success as a Function of Changes in Conceptual Complexity. *Journal of Personality and Social Psychology* 34(2): 169-178.

Suedfeld, P., P. E. Tetlock and C. Ramirez. 1977. War, Peace, and Integrative Complexity UN Speeches on the Middle East Problem, 1947-1976. *Journal of Conflict Resolution* 21(3): 427-442.

Teger, A. I. 1970. The Effect of Early Cooperation on the Escalation of Conflict. *Journal of Experimental Social Psychology* 6: 187-204.

Vallacher, R. R., P. T. Coleman, A. Nowak, L. Bui-Wrzosinska, L. Liebovitch, K. Kugler and A. Bartoli. 2013. *Attracted to Conflict: Dynamic Foundations of Destructive Social Relations*. Berlin, Germany: Springer Berlin Heidelberg.

Vallacher, R. R., P. T. Coleman, A. Nowak and L. Bui-Wrzosinska. 2010. Rethinking Intractable Conflict: The Perspective of Dynamical Systems. *American Psychologist* 65(4): 262-278.

Van De Vliert, E., M. C. Euwema and S. E. Huismans. 1995. Managing Conflict with a Subordinate or a Superior: Effectiveness of Conglomerated Behavior. *Journal of Applied Psychology* 80(2): 271-281.

Van Lange, P. A. M., A. Klapwijk and L. M. Van Munster. 2011. How the Shadow of the Future Might Promote Cooperation. *Group Processes & Intergroup Relations* 14(6): 857-870.

Vandenbroeck, P., J. Goossens and M. Clemens. 2007. Foresight, Tackling Obesities: Future Choices-Building the Obesity System Map. London, UK: Government Office for Science.

Williams, R. F. 1993. Claus von Bulow Case: Chutzpah and State Constitutional Law. *Connecticut Law Review* 26: 711-719.

Williams, R. J., R. A. Bush and D. Reilly. 1983. Objectives Perceived by Administrators within the 'Decision to Divert Network': Conflict and Resolution. *Drug and Alcohol Dependence* 12(4): 339-348.

Wolf, S. T., T. R. Cohen, J. L. Kirchner, A. Rea, R. M. Montoya and C. A. Insko. 2009. Reducing Intergroup Conflict through the Consideration of Future Consequences. *European Journal of Social Psychology* 39: 831-841.

Zaccaro, S. J. 2001. *The Nature of Executive Leadership: A Conceptual and Empirical Analysis of Success*. Washington, DC: American Psychological Association.

Zartman, I. W. and J. Z. Rubin (eds). 2002. *Power and Negotiation*. Ann Arbor, MI: University of Michigan Press.

ᘏ 85 ᘌ

Influencing Intractable Conflicts

Peter T. Coleman, Nicholas Redding & Joshua Fisher

Editors' Note: The final chapter of our complex-case trilogy describes techniques developed in recent years which promise greater effectiveness in the admittedly frustrating process of actually tackling an intractable conflict. It should be read not only in conjunction with Understanding Intractable Conflicts by the same authors and Getting in Sync by Coleman and Ricigliano, but also in conjunction with McDonald on Kashmir, in which a retired U.S. Ambassador describes what he actually did when drawn into working on the long-standing Kashmir problem.

In the previous chapter, we introduced dynamical systems theory (DST) as a paradigm for understanding intractable conflicts, and proposed a DST theory of practice for working with these conflicts constructively. We then described competencies and skills that allow one to prepare for engaging with these types of conflicts, before outlining approaches for

Peter T. Coleman is Professor of Psychology and Education at Columbia University, where he holds a joint appointment at Teachers College and The Earth Institute. Dr. Coleman directs the Morton Deutsch International Center for Cooperation and Conflict Resolution (MD-ICCCR) and the Institute on Psychological Science and Practice (IPSP) at Teachers College, and is Executive Director of Columbia University's Advanced Consortium on Cooperation, Conflict, and Complexity (AC4). He currently conducts research on optimality, adaptivity, and complexity dynamics in conflict contexts.

Nicholas Redding is a research psychologist with the Ulupono Initiative of The Omidyar Group, a social impact investment firm focused on encouraging sustainable energy, food and waste practices in Hawai'i. Prior to joining Ulupono, he was a research program coordinator with the Advanced Consortium on Cooperation, Conflict, and Complexity (AC4) at the Earth Institute, Columbia University. He holds a Ph.D. in Social-Organizational Psychology from Columbia University.

Josh Fisher is the Director of the AC4 consortium at Columbia University. He is also an Adjunct Faculty member in the School of Professional Studies, and an Associate Research Scientist at the Earth Institute, studying conflict management, natural resources, and extractive industry. His current work focuses on natural resource management as a tool for conflict prevention. He works with government, civil society, international organizations, and nonprofit partners to design strategies to constructively manage environmental conflicts. Dr. Fisher received his PhD in Conflict Analysis and Resolution from George Mason University.

comprehending systemic conflict dynamics. For the current chapter, we will continue our guideline series from Part One (see Figure 1), starting with approaches for engaging with intractable conflict systems. Systemic *engagement* is one of the least predictable and thus most challenging phases of nonlinear change processes. However, the study of complex systems of all types has provided important insights into this phase. The guidelines outlined in this stage focus on effectively *entering the system, engaging levers for change,* and *conducting proximal change experiments.*

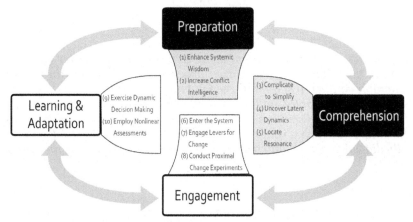

Figure 1: A Dynamical Systems Theory of Practice

Guideline #6: Entering Systems Mindfully

Begin Mindful of Initial Conditions

Research from three different conflict labs in the U.S. has come to the same conclusion: what happens at the onset of a conflict is critical. Studies conducted in Marcel Losada's Capture Lab, which studied conflict in executive work teams, John Gottman's Love Lab, which studies marital conflict and divorce, and Coleman and Kugler's Moral Conflict Lab, which studies difficult moral disputes, have shown that *what goes on in the first few minutes of a conflictual encounter has the most impact on everything that follows.*

This is consistent with other research on nonlinear systems, which consistently shows that they tend to be particularly sensitive to the initial conditions of the system. Computer simulations of conflict dynamics suggest that even very slight differences in initial conditions can eventually, after a delay, make a big difference in the experiences of the parties (Liebovitch et al. 2008). The effects of these small differences may not be visible at first, but they can trigger other changes that trigger still others, cascading over time to culminate in major changes in the structure and dynamics of the system. For example, at the onset of a negotiation, slight differences in the moods of participants or in the framing of the process by facilitators may be almost imperceptible at first, but can lead to qualitative shifts in the dynamics as the negotiation progresses. These initial differences can be the result of various factors: the attitudes or personalities of the people coming in; their openness to dialogue, or the level of complexity of their thinking; how the conversations are set up and facilitated; how the room and participants are arranged spatially; or history of the disputants' interactions together. But what is clear is that the initial encounters tend to matter more than what follows.

This has several implications for initiating change as a negotiator or mediator. First, setting a strong, professional tone at the outset of a session by getting consensus on clear ground-rules and establishing your credibility as a professional can build a strong base for respectful discourse. If you get a sense that the disputants are incensed and are likely to come out of the gate kicking and screaming, then it may be best to caucus right away to see if it's possible to de-escalate hostilities and start the joint discussion later on from a more reasonable place. In addition, the earlier you intervene into a potentially destructive, escalating conflict, the better. It is much harder to reverse a process of destructive conflict when the session has gone sour then it is to mitigate one before it goes bad.

Finally, when determining how to introduce alternative dispute resolution (ADR) initiatives into new settings (schools, human resource departments, labor-management grievance procedures, etc.) it is best to seek to integrate them into the initial designs of the undertaking or existing internal procedures, and not attempt to add them on later. Starting early and being cognizant of existing, and potentially latent, dynamics helps to shape the emerging culture of the initiative in a way that is conducive to constructive conflict. (See Honeyman et al. 2007; also NDR: McDonald, *Peer Mediation* and NDR: Groton et al., *Thinking Ahead*.) Bringing these procedures in later on will typically elicit much greater resistance.

Begin with What is Working

Peace and conflict resolution practitioners tend to focus on identifying and solving problems. While important, this approach tends to obstruct our view of what is already working in a conflict system, and of existing opportunities for solutions. Virtually every conflict system contains people and groups who are willing to reach out across the divide and work to foster dialogue and peace. These are what Laura Chasin calls *networks of effective action* (Pearce and Littlejohn 1997), and Gabriella Blum (2007) labels *islands of agreement*. For example, Blum has found that during many protracted conflicts, the disputing parties often maintain areas in their relationship where they continue to communicate and cooperate, despite the severity of the conflict. In international affairs this can occur with some forms of trade, civilian exchanges or medical care. In communities and organizations these islands may emerge around personal or professional crises (e.g. a sick child), outside interests (e.g. mutual work on common causes), or by way of chains of communications through trusted third parties. Recognizing and bolstering such networks or islands is job one.

For example, during the civil war in Mozambique, a critical actor in catalyzing the peace process was Catholic Archbishop Jamie Pedro Gonçalves who, being one of the first native and black bishops in the region, was respected by both major parties in the dispute and was tied to a broad network of contacts within the communities (Bartoli, Bui-Wrzosinska and Nowak 2010). Because he was perceived as neutral among the parties in the dispute, and was communicating directly with a diverse range of stakeholders, he was well-placed to influence the system toward positive change. Thus, initial systemic engagement should begin by identifying and engaging with these networks, carefully, and working with them to help alleviate the constraints on their activities in a safe and feasible manner. Ideally, a systemically competent practitioner will have processes in place through systemic *comprehension* (see Part One) to assist them in visualizing these networks and leveraging critical information to constructively engage them.

A more thorough scan of the system can help to locate its more functional components. These may include local norms and practices that prohibit aggression and violence beyond certain levels, indigenous grievance systems or other regulatory mechanisms considered impartial and fair, or widely respected members of families or communities that might be able to play a more actively constructive role in addressing disputes. Feedback-loop mapping can be particularly useful for identifying and understanding the more constructive aspects of social systems. Merely asking stakeholders, "Why doesn't the conflict get worse?" "Why did disputants settle in the past?" or "What provides a sense of hope today?" can orient the analysis towards the more constructive components or dynamics of the system. Or asking, "Where are the islands of agreement or the networks of effective action today?" Or "What types of taboos exist for destruction and violence here (places of worship, children, hospitals)?" This information—which is typically ignored in traditional conflict analysis—can help reveal the existing feedback processes in the system that inhibit destructive conflict engagement.

Leverage Instability

Intractable conflicts tend to be ultra-coherent, closed systems that steadfastly resist many good faith attempts at change. When absolute certainty about "us versus them" takes over in such systems and provides *the* foundation for understanding, then it's likely time to *seek instability*.

This entails either capitalizing on recent disruptive conditions or creating new conditions that in fact *destabilize* the system. (Note that our use of "destabilize" is a rigorous one, not the casual usage that implies that stability is always good.)

For instance, in research on the approximately 850 enduring international conflicts that occurred throughout the world between 1816 and 1992, over three-quarters of them were found to have ended within ten years of a major political shock (i.e. world wars, civil wars, significant changes in territory and power relations, regime change, independence movements, or transitions to democracy; Diehl and Goertz 2001; Klein, Goertz and Diehl 2006). From the perspective of DST, these shocks created fissures in the stability of the previous attractors, eventually leading to the establishment of the necessary conditions for the major restructuring and realignment of conflict landscapes (i.e. in the vernacular, for peace to break out.) This suggests that events such as those erupting in the Middle East today (e.g. the ISIL threat, instability in Iraq and Syria) may actually promote optimal conditions for dramatic realignment of socio-political systems—such as in Israel-Palestine—contrary to common assumptions. Similarly, a family system plunged into crisis by divorcing parents, a child's diagnosis of a terminal illness, a criminal conviction of a family member, or the need to quickly uproot and move out of state for work could all place a family system into a tenuous, high-anxiety state.

However political shocks can go either way—encouraging radical change or further intransigence. For example, precisely ten years after 9/11 and the American incursions into Afghanistan and Iraq (major political shocks), Tunisia and others states in the MENA region erupted into revolutions which, in the case of Tunisia, today offer the potential of a stable shift from an authoritarian regime to more pluralist democratic rule. However other states, such as Egypt, despite the temporary shift in political dynamics, seemed to return to the previous pattern of hardline military rule after one year. Thus, the results of destabilization can take months or years to become evident, as the initial shock most likely affects factors that affect other factors and so on until overt changes occur. It is also important to note that such ruptures to the coherence and stability of sociopolitical systems do not *ensure* radical or constructive change, or peace. They must therefore be considered a necessary, but insufficient, condition when working with intractability.

Guideline #7: Engage Levers for Change

Donella Meadows (2008) outlined a set of low to high impact levers for navigating change in complex systems. Below are five derived from DST.

Open up the System

Research shows that relatively high levels of emotional, cognitive, behavioral, and structural complexity characterize more constructive conflict relations. Thus, communities that maintain more complex crosscutting structures and social networks have been found to be more tolerant, less destructive, and less violent when conflicts do spark (Varshney 2003). Research also supports the idea that more constructive relations are often associated with an increased capacity for physical or psychological *movement* (Bartoli, Bui-Wrzosinska and Nowak 2010). From this perspective, sustainable solutions to difficult, long-term conflicts require establishing conditions that induce and allow for sufficient openness: complexity, movement, and adaptation.

Michelle LeBaron, Carrie McLeod, and Andrew Floyer Acland (2013) tell a story of how in 1993 a group of international diplomats gathered near Dublin to attempt to generate new ideas for addressing the Israel-Palestine conflict. A primary challenge for the facilitators was to figure out how to move this group out of well-worn ruts when speaking about the conflict: positional statements, repetitive framings, and limiting assumptions that tended to dictate how they defined and responded to the conflict in the Middle East. For the first two days, the process followed a standard problem-solving format, and little of value transpired.

On the third day, the diplomats took a bus trip to Belfast. Jostled in the old school bus used for transport, the previously restrained participants began to experience each other differently. As they uncovered commonalities and shared passions, they began to relate more playfully. Several discussions with Northern Irish peacemakers and visits to bi-communal projects deepened the camaraderie within the group. As the bus headed back to Dublin following a group meal, participants sang together in the darkness. One of the facilitators later wrote, "Only after this excursion did conversations enliven, originality emerge, and imaginative possibilities for shifting intractable conflict in Israel-Palestine begin to reveal themselves" (LeBaron 2014: 594).

The facilitators of the meeting were thrilled by the change in dynamics among the participants but struggled to understand what had happened. Then something stuck them. Human beings are physical entities, so ignoring or denying this when we try to talk things out and negotiate is a mistake. Physical changes—movement, jostling, speaking with outsiders, traveling to new places—is one way to shake up and perhaps alter our programmed chronic responses to conflicts and thus allow and encourage us to see, think, feel, and respond differently. (See also Honeyman and Parish 2013, suggesting that what may work best is to arrange for a change in the participants' *social context*—in other words, whom they are engaging with and about what—at the same time as the spatial movement.)

Work Upstream, Away from the Conflict

Recognizing that stakeholders in protracted conflicts often view peace-makers as also being players in the theater of conflict, some interveners attempt to work constructively upstream in these settings—away from the conflict—by circumventing the conflict.

The idea here is that attempts to address these conflicts directly, in the context of a peace process, typically elicit resistance, as they are seen as affecting the balance of power in the conflict (usually by supporting lower-power groups most adversely affected by the conditions). Interveners recognizing this will work to address conditions of hardship without making any connection whatsoever to the conflict or peace processes. Retired US Ambassador John McDonald's private effort in establishing a bus line across the Kashmir border is an example. [NDR: McDonald & McDonald, *Kashmir*]. To some degree, this is what many community and international development projects try to achieve. The difference is that this tactic targets the conditions seen as most directly feeding the conflict, and requires that every attempt be made to *divorce* these initiatives from being associated with any peace process (Praszkier, Nowak and Coleman 2010). This un-conflict resolution strategy can help address some of the negativity and misery associated with conflicts, without becoming incorporated (attracted) into the polarized "good versus evil" dynamics of the conflict.

For example, several years back a conflict-resolution and peace-building group arrived at a Palestinian school in Israel to work to promote peaceful coexistence among Muslims, Christians, and Jews in Israel-Palestine through an intensive educational program in peace and conflict resolution. It soon became clear that this intervention evoked negative feelings and attitudes among the local Palestinians. Some complained that the interveners simply did not have sufficient understanding of their circumstances; others expressed the opinion that by making the Palestinians the focus of the program, the interveners were implying that they, the Palestinians, were the source of the problem. Resentments built, and the result was that the school authorities were forced to terminate the program.

Later, an alternative group of activists, who worked closely with local residents and were familiar with the specific needs of the community, decided to focus their work on an area that crossed cultural lines and was a shared interest of both groups: information technology (IT). The group proceeded to establish an IT school for Arab and Jewish students. As they had surmised, the study of computer science proved to be a "bonding agent" among the students, without regard to religious and ethnic differences.

Seek Soft Power

Sometimes, however, more direct intervention into a conflict is necessary. Soft-power third parties are at times able to weaken resistance to change by carefully introducing a sense of alternative courses-of-action, hope for change, or even a sense of doubt in the ultra-certain status quo of "us versus them" conflicts. Through the unique influence of people and groups with little formal or "hard" power (military might, economic incentives, legal or human rights justifications, and so on) but with relevant "soft" power (trustworthiness, moral authority, wisdom, kindness, etc.), change does occur. Soft-power parties can also model and encourage other more constructive means of conflict engagement, such as shuttle diplomacy and indirect communication through negotiation chains.

This is the extraordinary role that the Women's International Peace Network (WIPN) played in the early 2000s, when they helped end Liberia's decades-long civil wars (Disney and Gbowee 2012). This ordinary group of women—mothers, aunts and grandmothers—organized amid the grueling armed conflict in Liberia, with no formal authority and few "hard" resources—helped to mobilize and shepherd the peace process between the government of strongman Charles Taylor and the rebels. For example, at one point in the war, UN peacekeepers were stuck in a protracted gun battle with rebel forces in the jungle, and could see no way out. They contacted the WIPN, who arrived at the scene in their white T-shirts and headdresses. The women then entered the jungle with hands raised, dancing and singing. After spending two days there, feeding and speaking with the rebels, the women brought the rebels out of the jungle, ending the stalemate.

Enhance Positive Latent Attractors for the Future

Seen from the perspective of attractor landscapes, finding common ground between parties, emphasizing shared goals and concerns, facilitating trust-building activities, and incentivizing cooperative trade initiatives—although they may appear to be largely ineffective in situations locked in an ongoing protracted struggle—may in fact be acting slowly and indirectly to establish a sufficiently wide and deep attractor basin for moral, humane forms of intergroup relations. One day, these initiatives may provide the foundation for a stable, peaceful future. The key is to work both to enhance factors that increase the likelihood of a shift to peace in the system, while simultaneously working to minimize the factors that perpetuate destructive conflicts. It is not possible to eliminate all factors that contribute to destructive conflict, but it may be possible to elevate just enough positive components so as to shift the ratio to favor factors promoting peace relative to those perpetuating more destructive dynamics.

In *Psychological Components of Sustainable Peace* (Coleman and Deutsch 2012), a group of distinguished scholar-practitioners of peace and conflict offered a review of empirical research on factors associated with peaceful individuals, groups, and societies. These factors can be viewed as components of a multilevel system of peace, and so used as a checklist of factors associated with increasing probabilities for lasting peace:

Individual Level
■ Recognition of the interdependence of all people, similar and different, local and global. ■ A strong self-transcendent value orientation committed to the welfare of others and society. ■ An optimal balance of openness to change and conservatism, responsive to changing times and circumstances. ■ Skills and behaviors promoting cooperation and trust. ■ nowledge, attitudes, and skills for constructive conflict resolution. ■ Higher levels of cognitive, emotional, behavioral, and social identity complexity. ■ Capacities for tolerance and realistic empathy (understanding how a situation looks to someone else). ■ A strong sense of global identity, along with a concrete understanding of the steps that need to be taken locally to act as a global citizen.

Organizational Level
■ Structures of cooperative task, goal, and reward interdependence in schools, workplaces, and politics. ■ Gender parity with a proportional number of women in the highest positions of leadership in business, politics, and the military. ■ Political and business ethics that are in harmony with nature and environmental stewardship. ■ Institutions that reflect and uphold self-transcendent values. ■ Programs and workshops in constructive conflict resolution and creative problem solving for children, adults, parents, and leaders of schools, businesses, and politics.

Cultural Level
■ Language for peace: a large lexicon for all aspects of cooperative and peaceful relations, and sufficient use of such terms to foster automaticity. ■ An appreciation of environmental stewardship and equitable sharing of the earth's resources among its members and with all human beings. ■ Strong norms valuing and nurturing children. ■ Early socialization of children oriented toward mutual care and nurturance. ■ Cross-cutting structures fostering common interests, activities, and bonds across different ethnic and religious groups. ■ Shared, accurate, and transparent collective memories of past events, conflicts and relationships between groups.

Societal Level
■ A societal idea of peace. ■ Societies that define themselves as internally and externally peaceful. ■ A transcultural elite with shared norms of tolerance, cooperation, and creative problem solving, who model for all the efficacy and value of constructive, non-violent action. ■ National governance structures tending towards egalitarianism and democracy. ■ Use of the Internet and other social technologies to mobilize broad social movements for humanitarian works and global peace. ■ Strong initiatives for communications, trade, and cultural and civilian exchanges between nations.

Table 1: Checklist of factors associated with increasing probabilities for lasting peace.

Together, these factors can operate in concert to constitute a *system of sustainable peace*—in other words, societal attractors for peaceful relations—distinguishing such societies from those locked in systems of destructive conflict. As mentioned above, other dynamical research has shown (see Gottman et al. 2002; Kugler, Coleman and Fuchs 2011; Losada 1999) that when the ratio of positive dynamics to negative dynamics in social systems is high (somewhere between 3:1 and 5:1), the odds of healthier, thriving relations and societies tend to increase markedly. When the positivity/negativity ratio is closer to 1:1 or lower, the relatively stronger effects of negativity will drive the system into either a sustained state of hostilities or lead to its disintegration. In other words, focusing resolution efforts on activities that do not directly confront the factors contributing to the conflict, but instead work to build or strengthen existing elements in the system that serve to strengthen the probabilities of sustainable peace, can be an effective strategy. What is critical is to work with these positive elements in the system in ways that stimulate movement toward a new attractor for sustainable peace.

Reverse Engineer Negative, Destructive Attractors

Even when systems de-escalate and appear to move into a state of peace, it is critical to recognize that the potential for destructive interactions (destructive attractors) is still functioning in a latent manner. Now, it is important to begin to deconstruct and dismantle the negative attractors. This entails decoupling some of the reinforcing feedback loops that perpetuate the conflict, or adding inhibiting feedback to lower the level of super-coherence in the system. We call this reverse engineering.

The following components for preventing and mitigating destructive conflict (Coleman 2012) can be used by communities as a checklist of aspects to address or enhance for decreasing probabilities for destructive conflict:

Individual Level

- Awareness of the causes, consequences, and escalatory tendencies of destructive conflict and violence.
- High levels of tolerance for, and openness to difference.
- Moderate levels of tolerance for uncertainty.
- Moderately high levels of self-monitoring, restraint, and regulation of internal impulses for destructive or violent acts.
- A capacity for forgiveness.

Organizational Level

- Early access to peace education and multicultural tolerance programs in preschool, elementary, and middle school.
- Establishing national political and social institutions that ensure the implementation and follow-through of negotiated settlements.
- Functional and accessible venues for constructive, non-violent action to seek recourse and address perceived injustices and other harms.

Cultural Level

- Satisfaction of basic human needs including physiological needs, safety, and dignity.
- Norms of gender equity and equality in the home, schools, and the workplace.
- Values, attitudes, and skills supporting non-violence.
- Opportunities for peaceful sublimation of aggression through competitive sports, occupations, creative arts, etc.
- Strong norms for procedural and distributive justice in schools, workplaces, marketplaces, and elsewhere in the community.
- Social taboos against corporal punishment and other forms of violence in the home, schools, workplaces, and public spaces.

Societal Level
<ul><li>Well-coordinated early warning systems operating through local governments and NGOs networked locally, regionally, and globally for efficient communication.</li><li>Use of crisis-mapping: an open-source platform for collecting and plotting local cell-phone accounts of the commission of violent atrocities, to inform the international community of emerging crises in a timely manner.</li><li>Use of the Internet and other social technologies to mobilize broad non-violent movements for social justice and corporate responsibility.</li><li>Coordination between local governments, civil society, and international organizations to prevent violent conflict.</li><li>Well-functioning global organizations and institutions such as the United Nations, the International Criminal Courts, Interpol, and the Universal Declaration of Human Rights.</li></ul>

Table 2: Checklist of factors for decreasing probabilities for destructive conflict.

Once the reinforcing feedback system of conflict escalation/stalemate is mapped, it can help to target specific links for the introduction of inhibiting feedback mechanisms.

Tables 1 and 2 are provided, not as exhaustive lists of peaceful and destructive systemic factors, but instead as a means for negotiators, and others working to influence positive change, to begin to explore the system from this perspective and start to identify and map existing processes that can be strengthened, to increase the probabilities for sustainable peace while simultaneously minimizing the impact of the more destructive elements. As described in the previous chapter, those working in the system can engage stakeholders in mapping activities and other methods of inquiry to begin to flesh out the factors and feedback loops perpetuating the conflict. These checklists can be used to complement that process by looking specifically for levers to shift the constructive and destructive drivers in the system.

Guideline #8: Conduct Prototype and Proximal Change Experiments

One strategy for cultivating and sustaining positive systemic change is through the identification or establishment of strong but isolated prototypes of the desired change—prototypes that can survive long enough to test and then facilitate the transfer of changes throughout the broader system (Morgan 1997). These experiments can be used as systemic probes to explore and learn about a system's reactions to the proposed change.

This is essentially what Laura Chasin and her organization, the Public Conversations Project (PCP), were able to do with the pro-life and pro-choice dialogue group in Boston. The initiative was launched in secret, and PCP was able to protect the anonymity of the group for several years, until the members themselves felt confident enough about their process and outcomes to go public. What was critical here was the facilitator's capacity to *protect the boundaries of the experiment* (and in this case the lives and livelihoods of the participants) as long as was necessary.

Alternatively, John Gottman (2014) describes the use *of proximal change experiments* with married couples. In these studies, the goals are much smaller than that of couples therapy. The proximal goals are to change specific aspects of a couple's relationship, such as how they enter or begin a conflict discussion or how they respond to their spouses' initial attempts at communication. The researchers then examine the effects of such adjustments on subsequent discussions between the couple, and may use these data to reinforce the value of the change. The idea is that by changing one smaller component of the system, observers and parties involved can experiment with potential levers for improving the system, learning more about how the system behaves over time. For a couple in distress, Gottman's group found that a brief intervention focusing just on improving friendship initially significantly reduced negativity in the future. Rather than committing to a lengthy and involved series of therapy sessions with an indeterminate outcome, couples were able to see small positive changes after one session (Gottman 2014). Although the goals of such interventions are smaller, they are informed by knowledge of complex systems (such as the power of initial conditions), and so target potentially significant "small" adjustments.

Summarizing the above, the following questions can be used to guide the systemic engagement approach:

- Are the initial conditions conducive to constructive change? Has a sufficient degree of professionalism and respect been established in the process? Should caucusing, shuttle diplomacy or other forms of one-on-one engagement be the next step?
- Where are the islands of agreement or the networks of effective action functioning in the system today? How might you support or bolster the work of these networks? What are some possible unintended consequences of engaging with these networks?
- Why doesn't the conflict get worse? What provides a sense of hope today?
- Are there local taboos against destructive action and violence (places of worship, children, hospitals) that might be leveraged?
- Where are the opportunities for "opening the door to instability?" (Either capitalizing on recent disruptive conditions or creating new conditions that *destabilize* the system)?
- Are there opportunities for physical changes—movement, jostling, speaking with outsiders, traveling to new places—to

shake up chronic responses to conflicts and allow participants to see, think, feel, and respond differently?
- Are there opportunities for working upstream—initiating *an un-conflict resolution strategy*—to help address some of the negativity and misery without becoming pulled into the polarized "good versus evil" dynamics of the conflict?
- Where are the soft-power third parties working? Will they benefit from your support?
- What are the venues and opportunities for reinforcing a system of sustainable peace?
- Where are the levers for inhibiting or reverse engineering a system of destructive conflict?
- When and where should the change experiments begin?

Finally, in order to leverage the power of proximal change experiments (described above), a system needs to be in place to learn from those experiments in order to assess:
- What changed in the system and in what direction.
- Which changes were expected, and what (if any) unanticipated factors or dynamics emerged as a result of the experiment.
- When things moved in unanticipated or undesired ways, what went wrong as a result of assumptions about the system, an inadequate understanding of the system, or new emergent properties of the system.

In order to learn about the system in this way, the last lap is systemic learning and adaptation through dynamic decision-making and assessment of nonlinear impact.

Guideline #9: Exercise Dynamic Decision Making and Action

In his influential book *The Logic of Failure: Why Things Go Wrong and What We Can Do to Make Them Right*, Dietrich Dörner (1996) presents his research on decision making and initiating change in complex environments involving "simulated communities." Dörner's research tells us a lot about decision-making, change, and leadership in complex systems and raises important considerations for fostering *sustainable* solutions. His findings suggest that well-intentioned decision makers working in complex systems typically commit a standard set of errors:
- They act without prior analysis of the situation, or clarification and prioritization of goals.
- They fail to anticipate the side effects or long-term repercussions of their actions.
- They assume that the absence of immediately obvious negative effects means their measures have worked correctly.
- They let over-involvement in subprojects blind them to emerging needs and changes on the ground.

Why? Because this way of thinking and acting is usually more efficient and less cognitively demanding in the short term, and it helps to bolster one's self-esteem by maintaining a feeling of control. Importantly, this happens across stakeholders and levels of power.

The good news is that Dörner's research also sheds light on more effective methods of decision-making and problem solving within complex systems. The research participants able to improve the well-being of the simulated communities did the following:

- **Made more decisions:** They assessed a situation and set a course, but then continually *adapted*, staying open to feedback to reconsider their decisions and alter their course as needed. They were found to make more, not fewer, decisions as their plans unfolded. They found more possibilities for enhancing the system's well-being as the situation evolved.

- **Demonstrated complexity of action:** They seemed to understand that the problems they were addressing were closely linked with other problems, so their actions would have multiple effects. Therefore, they made many more decisions and took a wider variety of actions while attempting to achieve one goal (e.g. "I'll increase revenues in Greenvale by creating new jobs, investing in product development, and advertising"). This was in contrast to those who failed, who would typically make one decision per goal (e.g. "I'll raise taxes in Greenvale to raise revenues").

- **Focused on the real problems first:** They took the time to gather enough information to determine the central problems to address, and did not jump into action prematurely or simply focus on the problems they *could* solve because that felt good.

- **Tested hypotheses more:** They tested their solutions in pilot projects, and assessed the effects before committing to them.

- **Asked *why* more:** They actively investigated the *why* behind events: the causal links that made up the *networks of causation* in their community.

- **Stayed focused on the prize...:** Effective decision makers identified the central issues early on and stayed focused on addressing them. Ineffective decision makers got easily distracted and diverted; they shifted from problem to problem as each arose.

- **...But not on one solution:** However, effective decision makers did not develop a single-minded preoccupation with one solution. If the feedback data informed them that a solution was too costly or ineffective, they altered their approach.

In other words, the best results, or the results that lead to more constructive engagement and more sustainable solutions over time, are those that result from a process of adaptation to changes in the system. This requires that stakeholders build structures and processes for decision-making that are both analytical and deliberative (National Research Council 1996; Balint et al. 2011). Under this approach, the *analytical* component enables stakeholders to collect information on systemic responses to action and decisions, in order to assess what is changing in the system and how. This requires collaboratively structuring means of monitoring the proximal change experiments as they are implemented, and cycling that information back to the stakeholders and decision makers. The deliberative component then provides a forum for stakeholders to engage each other constructively in order to understand how each party perceives and is affected by those changes, in order to design new proximal change experiments to adapt to the new system dynamics. Again, this deliberative process will likely be rife with the same conditions described in the preceding section on Systemic Engagement (i.e. high levels of complexity, uncertainty, and disparity in types of power or degree of impact from systemic changes). Thus increasing Systemic Preparation and Systemic Comprehension are required to enable stakeholders to engage in this process of engagement and learning, in order to adapt to new dynamics and maintain a new level of constructive dialogue and collaboration.

Guideline #10: Employ Nonlinear Assessments

The concepts of *cause* and *effect* are overly simplistic in complex systems and protracted conflict. While an action may have a direct (i.e. linear change) impact on certain associated factors, it will also have dispersed or indirect impacts on more distant factors and dynamics across the system. Further, the energy from those impacts can accumulate in the system and contribute to additional changes across time (i.e. non-linear change). In assessing change in a system, it is therefore more fruitful to operate in terms of *impetus, influence*, and *impact*.

Creating the adaptive and deliberative structures described above can enable assessment of linear change in a system, and result in enhanced adaptation in systemic *engagement*. However, nonlinear changes in systems typically belie assessment and outcome evaluation. Because they are inherently unpredictable, it is nearly impossible to anticipate specific outcomes—to plan for and then to monitor predicted outcomes of interventions. What is needed then are methods to augment linear change assessment in systems, in order to provide the full range of information back to stakeholders to continue refining their systemic comprehension and thus informing new approaches to systemic engagement, and to learning and adaptation.

Fortunately, an ever-expanding suite of tools is being developed to complement traditional approaches to monitoring and evaluation. These new approaches range from community-based monitoring to retrospective and forensic analytical techniques, and others that leverage the power of the data revolution and social media to gather real-time data. In this quickly evolving landscape, new analytical communities are forming to respond to the need for research and development in this area. An example of this is the Learning Lab at USAID (http://usaidlearninglab. org/) which develops, tests, and hosts a community around alternative methods for program planning and learning. Several of the approaches they employ, like the family of methods known as Outcome Mapping, suggest that what can be anticipated in nonlinear systems are eventual (high-level) qualitative changes in the patterns that are of interest in the given situation; in, for example, patterns of conflict or peace, negativity or positivity, destructiveness or constructiveness. Thus, these approaches recommend identifying the patterns of interest, and then selecting outcomes for measurement *en passant*, as the effects of the intervention unfold in the system, and only then identifying variables and dynamics that might inform the state of the changing nature of the pattern of interest. Further, several of these approaches recognize that change in a system is simultaneously produced by endogenous impetus (an impetus initiated by action inside the system and stakeholders), as well as by exogenous shocks (external forces that influence the factors or dynamics inside the system). In order to assess how change occurs in the system, it is thus important to account for influence and impact of both endogenous and exogenous stimuli.

As with all approaches to conflict management, identifying the correct suite of tools with which to collect information on changes in the system will ultimately depend on the specific context, the needs and capacities among decision makers, the resources available, and buy-in from the stakeholders. However, the DST approach relies on anticipating information needs to enable enhanced systemic preparation, improved systemic comprehension, and adaptive systemic engagement. It then relies on building structures and processes that are both analytical and deliberative, as well as able to assess the linear and non-linear changes that occur across the system.

The following set of questions is provided to guide this process of ongoing systemic learning and adaptation:

- What are the most general objectives of this initiative? Increase well-being? Reduce a sense of injustice-without-recourse? What qualitative changes would you hope to see in the system if the intervention were successful?
- What are the (possibly many) feasible actions a decision-maker could initiate that might have a positive impact on these objectives? What might be the unintended consequences of these actions?
- What has changed or is changing in the system as a result of previous change experiments and/or external events? Based on those changes, is your current comprehension of the system still accurate? Is your current strategy for engaging the system still appropriate and relevant? Do you need new indicators and strat-

egies for monitoring progress and learning about change in the system?

- What further proximal experiments, prototypes or pilot projects might be useful in testing the system?
- Do the funders understand the need for setting high-level objectives and conducting post-hoc evaluations?
- What is a realistic timeline for seeing the nonlinear impacts of the initiative? Ten years? Twenty?
- What are the generalizable learnings you take from this experience that might inform future change initiatives?

Conclusion

The state of the practice of working effectively with protracted conflicts and associated problems in the context of complex, nonlinear systems is nascent at best. However, if we as a field wish to have a constructive impact somewhere between doing no harm and sustaining peace, then this must be our next horizon.

The theory of practice outlined in this chapter and the preceding one is a work in progress. It pulls together insights from research and practice on addressing conflicts and related challenges in complex systems, and provides a parsimonious heuristic for thinking about social change in these contexts. It synthesizes insights and findings from our own labs and practices, as well as from those of our colleagues working in this area. As such, it offers a platform for research and practice that is itself simple and complex, stable and dynamic, old and new, and constantly evolving.

Our main objective for sharing this theory of practice at this stage in its development is to challenge, stimulate, and invite readers with whom the approach resonates to engage with us.

References

Balint, P., R. Stewart, A. Desai and L. Walters. 2011. *Wicked Environmental Problems: Managing Uncertainty and Conflict*. Washington D.C.: Island Press.

Bartoli, A., L. Bui-Wrzosinska and A. Nowak. 2010. Peace is in Movement: A Dynamical Systems Perspective on the Emergence of Peace in Mozambique. *Peace and Conflict* 16(2): 211-230.

Blum, G. 2007. *Islands of Agreement: Managing Enduring Armed Rivalries*. Cambridge, MA: Harvard University Press.

Coleman, P. T. 2012. Constructive Conflict Resolution and Sustainable Peace. In *Psychological Components of Sustainable Peace*, edited by P. T. Coleman and M. Deutsch. New York, NY: Springer.

Coleman, P. T. and M. Deutsch. (eds). 2012. *Psychological Components of Sustainable Peace*. New York, NY: Springer.

Diehl, P.F. and G. Goertz. 2001. *War and Peace in International Rivalry*. 1st edn., Ann Arbor, MI: University of Michigan Press.

Disney, A. and D. Gbowee. 2012. Gender and Sustainable Peace. In *Psychological Components of Sustainable Peace*, edited by P. T. Coleman and M. Deutsch. New York, NY: Springer.

Dörner, D. 1996. *The Logic of Failure: Why Things Go Wrong and What We Can Do to Make Them Right*. Cambridge, MA: Perseus Press.

Gottman, J. M. 2014. *Principia Amoris: The New Science of Love*. New York: NY: Routledge.

Gottman, J. M., C. D. Murray, C. C. Swanson, R. Tyson and K. R. Swanson. 2002. *The Mathematics of Marriage*. Cambridge, MA: The MIT Press.

Honeyman, C., J. Macfarlane, B. Mayer, A. Schneider and J. Seul. 2007. The Next Frontier is Anticipation: Thinking Ahead about Conflict to Help Clients Find Constructive Ways to Engage Issues in Advance. *Alternatives to the High Cost of Litigation* 25(6): 99-103.

Honeyman, C. and R. Parish. 2013. Choreography of Negotiation: Movement in Three Acts. in *Choreography of Resolution: Conflict, Movement, and Neuroscience*, edited by M. LeBaron, C. MacLeod, and A. F. Acland. Chicago, IL: American Bar Association.

Klein, J. P., G. Goertz and P. F. Diehl. 2006. The New Rivalry Dataset: Procedures and Patterns. *Journal of Peace Research* 43(3): 331-348.

Kugler, K. G., P. T. Coleman and A. M. Fuchs. 2011. Moral Conflict and Complexity: The Dynamics of Constructive Versus Destructive Discussions Over Polarizing Issues. *IACM 24TH Annual Conference Paper*. Available at SSRN: http://ssrn.com/abstract=1872654.

LeBaron, M. 2014. The Alchemy of Change: Cultural Fluency in Conflict Resolution. In *The Handbook of Conflict Resolution: Theory and Practice*, 3rd Ed., edited by P. T. Coleman, M. Deutsch and E. Marcus. San Francisco, CA: Jossey-Bass.

LeBaron, M., C. MacLeod and A. F. Acland. (eds). 2013. *Choreography of Resolution: Conflict, Movement, and Neuroscience*. Chicago, IL: American Bar Association.

Liebovitch, L. S., V. Naudot, R. Vallacher, A. Nowak, L. Bui-Wrzosinska and P. T. Coleman. 2008. Dynamics of Two-Actor Cooperation-Competition Conflict Models. *Physica A: Statistical Mechanics and Its Applications* 387(25): 6360-6378.

Losada, M. 1999. The Complex Dynamics of High Performance Teams. *Mathematical and Computer Modeling* 30(9): 179-192.

Meadows, D. 2008. *Thinking in Systems: A Primer*, edited by Diana Wright. White River Junction, VT: Chelsea Green Publishing.

Morgan, G. 1997. *Images of Organization*. London, UK: Sage Publications.

National Research Council. 1996. *Understanding Risk: Informing Decisions in a Democratic Society*. Washington D.C.: National Academy Press.

Pearce, B. W. and S. W. Littlejohn. *1997. Moral Conflict: When Social Worlds Collide*. Thousand Oaks, CA: Sage Publications.

Praszkier, R., A. Nowak and P. T. Coleman. 2010. Social Entrepreneurs and Constructive Change: The Wisdom of Circumventing Conflict. *Peace and Conflict: The Journal of Peace Psychology* 16(2): 153-174.

Varshney, A. 2003. *Ethnic Conflict and Civic Life: Hindus and Muslims in India*. New Haven, CT: Yale University Press.

෬ 86 ෭

Training a Captive Audience

Stuart M. Kirschner & Jack J. Cambria

Editors' Note: Let's say you've finished this book and would like to use some of it. But what about your more hardheaded colleagues, team members or other audiences? Using their experience in training the highly skeptical police officers of the New York City Police Department, psychologist Stuart Kirschner and longtime (2001-2015) NYPD Hostage Negotiation Team commander Jack Cambria discuss the design of training for a potentially resistant audience.

The practice of negotiation embeds a great deal of "teaching" activity. In any but the simplest of transactions or disputes, it becomes necessary to inform your counterpart, and your own team (if you work as part of a team), of information and possible new perspectives that you have and they do not have. The fact that you may have a body of knowledge, which you wish to impart to them, may create the trap of having to negotiate with the negotiator. To be sure, many of those who have been in the position of authority as negotiators do not like to be "taught," especially by someone they perceive as an opponent, outsider, or intra-team rival. Negotiators may have the self-perception that they are the *bearer* of

Stuart Kirschner is retired as an Associate Professor of Psychology at John Jay College of Criminal Justice. For over a decade he was principal instructor for the Emergency Psychological Technician (EPT) course, which instructs New York City Police Officers on communication with emotionally disturbed persons. Kirschner received his M.A. from Columbia University and his Ph.D. from the University of North Carolina, Chapel Hill. For 12 years he was an Administrator at Kirby Forensic Psychiatric Center (KFPC), a New York State Office of Mental Health maximum security psychiatric center. Dr. Kirschner has served as expert witness and consultant to defense counsel and prosecutors where psychiatric defenses have been entered, and writes regularly on psychiatric defenses and assessment of dangerousness.
Jack Cambria retired from the New York City Police Department in 2015 after nearly thirty-four years of dedicated service. For over sixteen years he served in the Emergency Service Unit (ESU), whose primary focus is to provide rescue, SWAT, and counterterrorism services to the City of New York. He ended his NYPD career as the longest-standing commander of the Hostage Negotiation Team, serving in that capacity for over fourteen years.

knowledge, not necessarily the *recipient*. Even when negotiators or team members clearly recognize the need to gather new perspectives or information, and to adjust their own thinking in relation to either or both, they certainly may resist being given a lecture. It is frequently the case that those who engage in negotiation can be very resistant to changing and/or expanding their thinking. This mind set is certainly true for police officers who are required to negotiate as an essential part of their job. It is inherent in the police culture that officers are figures of authority, and they are not inclined to take direction, especially from those they are tasked with policing. The perception is "I'm the cop and you will listen to whatever I have to say," lending an added impediment where the police culture often seduces an officer into believing that they are more than they are. This attitude presents a major obstacle to the training of police. It becomes even more salient when there is a civilian trainer. The officer needs to develop flexibility and openness during the training—the very same stance that the officer must adopt when negotiating. And while it is the task of the trainers to facilitate this change in perception, that is of course easier said than done. The abilities to listen, understand and receive the trainers' message are the same skills that will place the officer in a better position to assist the consumer. In fact, the mission of the trainer is not dissimilar to that of a psychotherapist who is treating a resistant patient. Breaking through the resistance to treatment is treatment in itself.

The officer's position, instead, should now be: "teach me how to better understand you." The hostage team commander has made this point many times, when teaching a new class of negotiators to embrace the difficult people of the world: ultimately, *they* will become your greatest teachers. It is perhaps those difficult or negative encounters where over time we derive our most powerful lessons, in learning what people in crisis would better respond to.

This chapter discusses the tension which may occur between those who need to transmit information and perspectives, and potentially resistant practitioners. This friction was exemplified when an explicit need arose to create an effective course in negotiation with emotionally disturbed persons for officers of the New York Police Department. The lessons learned from more than twenty years of experience in teaching that course may be helpful to other kinds of negotiators (and trainers) as they contemplate how to get their next audience to pay better attention to what they have to say.

Over the past few decades, there has been a dramatic increase in the number of chronically mentally ill people who are treated in the community. This trend has derived from a conscious policy to shift away from inpatient services, with a concomitant downsizing of inpatient facilities for the treatment of psychiatric patients. Deinstitutionalization, changes in the standard for the civil commitment of the mentally ill, and U.S.

Supreme Court decisions have all contributed to this shift from inpatient to outpatient treatment.

The rise in numbers of mentally ill people who live in the community has created a number of concerns. The decrease in the number of inpatient beds available for psychiatric patients makes it more difficult for such patients to receive inpatient services when they are in acute crises. In addition, there has been a failure of community-based mental health services to provide adequate out-patient care. One result of these changes is that large numbers of mentally ill people have found themselves among the homeless population. High concentrations of homeless mentally ill have become commonplace in large urban settings throughout the United States. Moreover, there has been a significant increase in the number of mentally ill people in correctional facilities. Estimates indicate that over 25% of the inmate population in county, state and federal prisons suffer from a major mental illness. The present trend has been termed the era of the criminalization of the mentally ill. This criminalization has also been considered, by some, to be a direct outgrowth of deinstitutionalization and a failure of the mental health system to provide adequate community-based services to released psychiatric patients (Kirschner 2001). In light of these findings, one attempt to help reduce the criminalization of the mentally ill has been the increase in diversion programs. Many jurisdictions now have mental health courts, where mentally ill defendants are diverted out of the criminal justice system to courts which mandate and monitor community-based treatment as part of a defendant's conditional release.

The presence of significant numbers of the severely and persistently mentally ill in the community poses challenges for the police. Police officers are the first line of intervention for individuals who present an imminent danger to themselves or others (whether they are mentally ill or not). With recent research indicating that a diagnosis of a major mental illness is, in fact, a risk factor for dangerousness (Webster et al. 1997)[1] there is clearly a need for police officers to become more proficient in dealing with those who suffer from psychiatric disorders. It is against this backdrop that the training of police to recognize, communicate and intervene with the mentally ill emerges as a major issue in policing. A basic philosophy of good police work is, "just because you have the stick does not mean you have to use it." When interacting with the emotionally disturbed or mentally ill, the officer should, when able, demonstrate compassion and empathy. Psychologists can also serve a critical function in implementing such training.

The Origin of Emergency Psychological Technician Training

In 1984, Eleanor Bumpers, an elderly and mentally ill woman, was shot and killed by New York City Emergency Service Unit (ESU) police officers as they entered her apartment. The police were unaware of her mental illness and believed they were there to effect what was presumed to be a routine eviction. However, Ms. Bumpers, who was an extremely obese women, was actively psychotic and in an acute paranoid crisis at the time. She charged at the police officers while wielding a knife and, as a result, was shot and killed.

The Eleanor Bumpers incident provided the impetus for the New York City Police Department (NYPD) to change its policy and procedures in regard to dealing with emotionally disturbed people (EDP's). Since then, whenever there is a call to the police and it is confirmed that it involves an EDP, the ESU would be required to respond and, in barricade or hostage situations, the Hostage Negotiation Team (HNT) would send a negotiator to the scene (Kelly). [NDR: Volpe et al., *The Unknown*] In light of this change, a new training program was implemented. The New York City Police Department contracted with John Jay College of Criminal Justice and the New York City Department of Mental Health to provide this training.

Structure of the Training Program

The program is referred to as Emergency Psychological Technician (EPT). The five-day, intensive program has evolved since its inception, and includes both experiential and didactic components. During the first half of each day, there are lectures explaining the various types of mental illnesses and personality disorders, with specific emphasis on the signs and symptoms of the various conditions. The second part of each day is devoted to communication skills. Each participant is involved in a role play situation where the officer is required to talk an EDP out from behind a door. The EDP may be barricaded or holding a hostage. (A free standing door is the only prop which is used in the training.) Actor/trainers play the EDP, who manifests a predetermined psychiatric condition (e.g. a person with schizophrenia, bipolar disorder, narcissistic personality disorder, etc.). The actor/trainer has no script and responds, in character, to the officer's verbal interventions. The dialogues are periodically interrupted so that the audience can offer comments and suggestions to the negotiator who is at the door. Thus, these trainings are much like other role-play and fish bowl experiences in other negotiation courses. The participants in the training are mostly police officers who are members of ESU and HNT.

ESU officers of NYPD provide specialized support to all units of the Department. The unit has a number of emergency response vehicles and the officers are highly trained to respond to many types of emergency and catastrophic situations. These situations include such things as construction accidents, water rescue, railway incidents, hazardous material concerns, rope rescue and rappelling, vehicle accidents and bombs. The unit is outfitted with various types of lethal and nonlethal tactical equipment and, while the unit can serve as a S.W.A.T. team, its mission is clearly more than that. The motto for ESU is "When civilians need help they call the police. When the police need help, they call ESU." ESU officers generally have a number of years of experience on patrol before they will be considered for ESU.

The Hostage Negotiation Team is also a specialized unit with a high prior-experience requirement. All prospective members of the HNT must have been previously promoted to Detective, Detective Sergeant or Detective Lieutenant. To be eligible for selection to this Team, they also must have a minimum of twelve years' experience within NYPD and an excellent department record. Higher education is important but not mandatory; the selection of HNT members emphasizes both job and life experiences. [See NDR: Volpe et al., *The Unknown*, for more on how these officers are selected] While individuals volunteer to become members of ESU or HNT, EPT is a mandatory component of the training they then receive.[2]

Problems and Concerns in Training Police Officers

A number of considerations govern the EPT course, which may provide some context for readers who are grappling with developing formal courses for other kinds of practitioners. Each of these factors constitutes an important consideration for the training of police officers; however, they are relevant for the training of many types of negotiators, or for that matter, many educators who are faced with "tough" audiences. Perhaps the toughest audience of all is the police audience, who would prefer being out on the street instead of sitting in a classroom. The training curriculum presented must be keyed to their environment so that it will motivate the officer-participant to want to learn. The following list, while not exhaustive, highlights some of the issues which have been dealt with in developing the course.

The Training Site

The first concern was whether the program would be conducted at an NYPD location (e.g. the Police Academy) or at a facility outside of the Department (e.g. John Jay College of Criminal Justice, which has a long-standing association with the NYPD, but is independent of it). It was concluded that John Jay College would be the training site, for a number of reasons. First, providing an academic atmosphere was thought to facilitate learning. Second, a setting which is not part of the Department gives the participants a sense that there may be something new rather than the usual, routine trainings which are offered by the Department. Third, and significantly for this "participant" population, a number of participants have a kind of "institutional paranoia." Training conducted at a Department facility increases the feeling that "the bosses" are overseeing the program and maintaining a watchful eye on all that takes place; using John Jay College offers a sort of sanctuary. Fourth, even though any number of "bosses," (Sergeants, Lieutenants, Captains, and two-star Chiefs) have attended the training sessions, all participants are in civilian clothes. The fact that rank is not obvious to others helps to create a forum which is conducive to freedom of speech.

The Participants

An important feature is the heterogeneity of the group. Participants who are from diverse racial, ethnic, cultural and educational backgrounds bring different perspectives to the group discussions. While most of the participants in EPT are police officers, there are often invited guests in attendance, who may include local, state, federal and foreign law enforcement officers from a variety of jurisdictions and agencies. There are also mental health workers from different disciplines, researchers and academicians frequently in attendance. Moreover, police officers themselves do not constitute a homogenous group of individuals. They bring to the training a wide range of educational backgrounds, interests and personal life experiences. For example, ESU officers are generally multi-talented and have a variety of technical and tactical skills, including some medical training. Some also have Doctorate or Master's degrees, with majors in a wide array of subjects. The heterogeneity of the group works well, allowing the participants to bring in their different views. Alternatively, the participants walk away from this training with greater sensitivity in understanding diverging perspectives that, when properly applied, eases their approach in managing difficult encounters, and further develops the officer's "working personality".

Group Size

The size of the group ranges between 25 and 30 participants. Larger groups would not afford an opportunity for every member to practice negotiation skills, and create too much of an impersonal environment. (Smaller groups place too much of a burden on each individual participant, forcing the members to become involved in too many role play situations, which is thought in this context to lead to resistance.) The moderate size of the group allows for better group cohesiveness, a very important aspect of the training. Members get to know each other personally and to work together as a team. It is worth noting that in a Department of close to forty thousand officers replete with Divisions, Bureaus, Offices and many other organizational subdivisions, the Hostage Negotiation Team is the only unit formally accorded the title "Team." It is for this reason that the hostage team commander has insisted that each class participant know the name, rank and detective squad assigned of each class member by the end of the week's training. His rationale is that in order to operate as a team, you must know your teammates. The commander facilitates this learning throughout the week by asking the participants at intervals to turn down their name placards, and then randomly quizzes the class for the names of other class participants. He also reassigns seating positions each day so that the participants are interacting with different classmates on a daily basis. Additionally, each class member is given a class roster, for their further study. After the first day, the class members start to cooperate with this endeavor, and the participants make a concerted effort to learn each team member's name, on which they will be openly tested. This process of interacting with those who were complete strangers at the commencement of the class serves to instill group cohesiveness.

Duration

The EPT program runs for five consecutive days. A critical part of the training is the experiential component. Each participant takes "center stage" and the group observes and critiques the participant's negotiation skills. The first day is usually the most difficult; at the outset, these individuals are generally reluctant to expose their shortcomings and vulnerabilities. It is the trainer's job to create a safe environment whereby the members of the group feel comfortable so they can candidly engage in the simulated negotiations. Usually, by midway through the second day, participants become relaxed enough to engage in a candid negotiation which is a true representation of how they would behave in an actual situation.

Communication

Communication skills and negotiation strategies are critiqued in an open forum. The negotiation trainees are also encouraged to critique the exercises and offer suggestions to the trainers (e.g. participants at times have stated that a given simulated situation is too artificial and not "true to life"). This is a conscious departure from much of police training, and helps to set a tone of collegiality—important in the context of the more "pedagogical" part, which follows. The class participants learn to appreciate the value of proper verbal communication. The group members come to realize that most people will respond positively when they are treated with respect, even if an EDP is evidently psychotic, during the negotiation. They quickly grasp that EDP, in addition to meaning "Emotionally Disturbed People," also means "Every Day People," just like themselves. In fact, this sentiment is instilled in the participants on the very first day of class. The HNT commander poses a question on the first morning of training, which is, "Who in the class has never had a serious problem in which your emotional levels have escalated?" Not surprisingly, no one in the class answers affirmatively. Then, throughout the week, each individual is invited to present a personal, emotionally-charged life experience to the group. Through this presentation, the person is now faced with the realization that, on at least one occasion, the presenter was an EDP. These personal vignettes help to enhance empathy in the other participants and creates an emotional bond between members, who may be their negotiation partner during a crisis. The class nurtures an ethos amongst its members that will become ingrained within each of them. By the end of the fifth day, the group has developed an identity of its own and the members have become palpably connected to each other.

The Problem of Standard Pedagogy

While much of the necessary learning is experiential or by demonstration, unfortunately some lecturing is unavoidable. Much of the structure (e.g. the split day) can be seen as part of a coordinated plan to help these participants to accept the "cod liver oil" part. The remaining risk is that the trainer can easily become too pedantic, leaving the participants with the impression that the material is irrelevant or not applicable to the work that the officer does. Even worse, the material could be presented in a fashion that is only comprehensible to professionals with advanced degrees in psychology. It is the trainer's job to present the material in an interesting and comprehensible fashion, demonstrating how the content is relevant to improving job performance by continuously presenting, throughout the training, how theory is translated into practice. It also underscores the fact that the scenes, which the negotiators have to navigate their way through, must depict actual circumstances or possible scenarios that the officer may encounter at work. But the didactic component must somehow cope with who these officers are. In a nutshell, this is an audience particularly maladapted to sitting in chairs and listening to a lecture.

The Need for Stimulation

The need for stimulation or excitement can lead to risk-taking behavior and is often associated aberrant conduct (Hare 1999).[3] However, police officers are also generally people of action (Lykken 1995).[4] This need to be on the move is one of the major reasons that they entered the profession. The ESU officers, particularly, have this trait in abundance. (Within the police department they are referred to fondly as "The boys with toys.") It is because of this perspective that they are not often mesmerized by an academic lecture. In addition, an officer's frequent instinctive reaction, to yet another provocative remark by the actor playing an EDP, is to move in tactically, "taking the door" and through the use of other (in normal circumstances, non-lethal) means, getting the EDP into custody. This also reflects the real-world imperfection of negotiation: the trainers must concede that a significant percentage of the cases may, in fact, be resolved in this manner. There is a shared understanding that the ESU officers have a variety of tools, and are proficient in using them. But this training is an exercise in improving verbal communication skills. It is emphasized that, in helping officers to tap and practice these skills, officers are acquiring yet another tool to be placed in their tool box. It is important that scenes create tension and drama. Intensity can be established only if the scenarios are "true to life." Therefore, scenarios are adapted from actual cases. They often have been modified to better meet the confines of the training situation. The situations are regularly critiqued by the participants so that their suggestions can serve as guidelines to improve the scenarios. The scenes also must create a dilemma for the officers that makes it extremely difficult for the officers to move in tactically. The situation is such that the officers have little choice but to communicate verbally with the barricade maker or hostage taker.

The realism of the scenes is reflected by the outpouring of the negotiators' emotions during the exercise. It is obvious that they are involved and focused on the task, to the point that officers become oblivious to the presence of an audience. Many officers have completed a negotiation with perspiration visibly soaking through a shirt. The sheer exhaustion has been expressed by many a negotiator who has commented how he or she is "emotionally spent" at the completion of the exercise. Needless to say, the officers' need for stimulation has usually been met.

Credibility of "Didactic" Trainers

What makes and keeps a trainer credible? History, honesty, humility and humor. The reputations of the civilian and department trainers precede them. Participants in a training generally have some advanced knowledge of who the instructors are. In the EPT program, police personnel and a psychologist serve as co-trainers and organizers of the program. The police co-trainers, who have had years of experience in hostage negotiating and working within ESU in the "trenches", are highly respected by their colleagues.

The psychologist in the program has developed a close professional alliance and, over the years, a personal friendship with the police co-trainers. As a result of these ties, the advance message to the participants is often positive. It also helps if the civilian trainer has made attempts to understand negotiation from the officer's perspective. While it is not mandatory or even recommended that the civilian trainer enter the "hot zone" of an actual police negotiation, the trainer can develop a better understanding of the process by going on a "ride-along" with police negotiators in order to observe crisis situations from the periphery. The trainer may also attend other police training sessions to learn about more tactical aspects of the job. As an outsider, it is important for the civilian trainer to develop and maintain such good standing. An advanced academic degree doesn't necessarily make one credible in every circle.

While police officers may respect that one has a degree, they often feel that "the professor" does not understand the world outside of academia, especially from a police officer's perspective. As officers relate their personal experiences, one cannot help being humbled by what they often have encountered while working on the job. It is important for the trainer not to rely merely on academic credentials. On one occasion, a police officer who participated in the training asked the civilian trainer if he knew what suffix "Ph.D." meant. When he indicated that it stood for "Piled higher and deeper," the trainer immediately adopted the line when introducing himself at future training. Police officers often speak about how they ventilate their emotions through humor. Years of working as a cop in New York can make one quite jaded and cynical. Humor often becomes a way of coping with the tragedies and the plight of humanity that they encounter on a daily basis. ESU officers and the seasoned detectives who comprise the HNT have witnessed the worst that life has to offer, and comic relief can be very therapeutic. They have a "gallows humor." While this can be viewed as callousness, it is important to understand this as a coping mechanism. Joining the participants in this type of humor is important way of connecting to the group. When the trainer is honest and open it sets the tone for the training. Sharing personal experiences helps, especially during the experiential part. The trainer can model how to engage people and develop rapport through the use of one's own humanness. The example that is set by the trainers, in developing a relationship with the group, sets the stage for how the trainees will relate to a barricade or hostage taker. It allows the officer to tap his or her own humanness, an extremely valuable resource.

Work Experience

For the seasoned police officer in New York, there is little that may be new. The breadth and depth of experience is usually great, and these are what the officer, in the end, relies on to do his or her job well. It is also a major component of what the officer brings to the negotiation with EDPs. While officers volunteer for ESU and the HNT, and they are usually quite enthusiastic about the new assignment, there is always the concern that some officers may be experiencing "burnout." [NDR: O'Shea, *Compassion*] Disillusionment, depression, anger and apathy are impediments to the negotiation process. These are private feelings which police officers do not readily volunteer.

However, within the context of a successful training program, officers often begin to feel comfortable enough to express their discouragement. At times, it enters into their negotiation when they are at the door. As they begin to resolve some of their own feelings about being a police officer, they are at the same time improving their skills as a negotiator.

Anxiety

It is often more difficult for an individual to present before a group of colleagues who are in the same profession because the audience possesses a similar fund of knowledge and has the capability of being more critical about the information which is provided. In the same way, it is difficult for police officers to expose their knowledge or lack thereof to their fellow officers. Trainers must be sensitive to the fact that the officer, during the simulated negotiations, is performing before his or her peers and is in a position to expose all of his or her shortcomings. However, the participant, who is engaged in the role-play, is actually the spokesperson of a support team. The participant negotiator is not alone at the simulated door, but is part of a team with three or four other members. The other members serve as additional "sets of ears", offer coaching or advice whenever the primary negotiator runs out of things to say, and help to assuage some of the primary negotiator's anxiety during the ordeal. At times, the trainer may call for a "time-out" to allow the participant to reflect on any emotions that may have been elicited and to assess how the negotiation is progressing. The class is then called upon to offer suggestions in furthering that support system that is at the door. Often times it was not a "brilliant" argument that wins the moment, but rather the empathy for the EDP that was demonstrated by the negotiator.

Stereotypes of Trainer

The differences in the way that mental health professionals are trained compared to those who work within the legal system has led to the stereotyping of mental health workers. Due to the fact that psychological theories are generally deterministic in nature, psychologists look for explanations of human behavior. However, within the context of the legal system, this may be viewed as providing excuses for individuals, especially when applied to criminal defendants who enter psychiatric defenses. As a result, psychologists may be viewed as overly paternalistic and "bleeding hearts" (Melton et al. 1997).[5] This stereotype is often held by police officers whose theoretical perspective is grounded in the legal system, where the assumption is that individuals possess "free will" (White and Honig 1995).[6] Their working concept is that people have a choice, and they can choose to be good or bad, even mentally ill or sane. It is important to address one's own philosophy and intrinsic assumptions about personality. To be sure, the way that an officer understands the development of personality and psychiatric disorders directly impacts on the approach that the officer takes to the negotiation. [For more on how these disorders relate to negotiation, see NDR: Jeglic & Jeglic, *Mental Health*]

Summarizing the Training

Teaching police officers how to negotiate with emotionally disturbed persons presents some unique challenges. The nature of this type of negotiation warrants a few considerations:

- In negotiating with a barricaded person or a hostage taker, the communication normally takes place through a closed door (certainly this is the way the training is done.) While other types of negotiation can be done without the use of visual communication (e.g. by telephone or e-mail), any agreement which is reached is done without having eye to eye contact. It is certainly important for the police officer to gain a knowledge of various psychiatric conditions, theoretical principles and hostage negotiation strategies; however, the key is for the negotiator to develop good listening skills. Active listening is emphasized throughout the training.

- In some negotiations, the negotiator may be an objective party who serves as a mediator in helping to reconcile differences between other parties. In such negotiations each side maintains a subjective perspective and has a vested interest in the outcome. In negotiating with EDP's, the police officer is involved in a two-party negotiation and while the officer, no doubt, has a vested interest in the outcome, he or she is also obligated to maintain a significant degree of objectivity. The officer must never lose his or her professionalism. In "talking down" an emotionally disturbed barricade maker or hostage taker the emotional investment and expenditure can be immense. In fact, the negotiation will rarely be successful if the negotiator does not make some emotional investment in the encounter. Yet, at the same time, the negotiator must remain objective and professional by being non-judgmental and non-threatening in their approach. Moreover, the officer must be able to move on to the next job which may be a few minutes away. The officer has to be capable of de-cathecting (withdrawing this emotional attachment) from what may have been an extremely emotionally exhausting experience.

- In the two-party negotiation between officer and EDP, there is a hierarchical relationship. One clearly can exercise legal power over the other in the performance of a duty. In this sense, the two parties who are involved in the negotiation are not on equal footing. How the officer deals with this inequality and communicates the understanding of his or her role becomes critical in the negotiation process. There is a delicate balance that must be maintained. The officer must be able to confine, contain and control; yet, at the same time, the officer must communicate an understanding of the EDP's distress—without being at all condescending. However, both parties are on equal footing inasmuch as they are humans; and everyone, at some time in their life, has been an EDP.[7]

- In the negotiation between officer and EDP, the stakes are as high as they can get. A successful negotiation can preserve life;

unsuccessful negotiations can result in death. It is certainly a rare type of negotiation where the failure to resolve the conflict can result in the death of one or more of the parties in conflict or, in fact, an innocent victim (e.g. hostage or bystander).

This chapter has addressed some of the issues and concerns relevant to developing a successful program for training police officers to better communicate with emotionally disturbed persons. One conclusion is that, while course content is certainly important, often not so much *what* is taught as *how* it is taught, and the context in which that is presented, are key to effective learning. Thus, the process is the message:

- The training is presented in an environment which is non-threatening and where the participants can practice their newly acquired information and skills, in what is often referred to during the training as a "laboratory setting". The trainers reinforce the fact that the classroom is a forum where trial and error interventions are encouraged.

- Rapport is established among the participants and between the trainers and the participants. The trust which is an outgrowth of the rapport develops over the course of the training.

- Within the context of a trusting relationship, barriers and defenses are lowered and participants allow themselves to become more vulnerable.

- They openly engage in dialogue in the role plays, allowing their true selves to emerge, while often revealing very personal stories to the actor-trainer in order to achieve their objective in having the EDP "come out that door".

- They make mistakes and accept the training as a laboratory where errors can be made without untoward consequences. In effect, the course that the training follows is the same path that a successful negotiation should follow. The officer establishes trust with the EDP by enhancing his own listening skills and making use of his own responsiveness as a human being, allowing the barricader's or hostage taker's "real" needs to become known so that they can then be addressed. As the psychological barriers fall, so do the physical barriers, and ultimately the EDP can safely walk through the door.

Conclusion: The Wider Adaptation of "EPT" Training

Most recently, the NYPD has recognized the importance of EPT training by developing two additional training programs. The first in the sequence is entitled "Smart Policing," which is then followed up by "Critical Incident Training." As of 2015, these training programs are mandated for all patrol officers. The concepts at the foundation of these programs are derived from the Emergency Psychological Training. These additional curricula were developed in response to the amassing discourtesy complaints that have been lodged against the NYPD rank and file, and in the wake of some other recent negative encounters between the police and public. Yet such complaints against police are not specific to NYPD. Over recent years, throughout the nation, there has been an increase in publicized allegations of brutality or the use of excessive force by the police. These accusations have also been fueled by technological advances such as the use of dashboard cameras, cellphone videos, social media and enhanced media coverage in general. Patrol officers are under increased scrutiny, and those who respond to citizens in a disrespectful, antagonistic or abusive manner can be readily observed and held accountable for any such unprofessional conduct.

These concerns have underscored the importance of providing patrol officers with basic hostage negotiation skills. The urgency of this mandate has been addressed by NYPD: for example, one of the authors, who had already announced his retirement as the HNT commander at the end of 2014 after a thirty-three-year career with the NYPD, was asked to delay his departure from the NYPD to assist in writing the "Smart Policing" curriculum. His part was to produce a short video, incorporated into a three-day program, that presented basic negotiation principles utilized by hostage negotiators. Its purpose was to teach patrol officers how to develop rapport during those difficult street encounters. The video demonstrates fundamental skills that negotiators rely upon to defuse conflict, such as communicating empathy and employing active listening techniques.

It is apparent that many types of everyday situations, which police officers encounter while on patrol, mandate them to have these negotiation skills in their repertoire, yet most do not. (Kirschner, 2006; Volpe et al. 2006. It is encouraging that now, this principle is being given more attention by police management. Also encouraging, and somewhat surprisingly (i.e., not necessarily the anticipated response of a "captive audience"), the feedback from the officers who have received this training, has been overwhelmingly positive. They appear to be accepting the message that just because they have "the stick" does not mean that they have to use it!

The EPT program and the Smart Policing and Critical Incident Training courses have proven to be highly successful for the training of police officers. In closing, we would like to emphasize our belief that the factors which have been addressed, and the methodology employed, in these programs would be relevant to the teaching of many difficult-to-reach and resistant participants or practitioners, in a variety of settings.

Notes

[1] The diagnosis of a definite/serious major mental illness is a risk factor for the re-occurrence of violence.

[2] Descriptions of the ESU and HNT provided by Lt. Jack Cambria, Commanding Officer of the NYPD Hostage Negotiation Team and Det. Spec. Anthony Favara, ESU: personal communications.

[3] A salient trait of the psychopath is the need for stimulation. Psychopaths become bored easily and seek action. Often the action is antisocial in nature.

[4] The same trait for high risk behavior which is often found in criminals can be cultivated to elicit socially appropriate or even heroic behaviors.

[5] The perceived attitudinal differences between lawyers and mental health professionals may be over-emphasized.

[6] They state that people in law enforcement generally come in contact with mental health professionals in one of four ways: (1) observing psychologists offer expert testimony in court on behalf of criminals, (2) dealing with psychiatric patients who were inappropriately discharged back into the community by mental health professionals, (3) viewing psychologists provide excuses for malingering police officers who are claiming psychological trauma, and (4) witnessing psychologists evaluate them for fitness for duty or pre-employment screenings. It is because of these types of contacts that many peace officers have little respect for, and a negative view of, psychologists.

[7] In fact, it is regularly emphasized throughout the training that EDP also stands for Every Day People.

References

Hare, R. D. 1999. Without Conscience: The Disturbing World of Psychopaths Among Us. New York: The Guildford Press.

Kelly, R. W. NYPD Hostage Negotiations Organizational and Tactical Guide.

Kirschner, S. 2001. The Mentally Ill in New York City: Treatment and Criminal Justice Management. In *Crime and Justice in New York City, Vol. 1: New York City's Crime Problem*, edited by A. Karmen. Belmont, CA: Wadsworth.

Kirschner, S. 2006. Tyraining a Captive Audience in *The Negotiator's Fieldbook*, edited by A. K. Schneider and C. Honeyman. Chicago: ABA Publishing

Lykken, D. T. 1995. The Antisocial Personalities. Hillsdale, NJ: Lawrence Erlbaum Associates, Inc. Publishers.

Melton, G. B., J. Petrila, N. G. Poythress and C. Slobogin. 1997. Psychological Evaluations for the Courts: A Handbook for Mental Health Professionals and Lawyers. New York: The Guildford Press.

Volpe, M., J. J. Cambria, H. McGowan and C. Honeyman. 2006. Negotiating with the Unknown. In *The Negotiator's Fieldbook*, edited by A. K. Schneider and C. Honeyman. Chicago: ABA Publishing.

Webster, C. D., K. Douglas, D. Eaves and S. Hart. 1997. *HCR-20: Assessing Risk for Violence (2nd ed)*. Burnaby, BC: Mental Health, Law, and Policy Institute, Simon Fraser University.

White, E. K. and A. L. Honig. 1995. The Role of the Police Psychologist in Training. In *Police Psychology Into the 21st Century*, edited by M. I. Kurke and E. M. Scrivner. New York: Psychology Press.

∝ 87 ∝

Religion in Cooperation and Conflict

Jeffrey R. Seul

Editors' Note: In the first of two chapters, the author argues that the relationship between religion and conflict is widely oversimplified. Recent and careful social science research has demonstrated that, contrary to the assumptions of some people, religion most often increases its adherents' ability to relate positively to others—and this can include adherents of another religion or none at all. In contrast, he reviews the research on extreme religious militancy, including the evidence on suicide and other violent attackers, and concludes that the most careful researchers have universally found that these actions are not principally propelled by religion itself, but by other factors. In his next chapter, Seul proceeds to analysis of how religion can help to transform conflict, and how it can be consciously invoked toward that purpose.

Religion and conflict sometimes mix, but perspectives on their relationship tend to be overly simplified. For some, religion is irrational and in tension with modern, liberal notions of democracy and collective problem solving; it is not merely a factor in some conflicts, it is a cause of conflict, and it offers little or nothing in the way of resources for conflict resolution. For others, religion, properly understood, is a benevolent force that promotes personal and collective peace and wellbeing, and all entanglements of religion and conflict stem from perversions of religion or cynical manipulations of it by unscrupulous leaders who are not genuinely religious, but who understand and exploit religion's capacity to bind and mobilize people. Still others see religion simply as a hopelessly complex, impenetrable mass of traditions, perspectives and social struc-

Jeff Seul is Lecturer on the Practice of Peace at Harvard Divinity School and co-chair of the Peace Appeal Foundation, an organization that helps local stakeholders launch and sustain peace and national dialogue processes to end or avoid war. Mr. Seul previously taught at Harvard Law School, and was a senior associate of the Program on International Conflict Analysis and Resolution at Harvard's Weatherhead Center for International Affairs. Much of his work is focused on approaches to transformation of conflict with a religious dimension. Mr. Seul is also a partner in the international law firm Holland & Knight, the former general counsel of a startup tech firm (Groove Networks), a Roman Catholic and a Zen practitioner.

tures; a feature of history and culture that must be superficially understood and acknowledged, but which must largely be quarantined as parties seek a resolution to their conflict in a political, social and conceptual space mostly free of its influence.

This chapter presents a different perspective on the role of religion in both conflict and cooperation, and the potential for transformation of conflicts involving religion. A clearer and more nuanced picture of the ways in which religion and conflict relate, and also how religion promotes cooperation within groups and can contribute to the transformation of conflict between groups, has begun to emerge over the past couple of decades—thanks, in part, to the efforts of a small group of social scientists who have approached these questions with genuine curiosity, largely steering clear of the polemics that too often attend them. This chapter provides an in-depth introduction to this emerging, interdisciplinary field of research. The next chapter, *Religious Prosociality for Conflict Transformation*, attempts to draw lessons from it, and from the fields of religious studies and conflict resolution, that can be employed to avert, moderate or transform destructive cycles of conflict in which religion is a factor. Violent conflict is the focus of these chapters, but the perspective on religion they present, and the lessons drawn, also are applicable to other types of disputes involving religion.

The Prosocial Character of Religion

Nineteenth and 20th century proclamations that religion was dead or dying are now themselves widely considered deceased. Data compiled by the Pew Research Center indicates that humanity now is approximately 31 percent Christian and 23 percent Muslim. The percentage of Christians is projected to be precisely the same in 2050, while the percentage of Muslims is projected to climb to about 30 percent. If current trends hold, by mid-century about 60 percent of the world's population will consist of roughly equal numbers of Christians and Muslims, and another 27 percent will identify with other religions. Just 13 percent of the world's population will be religiously unaffiliated, down from approximately 16 percent today (Pew Research Center 2015). Even many of these unaffiliated people say they hold religious beliefs; for example, 68 percent of unaffiliated adults in the U.S. and 30 percent of unaffiliated adults in France report believing in God or a higher power (Pew Research Center 2012). Following decades of official efforts in the Soviet Union to promote atheism, 82% of Russians identify with one religion or another (Pew Research Center 2014b).

As political scientists Pippa Norris and Ronald Inglehart sum up the data, "[t]here is no evidence of a worldwide decline of religiosity, or of the role of religion in politics" (Norris and Inglehart 2011: 212). Those who are confounded by these trends would do well to consider recent, interdisciplinary research on the prosocial dimensions of religion. Although some view religion principally as a divisive, and even malevolent, force, it seems few other features of human culture historically have been as effective at promoting cooperation among large numbers of people. Indeed, social scientists studying religious prosociality recognize that some secular institutions that promote social trust and cooperation, like the rule of law, can be seen as outgrowths of precursor religious institutions, serving many similar functions (Norenzayan 2013; Fox 2015).

When most religious and non-religious people think about religions today, they likely think of belief systems with associated practices, narratives, texts, norms, roles, and institutions. What impulses contributed to the development of these sources, beliefs, practices and other features of religion, and how do they serve individuals and groups today? Many people see their religious sources, beliefs, practices, and institutions as transcendently revealed or inspired, of course. And many religious adherents who link tradition with the transcendent also generally acknowledge that there are many aspects of religion, as it becomes expressed in social life across time and place, that are products of human influence. Indeed, some religious people would say this human agency and its accumulated consequences over time are a dimension of divine agency.[1]

A growing body of empirical research confirms that, however else a religion is understood by and serves its adherents, it helps them get along, promoting mutually beneficial trust and cooperation. According to currently prevailing evolutionary theory, as biological kinship becomes more remote, it becomes too attenuated to ensure cooperation (Hamilton 1964; Trivers 1971). Religion helps engender a sense of social kinship even among people who are not closely related biologically (Nesse 1999).[2]

We operate in groups, in part, because group membership confers benefits isolated individuals cannot obtain, or cannot obtain in equal measure, including increased protection from many types of harm (e.g., animal and human predators) and greater productive capacity. Much research—from biological, anthropological and historical work to game theoretical computer simulations—suggests that blood ties alone may not promote cooperation at a scale sufficient to develop many forms of coordinated human effort we now take for granted, like large-scale agriculture, life in cities, and maintenance of reliable trade networks spanning and joining continents (Axelrod 2006).

Life in groups of any size presents us more frequently and pressingly with a question with which even wanderers and hermits must struggle on occasion: Whom can I trust? Satisfaction of many individual needs and desires requires cooperation, but people sometimes exploit others. We all try to guard ourselves against exploitation, but it is not so easy to identify would-be exploiters. Researchers approaching these questions from an evolutionary perspective have developed evidence that family members generally are more reliable, and that closer family members tend to be most reliable, but what about the person at the opposite edge of the village, the stranger passing through, those in the next village, or potential trading partners half a continent away or across the ocean? How do we develop and maintain sufficient trust in others to confront and overcome collective action problems, so as to realize benefits wanderers and hermits largely choose to forego?

Recent social scientific work suggests that the widely-shared complexes of beliefs, practices, narratives, texts, norms, roles and institutions that we recognize today as the world's major religious traditions help solve this dilemma, facilitating social life at large scale (Norenzayan 2013).[3] People (religious or not) generally seem to be more trustworthy when they believe they are being watched (Shariff and Norenzayan 2007),[4] and so it arguably follows that felt awareness of a god that one believes is concerned with human moral conduct encourages compliance with social norms and lessens the monitoring burden borne by members of one's group (Laurin et al. 2012; Norenzayan 2013).[5] Ara Norenzayan and others argue that "Big Gods"—morally concerned gods that inspire exclusive commitment—are capable of engendering trust among large numbers of people, thus helping groups grow.[6] Religious practices (e.g., regular attendance at services and regular and/or extended periods of time devoted to prayer or meditation) and sacrifices (e.g., fasting, renouncing certain pleasures, and giving material support to the community) signal sincere commitment, thereby demonstrating one's trustworthiness (Henrich 2009). In addition, I would add, they genuinely deepen one's commitment to a way of life and to others who embrace it, thus helping one become the sort of person whom one means to be. This includes not only cultivation of the virtue of trustworthiness, but also cultivation of other, complementary virtues.

Pippa Norris and Ronald Inglehart have shown that religious participation and commitment are greatest "in societies in which survival is uncertain" because of poverty, weak or corrupt state institutions, unreliable food or water supplies, disease, harsh environmental conditions, or any of a host of other factors that are less prevalent in industrial and post-industrial societies (Norris and Inglehart 2011: 219). As Norenzayan explains,

> [i]n a society in which the rule of law is weak, and overall levels of trust and cooperation among strangers are quite low (that's indeed most people for most of history), credible signals of fearing a god are, and have been, the only game in town, and in those societies, it would be reasonable to rely on such religious badges as a trust cue (Norenzayan 2013: 74).

Some Iraqis and Syrians in territory controlled by ISIS,[7] though they never were fond of the group or its methods, initially appreciated the jobs, infrastructure improvements, and relative (even if minimal) sense of order it seemed to be providing in a region devastated by conflict that already had made life impossibly bleak (Hubbard 2015a) —conflict which is, in large part, a response to corrupt regimes (and their foreign patrons).[8] This is how some non-Taliban people in Afghanistan regard the Taliban (Atran 2010a; Ahmed 2015). The fact that many people remain religious in traditional and untraditional ways in the United States, Russia and other societies where survival is comparatively certain is evidence that religious perspectives, practices and affiliations still have salience for many people in those societies. The reasons for this no doubt include, yet extend well beyond, the social ordering functions religion can play.

Scholars debate whether the heightened trust, cooperation and generosity that characterize religious prosociality are persistent personality characteristics or preferences of religious people (Everett, Haque and Rand 2015) or whether they arise only in situations in which a person is reminded of God or religion (Malhotra 2010; Xygalatas 2013; Shariff et al. 2015). Scholars on both sides of this debate cite experimental evidence in support of their respective positions. They also debate whether religious prosociality is parochial (*i.e.*, favors members of one's own group) (Shariff 2015) or readily extends to members of other groups (Welch et al. 2004; Everett, Haque and Rand 2015), though it seems clear that situations can be shaped to increase the odds that prosocial conduct will extend to members of other groups (Clingingsmith, Khwaja and Kremer 2009; Pyszczynski, Abdollahi and Rothschild 2009). Finally, scholars debate whether religious prosociality is dependent upon an expectation of reciprocal benefit (Shariff 2015) or not (Xygalatas 2013; Everett, Haque and Rand 2015).

Whatever one might conclude in these debates, increased prosociality (including restraint when issuing punishments) is associated more with belief in a punishing God than with belief in a forgiving God (Laurin et al. 2012). "[R]eligions obey a well-known principle in human psychology (that the stick is often stronger than the carrot)" (Norenzayan 2015: 73). Norenzayan speculates, however, that religious "sticks" may be relatively more useful (in terms of promoting adherence to group norms) in societies with weak secular institutions, because religion generally is more responsible for producing prosocial behavior in those societies (Norenzayan 2015). Anthropologist Hillary Lenfesty and biologist Jeffrey Schloss accept this principle "[g]iven the overwhelming abundance of supporting empirical data," but they also place considerable stock in the ability of positive inducements associated with religion to elicit prosocial behavior. They point, for example, to the experience of connectedness it engenders and "the ability of some religious . . . cues to provoke empathy" (Lenfesty and Schloss 2014: 43-44).[9]

In sum, religion is adept at promoting trust and cooperation among members of a group. No other feature of culture seems to offer so many resources for establishing and maintaining positive, secure group (and individual) identity (Seul 1999). Indeed, the notion that there are separate religious and secular cultural spheres in some societies is a modern one, and the existence, nature and extent of these spheres remain contested (Taylor 2007; Calhoun, Juergensmeyer and Van Antwerpen 2011; Asad et al. 2013).

Religion and Conflict

Religious prosociality arguably is most evident from the in-group dynamics it generates (Norenzayan et al. 2014). The flipside of this phenomenon, of course, is competition with out-groups, and "[h]umans often use religion to cooperate to compete" (Atran 2010a: 456). Individuals form and cooperate within groups (including religious groups), in part, to gain advantages over and protect themselves against people outside the group. Even groups arbitrarily assembled and labeled in temporary experimental settings bond and compete (Tajfel 1970; Brewer 1979). Scholars debate the extent to which groups fight for material gains (Collier and Hoeffler 2004) or to address identity-based grievances (Keen 2007), but most acknowledge that both these and other motivations typically are at play in civil wars and other violent conflicts (Vinci 2006).

Attitudes toward religion in the West can be so hostile that the average person might be forgiven for considering it a factor in most violent past and present conflicts.[10] As best we can tell, however, this simply is not true. The few rigorous analyses available suggest that religion has been a factor in no more than 40% (Austin, Kranock and Oommen 2003), and perhaps even significantly less than 10% (Austin, Kranock and Oommen 2003; Phillips and Axelrod 2004), of violent conflicts from antiquity to the present day. Rarely is religion the primary factor. One recent study found that religion was a primary factor in just 14% of conflicts, but that it was not the lone primary factor in any of these (Institute for Economics and Peace 2014).

We nonetheless must ask why religion is associated with conflict at all. One reason that some conflicts involve one or more religious groups is that identity dynamics play a significant role in intergroup conflict and religion serves the identity-related needs of individuals and groups (Seul 1999). Religion supports a strong sense of *us*, generating a strong sense of *them*, and we know this us-them dynamic can turn violent when one group feels threatened by another.

The us-them dynamic, it must be noted, also is at play in conflict in which religion is not a significant factor, like conflict between ethnic identity groups, so this answer does not tell us whether religion contributes uniquely to conflict dynamics. Through cross-cultural lab experiments and field research, social scientists from varied disciplines are attempting to determine whether there is something peculiar about religion that makes religious groups more prone to conflict, makes conflict involving religion more intense, or both. Norenzayan reminds us that "[e]xclusivity, dogmatism, and fundamentalism are not the same thing as religion," even though "they are often seen as interchangeable with religion by its critics" (Norenzayan 2013: 158).

Based upon his own and others' research, Norenzayan tentatively believes there are at least three ways religion contributes to conflict. First, Norenzayan sees the phenomenon he and other researchers refer to as "supernatural monitoring" as a unique factor that can contribute to religious intolerance and conflict (Norenzayan 2013). This is the felt sense that a person is watched by God, and that God is concerned with human morality. For example, Norenzayan and fellow social psychologist Azim Shariff found in one study that their North American Christian research subjects, when prompted to think of God, were more generous toward other Christians when dividing a sum of money, less generous to those whose religious affiliation was unknown to them, and least generous to Muslims (Shariff and Norenzayan 2012). Norenzayan points out, however, that findings like this are merely evidence that "making supernatural monitoring salient" leads religious people to be less generous toward members of another religion, which is not necessarily "an indication of intense hostility toward religious outgroups" (Norenzayan 2013: 161).

Second, Norenzayan points to "the social bonding power of religious participation and ritual that could exacerbate conflict between groups" (Norenzayan 2013: 160; Seul 1999). Norenzayan and fellow social psychologists Ian Hansen and Jeremy Ginges conducted a series of experiments involving Palestinians and Israelis to determine whether practices that build strong ties within a religious community also widen the gulf between that group and other groups, making it more prone to intolerance and more likely to support violence. Because many types of identity groups not premised upon religion also build and strengthen bonds through gatherings, rituals and other practices, these researchers sought to determine whether religious belief itself causes conflict, as many critics of religion claim.

Their studies assessed support for suicide bombings and other extreme forms of parochial altruism among Palestinians and Israelis[11] and how support correlated to the frequency with which respondents attended religious services (as a proxy for strong commitment to the religious group) and prayed (which the researchers found to be a reliable indicator of strong commitment to religious beliefs). These two variables (attendance at services and prayer) are themselves weakly correlated (i.e., some people attend services frequently and pray frequently; others attend services frequently, but do not pray; and so on). The researchers found a strong correlation between support for violence and frequent attendance at services and no correlation among support for violence and prayer frequency (i.e., strong religious beliefs) (Ginges, Hansen and Norenzayan 2009). These results, which were replicated through surveys of respondents representing six different religions (Anglican, Catholic and Orthodox Christianity, Hinduism, Islam, and Judaism) in six different countries (Great Britain, India, Indonesia, Israel, Mexico, and Russia), discredit the religious belief hypothesis regarding the link between religion and conflict and suggest that "religious violence" is more attributable to the general human phenomenon of solidarity within a group that competes with other groups (as many other types of groups do) than to religious belief itself.

Finally, Norenzayan observes that values embraced by religious groups often are regarded as sacred—that is, they are "immune to trade-offs and seem insensitive to outcome" (Norenzayan 2013: 167). When values are regarded as sacred, trades involving them are considered taboo (Tetlock, Peterson and Lerner 1996). Indeed, even suggesting trades of material goods for things to which sacred value is ascribed (*e.g.*, land regarded as holy) increases opposition to compromise (Ginges et al. 2007).

This and other recent research regarding the relationship between religion and conflict seems to establish that religion is not the cause of conflict with a religious dimension.[12] Religion may well contribute to conflict in each of the three ways Norenzayan suggests, yet we see similar dynamics at play even where religion is not involved:

- What Norenzayan and other researchers call "supernatural monitoring" is unique to religion almost by definition, but a sense of being monitored promotes prosocial behavior even when the monitor is not believed to be transcendent (Bateson, Nettle and Roberts 2006) and even if it is associated with secular, rather than religious, institutions (Shariff and Norenzayan 2007).[13] Nationalists submit to, bond around, and die for abstract, romanticized, superordinate (if not supernatural) concepts of the nation (Connor 1994).

- While some studies indicate that co-religionists are more generous to one another than they are to outsiders, this same tendency has been observed in experiments among members of other types of groups, including members of the same ethnic group (Habyarimana et al. 2007). There also is evidence that religious prosociality is generalized and not parochial. In one study, for example, Christians were more generous both to other Christians and to atheists in a set of economic games, and more devout Christians were most generous, while atheists gave more only to other atheists (Everett, Haque and Rand 2015; see also Welch et al. 2004). Religious groups generate strong bonds and can generate strong oppositional identities, but other types of groups also do, including people with differing political perspectives (Waytz, Young and Ginges 2014). Although theists whose perspective is exclusivist (i.e., believing one's religion is the only true religion) generally are less tolerant of others, theism can also be non-exclusivist. Non-exclusivist theism is no more associated with intolerance than is atheism; in fact, non-exclusivist religious belief and devotion have been shown to reduce intolerance (Hansen and Norenzayan 2009).[14]

- Religion is effective at promoting sacred values, yet secular cultural influences also can sacralize values (Atran 2010a). For example, some adversaries in environmental disputes regard their values as sacred (Hoffman et al. 1999). Religious rituals can sacralize a group's values, but so can secular rituals (Sheikh et al. 2012). There is evidence that some religious people, more than non-religious people, are more likely to think about ethics in rule-bound ways not easily amenable to compromise solutions (Piazza and Landy 2013; Piazza and Sousa 2014), and this is a factor that might tend to intensify some conflicts involving religion. However, the same is true of political conservatives (Piazza and Sousa 2014).

As noted above, what religion does clearly provide is abundant support for the development and stability of group identity, and competition between identity groups of various kinds sometimes turns violent (Seul 1999). Religion certainly offers some distinctive resources for group development and cohesion. However, while it is a common perception that these resources or other features of religion make religious groups more prone to conflict, or to more intense conflict, than other types of identity groups, the existing evidence does not support such claims.[15]

Religion's distinctive features may well have helped religious groups grow larger and endure longer than other groups, with their expansion inevitably bringing them into conflict with new potential adversaries (Atran 2010a; Norenzayan 2013). The more we understand about the ways religion is associated with conflict—and especially about unique ways in which it is associated with conflict—the better able we will be to devise approaches for trying to avert or transform violent and otherwise destructive conflict in which religion is a factor. Where religion is a significant factor in a conflict, however, other factors almost certainly will be at play. Effective conflict resolution strategies must attend to all dimensions and drivers of a conflict.

In addition to providing insight into how religion is and is not entangled in conflict, research on religious prosociality has begun to provide useful insights about the ways in which religion can contribute to the promotion of tolerance and conflict resolution. Unlike many other cultural markers and worldviews that have contributed to conflict, religions also have resources that tend to promote tolerance and peacemaking.[16] As Norenzayan says, if religion is a maker of conflict, then it also is an unmaker of conflict (Norenzayan 2013: 160).[17] Religion's potential to help resolve conflict and promote peace is the subject of the next chapter, *Religious Prosociality for Conflict Transformation*. Before concluding this chapter, however, I wish briefly to address the issue of extreme militancy in the name of religion.

Extreme Religious Militancy

What are we to make of contemporary groups that sponsor suicide attacks and other acts of extreme violence in the name of religion, as opposed (or in addition) to engaging in conventional forms of armed conflict, like Al Qaeda and ISIS?

Like all paramilitary groups, they are comprised mostly of young men—and, increasingly, but still minimally, young women (Atran 2010a; Halliday 2015)—who use violent tactics that are shocking, and which are meant to shock.[18] Anthropologist Scott Atran, who has studied and interviewed suicide bombers and other violent extremists around the world, concludes from his extensive research (involving many interdisciplinary collaborations) that religiously affiliated militants, including jihadists, generally are, or emerge from, "cliques of youthful friends . . . on a moral mission" (Atran 2010a: 312). Research conducted by political scientist Marc Sageman supports this view (Sageman 2004; Sageman 2008). His "data shows that they are generally idealistic young people seeking dreams of glory fighting for justice and fairness" (Sageman 2008: 35). Political scientist Robert Pape and economist James Feldman distinguish between transnational suicide attackers, who act in defense of distant communities to which they are loyal, and national actors defending their own communities. Though their analysis suggests that transnational attackers work in tightknit groups and national actors more often are independent volunteers (Pape 2005; Pape and Feldman 2010), the latter often may be influenced by and seek the esteem of likeminded peers (Atran 2010a).

All of these scholars find that violent extremists' moral mission is not principally propelled by religion. Pape and Feldman, who analyzed a comprehensive dataset containing details about all suicide attacks occurring since 1980, including the timing of attacks in relation to the inception of associated foreign military occupations, conclude that, "[s]imply put, [resistance to foreign] military occupation accounts for nearly all suicide terrorism around the world since 1980" (Pape and Feldman 2010: 10). ISIS's bombing of a Russian commercial airliner in Egypt on October 31, 2015 and its attacks in Paris on November 13, 2015 seem consistent with this perspective; in September 2015, both countries began striking ISIS militants in portions of Syria controlled (albeit in contravention of international law) by ISIS. Even scholars like Marc Sageman (2008), who place more emphasis on processes of religious radicalization, including belief in a global war against Islam, see specific grievances, such as objection to foreign military occupation, as a necessary precondition to terrorist acts.

Most suicide attacks occur when the foreign military presence is from a country with a different predominant religion than the predominant religion of those in the place where the foreigners are present (Pape and Feldman 2010), but this likely describes the vast majority of contemporary foreign military occupations. Religion is among the features of culture these actors wish to defend; it is one of the sources of shared meaning that binds them together; and they ground their actions, in part, in religious doctrines and passages from texts that justified violent defense of the group centuries or millennia ago. Resistance to foreign occupation nonetheless holds greater explanatory power for suicide attacks, rather than religion as such.[19] Members of some militant groups, like Hamas's founder and leader, Khaled Meshaal, sometimes explicitly frame the group's violent tactics in these terms: "We are a resistance movement against an occupation. . . . We have never sought to kill a Jew because he was a Jew" (Atran 2010a: 399).[20]

Many of those recruited to Islamic militant organizations are recent converts, or come from moderate or largely secularized Muslim families (Sageman 2004; Sageman 2008; Atran 2010a). "[W]hat inspires the most lethal terrorists in the world today," Atran maintains, "is not so much the Koran or religious teachings as a thrilling cause and call to action that promises glory and esteem in the eyes of friends, and through friends, eternal respect and remembrance in the wider world that they will never live to enjoy" (Atran 2010b). Reflecting on the presumption that Islamic fundamentalist religion "independent of American and Western foreign policy" is the cause of suicide attacks, thus justifying military intervention to democratize Muslim countries, Pape and Feldman conclude that "the facts have not fit our presumptions" (Pape and Feldman 2010: 2-3).

While religion may not be the driving motivation of these militants, it would be a mistake to view religion only as cynically manipulated for instrumental purposes in these movements and to view their religious character as irrelevant to most recruits. For some—and perhaps for many recent converts, in particular—religion may be considered an antidote to the unmoored, debased existence the forces of secularization and globalization seem to promote (Atran 2010a). It was right for Muslim leaders to denounce both ISIS's militant and exclusivist form of Islam and the violence ISIS has done in its name (Kaplan 2015),[21] and western leaders' insistence that such extreme militancy has nothing to do with religion is to be applauded as a moral stand against such violence and in defense of the spiritually- and ethically-grounded forms of Islam practiced by the vast majority of Muslims around the world. Discrediting violence in the name of religion and validating and amplifying religious perspectives that encourage tolerance and moderation is imperative.

Nonetheless, we should acknowledge that religion is at least superficially entangled even with the most extreme forms of violence with which it plainly seems to be associated, and we should encourage more research about extreme militancy in the name of religion, as well as methods for addressing it. The strategies and methods useful for addressing this problem may be more about altering Western foreign and military policy, avoiding and reversing radicalization of youth, and other types of policies and programs that are largely beyond the primary focus of this chapter, but understanding the ways in which religion is associated with extreme militancy (ranging from cynical and disingenuous manipulation of religion to sincere belief) and supporting efforts by mainstream religious actors to counter them no doubt can contribute meaningfully to solutions.[22]

Conclusion

This chapter highlights the role of religion in promoting cooperation within groups and the ways in which it is—and is not—implicated in conflict between groups. Religion promotes trust and cooperation among members of a group. No other feature of culture seems to offer so many resources for establishing and maintaining positive, secure group (and individual) identity and, hence, group solidarity. Religion supports a strong sense of *us*, generating a strong sense of *them*, and we know this *us-them* dynamic sometimes can turn violent. Yet, the prosocial features of religion that help a religious group grow and thrive also can contribute to tolerance and the resolution of conflicts between groups. Tapping religious prosociality for conflict transformation is the subject of the next chapter.

Notes

[1] It should be noted up front that much of the research discussed in this chapter was conducted by social scientists who are atheists, but who nonetheless are respectful of religion. Needless to say, the veracity of religious metaphysical claims is beyond the scope of this chapter. Most of these researchers argue that belief in supernatural agents is a byproduct of specific features of human cognition, such as theory of mind, and some argue that the seeming improbability of a religion's metaphysical claims is a factor that increases trust among co-religionists (Atran 2002; Norenzyan 2013). One need not be an atheist, of course, to appreciate and contribute to the emerging science regarding the psychology of religious commitment, as the work of Christian experimental psychologist Justin Barrett demonstrates (Barrett 2004). Theologian Sarah Coakley and biologist and mathematician Martin Nowak, both Christians, nonetheless observe in their introduction to *Evolution, Games, and God: The Principle of Cooperation* (which is the culmination of a long collaboration among a group of theologians, philosophers, and religious and non-religious natural and social scientists) that "if it is simply assumed that 'religion' may be explained away in terms of something else, all attempts to clarify its workings will inevitably fall prey to the same reductive principles," a concern that has led them and collaborators to develop research protocols which "test genuinely *theological* motivations for 'altruistic' human behavior" (Nowak and Coakley 2013: 26). Nowak, Coakley and their collaborators have developed and begun to use such protocols (Rand et al. 2014). This research by scholars who do not share the atheistic orientation of others studying religious prosociality is significant, and perhaps it eventually will produce robust empirical support countering the strains of others' research that Coakley and Nowak consider reductionist. If so, it seems unlikely to me (nor do I think they would expect) that their new line of research would completely negate all findings of others' research, nor the utility of all of those find-

ings (alongside their own) for conflict resolution practice, which is the focus of this chapter.

[2] Biologists Martin Nowak, Corina Tarnita and Edward Wilson (2012) maintain that the biological basis for the evolution of cooperation extends beyond the limits predicted by the theory of kin selection. We might surmise that, in human populations, their theory suggests religion does not function to extend cooperation beyond kin, but rather that it is consistent with a broader, God-given tendency to cooperate, and perhaps has "goaded [groups] to further altruistic efforts" (Rand et al. 2014.) The Nowak, Tarnita and Wilson challenge to the theory of kin selection does not, however, appear to be holding up well to critique by other scientists (Liao, Rong, and Queller 2015).

[3] Primatologist and biological anthropologist Augustin Fuentes argues that development of our capacity for large scale cooperation precedes the development of religion (Fuentes 2014). There also is some counter-evidence suggesting that prosocial forms of religion are most prevalent in mid-sized populations (Brown and Eff 2010). Norenzayan himself suggests there may come a point in the largest societies when material goods and secular institutions are secure enough that religion is "no longer need[ed] . . . to sustain large scale cooperation. In short: secular societies climbed the ladder of religion, and then kicked it away" (Norenzayan 2013: 172).

[4] "A mountain of evidence in psychology and economics reveals how powerful social monitoring incentives are. . . . Experiments in social psychology have also shown that any cue that increases the feeling of being watched . . . increases prosocial tendencies, and those that encourage feelings of being hidden from view . . . license more selfishness and cheating" (Norenzayan 2013: 20). This is equally true whether or not the monitor one perceives is associated with religion (Bateson, Nettle, and Roberts 2006; Shariff and Norenzayan 2007). Economist Thomas Schelling, a pioneer of game theoretic approaches to conflict analysis, foreshadowed the findings regarding supernatural monitoring: "In a society that believes absolutely in a superior power that will punish falsehood when asked to do so and that everybody knows everybody else believes in, 'cross my heart and hope to die' is a sufficient formula for conveying truth voluntarily" (Schelling 1980: 116).

[5] In a meta-analysis of 93 studies on the effects of religious priming for prosocial behavior (i.e., reminding research subjects of God or religion before presenting an opportunity for prosocial behavior), Azim Shariff and colleagues found that "[c]ontrary to previous speculation, . . . religious priming produced no consistent effect on the non-religious," leading them to speculate that "responsiveness to religious cues depends to a significant extent on culturally transmitted beliefs . . .." (Shariff et al. 2015: 15). Many religious people no doubt would take umbrage with the suggestion that their prosocial conduct is primarily attributable to a sense of being watched by a divine agent whose vengeance they fear, and would instead attribute this conduct to elements within their religions that encourage amity, compassion, charity, forgiveness, generosity, and other prosocial values. One might fairly question whether prosocial conduct premised upon a sense of being watched (not to mention fear of punishment) can properly be understood as being associated with trust, as opposed to mere compliance behavior. Social psychologist Mariska Kappmeier has developed a more nuanced, multivariate theory that conceives of trust in terms of the presence or absence of indicia of seven super-ordinate personal and relational qualities (competence, integrity, predictability, compassion, compatibility, collaboration, and security), rather than something dependent upon a sense that one is being monitored (Kappmeier 2016). Kappmeier's approach can be used to identify and study other features of religion that promote prosocial conduct, and to do so in a way that is more broadly consistent with the self-understandings of religious people.

[6] Data from numerous cross-cultural laboratory and field experiments support the notion that individual prosocial behavior is causally associated with religion (Xygalatas 2013; Shariff et al. 2015). The theory that mass commitment to Big Gods explains the transition from small-scale group life to the large-scale group life we see in most places around the world today, however, relies heavily upon various studies conducted over the past 50 years that attempt to determine the correlation between group size and belief in a Big God (aka a "moralizing High God"), while controlling for other variables, like relative resource scarcity. The findings from these correlational analyses generally are consistent with the "Big Gods, big groups" theory, but there remain open

questions, particularly with respect to groups outside the Abrahamic religions, about which more, and currently more compelling, data exist (Atkinson, Latham and Watts 2014). Among the major religions, Buddhism seems least consistent with the Big Gods theory, though "counter-intuitive agents" exist within many strains of Buddhism (Pyysiäinen 2003). Norenzayan nonetheless sees "karmic eschathologies," such as those in Hinduism, Buddhism and Jainism, in which "[r]ebirth links up with the idea of ethical causation across lifetimes," as another mechanism promoting prosocial behavior that plays "a central role in the cooperative sphere" (Norenzayan 2015: 70). It is important to note that Norenzayan and his collaborators do not claim that Big Gods are the only prosocial feature of religion, nor, of course, that religion is the only prosocial feature of human culture (Norenzayan 2015).

[7] I use this acronym, rather than the phrase signified by its first two letters, because that phrase constitutes a claim by the group that is deeply problematic and offensive to many Muslims.

[8] Whatever modest sense of appreciation some inhabitants of territory controlled by ISIS initially felt has since been exhausted by ISIS's inability to continue to provide jobs and services, not to mention its onerous taxation and incredible brutality (Hubbard 2015b).

[9] Nowak and colleagues maintain that the role of punishment in the evolution of cooperation has been inflated (Dreber et al. 2008).

[10] Neuroscientist Sam Harris, one of the "New Atheists," calls religion "the most potent source of human conflict, past and present" (Harris 2005: 35). An empiricist, Harris cautions that "an insufficient taste for evidence regularly brings out the worst in us" (Harris 2005: 26). Like biologist and fellow New Atheist Richard Dawkins (Dawkins 2006), however, Harris nonetheless shows little interest in studying religion with the rigorous empirical orientation and methods he deploys in his work as a scientist. Writing about the causes of violence involving religious people, Dawkins says "[t]he very word 'religions' is bowdlerized to 'communities', as in 'intercommunal warfare'" (Dawkins 2006: 21). Like Harris, Dawkins thus advances the notion that religion is the cause of conflict involving religious people, which is a view that has been discredited by scientists studying conflict involving religion. Psychologist and prominent atheist Steven Pinker is no friend of religion, but does not go quite as far as Harris. In his 802-page, data-driven explanation of the historical decline in all types of violence, *The Better Angels of Our Nature: Why Violence has Declined,* Pinker acknowledges that "particular religious movements at particular times in history have worked against violence" (Pinker 2011: 677) and maintains that "[r]eligion plays no single role in the history of violence because religion has not been a single force in the history of anything" (Pinker 2011: 678). He nonetheless opens his book with a (textually accurate) litany of heinous acts reported or sanctioned in the Bible, then returns frequently to the theme of religious support for violence, cruelty and intolerance throughout his book. Pinker maintains that "[t]he theory that religion is a force for peace, often heard among the religious right and its allies today, does not fit the facts of history" (Pinker 2011: 677), but this position is not reached using the unbiased empirical orientation and quantitative methods with which he studies the history of violence more generally, nor the other subjects to which he has turned his attention, like human cognition. It is unsurprising that some of the (mostly atheist) social scientists studying religion in a comparatively unbiased manner distance themselves from these critics of religion (Atran 2010a). For example, as atheist experimental anthropologist Scott Atran muses (rather ironically) about the flimsy empirical basis underlying the New Atheists' crusade against religion, "Well, damn the facts; world salvation is on the march here" (Atran 2010a, 417).

[11] Suicide attacks by Israeli Jews are not common, so the researchers assessed attitudes among Israelis toward Israeli settler Baruch Goldstein's February 25, 1994 attack at a West Bank Muslim holy site, during which he killed 29 Muslims and died himself.

[12] Seul concluded previously that so-called "religious conflict" is "caused by the same material factors and social dynamics that incite and fuel conflict between ethnic, racial, and other identity groups. . . . Religion is not the cause of `religious conflict'; rather, for many, it still provides the most secure basis for maintenance of a positively regarded social identity, and it frequently supplies the fault line along which inter-group identity and resource competition occurs" (Seul 1999: 564). Atran, likewise, sees

"no evidence that with religion banished, science will reduce violence . . . Religions throughout history have tended to lessen social distance within a group as they have increased distance and occasions for misunderstanding and conflict with other groups. But so do other determinants of cultural identity, such as language, ethnicity and nationalism" (Atran 2010a: 414). Social Psychologist Jonathan Haidt, who also studies religious prosociality, says, "[r]eligion is . . . often an *accessory* to atrocity, rather than the driving force of the atrocity" (Haidt 2012: 268.) Norenzayan concludes that "[r]eligion is an important player, but rarely the primary cause of wars and violent conflicts" (Norenzayan 2013: 157). These views comport with Norris and Inglehart's belief that "[t]he expanding gap between the sacred and the secular societies around the globe will have important consequences for world politics, making the role of religion increasingly salient on the global agenda. It is by no means inevitable that the religious gap will lead to greater ethno-religious conflict and violence" (Norris and Inglehart 2011: 241).

[13] Citizens of the officially atheist former Soviet Union felt monitored to a degree that might approach the "supernatural," as perhaps do some people in the United States in the age of digital surveillance by the NSA.

[14] It must be noted, however, that Ian Hansen and Ara Norenzayan found that "[t]heists were 19 times as likely as non-theists to be exclusivist" (Hansen and Norenzayan 2009: 2). This suggests that efforts by religious authorities to promote pluralist (or, at least, inclusivist) understandings of their religious traditions are among the most effective things they can do to help reduce intergroup tension.

[15] One recent quantitative analysis of armed conflicts in developing countries over a 20-year period (1990-2010) may begin to shed some light on the question of when religious identities or other religious factors do and do not play a role in the onset of armed conflict (Basedau, Pfeiffer and Vüllers 2016). The study found that armed conflict between two groups is more likely when both their ethnicities and their religions differ (what the study calls "interreligious conflict"). It also found that, when a religious group has ideological differences with the state (what the study calls "theological conflict"), such as when the group wants to replace secular law with religious law, calls to violence by religious leaders have some predictive effect regarding the onset of armed conflict. When one religion is dominant (*i.e.*, at least 60% of a country's citizens adhere to the same religion), the study found that this can contribute to the onset of types of armed conflict other than "interreligious conflict" and "theological conflict" (*e.g.*, conflict between two religious groups with mixed ethnic identity or conflict between a religious group and an ethnic group). The study found, however, that both religious fractionalization (*i.e.*, high religious diversity) and religious polarization within a society (*i.e.*, the existence of religious groups that are roughly equal in size) reduce the likelihood of armed conflict.

[16] Political scientist Matthew Walton and conflict resolution practitioner Susan Hayward (2014) provide an excellent example of recent scholarship identifying tolerance promoting religious resources within a specific tradition (Theravada Buddhism) and conflict context (Myanmar's long-running civil war) and offering suggestions about how to employ those resources to help transform tensions among some Buddhists and Muslims.

[17] This point also has been emphasized by Casanova (1994), Seul (1999), Appleby (2000), Gopin (2000; 2012: 271-279), Seul (2006), and others.

[18] Suicide bombings and beheadings may be meant to shock, but Stephen Walt (Walt 2015) rightly encourages us not to "pretend that today's 'advanced' societies are uniformly genteel or moral either. An innocent blown up by an ill-aimed drone strike is just as much a victim as someone brutally beheaded by the Islamic State."

[19] Speaking about the assumptions he held as he began his research on suicide terrorism, Robert Pape says, "I thought I was going to figure out when an Islamic fundamentalist goes from being a devout, observant Muslim to somebody who then is suicidally violent. But there was no data available, so I put together this complete database of suicide attacks around the world . . . I was really struck that half the suicide attacks were secular. I began to look at the patterns and I noticed that they were tightly clustered, both in where they occurred and the timing, and that 95 percent of the suicide attacks were in response to a military occupation" (Balch 2015). Commenting on journalist Graeme Wood's March 2015 article about ISIS in *The Atlantic*, in which Wood

argues that ISIS's chief objective is to "[return all of] civilization to a seventh-century [religious] legal environment, and ultimately to [bring] about the apocalypse" (Wood 2015), Pape maintains that Wood is "just wrong. . . Wood is painting a picture of ISIS as all religious, all the time. Interestingly . . . he is talking about how the main difference with Osama bin Laden's Al Qaeda is that ISIS really wants territory. Wanting territory means there's a community that wants a state. ISIS, and most suicide groups, are driven by an ideal of nationalism; they want to control their destiny with a state. ISIS is composed of a leadership of about 25 people, which is one-third very heavily religious, for sure; one-third former Saddam [Hussein] military officers who are Baathists, who are secular; and one-third who are Sunni militia, Sunni tribal leaders. That just conveniently is lost in the Wood piece. It's definitely the case that ISIS wants to kill people who are not part of its community. But this is normal in nationalist groups" (Balch 2015).

[20] There are obvious differences between an organization with transnational ambitions, like ISIS, for example, and Hamas. ISIS seeks to build a theocratic state and to dominate the surrounding region from it, displacing a perceived hegemon to which it attributes many problems near its base and around the world (Bunzel 2015). Although Hamas once campaigned for imposing uniform religious standards, like requiring women to wear the hijab, on all Palestinians, and there have been some sporadic, though less ambitious, efforts to do so since, it never has officially declared imposition of a specific interpretation of Islamic law on all Palestinians to be among its policy objectives, nor does it advocate global jihad.

[21] Among many in the West and some smaller regions around the world, Muslims presently are viewed as more prone to violence than other groups, but data compiled and analyzed by political scientist Steven Fish dispel this invidious stereotype, clearly demonstrating that Muslims generally are not violent people. Non-Muslim countries average 7.5 murders per 100,000 citizens per year, for example, while the murder rate in Muslim countries is less than a third of that number, whether or not those Muslim countries have authoritarian regimes. Nor is large-scale political violence more prevalent in predominantly Muslim countries (Fish 2011). Muslims were, however, responsible for about 60% of the approximately 200 terrorist bombings that occurred between 1994 and 2008 (Fish 2011). Fish sees this statistic as a response by a small number of extremists to the fact that "in the contemporary world, Christians won big." As Fish explains, "Christians drew the boundaries of the states in which most Muslims live. . . . Currently, people in Christian countries make up one-third of the world's population, while holding two-thirds of its wealth and nine-tenths of its military might" (Fish 2015). Many Muslims feel frustrated and humiliated by this history and its legacy, Fish maintains, but only a small number of people express those feelings violently, as (according to Fish) we could expect to happen if the tables were turned (Fish 2015). Of course, Muslims in the Middle East and elsewhere generally have a negative view of groups that sponsor terrorism and their violent tactics (Pew Research Center 2014a).

[22] For example, Scott Atran (2010a: 415) observes that "Islam also stops violence. The only organizations I've found that have actually enticed significant numbers of voluntary defections from the ranks of would-be martyrs and jihadis—in Indonesia, Saudi Arabia, Pakistan, Egypt, and elsewhere—are Muslim religious organizations."

References

Ahmed, A. 2015. Taliban Justice Gains Favor as Official Afghan Courts Fail. *New York Times*, February 1, 2015. Available online at http://www.nytimes.com/2015/02/01/world/asia/taliban-justice-gains-favor-as-official-afghan-courts-fail.html (last accessed May 17, 2016).

Appleby, R.S. 2000. *The Ambivalence of the Sacred: Religion, Violence, and Reconciliation*. Oxford, UK: Rowman & Littlefield Publishers, Inc.

Asad, T., W. Brown, J. P. Butler and S. Mahmood. 2013. *Is Critique Secular? Blasphemy, Injury, and Free Speech*. New York: Fordham University Press.

Atkinson, Q. D., A. J. Latham and J. Watts. 2014. Are Big Gods a Big Deal in the Emergence of Big Groups? *Religion, Brain & Behavior* 1-9. DOI: 10.1080/2153599X.2014.928359 (last accessed August 13, 2015).

Atran, S. 2002. *In Gods We Trust: The Evolutionary Landscape of Religion*. Oxford, UK:

Oxford University Press.

Atran, S. 2010a. *Talking to the Enemy: Violent Extremism, Sacred Values, and What It Means to be Human.* London, England: Penguin Books.

Atran, S. 2010b. Pathways To and From Violent Extremism: The Case for Science-based Field Research. *Statement Before the Senate Armed Services Subcommittee on Emerging Threats & Capabilities, March 10, 2010.* Available at http://www.edge.org/3rd_culture/atran10/atran10_index.html (last accessed July 31, 2015).

Austin, G., T. Kranock and T. Oommen. 2003. God and War: An Audit and Exploration. Available at http://news.bbc.co.uk/2/shared/spl/hi/world/04/war_audit_pdf/pdf/war_audit.pdf (last accessed August 14, 2015).

Axelrod, R. 2006. *The Evolution of Cooperation.* Cambridge, MA: Basic Books.

Balch, E. 2015. Myth Busting: Robert Pape on Suicide Terrorism, ISIS, and U.S. Foreign Policy. *Chicago Policy Review,* May 5, 2015. Available online at http://chicagopolicyreview.org/2015/05/05/myth-busting-robert-pape-on-isis-sui cide-terrorism-and-u-s-foreign-policy/ (last accessed on September 7, 2015).

Barrett, J. L. 2004. *Why Would Anyone Believe in God?* Lanham, MD: AltaMira Press.

Basedau, M., B. Pfeiffer and J. Vüllers. 2016. Bad Religion? Religion, Collective Action, and the Onset of Armed Conflict in Developing Countries. *Journal of Conflict Resolution* 60(2): 226-255.

Bateson, M., D. Nettle and G. Roberts. 2006. Cues of Being Watched Enhance Cooperation in a Real-World Setting. *Biology Letters* 2(3): 412-414.

Brewer, M. 1979. In-group Bias in the Minimal Intergroup Situation: A Cognitive-Motivational Analysis. *Psychological Bulletin* 86(2): 307-324.

Brown, C. and E. A. Eff. 2010. The State and the Supernatural: Support for Prosocial Behavior. *Structure and Dynamics* 4(1): 1-21.

Bunzel, C. 2015. From Paper State to Caliphate: The Ideology of the Islamic State. *The Brookings Project on U.S. Relations with the Islamic World Analysis Paper No. 19.* Available online at http://www.brookings.edu/~/media/research/files/papers/2015/03/ideology-of-islamic-state-bunzel/the-ideology-of-the-islamic-stat e.pdf (last accessed July 30, 2015).

Calhoun, C., M. Juergensmeyer and J. VanAntwerpen (eds). 2011. *Rethinking Secularism.* New York: Oxford University Press.

Casanova, J. 1994. *Public Religions in the Modern World.* Chicago: The University of Chicago Press.

Clingingsmith, D., A. I. Khwaja and M. R. Kremer. 2009. Estimating the Impact of the Hajj: Religion and Tolerance in Islam's Global Gathering. *The Quarterly Journal of Economics* 124(3): 1133-1170.

Collier, P. and A. Hoeffler. 2004. Greed and Grievance in Civil War. *Oxford Economic Papers* 56: 563-595.

Connor, W. 1994. *Ethnonationalism: The Quest for Understanding.* Princeton, NJ: Princeton University Press.

Dawkins, R. 2006. *The God Delusion.* Boston, MA: Houghton Mifflin Company.

Dreber, A., D. G. Rand, D. Fudenberg and M. A. Nowak. 2008. Winners Don't Punish. *Nature* 452: 348-351.

Everett, J. A. C., O. S. Haque and D. G. Rand. 2015. *How Good is the Samaritan, and Why? An Experimental Investigation of the Extent and Nature of Religious Prosociality Using Economic Games* (February 27, 2015). Available online at SSRN: http://ssrn.com/abstract=2484659 (last accessed August 14, 2015).

Fish, M. S. 2011. *Are Muslims Distinctive? A Look at the Evidence.* Oxford, UK: Oxford University Press.

Fish, S. 2015. Why is Terror Islamist? *The Washington Post,* January 27, 2015. Available online at http://www.washingtonpost.com/blogs/monkey-cage/wp/2015/01/27/why-is-terror-islamist/ (last accessed August 29, 2015).

Fox, J. 2015. *Political Secularism, Religion, and the State: A Time Series Analysis of Worldwide Data,* edited by D.C. Leege, K.D. Wald, and R.L. Wood. New York: Cambridge University Press.

Fuentes, A. 2014. Hyper-cooperation is Deep in Our Evolutionary History and Individual Perception of Belief Matters. *Religion, Brian & Behavior* 5(4): 284-290. DOI: 10.1080/2153599X.2014.928359 (last accessed August 13, 2015).

Ginges, J., S. Atran, D. Medin and K. Shikaki. 2007. Sacred Bounds on Rational Resolution of Violent Political Conflict. *Proceedings of the National Academy of Sciences*
104(18): 7357-7360.
Ginges, J., I. Hansen, and A. Norenzayan. 2009. Religion and Support for Suicide At-
tacks. *Psychological Science* 20(2): 224-230.
Gopin, M. 2000. *Between Eden and Armageddon: The Future of World Religions, Vio-
lence, and Peacemaking.* Oxford, UK: Oxford University Press.
Gopin, M. 2012. Religion as Destroyer and Creator of Peace: A Postmortem on Failed
Peace Processes. In *Religion and Foreign Affairs: Essential Readings*, edited by
D.R. Hoover and D.M. Johnston. Waco, TX: Baylor University Press.
Habyarimana, J., M. Humphreys, D. N. Posner and J. M. Weinstein. 2007. Why Does
Ethnic Diversity Undermine Public Goods Provision. *American Political Science
Review* 101(4): 709-725.
Haidt, J. 2012. *The Righteous Mind: Why Good People Are Divided by Politics and Reli-
gion.* New York: Pantheon Books.
Halliday, J. 2015. London Schoolgirls among 60 Female Britons Thought to Have Joined
ISIS. *The Guardian*, March 1, 2015. Available online at
http://www.theguardian.com/world/2015/mar/01/london-schoolgirls-60-female-
britons-joined-isis (last accessed August 3, 2015).
Hamilton, W. D. 1964. The Genetical Evolution of Social Behavior, Parts I and II. *Jour-
nal of Theoretical Biology* 7: 1-52.
Hansen, I. and A. Norenzayan. 2009. *Does Religious Belief Promote Religious
Scapegoating?* Manuscript in preparation available at http://www2.psych.ubc.ca/
~anlab/pdf/Hansen%26NorenzayanScapegoating.pdf (last accessed August 29,
2015).
Harris, S. 2005. *The End of Faith: Religion, Terror, and the Future of Reason.* New
York: W.W. Norton & Company, Inc.
Henrich, J. 2009. The Evolution of Costly Displays, Cooperation and Religion: Credibil-
ity Enhancing Displays and Their Implications for Cultural Evolution. *Evolution and
Human Behavior* 30(4): 244-260.
Hoffman, A. J., J. J. Gillespie, D. A. Moore, K. A. Wade-Benzoni, L. L. Thompson and
M. H. Bazerman. 1999. A Mixed-Motive Perspective on the Economics Versus Envi-
ronment Debate. *American Behavioral Scientist* 42(8): 1254-1276.
Hubbard, B. 2015a. Offering Services, ISIS Ensconces Itself in Seized Territories. *New
York Times* (June 17, 2015). A1.
Hubbard, B. 2015b. Statehood Project is Troubled, Those Who Escaped ISIS Say. *New
York Times* (December 2, 2015). A1.
Institute for Economics & Peace. 2014. Five Key Questions Answered on the Link Be-
tween Peace & Religion: A Global Statistical Analysis of the Empirical Link be-
tween Peace and Religion. *Institute for Economics and Peace*, October 2014.
Available online at http://economicsandpeace.org/wp-content/uploads/
2015/06/Peace-and-Religion-Report.pdf (last accessed August 14, 2015).
Kaplan, M. 2015. ISIS Ramadan War: Muslim Leaders Condemn Islamic State Attacks,
Call Holy Month Time for Peace. *International Business Times*, July 1, 2015. Avail-
able online at http://www.ibtimes.com/isis-ramadan-war-muslim-leaders-
condemn-islamic-state-attacks-call-holy-month-time-1990904 (accessed on August
3, 2015).
Kappmeier, M. 2016. Trusting the Enemy: Towards a Comprehensive Understanding of
Trust in Intergroup Conflict. *Peace and Conflict: Journal of Peace Psychology*
22(2) 134-144.
Keen, D. 2007. *Complex Emergencies.* Cambridge, UK: Polity Press.
Laurin, K., A. F. Shariff, J. Henrich and A. C. Kay. 2012. Outsourcing Punishment to
God: Beliefs in Divine Control Reduce Earthly Punishment. *Proceedings of the
Royal Society B.* DOI: 10.1098/rspb.2012.0615 (last accessed August 14, 2015).
Lenfesty, H. L. and J. P. Schloss. 2014. Big Gods and the Greater Good. *Religion, Brain
& Behavior* 40-48. DOI: 10.1080/2153599X.2014.928359 (last accessed August 13,
2015).
Liao, X., S. Rong and D. C. Queller. 2015. Relatedness, Conflict, and the Evolution of
Eusociality. *PLOS Biology.* DOI: 10.1371/journal.pbio.1002098 (last accessed Sep-
tember 16, 2015).

Malhotra, D. 2010. (When) Are Religious People Nicer? Religious Salience and the "Sunday Effect" on Pro-social Behavior. *Judgment and Decision Making* 5(2): 138-143.

Nesse, R. M. 1999. The Evolution of Commitment and the Origins of Religion. *Science and Spirit* 10(2): 32-33, 46.

Norenzayan, A. 2013. *Big Gods: How Religion Transformed Cooperation and Conflict.* Princeton, NJ: Princeton University Press.

Norenzayan, A. 2015. Big Questions About Big Gods: Response and Discussion. *Religion, Brain & Behavior* 5(4): 327-342. DOI: 10.1080/2153599X.2014.928359 (last accessed August 13, 2015).

Norenzayan, A., A. F. Shariff, A. K. Willard, E. Slingerland, W. M. Gervais, R. McNamara and J. Henrich. 2014. The Cultural Evolution of Prosocial Religions. *Behavioral and Brain Sciences* (in press). Available online at http://sharifflab.com/wp-content/uploads/downloads/2015/06/Norenzayan_etal_BBS_preprint.pdf (last accessed August 14, 2015).

Nowak, M. A. and S. Coakley. 2013. Introduction. In *Evolution, Games, and God: The Principle of Cooperation*, edited by M.A. Nowak and S. Coakley. Cambridge, MA: Harvard University Press.

Norris, P. and R. Inglehart. 2011. *Sacred and Secular: Religion and Politics Worldwide.* New York: Cambridge University Press.

Pape, R. A. 2005. *Dying to Win: The Strategic Logic of Suicide Terrorism.* New York: Random House.

Pape, R. A. and J. K. Feldman. 2010. *Cutting the Fuse: The Explosion of Global Suicide Terrorism and How to Stop It.* Chicago: The University of Chicago Press.

Pew Research Center. 2012. *The Global Religious Landscape.* Available online at http://www.pewforum.org/2012/12/18/global-religious-landscape-unaffiliated/ (last accessed August 12, 2015).

Pew Research Center. 2014a. *Concerns about Islamic Extremism on the Rise in Middle East: Negative Opinions of al Qaeda, Hamas and Hezbollah Widespread.* Available online at http://www.pewglobal.org/2014/07/01/concerns-about-islamic-extremism-on-the-rise-in-middle-east/ (last accessed August 29, 2015).

Pew Research Center. 2014b. *Russians Return to Religion, But Not to Church.* Available online at http://www.pewforum.org/2014/02/10/russians-return-to-religion-but-not-to-church/ (last accessed August 29, 2015).

Pew Research Center. 2015. *The Future of World Religions: Population Growth Projections, 2010-2015.* Available online at http://www.pewforum.org/2015/04/02/religious-projections-2010-2050/ (last accessed August 12, 2015).

Phillips, C. and A. Axelrod. 2004. *Encyclopedia of War.* New York: Facts on File.

Piazza, J. and J. F. Landy. 2013. "Lean Not on Your Own Understanding": Belief that Morality is Founded on Divine Authority and Non-Utilitarian Moral Judgments. *Judgment and Decision Making* 8(6): 639-661.

Piazza, J. and P. Sousa. 2014. Religiosity, Political Orientation, and Consequentialist Moral Thinking. *Social Psychological & Personality Science* 5(3): 334-342.

Pinker, S. 2011. *The Better Angels of Our Nature: Why Violence Has Declined.* New York: Penguin Group.

Pyszczynski, T., A. Abdollahi and Z. K. Rothschild. 2009. Does Peace Have a Prayer? The Effects of Morality Salience, Compassionate Values, and Religious Fundamentalism on Hostility Toward Out-groups. *Journal of Experimental Social Psychology* 45(4): 816-827.

Pyysiäinen, I. 2003. Buddhism, Religion, and the Concept of "God". *Numen* 50(2): 147-171.

Rand, D. G., A. Dreber, O. S. Haque, R. J, Kane, M. A. Nowak and S. Coakley. 2014. Religious Motivations for Cooperation: An Experimental Investigation Using Explicit Primes. *Religion, Brain & Behavior* 4(1): 31-48.

Sageman, M. 2004. *Understanding Terror Networks.* Philadelphia: University of Pennsylvania Press.

Sageman, M. 2008. *Leaderless Jihad: Terror Networks in the Twenty-First Century.* Philadelphia: University of Pennsylvania Press.

Schelling, T.C. 1980. *The Strategy of Conflict.* Cambridge, MA: Harvard University Press.

Seul, J. R. 1999. "Ours is the Way of God": Religion, Identity, and Intergroup Conflict. *Journal of Peace Research* 36(5): 553-569.

Seul, J. R. 2006. Religion and Conflict. In *The Negotiator's Fieldbook*, edited by A.K. Schneider and C. Honeyman. Washington, DC: American Bar Association.

Shariff, A. F. 2015. Does Religion Increase Moral Behavior? *Current Opinion in Psychology* 6: 108-113.

Shariff, A. F. and A. Norenzayan. 2007. God is Watching You: Supernatural Agent Concepts Increase Prosocial Behavior in an Anonymous Economic Game. *Psychological Science* 18(9): 803-809.

Shariff, A. F. and A. Norenzayan. 2012. Religious Priming Effects Are Sensitive to Religious Group Boundaries. Unpublished data (referenced in Norenzayan 2013:161). University of Oregon.

Shariff, A. F., A. K. Willard, T. Andersen and A. Norenzayan. 2015. Religious Priming: A Meta-Analysis with a Focus on Prosociality. *Personality and Social Psychology Review* 1-22. DOI: 10.1177/1088868314568811 (last accessed August 13, 2015).

Sheikh, H., J. Ginges, A. Coman and S. Atran. 2012. Religion, Group Threat and Sacred Values. *Judgment and Decision Making* 7(2): 110-118.

Tajfel, H. 1970. Experiments in Intergroup Discrimination. *Scientific American* 223: 96-102.

Taylor, C. 2007. *A Secular Age*. Cambridge, MA: Harvard University Press.

Tetlock, P. E., R. S. Peterson and J. S. Lerner. 1996. Revising the Value Pluralism Model: Incorporating Social Content and Context Postulates. In *The Psychology of Values: The Ontario Symposium, Volume 8*, edited by C. Seligman, J. Olson and M. Zanna. Hillsdale, NJ: Lawrence Erlbaum Associates.

Trivers, R. L. 1971. The Evolution of Reciprocal Altruism. *The Quarterly Review of Biology* 46(1): 35-57.

Vinci, A. 2006. Greed-Grievance Reconsidered: The Role of Power and Survival in the Motivation of Armed Groups. *Civil Wars* 8(1): 25-45.

Walt, S. M. 2015. What Should We Do if the Islamic State Wins?: Live With It. *Foreign Policy*, June 10, 2015. Available online at http://foreignpolicy.com/2015/06/10/what-should-we-do-if-isis-islamic-state-wins-containment/ (last accessed August 29, 2015).

Waytz, A., L. L. Young and J. Ginges. 2014. Motive Attribution Asymmetry for Love vs. Hate Drives Intractable Conflict. *Proceedings of the National Academy of Sciences* 111(44): 15687-15692.

Welch, M. R., D. Sikkink, E. Sartain and C. Bond. 2004. Trust in God and Trust in Man: The Ambivalent Role of Religion in Shaping Dimensions of Social Trust. *Journal for the Scientific Study of Religion* 43(3): 317-343.

Wood, G. 2015. What ISIS Really Wants. *The Atlantic*, March 2015. Available online at http://www.theatlantic.com/magazine/archive/2015/03/what-isis-really-wants/384980/ (last accessed September 7, 2015).

Xygalatas, D. 2013. Effects of Religious Setting on Cooperative Behavior: A Case Study from Mauritius. *Religion, Brain & Behavior* 3(2): 91-102.

ೞ **88** ೞ

Religious Prosociality for
Conflict Transformation

Jeffrey R. Seul

Editors' Note: In the second of two chapters on religion and conflict, Seul reviews the research on religious prosociality, and the ability of religion to help people relate positively to others, and to help resolve conflict. He offers examples of specific strategies to encourage cooperative behavior when working with religious stakeholders in a conflict.

As we saw in the previous chapter, *The Role of Religion in Cooperation and Conflict*, religious beliefs and practices help bind people together in groups, and groups sometimes compete. Yet the prosocial features of our religions that help groups form and develop strong internal bonds also can and do help build bridges between people from different groups. Most contemporary conflict resolution theory and practice focused on conflicts that involve religion, particularly the work of religious peacebuilding scholars and practitioners, has given little or no attention to social scientific research on religious prosociality and what it tells us about the ways in which religion is and is not entangled with conflict and how it can and does contribute to conflict transformation.

The contemporary (and still largely Western) academic field of religious peacebuilding, one key strain of which is about religious actors working to prevent or end violent conflicts, has grown rapidly over the

Jeff Seul is Lecturer on the Practice of Peace at Harvard Divinity School and co-chair of the Peace Appeal Foundation, an organization that helps local stakeholders launch and sustain peace and national dialogue processes to end or avoid war. Mr. Seul previously taught at Harvard Law School and was a senior associate of the Program on International Conflict Analysis and Resolution at Harvard's Weatherhead Center for International Affairs. Much of his work is focused on approaches to transformation of conflict with a religious dimension. Mr. Seul is also a partner in the international law firm Holland & Knight, the former general counsel of a startup tech firm (Groove Networks), a Roman Catholic and a Zen practitioner.

past two decades, both in terms of theory development and in terms of number and scope of applied activities. This growth was sparked, in part, by the publication in 1994 of *Religion, The Missing Dimension of Statecraft* (Johnson and Sampson 1994) the first in-depth study in the modern West of religion's potential to contribute positively to official and unofficial diplomacy in the context of contemporary international relations. This was the year after Samuel Huntington's article *The Clash of Civilizations?* appeared in *Foreign Affairs* (Huntington 1993). That article and the book (Huntington 1996) that followed it tend to characterize religion as essentialist, reified, and conflict generating. The field's growth began to accelerate in 2000, with the publication of Scott Appleby's *The Ambivalence of the Sacred: Religion, Violence, and Reconciliation* and Marc Gopin's *Between Eden and Armageddon: The Future of World Religions, Violence and Peacemaking.*

While violence in the name of God grabs headlines, many religious actors are working quietly to avert or end conflict, whether or not it involves religion, and to promote peace in other ways (Smock 2001; Hayward 2012)—as, indeed, they have been doing for millennia. According to one study published in 2011, religious actors had played a mediating role in the vast majority of post-Cold War peace processes designed to end civil wars (21 of 25), playing a very direct and decisive mediating role in over half of these cases (11). Well-known examples include the successful mediation efforts by the Roman Catholic Community of Sant'Edigio and the work of Muslims and Christians through the Interfaith Mediation Center to reduce conflict in Nigeria. They also played significant roles in many of the reconciliation and transitional justice cases examined (Toft, Philpott and Shah 2011). There is resurgent interest among researchers and policymakers in religion as a positive force in international affairs, including interest in "very non-political notions such as reconciliation, forgiveness, healing of relations, and apology . . . connected with religious world views" that are increasingly "included in contemporary discourse on [international relations]" (Kulska 2015). Former United States Secretary of State Madeleine Albright asserts that religious organizations "have more resources, more skilled personnel, a longer attention span, more experience, more dedication and more success in fostering reconciliation than any government" (Albright 2006: 77).

Religions obviously have resources (texts, norms, rituals, etc.) that can be used to justify and promote cooperation or conflict (Appleby 2000; Gopin 2000; Seul 2006: 323-334). While resources that more readily can be used to promote cooperation often are deployed to expand and strengthen bonds within religious groups, and resources that more readily can be used to justify conflict sometimes are deployed to maintain and defend the boundaries of religious groups, examples of religion supporting tolerance and cooperation between and among groups are abundant.[1] One contemporary opportunity and challenge for those who wish to help prevent or transform conflict involving religion is to tap into religion's prosocial impulses more systematically in efforts to improve intergroup relations.[2]

Effective conflict transformation efforts can, and often must, be incredibly varied, encompassing different modes of advocacy, third-party and internal mediation, interaction within and between groups, and social action (Ricigliano 2012). [See also NDR: Coleman et al., *Intractable 1 and 2*; NDR: Coleman & Ricigliano, *Getting in Sync*] While the (mediated or unmediated) negotiation of a ceasefire agreement, peace accord or new constitution is a focal point activity in efforts to transform most violent conflicts, a document like this typically is just a milestone, however important it may be, in an ongoing process of building more functional structures and relationships within a society. Most peace processes that lead to long-term social and political stability are akin to social movements that involve diverse actors and diverse forms of action (Lederach 2003; Weissmann 2008; Ricigliano 2012). Key actors involved in any peace process must find direct and indirect ways to engage many more people in the process, not only through dialogue, but also through modes of communication and experiences that help to overcome differences, serve basic human needs, and unite and reconcile people who have been in conflict. Religious actors can engage in peace practice not only by participating in negotiations and political dialogue, but also through other forms of speech (e.g., preaching) and action (e.g., group ritual or provision of social services), however loosely or tightly connected to official negotiations and dialogues these activities may be.

The "Big Gods, Big groups" hypothesis introduced above in *The Role of Religion in Cooperation and Conflict* and contending theories will continue to be debated, but the potential value to the field of conflict resolution of this new strain of social scientific research regarding religious prosociality already is becoming apparent, whether or not a consensus regarding grand theories ultimately emerges. To date, most theory and practice directed at conflicts that involve religion, including work done by religious peacebuilders, has not systematically accounted for insights derived from the empirical research methods used by social scientists, nor has it routinely been evaluated by them.[3] Scholars and practitioners have advanced what would seem to be many valuable approaches to employing religious resources to promote peace, such as using practices of forgiveness and reconciliation in conflict resolution efforts (Gort, Jansen and Vroom 2002; Helmick and Petersen 2001) and amplifying pro-peace doctrinal strains within a tradition (Abu-Nimer 2003; Walton and Hayward 2014), but they have lacked rigorous ways to determine which approaches are most effective, to fine-tune approaches, and to develop new approaches. The new social science regarding the relationship among religion, conflict and conflict resolution already is beginning to produce insights that can increase the effectiveness of efforts to resolve conflicts in which religion is a factor.

The remainder of this chapter provides an overview of some early insights from the new social science on religious prosociality that should prove useful to conflict resolution practitioners and other peacemakers working to help prevent or transform a conflict involving religious actors. These examples mainly pertain to what Rob Ricigliano (2012) calls attitudinal (i.e., group perspective change) and transactional (i.e., negotiation interaction) contributions to peacebuilding, but research on religious prosociality also can make structural contributions to peacebuilding (for example, by influencing law and policy on such matters as free exercise of religion and religious militancy) (Ricigliano 2012: 35). Some of this research affirms current practices; some suggests refinements or new modes of practice. I see this research and the insights it offers as a complement to other perspectives and approaches within and beyond the social sciences, including more qualitative perspectives and approaches.[4] Practitioners have much to gain from this new line of scholarship, but effective practice must be multi-disciplinary, including careful attention to the history of a conflict (Thompson 2009).

Devoted Actors Defending Sacred Values

Much conflict resolution theory is premised upon the hypothetical "rational actor" model that dominates modern economic theory. This model has been tempered by findings from psychology about actual human perception and cognition, but this tempered view of rationality still assumes that individuals always seek to achieve outcomes that maximize net personal, worldly gains; sometimes, according to this perspective, we simply are prone to errors in perception and judgment that prevent us from optimally serving our self-interest (Bazerman and Shonk 2005).

Some conduct, from suicide attacks to forgone opportunities to resolve a conflict on terms widely judged by others to be beneficial, seems so to defy self-interest, however, that it strains the rational actor model to the breaking point. This sort of conduct makes more sense when viewed from the perspective of a *devoted actor* model, in which one is willing to defend what is at stake in the conflict at great, and even ultimate, this-worldly personal cost (Atran 2003). Devoted actors do not seek outcomes that maximize self-interest in mundane or material terms; they act to preserve and defend a moral order with which they and their compatriots identify completely (Atran, Axelrod and Davis 2007; Ginges and Atran 2009; Fiske and Rai 2015). Many religious people undoubtedly conceive of themselves and behave as devoted actors in many situations.

The devoted actor can, of course, be seen as an absolutely resolute rational actor; as a person who values one thing (like resistance to foreign occupation) much more than other things (like the prospect of continued this-worldly existence with family and friends) that most of us give comparable weight when making decisions (and which other theists believe God wills for them as much or more). In this sense, the devoted actor who resorts to violence is acting to maximize personal gain. He simply ascribes much higher value to outcomes that others either consider immoral or as entailing unacceptable costs.

This point highlights a major difference between a typical secular materialist worldview and a typical theistic religious worldview. Many religious people believe that acting in accordance with God's will, following ethical principles, and struggling for moral causes lead to nearness to God, salvation, and eternal well-being, all of which are, in a sense, considered personal gains consistent with one's worldview. A person with such a religious worldview may well consider the espoused religious justification for a suicide attacker's conduct to be theologically unsound (not a true expression of God's will) or disingenuous (not truly motivated by religion), yet she herself does try to discern and act in keeping with God's will in her own life, and she accepts and appreciates that other religious people also try to do so. To the extent she makes what she herself or others consider to be sacrifices along the way, these sacrifices are rational when considered from inside her worldview. The secular materialist, by contrast, regards the suicide attacker's conduct as irrational, not only because it fails to account for costs she believes the attacker should wish to avoid (like loss of one's own life and the likelihood of retaliation against members of one's family and community), but also because she considers the attacker's religious worldview to be false.

Some suggest that (religious or secular) sacred values may not really be incommensurable (non-tradable) with more mundane (religious or secular) interests. Some values that are deeply-held by some people may well be more subject to compromise when one's alternatives to negotiation are unattractive (Tenbrunsel et al.; Bazerman 2009). There is evidence, for example, that environmentalists are more open to compromise when they perceive significant litigation risk (Hoffman et al. 1999; Tetlock 2003). Studies by experimental anthropologist Scott Atran, political scientist Robert Axelrod and their colleagues (and the daily news streams from the fronts of civil wars and culture wars) indicate, however, that many conflicts with devoted actors involved in armed conflict and extremely polarized political disputes are likely to remain immune to negotiation so long as efforts to resolve them solely employ methods that treat sacred values as if they were readily tradable. From a practical perspective, we would be wise to assume in these situations that concessions involving sacred values cannot be bought with concessions on more mundane matters, even though, with careful attention to process, including the sequencing of moves, a package deal in which all parties to a conflict realize gains and losses on both sacred and mundane matters ultimately may be possible "within an overarching moral frame of social duties and (material) attempts to balance duties," rather than through trades that ask devoted actors to disregard felt duties imposed by sacred values (Atran and Axelrod 2008: 229).[5]

In one study, social psychologist Jeremy Ginges, Atran and other researchers assessed Israelis' and Palestinians' and other combatants' willingness to end their conflicts through material concessions and compromises on issues to which one or both of the communities in conflict attached sacred values (e.g., territory, the right of return, and the status of Jerusalem). They found that proposed trades in which one side would concede something to which it attached sacred value in exchange for material benefits (e.g., money) generated a "backfire effect," increasing resistance to resolution of the conflict. However, even the most hawkish members of each community were open to proposals in which each side made concessions involving sacred values (Ginges et al. 2007; Atran, Axelrod and Davis 2007). The conventional thinking among conflict resolution theorists and practitioners is that incremental progress on resolution of more mundane issues eventually can lead to willingness to compromise on major issues of symbolic importance, but this research suggests instead that symbolic gestures (like demonstrations of recognition and respect or an apology) may pave the way for negotiation of more mundane issues (Atran and Axelrod 2008). The implication, of course, is that peacemakers should invest at least as much energy in efforts to achieve early symbolic concessions as they invest in efforts to achieve material concessions.

Atran and Axelrod suggest numerous strategies for reframing sacred values to make trades involving them more tenable (Atran and Axelrod 2008; Atran 2010a: 382-389). These reframing strategies include the following (which I illustrate with examples):

- *Updating how sacred values are expressed to signal retreat from or revision of claims one knows are inaccurate or out-of-step with current realities.* For example, before the Boy Scouts of America (BSA) revised its policy on inclusion of homosexual youth and leaders, it progressively relaxed prior claims about the morality of homosexuality.
- *Expressing or operationalizing sacred values in ways that are creatively ambiguous.* The BSA's new membership standard says a person cannot be excluded from the organization based

solely upon "sexual orientation or preference," thus allowing those involved to "agree to disagree" on the nature of homosexuality, while paving the way for inclusion of homosexuals. Years before the 2000 Camp David Summit, Israeli legal scholar Ruth Lapidoth proposed that Jerusalem's Holy Esplanade (the Temple Mount to Jews, and Al Aqsa Mosque to Muslims) be regarded as subject to Divine Sovereignty (Lapidoth 1992), and Jordan's King Hussein later suggested many times that *all* holy sites in Jerusalem be regarded as subject to Divine Sovereignty, rather than the sovereignty of one party or divided into sovereign parts. This notion was seriously explored at the summit, but was rejected because religious leaders were not sufficiently involved in the process and the suggestion raises many complications regarding religious understandings of holy sites in general, and the Holy Esplanade in particular (Hassner 2009: 86). Nonetheless, Professor Lapidoth and King Hussein were suggesting a creatively ambiguous solution to the symbolic dimension of the disputes over Jerusalem's holy sites that was intended to open the way for compromise on more mundane matters.

- *Change the context or time horizon, so the stakes are lowered here and now.* The recent multi-lateral agreement regarding Iran's nuclear capacity is intended to delay (for 15 years), but not entirely eliminate, Iran's ability to develop a nuclear arsenal eventually. Assuming the agreement is respected by all parties, sanctions against Iran will be lifted, but Iran's leaders can credibly claim they still stand by Iran's "sovereign right" to develop a nuclear bomb.

- *Prioritize among sacred values without abandoning any of them.* Many environmentalists and other supporters of renewable energy and many supporters of fossil fuels likely agree that job creation is desirable (and, for some, even a sacred value), even if they do not agree on the scientific case for climate change. Policies that phase in renewable energy production and phase out reliance on coal in the nearer term and natural gas in the longer term, and which focus on creating jobs in the transitional fossil fuel and renewable energy sectors now and later seek a (shifting) balance among prioritized values, and thus might be negotiable among these staunchly opposed players. Laws creating buffer zones around abortion clinics and waiting periods and/or optional counseling prior to abortions balance pro-life and pro-choice perspectives on abortion and the principle of free speech, which both sides value.

■ *Seize low-cost opportunities to demonstrate respect for others'*
sacred values. During Nelson Mandela's first secret meeting
with South African President F.W. de Klerk, Mr. Mandela
opened with a respectful, in-depth summary of Afrikaner
history, experience and perspectives, as he understood them.
Mr. de Klerk later reported feeling utterly disarmed by this
opening gesture and completely disposed to listen to and work
with Mr. Mandela. Mr. Mandela's gesture cost him nothing, but
helped achieve much for all South Africans.

Other reframing strategies include appeals to shared values that will be
served through an agreement in which each side compromises on some
sacred value that is not shared and breaking a sacred value down into
smaller elements or steps. The abortion waiting period law discussed
above is an example of the latter strategy. It may result in fewer abortions, even if does not eliminate all abortions (a goal that pro-life advocates would continue to pursue). All of these reframing strategies have a
common logic and objective: They enable a party to enter and negotiate
within the other's frame of reference without leaving one's own frame of
reference, and they permit parties to retain (sometimes in a refigured
way) all, or nearly all, of the *symbolic value* associated with what they
hold sacred while enabling them to divide the *mundane or material*
value connected to what they hold sacred.

Tolerance-Promoting Texts and Doctrine

Religious peacebuilding experts often encourage religious leaders and
others to amplify texts and doctrine that encourage tolerance (Coward
and Smith 2004), but does spotlighting of pro-peace textual material and
ideas help? If so, in which circumstances? Social scientists may help
provide some answers to these questions.

For example, through decades of collaborative research, including
studies of Israelis and Palestinians and U.S. citizens reminded of the 9/11
attacks, social psychologists Sheldon Solomon, Jeff Greenberg and Tom
Pyszczynski consistently have found that "[d]eath fears inflame violence
toward others with different beliefs, especially those whom we designate
as evil" (Solomon, Greenberg and Pyszczynski 2015: 144). A fascinating
and encouraging study by Pyszczynski and other colleagues, however,
found that Iranian conservative Muslim and U.S. fundamentalist
Christian subjects were more likely to support violent action against the
other group when reminded of their mortality, but that support for
violence decreased to the same levels expressed by moderate citizens of
each country when they also were reminded of their religion's
compassionate values (for Muslims, the saying "Do goodness to others
because Allah loves those who do good"; for Christians, the saying "Love
thy neighbor as thyself") (Pyszczynski, Abdollahi and Rothschild 2009).

These priming studies are not conducted in the ordinary course of subjects' lives, but it seems reasonable to assume that reminding people frequently (in religious services, in daily life, and during conflict resolution activities) both of the transience of this earthly life (through, for instance, the Christian ethic and practice of *momento mori* or Buddhism's *Five Remembrances*) and of their tradition's compassionate values may promote a similar shift in perspective.

A recent set of studies by social psychologists Adam Waytz, Liane Young and Jeremy Ginges involving Democrats and Republicans in the United States (in one study) and Israelis and Palestinians (in a separate study) revealed that parties to intense political and ethnoreligious conflicts unconsciously attribute their own group's aggression more to love of their group and the other group's aggression more to hatred of the out-group, a bias they call "motive attribution asymmetry" (Waytz, Young and Ginges 2014). Interestingly, a material reward (in this case, money) offered to some study participants for accuracy in assessing the other side's true motivations "reduce[d] egocentrism through increasing effortful perspective-taking" (Waytz, Young and Ginges 2014: 15690). This suggests that structures and incentives designed to help a group see and experience the real, in-group focused motivations of the other group might help dampen this bias (and other biases). Interreligious dialogue that is structured and guided in keeping with findings from research on attitude change and the sort of perspective taking exercises that are standard fare in conflict resolution trainings are examples of these types of structures, and perhaps "effortful perspective taking" would be increased if small, appropriate incentives were deftly incorporated into the experience (e.g., facilitators might offer to pick up the tab for the group's dinner if participants effectively assess others' motivations).

Devotional Practices

An interesting study in the United States (where existential security generally is high) found that conservative Pentecostal Christians who attend church most regularly and report greater influence of religion in their daily lives are more trusting of people inside *and outside* their group than less committed co-religionists and atheists, other Christians, and Jews (Welch, et al. 2004). As noted above, a series of studies (conducted in environments with comparatively low existential security) found strong support for suicide attacks among those Israelis and Palestinians who attend religious services frequently, but do not pray frequently. However, these same studies found that "[r]eminders of prayer, if anything, decreased" support for attacks (Norenzayan 2013: 164). These latter studies suggest that devotional practices such as prayer may dampen out-group hostility, even where groups are under stress. There are many types of prayer in theistic traditions in which one could reflect upon peace-oriented textual material or values. Certain types of Buddhist meditation practice have been shown to increase empathy and compassion, as well as prosocial conduct in games that offer the opportunity to cooperate or compete (Klimecki et al. 2014). This research would seem to validate the efforts of some conflict resolution experts to incorporate mindfulness practices into their work (Riskin and Wohl 2015). Religious peacemakers should consider encouraging these types of devotional practices.

Group Ritual

The religious peacebuilding literature encourages the creative use of ritual in conflict resolution practice (Gopin 2000; Schirch 2015: 516-540). Recent social scientific research on religious prosociality validates this idea, while also offering insights about types and features of rituals that may particularly help promote tolerance and conflict transformation. For example, several studies indicate that *synchronized movement* is one key to creating feelings of affinity (Hove and Risen 2009; Wiltermuth and Heath 2009).[6]

Most studies of ritual have focused on in-group solidarity, but there is evidence that group rituals can help promote solidarity with and tolerance toward members of other groups. Economists David Clingingsmith, Asim Khwaja, and Michael Kremer studied effects on social attitudes of Pakistanis who either won or lost (through a lottery system) a spot to participate in the annual Muslim pilgrimage to Mecca (the Hajj). The Hajj draws more than two million Muslim men and women of all sects, races, ethnicities, classes, ages, regions, and cultures from around the world for a five-day pilgrimage that includes performance of a diverse set of rituals at a number of different locations. A one-time requirement (for those with financial and physical capability) symbolizing each individual's ultimate self-presentation before and return to God, the Hajj is an event of culminating spiritual significance and intimacy for the individual, and is intended to highlight the shared nature and equality of human beings' existential situation before God. Intentions and prayers, ranging from verbally recited prayers and prayers involving synchronous movements to individual, personal spontaneous supplications, are integral to the rituals. Many of the rituals, such as encircling the Ka'ba and running back and forth between the hills of Safa and Marwa, are understood to recapitulate prayers, activities, and events in the lives of beloved religious figures and spiritual-ethical exemplars. The Hajj is very strenuous physically, with much of the travel between locations taking place on foot, often in high temperatures. The pilgrims together undergo considerable hardships and physical risks, provide mutual assistance, engage in spiritual conversation, share meals and supplies, and stand side by side for prolonged periods while praying with many people different in physical appearance, languages, customs, and even styles of ritual practice.

The Hajj thus brings diverse people together for extended interaction and ritual activity. The researchers found that Hajj participation decreased observance of more parochial religious practices and increased observance of more global religious practices; increased attitudes of equality, peace and harmony toward other Muslims (including people from different Islamic sects and ethnic groups) and toward adherents of other religions; increased belief in the ability of people from different religious traditions to live in peace; and produced more favorable attitudes toward women (Clinging-smith, Khwaja and Kremer 2009). Cambodian Buddhist leader Maha Ghosananda's Dhammayietra (also known as the Walk for Peace and Reconciliation) (Skidmore 1996) and the Abraham Path initiative in the Middle East (abrahampath.org) are other examples of the simple power of group ritual for peacebuilding.

Shaping Situations to Promote Religious Prosociality

Religious prosociality is persistently "in the situation" (i.e., religious people tend to behave in prosocial ways when their present context encourages prosocial behavior), regardless of the conflicting evidence about whether it is persistently "in the person." This suggests that it may be possible to shape negotiation contexts and other situations in ways that encourage prosocial behavior. For example, if key members of negotiation delegations are religious, moderate religious leaders could be invited to offer words of encouragement (perhaps drawing upon scripture) before important meetings or negotiation sessions, reminding people of the loss of life the conflict has caused and will continue to cause if it is not resolved, and of values within their respective traditions that call for tolerance, compassion and reconciliation. Meeting spaces could contain or be situated around positive reminders of religion. For example, the offices of the Common Space Initiative in Beirut, where many key meetings that are part of Lebanon's national dialogue process have occurred, is surrounded by dozens of churches and mosques that broadcast their presence throughout the day with bells and calls to prayer (commonspaceinitiative.org).

One recent experiment involving Muslim youth in Gaza and the West Bank powerfully demonstrates the potential value of interventions that shape negotiation situations to promote prosociality across group lines. Study participants were asked how they would resolve a moral dilemma in which they had the choice to act to sacrifice the life of one Palestinian man to save the lives of several children who otherwise would be killed accidentally (a variant of the famous trolley dilemma). All respondents considered two versions of this dilemma: in one, the children they had the opportunity to save were Palestinian; in the other, they were Jewish

Israelis. Even the baseline responses of these Palestinian youth were not what many would expect: many of the respondents had serious reservations about allowing Jewish children to die to save a Palestinian. When the researchers subsequently asked them to think about this choice *from God's perspective*, however, they were almost 30% more likely to sacrifice the life of a Palestinian to save the Jewish Children—a hugely statistically significant shift. Those who facilitate discussions or negotiations among parties in conflict who are religious will recognize immediately how practically useful an insight like this can be in their work. Asking theistic negotiators to consider issues and options from God's perspective may well help spark creativity and break impasses.

Conclusion

This chapter highlights the potential of religion to promote cooperation between groups. Recent social scientific research regarding the prosocial nature of religion is producing a clearer and more nuanced picture of the ways in which religion and conflict relate, and also of how religion can contribute to the transformation of intergroup conflict with a religious dimension. This work is beginning to yield insights that can increase the effectiveness of conflict resolution practice, both by affirming or prompting modifications to existing approaches to practice and by inspiring new approaches. This new line of scientific inquiry into the social dynamics surrounding religion deserves the sustained attention of scholars and practitioners interested in conflict with a religious dimension.

Notes

[1] One will find numerous examples among the essays collected in the new *Oxford Handbook of Religion, Conflict and Peacebuilding* (2015).
[2] This project is not about excavating what supposedly is authentic and good in religion, sifting out what supposedly is inauthentic and bad, and essentializing these "good" elements apart from their historical, social and political contexts—a strategy justifiably criticized by religion, conflict and peace studies scholar Atalia Omer (Omer 2015: 3-32). Rather, it is about recognizing that the impulses and perspectives which often cause people to favor their own group—a tendency that cannot simplistically be characterized as good or bad, either for one's own group or for other groups— sometimes also can be tapped to help extend prosocial conduct beyond the boundaries of one's own group, possibly reducing intolerance and violence.
[3] Save one passing reference to one source in one author's contribution to the project, the *Oxford Handbook of Religion, Conflict and Peacebuilding*, an otherwise excellent and wide ranging 700-plus page survey of the field written by leading religious peacebuilding scholars, does not discuss, or even reference, any of the new social science on religious prosociality and its implications for conflict resolution practice, including evaluation of programs. The GHR Foundation recently made a large grant to the Alliance for Peacebuilding to enable it to systematically assess and improve the effectiveness of religious peacebuilding efforts using evidence based methods (Suchecki 2015).
[4] Political scientist Ron Hassner's study of conflict over sacred sites is an excellent example of interdisciplinary work on the relationship among religion, conflict and conflict resolution efforts that endeavors to be both "deep" and "broad." Deep

approaches to studying this relationship, such as those utilized by many scholars in disciplines such as religious studies, theology, and history, often rely upon detailed case studies to gain in-depth insight into very local perspectives and practices within a particular religious group or national or subnational geographic area. Broad approaches to studying this relationship typically utilize quantitative and qualitative social scientific research methodologies in search of insights that apply, and which may be capable of guiding policy and practice, not only within, but also across, local contexts. Each of these orientations has advantages and disadvantages. This article focuses mostly upon contributions made by broad approaches, because they are largely neglected in the literature on religious peacebuilding, but joining these orientations arguably is the most productive way to generate actionable insights regarding the relationship among religion, conflict and conflict resolution (Hassner 2009: 174).

[5] Deeply held values implicated in disputes that are brought to court in a well-functioning domestic legal system are effectively rendered commensurable, because both parties implicitly accept that the outcome of litigation may be a ruling that wholly or partially disregards one's values. A judicial system before which parties can bring a dispute involving sacred values simultaneously allows their values to be negotiated (by the judges who will debate and rule on the merits of the case) and ensures their values and the group's identity are (seemingly) defended without compromise (Seul 2004). In the context of many international armed conflicts and civil wars, as well as some domestic conflicts involving sacred values (e.g., free speech rights versus images of the Prophet in Denmark or France), however, there is no third party arbiter that all parties consider legitimate or sufficiently authoritative. The conflict must be resolved through negotiation by the conflict parties themselves, if it is to be resolved peacefully.

[6] Other examples include uniform, repeated rituals (which also may involve movement and song) performed regularly and less regular, high-arousal rituals performed under the supervision religious authorities (Atkinson and Whitehouse 2011; Konvalinka et al. 2011; Xygalatas et al. 2013). Group ritual evokes the sentiment Emile Durkheim famously described as "collective effervescence" (Durkheim 1995: vii). Social psychologist Jonathan Haidt (2012: 221-245) provides a more comprehensive list of activities that can evoke this sentiment.

References

Abraham Path. http://abrahampath.org (last accessed June 13, 2016).

Abu-Nimer, M. 2003. *Nonviolence and Peace Building in Islam: Theory and Practice.* Gainesville, FL: University Press of Florida.

Albright, M. 2006. *The Mighty and the Almighty: Reflections on America, God and World Affairs.* New York: HarperCollins.

Appleby, R.S. 2000. *The Ambivalence of the Sacred: Religion, Violence, and Reconciliation.* Oxford, UK: Rowman & Littlefield Publishers, Inc.

Atkinson, Q.D. and H. Whitehouse. 2011. The Cultural Morphospace of Ritual Form: Examining Modes of Religiosity Cross-culturally. *Evolution & Human Behavior* 32(1): 50-62.

Atran, S. 2003. Genesis of Suicide Terrorism. *Science* 299:1534-1539.

Atran, S. 2010. *Talking to the Enemy: Violent Extremism, Sacred Values, and What It Means to be Human.* London, England: Penguin Books.

Atran, S. and R. Axelrod. 2008. Reframing Sacred Values. *Negotiation Journal* 24(3): 221-246.

Atran, S., R. Axelrod and R. Davis. 2007. Sacred Barriers to Conflict Resolution. *Science* 317: 1039-1040.

Bazerman, M. and K. Shonk. 2005. The Decision Perspective to Negotiation. In *The Handbook of Dispute Resolution,* edited by M. Moffitt and R. Bordone. San Francisco, CA: Jossey-Bass.

Bennhold, K. 2015, Jihad and Girl Power: How ISIS Lured 3 London Girls. *New York Times, August 17, 2015.* Available online at http://www.nytimes.com/2015/

08/18/world/europe/jihad-and-girl-power-how-isis-lured-3-london-teenagers. html?_r=0 (last accessed August 29, 2015).

Clingingsmith, D., A.I. Khwaja and M.R. Kremer. 2009. Estimating the Impact of the Hajj: Religion and Tolerance in Islam's Global Gathering. *The Quarterly Journal of Economics* 124(3): 1133-1170.

Common Space Initiative. http://www.commonspaceinitiative.org (last accessed June 13, 2016).

Coward, H. and G.S. Smith (eds). 2004. *Religion and Peacebuilding*. Albany, NY: State University of New York Press.

Durkheim, E. 1995. *The Elementary Forms of Religious Life*, translated by K.E. Fields. New York: Simon and Schuster Inc.

Fiske, A.P. and T.S. Rai. 2015. *Virtuous Violence*. Cambridge, UK: Cambridge University Press.

Ginges, J., S. Atran, D. Medin and K. Shikaki. 2007. Sacred Bounds on Rational Resolution of Violent Political Conflict. *Proceedings of the National Academy of Sciences* 104(18): 7357-7360.

Ginges, J. and S. Atran. 2009. What Motivates Participation in Violent Political Action: Selective Incentives or Parochial Altruism? *Annals of the New York Academy of Sciences* 1167: 115-123.

Ginges, J., H. Sheikh, S. Atran and N. Argo. 2016. Thinking from God's Perspective decreases biased valuation of the life of a nonbeliever. *Proceedings of the National Academy of Sciences* 113 (2): 316-319.

Gopin, M. 2000. *Between Eden and Armageddon: The Future of World Religions, Violence, and Peacemaking*. Oxford, UK: Oxford University Press.

Gort, J.D., H. Jansen and H.M. Vroom (eds). 2002. *Religion, Conflict and Reconciliation: Multifaith Ideals and Realities*. Amsterdam: Rodopi.

Haidt, J. 2012. *The Righteous Mind: Why Good People Are Divided by Politics and Religion*. New York: Vintage Books.

Hassner, R. E. 2009. *War on Sacred Grounds*. Ithaca, NY: Cornell University Press.

Hayward, S. 2012. Religion and Peace Building. Reflections on Current Challenges and Future Prospects. *United States Institute of Peace Special Report* 313: 1-12.

Helmick, R.G. and R.L. Petersen (eds). 2001. *Forgiveness and Reconciliation: Religion, Public Policy, and Conflict Transformation*. Radnor, PA: Templeton Foundation Press.

Hoffman, A. J., J. J. Gillespie, D. A. Moore, K. A. Wade-Benzoni, L. L. Thompson and M. H. Bazerman. 1999. A Mixed-Motive Perspective on the Economics Versus Environment Debate. *American Behavioral Scientist* 42(8): 1254-1276.

Hove, M. J. and J. L. Risen. 2009. It's All in the Timing: Interpersonal Synchrony Increases Affiliation. *Social Cognition* 27(6): 949-961.

Huntington, S. 1993. The Clash of Civilizations? *Foreign Affairs* 72(3): 22-49.

Huntington, S.P. 1996. *The Clash of Civilizations and the Remaking of World Order*. New York: Simon & Schuster.

Johnson, D. and C. Sampson. 1994. *Religion, the Missing Dimension of Statecraft*. Oxford: Oxford University Press.

Klimecki, O., S. Leiberg, M. Richard and T. Singer. 2014. Differential Pattern of Functional Brain Plasticity After Compassion and Empathy Training. *Social Cognitive Affective Neuroscience* 9(6): 873-879.

Kulska, J. 2015. A Balanced Perception of Religion in International Relations. *E-International Relations* July 9, 2015. Available online at http://www.e-ir.info/ 2015/07/09/a-balanced-perception-of-religion-in-international-relations/ (last accessed August 14, 2015).

Konvalinka, I., D. Xygalatas, J. Bulbulia, U. Schjødt, E. Jegindø, S. Wallot, G. Van Orden and A. Roepstorff. 2011. Synchronized Arousal Between Performers and Related Spectators in a Fire-walking Ritual. *Proceedings of the National Academy of Sciences* 108(20): 8514-8519.

Lapidoth, Ruth. 1992. Sovereignty in Transition. *Journal of International Affairs*. 45(2): 325-346.

Lederach, J.P. 2003. *The Little Book of Conflict Transformation*. Intercourse, PA: Good Books.

Norenzayan, A. 2013. *Big Gods: How Religion Transformed Cooperation and Conflict*. Princeton, NJ: Princeton University Press.

Omer, A. 2015. Religious Peacebuilding: The Exotic, the Good, and the Theatrical. In *The Oxford Handbook of Religion, Conflict, and Peacebuilding*, edited by A. Omer, R. S. Appleby and D. Little. Oxford, UK: Oxford University Press.

Pyszczynski, T., A. Abdollahi and Z. K. Rothschild. 2009. Does Peace Have a Prayer? The Effects of Morality Salience, Compassionate Values, and Religious Fundamentalism on Hostility Toward Out-groups. *Journal of Experimental Social Psychology* 45(4): 816-827.

Ricigliano, R. 2012. *Making Peace Last: A Toolbox for Sustainable Peacebuilding*. Boulder, CO: Paradigm Publishers.

Riskin, L.L. and R. Wohl. 2015. Mindfulness in the Heat of Conflict: Taking STOCK. *Harvard Negotiation Law Review*.

Schirch, L. 2015. Ritual, Religion, and Peacebuilding. In *The Oxford Handbook of Religion, Conflict, and Peacebuilding*, edited by A. Omer, R.S. Appleby, and D. Little. Oxford, UK: Oxford University Press.

Seul, J. R. 1999. "Ours is the Way of God": Religion, Identity, and Intergroup Conflict. *Journal of Peace Research* 36 (5): 553-569.

Seul, J. R. 2004. Settling Significant Cases. *Washington Law Review* 79(3): 881-968.

Seul, J. R. 2006. Religion and Conflict. In *The Negotiator's Fieldbook*, edited by A. K. Schneider and C. Honeyman. Washington, DC: American Bar Association.

Skidmore, M. 1996. In the Shade of the Bodhi Tree: Dhammayietra and the Re-awakening of Community in Cambodia. *Crossroads: An Interdisciplinary Journal of Southeast Asian Studies* 10(1): 1-32.

Smock, D. 2001. "FBOs and International Peacebuilding," United States Institute of Peace Special Report, no. 76, October, pp. 1-8. http://www.e-ir.info/2015/07/09/a-balanced-perception-of-religion-in-international-relations/

Solomon, S., J. Greenberg and T. Pyszczynski. 2015. *The Worm at the Core: On the Role of Death in Life*. New York: Random House.

Steel, D. 2008. An Introductory Overview to Faith-Based Peacebuilding. In *Pursuing Just Peace: An Overview and Case Studies for Faith-Based Peacebuilders*, edited by Rogers, M., T. Bamat and J. Ideh. Maryland: Catholic Relief Services.

Suchecki, P. M. J. 2015. How Useful Is Religion in Defusing Conflicts? A Funder Gives Big to Find Out. *Inside Philanthropy*, February 27, 2015. Available online at http://www.insidephilanthropy.com/home/2015/2/27/how-useful-is-religion-in-d efusing-conflicts-a-funder-gives.html (last accessed on August 4, 2015).

Tenbrunsel, A. E., K .A. Wade-Benzoni, L. P. Tost, V. H. Medvec, L. L. Thompson and M. H. Bazerman. 2009. The Reality and Myth of Sacred Issues in Negotiations. *Negotiation and Conflict Management Research* 2(3): 263-284.

Tetlock, P. E. 2003. Thinking the Unthinkable: Sacred Values and Taboo Cognitions. *Trends in Cognitive Sciences* 7(7): 320-324.

Thompson, E .F. 2009. Justice Interrupted: Historical Perspectives on Promoting Democracy in the Middle East. *United States Institute of Peace Special Report* 225. Available online at http://www.usip.org/sites/default/files/Special%20Report%20225_ Justice%20Interrupted.pdf (last accessed December 14, 2015).

Toft, M. D., D. Philpott and T. S. Shah. 2011. *God's Century: Resurgent Religion and Global Politics*. New York: W.W. Norton & Co, Inc.

Walton, M. J. and S. Hayward. 2014. Contesting Buddhist Narratives: Democratization, Nationalism, and Communal Violence in Myanmar. *East-West Center Policy Study Series 71*. Available online at http://www.eastwestcenter.org/sites/default/files/private/ps071.pdf (last accessed July 31, 2015).

Waytz, A., L. L. Young and J. Ginges. 2014. Motive Attribution Asymmetry for Love vs. Hate Drives Intractable Conflict. *Proceedings of the National Academy of Sciences* 111(44): 15687-15692.

Weissmann, M. 2008. *The Missing Link - Bridging Between Social Movement Theory and Conflict Resolution*. GARNET Working Paper No. 60/08. Available online at http://www.diva-portal.org/smash/record.jsf?pid=diva2%3A780143&dswid=-966 (last accessed August 29, 2015).

Welch, M., D. Sikkink, E. Sartain and C. Bond. 2004. Trust in God and Trust in Man: The Ambivalent Role of Religion in Shaping Dimensions of Social Trust. *Journal for the Scientific Study of Religion* 43(3): 317-343.

Wiltermuth, S. S. and C. Heath. 2009. Synchrony and Cooperation. *Psychological Science* 20(1): 1-5.

Xygalatas, D., P. Mitkidis, R. Fischer, P. Reddish, J. Skewes, A. W. Geertz, A. Roepstorff and J. Bulbulia. 2013. Extreme Rituals Promote Prosociality. *Psychological Science* 24(8): 1602-1605.

♋ **89** ♌

A New Future for Kashmir?

U.S. Ambassador John W. McDonald (ret.)
with Christel G. McDonald

Editors' Note: Only rarely is the public privileged to track a major negotiation and see up close whether the theories actually get put into practice. A multitude of other chapters in the book are implicated here as Ambassador John McDonald talks about the prevailing assumptions, the intractable conflict, and a breakthrough move toward progress in the decades-old conflict between India and Pakistan over Kashmir. Because so few practitioners at this level have undertaken to write down what they actually did, we have elected to preserve the original 2006 text largely intact, with only a few clarifying changes. The McDonalds' updated (2016) assessment follows. [This chapter stands particularly as a practical illustration, by a consummate practitioner, of the principles explained by Coleman et al., in Intractable 1 and 2, as well as Adler's Protean Negotiator. For another view of how the field's theories apply, or do not, in a difficult environment, this chapter could be read in conjunction with NDR: Kaufman & Blanchot, Theory Meets Reality.]

In late November 1995, I was visited in my office in downtown Washington, D.C. by two three-star generals, one from India and the other from Pakistan. Given the animosity between these countries, the mere fact that they would travel across town together for such a visit was itself extraordinary. Within two minutes of their arrival, they asked me to solve the "Kashmir Problem"!

I was honored by their visit and stunned by their request. I laughed unbelievingly at their suggestion and then said, "No, I can't do that." But

U.S. Ambassador (ret.) **John W. McDonald** is a lawyer, diplomat, former international civil servant, development expert and peacebuilder, with twenty years in Western Europe and the Middle East and sixteen years working on United Nations economic and social affairs. He retired in 2017 as Chairman and CEO of the Institute for Multi-Track Diplomacy; he co-founded IMTD in 1992, and developed its systems approach on national and international peacebuilding.
Christel G. McDonald (M.A. History), former European Civil Servant, and experienced Historical Researcher, is deeply committed to furthering higher education for young people from around the world.

they were very serious career military officers and meant what they asked. We spent the rest of the day talking.

The two Generals told me that they had fought two wars against each other over Kashmir and did not want to fight a third one. I learned they had both recently retired from the military and had been invited by the renowned Stimson Center to come to Washington, D.C. for six weeks. They had heard about our Institute for Multi-Track Diplomacy (IMTD) from a mutual friend, learned about our systems approach to peace through conflict resolution skill building, and decided to visit us.

They said their two governments were "stuck in time" and did not know what to do. Both governments had repeatedly rejected help from other governments over the issue of Kashmir, saying they would resolve the problem themselves. But they had made no progress since 1947, and the problem was just getting worse. It was the Generals' belief that IMTD, being a small, not-for-profit, non-governmental organization (NGO) that would not be seen as a threat to anyone, might have some ideas that could move the two governments to take some positive action, or at least help reduce some of the ongoing violence.

The Province of Jammu and Kashmir has been a thorn in the sides of both Pakistan and India since 1947, when India broke away from the British Empire and the country of Pakistan was created as a new Muslim nation. Even though the Province was 85% Muslim, the then Maharaja decided at the last moment to remain a part of India.

The issue of who "owns" Kashmir became the root cause of the conflict and continues to be so to this day. The nuclear arms issue of recent years has only exacerbated the "Kashmir Problem."

In 1965, after the second Kashmir war, a "Line of Control" ("LoC") was established along the cease-fire line, dividing the province. The six million people in the south of the province are now a part of India and administered by the Indian government. The three million people in the north are a part of Pakistan and administered by that government. The two parts have been totally sealed off from each other since the LoC was created.

The purpose of this chapter is to show how, after many years of thinking not once, but many times, "outside the box," and with patience, perseverance, countless fundraising efforts and cooperation between governments and an NGO, a goal can be achieved that was once thought impossible. I will talk about how IMTD did, after all, get involved in the Kashmir question and how IMTD used a several-pronged approach: utilizing the role of business in peacebuilding; training in negotiation and conflict resolution skills of Azad (Pakistani) Kashmiri; bringing Kashmiri citizens from both sides of the LoC together for training in conflict resolution; and finally, establishing a People's Bus that allows families who were separated from each other for 57 years to come together. Each of these was an essential phase.

IMTD Responds

Two years went by with no action on our part to the Generals' critical invitation to get involved with Kashmir, because no one in the funding community was interested. We don't charge for our services overseas, so we have to raise funds to carry out the projects requested by the people in a conflict situation. Unfortunately, we could not raise any money for Kashmir.

Suddenly four things happened. In 1997, the McKnight Foundation in Minneapolis and later the Sasakawa Peace Foundation in Tokyo were intrigued about our proposal to involve the business communities in India and Pakistan in a Kashmir peace process, and came up with generous funding.

At about the same time, three other things happened. I was visited by the Indian Director of an NGO in Bombay who had done some excellent analysis of the Indian-Kashmir situation. We spoke at length and I put forward my idea of trying to involve some members of the business community in the Kashmir problem. I said there were three power centers in India—the government, the military, and business—and while business did not talk to the other two, they could play a key role in a peace process. I pointed out that in 1988 there were 800,000 visitors to Kashmir and a few months later the number dropped to zero because of fear. The economy collapsed because the conflict had become violent again. If business could take a long-term view of the conflict and become involved they could help reduce the fear, and as tourists returned to the Valley they could invest or re-invest in the region. He liked the idea and invited me to Bombay to meet some business leaders.

The very next day, through the State Department's International Visitors Program, I was visited by a distinguished parliamentary leader from Pakistan who was also a businessman. We had virtually the same conversation, and he invited me to Lahore to meet business leaders there and in Karachi. A week later, I received a letter from an Indian businesswoman who was a consultant to the PHD (Punjab) Chamber of Commerce[1] in New Delhi. She expressed interest in helping develop the role of business and peace and invited me to Delhi.

Dr. Louise Diamond (the co-founder of IMTD) and I talked. She said that in her belief system the coming together of this synergy was a powerful indicator that we should move, and so we started on a journey that continues to this day.

The Role of Business

We had funds on hand to continue our training with the Dalai Lama and the Government of Tibet-in-Exile in Dharamsala, in Northeast India. While we were there we visited New Delhi and Bombay and then Lahore and Karachi over the next several years, in order to build trust relationships with members of the business community in both countries.

IMTD also sent staff members to South Africa, Northern Ireland, Cyprus and Israel-Palestine to develop case studies on the positive role the business community in each of these conflicted areas played in furthering the peace process. In each instance business people, working quietly behind the scenes, away from the press and the TV, put their egos behind them and achieved remarkable changes. These case studies later proved very useful in the discussions with business leaders from India and Pakistan.

In 2001, we held a training session at the PHD Chamber of Commerce for 28 Indian business leaders on their potential role in the Kashmir conflict. A few months later we carried out the same program in Lahore for 50 Pakistani business leaders at LUMS University, which has the most important MBA program in the country. This session was opened by the three-star general from Pakistan who had started me on this path in 1995. He was brilliant in his presentation and totally dedicated to our cause.

We provided all participants with our four case studies to show these business leaders what was possible and to let them see that they were not the first to get involved in a peace process. We also had two distinguished American business leaders as a part of our team for both trainings. Both spoke eloquently about their efforts in the United States to build peaceful communities.

Our long-term plan was to work separately with business leaders and then bring both sides together in addition to working separately with the Kashmiri—and then to bring all four groups together to dialogue. Unfortunately this has not yet come to pass because our two funding organizations had a change of heart. The McKnight Foundation Board decided to support only projects in the State of Minnesota, and the Sasakawa Foundation said, "If they stop, we stop." So we had to look elsewhere for resources, and continue doing so.

Kashmir—Training for Azad Kashmiri

Pakistan-administered Kashmir, or as they say in Pakistan, Azad Kashmir, which means "Free Kashmir," is a semi-independent, democratic province of Pakistan with its own constitution, parliament, and justice system headed by a Supreme Court, and a multi-party political system with free, non-violent elections and a free press. In fact, in the early 2000s, as a result of a free election, the party in power lost, and there was a peaceful transfer of power to the opposition party.

India-administered Kashmir, however, is another story. Its six million citizens are "protected" by some 700,000 military, police and border guards from the militants across the LoC. Unfortunately, most Indian Kashmiri are quite uninformed about Azad Kashmir and think "they" are all "terrorists over there."

Both the Indian and Pakistan Governments do have one thing in common. For over 55 years neither government had ever asked the citizens of Kashmir what they wanted for their own political future. It seemed as though New Delhi and Islamabad always knew what was best for their Kashmiri. This has now begun to change for the better. I was visited recently by a newly appointed Minister for Kashmir Affairs and Northern Areas from the Government of Pakistan. He was a very personable and impressive individual who was truly concerned about the future of the people living in those areas.

In 1993, while attending an important conference dealing with existing international conflicts sponsored by the United States Institute of Peace in Washington, D.C. I met an exceptional man from Azad Kashmir, Shah Ghulam Qadir, the head of an NGO called the Kashmir Institute of International Relations (KIIR). He was on a panel at that conference talking about Kashmir and got on very well with the Indian panelist who was giving his views of the conflict. The three of us met for coffee afterwards, and I began a friendship with Shah Ghulam Qadir, which has lasted to this day. Shah was the first person I contacted when we decided to take on Kashmir as an IMTD project. He has been a major player in our work ever since as he has dedicated his life to the peaceful resolution of the "Kashmir problem."

In 2000, during one of my trips to the region, Shah asked me if it would be possible for IMTD to train parliamentary leaders from Muzaffarabad, the capital of Azad Kashmir, in negotiation and diplomatic skills. I was delighted at the invitation and asked when he would like us to go to Pakistan to begin the training. He answered, "You don't understand. I want the training to take place in Washington, D. C., so that we can learn more about the world. We are so isolated in Azad Kashmir."

Since that conversation, we have carried out five week-long training sessions for some 75 parliamentary leaders, cabinet ministers, members of the opposition party, NGOs, and university professors. We have taken these groups to the State Department, the United States Institute of Peace (USIP), the Federal Mediation and Conciliation Service, and leading NGOs like the Stimson Center and Center for Strategic and International Studies (CSIS), and time has proven that all parties have greatly benefited from these exchanges of ideas.

Bringing Kashmir Citizens Together in Nepal

Part of my long-term goal was to bring together Kashmiri from both sides of the LoC. After a long struggle, we finally got funds from a private donor and the USIP for a week-long dialogue and training session for ten civil society leaders from Azad Kashmir and ten civil society leaders from Indian Kashmir.

The meeting took place in August 2004 at a peaceful retreat, a lodge in Dhulikhel, an hour outside of the city of Kathmandu, Nepal. We had a great team, with Dr. Eileen Borris, Mr. Ladia Michalcik, IMTD's Program Officer, and me. We chose this resort away from the city because of its beauty, comfort, location and, most important, its reasonable cost and the fact that visitors from India did not need a visa to come to Nepal.

This historic coming together of Kashmiri from both sides of the LoC, the first of its kind since separation in 1947, was a great success. Yet some parts of our initiative were difficult to organize.

There was fear and concern on all sides. What finally made it happen, however, were the trust relationships we had built up over the years. Both sides knew we had no hidden agenda and were not pushing any particular "solution" to the Kashmir problem. The Pakistan side was easier for us to organize thanks to our contacts with Shah Qadir. KIIR, with whom we had worked for years, followed our guidelines on the selection of participants and chose all ten Azad Kashmir members.

The Indian side was quite different, and it took time and caused some anguish. There are no NGOs in Indian Kashmir, and we had to ask for recommendations from our many friends in India and Kashmir. We contacted those who were recommended, one by one, over the telephone, to tell them of our plan and convince them it was safe to participate. Our choice of location in Nepal was very helpful in this regard.

With great patience and skill the "Indian Ten" were finally selected. We were pleased that women from both sides of Kashmir signed up to participate. On the Indian side, six of the ten were women, and two were women from Azad Kashmir. This was quite an accomplishment in itself. Interestingly, neither side thought the other would show up in Kathmandu. All 20 participants did arrive, though, and our training began.

We met with each group separately for several hours to get acquainted and explain what we thought the week would be like. Then we all had dinner together. Breaking bread as a group has been a sign of peacebuilding across history. After dinner, we sat together and the trust-building process began. While they all spoke Kashmiri and English, they were separated by history for 57 years and had little accurate information about each other.

One little event really broke the ice and helped the 20 individuals begin to come together. One of the men from Azad Kashmir talked about his sister, who lived in the city of Jammu on the Indian side of Kashmir, and about how angry and frustrated he was because, although he only lived 50 kilometers away, he could never visit her as he could not cross the LoC. One of the Indian women said, "I live in Jammu. Where does your sister live?" He told her, and she said, "Why, that is only ten minutes from where I live. Why don't you write her a letter, and we will take some pictures together. When I get home I will visit your sister and tell her all about our time together and give her the letter and the pictures." That powerful little gesture of friendship changed the atmosphere completely.

At the end of our training session, we all went to the airport together and there were many hugs and some tears. The group had bonded. The promises to keep in touch have been maintained, a web page has been established, and the Indian side is trying to establish their own NGO in Kashmir.

We applied for additional funding to carry out a second "coming together" to build on the first successful approach to bring Kashmiri citizens from both sides of the LoC together. This has now occurred.

The People's Bus

In April 2001, during one of my trips to Azad Kashmir, Shah Qadir asked me if I would like to visit a refugee camp near the capital city of Muzaffarabad. I did not know there was such a camp and agreed to the visit. There were some one thousand people living in the camp, under miserable conditions, all of whom had fled from the Indian side of the LoC in fear of their lives. Many were injured and in poor health. I asked why UN agencies such as UNHCR, UNICEF, UNDP or WFP were not helping out. I was told that this was a delicate issue for the central government in Islamabad, which considered this an internal problem. I was shocked—and determined to do something about this very bad situation. After my return to the United States I had several conversations with the UNHCR in Geneva, which confirmed that the Government of Pakistan had, so far, turned down its offer of assistance. I have continued to pursue this matter, most recently with the new Minister for Azad Kashmir, and he has agreed to take a fresh look at the problem.

While at the refugee camp, I was asked to speak to the people in the camp. I started talking about IMTD and the small steps we were taking to reduce conflict in Kashmir; but then, as I was about to lose my audience, I had a great idea that immediately got their attention. I asked if they remembered the "politician's bus" the previous year when the Prime Minister of India took a bus from New Delhi to Lahore, Pakistan, to meet with the Prime Minister of Pakistan. They all said, "Yes," because out of that meeting came the Lahore Declaration which had positive language in it about the Kashmir situation. They also knew that Declaration had fallen apart a few months later and that nothing had happened since. I then said "I want to start a 'People's Bus' which will cross the LoC and bring divided families together from both sides of Kashmir for the first time in decades." They all agreed that this was a great idea and cheered me on, recognizing it would be a positive, practical sign of peacebuilding, which would allow many of them to finally see their families again.

With their encouragement to follow up on this idea, I returned to Washington, determined to make that "People's Bus" a reality. I did not approach the U.S. Government with this idea. I never wrote a grant proposal. We just got to work at IMTD to find ways to make it happen. The key challenge was to move the idea from Track II (citizen diplomacy) to Track I (government to government diplomacy) because governments were ultimately the only ones capable of taking the political step to open the LoC for this bus exchange.

It was a long three-year campaign that involved everyone pushing the idea during repeated calls on the Embassies of Pakistan and India in Washington, D.C., meetings with the press from both countries, and many talks with our friends in both countries. It was a hopeful sign when, as a result of my letter campaign, I actually heard back via the Pakistani Embassy from the President of Pakistan that he liked the idea and would raise it with the Indian Prime Minister when they next met.

The first major breakthrough came from the Indian side, however, when in November 2003 the Indian government proposed half a dozen "Track II" ideas to the Pakistan Government. The third item on the list was the "People's Bus." The Pakistan Government agreed four days later. I was ecstatic, but nothing happened. The two Foreign Ministries got stuck on the details. They could not agree on what kind of documentation for identification was needed for the bus passengers to cross the LoC and return.

In September 2004, after my return from Nepal, I got in the act again by writing both sides and telling them that three of our ten Indian Kashmiri came to Nepal with no passport, only an Indian ID Card. If Nepal would accept this documentation as proof of Kashmir identity, why not try it for the LoC? I was told, "We will handle this;" but they remained stuck. Finally, in December 2004, when the new Prime Minister of India and the President of Pakistan met, their Foreign Ministers were ordered to move the bus project forward. On February 15, 2005, the two Foreign Ministers announced the first bus exchange would take place on April 7, 2005, five years to the day after I had proposed the idea to the people in the refugee camp.

Despite some violence in Indian Kashmir the day before the planned event, the Indian People's Bus did leave on schedule. The high level of visibility given to the new "trust-building measure" between India and Pakistan was further heightened by the fact that the Indian Prime Minister and Mrs. Sonya Gandhi, the head of the Congress Party, the two most powerful people in India, flew to Srinagar, the Indian capital of Kashmir, to wave good-bye to the participants on this historic bus. The Prime Minister of Azad Kashmir in Pakistan, together with huge crowds, welcomed that bus in Mazaffarabad, while the Azad Kashmiri Bus was welcomed on the Indian side with great fanfare.

The high point for me personally was when the mayor of Muzaffarabad telephoned me that same day to thank IMTD and me for our role in making the "People's Bus" a reality.

In the United States the press highlighted this important action of peace building between groups of people, from countries that are strong allies of the United States. In fact, the front page of the *New York Times, The Wall Street Journal* and the *Washington Post* carried the same photograph of 20 passengers from Azad Kashmir crossing the recently re-built and re-named "Peace Bridge" and entering Indian Kashmir for a historic first in Indian-Pakistani relations.

Despite this very momentous success, much remains to be done. The impact of the initial exchange of buses continues to be positive and has stimulated several other people exchanges between the two countries. Experts have predicted the bus will eventually become a daily occurrence, and it is expected that truck traffic will start soon. I can only hope that relations will continue to improve. The positive political and economic impact on both sides will not only benefit the region and both countries but also can lead to reducing global tensions.

As a further note, in October 2005 as the original version of this chapter was being drafted, Kashmir was hit by a devastating earthquake, which caused much more destruction in Pakistan Kashmir than in Indian Kashmir. Over 80,000 people were killed and it is estimated that three million are homeless. Many countries, including the United States and India, responded quickly to this disaster. Thanks to the ties forged by the People's Bus operations since April 2005, the Indian and Pakistan governments worked closely together, and at least five additional border crossings along the LoC have been opened.

(Original, 2006) Conclusion

What lessons can be drawn from these different events? There are many, but here are a few of the most essential ones.

There is no such thing as an "intractable" conflict. To obtain positive results, the following are necessary ingredients at the government and citizen levels: building trust, demonstrating goodwill, deploying mutual peacebuilding skills, and having profound dedication to creating peace. Obtaining funds to work in the field of conflict resolution is one of the most difficult factors and can take a long time. Thinking outside the box is key, and risk-taking is also a critical element. Yet, in the end, by instilling hope, each individual and even a small NGO focusing on international peacebuilding can make an impact.

Ten Years Later: 2006-2016 and Beyond

Looking back at the ten years from 2006 to 2016, I am pleased to report that more positive action has taken place in the last 10 years, even though many problems and questions are still remaining. Yet, the efforts to find solutions continue on both sides of the Line of Control that separates Kashmir and Jammu (India) from Azad Kashmir (Pakistan). For example, elections are scheduled for March 2016 in Azad Kashmir, which, it is hoped, will lead to renewed dialogues between participants in Azad Kashmir how best to proceed.

Several of these participants—and newcomers—have repeatedly expressed interest in continuing the discussions that we organized in 2006. At that time, we were able to raise further funds to carry out a second training with Kashmiris from both sides, i.e., Indian Kashmir/Jammu and the Kashmiris in Pakistani. Following one of our principles

—training, if possible, on neutral ground—we organized the 2006 training in the Maldives Islands, off the coast of India.

We brought 27 Kashmiris from both sides together for a whole week. Many had taken our first training in Nepal and a few newcomers joined. For many it felt like a great homecoming since they had not met since 2004.

During this one week training, all participants were eagerly trying to make progress in finding ways where and how a closer collaboration could be developed, and ways found to reduce the tensions on both sides by better understanding the political, economic and social ramifications of the "Kashmir Situation".

On the last day of training a heartwarming event took place, which is testimony to the trust and confidence level that emerged among all participants. One of the women participants told the others in the group that she was originally from Srinagar, the summer capital of the State of Kashmir and Jammu on the Indian side. When she was still a young girl, she and some 200,000 Hindus living in Srinagar were shipped south to Jammu, the winter capital of Kashmir and Jammu, because the Indian government wanted to ensure that only Muslims were based in Srinagar so they could control them more efficiently.

The sad result was that the local Jammu citizens treated these Hindus from Srinagar as refugees, and they were never truly accepted even though they were also Hindus.

The woman told us that she finished her education in Jammu and got hired as a journalist by the Times of India. Because her bosses knew her background, they sent her to Srinagar to report from there to the newspaper. She had never told anyone her story until the last day of the training. Her story, and what it meant to her and so many others, touched the heart of everybody in the room and enhanced the bonding that had begun years ago.

After the training was over, she and a fellow journalist from Azad Kashmir, Pakistan, wrote numerous articles for their respective newspapers about the meaningful exchanges of ideas, points of view and individual contributions of the people on both sides in the economic and social sector—if only the Governments of India and Pakistan could agree on allowing a closer relationship to develop peacefully. The articles written by the two journalists from the two sides created a sensation, and they were reproduced all over India and Pakistan.

In 2009, Dr. Eileen Borris, our chief of training, and I were invited to carry out a "small training" session in Islamabad, Pakistan. Shortly after our arrival at the airport, we took a bus to the Convention Center for "a training session for some 30 Kashmiris". However, we did not believe our eyes when we entered this Convention Center. We were totally astonished to see that about 1500 people were assembled in the big conference hall. Mr. Shah Ghulam Qadir, the Chairman of the Kashmir Institute of International Relations (KIIR) had made changes in his plan for a "small training session", and organized a new event without being able to tell us beforehand about it. Many speeches were made for a larger part of the morning, including one by the Prime Minister of the Autonomous Region of Azad Kashmir. Then all of the attendees left the conference hall and a group of 30 stayed behind for lunch and invited us to join them. During this lunch, Mr. Shah Qadir asked me to chair the upcoming group meeting, which was planned for three days and would include a training regarding the development of plans for gradually creating a possible scenario to bring the people of Indian Kashmir and Jammu more closely together with the Azad Kashmiris. He added that he had planned that, as soon as the training session was concluded in the next three days, I would report back to the 1500 people who would be reconvened the afternoon after the training.

Our group began its discussions about the main issue (discussed, debated and considered for years already), i.e. should the Kashmir region on both sides of the border, be reunited and become an independent nation? A lively dialogue ensued which made it clear that at least these group representatives were ready to engage in the process of reunification, and felt that it should be pursued in a non-violent, peaceful way. When we reconvened in the convention hall, I was invited to address the 1500 people to present the findings of the group I had chaired. I informed the audience that the group wants to pursue a peaceful negotiation that would allow the Kashmiris to be united and follow an economic and social development course beneficial to all. In my presentation I formally pledged to make every effort for my dream and their dream to come true.

On November 13, 2015 I was visited by six parliamentary leaders from Azad Kashmir (Pakistan), including the Speaker of their autonomous parliament and three Ministers from the Azad government. The delegation had spent a few days in meetings at the United Nations in New York, before they flew down to Washington, D.C. to visit me. One member of this delegation had taken our training in the Maldives Islands in 2006 in conflict resolution skills. All of them were clearly in search for a peaceful resolution of the Kashmir conflict. We discussed at length our future dream, including more training in the near future, and I have recommitted myself to be helpful in any way we can at IMTD.

After my November 13, 2015, meeting with the Azad Kashmir delegation, I sent an e-mail to Mr. Shah Qadir at his NGO, the KIIR, to ask for his support for future training of Azad Kashmiris in Islamabad. He replied two days later that he liked the idea of future training, but as mentioned earlier, new parliamentary elections will be held in the Spring of 2016, so a future training could be planned for no earlier than the summer of 2016. (These kinds of real-world political, overarching factors are routine in all long-term conflicts and negotiations.)

I concluded that we at IMTD would follow our principle of always maintaining our hope and patience that things will eventually move forward. I learned shortly thereafter that Prime Ministers Narendra Modi and Nawaz Sharif had met on the sidelines of the Climate Conference COP-21 in Paris in the first days of December 2015. They spoke about the need to resume the dialogue between their two countries, the dialogue that had broken down a long time ago. On December 6, 2015, the leaders of the Indian and Pakistani National Security Agencies (NSA) then talked to each other while attending a meeting in Bangkok.

Unfortunately, on December 3, 2015, it was reported that three terrorists had infiltrated the Line of Control and were killed by the Indian Army, which insisted that these men were wearing jackets that identified them as coming from Pakistan.

Despite this setback, the Indian Foreign Minister Sushma Swaraj declared in Parliament on December 16, 2015 that going to war with Pakistan was not an option and that the NSA representatives of both India and Pakistan had agreed in Bangkok on a restart of a dialogue between the two countries. This dialogue would include also the topics of Kashmir and terrorism. On December 17, 2015, the Foreign Minister added that the Prime Ministers from India and Pakistan would meet as soon as a mutually agreeable date was set, and that *both* countries are committed to peace. However, it was also stated—as had been done in the past—that there was no room for the Hurriyat in the dialogue process. (Hurriyat is an alliance of 26 political, social, and religious organizations that formed a political front, the All Parties Hurriyat Conference (APHC) in Indian Kashmir. It has its origin in the 1993 Kashmir insurgency, and follows its ideology of finding a solution based on the aspirations of the people of Jammu and Kashmir. It sees itself as the sole representative of the Kashmir people.)

The balance of these statements, very recent at the time of this writing, of course means that there can be progress on many issues that will be placed on the agenda; but the exclusion of Hurriyat, at this point, reduces the chances of an enduring solution regarding Kashmir's future. [See NDR: Kaufman & Blanchot, *Theory Meets Reality* on the lessons of inclusion]

Yet, in my opinion, this does not need to mean that the Kashmir conflict cannot be solved. Between 1993 and 2015, a lot has happened within Hurriyat, with the effect of splitting the organization into two factions. This weakens its effectiveness and increases the Indian government's challenges in discussing the topic of Kashmir and Jammu's future with Pakistan.

The recent announcement of the renewal of a dialogue between India and Pakistan, with a long agenda on many topics of various priorities, is promising. It was reinforced by a surprise stopover of Indian Prime Minister Modi in Lahore, on his way home from Russia and Afghanistan, on December 25, 2015. He was warmly welcomed in the Pakistan Prime Minister's family home—for the first time. Most important, from our point of view, Kashmir was among other issues discussed during their friendly two-hour meeting, according to the Pakistani Foreign Secretary, Mr. Chaudhry. He added that the Indian Foreign Secretary, Mr. Subrahmanyan Jaishankar, would visit Islamabad in January 2016 to continue the dialogue.

We must eliminate this dangerous flashpoint between India and Pakistan. Soon it will be 70 years since a political boundary was created that separates families and friends. Yet the people's aspirations for unification will not disappear, especially if economic and social conditions do not improve. We at IMTD hope to be able to help shape constructive dialogues between all parties concerned. We believe IMTD's systems approach to peacebuilding can positively and substantially contribute to the path from Multi-Track Diplomacy to Track I. It can help the Kashmiris on both side of the Line of Control to prepare peacefully the ground for a reunification of its people through increased trade between the Pakistani and Indian side, through strengthening the social ties over the years to come, and through building stronger security links together against terrorist attempts. The future dialogues between the two countries, expanding their political process to a multi-track process, can explore and build trust-building measures beyond fighting terrorism, to establish a more peaceful relationship, one that will be exemplary for others in the 21st century.

Notes

[1] "The Chamber was established in December 1905 as the Punjab Chamber of Commerce and Industry to serve the cause of trade and industry in undivided Punjab. Since then it has traveled a long distance and now serves ten states of Northern Region India, i.e. Punjab, Haryana, Delhi, Uttar Pradesh, Himachal Pradesh, Rajasthan, Jammu & Kashmir, Madhya Pradesh, Chhatisgarh [sic] Uttaranchal and the Union Territory of Chandigarh. The acronym PHD stands for Progress, Harmony, and Development." PHD Chamber of Commerce & Industry, available at http://www.phdcci.org/introduction.html (last visited Oct. 31, 2005).

Section XVI: Getting It Done (Strategies)

"Getting It Done" is the topic of both of the last two sections of the book, but in different ways. Section XVI is about strategies, beginning with an analysis of how, for any resolution to be possible, many disputes and other negotiations will require some kind of sharing of power. Next is a chapter on the inevitability of situations in which the most effective solution possible for the parties is not to try—contrary to instinct—for absolute clarity, but instead to admit that a well-chosen ambiguity here and there may be the lubrication that allows the gears to move. A similar function is served by the next topic, contingent agreements, in which the parties agree to disagree about the future, to their mutual benefit.

The remaining three chapters of this section address the late stages of a negotiation, beginning with what to do when the common "final gap" presents itself, at the tail end of an arduous negotiation. But sometimes, despite all of the advice in that chapter, a deadlock ensues; and the next chapter is about how to deal with that situation, and unlock the dead-lock. The last chapter in this group analyzes what it takes to make sure that when you and your counterparts finally do "sign on the dotted line", the result sticks.

❧ 90 ❧

Making Deals about Power Sharing

John H. Wade

Editors' Note: Power-sharing is an intrinsic element of many negotia-
tions, particularly those which involve some kind of continued interac-
tion in the future. The need to provide for future decisions to be made
without resort to open conflict creates a series of questions, about who
will make each decision or type of decision, what the criteria will be,
and what essential or ancillary conditions might apply. Clear thinking
is essential, and here Wade offers a gradation in 13 steps from total
power held by one party to total power held by the other. Somewhere
along the 11 steps in between, perhaps, is your best solution to your
particular problem in negotiating today, for what must happen next
week or next year.

Future Decision-Making Power

This chapter will set out a "gradation" of legal decision-making power
ranging from total to zero. Such a gradation provides a useful template
and a form of "expert power" for any negotiator.

Founding fathers and mothers of clubs, churches, organizations and
nations are particularly adept at negotiating balances of power in the
form of "constitutions". The founders usually negotiate with passion and
persistence as they have experienced absolute power corrupting absolutely. Power sharing deals also commonly include power over budget
spending; relocating children; appointing judges; hiring and firing employees; and implementing medical research, prisoner releases and
military invasions (Bosquet 2008; Tuchman 2009; Savoie 2015).[1]

John Wade is an emeritus professor of law of Bond University, Queensland, Australia. He
practiced as a lawyer in Australia between 1987 and 2012, and also had an active
mediation practice in organizational, family and commercial conflicts during those years.
He has taught over 300 mediation and negotiation courses in Hong Kong, New Zealand,
London, Canada, the U.S. and Australia. John has published over 100 books and articles
(see epublications@bond.edu.au). His teaching awards include best law teacher at Sydney
University (1989); at Bond University (1990); and in Australia (1998). John now lives in
Vancouver, Canada with his growing family, and teaches intensive negotiation courses
there.

Negotiations about decision-making power raise a challenge. What is the predictable "range" of non-numerical offers, counter-offers and solutions from total to zero legal power? Generic negotiation agenda questions about power often take forms such as:

- *How* will future decisions be made about the following different topics—(expenditure, medical care, armament restrictions, holidays etc.)?
- Or, *who* will have the power to make future decisions about—?
- *What* conditions, if any, should be followed before or after each type of decision is made?[2]

Gradations of Legal Decision Making Power

What follows is a gradation or scale which gradually moves future decision making power from total power for one person, to a solution of total power in the hands of the other negotiating party. A negotiator or mediator who has ready access to such a gradation or range adds normalcy, structure, visibility and predictability to the negotiation. As with a "numbers" negotiation (dollars, acres, steak knives), each party can prepare on a confidential chart its preferred starting solutions about future power, what moves to make and how quickly to make them, and where resistance will probably occur based on current "facts" and emotions. Moreover, guesses can be made about the same concepts for the other negotiating parties, who may be moving from somewhere near to the opposite end of the range.

Of course, a "loss" of decision-making power "down" the gradation scale will often be, and can be reframed as, a potential "gain." For example, negotiating some degree of power sharing with another may:

- Placate a disruptive dissident and tribal supporters
- Add new expertise for future decisions
- Test abilities of and educate potential future leaders
- Enable blame shifting for future decisions
- Create an obligation to return favors later
- Distribute exhausting work loads
- Create mutually shared "agreement" language
- Encourage commitment to an organization

In summary, a gradation from *total* "legal" power via thirteen incremental losses to *no* "legal" power is as follows:

- Total Power
- Time-Limited Total Power
- Rotation of Power
- Duty to Report
- Criteria as Guidance to the Exercise of Power
- Division of Topics and Categories of Power
- Mandatory Consultation Processes—Secret or Publicized
- Entrenchment of Restrictions on Future Decision Making

- Deadlock: Agreed Mandatory Negotiation or Mediation Process
- Deadlock: Agreed Mechanisms to Trigger Resolution:
    - automatic formulae;
    - an independent arbitrator or judge;
- Qualified Veto Power by Other
- Veto Power by Other
- Total Power to the Other Party

Each of these gradations will be expanded shortly in what follows:

Total Power

One party has or claims complete power to decide in the future—what repairs to the apartment complex, by whom and at what cost; how much will be spent on marketing; who will be appointed as employee or judge; who decides about children's medical treatment.

Where one party trusts another, they may be willing to grant total power to that trusted other in certain areas of decision-making (Maister, Green and Galford 2000; Lewicki 2006).

Conversely, a claim (and inherent threat) of absolute power may be disguised by veneers of nominal consultation, rigged elections, a history of benign dictatorship, the smile of a crocodile, or reassurances of wisdom and expertise. Some long term bosses, rulers, spouses and chiefs are experts at recycling smiling veneers during negotiations.

Time-Limited Total Power

One gradation less than total decision-making power is where that capacity is limited in time. The president/boss/spouse/business partner/parent/tribe agrees to be "in charge" for x years, whereupon power will shift to another named person automatically, or an unnamed person via an election process.

Of course, this model of time-limited total power has been negotiated into many national constitutions by the founding parents of those nations.

Rotation of Power

A further diminution of decision-making power can be agreed upon whereby that power mandatorily rotates every X years between tribes, factions, university departments or individuals. Today's boss will be tomorrow's servant until his/her turn comes around again. So be kind today, in order to avoid payback tomorrow. This solution is adopted in some families where children or separated parents feud over holiday destinations. Therefore the parents agree that child one decides in year one; child two decides in year two; child three decides in year three; and then start again. This solution has also been adopted in some tribal societies, where automatic leadership rotation between tribes provides an attempt to modify nepotism. It also operates in academic departments where the chair position might regularly rotate.

Duty to Report

A minor though important qualification on total legal power is a duty to report after certain decisions are made. This is not as onerous as certain duties to consult, but the two are often combined.

The duty to report:

- can be to the other interested parties, or to a neutral accountant, engineer or other go-between;
- may arise daily, weekly or yearly;
- and may be paid for by one or all parties. (Note how these last two variables introduce numbered negotiation lines again. For example, report once, or 52 times a year; or share reporting costs 90/10, 50/50 or 10/90; etc.)

Thereby a mechanism for some degree of transparency is set up, and also an early warning system for possible misuses of total power. For example, where partners or separating spouses agree to the sale of a business, it is common for one partner:

- to insist on interim control of the business and sale process in order to sustain efficiency;
- to insist on minimum "interference" or access to the business by the other party while the sale is being negotiated;
- and in return, to authorize provision each week of records of the business income, expenditure and bank accounts to the other partner(s), in order to reduce suspicions that money or assets might "disappear."

Similar regular obligations to account publicly to boards, shareholders and electors for financial decisions are imposed on managers, corporations and government departments. These obligations may arise from agreement or legislation.

Criteria as Guidance to the Exercise of Power

The next gradation in the diminution of absolute power is effected by a list of agreed criteria which allegedly modifies the decision maker's broad discretion. For example, a major tenant in a shopping mall can negotiate with the owner-lessor that future adjoining stores shall *not include* food or clothing shops; but should if possible *include* only those stores which are selling technology, camping or electrical goods. Or, the power of a parole board or government to release prisoners early could be qualified by the board or national government agreeing *not* to release those convicted of crimes of terrorism or murder; and to *favor* early release of those convicted drug use or seditious speech offences.

Notoriously, long and vague criteria lists provide little restraint on power and discretion as the criteria are not ranked.

Division of Categories of Topics and Power

It is a classic pattern of bargaining for parties to divide or swap resources. "If you take charge of marketing decisions, I am willing to manage research"; "if you will control budgetary allocations, I am willing to manage day-to-day expenses." Famously, the negotiated constitutions of various federated countries, including the USA, Canada and Australia, include a *list* of topics over which the federal government has exclusive power, while the states or provinces pick up the residue—or vice versa. Of course, boundary disputes are frequent, at least because such lists cannot foresee new topics which emerge in complex societies. These boundary disputes are occasionally "resolved" by decisions of "high" courts.

In conflicted organizations, it is common for one of the disputants (a.k.a. "troublemakers") to be pushed into the "negotiated" solution of a work transfer to a distant office or minor portfolio, where, pending retirement, the categories of decisions made will be uncontroversial or unnoticed.

Another illustration of a starting division of power by vague "topic" can be found in local statutes, or in agreements between separating parents about their children. The topics can be bunched under four vague colloquial categories of "little," "emergency," "big," and "irreversible decisions."

- **Little Decisions:** The parent who has daily care of the child legally can make little decisions, which might be listed, such as food, clothing, friends, books, screen time; or left unspecified, under the vague label of "day to day" decisions.
- **Emergency Decisions:** The parent who has daily care at the moment of the emergency (e.g. car accident, swallowing poison, breathing difficulties etc.), can decide immediately what response is appropriate.
- **Big Decisions:** Obviously this topic has murky borders with the preceding two categories, but commonly includes decisions about church attendance; which kind of school; relocation to another residence; travel out of the country; contraception; name change. This category of decisions often requires, as a starting point, the written consent of both parents, or a court order allowing one parent to make such unilateral decisions.
- **Irreversible Decisions:** Again this category has overlap with "big" decisions, but classically includes a therapeutic decision to sterilize a child; or allow a child to donate organs to a sibling or parent; or permit gender reassignment of a teenage child. Such decisions, due to dark histories of exploitation of children, may be taken away from parents by statute or agreement and given to courts (Secretary, Department of Health and Community Services v JWB and SMB 1992).

Disputes over "parental rights" also illustrate a related dynamic: the instability of such power sharing agreements with the passage of time and circumstance. The above decision making powers of parents over children's lives *fade* gradually as children reach teenage years, and power shifts to the child, practically, culturally and legally. Additionally, where patterns of "neglectful" or "abusive" parental decision making come to the attention of a state child welfare department, a child may be made a ward of the state, and all decision-making power about the child *shifts* to that department.

One variation of separated categories of power which may provide an extra degree of concession is that of *overlapping* powers, which are a common feature of national constitutions. One negotiator is conceded priority to make decisions in a certain area, but at a later stage, the other party can choose to intervene and trump them. For example, local branch managers of restaurants or schools can decide how to market their services, unless and until the emerging national head office decides to create uniform marketing policies.

Mandatory "Consultation" Processes

A further diminution of centralized decision-making power is often effected by an agreement to "consult" with other interested or expert people before a decision is made. This process has a number of benefits:

- Importantly, consultation also reduces ambush and marginalization for the consultee.
- The pause, wisdom and diverse opinions involved in the consultation process may (or may not) modify a hasty, foolish or self-interested proposal.
- Shallow or deep consultation also provides someone else to blame if the ultimate decision turns out to be foolish or illegal.
- Moreover, where the volume of decisions is huge (e.g. employment, funding, immigration and social security applications), routine delegation and rubber-stamping of the decisions of consultees becomes normal practice.

Although the *process* of consultation is usually mandatory in such agreements, the ultimate decision-maker rarely agrees to be legally bound by any substantive recommendations of the consultees. Such loss of control would be a large leap in the gradation of possible concessions during a negotiation. In some situations, such an agreed delegation of complete decision-making power ("passing the buck"; or "routine rubber-stamping") is itself illegal, as statutory or contractual rules require that the consultor make the final decision on criteria, rather than others' opinions, or majority vote of a committee.

Some courts or agreements notoriously impose a vague duty to "consult" in order to complete some compromise judgement or contract. Cheap momentary peace in exchange for conflicted futures? These ticking clauses quietly pass the buck to decades of future disputes and con-fusing "precedents" to fill in the details of how many meetings (two meetings or one hundred and two?), of what kind, duration and with whom are sufficient to safely pass the test of "enough" consultation? (Tsilhquot'in Nation v British Columbia 2014)[3]

The process has the following basic and important distinction be-tween *secret* and *publicized* consultation, as the former only marginally modifies "total legal power".

Secret Consultation

Many powerful individuals, organizations and nations do not want a publicized obligation to consult anyone outside their own tribe about placement of retail stores, prisoners, armaments, crops, land boundaries, investments or staff appointments. Any such publicized obligation to one person inevitably leads to requests or demands from others. A consulta-tion floodgate is opened. Accordingly, a common practice is to placate another negotiator with a confidential verbal agreement to consult se-cretly, perhaps over coffee in Vienna. These are sometimes referred to as "sidebar" or collateral agreements. The side agreements are occasionally embodied in a letter so that the negotiator can show this document confi-dentially to disgruntled hawks and constituents. An added ubiquitous term is that if the duty to consult secretly is ever publicized, then the process and letter will be denied, and the promise to consult will instantly terminate.

Publicized Consultation

As a matter of degree, the more consultation obligations become detailed and publicized, the more they erode total decision making power.

However, the alleged power of the consultees can be readily weak-ened if the dominant decision-maker uses standard devices such as:

- Only consulting a small committee or a few friends
- Appointing a majority of sycophants and allies to the consul-tancy committee
- Requiring consultants to sign lengthy and onerous confidential-ity agreements
- Denying the consultees any permission to consult others, or to report to constituents
- Demanding secrecy around all consultations
- Prohibiting any written or published report by those consulted
- Prohibiting ranking of proposals by the consultees
- Blandly stating that the majority of those consulted "agreed" with the eventual decision-maker

In order to hamper such standard power shifting strategies, negotiators can push for documented *details* in advance about: which individuals or organizations must be consulted; for what kinds of decisions; in what time frame; what proportions of each kind of individual or faction will make up on any committee; how many hours of consultations; with limited or no restraints on publicity; permission for consultees to report to constituents; and/or a requirement for a public written report (including any dissenters) on process, opinions and rankings by those who are or should have been consulted.

Each of the above details in the consultation process represents another possible shift of power, which may be sufficient concession to enable an initial agreement.

Entrenchment of Restrictions on Future Decision Making

Some negotiators push for an extra layer of restrictions upon the use of certain power by a faction or future leader. They attempt to "entrench" or "solidify" various gains, assets or "rights". Accordingly, certain types of decisions are prohibited unless visible and perhaps onerous procedures are followed. These restrictions are sometimes embedded in the language of "rights".

For example:

- A sporting club, school, university or aboriginal band may agree to prohibit the sale of land unless such proposals are supported by 70% vote of alumni or "members".
- A new government may be elected, after "negotiations" with voters, and after assurances to enact entrenched "human rights" legislation. For example, that government could legislate that no law can modify freedom of the press, speech, religion or of association without a specified form of notice to the public; a specified period of delay; and parliamentary approval by at least two thirds majority; or perhaps even by approval in a referendum of two thirds of voters.

Deadlock: Agreed Mandatory Negotiation or Mediation Process

Once absolute legal power is qualified, modified or divided in any way by law or by agreement such as the gradations above, there arises the probability of boundary disagreements about the modifications. For example: Is it time to "rotate leadership"? Have the requirements for an adjoining "clothing" shop been adequately considered? Is this a "marketing" or "research" decision? Is this a "defense", "emergency" or "immigration" decision? Who can decide whether to start a child on karate classes, vegetarian meals or alternative medicine? Were the opinions of all the consultants properly gathered and considered?

Much has been written on "dispute system design" (Ury, Brett and Goldberg 1988). How to create an agreed series of publicized and accessible bus-stops where disputes can find resolution? The steps tend to increase in formality, expense and delay, though parties are free at any time to return by agreement to simpler procedures in the chain.

The first few steps involve a *minimal* surrender of power by any of the parties to the dispute—namely the use of negotiation or some kind of mediation. In order to be legally binding, agreements to negotiate or mediate about division of powers require *detailed* machinery clauses. For example, how to trigger the process? What time limits to prepare? How to appoint a mediator? What time limits for the meetings to begin? What minimum length of meetings? Such machinery clauses now have many accessible precedents.

How does agreeing to a mandatory negotiation or mediation clause amount to a "loss" of power? Particularly in employment contracts, such clauses may involve management losing time, money, mystery, information and status in a semi-public meeting which may include lawyers, accountants and board members as observers or participants. Anecdotally, some humiliated bosses resign soon after such mandatory processes, which place a spotlight on their alleged incompetence, or unearth scandals. If the contractual obligation specifies "good faith" negotiation, this may also require interpretation of the complex case law which requires different degrees of co-operation and disclosure depending on the topic in dispute.

Deadlock: Agreed Mechanisms to Ensure Resolution

Negotiation or mediation may not resolve the boundary disputes which inevitably arise under the power division solutions listed above. Accordingly, disputants can agree in advance or on the occasion of a dispute to more drastic measures. These mechanisms all involve giving up power and control over a particular boundary decision. This is not a choice which control freaks, experienced leaders or zealous reformers readily embrace. Such humans have an array of well-practiced strategies to undermine the agreed resolution mechanism so that power and control reverts to them.

Two examples of agreed deadlock breaking mechanisms are as follows:
- Automatic formulae
- Independent arbitrator or judge

Automatic Formulae

Some predictable borderland conflicts can be resolved by an agreement in advance to apply a mathematical formula if and when the conflict occurs (numbers emerge again!). A frequent example arises again where partners or separating spouses agree to sell a business or real estate, but no buyers emerge at the hoped-for price. How to decide on price reductions and sale process without months of further damaging negotiations between the sellers? A common solution is a "self-performing" agreement which states to the effect:

- The parties agree to sign all documents necessary to advertise and sell the business at a list price of $X;
- If the contract of sale is not signed for that price or at another price within 3 months;
- Then unless the parties agree otherwise in writing, the business will be auctioned under the control of auctioneer Y with a reserve price of $X minus 15 percent, such an auction to take place within a further 6 weeks.
- [If no sale, progressive percentage reserve price reductions at subsequent auctions, until sale etc.]

Independent Arbitrator or Judge

Failing a negotiated solution, a disputed interpretation of an agreement which divides decision-making power can of course be referred in advance or in the moment to one of the many forms of independent arbitration (Wade 1999). Obviously, this involves a substantial loss of control to a third party. Especially where competing decision-makers have a history of trickery and distrust, surrendering power over decision-making boundaries to an arbitrator may be considered dangerous, due to use of "litigation strategies", and the possible creation of an unfavorable precedent.

Predictably, the disputants may use a range of standard strategies to regain control such as appointment of a friendly arbitrator, hiding information, organizing procedural skirmishes and delay, multiplying expenses and paper, or seeking disqualification of successive arbitrators.

In 1215, King John and his barons entered into a famous power sharing agreement known as Magna Carta. However, less well known is that this "peace agreement" contained a one-sided arbitration clause, which immediately discredited the whole agreement: The 25 arbitrators chosen to adjudicate future disputes were *all* barons, and the king had not a *single* representative on the panel. Civil war followed three months later. (Danzinger and Gillingham 2003).[4] Even arbitrators who are hired and paid repetitively by one wealthy client, such as a corporate employer, have lost the appearance of neutrality and independence. Why would a wealthy client repetitively rehire an arbitrator unless that arbitrator had a record of rendering favorable, or at least tolerable decisions? (Cole 2001)

In some jurisdictions, where the judiciary has a reputation for independence, the parties may agree to use, or in the moment actually use, the state courts as a process to resolve borderland disputes. However, the slippery slope of loss of power increases as state courts become involved. In some areas of dispute, a court does not merely *interpret* the agreed division of powers. More dramatically, the court can *create* an entirely new division of powers. In such cases, each decision-maker's status quo of existing power becomes fragile if (s)he chooses, or is pushed, to buy into the lottery of litigation (Wade 2001b).

Examples of this "increase" in judicial power from "interpreter" to "legislator" include:

- A parental agreement about who makes which future decisions in relation to a child can be entirely overruled and be replaced by a new division of powers between parents and relatives, which a judge considers to be "in the best interests of the child" among the limited options available.

- A public body such as a court, law society, licensing board or environmental protection agency may have divided or delegated some powers to certain employees, to a committee or tribunal, or to a referendum of members, for the sake of efficiency, or in an attempt to avoid blame for unpopular decisions. A court may decide that parts of this division or delegation are beyond statutory authorization or are even "unconstitutional" (Boilermaker's Case 1956; Harris v. Caladine 1991).[5]

Qualified Veto Power by the Other Party

The transfer of decision-making power becomes more effective where one person, faction or nation is given the legal power to veto the other's proposal on a limited number of occasions. For example:

- A staff association may have negotiated a right to veto a maximum of two recommendations on a short list for management positions.

- A defense lawyer may have a right to reject up to eight jurors proposed by the prosecution without giving reasons for such rejection.

- An upper house in parliament may have the constitutional right to reject a financial bill up to three times before parliament is dissolved for new elections.

Veto Power by the Other Party

The penultimate loss of decision-making power occurs where one party confers an unqualified right of veto on another. That is, one party can legally block *any* proposal by another. This unlimited power to say "no" may be the only method to entice a powerful person into membership of a young organization. For example:

- A permanent member of the Security Council of the United Nations can veto any decision proposed by other members.

- An eminent researcher can veto any proposal by a research department of which he is a member to spend funds of more than one million dollars.

- The current elected head of a church denomination or sporting club can veto any number of proposals to change that organization's constitution or code of fundamental beliefs.

Obviously, an unlimited right of veto gives power to the holder to conduct endless negotiations and lead an organization into passivity, new directions or closure. Moreover, the power to block another person's proposals and decisions leads indirectly to the veto-holder having power to *make* alternative proposals. Sometimes, negotiated or legislated power sharing is couched in optimistic phrases which are intentionally or accidentally vague—for example, "equal partners"; "joint custody and guardianship"; "equal responsibility"; and "co-operative management". When conflicts later arise, there will be a debate about whether the vague terminology means "unlimited rights of veto", "limited right of veto", or some gradation of "duty to consult."

Total Power to the "Other"

Be careful, or you may get what you wish (negotiate) for.

The final transition in the gradation of shared power reaches the opposite end of the starting point of "total power". The tables are turned. This occurs where one party "wins" by attrition or other means and "negotiates" a total power transfer. The winner may achieve his/her goals of a relatively efficient or dysfunctional dictatorship; a resources grab; tribal revenge; status as boss; "removal" of dissenters who tried to achieve a more power-sharing venture or nation; control during a "short term" emergency or transition.

Conversely, it is arguable that to function "well", most families, organizations and nations require a mixture of co-operation, tolerance, power sharing, independence, non-conformist ingenuity, resources, skills, motivation and morale. It may be a Pyrrhic victory where one faction achieves total power, unless that transition is replaced subsequently with a model lower or higher on the power- sharing gradation.

Caveat: Paper Agreements & Their Non-Performance

These gradations of legal power may well assist parties to reach a *paper* "agreement" on future division of powers. However, if a power struggle has escalated prior to "settlement", then the paper agreement may give only shallow and temporary peace. The residual dynamics of conflict may be entrenched (Pruitt and Kim 2004).[6]

Nevertheless, even a paper division of power has potential benefits such as:

- A moment of peace.
- Reduced intensity of emotions for some of the disputants.
- "Back to business" activities for some of the disputants.
- A new mutual narrative of "satisfactory settlement".
- Expenditure of money elsewhere than on the dispute.

- Placation of tribal supporters, perhaps even some hawks (Wade 2006).
- Sometimes, time and experience enough to demonstrate that in the long run, the agreed division of "legal" powers does not matter, or does not work, and will be replaced by another "practical" and perhaps more advantageous reality.

Illustrative of all these benefits are the many thousands of intensely negotiated formal and informal agreements between family tribes each year about the division of parental power over (and "time-with") children. The vast majority of these agreements are soon ignored, technically "breached", or altered due to weariness, lack of funds, new parental employment, relocation, and relationships; and independent teenagers voting with their feet.[7] Life goes on. However, the gradation of powers discussed in this chapter can still assist the renegotiation (or rationalization) of an emerging and normal statistical reality.

Conclusion

Negotiators and mediators who know about, and can recite, the gradations of solutions which lie between offers and counter-offers can assist disputing parties to consider the range and find a mutually "satisfactory" choice. They can plan, predict and manage the sense of loss which all parties experience as their initially preferred solutions fade. An elusive gradation of shared (or not shared) decision-making powers has been set out in this chapter. This knowledge is a worthwhile addition to the repertoire of a skillful negotiator, mediator, politician, parent, manager, or other decision-making human being.

Notes

[1] Trends toward centralization of power in allegedly democratic governments and universities in first world nations ("corporatization" or "managerialism") have led to frequent disputes about where decision making power does and should fall.
[2] Examples of three standard power questions used in negotiations about the interim management of a business which is proposed to be sold are set out later in the section under "Duty to Report."
[3] For example, this practice is notorious in court judgments which allegedly "decide" claims by indigenous tribes to ownership of land. A dramatic illustration is found in the Supreme Court of Canada decision of *Tsilhquot'in Nation v British Columbia* (2014). This decision confirmed that the government has a duty to "consult" and "accommodate" aboriginal "interests", whenever aboriginal title is asserted, even though the claim to such title is *unproven*.
[4] D. Danzinger and J. Gillingham, *1215: The Year of Magna Carta*, (2003) at 262-262. Clause 52 of the Charter stated boldly "If without lawful judgement of his peers, we [the king] have deprived anyone of lands, castles, liberties or rights, we will restore them to him at once. And if any disagreement arises on this let it be settled by the judgement of the twenty five barons." Clause 61 goes on to confer unlimited remedial powers on the 25 barons.
[5] For example in Australia, *Boilermaker's Case* (1956) (the popular political practice of granting vote-catching "judicial" powers to a friendly tribunal was limited by the Australian constitution); *Harris v Caladine* (1991) (the practice of delegating certain "mi-

nor" judicial powers to court registrars was narrowly held to be constitutionally permissible, so long as limiting conditions were attached to the delegation of powers).
[6] In D.G. Pruitt and S.H. Kim, (2004) chapters 5-8 set out the emotional and structural changes which occur as conflict "escalates". When these changes have occurred, the toothpaste is out of the tube, and cannot be easily restored to a previous state by an agreement.
[7] See Australian Institute of Family Studies, *Evaluation of the 2006 Family Law Reforms* (2009). This is a remarkable Australian study of 28,000 people involved in separating families with children, and what happened to their formal and informal "child arrangements" about time and power over children over a 3 year period.

References

Australian Institute of Family Studies. 2009. *Evaluation of the 2006 Family Law Reforms*. Melbourne: Australian Institute of Family Studies. Available at www.ag.gov.au/cca

Blum, G. and R. H. Mnookin. 2006. When Not To Negotiate. In *The Negotiator's Fieldbook: The Desk Reference for the Experienced Negotiator*, edited by A.K. Schneider and C. Honeyman. Washington, DC: American Bar Association.

Boilermaker's Case (1956) 94 *Commonwealth Law Reports* 254 (Australia).

Bosquet, M. 2008. *How the University Works: Higher Education and the Low Wage Nation*. New York: New York University Press.

Cole, S. 2001. Uniform Arbitration: One Size Fits All Does Not Fit. 16 *Ohio State Journal on Dispute Resolution* 759-790.

Danzinger, D. and J. Gillingham (2003) *1215: The Year of the Magna Carta*. Great Britain: Hodder and Stoughton.

Harris v Caladine (1991) *Family Law Cases* 92-217 (Australia).

Lewicki, R. J. 2006. Trust and Distrust. In *The Negotiator's Fieldbook: The Desk Reference for the Experienced Negotiator*, edited by A.K. Schneider and C. Honeyman. Washington, DC: American Bar Association.

Maister, D.V., C.H. Green, and R.M. Galford. 2000. *The Trusted Advisor*. New York: Touchstone.

Mayer, B. 1987. The Dynamics of Power in Mediation and Negotiation. 16 *Mediation Quarterly* 75-86.

Pruitt, D. G. and S. H. Kim. 2004. *Social Conflict: Escalation, Stalemate and Settlement*. New York, Mc Graw-Hill.

Secretary, Department of Health and Community Services v JWB and SMB (Marion's case, 1992) *Family Law Cases* 92-293 (Australia).

Savoie, D. 2015. *What is Government Good At?: A Canadian Answer*. Montreal: McGill-Queens University Press.

Tuchman, G. 2009. *Wannabe U: Inside the Corporate University*. Chicago: University of Chicago Press.

Tsilhquot'in Nation v British Columbia. 2014. SCC 44 (Canada).

Ury, W., J. Brett, and S. Goldberg. 1988. *Getting Disputes Resolved*. San Francisco: Jossey-Bass.

Wade, J.H. 1994. Forms of Power in Family Mediation and Negotiation. *Australian Journal of Family Law* 8: 40-57. Available online at epublications.bond.edu.au.

Wade, J.H. 1999. Arbitration of Matrimonial Property Disputes. 11 *Bond Law Review* 395-434. Available online at epublications.bond.edu.au.

Wade, J.H. 2001a. Systematic Risk Analysis for Negotiators and Litigators: But You Never Told Me It Would Be Like This. *Bond Law Review* 13: 462-485. Available online at epublications.bond.edu.au.

Wade, J.H. 2001b. Don't Waste My Time in Negotiation or Mediation: This Case Needs a Judge: When is Litigation the Right Solution? *Mediation Quarterly* 18: 259-280.

Wade, J.H. 2006. Bargaining in the Shadow of the Tribe and Limited Authority to Settle. In *The Negotiator's Fieldbook: The Desk Reference for the Experienced Negotiator*, edited by A.K. Schneider and C. Honeyman. Washington, DC: American Bar Association. A version is also in (2003) 15 Bond Law Review 115-143.

ೞ 91 ೲ

The Uses of Ambiguity

Chris Honeyman

Editors' Note: The reality sinks in: everybody's now trying to reach an agreement, but on some fundamental things, the parties really don't agree. Some of those involved see themselves as reasonable people, others are Standing On Principle without any thought of what that will mean in practice. Is there anything you can do to get this dispute over with before it spirals completely out of control? Yes, says Honeyman: you can allow, or even consciously design in, a bit of ambiguity here and there. Doing this knowledgeably can preserve your principles, while allowing for an agreement that works well enough for an imperfect world. This can be read with Moffitt's chapter on Contingent Agreements and Wade's on the Final Gap.

Go to work under any of thousands of labor-management contracts, and you can be fired only for "just cause"—whatever *that* means. A truly vague statement, it's pretty well guaranteed to generate disputes under the contract later, as the parties naturally see a marginal employee differently. So it's a classic example of ambiguity in action. But why on earth would any sane pair of labor and management negotiation teams leave the all-important discharge clause so up-in-the-air?

There is, I think, a very good reason. It starts with the notion that a matter of principle really is often at the root of a dispute—even though experienced negotiators are familiar with the counterpart who takes a strong and seemingly unalterable stand on a point of principle, only to exchange it for money when the price is right. An explicit confrontation over a question of principle can result in a total inability to work out a settlement; so it should not be surprising that negotiators and mediators

Chris Honeyman is managing partner of Convenor Conflict Management, a consulting firm based in Washington, DC. He is co-editor of *The Negotiator's Desk Reference* and five other books, and author of over 90 published articles, book chapters and monographs. He has directed a 25-year series of research-and-development programs in conflict management (see www.convenor.com/projects). Chris has also served as a consultant to numerous academic and practical conflict resolution programs, held a variety of advisory roles with the ABA, IMI and other organizations, and served as a mediator, arbitrator and in other neutral capacities in more than 2,000 disputes.

sometimes paper over these cracks with calculated or innocent ambiguities. This chapter will examine the function of ambiguity in agreements, and defend its deliberate use under certain circumstances. I will argue in particular that under certain (quite common) circumstances, ambiguity can be employed with a reasonable confidence that its use will moderate some otherwise unacceptable risks.

There will always be those who value the effect of ambiguities on their earnings, such as a full-time labor arbitrator of my acquaintance who once declared happily that "There's no such thing as clear contract language." But most negotiators and mediators seem to have a vague disapproval of ambiguity. This is excusable. Most professional negotiators, most of the time, seek agreements that will be clear, easy to administer, and durable. [NDR: Wade & Honeyman, *Lasting Agreement*] A general preference for wrapping up loose ends fits with the notion of "settlement," and a neat and tidy job seems consistent with professionalism.

The principals in many negotiations may bring to bear a different perspective. Even while negotiating an agreement, they are looking down the road to the later interpretation of that agreement; and in the case of permanent relationships like those between labor and management or one nation and another, they are quite likely to be engaged in the arbitration of one dispute, the litigation of another, and the negotiation of a third at the same time.

Much of what happens in complex negotiations can be seen in terms of a struggle between radical and moderate elements within each party (Bellman 2006; Matz 2006). In a multi-faceted negotiation, the fact that the moderate element on one issue may be the radical element on another obscures, but does not change, the essential relationship between moderate and radical. Bear with me if for simplicity I encapsulate a typical negotiating group as consisting of a radical minority and a moderate majority. (Where the situation is reversed, effective negotiation or mediation is unlikely).

In such a group, the radicals can be expected to emphasize philosophical and ideological purposes, partly out of conviction, but also because this gives them a platform in the continuing attempt to garner public support, and perhaps become the dominant faction. The moderates, meanwhile, are likely to emphasize the practical results of accommodation as opposed to confrontation. I have elsewhere commented [NDR: Honeyman, *Working with Mediators*] that when a mediator is presented with such a situation, the mediator's tendency, or even function, is to help the moderate out-argue the radical within a given party. Mediators, however, are not alone in seeing it as generally preferable to divert an argument over "principle" into a "pragmatic" channel, so that an explicit agreement can be reached. Yet this cannot always be accomplished. The best alternative may sometimes be to leave a deliberate gap or other ambiguity in the agreement: clarity emphasizes the differences, while ambiguity can serve to let each faction maintain its position and self-image in principle, if not necessarily in practice. But does this merely store up trouble for the future? Is it, in some sense, immoral? [See also NDR: Menkel-Meadow, *Morality*]

The traditional view of ambiguity in an agreement is that it implies either the presence of an unconsidered point, or a deliberate failure to come to grips with the problem. In either case, that view amounts to a belief that where there is ambiguity there is no agreement. A classic example is one presented by Sanda Kaufman. [NDR: Kaufman, *Interpreters*] The word *"ceasefire"* carries critically different meanings in Arabic (*hudna*), in Hebrew (*hafsakat esh*) and in English. In English, it means an end to aggressive acts; in Hebrew, *hafsakat esh* means to Israelis that Palestinians must stop all attacks against them, but that if Israel gets wind of a pending terror attack, an anticipatory response is permissible; in Arabic, *hudna* means a temporary scaling down of hostilities, but that a true enemy remains. When any agreement must be rendered in three languages, this particular ambiguity is conspicuously likely to cause trouble.

But I believe there's more to it than that. As every arbitrator knows, agreements are to be read as a whole. And there is a strong impetus on others, as well as arbitrators, to find a way to *interpret* an agreement rather than declare that for the purpose under review, there isn't one—a stance that may be intellectually defensible, but which can have alarming practical results.

The potentially calamitous consequences of an untimely declaration that "Gee, now I look at it closely, there's no agreement after all" can often be predicted by the parties. I take the view that they often *have* predicted such consequences. Parties have impliedly anticipated that agreement-readers will strive to interpret the agreement as a whole to resolve the ambiguity for immediate purposes. In turn, parties have often built in implicit mechanisms for doing so, such that the interpretation of an ambiguity depends partly on the enforcement mechanism specified in the agreement.

Suppose, for instance, that you are negotiating two different matters with different parties at the same time. Each party sends you a draft agreement on the same day. In the event of a later dispute over its interpretation, one proposed contract calls for mediation, followed by arbitration if necessary, with both clauses specifying mainstream firms as the neutrals. The other draft contract specifies good-faith negotiations over any differences of interpretation but provides for either party to sue in the courts of, say, Singapore for enforcement at any time. By chance, in another section, both drafts also contain the exact same clause—a rather ambiguous one. But will that clause, in practice, mean the same thing in both contracts?

Every agreement contains at least one express or implied means of securing compliance with its terms. Different mechanisms of enforcement generate different results when exposed to ambiguity, and this can be predicted by anyone who possesses a working knowledge of the several mechanisms. For this reason, an agreement, read as a whole, can in fact provide a functional interpretation to the ambiguity.

A moment's thought about the characteristics of the various enforcement mechanisms will suggest that the choice of negotiation, mediation, arbitration, fact-finding, litigation or unilateral action implies something about the balance of power *within* each party as well as that *between* the parties. Negotiation, for instance, inherently preserves to the parties the power to create something new; but it always requires a backup process, since settlement cannot be guaranteed. Mediation is similar in this respect. But both processes imply more. They anticipate some give-and-take, suggesting that parties specifying these processes are willing to settle for a moderated result in a given case, one that is likely to draw as much from the exigencies of circumstance as from principle. In non-Western cultures such flexibility is often a basic expectation [see NDR: Liao, *Style & Culture*, and NDR: Goh, *Cultural Errors*] But even in the West, when compared with the rights-only implication of specifying litigation, or the raw power-display of unilateral action (such as, in a labor context, the right to strike over grievances) the expectation of give-and-take is likely to result in significant differences in the practical interpretation of ambiguous language.

Litigation, when selected as the "bottom line" in the event of disagreement over interpretation, implies that the parties have adopted the rules and mores of the society-at-large as their working standards; but because of its expense and the burden of proof, it implies more than that. In ambiguous circumstances, it suggests a larger sphere of unilateral discretion flows to the "acting party," and correspondingly less to the "responding party." And so on. Thus which process, or combination of processes, the parties choose can be an index to the interpretation of other parts of the agreement.

For a couple of illustrations of how this works in practice, I will use labor agreements;[1] not only have they long provided explicit grievance mechanisms for negotiating subsidiary disputes, but they also have a long history of using mediation and arbitration as well, often as steps in the same dispute. Rounding out the menu, labor and management are also no strangers to litigation or to unilateral action. But I will focus on arbitration, because in this context it is particularly revealing. Atypically, in the often-confidential world of ADR, this history is thoroughly documented, with thousands of arbitration awards published and codified, and with many prior grievance settlements discussed in those awards. Also, arbitration alone combines the terminating force of an imposed decision with a value system theoretically drawn from the agreement itself. So it's significant, I think, that almost all of these agreements use arbitration as the final step in subsidiary disputes.

If in fact ambiguity implied the absence of an agreement, the thousands of reported pronouncements of labor arbitrators on ambiguous clauses should reflect that. The fact that they typically do not is instructive as to the underlying intent of the amorphous mass of contending factions often called, in an oversimplification, "the two parties." Meanwhile, labor arbitration proceedings are widely recognized as governed by principles that combine an injunction to the arbitrator to arrive at an award which "draws its essence" from the parties' agreement with an underlying set of nonlegal expectations, expressed in labor cases as "the law of the shop." Labor arbitrators can regularly be heard to denounce the notion that they should apply external law in their decisions, and the system of labor arbitration has continued with surprising stability of attitudes for many years. This is a system that comes as close to pure reliance on the perceived intent of the parties as decision-making systems get. It is significant, therefore, that the bulk of labor arbitration awards concerned with ambiguous contract language in effect apply a general rule that *ambiguity implies moderation.*

To return to the opening example, the common and above cited clause in labor contracts, providing that an employee may be discharged (or disciplined) for "just cause," is not ubiquitous. Some parties have been able to agree on a laundry list of circumstances that warrant discharge or don't, and have written that into their agreements. But such an effort generally runs into roadblocks of principle that tend to exacerbate the dispute. Consider, for instance, even so "obvious" a standard for discharge as proven theft: the company says "Theft is theft," the union says "What if it's just a pencil?" Or lateness: the union says "You can't fire someone for being late," the company replies "Then we'll get a few employees who take advantage of that, and we'll be stuck with them for years while they screw up the production schedule any time they feel like it."

In the practical result of countless labor negotiations, the phrase "just cause" is preferred to the divisive thrashing-out of the possible permutations and combinations of circumstance. The phrase is ambiguous, in this instance, because of its vagueness. (Empson 1949)[2] The company agrees to "just cause" because it is hard to maintain a claim that it should have the right to discharge employees for unjust reasons or no reason at all. The union agrees to it because it is hard to maintain that employees who by definition are getting what they deserve should be kept on the job. Even a cursory review of the vast profusion of cases decided under this standard shows that the awards are generally moderate in tone and fact-driven. And the parties routinely complain about the result, but rarely change the underlying standard.[3]

The long line of subcontracting (or in more recent parlance, "outsourcing") cases supplies a second illustration, which draws from a different kind of ambiguity. In theory, nothing could be simpler than for the parties to a labor agreement to write such language as "The employer may subcontract work" or "The company may not subcontract work." However, either phrase will conflict with a basic principle of one of the parties. In the union's case, the principle is that the union represents those who perform certain work, and by strenuous efforts it has managed to raise their wages. The last thing a union can accept is the notion that an employer can, without restriction, give away the employees' work to the cheapest labor it can find through a subcontractor. But at the same time, the question of "make or buy?" is basic to the manufacturing process of any complex product. Industries have a long history, predating any organization of the employees, of routine decision-making as to the best method of obtaining any given component of a product or service. Management therefore finds a principled obstacle to agreeing to give up the right to make such decisions.

Some parties have been able to agree on specific language providing for the right to subcontract under certain circumstances and not under others. But of greater interest here is the plethora of labor agreements that are *silent* as to subcontracting, even though both parties have been aware for decades of the potential or actual issue. These contracts, however, often contain a seniority clause, a recognition clause and a general management rights clause. Typically in subcontracting cases, the union will argue that the recognition clause, combined with language protecting seniority rights and the specified wage scale for the performance of certain work, shows clearly that in the absence of language specifically allowing subcontracting, the agreement must be read as preserving work to the employees represented by the union. The company, in turn, will argue that the management rights clause (generally using a formula something like "the company shall have all rights of management except as limited by this agreement") clearly shows that, since the union has not managed to negotiate language expressly restricting subcontracting, the company has plenary rights to subcontract any work it chooses in the best interest of the business. And then both parties will get down to brass tacks and try their case based on the ambiguity customarily recognized to arise from these conflicting clauses.

The standard desk reference of the labor arbitration trade, universally called *Elkouri* (Elkouri and Elkouri 2012), accurately describes the various tests used by different arbitrators where no specific contract language (or conclusive evidence of bargaining history) exists concerning subcontracting. These general tests, all of which discuss the common clauses favoring the union and favoring the company, are less interesting than the fact that they converge on the same practical considerations. Elkouri summarizes these standards as past practice; justification of the present instance; effect on the union or the bargaining unit; effect on individual employees; the type of work involved and its relation to employees' usual work; whether suitable employees or equipment are available in-house; whether the subcontracting will be regular or long-lasting; and special circumstances, such as an emergency. (Elkouri and Elkouri 2012: 13-126-13-131).

What is significant to this discussion is that every one of these standards tends to secure a moderate answer. The resulting fact-driven awards have, of course, regularly prompted the "we was robbed" reaction almost expected of a losing party to a labor arbitration; but in the larger sense, they have found acceptance. This is proven by the simple fact of the longevity of these standards, and by thousands of pairs of parties' bilateral if tacit agreement not to renegotiate the underlying contract language over a long period of time.

In either example, the negotiators who constructed the agreement and the arbitrator who interprets it all show their relationship to the moderate and radical elements on both sides by the practical and predictable result of their actions. The arbitrator in particular—a creature of the agreement and, one hopes, uniquely sensitive to its nuances—serves the moderates' goals by distinguishing between tolerable and intolerable incursions into each party's "principles." The arbitrator couches her decision in terms of the agreement, and strains to avoid using the term "equity" in order to escape the accusation of the radicals on the losing side that the award does not "draw its essence" from the agreement. And in turn, the courts refrain from second-guessing the arbitrator by applying general legal principles, adopting instead the Supreme Court rulings in the "Steelworkers' Trilogy"[4] and related standards for deferral to arbitration's results.[5] At the same time, the "bargaining in the shadow of the arbitrator" [NDR: Gross, Arbitration's Shadow] that takes place in the earlier stages of grievance processes ensures that the vast majority of grievances are resolved at relatively low transaction costs, preserving to both parties the financial ability to contest a grievance to the point of arbitration when they feel they must. From the point of view of the moderate on either side who desired a workable if not ideal agreement, *the various processes of dispute resolution thus form an intricate ecology, in which each process depends on the others for the success of the whole.*

Some may object that the moderating effect I describe is instead an indication of the alleged tendency of arbitrators to compromise.[6] But an award that does not clearly give the whole issue to either party is not proof of the arbitrator's lack of integrity, nor does it demonstrate that the arbitrator was prejudiced. In a "compromise" decision, the arbitrator presumably is motivated by a desire not to offend anyone; but in the awards under discussion here the arbitrators are properly performing their function, which is to interpret conflicting or vague provisions so as to give meaning to the whole agreement.

The net result for negotiators and mediators is that ambiguity can be employed as a tool in achieving an adequate, if imperfect, settlement of a dispute. *Provided that the agreed-on enforcement mechanism is appropriate to this end*, leaving ambiguities can imply that the disposition of

THE USES OF AMBIGUITY

subsidiary disputes will be fact-driven and moderate in overall effect. This enables the moderates in either party to compel discourse on terms acceptable to them, and to retain control of their party by avoiding reliance on rhetoric and ideology. A judicious bit of ambiguity therefore becomes a sophisticated means of ensuring that the general philosophy of the party does not have to be compromised explicitly (which would allow radicals to claim that the moderates had "sold them down the river"), while allowing enough putative "wins" by the opposing party to make agreement possible.

Negotiators are employed to create agreements, and should not sneer at an ambiguity when that is a necessary element in obtaining an overall agreement—as long as any subsidiary disputes that result seem likely to be manageable. (A possible exception, beyond the scope of this chapter but worthy of discussion in terms of its ethics, is the situation where a negotiator or mediator suspects that a proposed ambiguity will not be interpreted according to the kinds of standards applied above, but will instead be subject to unilateral action. That involves a technically difficult and morally problematic calculation of the "mutual best interest" of conflicting parties.) [See e.g. NDR: Coleman et al., *Intractable—2*]

But where a "moderating" system obtains for the disposition of subsidiary disputes, there is nothing inherently wrong with gracefully admitting the impossibility of reaching, in every instance, a complete "meeting of the minds." Allowing an ambiguity to pass into the agreement, when there is a reasonable expectation that it will later be interpreted in terms not likely to cause a wider dispute, is just another way to get the agreement done.

Notes

This chapter is adapted from the author's *In Defense of Ambiguity*, 3 NEGOTIATION JOURNAL 81 (1987).

[1] This discussion is based on U.S. practice; the underlying legal rights and other expectations of these types of parties vary by country.

[2] See Empson 1947. Empson distinguished a series of different types of ambiguity, though Empson, who was writing about poetry, identified some types not relevant to disputes. (A "fortunate confusion" is a concept of ambiguity attributable, in the context of an agreement, only to someone who hopes to make a living from it.) Of Empson's list, these seem applicable to disputes: "when a detail is effective several ways at once;" "simultaneous unconnected meanings;" "a contradictory or irrelevant statement, forcing the reader to invent interpretation;" and "full contradiction, marking a division in the author's mind." All of these are consistent with a condition not normally present in poetry—the opposing purposes of plural authors.

[3] In the years since this was first written, there has been a widespread political shift in the U.S. toward weakening unions. The supposed injustice to employers of having the burden of proving "just cause" for discharges of, say, teachers has been part of the case urged by conservatives. The rights and wrongs of this shift are beyond the scope of this chapter, but the direct parties themselves still appear to rarely change this standard clause, politically challenged though it now is. Thus I believe the argument made here remains true.

[4] These three U.S. Supreme Court decisions set the standards for federal courts to use in determining both arbitrability of a given dispute and whether or not an award should be overturned on the merits. See United Steelworkers of America v. American Mf. Co., 363 U.S. 564 (1960); United Steelworkers of America v. Enterprise Wheel & Car Corp., 363 U.S. 593 (1960); United Steelworkers of America v. Warrior & Gulf Nav. Co., 363 U.S. 574 (1960).

[5] In more recent years, the U.S. courts' friendliness toward deferral to arbitration has gone well beyond this, to a point where there is increasing concern about wholesale deferral to one-sided arbitration structures that are attached to contracts of adhesion. [NDR: Gross, *Arbitration's Shadow*, in this volume] But this disturbing trend does not disturb the logic behind the original example.

[6] It is often argued that arbitrators have a tendency to "split the baby" in order to remain acceptable to both sides. I doubt the truth of that assertion, but must note that the fact that it is so often made implies that it is at least widely believed by parties using arbitration. From this, however, it could be inferred that parties holding such suspicions enter into their agreements "knowing," and implicitly tolerating, so widely expected an outcome—also, of course, a form of moderation-by-ambiguity.

References

Bellman, H. 2006. Internal Conflicts of the Team. In *The Negotiator's Fieldbook: The Desk Reference for the Experienced Negotiator*, edited by A. K. Schneider and C. Honeyman. Washington, DC: American Bar Association.

Elkouri, F. and E. A. Elkouri. 2012. *How Arbitration Works*, 7th edn. edited by Kenneth May. Washington, DC: BNA/American Bar Association.

Empson, W. 1949. *Seven Types of Ambiguity*. London: Chatto & Windus.

Matz, D. 2006. Intra-team Miscommunication. In *The Negotiator's Fieldbook: The Desk Reference for the Experienced Negotiator*, edited by A. K. Schneider and C. Honeyman. Washington, DC: American Bar Association.

❧ 92 ❧

Contingent Agreements

Michael L. Moffitt

Editors' Note: What if you and the other side have very different views of the future? Should this make it harder to achieve an agreement? In fact, as Moffitt explains, these different views can provide exactly the lubricant needed for the gears to mesh. Contingent agreements can help negotiators move toward an overall agreement, even (or particularly) when they disagree. As one of several chapters discussing particular techniques for use when things get sticky, it should be read in conjunction with Wade's chapter on the Final Gap and Honeyman's on Ambiguity.

"That won't happen." "Yes, it will." "No, it won't." "Will too."

Negotiators generally find no shortage of things about which to disagree. For example, negotiators seeking to resolve a dispute often have sharply differing perceptions of the past. What happened? Whose decisions and actions caused the effects in question? How does their conduct compare with expectations or duties? In some circumstances, settlement is impossible without resolution of these backward-looking questions. Classical dispute resolution theory suggests that one might overcome impasse by shifting the focus of conversations toward the future (Stulberg 1987; Menkel-Meadow 2000; Alfini et al. 2001). Sometimes, however, the shift to a forward-looking exploration merely provides fertile, new grounds for disagreement. Rather than arguing about what happened, the negotiators argue about what will happen. A wholesaler asserts that demand for the product will skyrocket, and the retailer suspects otherwise. A defendant points to the relatively minor and temporary injuries caused in a car crash, but the victim fears that later on, new injuries may manifest them-

Michael Moffitt is the Philip H. Knight Chair in Law at the University of Oregon School of Law, where he has been a professor since 2001 and served as Dean from 2011 through 2017. He was formerly a Lecturer on Law at Harvard Law School and served as the Clinical Supervisor of the Harvard Mediation Program. A graduate of Harvard Law School and Marietta College, he has worked in more than twenty countries on public and private sector negotiations.

selves. Instinct may suggest that one negotiator will need to persuade the other about the likelihood of future uncertain events. Instead, genuinely held disagreements about the future present an important opportunity for negotiators to discover an attractive exchange. The vehicle for capturing this potential is the contingent agreement.

All contingent agreements share a basic structure: the parties identify the universe of possible future conditions and agree to take on different obligations in each of those conditions. The simplest contingent deals are those in which the future has only two possible relevant conditions. X will happen, or it will not. If X happens, the terms of our deal are ABC; if not, we will do DEF. If I think X is unlikely to happen, I will be happy to give you terms you prefer for ABC, in exchange for terms I favor for DEF. Believing that she will get the work finished on time, an author signs a lucrative book contract with a very harsh penalty for late completion. Buyer loves Seller's house, but really wants a property with off-street parking. Seller firmly expects that the city council will approve a variance required for construction of a new garage, but Buyer is less confident about the likelihood of getting approval. Buyer agrees to purchase the property from Seller at a reduced price, with a substantial additional payment to Seller if the City Council grants a variance within the next twelve months. Negotiators can craft attractive trades by establishing obligations that are contingent on a future uncertain event that affects each side's valuation of the agreement.

Contingent agreements can also include variable terms, pegged to some benchmark to be measured in the future. I think interest rates will increase over the next few months, and you think they will go down. If I am loaning you money today, we will each be happy to agree to a deal with a floating interest rate. Neither of us knows what the rate will be, but we can agree on the external measure to which we will look when the time comes. The plaintiff believes that he may suffer long-term negative health effects from exposure to the defendant's product, while the defendant believes no significant health risk exists. The defendant agrees to pay for specified medical monitoring expenses for the plaintiff and to assume any future medical costs associated with exposure.[1] A school board is nervous about the future levels of state funding available for school districts, while the teachers' union is optimistic. The two sides agree to a contingent wage package that is tied to a particular line item in the upcoming state budget. Two businesses entering a complex joint venture agree to final, binding resolution of their intellectual property dispute by an appointed arbitrator.[2] Without the possibility of contingent agreements, uncertainty regarding future conditions can make distributive decisions (for example, who gets how much money) difficult. By linking the allocation of resources to an externally measurable variable, negotiators can sometimes overcome otherwise paralyzing disagreements about the future.

Contingent agreements also present an opportunity to shape the incentives under which one or more of the negotiators will operate going forward. Some negotiated deals involve no future relationship between the negotiators and are self-executing. Buying a trinket in a marketplace involves a simple exchange of money for goods. In more complex circumstances, however, ongoing relationships exist and implementation of the agreement takes place over time. When the negotiated deal involves more than a simple, one-time exchange, parties' behavior after the agreement is relevant. Contingent agreements can help to create incentives for parties to behave well after the terms of the deal are fixed. A company may agree to tie a sales executive's compensation to sales performance, thus promoting sales-maximizing behavior out of the executive after the deal is signed. The health ministry of a developing country approaches a prospective donor, seeking support for particular health sector programs. Both the prospective donor and the developing country want to see multiple sources of funding. They agree to a matching program under which the donor will contribute an amount equal to the funds the ministry secures from other sources, giving the ministry officials added incentive to garner resources. In some contingent deals, one party can affect the likelihood of the contingent trigger—the salesman can make more sales calls, the ministry officials can approach more donors. In these types of deals, contingent agreements can affect parties' behavior after the agreement.

At the same time, precisely because contingent agreements can affect parties' behaviors, some contingent agreements risk creating conditions of moral hazard. Moral hazard is a condition in which one party, under the terms of an agreement, may undetectably or uncontrollably behave in a way that is adverse to the other party (Mnookin et al. 2000).[3] How quickly do you take the speed bumps when you are driving a rental car? Moral hazard suggests that many drivers will drive more cautiously over the bumps if they are driving their own cars because they consider the long-term effects of their driving behavior. Athletes' contracts often contain contingent incentive clauses. If the athlete scores a certain number of points, for example, he or she receives additional money. Such arrangements are a classic example of using contingent agreements to create favorable incentives for the player to perform. Moral hazard arises when, toward the end of the season, a team notices that the athlete is only a few points away from the triggering contingent event. Will the team structure its play to enable the athlete to achieve the statistical goal, or will the prospect of this contingent payment encourage the team's management to focus its efforts on a different player during the remaining games? If a salesperson's contract provides for a thirty percent commission on sales this year, but only a ten percent commission in future years, the salesperson will have an incentive to push deals into the current year—even if the deal he or she could have struck next year would have been on terms more favorable to the company. If a developing country knows that the international community will bail it out if the country's risky currency strategy winds up going poorly, will the country take on an inappropriate risk?[4] Negotiators crafting a contingent agreement should foresee the possibility of moral hazard and, where appropriate, structure incentives and disclosures to minimize the incentive for subsequent adverse behavior.[5]

One challenge in crafting a contingent agreement is identifying the boundaries of future possible conditions with sufficient clarity to know what obligations attach. A married couple might agree, "If the weather is nice tomorrow, we'll hike. Otherwise, we'll go shopping." The next morning, when it is cloudy but not raining, the spouse who wants to hike is likely to declare it "nice," while the person preferring to shop will argue the opposite. Rather than premise future obligations on something difficult to define with precision—the weather, the economy, one's health, political stability—wise contingent deals depend on easily-measured external variables. Did the airport weather station register precipitation in the past twenty-four hours? Did the unemployment rate for the state increase last month? Did the lab results show a drop in the level of "bad" cholesterol in your blood? Did the local elections take place on the pre-specified date? Answering such questions is relatively reliable and low-cost.

Still more complications arise when the contingent variable being measured is under the interpretive control of one party. For example, a mid-level executive may not want to have her bonus tied to the performance of the business unit she oversees if she has concerns that the company may subsequently adopt accounting methods that shift credit from her unit to another unit.[6] Similarly, a screenwriter is more likely to favor a percentage of the box office take over a percentage of the profits a studio reports on a film. Contingent agreements containing unambiguous, external triggers are less likely to produce post-agreement disagreements.

Crafting contingent deals also raises considerable questions about strategic disclosure.[7] Without any disclosure regarding forecasts and preferences, negotiators will not spot the possibility for a contingent agreement. Such disclosures, however, inevitably produce a risk of exploitation. Assume that I am virtually certain that X will happen, and you are virtually certain that X will not happen. If I begin our negotiations by declaring that I am "virtually certain X will happen," you may have an incentive to misstate your actual forecast. Rather than tell me that you are virtually certain of the opposite, you may tell me that you think there is "a decent chance" that X will not happen. You then may have an opportunity to demand a more favorable premium for being the party to take on the apparently greater risk. Contingent agreements are not different from most other aspects of bargaining; this presents opportunities both for mutually beneficial value creation and for one-sided efforts to skew value distribution.

And, once agreed upon, contingent agreements may affect negotiators' perceptions of "winning" and "losing." Classical negotiation theory counsels negotiators to conceive of negotiations in terms other than win-lose, pointing to the risk that competitive behavior may cloud opportunities for joint gains.[8] In one respect, contingent agreements may present an opportunity for negotiators to avoid the necessity of identifying a winner. Rather than forcing one side to concede on its forecast, contingent agreements permit (in fact, depend on) both sides to maintain their conflicting predictions about the future. At the time of the agreement, therefore, each side can declare "victory," to the extent such a declaration is important.

At the same time, contingent agreements have the nature of a wager. Unless one counts the sheer joy of gambling as a victory, both sides cannot win a wager. The contingent event either happens or it does not. Either way, one side may be disappointed.[9] In some organizational cultures, failure is punished more harshly than success is rewarded. How likely is a mid-level bureaucrat to agree to take on the prospect of a contingent agreement if the unlikely-but-possible "bad" outcome will be attributed to him personally? Even if the contingent agreement is rational from an expected-value perspective, the fear of "losing" the wager involved may lead a negotiator to reject an otherwise elegant contingent arrangement in favor of a non-contingent deal.[10]

Certain contingent structures may help to reduce the risk of visibly "losing." For example, if a plaintiff fears that a jury may award him nothing and a defendant fears a runaway jury award of millions, the two could agree to a small guaranteed recovery in exchange for a cap on the maximum recovery.[11] The losing party at trial will then be grateful to have made the contingent agreement, and the winner's regret will be dampened by having won a favorable verdict.

Given that two people virtually never agree entirely on the likely shape of the future, why aren't all deals contingent? Part of the answer lies in the transaction costs associated with identifying differences and crafting elegant contingent agreements. Two parties crafting the terms of a joint venture cannot imagine that they will plan for every possible contingency. At some point, they will agree to resolve future uncertainties when/if they arise. Even in circumstances without trust or a structural incentive for cooperation, the contingent stakes may simply be too low to justify the effort of crafting and implementing the deal. The costs of crafting a contingent agreement may, in some cases, outweigh the possible benefits of a contingent arrangement.

Another factor dissuading parties from crafting contingent deals is the value some parties place on certainty and finality. Particularly for negotiators embroiled in a dispute, achieving resolution may have an inherent value independent of the terms of the deal. Many disputants find it emotionally costly to carry around uncertainty. A contingent agreement does not represent complete finality, as at least some of the terms are yet to be determined. Uncertainty also can be costly for economic reasons. A company with an uncertain liability or benefit on its books faces considerable challenges in planning appropriate reserves of money, for example. If a company has a large collection of similar contingent agreements, it may be able to spread the risks and allocate money accurately in the aggregate. Similarly, some circumstances may permit parties to manage risks through the use of hedging instruments such as futures or options. Such allocations are not generally available to all individual negotiators, potentially making contingent agreements less attractive. For a contingent agreement to be appropriate in a given context, therefore, the perceived benefit it captures for each negotiator must exceed the transaction costs of discovering and implementing the agreement.

Negotiators arguing about the past sometimes "agree to disagree," preferring instead to focus on what they will do moving forward. Negotiators with differing perceptions of the future should similarly agree to disagree—using contingent agreements to capture the potential benefits of their differences.

Notes

[1] Such an agreement raises certain risks related to the precision with which the triggering event is defined. Which tests are necessary for monitoring? The plaintiff may want many more tests than the defendant considers appropriate. Even more significantly, who will determine whether the need for particular medical treatment was caused by exposure?

[2] An arbitrator's award is a measurable, external variable to be fixed in the future, on which the parties might agree to base the terms of their agreement. In this sense, arbitration agreements are a form of contingent agreement. (Lax and Sebenius 1986; Bazerman and Gillespie 1999) In some sense, parties may also purposefully agree to a currently ambiguous term in a contract, with an understanding that in future conditions a non-party will interpret the term. In his article, Christopher Honeyman (1987) described the pragmatic considerations of including ambiguous language in agreements—for example, a labor agreement permitting termination only for "just cause".

[3] Robert H. Mnookin (2000: 26) defined moral hazard as "the problem created when a contract shifts risk from one party to another party and information asymmetries permit the non-riskbearer to behave adversely under the contract without detection or consequence."

[4] Laura Tyson (1998: 21) observed that, "Without question, the most serious concern about the IMF's intervention is that it contributes to the so-called moral hazard problem, whereby economic actors reap the benefits of their decisions when things go well but are protected when things go poorly. If borrowers and investor do not suffer the costs of bad decisions, won't they be encouraged to make more bad decisions in the future? If the system spares the financial market rod, won't it spoil the financial market child? To some extent, the answer is yes."

[5] Additional factors may affect the question of implementation after the fact, beyond simple incentives or monitoring (Mislin et al. 2011). Moreover, Alexandra Mislin (2011: 55) discussed the apparent impact of "cheap talk" and trust building as having positive effects on the likelihood of favorable implementation in conditions of contingent agreements.

[6] Lax & Sebenius (1986) give another example by describing a union's reluctance to tie wages to a company's profit margin.

[7] Howard Raiffa (1982), G. Richard Shell (1999), David Lax and James Sebenius (1986), and Robert Mnookin (2000), offer more on strategic disclosure and the tactical considerations raised by information exchange in negotiation.

[8] Roger Fisher (2011) is perhaps the most widely cited authority for this proposition. While the authors of "Getting to Yes" do not label it so, many describe a particular stance toward negotiation as "win-win." The label is problematic, but widely recognized.

[9] This assertion is modestly overbroad. On a business trip some time ago, a colleague and I were dashing between gates, trying to make a connecting flight. My colleague expressed confidence that we would make it, while I was convinced we would not. We placed a small wager on our fate. We made the gate with seconds to spare, and as we boarded the plane, I handed over the $1 wager I had lost. I was not in the least disappointed to have been wrong in my prediction. The nature of my position in the wager, however, was uncommon in that I was sure to experience some measure of success in either event.

[10] Factors beyond fear of conspicuous losses may also affect the decision about whether to enter a contingent agreement. Laura Kray (2005) summarizes research showing that negotiators' relationships and the effects of accountability to external parties affect the rate with which problem-solving moves like contingent agreements are explored in negotiations.

[11] Samuel Gross (1996) and Chris Guthrie (1999) offer more on high-low agreements.

References

Alfini, J. J., S. B. Press, J. R. Sternlight and J. B. Stulberg. 2001. *Mediation Theory and Practice*. New Providence, NJ: LexisNexis.

Bazerman, M. H. and J. J. Gillespie. 1999. Betting on the Future: The Virtues of Contingent Contracts. *Harvard Business Review* 77(5): 155-160.

Fisher, R., W. L. Ury and B. Patton. 2011. *Getting to Yes: Negotiating Agreement Without Giving In*, 3rd edn. United Kingdom: Penguin Group.

Guthrie, C. 1999. Better Settle Than Sorry: The Regret Aversion Theory of Litigation Behavior. *University of Illinois Law Review* 1999: 43-90.

Gross, S. R. and K. D. Syverud. 1996. Don't Try: Civil Jury Verdicts in a System Geared to Settlement. *UCLA Law Review* 44(1): 1-64.

Honeyman, C. 1987. In Defense of Ambiguity. *Negotiation Journal* 3(1): 81-86.

Kray, L. J., L. Thompson and E. C. Lind. 2005. It's a Bet! A Problem-Solving Approach Promotes the Construction of Contingent Agreements. *Personality and Social Psychology Bulletin* 31(8): 1039-1051.

Lax, D. A. and J. K. Sebenius. 1986. *The Manager as Negotiator: Bargaining for Cooperation and Competitive Gain*. New York, NY: Free Press.

Menkel-Meadow, C. 2000. *Mediation : Theory, Policy and Practice* London: Ashgate.

Mislin, A. A., W. P. Bottom and R. L. Campagna. 2011. After the Deal: Talk, Trust Building and the Implementation of Negotiated Agreements. *Organizational Behavior and Human Decision Processes* 115(1): 55-68.

Mnookin, R. H., S. R. Peppet and A. S. Tulumello. 2000. *Beyond Winning: Negotiating to Create Value in Deals and Disputes*. Cambridge, MA: Belknap Press.

Raiffa, H. 1982. *The Art and Science of Negotiation*. Cambridge, MA: Belknap Press.

Shell, G. R. 1999. *Bargaining for Advantage: Negotiation Strategies for Reasonable People*. New York, NY: Viking.

Stulberg, J. B. 1987. *Taking Charge: Managing Conflict 101*. Lexington, MA: Lexington Books.

Tyson, L. D. 1998. If There Was No IMF, They'd Have to Invent One. *Bloomberg Businessweek*, March 9, 1998, 21.

93

Crossing the Final Gap

John H. Wade

Editors' Note: It's three o'clock in the morning. You've been negotiating or mediating since 9 a.m. and everybody is exhausted. Each side has made more concessions that it really thinks it should have had to, and the gap between the parties has narrowed to millimeters. But there it has stuck, and will stay stuck unless you do something new. Every sophisticated negotiator or experienced mediator has a personal answer to this problem, a private stock of a few gambits, often tried and sometimes successful. But John Wade has the longest list we have ever seen, 16 techniques in all. Not one of them works all the time, but together they can materially improve your batting average.

What is the last gap in a negotiation? It is the last step necessary to reach an agreement between the negotiating parties. Often that last gap or last increment emerges after long and exhausting negotiations which have led to agreement on all issues but one. For example, that one issue may be: who gets the grandfather clock? How should the last 10% of the pool of assets be divided? How should the outstanding credit card debt be paid? How to cross the difference of $600 or $1 million in the parties' "final" offers? Will the lease have a five year renewal option attached?

Most lawyers and business people can relate horror stories with humor and/or anguish about clients becoming stuck on the last issue of a lengthy negotiation. Some lawyers can tell how they themselves have offered to write a check to cover the last gap in order to help disputants end the drawn out negotiations, and almost invariably the disputants refuse the offer "as a matter of principle."

John Wade is an emeritus professor of law of Bond University, Queensland, Australia. He practiced as a lawyer in Australia between 1987 and 2012, and also had an active mediation practice in organizational, family and commercial conflicts during those years. He has taught over 300 mediation and negotiation courses in Hong Kong, New Zealand, London, Canada, the U.S. and Australia. John has published over 100 books and articles (see epublications@bond.edu.au). His teaching awards include best law teacher at Sydney University (1989); at Bond University (1990); and in Australia (1998). John now lives in Vancouver, Canada with his growing family, and teaches intensive negotiation courses there.

The Importance of the Last Gap

Why does the last increment or last issue assume such importance and so often (anecdotally) provide a stumbling block to a negotiated settlement? There are a number of possible explanations, which include:

- The last dance—Negotiations are often compared to a dance, where one or more parties circle each other apparently reluctant to end the process or relationship. The most clinging form of the last dance is sometimes referred to as "negative intimacy," where one or more of the parties find meaning to life in the ongoing conflict. No matter how satisfactory is the emerging deal, such intimacy leads to the ubiquitous add-on—"there is one more thing I want to raise—".
- Unfinished emotional business—Commercial "common sense" sometimes does not prevail at the last gap as one or more parties have a deep hurt or loss which has not been acknowledged or "resolved."
- The last straw—"I have given up so much already"—A common method of negotiation is for each party to open with extreme claims and then gradually make small moves toward a settlement between those extremes. This process often leaves one or both parties with an increasing sense of "loss" and anger.
- Sense of having been tricked—When the last gap is reached, the party who opened with what they perceived to be a "reasonable" offer, often feels tricked as the bargaining range has been dragged towards the person who started with an extreme or "unreasonable" offer.
- Skilled helpers attempt to prove worth—Sometimes lawyers (or union officials, etc.) negotiate aggressively about the last gap as a form of theater to justify the fees they will be demanding from their already disappointed clients.
- Recriminations for lost time and money—Sometimes the last gap triggers anger, as the negotiator realizes that he could have settled for the same amount two years earlier. Instead, he has invested two years of time and money to achieve "nothing."

How to Cross the Last Gap in Negotiations

What strategies are available to cross this hurdle in negotiations or mediation? One aspect of an adviser's role is to be an expert in the dynamics of negotiation and to educate the disputants concerning these dynamics. Parties can then have some confidence, even though they may feel in the wilderness, that there are well trodden paths which they have some power to choose between. A negotiator can give information concerning the range of options which are available. What follows is a list of options on how to cross the last gap.

Options for Crossing the Last Gap in Negotiations

The sixteen methods are as follows:

- Talk—Try to convince.
- Split the difference.
- Expand the pie by subdividing the last gap.
- Expand the pie by an add-on offer—"What if I moved on.....?"
- Refer to a third party umpire.
- Chance—Flip a coin.
- Chance—Draw gradations from a hat.
- Transfer the last gap to a third party.
- Conditional offers and placating incremental fears—"What if I could convince client to...? How would you respond?"
- Pause—and speak to significant others.
- Pause—and schedule time for a specific offer.
- Defer division of last gap; divide rest.
- Sell last item at auction; split proceeds.
- Pick-a-pile; you cut, I choose.
- Skilled helper has a face-saving tantrum.
- File a (further) court application—pursue pain and hope.

Talk—Try to Convince

A common response at the last one million dollars or $10,000, at the last set of paintings, or the last car, is for one or both disputants to talk—to rehash old arguments in an attempt to convince the other party to give in. These arguments take various forms:

- "I have given up so much in these negotiations; now it's your turn."
- A lengthy filibuster reiterating all the merits of the speaker's claims, and the weaknesses of the agitated or glassy-eyed "listener."
- An angry speech about how the listener's first offer was outrageous, so (s)he should make the last incremental concession "to be fair."
- A lengthy speech about the cost of litigation, the costs already incurred and the likelihood of settlement at the door of the court.
- A detailed historical version of the concessions made to date in the negotiation leading to the predictable conclusion that it is the listener's turn to be reasonable and make the last concession.
- A short but angry speech with express or implied threats of walking out, stonewalling, buying elsewhere, scorched earth, subpoenaing relatives or business associates, or advising the Commissioner of Taxation about unpaid tax of some kind.
- A combination of some or all of these speeches.

Anecdotally, these speeches rarely appear to be directly successful in crossing the last gap. The listeners may become inflamed to hear such a one-sided presentation (yet again) so late in the day and deliver a counter speech, or the speaker may back himself/herself into a positional corner. One negotiator strategy is to interrupt the flow of words with an attempted educational comment, and redirect the disputants to the remaining list of options on the board. "I don't think that these arguments are going to convince any of us as we've all heard them before. The last gap is never crossed by logical argument, so I'm going to ask each of us in turn, which one of the other options on the board you could live with."

Nevertheless, some degree of managed speechmaking at the last gap may serve latent functions of catharsis, boredom, the last dagger, further emotional pain, attempted justification of perceived role and fees of a skilled helper, or the farewell address. A managed last speech may be important given the complex psychological functions which the last gap appears to serve.

Split the Difference

This method is commonly suggested where the last gap consists of money or other divisible items—such as time with a child. It has the merits of simplicity, that both parties "lose" equally and that it is culturally commonplace.

However, given the complex psychological dynamics surrounding the last gap, "splitting the difference" may be seen as too quick, part of an orchestrated plan of attack, or involving another painful "loss."

Double Blind Offer—Split the Difference via Formulae

This method is used in a number of computer based negotiation programs. Each disputant agrees in writing to make one or more confidential offers to a mediator (or to a computer), on the condition that if the offers are "close" ("close" being agreed upon as a percentage), then the mediator (or computer program) will split the difference and both will be bound. [See NDR: Rabinovich-Einy & Katsh, *ODR*]

For example, the parties may be stuck at offers of $300,000 and $200,000 with a gap of $100,000 between them.

They can agree to each make a confidential offer; and that there will be no agreement unless and until one confidential offer is say at least 75% of the other (or perhaps unless and until parties are only $65,000 or less apart).

Thus if each confidentially moves $10,000 and offer $290,000 and $210,000, then there will be no automatic splitting the difference, as $210,000/$290,000 = 72%.

However, if each agrees to another round of confidential offers, and one moves $5,000, and the other moves $10,000, then there is a settlement as $215,000/$280,000 = 77%.

Splitting the difference between \$280,000 and \$215,000 means that the payout figure is \$247,500.

Expanding the Pie by Subdividing the Last Gap

The last increment can sometimes be divided in ways apart from an equal split by dividing the time of use or time of payment. For example, the last \$10,000 can be paid over time with or without interest or a painting can be used for alternative months by different parties, with one or the other paying shipping and insurance.

Expanding the Pie by an Add-On Offer

One party can attempt to overcome an impasse on the last increment by re-opening a "decided" issue, or adding another issue to the negotiating table. In these ways, there is an attempt to prevent the "last" issue from being the last. For example:

- "I would be willing to give up my lounge room couch if you re-turn the children's bikes to my house."
- "If that last \$10,000 is paid to me, I would be willing to redirect all old customers to you."
- "We have already agreed that you will occupy the house for 3 years, but I'm willing to reconsider that time period if I can have that painting."

Obviously, it is not always easy to re-open or to discover extra value to place on the bargaining table. One of the clear benefits of questioning and listening skills is that a negotiator can develop ideas on the needs, concerns and interests of the other disputant so that extra value can be put on the table. Some negotiators *begin* bargaining with a positional style. When an impasse is reached, they switch (or have a fellow negotiator switch) to an interest-based problem-solving approach.

Refer to a Third Party Umpire

The impasse of the last item can be "resolved" by:

- Agreeing to refer the whole dispute to an arbitrator or judge.
- Agreeing to refer just the issue of crossing the last gap to an arbitrator. A respected expert can be paid for two hours of her time to come to a binding oral or written decision only on the last \$20,000, car, Christmas Day or the terms of a leasing option.

In mediation, the disputants may request that a trusted mediator make a *recommendation* or a binding *decision* on how the impasse should be resolved. Most mediators respond to such requests with reluctance and make speeches about neutrality. However, occasionally the parties manage to persuade the mediator to accept one or both of those roles.

The writer once assisted a husband and wife in negotiating the division of a sugar cane farm, and then saw them " jam" on the final embittered topic of how much in retrospective wages should be paid to the son and his wife for 18 years of work on the farm. This final volatile topic was referred to a time-limited, "on-the papers" arbitration. Thereby the parties could (and did) blame the arbitrator for the outcome.

Chance—Flip a Coin

Chance provides an important option for deciding who gets the last gap. This is because flipping a coin:

- Is cheap and fast.
- Involves equal chance of winning or losing.
- Avoids loss of face by being "beaten" by other, more personal strategies.
- Is sometimes culturally acceptable in a gambling society.
- Provides a stark visual metaphor of the lottery involved in "going to court," and also reflects the educational conversations of many lawyers and clients. (Griffiths 1986; Sarat and Felstiner 1986; Sarat and Felstiner 1988; Wade 1989)
- Is so abhorrent to some risk-averse disputants that they return to the remaining list of options with enthusiasm!

Chance—Draw from a Range of Solutions

This is an alternative version of chance which avoids the all-or-nothing result of flipping a coin. The disputants agree that several solutions will be written out on slips of paper, placed in a hat, and the one drawn out will prevail.

For example, if the last increment is $20,000, then ten slips of paper can be placed in a hat beginning with "$2000" and ending with "$20,000" with gaps of $2,000 written on each slip of paper. The person drawing the slip receives whatever number is on the drawn piece of paper; the residue of the last gap goes to the other disputant. The writer and some colleagues have used this method successfully on several occasions in business disputes.

Of course, this method can be extended to a range of more complicated alternative solutions.

Transfer the Last Gap to a Third Party

This option involves both parties agreeing to transfer the last gap to a child, a charity, to pay the fees of skilled helpers, such as lawyers or mediators, or to pay for renovating a house or business before a sale.

For example, last increments from the division of a pool of assets in a matrimonial or deceased estate have been transferred:

- To a trust fund to pay for future child support or private school fees.
- In the form of an antique car to a husband on the condition that he bequeath it to his children.

- To pay a mediator's fees.

Such transfers to third parties may have the clear benefits of mutually avoiding a "loss," and of wedding a third party to the solution chosen.

Conditional Offers and Placating the Incremental Fear

Where a pattern of incremental bargaining has been established, each disputant will usually be concerned about the consequences of initiating any offer across the last gap. Why? Because any offer is likely to be whittled away by an incremental counteroffer. For example, if the last gap between A and B is $20,000, and A offers to split the difference ($10,000 to A) how is B likely to respond? B is likely to respond, split the difference again—only $5,000 to A. Thus there is a reluctance to make the first move, and the impasse remains intact.

Accordingly, some negotiators make exploratory conditional offers in an attempt to placate the fear of incremental counteroffers. This works best if there are at least two negotiators (e.g., lawyer and client) on each negotiating team.

> Lawyer: What if I could persuade my client to make a split-the-difference offer, would you guarantee that you wouldn't try to cut down her offer?
>
> Opposing Disputant: What do you mean?
>
> Lawyer: Well I'm not willing to put the effort persuading my client against her wishes to modify her position if you're going to try to cut her offer in half. She will then feel betrayed. I'm not willing to put in the work to attempt to persuade her unless I know what your response will be. And there are no guarantees I can persuade her.
>
> Opposing Disputant: "Let me talk to my lawyer about this in private for a moment. We'll be right back".

Obviously, this option can be manipulated by a negotiator attempting to discover the other side's willingness to settle for a hypothesized offer. Moreover, the offeree's response is also clearly conditional ("if your client makes that offer....") and can be withdrawn readily. However, raising any suspicion of reneging will usually be counter-productive at such a late stage of nearly successful negotiations.

The writer has used, and seen this method used, successfully on many occasions.

Pause—And Speak to Significant Others

The intensity of a negotiation session means that it is easy to become weary, to lose perspective and to make "a mountain out of a molehill."

Additionally, some people are cautious and are accustomed to reflecting upon options available before making a commitment.

Accordingly, it is a helpful strategy to suggest a break to consider one or more written options, with a clear appointment to resume negotiations, and with encouragement for each disputant to speak to specified trusted third parties. [NDR: Mayer, *Allies*] Where a mediator is being used, it is often helpful for all disputants to make contact with the mediator during the break to clarify, brainstorm and hypothesize on negotiation dynamics (e.g., "What will be the likely response if I make this offer...?")

A skilled "significant other" can also assist an entrenched person to work through a visual risk analysis (again). What are the risks if the gains from the negotiation are "lost" due to a relatively minor last goal or gap? (Wade 2001) The writer has found that a renewed, visual, and private risk analysis is helpful with parties jammed on the last gap. "What are your goals; what have you gained so far; and what will be lost if you leave here without an agreement?" For example, here is a common "life goal" list prepared by the writer as mediator while sitting with each disputant during family property negotiations which are "jammed" over a last monetary gap.

LIFE GOALS?	THIS OFFER??
To get on with life	
To open a new business	
To invest money	
To stop paying lawyers	
To stay healthy	
To minimize contact with "x"	
To reduce stress on colleagues	
To take a holiday	
To focus on my work	
To avoid becoming bitter	
To regain "control" of my life	
To settle "in the range"	

To reduce risks of paybacks	
To receive [$540,000]—current offer $500,000	
Other??	

Once the goals are visualized and reflected upon, anecdotally most clients are reluctant to lose the 14 dangling gains for the chance of acquiring one missing goal (the last gap).

Pause—And Schedule Time for a Specific Offer

As a variation on the previous procedure, the parties can actually draft a precise or general form of offer before the break is taken. This may, for example, represent a predictable outcome of "splitting the difference" which is too difficult to swallow during the negotiations.

A time and place is then agreed upon for one party to contact the other and make the offer as drafted (e.g., phone on Wednesday night between 6-8 pm). Both agree not to haggle, but either to accept or reject the ritual pre-planned offer and to return to the negotiation/mediation table at a specified time with the result.

This procedure gives a concrete proposal, reduces the fear of incremental haggling during the break, ritualizes conflicted conversations, provides a deadline, and allows the parties to return to the negotiation table knowing what has been decided.

Defer Division of the Last Gap; Divide the Rest

Where parties are in dispute over a pool of assets, it is possible for a portion to be divided as agreed, and for the last gap to be set aside for division at some later time. For example, a wife could take 50%, a husband 40% and the contested gap of 10% be invested in a joint account until the parties are "ready" emotionally or otherwise, to deal with that 10%.

Sell the Last Item at an Auction; Split the Proceeds

This option involves an agreement to sell the last contested item(s) at a without reserve auction, usually with all parties free to bid. The most determined bidder "wins" the item and the net proceeds of the auction are then divided in portions agreed to beforehand.

Recently, the writer was mediating a conflict which jammed on the last gap of who would receive an emotionally important house. The mediator offered to conduct an instant auction, if both parties agreed that the highest bidder would receive the house. They did, and the negotiations concluded successfully.

Pick-a-Pile

Where the last gap consists of a number of items such as "all the furniture," "all the stamp collection," "all the paintings," then the parties can be offered the "pick-a-pile" option, which is well known to family lawyers, and to parents cutting up children's birthday cakes.

One party agrees to divide the chattels into two lists of approximately equal value and submit these lists to the other party by a deadline. The other party then has a specified time in which to choose one list as his/her share (Australian Family Law and Practice (CCH) at 43-400 and in W and W (1980), Family Law Cases 90-872 at 75, 531 (Australia)).

Like dispute resolution by chance, this pick-a-pile option is so filled with risk and tension that some disputants quickly reject it and return to the list of remaining options with some relief.

Skilled Helper Has a Face-Saving Tantrum

This option is rarely chosen by the disputants. However, some parties comment confidentially during or after a mediation to a mediator, "I wish you would apply more pressure to us both; we are stuck."

Accordingly, when the last gap persists, some mediators, lawyers, or other team members try this option from their box of tools. For example, with varying degrees of simulated anger, the mediator, or other "helper" comments: "I cannot believe it. We have all sat here for three hours and patiently and successfully negotiated through four issues. Now you're about to throw it all away on this miserable pile of furniture. You all really disappoint me. I'm not going to let you out of here until we do the right thing and ...... etc., etc."

This option may cause the tantrum-thrower to lose reputation and clients, or may enable both parties to avoid any loss of face by making the last concession. They can blame the ballistic person for "forcing" the last concession (and rescuing them both from their painted-in corners).

This dramatic option may be particularly successful if the aggressor has gained the respect and trust of all parties (both lawyers and disputants) over a period of time. (Cialdini 1984; Shell 1999)

File a Court Application—Pursue Pain and Hope

Sometimes, the last gap is too difficult to cross amidst the sense of loss arising from a day or years of concessions. Accordingly, one of the negotiators delivers a mixed message of pain and hope "I believe that this dispute will settle. We have made progress today and, in my opinion, we are not diagnostically in the 1-3% of disputes which need a judicial decision. However we both may need to suffer more pain and expense of filing (further) court applications, open offers, and paying lawyers. Could we now agree to a time to talk over the phone in say 14 days time? etc." (Competent negotiators always organize face-saving methods to re-open negotiations).

Various versions of this pain and hope speech have sometimes led to awkward silences, and then positive responses to the question, "Would you like to take a short break, then try for another 15 minutes to see if this can be concluded today?"

Conclusion

Conflict and transaction managers are becoming more sophisticated in their knowledge of negotiation dynamics. This chapter has attempted to systematically explain some of the reasons for the difficulties experienced in crossing the last gap.

Sixteen ways of crossing the last gap have been described. Visually setting out some or all of these sixteen strategies is a useful addition to a negotiator's repertoire for working with disputants and negotiators to cross the last gap.

References

Australian Family Law and Practice (CCH) (1980), Family Law Cases 90-872 (Australia).

Cialdini, R. 1984. *Influence: The Psychology of Persuasion*. New York: Harper Business.

Griffiths, J. 1986. What do Dutch Lawyers Actually do in Divorce Cases? *Law & Society Review* 20: 135.

Sarat, A. and W. Felstiner. 1986. Law and Strategy in the Divorce Lawyer's Office. *Law & Society Review* 20: 93.

Sarat, A. and W. Felstiner. 1988. Law and Social Relations: Vocabularies of Motive in Lawyer/Client Interaction. *Law & Society Review* 22:737.

Shell, R. 1999. *Bargaining for Advantage*. New York: Penguins Books, 111-13.

Wade, J. H. 1989. The Behavior of Family Lawyers and the Implications for Legal Education. *Legal Education Review* 1: 165.

Wade, J. H. 2001. Systematic Risk Analysis for Negotiators and Litigators: But You Never Told Me It Would Be Like This. *Bond Law Review* 13: 462.

ෆ 94 ෨

Dobermans and Diplomats: Re-Opening Deadlocked Negotiations

John H. Wade

Editors' Note: One of the clear roles of negotiators, mediators, lawyers, managers, parents and human beings is to attempt to re-open "jammed" negotiations. Lawyers, negotiators, managers and mediators are paid to be competent, even expert, at recommencing communications and negotiations which have reached a stalemate or a tense stand-off. Yet many otherwise competent professionals find this difficult. This chapter sets out seventeen common strategies used by the most skilled "problem-solvers" to re-open negotiations between deadlocked disputants.

This chapter sets out seventeen common strategies used by skilled "problem-solvers" to re-open negotiations between deadlocked disputants. It raises the question of where such knowledge can be included in the already over-crowded lifelong education of lawyers (and diplomats, mediators, negotiators and parents). One of the clear roles of negotiators, mediators, lawyers, managers, parents and human beings is to attempt to re-open "jammed" negotiations. Lawyers, negotiators, managers and mediators are paid to be competent, even expert, at recommencing communications and negotiations which have reached a stalemate or a tense stand-off.

Yet the task is difficult, primarily because people in long-term conflict usually do not want to attempt to re-open negotiations if the attempt will involve loss of position, image or information. That is, they do not

John Wade is an emeritus professor of law of Bond University, Queensland, Australia. He practiced as a lawyer in Australia between 1987 and 2012, and also had an active mediation practice in organizational, family and commercial conflicts during those years. He has taught over 300 mediation and negotiation courses in Hong Kong, New Zealand, London, Canada, the U.S. and Australia. John has published over 100 books and articles (see epublications@bond.edu.au). His teaching awards include best law teacher at Sydney University (1989); at Bond University (1990); and in Australia (1998). John now lives in Vancouver, Canada with his growing family, and teaches intensive negotiation courses there.

want to be, or be perceived to be, weak. The negotiator wants to give out *double* messages of aggression and peacemaking. For example, lawyers commonly say on the telephone "Before our clients start up World War III again, should they talk first?" Words are important. Experienced lawyers do not usually say "My client would like to avoid World War III, can we talk?" This raises the other major difficulty in this process of re-opening jammed negotiations—it requires uncommon skills and character.

This chapter identifies a range of strategies and skills to re-open negotiations. These are based predominantly on the work of Pruitt and Kim (2004). Examples are given particularly from the writer's practice as a mediator and as a family lawyer.

Seventeen possible methods to re-open negotiations are:

- Back channel contacts
- Use of intermediaries
- Giving conciliatory signals
- Superordinate goals
- Expressing vigorous "no surrender" on interests
- Willingness to discuss procedure
- Admitting flexibility on specific solutions
- Refusing to make any unilateral concessions
- Identification of division between hawks and doves
- Acknowledgement of other's interests
- Mild threats or consequences
- Clear rejection of unacceptable past solutions
- Assembly of an expert problem solving team
- Rewarding others for any helpful initiatives
- Keeping communication open
- Prioritising of interests
- Filing a formal claim

No doubt there are a number of other strategies to re-open deadlocks. A negotiator or facilitator who has a large repertoire of available interventions becomes a powerful person—like a tennis player with a wide repertoire of shots.

The above seventeen will be discussed in turn.

1. Back Channel Contacts

While the official and public negotiators are posturing, threatening and expressing righteous indignation, unofficial meetings can take place in coffee houses (not necessarily in Vienna). The back channel personnel may be friends, relatives or technicians (e.g. accountants in family feuds).

They have no authority to settle and they speak "as individuals" *not* for the organizations or tribes. The back-channel meeting may have a real or feigned secretiveness—"I don't want my relatives to know that I've phoned you, but I would like to meet to see if anything can be done about this disastrous situation".

If the people at the back-channel meeting brainstorm some possible processes, solutions, or reframe the problem, then the official and public disputants may be able to explore publicly this ray of sunshine—without loss of image, position or data.

However, official negotiators may vigorously seek to undermine back channel contact (not just as a "good cop—bad cop" strategy). This is because some official negotiators are insecure, or unskilled, or want the personal kudos of arranging agreement, or have monetary or psychological needs to continue the long term conflict.

For example, the writer has been involved as a mediator between two charities arguing over large sums of money used for the care of seriously ill children. Certain individuals in the "anti-professional" faction vigorously prohibited their constituents from speaking to members of the "professional" faction on any social occasion. They clearly feared that in social conversations, the less embittered new members of their own organisation might fashion solutions.

Similarly, in a cross-cultural commercial negotiation about the ownership and use of land, the writer attempted to open back-channel discussions with Japanese corporate officers. The official local negotiator, a large Australian accountancy firm, heard about these attempts and (predictably) "prohibited" any of his client's officers from talking to people who did not have "authority to settle". Secrecy may sometimes be essential! Lack of authority to settle is the very reason why this strategy may be successful.

2. Use of Intermediaries

Use of an intermediary is one powerful possible intervention in a deadlock situation. The intermediary may act on his/her own initiative, actual or feigned—"I would like to talk to you both as I am very concerned about the damage you are inflicting on one another, and upon other bystanders."

Or he may insert personal interests as an added form of "authority"—"If you each fail to make some constructive offers in the next month, I will withdraw my vote/subsidy/weapons supply/testamentary provision etc from you." Or she may be approached by one party as a person perceived to have moral authority, neutrality and wisdom by the other disputant(s)—such as a respected cousin, or family accountant.

For example:

a) When enquirers discuss the possibility of mediation over the telephone, one of the writer's first questions is "how can mediation be raised with the other side without a loss of face?" After some discussion, a trusted uncle, accountant or manager is identified who could be asked to approach all the disputants to recommend mediation. This is a process intermediary to facilitate another process intermediary.

b) At the writer's university, one manager has a recurrent, and very successful, strategy used for entrenched conflicts between staff members. He whispers in the ear of one of a group of respected and grey haired academic colleagues. This go-between "casually" shuttles between the conflicted individuals or groups over coffee and lunches, listens, helps to define the problems, defuses intensity, and encourages the disputants to brainstorm potential solutions. The manager thereby gratefully avoids his necessary fallback role of imposing a solution upon the disputants.

c) Of course, there is now a world-wide proliferation of voluntary and mandatory mediation schemes particularly in areas of employment, discrimination, personal injury, family, native land and workers compensation disputes. (Boulle 2011; Moore 2003; Galanter 2006)

It should be emphasised that problem-solving intervention by an intermediary (like going to a dentist) is not a popular option, for a variety of complex reasons. However ironically, when chosen or mandated, the various types of mediation seem to have fair to very good outcomes on a variety of measures of "success".

3. Conciliatory Signals

A conciliatory signal is a small, often subtle, comment or action which indicates a willingness to be helpful, even co-operative. It may amount to a minor act of politeness or kindness amidst a long term battle.

One function of these signals is that it may create cognitive dissonance (Festinger 1957) for both the sender and receiver. The dehumanised and deindividualised opposition ("management", "union"; "corporate pigs"; "greenies"; "typical male"; "typical woman") may momentarily behave as a reasonable or even a kind human being. The demonised stereotype may momentarily "act out of character".

During long term conflicts, the writer has seen the following "conciliatory signals" re-open problem solving negotiations:

a) Unsolicited, a mother sent copies of school reports about children's improved academic progress to the father after years of vitriolic communication.

b) A man sent a two sentence "thank you" note to his estranged spouse for an act of kindness she had shown to his mother.

c) A lawyer carried a bottle of wine and some glasses into a tense commercial negotiation and placed them conspicuously at the end of a board room table. When asked what he was doing, he replied "That's to celebrate when this dispute is finally over".

d) Some cultures have a tradition of use of the small gift and its power to both prevent conflicts, and to re-open jammed communications. Another powerful conciliatory signal is an indirectly or directly conveyed qualified "apology"[1]. For example, during an intense conflict between a logging company and a government forestry department, a lawyer commented" "My client acknowledges that there has been very poor communication between the two groups in the past. Is there any way to avoid repeating those mistakes now?" [See NDR: Brown & Robbennolt, *Apology*]

4. Superordinate Goals

It is common during a stalemate for a disputant to announce to the media, or to one of the parties on the other side, that "despite our differences, we do have a number of things in common". These speeches, letters or diagrams may need to be repeated at strategic moments by key parties on all sides of the conflict in order to challenge entrenched beliefs, emotions and language about rivalry.

Examples of attempts to emphasise common or overarching goals are "Despite our history of differences, we both agree that:

- Our dispute is scaring new customers away
- We want our children to flourish
- We want restoration of civil order
- Our armies/lawyers are getting richer
- Judges will not understand the complexity of our disputes
- While we fight, our competitors prosper
- We will have to work together in the future"

5. Expressing Willingness to Discuss Procedure ("Negotiating about Negotiating")

Moderate members from each side can often reopen negotiations on *procedural* topics. A request for better negotiation procedural rules is not usually interpreted as weakness. The implication can be preserved that "we will still be tough when and if the *substantive* negotiations resume".

Lewicki (2005) has set out a useful list of preliminary procedural topics to begin a thaw between entrenched negotiators:

- "Determining a site for a meeting (changing the site or finding a neutral location).
- Setting a formal agenda outlining what may or may not be discussed and agreeing to follow that agenda.
- Determining who may attend the meetings. (Changing key negotiators or representatives may be a signal of the intention to change the negotiation approach.)
- Setting time limits for individual meetings and for the overall negotiation session. (As we have pointed out, progress in negotiation is often paced according to the time available; therefore,

setting limits is likely to yield more progress than not setting them.)

- Setting procedural rules, such as who may speak, how long they may speak, how issues will be approached, what facts may be introduced, how records of the meeting will be kept, how agreements will be affirmed, and what clerical or support services are required.
- Following specific dos and don'ts for behaviour (e.g., don't attack others).
- Finally, the parties may agree to set aside a short period during negotiations to critique how they are doing" (Lewicki, Saunders and Barry 2005: 450).

[See also NDR: Coleman et al., *Intractable—2*]

6. Vigorous "No Surrender" on Interests

This strategy consists of one or both parties making public or discreet statements that whatever solution is reached, it *must* incorporate certain vital interests. The speaker has thereby communicated that (s)he is willing to move off an initially preferred solution, as long as any suggested alternative embraces her/his interests and goals.

For example, after long stalemates in conflicts:

a) A wife who had insisted that she must receive *ownership* of a large historic house, stated that she must have complete *access* to that house for her daughter's 21st birthday celebrations.

b) A government official who had refused adamantly to allow a forest to be logged, said "whatever the solution, these kinds of trees must be preserved for future generations." This interest identification allowed agreement in principle and a new range of solutions to be proposed based on replanting and selective cutting.

c) In Australia in 1996, an inevitable stalemate between the Federal Parliament and pro-gun lobby groups, over a government proposal to ban hand guns and automatic weapons, was eventually ended. A key element was when Federal politicians publicly and frequently restated their interests in language such as "We must prevent another massacre ever taking place"; "We must keep high powered weapons away from potentially angry people." This appeared to be a successful strategy as it was difficult to disagree with the stated interests, as compared to the initially contentious solutions.

7. Flexibility on Specific Solutions

This is a signal given by one or both of the disputants that there may be several acceptable solutions, not just the single historical entrenched demand. This is often coupled with a restating of interests.

Examples:

Historic Demand	Eventual Indication of Flexibility
"My client wants $1 million."	"My client will only consider a settlement which is at least at the mid-range of figures for an injury/marriage of this kind."
"He cannot see the children."	"There will need to be some clear safeguards and changes in place before he sees the children."
"Her valuer is entirely unacceptable."	"I am seriously concerned that her valuer will escalate the conflict as he does not have experience valuing this type of business."
"He cannot, in any circumstance, take the antique furniture."	"Almost all of those antiques are of special sentimental value to me."

8. No Unilateral Concessions

This is a powerful-face saving strategy for the person who has backed himself/herself into a corner by insisting over years that there is only one possible solution—mine.

The message of tit for tat is conveyed by party, lawyer, business associate or relative. "If x is going to move off his/her historic offer, (s)he must be given something in exchange," or "we do not expect you to budge any more than us. Do we have anything of value which we could exchange?"

This strategy can be very helpful for a wide range of entrenched conflicts including nuclear disarmament or custody disputes. For example, after a lengthy stand-off, one parent makes a small unilateral concession on the time of pick-up of a child together with the clear statement that (s)he expects help with homework in exchange.

A minor risk-taking move by one party, if it attracts an appropriate response from the other, provides encouragement to try a series of small trust-building exchanges. However, one double-cross or perceived double-cross by either will again escalate the conflict and the stereotype that the other is unreasonable, crazy or vindictive.

9. Identify Division Between Hawks and Doves

This is another potentially very successful strategy for saving face and re-opening jammed negotiations. One disputant speaks to the other directly or through an intermediary. The message is—"It's not my fault that I'm being so unreasonable and entrenched. You need to understand that I'm trying to satisfy a whole team, some of whom want to fight to the death (the hawks), and others who are eager at least to explore a range of possible solutions (the doves)." To this speech may be added the confidential or pretended confidential plea—"If we ever are going to reach a settlement, you'll have to help me satisfy both the hawks and the doves in my camp."

It should be emphasised that this speech may be entirely orchestrated or may reflect one disputant's real position. Either way, it can still be very effective to help break the deadlock. It may provide a new perception about a totally belligerent negotiator, and may create for a moment, a joint problem solving team. What can be done about the hawks? Sometimes a subtle message hides the request "Please be patient with me and my rhetoric. I need time to placate my hawks, then to control and isolate them."

I have seen this strategy used successfully in epic disputes, where the "hawks" on one side were:

a) Middle managers fearful of losing their jobs if they took responsibility and made a decision to settle.

b) Parents who wanted to punish a son-in-law in a custody dispute.

c) Senior lawyers or valuers who had given professional opinions about money, and who "refused" to allow a client to settle on any basis other than their own expert evaluation (sometimes referred to as "dueling experts' syndrome") [NDR: Wade, *Dueling Experts*].

d) Middle managers in organisations who insist upon following policy rules to the letter.

e) A belligerent tenant—who went on vacation, thus enabling the remaining parties to settle the dispute in his absence.

10. Acknowledge Other's Interests

Often in the "fog of war", or the "blindness of involvement", entrenched negotiators cannot accurately articulate what is important to the "other side". Obviously, a fundamental negotiation skill is to listen, and then to demonstrate to the other person that (s)he has been heard by attempting to re-state what has been said. (Egan 1994; Eddy 2005) [See also NDR: Itzchakov & Kluger, *Listening & Understanding*] This basic skill provides another strategy for recommencing negotiations between entrenched disputants. For example, one party says to the other:

- "I recognise that you would like enough money to buy a 4 bedroom house".
- "I acknowledge that you don't want to be marginalised as a parent".
- "Correct me if I'm wrong, but I understand that you are interested in three particular concerns, namely...".
- "You see the facts this way...".

The process of listening and reframing may also help to clarify ubiquitous rhetoric such as "it's a matter of principle"; "I'm not going to give in"; "it's your fault...".

Such acknowledgement does not suggest surrender, but rather a willingness to listen, to be corrected and to understand the other's interests and feelings.

11. Mild Threats or Consequence

It is sometimes possible to break a long-standing deadlock by one or both disputants making a mild threat such as "If we both continue to come up with no solution then:

- "We will settle at the door of the court in 2 years' time".
- "My lawyer insists that I conduct a full scale investigation into your business affairs".
- "We will both be distracted from our work for the next 2 years and our competitors will overtake us".
- "Both our families will be subpoenaed to appear in court and face public humiliation at the hands of aggressive lawyers".
- "Our supporters will see us as incompetent parents/managers/ people".

This strategy is dangerous as it readily appears to be a tired repetition of the past history of threats and counter-threats. The subtle differences are that the tone is not hostile, there is often an element of *mutual* harm and the consequences are not presented as cataclysmic, but still painful. Somehow the "threatened" consequences are presented as systemically inevitable (distraction from work; alienation of relatives; investigation by tax officers; escalation by hawks; the children will become alienated from us both), rather than as an *intended* or *chosen* harm (e.g. "I'll cut off access"; "I'll sue you for damages"; "I'll ensure that you are reported to the tax authorities".)

12. Clearly Reject Unacceptable Past Solutions

Strangely, an unwillingness even to negotiate may be altered by insisting that a particular solution proposed in the past is totally unacceptable and should not be even mentioned again. "We are willing to talk again but want to clarify that proposed solution *X* was, is and forever will be totally unacceptable. We should look for answers among the various alternative solutions which are available".

This message communicates strength, may placate hawks in one's own negotiating team, warns about the potential exasperation caused by recycling rejected solutions, and yet indicates some flexibility.

The writer has seen this strategy used successfully in the following deadlock situations:

- "Whatever other discussions we have, in absolutely no circumstances will I contemplate moving the children from their present schools for the next 2 years."
- "These assets can be divided. However, if we resume negotiations, my client will not accept the continued involvement of his wife in the business in the long term. To even raise that possibility again will be inflammatory and unrealistic."

13. Assemble Expert Problem Solving Team

This is a time-honoured approach to a deadlock. One or both disputants announces publicly that a team of experts has been or will be assembled to study the problem and come up with a range of alternatives and recommendations. Such a statement:

- Shows that the problem is being taken seriously.
- Creates time for passions to cool, perspectives to change and for zealots to move onto other conflicts.
- Removes individuals from the negotiations who are clumsy communicators, or who need to rationalise their hostile feelings and past aggressive behavior.
- Reserves some power to the disputants to accept or reject the report of the expert team.
- Gives the disputants a period of time to attend to other business, or get on with their lives.
- Raises the possibility that the expert team will discover new data, interests and creative solutions.
- Raises the possibility that the team may be able to recommend preventive or management systems for *future* conflicts.

The writer has seen this approach used constantly in law firms and universities where there is deadlocked conflict over promotion, distribution of money, allegations of cheating and methods of evaluating staff performance. It is also a relatively common method to attempt to break up "dueling valuation experts" in large matrimonial property disputes. However, there are potentially serious disadvantages with the over-use of this strategy in organizations and communities which actually leads to an escalation of the deadlocked conflict.

These disadvantages include the perception that "expert teams" (or dreaded committees):

- Provide a convenient excuse for inept negotiators to avoid difficult situations.
- Provide a means of putting a conflict on the shelf for a long time in the hope that disputants will give up.
- Are not experts at all. Rather they will gather only biased data, and then process that incomplete information through their inexpert process and values.

- Will manage their process so badly that they will create a whole litany of new grievances based upon a series of predictable failures—to consult widely, to be polite, to be unbiased, to question vigorously, to collect adequate evidence, to report quickly, to write clearly, to justify recommendations.
- Will have their months of hard work and considered recommendations totally ignored by the disputants.

Despite these considerable risks when assembling expert teams, the process may still re-open conversation, at least temporarily, with new dynamics.

14. Reward Others for Helpful Initiatives

This strategy represents the other side of the coin to sending subtle conciliatory signals while trying to avoid sending a message of weakness. Whenever a member of the "opposition" does anything helpful, then an effort is made to express thanks or be helpful in return. This act encourages repetition of a co-operative cycle, and undermines dehumanised and demonised stereotypes of the opposition. [See NDR: Coleman et al., *Intractable—1*]

Examples of "rewarding" an act of helpfulness include:

- A lawyer's letter which begins "Thank you for sending us a summary of your client's goals. It was helpful to gain some understanding of your client's perspectives. We will send a similar document to you within the next 14 days."
- "Thank you for looking after the children for an extra two nights while I was ill last week. Your flexibility in that crisis was appreciated."
- "I appreciate the way you return phone calls so promptly. I will try to do the same for you."

15. Keep Communication Open

This strategy is often closely associated with "back channel contacts." It may appear to be platitudinous and somewhat ridiculous to suggest this approach where disputants have been in a long term deadlock. However, the suggestion has subtle and powerful applications.

Features of long term conflict and of a conflict spiral are that disputants gather tribes of supporters around them, psychological states of the tribes change, moderates in a tribe become hawks, dehumanisation and deindividuation take place (e.g. "typical male", "fascist cop"; "fat-cat bureaucrat" etc.).

Knowing these standard dynamics will occur, a wise conflict manager will preserve a line of communication ready for the "eventual" settlement.

For example:

■ A family lawyer friend has the following routine in her experienced repertoire: She sometimes advises clients that their conflict over property or children has escalated, and will continue to
escalate for another two years particularly if a gladiatorial lawyer
is "on the other side". Therefore the client must preserve a line
of communication with his/her partner, ready for the "right
moment to negotiate". The client is coached to send birthday
cards and school reports, and to be polite to his/her partner.
One or two years later, after a particularly aggressive and expensive round of public posturing and litigation, the coached client
makes a well-rehearsed "what can we do about---" telephone call
to his/her partner. A problem solving private luncheon is suggested between the clients. At that luncheon, the client expresses
concern about his/her own lawyer's rampant aggressiveness and
expense, (a variation of the good cop/bad cop negotiation routine), and an agreement is reached between the clients.

16. Prioritize Interests

This approach involves one or both parties acknowledging the deadlock,
but nevertheless agreeing to list issues from most important to least
important from his/her team's perspective. The disputants then agree to
return to the negotiating table with their respective lists of priorities in
the hope that trade-offs are possible in the light of this new information.
In conflict management terminology, prioritising of interests is sometimes labelled "bridging" or "logrolling".

This prioritizing approach has the benefits that:

■ It requires self-examination and self-insight in each negotiating
team.
■ It commonly will clarify claims and the interests behind claims
(and often will create *constructive* conflict within negotiating
teams).
■ The exercise reflects the negotiation reality that rarely does one
party achieve *every* goal; and therefore to identify that which
can be given up is realistic.

One disadvantage is that merely participating in the exercise may be
perceived to be a caving in on an original position "everything is important"—"we will surrender nothing".

This exercise is often helpful in the writer's experience in matrimonial property disputes where each party wants to "win" on the issues of
valuation (my values, not yours); percentage (higher percentage to me,
lower to you); timing (property transferred sooner versus property transferred later); debts (you pay the debts; not me); periodic payments (low
or none versus high); particular assets ("I want the furniture, versus, my
mother gave it to me"). When a mediator asks each disputant (and team

of supporters) in private, "what is most important to you in order of priority?", some helpful differences emerge. For example, males often want the valuations of their experts accepted as a first priority; whereas females often want a percentage division at least in the mid-range as advised by their experts. This leads *eventually* ("the right offer at the wrong time is the wrong offer"), to a predictable swap—"my valuation(s) for your mid-range percentage".

17. Make a Formal Claim

This is a common strategy used by lawyers which has some benefits and some clear disadvantages. Where negotiations drag on and appear to be getting nowhere, then one, or all disputants prepare formal claims and file them in a court or tribunal. In this situation, the claimant is not formalising a claim with the aim of obtaining a third party decision, but rather to gain from some of the incidental procedures attached to filing (Wade 1995; Wade 2001).

The step of filing a formal claim potentially provides these benefits:

a) A series of sanctioned deadlines for the exchange of information, backed by a mandatory process of disclosing requested information (by discovery or subpoena).

b) A series of official forms to complete by certain deadlines which may create a degree of sworn clarity about positional claims, counter claims, alleged facts and evidence to support the alleged facts.

c) Usually, an additional pressure to settle due to requirements to spend money, shift paper, lose work time, and inconvenience associates and relatives.

d) A degree of time, ritual and orderly process whereby passions may cool (or whereby the grieving process may operate).

e) An ultimate deadline (the door of the court) to complete negotiations and terminate procrastination about the final "loss".

f) An extensive code of ethics governing reasonable behavior during conflict.

g) The involvement of an expert lawyer or conflict manager who brings the new perspective of "this is how these conflicts normally are settled".

h) The convenience of eventually embodying the settlement in a consent order rather than in a "mere" contract. A consent order can be quickly supervised by a court if there are problems with performance, whereas an alleged breach of a contract may take years to be listed before a judge. For example, consent or contested orders commonly include a clause such as "With liberty to apply to the court with 14 days notice in relation to performance of these orders" (Wade 2001a).

However, the potential disadvantages of this filing strategy are also many. They include:

a) Filing a formal claim may well be interpreted as another unreasonable and confrontational step in the long-standing dispute. The "filer" may reinforce his/her image as someone who is an enemy worthy of destruction.

b) Because of scarce resources, most courts are engaging in aggressive case management practices. Therefore the disputants will lose control of the timing of negotiations and will be pushed quickly towards an actual hearing.

c) Following the previous disadvantage, the disputants may be pushed quickly into a series of procedural appearances before a judge or third party decision-maker, and perhaps even a final hearing before a judge. The litany of notorious disadvantages of placing the "resolution" of conflict in the hands of a third person may be far too great for one or both of the disputants to risk.[2] Moreover, it is difficult to extract and weigh up these disadvantages and risks "rationally" (Wade 2001b; Kahneman 2011).

d) In some cultures (particularly, certain Asian cultures) filing a formal claim is considered to be a form of public insult and foolishness. It necessarily adds a layer of offence to an existing history of dysfunctional communications.

Conclusion

This chapter has set out seventeen standard strategies in a negotiator's repertoire for recommencing communications where a deadlock has occurred. These strategies are essential to the daily work of litigation lawyers, managers, politicians and diplomats—otherwise known as "conflict managers".

This smorgasbord of approaches raises again the questions of when and how should such knowledge be acquired by "lawyers" and other professional groups of politicians, diplomats and parents. (Honeyman, McAdoo and Welsh 2001) Redefining lawyers by labels such as "conflict managers" opens up vistas of basic knowledge and skills which need to be mastered somewhere and sometime, in a profession already challenged by ubiquitous multi-skilling and by the pace of social change (ABA 1992; Sullivan 2007; Susskind 2013).

Notes

[1] Most people in high conflict are reluctant to make an "apology". However, as defamation lawyers know, there are at least eleven gradations of "statements about the past" which fall moderately or dramatically short of a "mea culpa" or "it was all my fault". [See NDR: Brown & Robbennolt, *Apology*]

[2] For example, lack of judicial time and resources, unpredictability of outcomes, lack of judicial expertise and patience, expense for parties, inaccessibility for middle class, judicial tendency to pressure for settlement, or to split the difference, long delays;

diversion from life opportunities; process games, publicity for disputants, inconve-nience for witnesses who are friends or associates, loss of business secrets, referral to governmental, tax, social security, and immigration investigative bodies etc. See V. Aubert, Competition and Dissensus: Two Types of Conflict and of Conflict Resolution, (1963) Vol VII *Conflict Resolution* 26; J. H. Wade, Don't Waste My Time on Negotiation and Mediation: This Dispute Needs a Judge (2001) 18 *Mediation Q.* 259; R. L. Kiser, M. A. Asher, B. B. Shane, Let's Not Make a Deal: an Empirical Study of Decision Making in Unsuccessful Settlement Negotiations (2008) 5 *Journal of Empirical Studies* 551.

References

American Bar Association. 1992. *Legal Education and Professional Development-An Educational Continuum* ("the McCrate Report"). Chicago: ABA.

Aubert, V. 1963. Competition and Dissensus: Two types of conflict and conflict resolu-tion VII. *Conflict Resolution*: 26-42.

Boulle, L. 2011. *Mediation: Principles, Process, Practice.* 3rd ed., Sydney: Butterworths.

Eddy, B. 2006. *High Conflict People in Legal Disputes.* USA: Janis.

Egan, G. 2007. *The Skilled Helper: A Problem-Management and Opportu-nity-Development Approach to Helping.* 8th ed, California: Thomson.

Festinger, L. 1957. *A Theory of Cognitive Dissonance.* Stanford: Stanford University Press.

Galanter, M. 2006. A World Without Trials? 2006 *Journal of Dispute Resolution* 1: 7-33.

Honeyman C., B. Mc Adoo and N. Welsh. 2001. Here There be Monsters: At the Edge of the Map of Conflict Resolution. In *The Conflict Resolution Practitioner. Mono-graph*, Office of Dispute Resolution, Georgia Supreme Court.

Kahneman, D. 2011. *Thinking Fast and Slow.* New York: Farrar, Straus and Giroux.

Kiser, R. L., M. A. Asher and B. B. Mc Shane. 2008. Let's Not Make a Deal: An Empirical Study of Decision Making in Unsuccessful Settlement Negotiations. 5 *Journal of Empirical Studies*: 551-591.

Lewicki, R. J., D. M. Saunders and B. Barry. 2005. *Negotiation.* New York: McGraw-Hill Education.

Moore, C. 2003. *The Mediation Process: Practical Strategies for Resolving Conflict,* San Francisco: Jossey-Bass.

Pruitt, D. and S. H. Kim. 2004. *Social Conflict—Escalation, Stalemate and Settlement.* New York: McGraw-Hill.

Sullivan, W. M., A. Colby, J. W. Wegner, L. Bond and L. S. Shulman. 2007. *Educating Lawyers: Preparation for the Profession of Law.* San Francisco: Jossey-Bass.

Susskind, R. E. 2013. *Tomorrow's Lawyers: An Introduction to Your Future.* Oxford: Oxford University Press.

Wade, J. H. 1995. In Search of New Conflict Management Processes. 10 *Australian Family Lawyer*: 23-28.

Wade, J. H. 2001a. Don't Waste My Time on Negotiation and Mediation: This Dispute Needs a Judge. 18 *Mediation Quarterly*: 259-280.

Wade, J. H. 2001b. Systematic Risk Analysis for Negotiators and Litigators: But You Never Told Me It Would Be Like This. 13 *Bond Law Review*: 462-485.

⚘ 95 ⚘

An Agreement that Lasts

John H. Wade & Chris Honeyman

Editors' Note: So, you finally have a deal! How can you make the deal stick? This straightforward chapter shows why deals regularly fall apart, and provides specific advice on what you can do in order to increase the likelihood that your agreement will survive the slings and arrows of outrageous fortune.

> Peace, peace, they say, when there is no peace
> *Jeremiah*, Chapter 8, Verse 11

It is usually a primary goal of a negotiator not merely to reach an agreement, but also to create an agreement which is durable, along with a mutual sense of commitment to its performance among those signing it.

Agreements which are performed in substance by all parties, which no one walks away from, and which do not require enforcement proceedings can be described as "durable," "final," "stickable," or "committed."

John Wade is an emeritus professor of law of Bond University, Queensland, Australia. He practiced as a lawyer in Australia between 1987 and 2012, and also had an active mediation practice in organizational, family and commercial conflicts during those years. He has taught over 300 mediation and negotiation courses in Hong Kong, New Zealand, London, Canada, the U.S. and Australia. John has published over 100 books and articles (see epublications@bond.edu.au). His teaching awards include best law teacher at Sydney University (1989); at Bond University (1990); and in Australia (1998). John now lives in Vancouver, Canada with his growing family, and teaches intensive negotiation courses there.
Chris Honeyman is managing partner of Convenor Conflict Management, a consulting firm based in Washington, DC. He is co-editor of *The Negotiator's Desk Reference* and five other books, and author of over 90 published articles, book chapters and monographs. He has directed a 25-year series of research-and-development programs in conflict management (see www.convenor.com/projects). Chris has also served as a consultant to numerous academic and practical conflict resolution programs, held a variety of advisory roles with the ABA, IMI and other organizations, and served as a mediator, arbitrator and in other neutral capacities in more than 2,000 disputes.

We are using this as a working description of a durable agreement in order to sidestep a historic legal debate over whether a contract actually gives each party a choice—to perform the expressed obligations, or to "perform" in a secondary sense, by breaching the contract and paying damages (or accepting other consequences of a breach). This chapter works on the assumption that choosing "secondary" obligations such as damages is not "performance."

What percentage of negotiated agreements in various types of transactions, types of conflict, or in various "cultures," are actually performed as written or promised? For how long do agreements in these varieties of areas "endure" or "stick?" To use more narrow legal language, what percentage of negotiated agreements in these various areas are seriously "breached," or allegedly seriously "breached?"

Various levels of courts ask similar questions about consent or litigated orders. What percentage of judicial orders is complied with, and for how long, in different areas of culture and conflict?

With only anecdotal evidence to rely upon, it is probable that the actual durability rate of agreements varies enormously across class, culture, wealth, and type of transaction or conflict. With extensive research, these patterns of breach could be made visible by "durability graphs" or "performance rates" which may assist to change people's expectations of finality.

For example, low rates of durability (only 10%-20% lasting more than 12 months) would possibly attach to child visitation agreements in certain categories of families. Conversely, high rates of vendor-purchaser durability (85%-90% lasting indefinitely) would possibly attach to house purchases in Australia or America. Purchaser—bank mortgage contracts may also have high rates of performance amongst the middle class, until recession and job losses escalate. Again, such studies of performance and non-performance would assist to modify expectations of "finality" of negotiated agreements.

Many of the factors which hinder *initial* commitment to reaching an agreement also contribute to undermining *ongoing* commitment to performance. Set out below are some of the anecdotal reasons why negotiated agreements are "breached," or are not durable.

Cultural Expectations of Flexibility

In some cultural groups, a written or oral contract is perceived to be only an agreement to work together in the future. It is a symbol of a relationship, not of obligation to perform its detailed terms (Lewicki, Saunders and Barry 2005). [NDR: Goh, *Cultural Errors*] The agreement has implied terms that if any party has difficulties in performing, then everyone will assemble again and negotiate ways to preserve the relationship, and vary the "obligations."

This interpretation of the impermanence of a contract or agreement may come as a shock to an inexperienced person from a Western or legal culture where legal finality is assumed, and where relationship does not trump commercial certainty.

This leads to the predictable pattern of the economically more powerful party attempting to negotiate that all breaches or variations will be dealt with ultimately by courts or arbitrators from their own culture, and applying their own cultural and legal rules.

Complexity of Ongoing Obligations

The more complex the terms of any negotiated agreement, then the higher the likelihood that various obligations will "break down" with the passage of time and circumstance. The fragility of an agreement increases with multiplication of parties, vague language, period of performance, and number of obligations on human behavior (e.g., "use best endeavors;" "take reasonable steps to refer customers;" "delays caused by inclement weather or unforeseen circumstances").

Of course, many negotiators attempt to reduce ongoing complexity by lengthy definition of vague terms, reference to industry standards, self-enforcing arbitration clauses or decisions by a specified "authority," liquidated damages clauses, and clean-break swaps of money for a defined act.

Shallow Peace

Agreements, treaties or litigation may momentarily provide an outcome, while the underlying causes of conflict remain, together with the emotional and structural changes associated with escalation (see Pruitt and Kim 2004; Cheldelin, Druckman and Fast 2003). The parties achieve shallow "settlement," but not deep "resolution." In those circumstances, the agreement is unlikely to endure. The aggrieved party will find a moral or legal justification to breach it in the next week or decade. Successive agreements may be entered into and breached many times during ongoing family, international or tribal disputes (see Honeyman 2001; Wade 2004: 283, 299, 302). Eventually, if underlying causes of conflict, emotional and structural changes are addressed satisfactorily, one of these agreements may be substantially performed by all the involved and still surviving parties.

The same reasons which cause conflict also cause the collapse of settlements; it is therefore worth reviewing these reasons here. Christopher Moore has categorized the five causes of conflict as data, interest, structural, value and relationship conflicts (Moore 2003: 64). These are represented by the following chart:

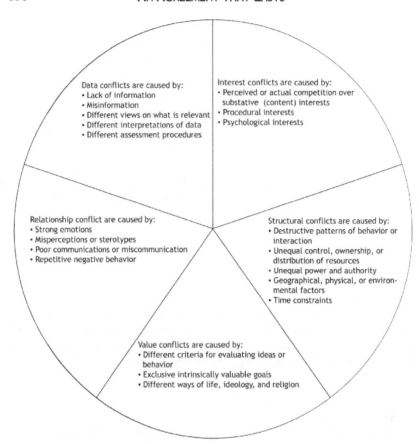

Data conflicts are caused by:
• Lack of information
• Misinformation
• Different views on what is relevant
• Different interpretations of data
• Different assessment procedures

Interest conflicts are caused by:
• Perceived or actual competition over substative (content) interests
• Procedural interests
• Psychological interests

Relationship conflict are caused by:
• Strong emotions
• Misperceptions or sterotypes
• Poor communications or miscommunication
• Repetitive negative behavior

Structural conflicts are caused by:
• Destructive patterns of behavior or interaction
• Unequal control, ownership, or distribution of resources
• Unequal power and authority
• Geographical, physical, or environmental factors
• Time constraints

Value conflicts are caused by:
• Different criteria for evaluating ideas or behavior
• Exclusive intrinsically valuable goals
• Different ways of life, ideology, and religion

In the comparatively well-researched area of family disputes, many reasons have been identified for the particular difficulties of responding constructively to serious interspousal conflict. Ken Kressel has commented:

Nine shared obstacles to a constructive negotiating experience can be identified:

1) High levels of intraparty conflict
2) Well-established and rigid patterns of destructive interaction
3) Inexperience in the art of negotiating
4) Scarcity of divisible resources
5) Complex issues which threaten loss of face or self-esteem
6) Elevated levels of stress and tension
7) Social norms and institutions for conflict management that are weak or that unintentionally provoke destructive interaction
8) Disparities in the parties' relative power
9) Disparities in the parties' degree of interpersonal sensitivity

The last two of these obstacles are closely associated with the male-female context in which divorce negotiations occur (Kressel 1985: 31; see also Johnston and Campell 1988; Kubler-Ross 1969; Weiss 1975; Jordan 1985). By itself, signing a piece of paper rarely modifies any of the above hovering and entrenched causes of conflict. But it may be an important step in a longer journey toward that goal.

Buyer's Remorse

There is a well-researched post-agreement emotional state sometimes labeled "buyer's remorse," or "post-settlement blues," or the "winner's curse" (Lewicki, Saunders and Barry 2005: 148). This is a state of regret and even depression which strikes many (not all) negotiators who have "lost" an actual or imagined better deal, for a perceived ordinary deal. "What if we had held out for longer, would we have received more?"

This personal sense of loss and regret can be reinforced by armchair critics. [NDR: Wade, *Tribe*] Someone experiencing buyer's (or seller's) remorse may refuse to perform the agreement, and can readily create a list of moral and legal justifications for this withdrawal.

Changed Circumstances—"Occupational Morality"

There are some agreements which through custom or market pressure will be renegotiated regularly because "things change." This is similar to the previous discussion of "cultural expectations of flexibility." However, that heading related to national or regional culture, whereas this category relates to common industrial practices, or common practices of flexibility in particular transactions. One example is an agreement between separated parents about times of access or visitation with their children. A carefully negotiated schedule always is varied/breached/not performed as a child is busy, sick, away on an excursion; or a parent is busy, sick, or sent away by an employer. Another example is employment contracts in research, exporting, military and technological industries. The original "understandings" or contracts for both employer and employee may be subject to constant renegotiation in order to adapt to mandated behavior in competitive fields.

In 1963, a classic study in Wisconsin found firstly that the majority of business "exchanges" were vague and therefore not legally enforceable; and secondly, the majority of business disputes are settled with no reference to the written "contract," much less to lawyers. The study further hypothesized on why the majority of business exchanges are considered by occupational custom and morality to be relatively binding, without being legally contractual.

> Even where agreement can be reached at the negotiation stage, carefully planned arrangements may create

undesirable exchange relationships between business units. Some businessmen object that in such a carefully worked out relationship one gets performance only to the letter of the contract. Such planning indicates a lack of trust and blunts the demands of friendship, turning a cooperative venture into an antagonistic horse trade. Yet the greater danger perceived by some businessmen is that one would have to perform his side of the bargain to its letter and thus lose what is called "flexibility." Businessmen may welcome a measure of vagueness in the obligations they assume so that they may negotiate matters in light of the actual circumstances (Macaulay 1963; see also Macaulay 1977).

Legal Rules Allow Variation Due to Changed Circumstances

Different legal rules exist in every country which enable contracts to be set aside or varied, based on a limited range of events which occur *after* the negotiated agreement.

So the phrase "But I thought we have a concluded agreement," is met by "We did, but we are legally justified in setting it aside because X (a fire, war, death, strike, etc.) has occurred."

The list of legal exceptions to finality of contracts varies from one jurisdiction to another, and is often placed under the label "frustration of contracts." These lists are studied assiduously by national and international lawyers and insurers who are trying to define the risks of nonperformance in each country. Then these lawyers engage in an ongoing industry of drafting standard clauses which narrow or expand those legal loopholes.

The broad cross-cultural legal exceptions to finality based on post-agreement events include:

- The doctrine of frustration.
- Protection of the public purse. For example, child support agreements in some jurisdictions can or must be re-opened once a child is receiving state welfare payments.
- Legislative destabilization based on a new "public policy."

There are many examples where a class of contracts is rendered invalid or unenforceable due to retrospective legislation which is purporting to protect some version of the "public good." For example, legislation invalidating existing contracts with certain classes of people or businesses considered at various times of history to be "the enemy" or "needing protection," such as German, American, Aboriginal, Roman Catholic, Protestant or female; or contracts which involve exportation of diminishing timber stocks, whales, or native animals; or contracts for the sale of newly discovered "dangers"—such as certain drugs, asbestos materials, explosive fertilizers, off-shore tax evasion schemes, or politically incorrect films or literature.

Legal Rules Which Allow for Setting Aside a Contract Due to Pre-Agreement Events

Following the previous legal exceptions to finality based on *post-agreement* events, there are many categories of legal rules (which again vary from country to country) which allow contracts to be challenged based on *pre-agreement* factors.

Once again, these lists of fluctuating rules are studied and systematized daily by armies of lawyers around the planet. These workers are attempting to give some clarity to the loopholes to finality in a wide range of transactions and disputes. These loopholes and attendant risks can then be partly closed by careful drafting of contracts; by insurance; and by adjusting price in favor of the risk-taker. There are some pre-agreement legal loopholes, such as lying, which are difficult to close by drafting or insurance in most countries. For example, a clause which tries to enhance finality by stating to the effect that "one or both parties are free to lie overtly during negotiations with no consequential legal liability" is unlikely to reduce the legal risks attached to overt lying.

Broad cross-cultural legal exceptions to the finality of agreements, based on pre-agreement events, include:

- Innocent, negligent and fraudulent misrepresentation (Korobkin 2002: 375-416; Spegel, Rogers and Buckley 1998: 189-202).
- A limited range of mistakes, or unconscionable dealings.
- Non-disclosure of "material" facts in certain classes of agreements such as insurance or family property contracts.
- Entering contracts at a time when such arrangements are illegal by statute (e.g. sale of weapons, drugs, state secrets, or unduly monopolistic sales, as well as sales prejudicing protected farming industries) or against fluctuating public policy at that time (Williston 1957; Carter and Harland 2002: 555-641).
- Entering negotiations and a resulting contract at a time when one of the parties does not have sufficient *capacity* to consent, due to youthfulness, junior status, depression, undue market pressure, inexperience, lack of information, lack of independent advice, haste, inappropriate threats, or undue influence.
- Consumer protection laws which in some countries give consumers mandatory cooling off periods; warranties which enable return of defective products; independent financial and legal advice; criminal sanctions against marketing tricks such as bait-and-switch advertising; or mandatory disclosures of information.

Efficiency and Accessibility of the Legal "System"

The previous two exceptions to finality of agreements concentrated on legal rules. But rule analysis by itself is unhelpful. It should be complemented by a cultural study of the "law in action." Obviously, access to efficient lawyers, courts and judges differs dramatically across the world, and within countries. There are gradations of expense, uncertainty, delay, and corruption. For example, one yearly study of large international businesses indicates that currently these businesses perceive Finland and New Zealand to have the least corrupt, and China and Indonesia to have substantially more corrupt, court systems and judiciary (Transparency International 2004).

Accordingly, where the legal (as compared to market) enforceability of a contract is unpredictable and/or unavailable, then finality of agreements due to "the law" diminishes.

On a shifting scale, where law enforcement is weak, delayed, uncertain, clumsy, or corrupt, then relationships and market power become more influential in either encouraging or diminishing finality. A subcontractor on a large building site will probably acquiesce when his/her boss reneges on the employment contract, and hope for a job on the next construction site. Even where legal enforceability is accessible, many "innocent" contractors do not bother with the delay and expense of enforcement proceedings. They prefer to invest their time and money in other business ventures, and punish the party allegedly in breach with business isolation.

Nevertheless, it is predictable that China will work hard to improve the image, rule of law, accessibility and independence of its own courts; and that meanwhile foreign businesses will attempt to add legal finality and western values to Chinese trade agreements by negotiating for off-shore arbitration or litigation enforcement clauses.

Lack of Informed Consent

Many agreements, notably settlements at the door of a court, are entered into under pressures of limited time, money, exhaustion, and exhortations to settle from lawyers and some tribal members ("Tribal" is used here in the sense of relationship to a negotiator's constituents or supports, not to ethnicity). [NDR: Wade, *Tribe*] Accordingly, some negotiators look back in anger at their confused state, chaotic information, and the pressure-cooker negotiating environment. [NDR: Nolan-Haley, *Agents*]

This sense of grievance may erupt later in a search for legal or moral justification to "get out of" the deal. For example:

- "My lawyer failed to explain the meaning of that clause."
- "I didn't know that the terms of the agreement were final."

- "I was so confused and distressed on that day that eventually I signed anything put in front of me."
- "My lawyer pressured me into signing by a barrage of threats about court costs and the uncertainty of litigation."

A landmark study in Australia has recorded the early distress of 723 separated spouses. "Property applications can now be made ... during the first year of separation. This may have unfortunate repercussions for those who are so distressed about the event that they can't think rationally, or for those whose animosity towards their spouses or whose guilt influences their decisions." A few of the spouses' comments follow:

- "When the marriage first breaks down, you're not in a proper frame of mind to face the Court etc. One is at a disadvantage. It's not the best time for making decisions." (man)
- "People are so mixed up after separation. The settlement should be decided by independent people." (man)
- "I signed away custody of the children while under stress and medication. I have no chance at present of getting them back." (woman) (McDonald 1986: 295)

These grievances sometimes trigger refusal to comply with the terms of family property settlements. As a matter of legal principle, they rarely are successful as a defense to an enforcement action (Public Trustee v. Gilbert 1991). But this begs the question whether the "successful" enforcement litigation actually produced promised dollars or performance in the hand.

Judges have consistently taken the view that a client advised by a lawyer is strongly presumed both to have a basic understanding of legal principle, and to have given consent (In Marriage of Holland 1982; In Marriage of Gebert 1990. In the latter, husband settled for 10% of assets against his probable entitlement to 40%; court held that there was no miscarriage of justice, as the husband acted freely and was advised to seek legal advice.)

In Australia, the most notorious documented "misunderstanding" of family clients occurred in the early 1980's. A survey conducted by the Australian Institute of Family Studies showed that the majority of family clients had settled without a proper understanding of the relevance of superannuation and pension entitlements to the division of property (McDonald 1986: 199-200; Wade 1993).

All Drafting Has Loopholes

This is particularly apparent where agreements are drafted late at night, or under severe time pressures—smaller time, bigger loopholes. Those professionals who draft agreements regularly know that there are no watertight documents. Even encyclopedic contracts do not allow for every exigency in human affairs, as many words are capable of multiple interpretations. Of course, most negotiators do not have the time, patience, money or inclination to negotiate multi-page documents. They perhaps realistically hope that goodwill, reputation and ("cheap") short documents will encourage performance of 90% of agreements, and tolerate the risk that the other 10% may not be performed when the unexpected occurs.

Fine Tuning "Later"

The dynamics of some negotiations include late night deadlines; presence of tired leaders; hurried general "heads of agreement" drafted and signed, so that important people can go elsewhere; and delegation to lawyers or junior bureaucrats to "fill in the details" or "complete the technicalities," sometime in the future.

This common and allegedly "efficient" process obviously leads to some almost "finalized" treaties, litigation settlements and commercial leases not actually becoming finalized. This is at least because the devil is in the details, the junior delegates are competitive and fearful for their own reputation, new key unresolved interests arise during drafting, and hawks use the drafting meetings as opportunities to re-open even the "settled" principles (Honeyman 2001).

Any Agreement is Better than None

Related to the previous point is that sometimes negotiators' goals evolve towards a "quick fix;" or any signed document; or any agreement is better than none. They realize that fine tuning will take too much time; that constituents are becoming restless; that their short-term reputation needs a signed document, even if performance will probably not happen. Managers sometimes sign off on unrealistic agreements with employees as they want to pay attention to other impending crises; peace treaties are often signed even though key clauses are missing, or unrealistic. After the First World War, the Treaty of Versailles was eventually signed in 1919 despite obviously unworkable realignment of borders for many minority groups in Europe, Africa and Asia. Signing something was considered essential as negotiators were exhausted, political leaders needed to get home for forthcoming elections, anxious electorates wanted to celebrate "the" peace, militia were engaging in violent self-help, and creating some stable buffers against Bolshevism had become a priority (MacMillan 2003: 181, 192, 254).

Conditional Agreements Subject to State Ratification

Some agreements require ratification, not only by constituents or tribes, but also by the state. This is because government policy or legislation has declared that certain "private ordering" affects important public interests. Therefore a right to veto exists until a public official is convinced that the private agreement has recognized community interests.

Sometimes, this community oversight reduces to a mindless, routine rubber-stamping by a state official or judge. But such low hurdles climb gradually towards expensive, time-consuming and uncertain hearings before an aggressive state judge, tribunal or official who is vigorously protecting actual or perceived public interests. Necessarily, any agreement lives in precarious limbo, subject to buyer's remorse, vengeful hawks, tactical maneuvers, and evidentiary uncertainty while waiting for this second round of public approval.

Examples of private agreements which need court or "official" approval to become relatively "final" or "binding" include:

- Building or forestry contracts which affect the environment.
- Child support agreements which affect the amount of social welfare paid to a custodial parent.
- Media, film, or literature contracts which import racist or pornographic views into the community.
- Private family agreements for the use of finances of a mentally disabled person.
- International treaties entered into by the executive, which legally require ratification by the legislature.
- Family property settlements which intentionally (a "sweetheart deal") or otherwise may result in a spouse becoming dependent on state welfare payments.
- Mergers of large corporations which potentially create monopolies of supply to the public.

Wealth

Wealth of one or both parties may destabilize an agreement. Money and the chance of "success" gives an aggrieved person the capacity and willingness to allege various legal justifications for breach when a future dispute occurs. Among the wealthy, a few years of legal expenses may only represent 1% of the aggrieved person's empire, and the resulting attrition and disparate investment may eventually encourage other parties to renegotiate the now disputed clauses.

Lawyers are instinctively aware of this pattern and that they may also become the target for the subsequent grievance. Accordingly, considerable time and consultation occurs when drafting contracts for the wealthy in order to minimize the chances of a subsequent professional negligence claim (as well as to attempt to close loopholes and thereby discourage subsequent legal sorties by an affluent party).

How to Increase the Durability of Negotiated Agreements?

If the above is a catalogue of hypothesized and anecdotally observed reasons for agreements being "breached," or being less than durable, how then to make negotiated agreements more durable?

In simplistic terms, as with the original perceived incentives to *enter* the agreement, *performance* can also be made attractive, and non-performance made unattractive, via economics, emotion, various versions of morality, reputation, legal rules, and accessible, affordable and honest legal enforcement mechanisms applying to the various contracting parties.

If some of the "durability" or "stickability" elements cannot be added to the dynamics of the agreement, then expectations should be lowered. The parties may have achieved one "success" criterion, namely a (signed) agreement. But they may only have a low or moderate chance of another measure of "success," namely performance. Many risk-taking negotiators are willing to buy the chance of performance, and then experience the rollercoaster of performance and breach as the predicted ratio of performed to non-performed agreements is still considered to be a worthwhile investment.

Reversing the above list of factors which encourage breach, the chances of performance of an agreement are enhanced by the following:

- Try to enter contracts with people, groups or nations with whom there are strong long-term relationships. This provides a layer of incentives to perform promises rather than alienate friends and future business.
- When negotiating with cultural groups which perceive an agreement as mainly the beginning of a relationship, be prepared for a lengthy series of rounds of negotiation in exchange for the promise of a long-term relationship.
- Attempt to clarify across cultures whether "yes" means "maybe" or even "no," and whether signed and detailed documents are considered to be "binding," morally, legally, and/or in reputation—or just amount to the declaration that a working relationship now exists, with the actual commitments subject to continuous renegotiation. [NDR: Goh, *Cultural Errors*; NDR: Miller, *Codes of Culture*]
- Include a serious discussion and contractual clauses (more than boilerplate) on how future misunderstandings and problems will be addressed procedurally and emotionally by skilled people ("dispute resolution" clauses). (Honeyman et al. 2007). [See also NDR: Groton et al., *Thinking Ahead*]
- Attempt to agree early on that final determination of any future "problems" with performance will be in an accessible court or

arbitration venue which is, first, not corrupt, second, governed by stable and clear legal precedents, and third, has legal precedents which have minimal scope for varying or setting aside the particular type of agreement.

- Where possible, convert a negotiated dispute settlement into a court order so that any breach of the agreement immediately opens additional enforcement mechanisms.

- Draft the agreement in detail, if possible, in accordance with standard industry practices.

- Contract with "stable" countries and people, cultivate back-up suppliers and take out insurance as risk management for non-performance or currency fluctuations.

- Include carefully planned procedures for managing hawks and armchair critics in the background. [NDR: Wade, *Tribe*]

- Lower expectations, where there is long-term escalated conflict with some of the emotional and structural changes attached to such entrenched conflict (Pruitt and Kim 2004; Cheldelin, Druckman and Fast 2003). This particularly applies to tribal conflicts in Northern Ireland, the Balkans, Rwanda, Israel and parts of Africa, but also within many families and businesses. The first year, decade, or century of agreements will undoubtedly not be durable with such dynamics in the background. [NDR: Coleman et al., *Intractable—2*]

- Attempt to enter agreements which recognize procedural, emotional and substantive needs of all parties. An aggrieved negotiator at any of those levels will probably be looking for payback or exit at a strategic moment. [NDR: Welsh, *Fairness*]

- Where a negotiator is on an emotional rollercoaster, try to include his/her long-term friends, doves, moderates, associates, allies or business partners in the negotiations. [NDR: Mayer, *Allies*] For years after the initial agreement is signed, they will exert pressure (ongoing negotiations) on the wavering party to "honor his/her commitments," or risk losing their friendship.

- Do not walk close to the line on any of the legal rules, such as duress, deceit, vague terminology or illegality, any of which gives other parties opportunity to allege a loophole to finality (Macaulay 1963: 62-65). [NDR: Hinshaw, *Ethics*]

- Use experienced wordsmiths (a.k.a. lawyers) to include a range of standard clauses which attempt to negate duress, misrepresentation, and/or illegality, and which make specific allowances for future contingencies.

- Try to avoid complex agreements with multiple long-term obligations of performance; try to create "clean-break" obligations where one performance is swapped for another (e.g. bank check upon delivery of goods); try to include self-enforcing clauses so that the transaction costs of enforcement are reduced (e.g. interest of 12% runs on payments in default; security is held by a bank or by one party until performance occurs; payments are released upon progressive certification by an architect; liquidated damages; 1% extra for each day early; 1% less for each day late, etc.).

- Discover and perform an appropriate ritual of commitment—in some places, it is eye contact and a handshake. In others, it may be an alcoholic celebration, or a vow in the presence of a holy book or priest.

- Attempt to reduce buyer's remorse by making congratulatory speeches about the benefits of the agreement, mentioning the list of risks which would follow no agreement; and by never agreeing quickly to any clauses; and by theatrical displays of anguish and pained speeches about the "tough terms," "special deal" or "hard bargain" which is being imposed; and by adding post-agreement gifts and bonuses (corner office, luggage racks, set of steak knives, 12 months' free warranty).

- Publicize the deal by mutual agreement. Then a wider audience places an expectation on all parties that they should perform, or lose face and credibility in future arrangements. Most people have a strong desire to act consistently with their own clear commitments (Shell 1999: 196-199; Cialdini 1984: 52-97). Thus a media announcement of a treaty, a takeover, or a trade agreement is more than a celebration; it is aimed at moving at least the visible parties from agreement to a deeper level of commitment.

Conclusion

Most negotiators want more than an agreement. They want commitment and performance. It is helpful for negotiators, first, to be aware of the smorgasbord of factors which present warning signs of impending breaches; and second, to be aware of, and skilled at working on, those factors which increase the likelihood of commitment and performance.

References

Carter, J. W. and D. J. Harland. 2002. *Contract Law in Australia*. Sydney: Butterworths.

Cheldelin, S., D. Druckman and L. Fast (eds). 2003. *Conflict: From Analysis to Intervention*. London: Bloomsbury Publishing.

Cialdini, R.B. 1984. *Influence: Science and Practice*. Glenview, IL: Scott-Foresman.

Honeyman, C. 2001. The Wrong Mental Image of Settlement. *Negotiation Journal* 17(1): 7-15.

Honeyman, C., J. Macfarlane, B. Mayer, A. K. Schneider and J. Seul. 2007. The Next Frontier: Thinking Ahead about Conflict. *Alternatives*, CPR/New York, 6/2007.

In Marriage of Gebert. 1990. Family Law Reports 14: 62.

In Marriage of Holland. 1982. Family Law Reports 8: 233.

Johnston, J. R. and L. E. G. Campbell. 1988. *Impasses of Divorce: The Dynamics and Resolution of Family Conflict*. New York: Simon & Schuster.

Jordan, P. 1989. The Effects of Marital Separation on Men. *Journal of Divorce* 12(1): 57-82.

Korobkin, R. 2002. *Negotiation Theory and Strategy*. New York: Aspen Publishers, Inc.

Kressel, K. 1985. *The Process of Divorce: How Professionals and Couples Negotiate Settlements*. New York: Basic Books.

Kubler-Ross, E. 1969. *On Death & Dying: What the Dying Have to Teach Doctors, Nurses, Clergy & Their Own Families*. New York: Scribner.

Lewicki, R. J., D. M. Saunders and B. Barry. 2014. *Negotiation*. New York: McGraw-Hill Higher Education.

Macaulay, S. 1963. Non-Contractual Relations in Business: A Preliminary Study. *American Sociological Review* 28(1): 55-67.

Macaulay, S. 1977. Elegant Models, Empirical Pictures, and the Complexities of Contract. *Law and Society Review* 11(3): 507-528.

MacMillan, M. 2003. *Paris 1919: Six Months that Changed the World*. New York: Random House Trade Paperback Edition.

McDonald, P. (ed). 1986. *Settling Up: Property and Income Distribution on Divorce in Australia*. Melbourne: Prentice Hall of Australia.

Moore, C.W. 2003. *The Mediation Process: Practical Strategies for Resolving Conflict*. San Francisco: Jossey-Bass.

Pruitt, D.G. and S.H. Kim. *2004. Social Conflict: Escalation, Stalemate and Settlement*. New York: McGraw-Hill Higher Education.

Public Trustee v. Gilbert. 1991. *Family Law Reports* 14: 573.

Shell, G.R. 1999. *Bargaining for Advantage: Negotiation Strategies for Reasonable People*. New York: Viking.

Spegel, N. M., R. Rogers and R. P. Buckley. 1998. *Negotiation: Theory and Techniques*. Sydney: Butterworths.

Transparency International. 2004. *Corruption Perceptions Index 2004*. Available at http://www.transparency.org/research/cpi/cpi_2004 (last accessed May 12, 2016).

Wade, J. H. 1993. Deals which Come Unstuck: Reasons for the Breakdown of Family Settlement. *Australian Family Lawyer* 9: 14.

Wade, J. H. 2004. Representing Clients Effectively in Negotiation, Conciliation and Mediation of Family Disputes. *Australian Journal of Family Law* 18: 283-302.

Weiss, R. S. 1975. *Marital Separation*. New York: Basic Books.

Williston, S. 1957. *A Treatise on the Law of Contracts* Vol. 14, edited by W. H. E. Jaeger. Mount Kisco, NY: Baker, Voorhis.

Section XVII: Getting It Done (with "Helpers")

The last section of the book acknowledges that sometimes, agents and principals by themselves are not enough, and some kind of "helper" is going to be needed. This section begins with three chapters on mediation: a general overview of mediation's uses is followed by a chapter analyzing why one mediator is frequently so different from another, and what you might need to watch out for. The set concludes with a famous mediator's reflections on how mediators, who routinely demand that the parties be more transparent, are often opaque about their own thought processes.

Yet mediators are not the only outside people who might become useful in a difficult conflict. The next chapter analyzes a whole series of non-neutral (and yet not classically "agent") roles, under the general heading of "allies" who might be invoked by a party. This is followed by a close review of one particular type of intervener whose subtle role (and influence) is frequently underestimated: the interpreter. And finally, sometimes what a situation needs is somebody who will really shake things up. The last chapter in the book assesses the possibility that an activist may not (always) create conflict, and instead may sometimes be essential to resolving it.

ೞ **96** ೞ

The Uses of Mediation

Lela P. Love & Joseph B. Stulberg

Editors' Note: How's your negotiation going? Would using a mediator perhaps be helpful? This chapter shows why and when mediation can help negotiators reach an agreement. It also explains the different types of mediation goals, and how each of those goals can affect the process. This should be read in conjunction with Honeyman on Working with Mediators.

Imagine a time when you negotiated with someone, either for yourself or as someone's representative, and it ended in an impasse. You walked away from the discussion even though you sensed that a negotiated outcome was in your best interest or that of your client. Perhaps your negotiating counterpart called you a name or accused you of something that you or your client did not do. Maybe an insulting offer was made. You may have been tired or depressed and working on a "short fuse." Perhaps it was simply too hard, acrimonious or polarized even to establish a time to meet again with your counterpart. For whichever reason, the negotiation did not succeed. In that same scenario, something different might have happened if you had added a mediator.

Lela Porter Love is a professor of law and director of Cardozo Law School's (NYC) conflict resolution program. She is Past Chair of the ABA Section of Dispute Resolution, where she initiated the first International Mediation Leadership Summit in The Hague. In addition to numerous articles, her writing on mediation includes law school textbooks (co-authored with Carrie Menkel-Meadow and Andrea Schneider); *The Middle Voice: Mediating Conflict Successfully* (co-authored with Joseph Stulberg); Stories Mediators Tell (co-edited with Eric Galton) and Stories Mediators Tell—World Edition (co-edited with Glen Parker). She is an active mediator and trainer of mediators in the U.S. and abroad.
Joseph B. ("Josh") Stulberg is the Michael E. Moritz Chair in Alternative Dispute Resolution at The Ohio State University Moritz College of Law. A former Vice President of the American Arbitration Association in charge of its Community Dispute Services, Josh has mediated disputes of national significance, including Native American land-claims, police-community group confrontations, and state budget negotiations; trained people to serve in court, agency-based, or community-based dispute resolution mediation programs; and published 15 books and manuals and more than 65 articles on conflict resolution topics. He served as Reporter for the Model Standards of Conduct for Mediators (2005).

Why Add a Mediator to Negotiations?

Negotiations are neither self-generating nor self-sustaining. One party might want to talk, but others refuse to do so. Some talks never start—or collapse—because participants lack effective negotiating skills or advocates engage in strategic but misleading posturing. Other discussions reach impasse due to misunderstandings, hostile comments or perceived rigidity. These familiar dynamics can disserve parties whose interests lie in resolving their dispute. Understandable—all too human—reasons cause negotiation meltdown.

Negotiators can be trapped by other pitfalls. Sometimes participants refuse to initiate direct negotiations (or to request mediation) for fear that their counterpart would interpret that move as a sign of weakness. Some take extreme public positions to protect themselves and their reputations, but in so doing undermine consideration of workable options. Some make inaccurate assumptions about aspects of the situation or their counterpart's motivation. Some fail to determine their priority interests. And some, because of such psychological phenomena as loss aversion or overconfidence in their own judgment, make sub-optimal decisions.

A skilled mediator, particularly with assistance from an insightful, strategic advocate, can defuse or transform these roadblocks into building blocks for movement by promoting constructive participation, minimizing misunderstandings, crystallizing significant interests, framing issues thoughtfully, urging parties to be realistic, and expanding discussion of possible outcomes. How?

What Does a Mediator Do?

A mediator is a neutral intervenor committed to assisting each negotiating party and their representative to conduct constructive conversations. She helps structure discussions. She stabilizes dialogue. She injects an attitude of hope and "going the distance." She prods participants to clarify interests, establish priorities and transform rhetoric into proposals. She develops discussion strategies that minimize misunderstandings when tensions run high. She helps parties understand one another when ill-chosen words create bitterness between them. She uses reframing and reality-testing to encourage participants to examine and evaluate their assumptions and conclusions. She performs these basic tasks in order to help all parties involved enhance their collective understanding, spark creative problem solving, and settle the controversy.

A Posture of Optimism

Former Senate Majority Leader George Mitchell, when referring to his intervention as a mediator in Northern Ireland and the Middle East, states, "Conflicts are created and sustained by human beings. They can be ended by human beings." (Mitchell 2002: 4, 6). In mediating the conflict in Northern Ireland, Mitchell describes 700 days of failure followed by one final day of success. Though he became disheartened at times, he did not give up. The mediator is the very last person to give up. Desmond Tutu, the Nobel Peace Laureate who helped negotiate the transition of South Africa from the horrors of apartheid towards black political leadership and racial dignity, concludes that "no problem anywhere can ever again be considered to be intractable." (Tutu 2004: 396) A mediator is not naïve, but she is persistently optimistic that negotiations—even difficult and stalled negotiations—can be set on course.

Most of us faced with a negotiation that is not working tend to feel that the other person involved is stubborn, selfish, uncooperative, or unreasonable. The presence of an upbeat, optimistic third person can transform the environment of a negotiation. Once the mood is changed, positive momentum can be created.

A Variety of Applications

From disputes on the Internet to controversies erupting on city streets or in school settings to cases filed in court, mediation is increasingly used to address and resolve problems. Situations in very diverse arenas—divorce, labor and employment, construction, landlord-tenant, commercial matters, public policy, and international disputes—all regularly benefit from mediation.

Consider the following:

- A single parent with teenagers moves into an apartment above an elderly couple. The teenagers make noise walking around their apartment, playing loud music and entertaining friends, sometimes late at night. When the downstairs neighbors complain to the teenagers, they respond with crude comments. The elderly couple bangs a broom against the ceiling to signal that the sounds should stop, but this results in the volume increasing. When one of the downstairs neighbors goes upstairs to try to talk with the parent, no one answers the door despite the presence of sounds in the apartment. Vigorous knocking on the door results in a door panel breaking. The upstairs neighbor demands money to replace the door. When the neighbors do talk, conversation results in angry accusations. How will the spiral stop?

- Cheryl is an associate in a large law firm. An African American, she is the only lawyer in the group who is not Caucasian. When other office attorneys socialize, gossip and chat in the corridors, she feels excluded and isolated. She notices that she is not given training opportunities that others are offered and she is not called on in meetings as frequently as others. After her supervising attorney tells her that "B+ work is ok," when an assignment is slightly late, Cheryl believes that she is being set up to fail.

When she raises any of these issues, she is given an unsatisfactory explanation. Is her only option to file a racial discrimination complaint against her employer?

- In an Eastern European town, members of the Roma (gypsy) community regularly go through the town dump to scavenge for useable material that has been discarded by others. Various ethnic and religious groups in the town are upset because such scavenging results in the garbage being strewn in disarray, thereby making it impossible for recycling efforts to succeed. Feelings of distrust, hostility, and discrimination create a tinderbox environment capable of exploding instantly into violence. Efforts to identify a Roma group to talk with have proven futile. Is this situation simply a "law enforcement" problem?

For each situation noted, using a mediator would be helpful. How? A short list of negotiating dynamics that result from a mediator's intervention includes:

- The presence of an energizing, yet calming, optimistic intervenor.
- A meeting site and environment that is safe, equitable, comfortable and inspiring for all participants.
- An opportunity for voices to be heard in a respectful way.
- A discussion format and agenda that guides participants to "tell their story" and organizes discussion topics in a clear, targeted manner.
- Procedural and communication tools designed to enhance understanding and movement. Examples of such tools include separate meetings (caucuses) and active listening or reframing.

It is easy to envision how a mediator's attentive presence at a comfortable meeting site would enhance communications between the upstairs and downstairs neighbors. In the second scenario, the mediator transforms an adversarial contest over allegations of racial or gender discrimination into a constructive negotiation discussion by simply and accurately identifying the negotiating issues to include social interaction at the worksite, training opportunities, professional meeting protocols, and performance standards—i.e. items about which the parties can, indeed, bargain. And a mediator's affirmative intervention in the final scenario—often by meeting separately with the various stakeholders to identify the necessary parties to a resolution and explore the concerns that must be addressed to secure stability and respect—can be the first step towards addressing differences. Sometimes such separate meetings provide a constructive "safe haven" through which persons with a history of profound conflict can communicate forcefully with one another without violence erupting.

Different Destinations and Many Paths

In one sense, mediation can be boiled down to a simple target shared by all mediators. Mediators help parties to negotiate more effectively. That often means helping parties communicate more constructively and, in many cases, reach agreements. Beyond that simple target, though, mediators have different goals and different means for achieving them.

What goals—or destinations—do different mediators and different schools of mediation have? Among the most often cited mediation goals are:

- Better understanding for each party of her own goals and interests (empowerment)
- Better understanding among parties (recognition of each other)
- Creative problem-solving and option generation
- Agreements that are durable and optimal
- Settlements acceptable to all parties

One school of mediation only embraces the first two goals (empowerment and recognition). Other mediators only target settlement—an end to the dispute. And others will include all of these goals. Here is a continuum of mediation approaches (above the line) together with a continuum of goals (below the line). The continuum roughly matches mediation approaches or schools with corresponding goals or targets. In real cases, however, it is important to note that any linear depiction is a simplification of a dynamic and complex process.

Transformative		Facilitative		Evaluative
empowerment and recognition		creative problem-solving		settlement
	understanding		agreement (durable optimal)	

Let's examine these goals.

Empowerment and recognition means that disputing parties come away from mediation stronger in two important respects. They "can recapture their sense of competence [empowerment] and connection [recognition]" (Bush and Folger 2005: 53). These goals are closely linked to the goal of *understanding* the overall situation better. It is easy to understand how Cheryl, in the employment scenario, imagined she was being excluded. Through mediated discussion about this potentially volatile situation, she can come to realize that others in the office wanted her participation in social life, but her own frequently closed office door deflected attempts to include her. Also, it might be that Cheryl's supervisor's comment about "B+ work" was meant to lessen any pressures Cheryl felt to get things perfect. The supervisor, in turn, might come to understand the adverse impact of his remark. Each party can feel sufficiently safe in mediation to "tell their story"—a more "empowered" state than letting confusion and anger fester. And each can come to understand the other.

The mediator who has *problem-solving* as a goal hopes to engage participants in a forward looking exercise of developing options to address the concerns raised by the parties. Ideally, these options will represent creative—sometimes "out of the box"—solutions to the concerns raised. If the amount of money that a defendant will pay in a personal injury situation is an issue, the mediator might encourage the parties to determine whether there are things the defendant can do for the plaintiff in lieu of money—provide a job, insurance, housing, a vehicle, as a partial or total alternative to an immediate payment or payment over time—that will cost the defendant less and still promote the plaintiff's interests. Or, in the Roma situation described above, perhaps the parties can achieve an arrangement where needy Roma citizens can help the recycling effort while obtaining necessary items for themselves. Any such resolution would build a better relationship and a capacity to engage in future problem-solving should other issues arise.

For many mediators, *agreement* among the parties is a goal of mediation so long as agreement provisions are "reality tested" by the mediator to ensure that commitments are as durable [NDR: Wade & Honeyman, *Lasting Agreement*] and optimal as possible. For example, the upstairs and downstairs neighbors might quickly agree to the following terms: "no communication, the upstairs neighbors will wear soft-soled shoes walking around in their apartment, the teenagers will have parties only on Saturday nights, no music after 11 pm, and no banging on the ceiling." Given the parties' proximity as neighbors, some of these proposed arrangements appear implausible (*no* communication between neighbors?), even if well-meaning, so many mediators would want to test these terms for precision (what does "parties" mean?) and workability (will soft-soled shoes alone solve the problem?) and explore a solution that provides the neighbors with some method of communication and constructive interaction.

Other mediators keep a sharp focus on *settlement*—coming to a resolution with respect to contested matters, so long as the settlement is acceptable to all parties. Mediators in pursuit of this goal might use a very forceful style to achieve the goal of settlement. One scholar has described that approach as mediator "trashing" and "bashing" (Alfini 1991). "Trashing" means tearing apart each party's case to encourage them to put realistic numbers on the table (Alfini 1991: 66). "Bashing" means trying to get parties to move from their entry settlement offers to some mid-point (Alfini 1991: 69). Settlement-oriented mediators consider the mediation successful if the parties can reach a number they will both endorse.

How Goals are Linked to Process Design

Different mediator strategies and techniques follow from different goals.

- Will the mediator encourage active *participation by the parties*, instead of allowing the lawyer or other professional representatives to dominate the session? If the goal is empowerment and recognition or creative problem-solving, the mediator would want to maximize party participation.

- Will the mediator use the *caucus* (individual meetings with each side)—never, sometimes, or exclusively? If the goal is for the parties to have an enhanced understanding, some schools of mediation encourage no caucus at all.

- What types of *settings* and *time frames* should be employed? In a settlement approach, twenty minutes in the hallway of a courtroom might be deemed an adequate attempt at mediation by mediators who are "trashing and bashing" their way toward a settlement.

Choosing and Using a Mediator

You must be clear about your goal when choosing a mediator. Various benefits outlined above may be available from some mediators, but not all. Some mediators, for instance, stress stakeholder participation to generate understanding and collaboration, even when hostile responses might jeopardize settlement. Others convert controversies to a discussion of money damages only, and then try to help parties find an acceptable "number" on which to settle, thereby minimizing opportunities to enhance understanding and improve relationships.

Whatever one's goal, though, and whatever the mediator's orientation, the astute advocate uses the mediator strategically to assist her in securing acceptable outcomes. How does she do that? Here is an illustrative list. These tactics are not secrets to the mediator or an abuse of her role—rather, they reflect a savvy use of this resource.

a) *Mediator selection.* What personal characteristics and traits of a mediator would be most helpful to you or your client? Does the mediator's gender, race, age, professional training or expertise make a difference? If so, select or propose accordingly. Many advocates select a mediator by saying to their counterpart: you pick whomever you want (presuming the selected individual is a professional mediator) and we will agree to that appointment; that strategy reflects a desire to make one's bargaining counterpart completely confident that the selected mediator does not favor you, their perceived adversary. But perhaps cost, or immediate availability, is the advocate or client's most important consideration; if so, one selects accordingly. The lesson is clear: a careful negotiator finds the type of mediator—and mediation—she wants. [NDR: Honeyman, *Working with Mediators*]

b) *Agreement to participate.* Everyone values his or her time. One does not want to prepare for and appear at a mediation only to learn that the bargaining counterpart has no intention of engaging in meaningful participation. The advocate can signal to the mediator that she is prepared to participate only if the mediator can confirm, based on conversation with the bargaining counterpart, that the meeting will not be worthless. No mediator, of course, will guarantee potential participants that they will reach agreement in mediation, but no mediator wants a reputation of setting up conversations that waste his time as well as that of the participants.

c) *Process design.* Advocates use the mediator to establish—i.e. negotiate—matters of procedure: Who will participate? Will the parties or their representatives assume a primary role in the discussion? How long will sessions last? Will persons meet physically in one spot or conduct the conversation via technology? Will persons meet in joint session or "separate" meetings called caucuses? Negotiation procedures and protocols are crucial to conducting an effective negotiation; while each mediator operates with her presumptive template for conducting a session, a good mediator values suggestions and ideas from participants and converts their proposals into negotiable topics regarding procedure.

d) *Communicating priorities.* Often negotiating parties deliberately camouflage their priorities from their bargaining counterpart ("these matters are all equally important to me") or communicate them in a way that is not understood clearly by the other party. A party or her representative can use a mediator, particularly in a caucus setting, to clarify priorities: "Madam Mediator, if our upstairs neighbors would exert effective control over the parties that their teenage children host, we would be willing to pay something—perhaps 50%—of the replacement cost of their damaged door panel. The noise is simply driving us crazy."

e) *Signaling flexibility without being perceived as "weak."* When a negotiator makes an initial settlement proposal, she is communicating her preferred outcome: "I will not pay you anything to replace the damaged door panel." If her bargaining counterpart rejects that proposal, she confronts the following dilemma: if she proposes another figure—e.g. "OK, I will pay a maximum of $100 for the damaged door"—she cannot, under conventionally accepted bargaining protocols, "go back" to her initial position of "no payment at all." A negotiator, of course, can signal flexibility by using many locutions, such as: "let's defer discussion on payment for the door until we resolve the matter of the number of parties your children host each month." But another effective way to signal firmness but not intransigence is for the negotiator to inform the mediator in a private caucus that she is willing to pay some restitution for the damaged door but at the moment is not going to change her public, official position of "no payment." The mediator takes this information to work in caucus with the other party, knowing there is bargaining flexibility.

f) *Party expectations.* Sometimes a person represents a party to the dispute who has exaggerated expectations regarding the strength of her particular claims or desirability of potential outcomes. That party needs a "reality check" about what might be possible, but she will not respect that assessment if it comes from the person "who is supposed to be on my side." However, if the representative and her client can meet with a mediator in a private session, there are ways for the representative to signal to the mediator that the party (their client) may have unrealistic expectations, and the mediator, not the advocate, can execute the "reality-testing" task in an attempt to pierce an impasse.

Mediation and Justice

Mediation allows parties to find resolutions that are in keeping with their own preferences and values.

Some mediator approaches—transformative or facilitative—systematically support democratic dialogue and decision-making, improving relations and building communities. Imagine:

- upstairs and downstairs neighbors able to communicate respectfully with one another, developing both an added degree of sensitivity and tolerance;
- an office which can set a precedent for displaying inter-racial and inter-gender cooperation, with Cheryl communicating more clearly her desire for inclusion and training, and a supervisor who comes to understand her perspective; and
- a community where different ethnicities find ways to appreciate their differences and resolve issues which are potentially divisive.

Other approaches to mediation, such as when an evaluative mediator presses parties to settle, are designed to secure speedy and cost-saving closure, thereby advancing the administrative goals of a justice system.

Conclusion—An Experiment Worth Trying

Perhaps the most important thing that negotiators should know about mediation is that it works. Frequently, it brings disputing parties a better understanding of each other and closure to their dispute. Given the emotional and financial costs that conflict can levy, a thoughtful negotiator should not ignore that mediation might provide a promising road out of a dispute.

President Theodore Roosevelt was the first American to be awarded a Nobel Prize for Peace. Like many recipients of the Nobel Peace Prize, he tackled a dispute which seemed intractable and was immensely costly—the war between Russia and Japan at the dawn of the 20th century. Writing to his son in 1905 about his efforts as a mediator, Roosevelt said:

> I have finally gotten the Japanese and Russians to agree to meet to discuss the terms of peace. Whether they will be able to come to agreement or not I can't say. But it is worthwhile to have obtained the chance of peace, and the only possible way to get this chance was to secure such an agreement of the two powers that they would meet and discuss the terms direct. Of course, Japan will want to ask more than she ought to ask, and Russia to give less than she ought to give. Perhaps both sides will prove impracticable. Perhaps one will. But there is a chance that they will prove sensible, and make a peace, which will really be for the interest of each as things are now. At any rate[,] the experiment was worth trying (Roosevelt 1926).

Thanks to Roosevelt's persistent efforts, enormous tact, and thoughtful prodding, an agreement was reached that ended the war. As testament to the significance of the accomplishment, the mayor of Portsmouth, New Hampshire, where the treaty was signed, rang the town bells for a full half hour (Fender 2005: 68-72).

While we should not expect town bells to toll when private disputes are resolved, we can nonetheless celebrate the impact on neighbors when a tense and volatile situation—like that of the upstairs and downstairs neighbors—is transformed into a neighborly relationship. We can celebrate the impact on a workplace when employees feel understood, included and supported by their colleagues and supervisors. And, for public disputes, we can celebrate the impact on a community when diverse ethnicities can collaborate with one another to address issues that divide them.

In many scenarios, mediation—a way to generate a possibility for negotiating success—is, as Teddy Roosevelt said, an experiment worth trying.

References

Alfini, J. 1991. Trashing, Bashing and Hashing It Out: Is this the End of "Good Mediation"? *Florida State University Law Review* 19: 47-75.

Bush, R. A. B. and J. P. Folger. 2005. *The Promise of Mediation: The Transformative Approach to Conflict*. San Francisco: Jossey-Bass.

Fender, J. 2005. Roosevelt, The Mikado and The Czar: Theodore Roosevelt's Mediation of the 1905 Treaty of Portsmouth. *New Hampshire Bar Journal.* Concord, NH: New Hampshire Bar Association

Mitchell, G. 2002. Peace Can Prevail. *Dispute Resolution Magazine.* Washington, DC: American Bar Association Section of Dispute Resolution.

Roosevelt, T. 1926. Letter from Theodore Roosevelt to Kermit Roosevelt. In *XXI The Works of Theodore Roosevelt,* edited by H. Hagedorn. New York: Charles Scribner's Sons.

Tutu, D. 2004. No Future Without Forgiveness. In *The Impossible Will Take a Little While,* edited by P. R. Loeb. New York: Basic Books.

☙ 97 ❧

Working with Mediators

Chris Honeyman

Editors' Note: Perhaps you've reached the point in the negotiation where it's time to bring in a third party. This chapter helps you make wise choices about whom to hire as a mediator. It's designed to help the negotiator understand how mediators actually operate, and to be aware of the skill set and biases within which any given mediator must operate. This should be read in conjunction with Love and Stulberg on Using Mediation.

Mediators regularly make claims of neutrality, as well as claims of producing qualitatively better results for parties than they can expect to get in other dispute resolution processes; indeed, neutrality is a foundational claim of the field.[1] Both kinds of claim have been opposed before, but generally in terms that are either polemical, or specialized as to subject matter. The notion has been under-explored that there might be limitations on neutrality and on quality of service that on the one hand are generally applicable, and on the other are not, or at least should not be, particularly alarming. This chapter will pull together and update several previous writings of my own to try to provide an integrated look at some limitations on mediators' quality of performance and neutrality.

Even an experienced negotiator can be rather surprised by the orientations and actions of mediators, particularly when encountering a mediator she has not worked with before. Leonard Riskin's thoughtful series of "grid" explanations (the most recent of which is Riskin 2005) has been helpful in explaining the differences, but they have concentrated on trying to make clear the nature of the differences themselves, rather than the "why." The simplest way to describe the relationship of this chapter

Chris Honeyman is managing partner of Convenor Conflict Management, a consulting firm based in Washington, DC. He is co-editor of *The Negotiator's Desk Reference* and five other books, and author of over 90 published articles, book chapters and monographs. He has directed a 25-year series of research-and-development programs in conflict management (see www.convenor.com/projects). Chris has also served as a consultant to numerous academic and practical conflict resolution programs, held a variety of advisory roles with the ABA, IMI and other organizations, and served as a mediator, arbitrator and in other neutral capacities in more than 2,000 disputes.

to Riskin's (newest) grids is that the two approaches represent different layers of an overall image of mediation—though the notion of such overlays, admittedly, draws more from graphic arts or Photoshop than from legal or ADR imagery.

Sometimes, the circumstances are such that the canny negotiator would be surprised if there were no surprises in working with a new mediator—e.g., when working in a different culture. But unless a negotiator is a "repeat player" with the same pool of mediators, so that individuals become known to each other, sooner or later a surprise is almost inevitable. Many writers have referred to variations among mediators as a matter of "style." That term, however, connotes some kind of choice by the mediator to adopt one style rather than another, and its use is often promptly contradicted by the same writer noting that a mediator usually seems to be unconscious that she has a "style." I believe that term would be better replaced by a matrix of three types of criteria—one conscious, and two, largely unconscious. The variations fall into three main categories:

- skill differences, which tend to be large in a largely unregulated profession;
- policies and philosophies, which are generally overt and therefore predictable; and
- biases, which are often unrecognized by the mediator but correspond to a variety of different kinds of pressures to which the mediator is subject.

Using that matrix, this chapter will describe the main variations among mediators, and briefly explain why they occur.

In part, the level of surprise among negotiators is an artifact of mediation's relative novelty in most parts of the negotiation market. In the two negotiation domains that have been using mediators for many decades—labor relations, and traditional diplomacy—such surprise is less common; a definable set of expectations has become part of the culture of each of those fields.[2] Yet even in labor mediation, the supposed autonomy of the practice was one of its most prized attributes. In the mid-1970s, when I first sought employment as a labor mediator, the highly experienced federal mediator who interviewed me remarked (or bragged) that the great thing about working in mediation was that it was the only profession that had no tools, and no rules. The concept was certainly attractive. But was it true?

Skills: She Does What She Can

Much has been written about the capabilities of mediators, without great consistency; even within Western culture, the set of skills thought important varies from program to program and setting to setting. (Honeyman 1988, 1990a and 1990b; Honeyman et al 1995). But a reasonably "vanilla" set of skill definitions, for a "mainstream" program operating in the U.S., might start with something like the following list, which also includes a sample set of rankings for the first skill:[3]

1. *Manage the Startup:* Effectively begin a productive relationship with the parties.

   9, 8, or 7 Evidence of pre-planning and "homework done" (where appropriate) was strong. Opening statement was thorough, clear, concise, and set a tone encouraging collaboration.

   6, 5, or 4 Some evidence of forethought and preparation. Opening statement was adequate but could have been more thorough, clear or concise.

   3, 2, or 1 Mediator did not appear to have prepared for the case or to have read the file (if applicable). No opening/closing statement, or the explanations given were cursory or inaccurate.

2. *Gather and Comprehend Facts:* Effectively identify and seek out factual information relevant to the case, and sift and organize information that has been gathered.

   (Descriptors ranked 9 through 1 for this and remaining characteristics omitted for space reasons. See note 3 above.)

3. *Understand Underlying Positions and Interests:* Draw out and understand the parties' essential concerns and needs, whether or not verbal or articulated in factual information.

4A. *Express Empathy Verbally:* Be consciously aware and considerate of the needs and values of others.

4B. *Express Empathy Nonverbally:* Be conspicuously aware and considerate of the needs and values of others, in body language and other ways not captured by Scale 4A.

5. *Convey Impartiality:* Convey a sense of neutrality to the parties.

6. *Manage the Personalities:* Effectively cope with strong personalities and conflicts between clients and professional representatives.

7A. *Assist Parties in Generating Options:* Pursue collaborative solutions, and assist parties in generating ideas and proposals consistent with the facts and workable for opposing parties.

7B. *Generate Options:* Generate ideas and proposals consistent with the facts and workable for opposing parties.

8A. *Assist Parties in Generating Agreements:* Effectively help the parties move toward finality.

8B. *Generate Agreements:* Effectively move the parties toward finality and "close" an agreement.

9. *Move the Parties Toward an Improved Relationship:* Effectively help the parties move toward better relationships with each other and third parties.

10. *Manage the Interaction and Conclusion:* Effectively manage the concluding process.

Is Anyone Perfect?

It should be immediately apparent that no normal human being has all of these qualities in abundance. In fact, one of the most highly regarded labor mediators in the U.S. once studied a similar list (tailored for labor mediators) and remarked that he thought he could hit the top note on two or three of the scales—on a good day. The top level of description for each of these characteristics thus represents an aspirational ideal for a mediator, not the expected capability of a typical mediator. What is important to the present purpose is that to the best of my knowledge, every mediator ever tested under controlled conditions (several hundred, at least), who was perceived in other ways as good at the work, has been found to score highly on at least one or two of these characteristics, and at least acceptably on the rest. But the exact balance has never been the same twice.

To anticipate what comes next, it is necessary only to reflect on the fact that every professional, in every profession, hopes to achieve something for the clients. If every mediator does what she can, and every mediator has a different balance of skills, the mere exercise of those skills is going to produce different styles of practice, different frames of reference, different options that are truly open to the mediator (versus those that are effectively closed because of incapability) and most important, *different results for the parties.*

The most obvious example, because it was for a time the subject of vigorous debate within the field as to whether the result should even be called mediation, is that of a mediator whose particular strengths are those articulated in items 7B. and 8B. above. That is an "evaluative" mediator in the making.[4] There are many mediators who combine those qualities with impartiality, high skills at gathering facts, and ability to manage the interaction and close up the case. All of these are skills that are likely to be developed in the course of a judicial career. Among the remainder of the list, however, such skills as empathy, or the ability to guide parties more subtly by assisting them to generate options and agreements rather than taking the lead in that process, are skills some judges have developed, while many others have not. [See NDR: Brazil, *Mediators & Transparency*] Yet if every mediator seeks to be effective, that pressure to be effective, in some sense, guarantees vigorous use of the skill set already possessed. Thus it should be no surprise that mediators who are particularly strong in the skills of evaluation find more moments to call upon those skills than mediators whose skill set is more rounded.

A party whose claims are grounded in arguments based in concepts of societal fairness, and whose proposals for resolution are not easily reduced to numbers (such as dollars) is likely to consider such a mediator biased against it. And this is not an uncommon scenario in major cases, such as where the rights and interests of Native American tribes compete with development interests. Conversely, in a case where the parties have different frames, a party which believes its argument is based in black-letter law and its dollar claim is "in the range" is also apt to believe the mediator is not neutral—if it finds itself in the hands of a mediator whose strengths are in empathy and intercultural understanding, and who flatly refuses to provide any hint of how the mediator views "the merits."

A similar problem can arise for any other common combination of skills. I leave it to the reader's imagination (or prejudice) which combination, and what perceptions of failed neutrality, might most logically be expected with a mediator with a background in, say, traditional diplomacy, or engineering, or psychological counseling. The point is that with some knowledge as to the full range of skills that have been found relevant in mediation, and with some forewarning of the likely skill set of the particular mediator you expect to encounter, the reader is in a better position to know what to expect—and also, significantly, to help the mediator perform those functions in which the mediator could use such help[5] (Honeyman 1990b).

Intent: She Does What She Wants

The reader may have wondered in passing why the list of skills above includes several with "A" and "B" variations. These, the major innovation of the second-generation definitions of a mediator's functions, correspond not merely to differences in skill but also to differences in intent. Up till the mid-1990s, it was widely known among experienced mediators, but not particularly remarked on, that some mediators seemed to have a different orientation to what they were trying to achieve than others (see, for example, the discussion of differing mediators' orientations even within the same program, in Honeyman 1988). Typically, this revolved around dimensions described as whether the mediator was more concerned with helping the parties to reach an immediate settlement, or to improve their future relationship. This dichotomy was given its sharpest delineation with the publication of an influential book which strongly argued that mediation was best suited for, and should be used primarily towards, generating (or regenerating) parties' respect for each other and ability to cope with disputes with each other and third parties in the future, rather than with settlement of the immediate dispute—a result that was seen as obtainable from other dispute resolution processes (Bush and Folger 1995, 2005).[6]

It is possible, of course, that the choice by a given mediator of what has come to be known as the "transformative" model is not in fact as policy-driven as it would appear, but instead reflects in small or large part the desire for effectiveness already noted. Some combinations of the typical skill set favor effectiveness at transformative approaches, and disfavor venturing far into evaluation, or even into some of the demands of "facilitative" mediation; others, as noted above, favor the reverse. There is thus no bright-line test to be had of whether a transformative, facilitative or evaluative mediator is operating primarily on conviction or on capacity. Furthermore, there is careful research that supports the dismaying finding that all mediators are more evaluative than they think (See e.g. Greatbatch and Dingwall 1989; Cobb and Rifkin 1991). Nevertheless, the distinction is useful in the attempt to understand what a negotiator is likely to experience, not least because mediators are often quite open about what they regard as deliberate policy choices, even while being guarded about any skill deficiencies—and, frequently downright ignorant about their biases.

Bias: She Does What She Must

Of course, a deliberate choice in favor of the transformative model, or the evaluative or facilitative, might be described as a bias toward a certain way of operating—with, more to the point, an associated bias towards certain kinds of results. But so openly stated a preference is the least problematic kind of bias, and barely deserves the word. Biases which are unstated or unknown are much more threatening to the negotiator's interests and to the mediator's integrity. There are, unfortunately, a number of them.

Once a mediator undertakes to interrogate parties as to their reasoning or to develop alternative proposals, it is axiomatic that the mediator has a degree of choice over which possibilities will be emphasized and which downplayed. Mediators' claim that "we don't make decisions" is true only to a degree, because often there is more than one set of terms that will make for an acceptable deal, and the mediator can exercise great influence as to which combination of proposals is adopted. In these situations, the sophisticated negotiator demonstrates a practical understanding of how to use knowledge of the pressures on mediators to obtain an advantage.

For convenience and without rigidity, biases can be classified into three groups: personal, situational, and structural. Of these, personal bias is by far the most widely recognized form.

Personal Bias

Most people would describe a palpable preference for the negotiator or principals of one party as a personal bias. Also, in disputes where a serious philosophical gulf exists, a mediator may have a propensity to think along the general lines of one of the parties. In addition, past associations or a partisan employment history of the mediator can give the appearance of bias. Apparent bias, though, does not have the same results as actual bias. An axiom, borrowed from an ancient legal principle, states that it is as bad for a mediator to seem biased as it is for an actual bias to exist. But this is not an accurate statement of the effect. Even though it affects the mediator's actions and proposals, an *actual* personal bias may remain unknown to all participants. The *appearance* of personal bias, however, may leave the mediator blissfully ignorant of any problem, while causing one party to act based on its perception that the mediator is biased against it. It is quite common for a party to complain to the mediator's appointing agency, independently seek a different mediator, or return quietly to direct negotiations, without ever confronting the mediator with its suspicions or giving the mediator an opportunity to allay its fears.

It is increasingly accepted practice for a mediator to disclose any known personal conflict, including friendships and past associations. While there is disagreement over what may reasonably constitute a potential conflict, the growing acceptance of the principle of disclosure (Honeyman 1985; Honeyman 1986; CPR/Georgetown Commission 2002) acts as some reassurance that potentially disadvantaged parties will be given an opportunity to object, or at least investigate further. It also helps the mediator's perceived objectivity, by showing that she has nothing to hide.

Provided that the accepted disclosure rules are applied conscientiously, there is nothing about personal biases that threatens to cause a negotiator general concern, let alone enduring resistance to the use of mediation as a process. That is not the case, however, with the other, more subtle types of bias.

Situational Bias

Situational bias refers to those biases that result from a mediator's source of appointment and obligations to persons or parties other than those immediately involved in the dispute.

Most lay people, if asked, would probably guess that mediators are selected by the parties jointly. In reality, this ideal is rarely achieved, because such a direct mutual selection process calls for a fair degree of mutual trust and willingness to negotiate in the first place. In many types of disputes, the intercession of some organizational third party is necessary to enable the parties to accept a given mediator. Depending on the type of dispute, the appointing or recommending agency may be a court, a nonprofit or for-profit firm that maintains a private roster, a state or federal labor mediation agency, an international body such as the United Nations, or another organization. Although each of these bodies has a pluralistic constituency, none is without an organizational interest of its own. This interest can affect both the mediator's actions and the parties' perceptions, because a mediator with enough of a relationship to an appointing agency to be selected may be presumed to have some degree of fealty to that agency.

Because of universal familiarity, the United Nations is a good example. Suppose that the Secretary-General, upon hearing of a border clash between countries X and Y, fears that a wider war will ensue and wishes to send someone to attempt mediation. Suppose further, in the interest of simplicity, that the major world powers are ignoring the matter, and that both X and Y indicate that mediation would be acceptable. The Secretary-General appoints Ibsen, a recently hired UN civil servant of Swedish extraction. Ibsen has a good reputation, a neutral background as a newspaper editor, and no prior connection with either disputing country.

Can Ibsen be presumed neutral by both parties? Of course, says the observer, from a safe distance. But neither President Smith of X nor Prime Minister Jones of Y is quite so sure. Ibsen comes from an organization that has little or no independent military power, and X has lost control of a border village. Smith feels that when push comes to shove the UN will not send troops, and fears that Ibsen may emphasize settlement terms that involve the de facto cession of that village to Y. The capital of Y, meanwhile, is awash in reporters, and it occurs to Jones that Ibsen could easily use his many press contacts to leak information in such a way as to put substantial international pressure on Y to return the village, which Y has considered properly its territory since 1842.

Even ignoring the many other possible complications and the myriad of rumors which attend any serious clash, both Jones and Smith will probably view any discussion with Ibsen regarding the disposition of the village with some misgivings. Is it surprising that neither is willing to trust Ibsen with his innermost thoughts as to what might be a minimally acceptable settlement? And yet in conventional terms Ibsen is as talented, blameless, unbiased and public-spirited a mediator as anyone could want.

In other circumstances, situational bias has an actual, rather than perceived effect. For a wholly innocent example, consider what happens when an attorney, acting as a mediator, realizes that a settlement which is mutually acceptable to the parties may infringe the law even though it lacks both a bright-line test and ready enforcement; for example, some kinds of environmentally-sensitive but small land development deals. An attorney with ethical standards high enough to make her acceptable as a mediator may find it difficult to give herself whole-heartedly to her role as mediator in this situation, even if the impact of the illegality would be minor compared to the result of unsuccessful mediation. (Note, however, that many observers have regarded this type of bias with such equanimity that they advocate the *assumption* of a "public interest" role by the mediator.)

Structural Biases

Structural biases, which stem directly from the nature of mediation, are the most obscure and the least avoidable. There are several of them, so that in given cases they may cancel each other out. They are probably not often conclusive as to the nature of the agreement reached; but that does not mean that they are not real, nor does it mean that a perceptive mediator or negotiator will not notice their subtle effect. Among these biases are tendencies for the process to benefit weaker parties over stronger ones, moderate factions over radical, and negotiators over principals. Another bias, which has no reliable preference for any particular kind of participant, is the tendency for the process to favor a quick or easy way out instead of a real and enduring solution. Finally, the most pernicious problem is that mediation can be an effective tool for a party determined to negotiate in bad faith.

In Joint Gains, the Weaker Party Gains Disproportionately

In any unequal negotiating relationship, the stronger party is in a better position to act unilaterally, while the weaker party seeks to claim some form of perceived equity. (Korobkin 2006) An agreement to proceed to mediation, however, exposes both parties to some skeptical examination, no matter how polite or restrained, by the mediator. In addition, the agreement to accept mediation also signals an acceptance of the legitimacy of the opposing party's existence, if not of its position. Because a mediator is endowed with a degree of moral authority, no one wants to defend a negotiating position solely on the basis of power; therefore, some claim to law, moral standing or common sense invariably is made. In the process of altering positions (which occurs to some degree even in an unsuccessful mediation attempt), the stronger party is thus led toward positions and proposals based on "defensible" criteria. In other words, the stronger party loses ground because she is led to compete more within the weaker party's frame of reference.

Sensitivity to this tendency seems to vary from place to place, and reduced sensitivity to it may be a mark of greater sophistication among negotiators. In American labor disputes, for example, there has long been a widespread willingness among stronger parties to join in a request for mediation, perhaps on the expectation that the mediator will help knock some sense into the other fellows and make them realize what a poor position they really occupy. By contrast, an official of the British Advisory, Conciliation and Arbitration Service told me, in the mid-1980s, that they found it difficult to get anyone to agree to mediation, since parties felt that to be first to ask for or accede to a mediator's assistance was an admission of weakness. Contemporary practice by attorneys in court-connected mediation seems, fortunately for mediators and parties alike, to be following the American rather than the British labor-management model in this instance.

The Diverse Factions Constituting Each Party Are Not All Treated Equally

In many types of disputes (with the obvious exception of divorces) groups of people are involved on one or both sides. A group may be as small as the tenants of a single building or as large as all consumers of a drug now suspected to have undisclosed side effects; but the interests of all the participants on the same side are never identical. Often the rift between nominally allied factions may be as wide as the gap between the opposing "parties" (Bellman 2006; Matz 2006). [See also NDR: Wade, *Tribe*] Different proposals and trade-offs may benefit these factions disproportionately.

If a given party contains both moderates and radicals, mediation tends to benefit the moderates at the radicals' expense. This is partly because the *process* of mediation, with its emphasis on reasoned dialogue and its implied promise of moderation to all, inherently opposes the radical's prescribed sequence, of disruption followed by massive change. The limited nature of concessions obtainable at any bargaining table, along with mediation's typical confidentiality, apparent legitimacy, and nominal acceptability to the public, also work to legitimize the gradualism of the moderate. Therefore, even at the start a mediator is by no means everyone's friend, and no matter how well-meaning her efforts, should not expect to be treated as such.

A parallel tendency is for mediation to submerge minority interests in general. The pressure to obtain an agreement which will get a majority vote or other form of "pass" within two (sometimes more) opposing groups, combined with the customary emphasis on confidentiality, can leave a dissident faction boxed in with little ability to keep effective contact with the opposing party or its own constituency. Sometimes such a faction's first opportunity to affect the outcome occurs when ratification by the entire constituency is required. [NDR: Wade & Honeyman, *Lasting Agreement*] By that time, the dissident faction can become militant after being pressured by the mediator and its own "allies," while the majority of the party has become complacent after having prevailed at the bargaining table. The resulting refusal to ratify an agreement has occurred at every level, from local labor unions to the U.S. Senate and the General Assembly of the United Nations.

In Conflicts of Interest Between a Negotiator and the Principals, Mediation Gives the Negotiator an Advantage

Be the negotiator an ambassador, lawyer, union business agent or king, there is often some level of conflict of interest with those he represents. In mediation an advantage accrues to the negotiator because he may be able to block a mediator from direct access to his principals, or at least limit that access. [NDR: Nolan-Haley, *Agents*] Furthermore, a negotiator often has broader access to sources of information than his principals, and can also communicate with a mediator on a one-to-one basis, out of his principals' hearing. A mediator, on the other hand, may have to bear in mind the likelihood of dealings with a particular negotiator on another day, in another context. These factors enable a negotiator to use a mediator, at least to a degree, to cloak proposals and deals that support the negotiator's interests as opposed to those of the constituents. This is a particular problem when the "mediator" is appointed by, or is an official of, a powerful third party with favors to bestow.

The First Possible Agreement Is Not Always the Best Possible Agreement

There is almost always more than one set of terms that can make for a mutually acceptable settlement; "give" on one item may compensate for "take" on an apparently unrelated one. However, many mediators are under some degree of time pressure, from the press of other work, the need to show progress to the mediator's appointing agency or peers, and for many other reasons. This pressure encourages a mediator to search for the *first* mutually agreeable settlement package rather than for some conception of the *best* agreement. Often the parties are aware of this. Despite the theoretical existence of an agreement, it is not unusual for negotiators to meet afterwards, with or without the mediator, and modify the original set of terms to their mutual benefit. It is as if these parties needed the mediator's assistance to get within hailing distance of each other, but once that is accomplished, the parties' superior knowledge of their own needs makes direct negotiation fruitful again. Under the same heading, "Never give a mediator your bottom line" is a wise admonition for those who intend to get a better than bottom-line deal if possible (See Brazil 2006). [NDR: Schneider, *Productive Ambition*]

Mediation Can Actually Abet Bad-Faith Bargaining

The problem of bad-faith bargaining or "playing games" is endemic. Here mediation has two, somewhat contradictory, tendencies. On a personal level, a mediator can conscientiously apply pressure against playing games, and a searching inquiry into a party's justification for its proposals can be quite effective. [NDR: Craver, *Distributive Negotiation*] However, if the party that the mediator suspects of bad faith has the power to block a settlement, the mediator may find himself forced to defend and cover for that party rather than expose the bad faith to the full wrath of the opposing party or general public and risk that negotiations will break down entirely. A similar effect may obtain without conscious manipulation by the mediator.[7]

It is natural for mediators (generally optimists by temperament, if not professional requirement) to assume that both parties are acting in good faith, and as already noted, parties usually take care to present some rationale for any position they adopt. Even the most skeptical mediator needs to retain the confidence of both parties, including the games-player, to be effective. In addition, the principle of confidentiality restrains the mediator from attempting to use her influence on public opinion to enforce genuine negotiation. Thus there is, sad to say, at least a degree of potential bias in favor of a party who is negotiating in bad faith.

The upshot of this last set of biases is that any negotiator dealing with a mediator must consider that there is a whole series of possible influences on the mediator which the latter, in maintenance of a self-image of neutrality, may be but dimly aware of.

Conclusion

To say that a profession has biases is not to decry its usefulness. To say that a professional is not superhuman is not to deny her talent or her assiduousness. Both biases, and differences in talents, are facts of life, and those described here should be no more alarming than such legal biases as the presumption of innocence and the burden of proof. The widespread use of mediation, along with its frequent success, shows that the effects of bias are limited, that the talents available are considerable, and that parties can learn to live with imperfection. Through under-standing and experience, good negotiators have been able to reduce most of the concerns described here to little more than a *caveat* to be kept in mind when discussing options with a mediator.

But the fact that the biases not only exist, but apply in different ways to mediators with different balances of skills, different personal histories and different sources of appointment, adds to the differing policy choices among even rather competent mediators to produce a truly awe-inspiring range of possible conduct. In the face of so complex a matrix, it might be worth challenging the over-reliance on "neutrality" by asking if any two mediators, assigned identical cases, could ever produce, or should ever have been expected to produce, exactly the same result for the parties.

Since no two real cases are ever identical, we will never know the answer to the "could" question, at least. But while wisely shelving this metaphysical issue, the savvy negotiator might profitably make a mental note to ask lots of other questions of, and about, any new mediator she is considering hiring.

Notes

[1] Not untypical is the definition "A mediator is a neutral intervener committed to as-sisting each negotiating party and their representative to conduct constructive conver-sations." [NDR: Love & Stulberg, *Using Mediation*]

[2] It was a surprise to many long-established players when Deborah Kolb—correctly, in my view—defined two quite different cultures of U.S. labor mediation, sharply differ-entiating practice in the public sector from the private. See Kolb (1984.)

[3] The list that follows shows the detailed descriptors only for the first item, to save space. (This full set of descriptors can be found in D'Alo 2003.) The list was prepared

by the author and Grace D'Alo in collaboration with the mediators of a Pennsylvania state agency concerned with mediation of disputes between parents of special needs children, and school boards and officials. It is a "second generation" set of descriptors, which makes a number of distinctions not recognized in the late 1980s, when the initial performance-based selection tests of mediators required development of the skills lists and performance criteria in the articles cited *supra*.

[4] Even some practitioners whose approaches might (rightly or wrongly) be lumped in with this style are diffident about whether it should be considered mediation. See Brazil 2006. This has its ironies, because in all probability mediators (and settlement judges) who have enough sensitivity to be concerned about this also demonstrate that sensitivity in daily practice, which ought to *reduce* the concern that they will rely excessively on the ability to evaluate.

[5] There is reason to believe that many parties, particularly repeat players in complex cases, have in effect internalized this point in the way they structure a case and make available different kinds of experts. *See* Honeyman 1990b.

[6] *See generally* Bush and Folger (2005.) In this second edition of the 1995 book, Bush and Folger significantly refined their concepts, and in the process reduced the starkness of the apparent policy choice. But a choice it remains.

[7] In his second autobiography *Ways of Escape* (1980), Graham Greene described the U.N. Middle East mediation machinery as the indirect cause of an hour of shellfire he once endured while traveling along the Suez Canal. In his view, Egypt was using its ready access to mediation to stage brief incidents of shooting which it could terminate through the U.N. before things got out of hand. Greene's description of the use of the ponderous United Nations chain of communication in the hands of a (then) "bad actor" should not be dismissed lightly.

References

Bellman, H. 2006. Internal Conflicts of the Team. In *The Negotiator's Fieldbook: The Desk Reference for the Experienced Negotiator*, edited by A. K. Schneider and C. Honeyman. Washington, DC: American Bar Association.

Brazil, W. 2006. Professionalism and Misguided Negotiating. In *The Negotiator's Fieldbook: The Desk Reference for the Experienced Negotiator*, edited by A. K. Schneider and C. Honeyman. Washington, DC: American Bar Association.

Bush, R. A. B. and J. Folger. 2005. *The Promise of Mediation*. San Francisco: Jossey-Bass.

Cobb, S. and J. Rifkin. 1991. Practice and Paradox: Deconstructing Neutrality in Mediation. *Law & Social Inquiry* 16(1): 35-62.

CPR/Georgetown Commission on Ethics and Standards of Practice in ADR. 2002. *Principles for ADR Provider Organizations*. New York: International Institute for Conflict Prevention & Resolution.

D'Alo, G. 2003. Accountability in Special Education Mediation: Many a Slip 'Twixt Vision and Practice? *Harvard Negotiation Law Review* 8: 226.

Greatbatch, D. and R. Dingwall. 1989. Selective Facilitation: Some Preliminary Observations on a Strategy Used by Divorce Mediators. *Law & Society Review* 23: 613.

Greene, G. 1980. *Ways of Escape*. New York: Simon & Schuster.

Honeyman, C. 1985. Patterns of Bias in Mediation. *Journal of Dispute Resolution* 1985: 141-149.

Honeyman, C. 1986. Bias and Mediators' Ethics. *Negotiation Journal* 2(2): 175-178.

Honeyman, C. 1988. Five Elements of Mediation. *Negotiation Journal* 4(2): 149-160.

Honeyman, C. 1990a. On Evaluating Mediators. *Negotiation Journal* 6(1): 23-36.

Honeyman, C. 1990b. The Common Core of Mediation. *Mediation Quarterly* 8(1): 73-82.

Honeyman, C. et al. as Test Design Project. 1995. *Performance-Based Assessment: a Methodology for Use in Selecting, Training and Evaluating Mediators*, available at www.convenor.com/uploads/2/3/4/8/23485882/method.pdf (last visited May 2, 2016).

Kolb, D. 1984. *The Mediators*. Cambridge, Mass: MIT Press.

Korobkin, R. 2006. On Bargaining Power. In *The Negotiator's Fieldbook: The Desk Reference for the Experienced Negotiator*, edited by A. K. Schneider and C. Honeyman. Washington, DC: American Bar Association.

Matz, D. 2006. Intra-Team Miscommunication. In The *Negotiator's Fieldbook: The Desk Reference for the Experienced Negotiator*, edited by A. K. Schneider and C. Honeyman. Washington, DC: American Bar Association.

Riskin, L. L. 2005. Replacing the Mediator Orientation Grids, Again: Proposing a New Grid System. *Alternatives* 23(8): 127-132.

Mediator As Medium:
Reflections on Boxes–Black, Translucent,
Refractive, and Gray

Wayne Brazil

Editors' Note: One of the U.S.'s most experienced mediators here discusses a striking difference between his own view of one critical feature of practice, and that of most of his peers. Most high-end litigators and their clients, he argues, have found most mediators to be anything but transparent as to their own thinking processes, even while pressing the parties to be more transparent about theirs. Brazil discusses the pluses and minuses of this way of working, offering his own take on transparency as an alternative. Delving further into the motivations, however, he concludes ultimately that his own practice is a bit less transparent than he thought—more "gray box" than either black or translucent box. The resulting reflection, stands as one of the most transparent discussions of a mediator's motivations and methods offered by a prominent practitioner.

A couple of years ago, a "high-end" litigator who had represented one of the parties in a caucus-dominated mediation I had hosted told me that my approach was very different from the approach taken by other mediators he had used in high stakes cases (he measured "stakes" by the amount of money involved). He said that other mediators remained "black boxes" throughout the process—meaning that what they were thinking and how they were going about trying to move the parties toward settlement remained shrouded in mystery, entirely hidden from the other participants' view. He was quite surprised (maybe even unnerved) by how freely I disclosed and discussed what I was thinking, about what I thought was happening in the negotiating process, and about how

---

Wayne Brazil has been a judge (for 25 years), law professor, litigator, and, for the past five years, has been affiliated with JAMS, Inc., serving as a mediator, arbitrator, special master, and neutral evaluator. He is the author of four books, three of which focus on settlement dynamics and ADR processes. He received the D'Alemberte-Raven Award from the ABA's Section of Dispute Resolution in 2009.

various behaviors or "moves" the parties were considering might affect (positively or negatively) the health of the mediation process.

The metaphor of the mediator as black box was new to me. [NDR: Gadlin et al., *Metaphors*] It got me thinking about the pluses and minuses of degrees of openness by mediators. As I ruminated about this, I extended the metaphor to include "translucent box" mediators and "refractive box" mediators. It occurred to me that it might be useful for negotiators to use this set of metaphors as one tool to help understand the ranges of roles that mediators can play, to identify the essential character of the approach a mediator is taking as a specific mediation unfolds, to anticipate more accurately the effects that different mediator styles or approaches may have on the character of the mediation process, and to make more refined judgments about the kind of mediator, or mediator behavior, that is likely to fit best the circumstances of particular cases, circumstances that include, of course, the personalities, negotiating styles, and expectations of all the participants in the process. [NDR: Honeyman, *Working with Mediators*]

Learning by Acknowledging Distances Between Theory and Practice

Before proceeding with this exploration, however, it is important to squarely acknowledge that the role that a black box mediator plays, and the character of the process he or she conducts, diverges radically from the vision of a mediator's role and the mediation process that many mediation theorists would endorse. [NDR: Love & Stulberg, *Using Mediation*] To advocates of the most philosophically attractive, humanistic forms of mediation, the black box process is not mediation at all—but a perversion produced by unfettered adversarial instincts, primitive values, and a runaway capitalist culture. These are important points—but it also is important not to ignore the sizeable corner of negotiation reality in which the behaviors and expectations of the participants do not follow the models that we theorists wish they would. Moreover, by examining this black sheep of the mediation herd, we might gain some insights into, and elevate our honesty about, the more widely endorsed forms of mediation with which we are most philosophically comfortable.

Nature of and Nurture Through the Black Box Approach

According to the lawyer who introduced me to the black box metaphor, mediators in his high end cases generally play their own analytical and process cards very close to their vests. They do not disclose their own views about the substance of the parties' positions under the law and evidence, about what the other parties are thinking or communicating to the mediator in their private caucuses, or about the participants' underlying interests, personal values, or long term goals. These mediators listen, but disclose little. They appear to absorb what they are hearing, but very little light (about the other side, the state of the negotiations, or about the mediator's views) passes through them. These black box mediators do not try to engage parties or lawyers in assessing the health of the negotiations or in analyzing (in caucus) the pros and cons of various process options or moves that might be under consideration. After listening and silently digesting what they hear, they are likely to say, without explanation, "This is what you should do next" or "This is what you're going to have to do."

My experienced informant told me that many sophisticated lawyers and clients are quite comfortable with the black box approach. They only engage mediators whom they trust—and in whose worldliness and negotiation-wisdom they have confidence. They want their mediator (not the parties) to remain in control of the process—because they believe that it is by capitalizing on their mediator's experience, on his or her familiarity with the music and understanding of the dance, that they have the best chance of striking a deal. To change metaphors yet again, they view the negotiation process in high stakes commercial cases as ritualized games —chess matches in which no one expects her opponent to be forthcoming (even with the mediator in private caucus) about what she really thinks, about which moves she is contemplating in the near term, about what her long range strategy might be, or about what factors or forces are playing the biggest roles in determining her goals. So, they hire mediators in whose canny guidance and experience-based judgment they have confidence.

The Black Box Mediator: Ring Master of Big Gamers

They want mediators who can read deep between the lines, who are fully aware that each of the other participants might be trying to "play" them—or at least that the other players probably are not disclosing important information about the case, about what is informing their decision-making, and about how much they might pay or accept in settlement. They want mediators who can spot and accurately interpret very subtle, oblique (sometimes unintentional) signals (verbal and non-verbal), who will hear everything parties tell them in caucus with a skeptical, filtering ear and who simply will not believe what parties say their absolute bottom lines are. They do not expect (or even want) their mediators to explain what they are thinking or doing at any juncture. They seem to believe that mediators who expose their thinking and engage the parties in analytical debates about the merits of the case are wasting time, artificially delaying entry into the only part of the negotiations (the money part) that really matters, or, worse, creating opportunities for parties to find analytical fault with the mediator's reasoning and to use that perceived or feigned fault as an excuse or rationale for refusing to make further concessions or refusing to change their offers or demands. They want their mediators to be both the navigators and the captains of the mediation ship, to lead them through opaque waters, to tell them, at each juncture, how many oars to put in the water and how hard to pull. They look to their mediators for all this help because they assume their mediators will understand the dynamics between the participants much better than any one of the caucusing parties could—and well enough to be the most sophisticated source of guidance about how to move the negotiation dynamics forward.

They even welcome being pushed or pressured by their mediators —as they assume that their mediators also will be pushing and pressuring all the other participants. They believe that it is only by exerting sustained pressure on all parties that their mediator will be able to reliably identify, for them, the real limits on the parties' willingness to compromise. In short, they want mediators who will do whatever it takes to keep the parties in the game well into extra innings, and who will push well past the points the parties have told them they would ever be willing to go. They want their mediators to keep pressing forward with the process until the deal gets done—or until everyone finally concludes that there is zero chance the parties will reach an agreement.

Hidden Informational Balls Undermine Analysis

Perhaps one reason some negotiators in high states cases can endorse a black box approach by their mediator is that they know that they and the parties in the other rooms also are being black boxes—not only in their interactions with one another, but also (significantly) in their private interactions with the mediator. A negotiator who knows that she is hiding important information from the mediator and "managing" what she communicates in private sessions, and who expects the players on the other side to be doing the same thing, might well feel that analytical openness by the mediator is valueless.

Or worse. A mediator who purported to offer substantive feedback to the parties (about the strengths and weakness of the case on the merits, or about the parties' assessments of case value) that was based on intentionally incomplete or unreliable inputs from them might end up skewing a dynamic in directions for which the parties are not prepared, thus upsetting the artificial balance that is necessary to make parties feel comfortable enough with final offers and demands to make a deal.

Gaming the Mediator

These kinds of negatives can be more threatening (to prospects for sustaining and succeeding in a fragile mediation process) when negotiators believe that some or all of the parties and their lawyers will be trying to "game" the mediator, i.e., trying to actively manipulate him or her into misplaced substantive assessments of the case or into behaviors that the "gamers" believe will produce negotiation advantages. Gaming goes beyond black boxing. It can include efforts to play on a mediator's emotions, attachments, ambitions, or needs. It can include actively misleading the mediator (by lying or otherwise) about anything that might get play in the negotiation dynamics: about the evidence, the assigned judge, the parties and their circumstances outside the litigation, about what terms the party might be willing or unwilling even to consider, or about other matters, e.g., a big firm's interest in hiring the mediator in other cases, or for another mediation session in the case at hand. When negotiators believe that gaming is infecting the process, they will worry even more that mediators will do harm to prospects for settlement if they insist on interjecting their own substantive "analysis" into the process, or on purporting to explain another party's views or plans.

How Will Black Box Negotiators React to Translucent Mediators?

For these and other reasons, negotiators and mediators need to consider how lawyers and clients who have been acculturated to black box approaches are likely to react when they encounter a mediator who, to their surprise, plays his or her role with much greater transparency. How will sophisticated and sometimes cynical lawyers (and clients) react when their mediator explicitly, and with apparent honesty, tries to engage with them (in caucus) in analysis of law and evidence (including the support for the other parties' positions), in exploring all parties' underlying interests and concerns, in assessing external circumstances, and in deciding, through open discussion in caucus, how best to advance the negotiating ball (what to do next in the mediation process)?

There is a distinct possibility that participants who have been acculturated to the black box approach will view a mediator who adopts an apparently "open" style as naive—and not as a reliable source of worldly wisdom about any factor that bears on settlement strategies or decisions. There is a substantial risk, in other words, that parties who encounter an open approach when they are accustomed to a black box will infer that their mediator just doesn't get it, doesn't understand how negotiations among sophisticated parties to big cases really work, how "elite" negotiators behave in this rarefied professional zone, what their signals and omissions and moves really mean, or what kinds of terms might be "business viable." Ironically, this fear of naiveté could make negotiators more distrustful (of the wisdom) of a translucent box mediator than they would be of a black box mediator with whose approach they have become comfortable.

Lawyers who think of themselves as skilled and sophisticated negotiators, and who have had considerable experience negotiating in similar kinds of cases with similar kinds of adverse parties, also might feel that their ability to capitalize on their skills and techniques, and to manage the dynamic between the parties, would be threatened and compromised by an intellectually open and energetically engaged mediator. They might assume that a black box mediator is much less likely to interfere artificially with the "natural" negotiation dynamic between sophisticated opponents—and thus less likely to disrupt its sub-cultural rhythm and damage prospects for an acceptable outcome.

At a more nuanced level, there also is a possibility that cynical business case negotiators will fear that what a mediator who is purporting to use a transparent style is really trying to do is game the lawyers and their clients. Lawyers who are accustomed to working with black box mediators might view "transparency" and "inclusiveness" by the mediator as calculated and disingenuous, as a cover for a clever effort to get inside their heads and manipulate them into a settlement that they otherwise would never accept. Stated differently, they might fear that the mediator's transparency is feigned, a device for gaining access to the parties' most sensitive and pivotal information or concerns, a verbal smoke screen intended to hide a more subtle form of "black boxism." Parties who fear this kind of subtlety are likely to be even more secretive about their real views and positions.

Gaps Between Reality and Any One of the Box Metaphors

On the spectrum of box metaphors, I tend to view my approach as close to the translucent end. I constantly urge the participants in mediations I host to be as open and honest with me as they can bring themselves to be, to share more information (with me, and, through me, with the other parties), to process in my presence (in caucus) their thinking about the negotiations, and to assume as much responsibility as possible for the health and productivity of the mediation dynamic. I take this approach because it fits my personality and values—and because, as I explain with emphasis to the parties, there is substantial support in social science research for the view that the more the negotiators adopt these kinds of practices, the more likely they are to reach an agreement (and the more likely that agreement is to approximate what, in theory, would be the best possible negotiable outcome for the parties) (Brazil 2014).

Is Any Mediator Truly Translucent?

Even as I urge the parties to adopt these practices, however, I worry that my words do not track as closely as I would hope the realities of negotiation behavior. As important (and instructive), as I watch the mediations I host unfold, it is not at all clear that the way I behave as a mediator, or my "cheerleading" in the direction of openness, has much, if any, effect on how the other participants in the process conduct the negotiations. These observations incline me toward the view that most lawyers and business clients would reject the notion that the choice to be made is between a black box approach and a translucent box approach—either by the mediator or by the other participants in the process. No matter what I say about how I intend to conduct myself, the other participants (at least when they are seasoned business negotiators or repeat institutional players) seem to believe that I will remain something of a "gray" box, i.e., translucent at times and in part, black at times and in part, but, for the most part, refractive.

In this context, "refraction" would be understood, perhaps not altogether consciously, the way *Webster's New Collegiate Dictionary* (1980) defines it: "1: deflection from a straight path undergone by a light ray or energy wave in passing obliquely from one medium (as air) into another (as glass) in which its velocity is different. 2: the change in the apparent position of a celestial body due to bending of the light rays emanating from it as they pass through the atmosphere; also: the correction to be applied to the apparent position of a body because of this bending." Refraction, so understood, attaches with uncanny exactitude to the role many lawyers seem to assume their mediator will play (protestations to the contrary notwithstanding): re-directing, re-framing, and reducing the velocity of emanations from one party to another; "correcting" and de-energizing communications and positions, thus reducing the damage they would cause if they did not pass through the mediator as medium.

Reflecting on how "savvy" business litigators expect me to play my role, regardless of what I tell them my intentions are, has led me to wonder whether there are any mediators who remain pure black boxes or pure translucent boxes throughout any one mediation—or, stated differently, whether there are any mediators who even attempt to sustain adherence to any one style or approach in any given case. I suspect that even the mediators whose role capes are darkest (or lightest) use multiple approaches, that at least to some extent they mix and match or blend techniques. The best mediators, even in the narrow world of high-end cynical litigation, probably try to remain flexible and to tailor their conduct to the personalities, circumstances, and individuated dynamics that they encounter in particular cases.

The Ubiquity of Refraction

Perhaps most significantly, most mediators act as refractors—bending light that is too bright, too hot, too linear, and ultimately too simple as it moves through them from one caucus room to the next. While not true to purist mediation theory, the refraction function likely is perceived as essential and invaluable by many participants in mediations in litigated cases. Refraction is an assumed, expected, even demanded feature of the skilled mediator's role. It is for this skill in refraction, and in knowing when (or if) to dawn their black capes or their white capes, that parties pay.

These conclusions are partly the product of thinking I have been doing about the gap between my actual conduct during mediations, on the one hand, and, on the other, the translucent model to which, in theory, I think I should adhere. The first discoloration became apparent when I considered the mandate of confidentiality. At the beginning of each mediation I explain (to all participants assembled) that California law prohibits anyone from disclosing outside the mediation itself any mediation communication—unless all participants formally stipulate otherwise. Then I explain the confidentiality rule that I will follow as I move between caucuses during the mediation:

> You must assume that I will communicate to the other parties everything that any of you tell me in caucus— except what you explicitly identify as a secret. I will not disclose information that I have been asked to keep confidential. If I have a secret from one side and then I'm asked about the matter when I caucus with the other side, I say: "I am not going to answer that question." Or "I have a secret about that and I'm not going to tell you." This is how I keep my conscience clean.

One purpose of this statement is to encourage the parties to trust me—to feel confident that they can share their secrets with me without risk of betrayal. This message is reinforced when, during the negotiations, I tell one set of participants in a caucus that I won't tell them something because it is a secret that has been shared with me by the opposing party.

Refraction and Boxes Ultimately Gray

While this is one form of process transparency, it also teaches or reminds the parties that my mediator box is not entirely translucent—that I am likely to know things, sometimes important things, that I am not telling them. When I know important things that I am not telling a party to the mediation, the box that I am is not refractive, but gray.

The gray takes on a darker hue when the parties assume (most often with justification) that the people in the other caucus room also are not telling me everything that is actually relevant to their case valuation or to their settlement decisions, or that they are telling me things that they do not really believe, or that are based only on unsupported hope. They assume that the other side is manipulating the flow of information to me to try to influence my thinking not only about the merits of the dispute, but also about limits on the offers or demands they would even begin to view as credible or worthy of a response.

In these senses, each side believes the other side is "playing" me —trying to manipulate me in order to gain leverage in the negotiations. Thus, each side assumes that the other side will remain, in some measure, a black box to me. So even if my promises of confidentiality did not distort the light that flows through my box from one side of the dispute to the other, each party believes that the managed and manipulated flow of inputs to me makes the promise of translucence a mirage.

Ironically, some of the means I use to try to illuminate the negotiation process might in fact shroud its reality deeper in darkness, at least when the parties are self-consciously examining the negotiation process and looking for ways to find leverage in it. In pursuit of translucence, I often try to explain or describe things that have happened, or sentiments that have been expressed, or moods that prevail in one caucus room to the people in the other caucus room. In effect, I say "Here is what you need to know about what's going on over there (in the other room) in order to make the best decisions about how you could advance the negotiation ball with your next communication or with your next move."

This kind of effort to be more open about the situation in the other room than a black box mediator would be, however, might well have the perverse effect of making each group with which I caucus less open with me. Each group might fear that I will naively disclose too much, or something whose sensitivity I do not really understand. Or, they might fear that I would unintentionally mis-characterize or misread the tone or implications of conversations that feel private but in fact, under my rules about confidentiality, often are not, because no one has attached the label "secret" to the communications I share or because it has not occurred to anyone to ask me to keep secret something as nebulous and variable as the "tone" or "mood" in a room. So a savvy and cautious negotiator who watches me talk more openly than other mediators do about the situation in the other room might well react by retreating into non-communicative modes and counseling her client to do the same.

The assumption (by the parties) that I also am performing my refraction function can cloud the translucent box even further. Even parties who have no experience with or would have no affinity for the black box approach often expect and want me to refract. They expect me to have a better feel than they do for the personalities and dynamics in the other room, and, therefore, to be in the best position to determine which kinds of messages would be most productively received at which points—and how to adjust their delivery. They expect me to be in the best position to decide what to emphasize, how to lubricate communications that might generate friction, and how to soften the landing of heavy shells. They expect me to know what to say and what to leave unsaid, and through all this "management of messages," to smooth edges, blunt knives, and prevent grievous wounds (to parties or process) from being unintentionally inflicted.

I expect no less of myself. But when I take on this responsibility, I darken the hue of my box, distancing myself even farther from the translucent model to which the foundational philosophy of the mediation movement and my conscience make me feel I ought to bear allegiance.

Conclusion—of Sorts

Where do these reflections leave me? Confused. Uncertain. Perhaps farther than I have ever been from feeling that I know how best to serve parties' negotiation needs or how to handle my role so as to deliver the most value to the people who engage my services. The best I can say is that I understand better that my "mediator box" is never purely translucent. While it varies from case to case, it is always some blend of gray and refraction.

Thinking about my role through these box metaphors has helped me understand more clearly that there is a wide range of expectations and preferences for mediator behavior among lawyers and clients—and that part of my job is to identify the place on the box spectrum, or the blend of approaches and techniques, with which the participants in each mediation will be most comfortable and that they will find most productive.

In the end, I can find some solace in the knowledge that the blend of gray and refraction that is my mediator box will be the blend that I have crafted. It will be the blend that is truest to who I am and who I want to be as a human being. I will be real as a mediator because my particular blend of hue and refraction will be rooted in who I am—and that will be obvious. Because its roots in who I am will be both real and obvious, I will be credible. I may not be subtle or sophisticated, but my work for the parties will not be encumbered by an effort to be something I am not, to play a role for which I could never be typecast. Indeed, my hope is to separate "role playing" as much as possible from my service—and that parties will feel the genuineness that I strive to keep intact. If it is true that we serve best when we maintain an integrity that flows from remaining true to ourselves, I will be serving as best I can.

References

Brazil, W. 2014. Reciprocal Coaching to Reduce the Risk of False Failure in Mediation and Support from Social Science for Coaching Ideas. 29 *Ohio State Journal On Dispute Resolution* 167.

Webster's New Collegiate Dictionary, 1980, s.v. "refraction."

ℭ𝔰 **99** ℭ𝔰

Allies in Negotiation

Bernard Mayer

Editors' Note: In a thought-provoking book, Mayer analyzed new roles that experienced mediators and other conflict specialists might play, and suggested that they think more broadly about how they can best assist disputants. Here, he focuses specifically on how negotiators can enlist these specialists as allies instead of as third party neutrals. Just for openers, this could help you to get a complex negotiation framed properly, or to approach the other side in ways that will put them in the right frame of mind. But a decade after first analyzing the possible roles, Mayer has extended the reach of the underlying idea to a long list of "ally" roles which today often go unfilled—to the negotiator's and principals' disadvantage,

Arden is the principal of a private school in the Midwest. Several years ago the faculty was engaged in a rancorous discussion about policies regarding admission criteria. A division existed between the "old guard" who wanted admission based solely on grades and aptitude test scores, with a weighting for the academic standing of previous schools, and those who argued for a broader set of criteria, including diversity. Arden was in a complicated role conflict since she was a critical party to these discussions, a facilitator of faculty meetings, and a decision maker. She had a strong personal view that diversity needed to be included as a criterion, but felt that voicing that belief would undermine her role as a facilitator and leader of the whole faculty. I had been working with her as an advisor on a number of issues, mostly concerning personnel deci-

Bernard Mayer, Ph.D. is Professor of Dispute Resolution in the Negotiation and Conflict Resolution program at Creighton University's Department of Interdisciplinary Studies, and a founding partner of CDR Associates. Bernie has provided conflict intervention for families, communities, NGOs, unions, corporations, and governmental agencies throughout North America and internationally for over 35 years. Bernie's latest book (2015) is *The Conflict Paradox: Seven Dilemmas at the Core of Disputes*. Earlier books include *The Dynamics of Conflict; Beyond Neutrality*; and *Staying With Conflict*. Bernie received the 2015 John Haynes Distinguished Mediator Award presented by the Association for Conflict Resolution, and the 2013 President's Award presented by the Association of Family and Conciliation Courts.

sions, but she wondered if in this circumstance it might be appropriate for me to act as facilitator. After several conversations, we decided that it was best that I remain as her advisor, her ally, as she continued to both participate in and facilitate the negotiations among the faculty about this issue. She needed someone who was her "go to" person on these issues, and I felt I could be more effective in that role than as an outside facilitator.

As conflict professionals, how can we be most effective in promoting productive, constructive, and ethical negotiations? Historically, the conflict resolution field has taken three approaches to this. We have provided negotiation training; we have helped design negotiation procedures; and we have provided third parties to conduct negotiation processes. All of these can be valuable contributions—but they are also relatively sparsely used in the universe of significant negotiations. Often the most effective—and available—role for a conflict specialist is as a support person to negotiators. In the above scenario, while I had the opportunity to intervene as a third party, I chose a different role, for two reasons. Given my prior work with the principal, I felt that I would have to expend a great deal of time and perhaps credibility to gain acceptance in the facilitator role, and in doing so I might have undercut the capacity of the principal to exert the kind of leadership the school was looking for at that point. But more important, I thought I could play a more powerful and effective role by working to enhance the principal's capacity to meet the demands of being simultaneously a leader, a negotiator, and a facilitator.

Negotiators need allies, and the support that is available to them is often limited in scope and sometimes counterproductive. The allies that are most frequently available are substantive experts, particularly legal professionals, or non-involved emotional supporters. What is often missing in this picture is someone who can assist the negotiator by taking a systemic look at the conflict, who has a clear understanding of negotiation dynamics, and who can help negotiators deal with the dilemmas and paradoxes that all negotiators face. Negotiators want help, they want coaching, and they want advice, but they are frequently reluctant to turn over a process to a third party. Often, however, they are more open, and better able to use, an ally. This role, which conflict specialists fulfill under a range of labels (e.g., strategist, advisor, consultant, coach, counselor, or advocate), is both an ancient one and a growing one in the world of negotiation. One sign of this is the growth of graduate programs in conflict studies. The great majority of students going through these do not and will not work as either third parties or direct advocates, but they nonetheless play a critical role in how conflict is handled, either as allies or systems players. Far from being peripheral to the conflict intervention field, allies are its most dramatic area of growth.

Four questions arise: (1) What does it mean to be a negotiation ally? (2) What competencies can allies provide to assist negotiators? (3) How do allies fit into the negotiation system? (4) How can ally services be made available to negotiators in a practical and acceptable way?

What Are Negotiation Allies?

As with the third party role in conflict, the ally role is one we find wherever there is conflict. Allies can help people handle conflict more effectively and pursue their goals in a more intentional and strategic manner. Negotiation allies are specifically focused on helping parties prepare for, conduct, and follow up on a negotiation process. Allies come in many forms and with widely different skills and purposes. Advocates, lawyers, labor representatives, real estate agents, community organizers, and human resource professionals, for example, all act as negotiation allies as part of their larger role. In this respect, there is nothing particularly new about the concept of a negotiation ally.

The most visible and acknowledged functions of negotiation allies are as advocate, spokesperson, or substantive expert who either participates in a negotiation or actually conducts the negotiation on behalf of a party. One way allies assist parties is to help them to develop more powerful alternatives to negotiation (e.g., through developing a strong legal case, political alternatives, or substantive choices). But while these are the most prominent roles of negotiation allies, they are not always the most powerful or durable ones. For example, negotiators often need assistance in developing their own capacities to be effective, and help in understanding the dynamics of the negotiation process itself. They frequently need help with the emotional demands of negotiation. And sometimes, the most important challenge for an ally is to help parties reexamine their very basic thinking about their conflicts and the negotiation process itself.

Negotiation allies can be vital to the effectiveness of a dispute resolution process. This is a role, however, that is often overlooked, or understood only in a very narrow and limiting way. In many grievance procedures a step involving a direct face-to-face meeting between the grievant and the manager is required. If this does not resolve the dispute, then there are usually later steps involving more formal negotiations, mediation, or arbitration. The focus in most dispute resolution systems is on how to make the latter steps more effective. Usually, very little attention and resources are given to the informal negotiation stage, but these may well provide the best opportunity to resolve the issues involved with a minimum of long-term animosity. The more common negotiation assistance is formal, substantive, and representational, as opposed to informal, procedural, and supportive.

Negotiation allies seldom operate from a conflict paradigm. That is, they do not generally see their role as conflict specialists whose task is to help people engage in conflict productively, creatively, powerfully, and wisely. Their focus is instead on substance, rights, technical issues, or

political advice and, as a result, the actual dynamics of the conflict interaction are not dealt with as intentionally or wisely as they might be.
While many allies in negotiation are in fact quite experienced in dealing
with conflict and often excellent at helping people be effective negotiators, the absence of a conflict perspective means that many potentially
useful approaches, analytic and practical, to negotiation are not systematically and consciously brought to the table.

So while negotiation allies are prevalent in most significant negotiation settings, there is a great variety of ways in which this role is perceived, fulfilled, and understood. People in ally roles may view themselves as representatives, advocates, counsel, advisors, organizers,
friends, coaches, strategists, substantive experts, supervisors, teachers,
or therapists. But what is often missing is a conscious understanding of
these roles and a set of conceptual and practical tools that can help them
focus on serving to enhance others' negotiating capacity. We can understand the nature of how allies fulfill their roles by considering six variables.

Intentional—De Facto

How aware are allies of the role they are playing, and how aware are the
negotiators of what they are asking from an ally? Further, how aware are
allies of the specific approach they are taking to the role, and how aware
are negotiators of exactly what they are asking or wanting from an ally?
If I am negotiating a salary from a prospective employer, what kind of
advice will I seek, and how conscious will I even be of asking for advice?
When I approach friends, colleagues, or agents, do they see themselves
as providing negotiation assistance, or do they see their role in a different light? We have all used allies and we have all been allies in negotiations, but we are not always aware that this is the assistance we are asking for or offering.

Supportive—Directive

Is the assistance offered in the spirit of advice and support for the negotiator, or does the ally take over the negotiation process? (Macfarlane
2016) For example, if I go to a lawyer for assistance with a divorce negotiation, will the lawyer take charge of the negotiation and act primarily as
my agent, or will the lawyer act more as my advisor and assistant in
conducting the process? To what extent is the ally a partner and
co-participant in negotiation, a representative who acts as an agent, or
an advisor who assists the party in a supportive way but without actually
conducting the negotiation?

Substantive—Procedural—Emotional

Does the ally offer advice about the substantive elements of the negotiation, e.g., likely outcomes, precedents, options, legal alternatives, etc.,

does the ally focus more on the negotiation and communication process, or does the ally primarily offer emotional support? Does a seller, for instance, mainly rely on her real estate agent for information about market value and financing or for assistance with setting a reasonable price, deciding when to reject, accept, or make a counteroffer, or when to try to communicate further with the prospective purchaser? Does an ally to someone going through divorce focus on financial or parenting issues, on how to negotiate effectively, or on how to handle the stress of dealing with an emotionally challenging interchange? If the focus is procedural, what is the lens through which the process is viewed? Does the ally understand negotiation as a communication process, a problem-solving effort, a conflict management procedure, a relationship building effort, all of the above, or none of the above? Of course, many allies, perhaps most, focus on more than one aspect of the process, but it is helpful to consider which of these predominates at any given time or interaction with the negotiator.

Individual–System Focus

Is the commitment, focus, and accountability of the ally to the individual negotiator, to a group, or to a system? As a labor representative in a grievance, one's obligation is to promote the interests of the individual grievant, but it is also to protect the rights of the collective bargaining unit as a whole and to advance the interests of the union. In providing advice to someone negotiating a divorce agreement, whether as a lawyer, counselor or friend, one's focus may be on the specific needs of the divorcee, on the needs of the children, or on the overall family system.

Tactical–Strategic

Allies are sometimes valuable in helping negotiators see the big picture, but is a given ally's focus more likely to be on specific moves at specific moments in a negotiation? Will an ally focus more on how to frame particular offers, and how to respond to threats or proposals, or will she be more tuned in to the structure of the negotiation and the nature of the relationships among the participants? Will the ally take a short-term view of what can be accomplished in a negotiation, or will she focus on the way a particular negotiation can alter a long-term relationship or open up new opportunities over time?

Specific–General

Allies most often focus on a particular conflict or negotiation, but others may focus on helping people develop their skills as negotiators or disputants more generally—teaching people to fish, as it were. This is particularly the approach associated with conflict coaching (Jones and Brinkert 2008; Noble 2011). Related to this is the time frame that allies adopt. While negotiators are often focused on a particular round of interactions, most intense conflict extends beyond any one set of interactions, even if those interactions end in an agreement. Disputants often need help with the enduring element of a conflict—the ongoing interactions and negotiations that will extend over time and the implementation and healing process that is necessary after even the most successful of negotiations (Mayer 2009).

Of course, in practice, allies act in a variety of ways and these should not be seen as either/or choices. But we can understand the role of allies in terms of how they operate along each of the continua described by these variables.

What Allies Bring to Negotiations

Informal, de facto allies are everywhere and are essential players in negotiation. Their role can be both constructive and problematic. Allies can give wise advise about how to pursue a negotiation, or they can project their own needs onto the negotiator in a destructive manner. We have all probably received (or given) well intentioned advice on how to handle a conflict that would only have led to an unproductive escalation if we followed it. In fact, one of the key skills of negotiators, and therefore of negotiation allies, is to identify the allies for all participants in the negotiation system, the roles they are playing, and the way they can be used effectively. In this chapter, however, we are most concerned with those allies who function intentionally and supportively, with an eye to understanding the dynamics of conflict and negotiation, because the conscious use of allies in negotiations has great potential to have a constructive impact. What conscious and intentional perspectives and skills can allies bring to the table to enhance the negotiation process? Let's focus on several specific perspectives that an ally can add that are essential across a wide range of negotiation settings.

Conceptual Perspective

Perhaps the most important asset an ally can bring is a conceptual perspective that helps negotiators look at their challenge in a more flexible and therefore more powerful way. One element of this is to help negotiators look beyond their personal opinion about other parties to what is genuinely motivating others, and to look more deeply into their own motivations as well. I may think that my opposite in a negotiation is greedy, selfish, and primarily interested in increasing his own power, but an effective ally should help me to understand how others view themselves, and to take a broader view about what may be motivating them.

Another element is what we can think of as "the larger picture." Allies may be there to help one party to advance their particular interests. And in doing so, it is enormously helpful to be able to look at the needs and relationships among all parties, at the larger environment within which a negotiation is taking place, at the historical and relational background giving rise to the negotiations, and at the long term implications of whatever immediate agreements are being negotiated. In other words, the capacity of allies to take a systems perspective is an important element of what they offer (see below).

Effective conceptual perspectives must in some way address what I have called elsewhere "the conflict paradox" (Mayer 2015). As conflict escalates, as negotiations become more intense, and as we become more immersed in a conflict, we tend to see our choices in more polarized ways. The more intense a conflict, the more likely we are to feel that we must either focus on protecting our interests or building relationships, on competing or cooperating, on compromising or standing on principle, on being realists or optimists, and our way of thinking therefore becomes more simplistic. But to work our way through conflict, we have to avoid thinking of our challenges in terms of either/or choices and to adopt a more nuanced and complex approach to understanding our choices. An effective ally helps us understand how we can move beyond these polarities, and to appreciate that they are not really polarities at all. For example, we can't truly advance our principles without compromising, and effective cooperation requires a capacity to compete.

Many of the specific skills discussed below are in fact manifestations of the fundamental conceptual perspectives that allies can bring.

Communication Skills

Communication is at the heart of effective negotiation, and good negotiators are usually good communicators. Allies can help negotiators hone their communication skills, become conscious of how they are communicating and what they are communicating, and become better listeners and observers. Allies also help by providing direct assistance in communicating and by directly observing the communication that occurs during a negotiation. While negotiators can use assistance with a broad range of communication skills, four elements of communication particularly call for the help of allies.

Listening

Allies can help by listening to what is being said in negotiations, by working with the negotiator to understand what is being communicated by others, by emphasizing the importance of hearing both spoken and unspoken messages, by helping negotiators separate out their reactions to what is being said from the actual message that is being communicated, by encouraging negotiators to provide the time and space in negotiations for listening, and by working with negotiators to develop an atmosphere in which communicating is encouraged and listening is valued. [NDR: Itzachov & Kluger, *Listening & Understanding*] Allies can also help overcome barriers to listening such as selective perception (only hearing that which confirms our initial views) and attributional bias (assuming that actions or statements we dislike are a result of someone's personality rather than a reflection of the circumstances they find themselves in).

Framing and Naming

How people present their ideas, thoughts, needs, suggestions, reactions, proposals, information, and arguments in negotiation is a second key communication skill. Very important ideas or proposals are often poorly presented, and this is particularly true when there is a lot of tension or anxiety associated with the communication. Allies can help negotiators frame their comments for maximum constructive effect. Sometimes the most difficult element in framing involves presenting a very hard issue in a way that does not diminish its importance or intensity in any way, but that also does not provoke a defensive reaction, in order to ensure that there is a genuine engagement around it. Negotiators frequently avoid engaging with the most important issues they face, perhaps because these are often the most complex, demanding, and emotionally challenging. They may do this by focusing on smaller, more easily resolvable issues, by rushing to premature solutions, or by a escalating an interaction in an effort to avoid having to face a morally or emotionally demanding problem. Allies can help us think through what we want to avoid, what we want to take on, and how.

Establishing a "Communication Loop" (Mayer 2012)

Effective communication is not about listening and framing as linear and sequential processes. The heart of good communication is the establishment of a *loop* of communication, whereby one is listening while talking and communicating while listening. Sometimes the most important information available to a negotiator can be understood from the reactions of the other party to what the negotiator is saying, while he or she is still saying it; but often we are so focused on what we have to say that we don't notice the reactions of others. Similarly, we often do not understand that how we communicate, especially in the way we listen, is often far more important than what we actually say. These are subtle but ever present dynamics in negotiation of which an ally can help the negotiator become more aware and adept at managing.

Establishing Systems of Communication

Communication in negotiation is not just about what is directly said at the negotiation table but also about establishing a system of communication away from the table. Paying attention to the totality of the communication system is challenging when we are involved in an intense or demanding interaction and is, therefore, one of the ways in which allies can be most helpful.

Integrative—Distributive Wisdom

In one way or another all negotiators must face the essential challenge—how to attend to both the distributive and integrative aspects of negotiation, (Thomas 1976; Axelrod 1984; Lax and Sebenius 1986; Fisher, Ury and Patton 1991) [NDR: Batra, *Integrative & Distributive*] that is how to work effectively for mutual gains while protecting one's own separate interests as well. As Lax and Sebenius (1986) have suggested, there are very different tactics that negotiators use when trying to create value than when claiming value, and at times these tactics are contradictory. For example, how much information should one share in the service of exploring the possibility of a creative solution that will be built upon our different needs, knowing that this information can make one more vulnerable?

Negotiators often struggle with how to create the right balance here, [NDR: Adler, *Protean*] and there is no one right approach to solving what is sometimes presented as the "negotiator's dilemma." In practice, this means it is hard to know how to pay attention to maintaining good relationships, establishing open communication, sharing information fully, and being willing to discuss a range of proposals while holding firm on key values and concerns, responding to provocative behavior effectively, and defending ourselves against aggressive negotiation tactics. The more intense, complicated, intractable, and long-lasting a conflict is, the more difficult it is to handle this dilemma. This dynamic is present in all difficult negotiations, whether interpersonal, inter-organizational or international. For many, the choice feels like it's between acting in a way that violates important values about interpersonal relationships and acting in a way that feels weak and vulnerable. Allies can help negotiators understand the interplay of these dimensions of negotiation, and they can be particularly useful in encouraging people not to act simply and uncritically along either the distributional or integrative dimension but instead to consider how to act wisely along both at the same time.

The tension between these two dimensions is an expression of a much more basic human struggle—one that is the foundation of all evolutionary processes—and that is the tension that is always present between the need for cooperation and the reality of competition (Dawkins 1989). Every move that is made in a negotiation involves finding a way to reach for cooperation and be prepared for competition. Yet negotiators often perceive the choice they face as whether to act in a cooperative manner or to take a competitive stance. In reality, it's impossible to have one without the other and still be effective. Perhaps the most fundamental challenge for allies is to help negotiators cope with this paradox.

Emotions and Logic

Significant negotiations can easily stoke up participants' emotions, and emotional exchanges are often key to effective negotiations. The challenge for negotiators is not to suppress their emotions but to use them responsibly and effectively. Another challenge is how to stay creative and focused when one is feeling threatened, angry, frustrated, or even excited. Negotiators need both emotional support and perspective. They need allies who will accept their emotions and provide an appropriate expressive outlet, but they also need allies who can maintain some distance from the emotions, to help negotiators see past their immediate feelings to the larger picture. Often people think that the goal is to "get over" ones emotions and take a logical approach to a problem. But this is a false choice. Emotions are necessary to logic, and our logical processes help us deal with our emotions. They can't be separated (Damasio 2005). Sometimes those personally closest to the negotiator, such as friends, other team members, or constituents, are best able to find the right path through this challenge. But these informal allies, in the name of friendship or because of their own feelings about the negotiation, sometimes reinforce the most reactive, destructive or negative emotions, and thereby fail to help the negotiator find a means of using their emotional energy in a constructive way.

A Process Sense

In most negotiations, the relative amount of time planning and strategizing about substantive issues far outweighs the amount of thought given to procedural issues (if any planning occurs at all). This is true before, during, and after negotiations. If thought is given to process, it is often very limited and tactical in nature. Yet poor or inadequate process may impede negotiations more often than substantive impasse. Maintaining an awareness of process and considering procedural alternatives can be key to moving negotiations forward. Allies with a background in conflict intervention and negotiation can help negotiators consider a whole range of procedural issues such as table formulation, agenda development, in-team processes, information sharing procedures, option generation, incremental exchanges, psychological needs, communication mechanisms, agreement identification and testing, exploring interests at the appropriate level of depth, looking for agreements in principle, and so forth. This is where the availability of allies with experience and training in conflict can be especially valuable.

Understanding Power Dynamics

All negotiations involve the application of power. However, what type of power is applied, and how, are critical to how a negotiation unfolds. The crude application of a coercive source of power can lead to an impasse. Good negotiators develop an ability to use their power wisely, subtly, sparingly, and constructively. They also know how to respond effectively to the coercive application of power by others. But in the middle of negotiations, it is easy to get drawn into an unproductive competitive display of power that is neither effective nor actually very powerful. Negotiators often need advice or at least feedback on how to use power in negotiations and how to respond to the power of others, to prevent the interaction devolving into a primitive "tit for tat" sequence of responses. It helps to have some good analytical tools for understanding the sources of power, the nature of its application, and the consequences of different applications (Boulding 1962; Axelrod 1984; Mayer 2012).

A System Perspective

As discussed above, it is easy for negotiators to lose sight of the system in which a negotiation is embedded and to focus almost exclusively on the specific relationship being played out at the negotiation table. Yet what happens away from the table and the way the negotiation interacts with the larger system of which it is part are critical. This is true whether one is considering a nuclear deal with Iran, a labor management contract, a divorce negotiation, or a commercial dispute. We often do not realize how much our actions and perceptions are governed by the system within which a negotiation is occurring and how limited a set of choices negotiators may realistically have. [NDR: Miller & Dingwall, *Dispute Domains*] An adequate understanding of systems theory, of system maintenance dynamics, and of the way energy travels through systems is not an abstract mental exercise, but an essential aspect of what makes negotiations work. [NDR: Coleman & Ricigliano, *Getting in Sync*] But this is not the natural focus or orientation of most negotiators, and it is another element of the role allies can play in enhancing a negotiator's capacities.

Cultural Awareness

Most negotiations involve issues of diversity and culture. Negotiations usually require working across some cultural boundary such as gender, sexual identity, age, race, ethnicity, religion, geography, organization or profession. As a result, an often hidden but fundamental factor in negotiation involves different norms about communication, problem-solving, face, power, direct dealing, rapport building, time, authority and status (Moore and Woodrow 2010). Particularly when negotiating in a new cultural environment or when struggling with how much to try to adapt to another culture or remain within one's own cultural comfort zone, people need assistance in understanding and adapting to the cultural dynamics in a negotiation. [NDR: Miller, *Codes of Culture*; NDR: Goh, *Cultural Errors*]

Permission to Settle or Not to Settle

In the end, the decision as to whether to arrive at an agreement or stay in conflict can be a very lonely and frightening moment for negotiators. They often need someone they trust and who they feel has their best interests at heart to talk to at the critical moment when a settlement is in sight. [NDR: Wade, *Tribe*] Negotiators often need someone on their side, whom they respect and have confidence in, to in effect give them emotional permission to settle, if that is what they choose to do, or to decline to settle. Effective allies don't make this choice for negotiators. They can't—even if they have a lot of influence. They may choose to make a strong recommendation, even to exert considerable amount of pressure, but the wise ally helps negotiators think through their genuine choices, consider alternatives broadly and with a view to the entire system, and assess how to choose the best of all of their alternatives. Allies also provide a kind of psychological reinforcement that can allow a negotiator to make a decision, whatever that may be, with a certain amount of confidence and with a minimum need to second guess. In the role of a mediator, I have seen lawyers provide this function over and over for their clients. And sometimes allies help negotiators decide whether and how to conclude the negotiation without an agreement.

Alternatives Management

The power of a negotiator is to a great extent defined by the alternatives he or she has. When we have no alternative but to settle, our power is very limited (often dependent on our ability to act *as if* we have no need for an agreement). So developing effective alternatives within negotiation and as an alternative to negotiation is one of the main ways of increasing our power and flexibility in the negotiation process. Used effectively, this can contribute to a creative and positive negotiation stance. But when negotiators use their alternatives as a bludgeon or in a crude way, they often bring about a breakdown of the negotiation process. This is an expression of the dilemma disputants face about whether they can or should prepare for war and peace at the same time, as well as a concrete manifestation of the challenge of working with the competitive and cooperative dimensions that are always present in conflict.

Attending to Team Dynamics

When negotiations involve teams, as they frequently do, attention needs to be given to team dynamics. Sometimes, an internal facilitator is needed to deal with in-team processes and problems. However, whether this particular function is needed or not, paying attention to team dynamics, decision-making, communication, and morale is an important and often neglected aspect of effective negotiation. Mediators often find themselves having to try to help a negotiation team work together more effectively, but their role in this is limited by their third party status. Allies are often better positioned to help with this and often find themselves as de facto within-team mediators.

The Negotiation System

Few significant negotiations occur without the involvement in some way of multiple players. Negotiations often involve bargaining teams. [NDR: Sally et al., *Teams*] Third parties may have a role, and advocates are often involved as well. The success of a negotiation is often dependent on the cohesiveness and functionality of the whole negotiation system, of which allies are only one part. The effectiveness of allies, therefore, is very dependent on how they fit into the whole system, whether they enhance the functionality of a negotiation group or make it more unwieldy, whether their roles are clear or murky, and how they interact with advocates (who are also allies) and third parties.

Role Clarity

Since the ally role is really an amalgam of different possible roles and functions, role clarity is often elusive. The clearer allies are that they are in fact functioning to *support* negotiators and to enable them to be more effective in identifying and meeting their negotiation goals, the more likely it is that they will be able to fit into the negotiation system in a constructive way. The skills that an effective ally brings to the table are in many respects very similar to the skills required for negotiators to be effective. But negotiators are subject to different demands and, in particular, have to be focused on the substance of the negotiation and the decisions that have to be made constantly throughout a negotiation process. If allies are clear that they have a different set of roles and if those roles can be clearly articulated, then they are likely to have an easier time finding a constructive place in the negotiation system.

Some ally roles are easier to define then others. Allies acting as spokespersons, technical or legal consultants, or bargaining agents, may be familiar to negotiators, and their role readily understood. An ally who focuses on communication, process, and systems issues is often playing a less easily defined role. Negotiators may be more comfortable asking for help of a kind that is familiar and easy to define, but the most significant way in which allies can assist with difficult negotiations often lies with the more subtle aspects of their role.

Allies as Advocates and as Coaches

Two very different approaches that allies might take to their role are as advocate and as coach. Advocates are one important kind of ally, and in its broadest sense, advocacy can include a wide range of the ally contributions discussed above. But advocates usually see their role in a more limited way. An advocate's job is in some way to articulate and try to achieve the goals of their client. Advocates usually see their role as trying to get as much as they can for their clients in a distributive context (Kronman 1993; Macfarlane 2016). To some extent, all allies must share the goal of helping negotiators achieve their most essential objectives. But the specific way in which they see themselves doing this and the attention they give to overall system dynamics are different from how traditional advocates do this. Allies do not necessarily represent or speak for the negotiator, but as described here, fulfill a whole series of functions that are intended to assist negotiators to be more effective as their own best advocates. In fact, advocates often need the same kind of assistance from allies that primary negotiators do. Allies with the focus that I have described are not just looking at the particular substance or negotiation interaction but the whole constellation of dynamics that surround it.

Coaching is another role that allies often play. The last twenty years has seen a proliferation of coaching services—for example, life coaching, drama coaching, personal coaching, executive coaching, divorce coaching, and conflict coaching. The popularity of this approach, and its diversity, says something about the types of allies that people need. Coaching is essentially a metaphor drawn from sports, and it implies working to help others be more effective and competent in some aspect of their lives and taking a developmental perspective on skill enhancement. A coach may concentrate on a particular task, interaction, or conflict, but the more fundamental purpose is to help people develop their general skills in the area of focus. In this sense a negotiation coach is at least as concerned with the long-term capacity of a negotiator or a negotiation team to develop their capacities as negotiators as they are with the outcome of any particular negotiation. A number of disputants I have worked with as a consultant over the years have spontaneously started referring to me as "Coach" in what I believe has been a de facto recognition of the importance of this aspect of what I have been trying to do.

Allies and Third Parties

The value and potential of allies does not in any way diminish the importance of what third parties offer. As is true with negotiators, the skills of mediators and of effective allies overlap considerably. The need for someone who can facilitate the interaction among the parties to a dispute and help manage the communication and problem-solving process is not always obviated by the presence of effective allies. While needing some of the same skills as third parties, the ally role is fundamentally different. The goal of allies is to help negotiators be more effective and powerful in achieving their interests. When the best way for negotiators to meet their interests is to ensure that the others involved in the negotiation also achieve their goals, then the fundamental purpose of the ally and mediator will be similar. But that is not always the best way for negotiators to meet their own interests, and even when it is, that is usually not a reasonable/automatic assumption going into the negotiation. The ally's role is to be part of the negotiator's team in a way that mediators cannot be if they are to maintain their own overall role as facilitators of the negotiation process. [NDR: Love & Stulberg, *Using Mediation*; NDR: Honeyman, *Working with Mediators*]

The dilemma for the mediator is how to maintain everyone's trust and confidence without taking any one party's side or adopting their party's interests in the sense that an ally must. Mediators are trusted because they do not take sides—and are mistrusted for the very same reason. The challenge that an ally faces is the mirror image of this: how to stay very clearly on the side and in the corner of the negotiator while always helping the negotiator look at the larger picture. They are trusted because of that commitment, but this also defines the limit of their role.

If third parties, because of their role and perhaps their training, are more likely to focus on cooperation and the integrative dimension of negotiation, then allies are more likely to focus on the distributive and competitive elements. The parallel challenge they both face is to help parties take a constructive and wise approach to both aspects of conflict, albeit from a different perspective.

When a third party is present, allies have a particular role to play in helping negotiators use her effectively. They may speak the third party's language, may have worked as third parties themselves, and may find that they can help the interaction between the negotiator and the third party. But to remain effective, they must remember that they are allies of the negotiator, not of the third party.

Making Allies Available to Negotiators

Allies in one sense or another are usually present in complex negotiations, but they are not generally selected with the particular purpose of fulfilling the role as I have described it here. Negotiators ask for help, advice, counseling, and advocacy. They do not normally ask for the process oriented systems role that may be the most powerful way conflict specialists can assist with difficult negotiations. But negotiators do ask for allies. Consider these examples of how negotiators have reached out for assistance to just one practitioner group:

- State agency facing a class action suit. I was asked to train the negotiation team, help plan negotiation strategy, and offer ongoing consultation as the state and the plaintiffs successfully negotiated a consent decree on child welfare issues.
- University administration and students. I provided consultation over several years to university administrators as they considered how to work with student organizations around a number of issues, mostly political in nature.
- Partnership dissolution negotiation. A profitable business partnership was being dissolved and the negotiation was bogging down because of poor interpersonal relationships and high levels of resentment. I worked with one of the parties to help him think through an appropriate approach. He was being advised

that he had a strong legal case and should not agree to too great a compromise, but there was a danger that if he emphasized the strength of his legal case the whole negotiation would break down.

- Labor union negotiations. In preparation for a round of collective bargaining, particularly after difficult negotiations, I have been asked on several occasions to work with the management team or with the collective bargaining unit, and sometimes with both, to prepare for negotiations.

- Superfund project manager. A federal employee managing a Superfund clean-up requested ongoing support in strategizing how to deal with the many different interests and stakeholders involved. Originally we were asked to facilitate a stakeholder process, but at later stages of the project our work primarily involved coaching the project manager.

- Professional service delivery organization. The administrator of a service organization was contending with challenging and often inappropriate behavior from senior level professionals and asked for my assistance in preparing for a series of negotiations in which the administrator had a great deal of theoretical power but not much practical power.

None of these involved negotiators specifically asking for negotiation allies, yet that was our role in all of these situations. Sometimes, the initial request was for what appeared to be third party assistance, but it quickly became clear (as in the example in the beginning of this chapter) that this was not feasible or optimal, it was just what people knew how to ask for. Many conflict professionals working on large and complex issues find themselves involved mostly in the role of an ally, consultant, strategist, internal facilitator, process consultant or trainer. Often we are asked to play a combination of these roles.

The challenge is how to make negotiation allies more readily useful, credible and available. While some of this may be a marketing challenge, the more profound issue is whether conflict specialists can understand this role thoroughly and can see its potential for themselves. If conflict specialists understand this, if they can look at how often they are asked, in effect if not overtly, to function as advisors or coaches and at how often they may be asked to fulfill a different role, but where the ally role is what is really needed, then they will be more likely to put themselves forward as an ally and will increasingly be utilized as such.

Another challenge is whether individuals and systems that support and manage negotiations (corporate counsel, labor unions, advocacy groups, human resource departments, equal employment offices, courts, federal agencies, etc.) can see the need for allies and can begin to build more resources and structures to make them available to their constituents or to the parties to the negotiations that they manage. One of the challenges here is to get over a mindset that automatically assumes that the solution to all negotiation problems is to provide either more elaborate "legal" services or some form of third party assistance. [NDR: Wade, *Dueling Experts*] While these will always be important tools, negotiation managers should also ask—perhaps first—what kinds of allies could be useful and how they might be provided. There are encouraging signs that these system agents are increasingly understanding the importance of taking a broader look at the kind of help they need and are less likely to be simply turning this function over to legal allies. One sign of this is the growing number of organizations that are formalizing some sort of coaching role as part of their internal dispute resolution process and even how this coaching is being included in online dispute resolution platforms. [See NDR: Rabinovich-Einy & Katsh, *ODR*]

Finally, conflict specialists should consider how to work with existing allies, such as advocates, organizers, human resource staff, shop stewards, technical advisers, ombuds offices, corporate counsel, and community leaders. Sometimes the most effective way to contribute to negotiations will be to support existing allies in their work with negotiators. If we recognize the widespread need and general presence of allies in conflict, we can work on helping them enhance their effectiveness.

The ally role is not a speculative one: it exists in almost all conflict systems, and allies of all types are increasingly viewing themselves as conflict specialists. As the conflict field embraces the critical importance of the ally role, its reach and capacity to have a constructive impact on the most important conflicts our organizations, families, and communities face will significantly increase. And the more allies come to view themselves as conflict specialists, the better able they will be to help their communities, clients, and organizations address the most difficult elements of the conflicts they face in a wise and effective way.

References

Axelrod, R. 1984. *The Evolution of Cooperation*. New York: Basic Books.

Boulding, K. E. 1962. *Conflict and Defense*. New York: Harper & Brothers.

Damasio, A. 2005. *Descartes' Error: Emotion, Reason, and the Human Brain*. New York: Penguin Books.

Dawkins, R. 1989. *The Selfish Gene*. Oxford: Oxford University Press.

Fisher, R., W. Ury and B. Patton. 1991. *Getting to Yes: Negotiating Agreement Without Giving In*. New York: Penguin Books.

Jones, T. S. and R. Brinkert. 2008. *Conflict Coaching: Conflict Management Strategies and Skills for the Individual*. New York: SAGE Publications, Inc.

Kronman, A. T. 1993. *The Lost Lawyer*. Cambridge: Harvard University Press.

Lax, D. and J. Sebenius. 1986. *The Manager As Negotiator: Bargaining For Cooperation and Competitive Gain*. New York: Free Press.

Macfarlane, J. 2016. *The New Lawyer: How Settlement Is Transforming the Practice of Law*. 2nd edn. Vancouver, British Columbia: UBC Press.

Mayer, B. 2009. *Staying with Conflict: A Strategic Approach to Ongoing Disputes*. San Francisco: Jossey-Bass.

Mayer, B. 2012. *The Dynamics of Conflict: A Guide to Engagement and Intervention*. 2nd edn. San Francisco: Jossey-Bass.

Mayer, B. 2015. *The Conflict Paradox: Seven Dilemmas at the Core of Disputes*. San Francisco: Jossey-Bass.

Moore, C. W. and P. Woodrow. 2010. *The Handbook of Global and Multicultural Negotiation*. Hoboken: John Wiley & Sons, Inc.

Noble, C. 2011. *Conflict Management Coaching: The CINERGY Model*. Toronto, Ontario: CINERGY Coaching.

Thomas, K. 1976. Conflict and Conflict Management, in *Handbook of Industrial and Organizational Psychology*, edited by Marvin D. Dunnette. Chicago: Rand-McNally.

☙ 100 ❧

The Interpreter as Intervener

Sanda Kaufman

Editors' Note: You're about to start negotiating in a language where you can't even read the alphabet. What to do? This chapter is essential for anyone about to engage in a negotiation involving multiple languages—which could include many "domestic" negotiations in Singapore or Chicago or London or Paris. Kaufman explores how translators are neither perfectly neutral third parties, nor part of a team (contrary to common assumptions). She then shows how they are often powerful and autonomous actors in the negotiation, and demonstrates how important it is to think about the use of interpreters before *the day they are hired.*

> The most dangerous of all falsehoods
> is a slightly distorted truth.
> *G.C. Lichtenberg*, physicist (1742-1799)
>
> Any translator who intends to render a work from
> one language to another merely by rendering word
> for word, and slavishly following the order of the
> chapters and sentences in the original, will come to
> grief. The product of his labor will be unintelligible
> and ludicrous.
> *Maimonides*[1] (1135-1204)

Sanda Kaufman is Professor of Planning, Public Policy and Administration at Cleveland State University's Levin College of Urban Affairs. Her research spans negotiations and intervention in environmental and other public conflicts; social-environmental systems resilience; decision analysis; program evaluation; and negotiation pedagogy. Her articles have appeared in the *Journal for Conflict Resolution*, the *Negotiation Journal, Conflict Resolution Quarterly, International Journal for Conflict Management, Negotiation and Conflict Management Research, Revue Négociations*, and others. B. Arch. and M.S. in Planning, Technion; Ph.D. in Public Policy Analysis, Carnegie Mellon University.

Language Barriers to Negotiations

The word "ceasefire" carries critically different meanings in Arabic (*hudna*), in Hebrew (*hafsakat esh*) and English, in which negotiations are often conducted in the Israeli-Palestinian conflict. The parties to this conflict also differ over the meaning of *tahdiah*, designating in Arabic the period of calm on which sides agreed informally in 2005, in Sharm el Sheik (Al-Ahram 2005). The *hudna* example led Micah D. Halperin (2003) to observe that:

> One of the most significant obstacles to be overcome in the Israeli-Palestinian peace process is language. The cultural, conceptual and language barriers that separate the negotiating partners are greater than their negotiation over land and far more difficult to resolve.

UN Resolution 242 (1967) famously carries significantly different meanings in English, Russian, French, and Spanish, hinging on one word—

"the"—whose absence in English and Russian leads to the interpretation that Israel should return [some of the] occupied territories, while French and Spanish versions arguably call for a return of [all] *the* occupied territories (Rosenne 1971). Noticed from the outset and neatly lining up with the respective countries' political stands, this discrepancy is only partly intentional since to align meanings with the English original would have required negotiating additional clarifying words which were not part of the English text.

Anecdotal examples from other places and times abound. For instance, due to a mistranslation, journalists interpreted Pope John Paul II's farewell words to his compatriots in 2002 as an endorsement of Poland's membership in the European Union, instead of the broader European community he really meant. In 2005, six-party talks regarding North Korea's nuclear program were bogged down by the need to translate to and from English, Russian, Korean, Chinese and Japanese.

Since interpreting is one of the oldest professions, we can find anecdotes going back to the Tower of Babel, itself a metaphor crying out for competent intervention. For example, translation diplomacy was exercised, as was apparently the norm, in rendering to Queen Elizabeth the meaning of a letter from the Sultan of Turkey, in the late 16th century (Lewis 2004: 28-29). The Sultan's exhortation to the Queen to demonstrate loyalty and subservience to him was translated in English as "sincere friendship." While this may well have been the gist of the formal message, because the Sultan may only have addressed his "friends" in this manner, and while the world may have been well served by the liberty translators took with the original text, we are left to ponder what is preferable in such situations—a literal translation alone, one accompanied by a cultural interpretation, or the one actually favored by diplomats at that time.

The 16th century, however, did not yet feature the complicating factor of a free, multinational and vigorously critical press. In March 2015, in the aftermath of negotiations between Iran and the so-called P5+1 countries seeking to craft a framework for the agreement to be concluded in June 2015 regarding Iran's nuclear capability, the communiqués in English, Persian and French regarding the content of the framework diverged in meaningful ways. It almost seemed as if the parties had not participated in the same negotiations. While arguably the discrepancies went beyond translation issues, their reporting in different languages allowed all parties to claim that their own version was correct despite what was being reported elsewhere in a different language. But within hours, newspapers, radio and TV in numerous countries cross-compared those versions, using their own interpreters, and reported or even exaggerated the differences. As in previous instances of international treaties written and reported in different languages, a space was created for imprecisions that could subsequently impede implementation or even conclusion of a treaty. Of lesser global import than negotiations among disputing nations, business negotiations among parties speaking different languages are both increasingly frequent and difficult. For example, at the White House Conference on Trade and Investment in Central and Eastern Europe (held in Cleveland in 1995) I interpreted talks between an American businessman and another country's representatives refusing to pay for services he had delivered. In that situation, by no means uncommon, my choice of words and of what to translate may have affected the outcome. Recognizing a need, how-to negotiation texts (e.g., Trenholm and Daggatt 2001; Brett 2001) have responded with advice to business negotiators on handling such situations. They have warned, for example, that as English is fast becoming lingua franca, English speakers may be at a disadvantage: their counterparts may well be fluent in English and still insist on speaking through interpreters, to gain precious time as they think about their responses.

Communication is the currency of negotiation (Putnam and Roloff 1991; Putnam 2016): "You say what you want, I say what I want and we go back and forth until we find a way to resolve our differences." (Lewicki, Hiam and Olander 1996). Evolutionary psychologists have even argued that language emerged in response to early humans' need to enter into non-aggression or cooperative agreements to avoid mutual destruction through violent acts (Pinker 2003). Negotiators should, therefore, wish to have full control over the clarity and precision of words they use to convey interests, make offers and promises, persuade, or threaten; for the same reasons, they should also seek to understand precisely what others are telling them.

Ideally, then, negotiations are best conducted in one shared language. Even then, subcultures—geographic, professional, experiential, education-or age-related—yield vocabulary differences that impede communication in obvious and easily correctable ways, as well as in more insidious ways that leave parties unaware of their differences. One consequence is confusion between substantive disagreements and mere vocabulary differences. This may also fool parties into believing they disagree less than in actuality. However, increasingly negotiators do not even share a language. When they do, their mastery levels may differ, undermining the ability to distinguish nuances, decode metaphors, or decipher cultural subtleties key to understanding the full import of what is said, or avoiding misunderstandings (Brett 2007: 145-47). Getting across exactly what we mean engages our ability to express our ideas in words, but also entails the listener's ability to decode our messages, a challenge that increases as parties communicate across language barriers. What recourse then? Until electronic devices reach adequate sophistication,[2] interpreters remain the answer.

I discuss next the need for interpreters, how they operate, and how they interact with their clients. I propose that, far from being a passive, inconsequential service, interpreting is active intervention. So it is important for negotiators to recognize it as such and to become aware of all the ways it can affect process and outcomes. Specifically, all involved tend to perceive the interpreters as being partial to, and acting on behalf of, the party whose native language they share. That perception generates a strategic space for interpreters interested in exploiting it. It is a "dark side" of this service, because it is difficult to detect or control. I also argue that the relationship between negotiators and their interpreters shares some, but not all, the characteristics of principal-agent relationships. Therefore, though this relationship is typically not negotiated, maybe it should be.

Who Needs Interpreters?

> The language of negotiations may be English, but each partner in the process thinks in his mother tongue, translates for his citizens in his mother tongue and consciously and subconsciously negotiates through his own cultural bias.
>
> *M.D. Halperin,* (2003) referring to the Israeli-Palestinian conflict

For simplicity, in what follows I will refer to two negotiators, although the arguments extend to multiparty situations. Even when they do not share a native language, parties may still negotiate directly in a third language, or one of them may negotiate in the other's native language, depending on levels of fluency and comprehension. For example, Indians speaking different languages conduct their affairs in English. So do Palestinians and Israelis. Portuguese negotiators can negotiate in Spanish with Spanish counterparts. Dutch and German negotiators occasionally interact in German.

The foreign language instruction methods combined with the type of starting point (one's native language) yield different results. Some people's understanding of a spoken or written foreign language is better than their ability to express themselves in that language; others are better speakers than listeners. Therefore, even when the parties can understand each other in a shared language, they may request an interpreter's assistance especially if the stakes are high and/or if precision is important, as in business negotiations, exchanges among scientists and engineers, conversations across different cultures, or discussions involving legal issues. Note that people's assessment of their own skill level in another language does not necessarily correspond to reality, and is not easily corroborated. Only their responses to direct questions that require precision may reveal misunderstandings. If neither party can understand the other's language or share a third, interpretation is obviously no longer optional.

Even when speakers are linguistically competent, they might not understand or utilize nuances or be culturally competent. Language is suffused with metaphors, old and new sayings, and cultural references transparent to native speakers, especially in the absence of geographic, professional or class differences. Some metaphors have become part of the vernacular, while we craft and use others intentionally, to clarify and to persuade, and to enhance the sense of what is shared and induce cooperation. Should we be forced to communicate without these linguistic adornments, we would feel hamstrung and less able to convey precisely what we mean. However, these rich devices are the most difficult to export to another language, and may require interpreter assistance, assuming the latter understands such subtleties. Cultural differences embedded in language may cause misunderstandings even among seasoned professionals. One example is the US-Chinese diplomatic fallout of 2001 surrounding the proper choice of words to express regret for the collision of an American plane with a Chinese one (Avruch and Wang 2005). Although career diplomats share a professional subculture that overrides cultural particularities, languages still trap them in misunderstandings avoidable to some extent through capable interpretation.

The English language has become special in the last decades. People around the world study it in schools and we have come to expect that wherever we go others will understand and respond in English. In one telling example, a ten year-old boy in North Uganda gave an interview in excellent English about the plight of the local population to an NBC journalist (Dateline NBC 2005). One consequence of the penetration of English in the world's furthest recesses is that native English speakers see little need to become skilled in other languages. As a result, they are possibly disadvantaged in multi-lingual negotiations, needing interpretation while being transparent to their counterparts. It is quite likely that in negotiations involving native English speakers, other negotiators, whether they acknowledge it or not, have weak to excellent understanding and exploit their advantage.

Given their effect on negotiation process and outcomes, it is important to examine how interpreters become messengers, agents, or interveners.

What Do Interpreters Do?

> Translation can provide semantic meaning, but not pragmatic meaning. Pragmatic meaning, however, is extremely important in diplomacy. Not being competent in the language of other nations, therefore, severely limits diplomats' and national leaders' ability to understand other nations and accurately predict the behavior of representatives of those nations.
>
> *William Gudykunst* (1990)

Interpretation ranges from literal renditions, which may fail to capture the spirit of what is being said, to conveying the gist and spirit of exchanges, using words that express the sense even if not entirely equivalent to the source.[3] At times, literal translations are explicitly requested, as in US court depositions or appearances of non-English speakers in court. Sometimes the choice on the continuum between literal and interpretive translation is left to the interpreters. The choice may be rooted in their professional philosophies, and occasionally in other considerations—as we shall see in an example below.

If they have speaking fluency in one (usually native or strong second) language, interpreters can engage in one-way interpretation, as when simultaneously translating a speech to an audience. For instance, a host of UN interpreters translate simultaneously speeches delivered in one of a small number of official languages. Speaking fluency in two languages allows interpreters to perform two-way, semi-simultaneous (by turns) interpretation among parties. As stakes increase, so does the professional level of interpreters, who have to be fluent in the requisite languages, adhere to interpretation codes of ethics, and have a good grasp of intercultural issues that might crop up during negotiations, to help the parties distinguish between substantive and language differences.

When interpreters are present, it is often unclear whether a negotiator actually understands the other directly, and to what extent. The higher the stakes, the more prudent it is for parties not to negotiate directly in a language not their own, to reduce the risk of misunderstandings. Just as negotiators are well-advised to assume their opponents are at least as smart as they are, they should also assume their counterparts have a working understanding of the language for which they are using interpreters, and never say anything they do not mean others to hear.

Although some professionals and some of their clients believe any mediator is able to intervene in disputes ranging from interpersonal to international, other professionals believe that, in practice, knowledge of content, rules, and practices in specific contexts is necessary. The same holds for interpreters, as language can become quite specialized. Using technically equivalent terms different from those employed in a specific context can detract from negotiations by unnecessarily increasing the time spent on establishing the equivalence. It can also add a layer of misunderstandings in situations that hardly need any more communication obstacles. As well, interpreters' hesitation around choice of words attracts attention to their presence as parties attempt to help clarify context-specific terms. Professional interpreters prepare for assignments by reading their clients' literature and by bringing themselves up-to-date on issues to be discussed, in order to enhance the smoothness of cross-language interactions. It is not uncommon, for the United Nations interpreters for example, to specialize, and be repeatedly assigned to organizations or agencies whose issues and vocabularies they have learned.

Another challenge interpreters encounter as they try to convey the sense, intensity, intent and depth of their clients' conversations is mapping words and expressions from one language into another, while minimizing interference with the process to preserve to the extent possible the feeling of direct communication. In that sense, the more invisible they make themselves to negotiating parties, the more successful they are, not unlike other interveners such as mediators. Many interpreters do succeed in their quest for invisibility, the hallmark of skill—all the more reason for negotiators not to forget their presence or the impact they may have on process and outcomes. The interpreters' "dark side" is their hard-to-control capability of becoming active interveners or agents on one side's behalf, with a point of view on the substance of issues discussed during negotiations.

Interpreters may have no initial stake in the process or outcome of a multilingual exchange. However, if they develop preferences during negotiations, they can exercise them, without necessarily infringing on interpretation ethics. Selecting their location on the literal-to-interpretive continuum,[4] choosing to render various utterances that may or may not be intended for translation, and conveying at will emotional cues may all predictably affect process and outcomes.

In the business negotiation example mentioned earlier, despite what the three negotiators were saying to the American businessman, what they were saying to each other in their native language indicated that they had no intention of honoring their commitment and were not taking his complaint seriously. To convey this to the businessman, I chose a literal extreme, translating flatly everything anyone said. Had they specifically asked me not to translate parts of their conversation not directed at the businessman, I would have had to honor the request. However, as happens in such situations, they wrongly assumed where my loyalties lay,[5] and their lack of knowledge of English robbed them of any measure of control. While partial comprehension of the other's language affords some oversight, it can also mislead. It still leaves room for interpreter discretion, but may cause the negotiator to second-guess and mistrust the interpreter even when this is unwarranted. It is important to note that my choice, as long as uniformly applied, was consistent with interpreter duties, as would have been any other choice along the literal-interpretive continuum, since interpreting means legitimately processing the raw input from one language to render it comprehensible in a different language.

My example illustrates one way for interpreters to alter the negotiation outcomes. In general, such actions can affect the tenor of negotiations, mutual trust, good will, and the readiness to share information. While in direct negotiations the parties have some control over their own messages and can interpret in unmediated fashion what they hear, interpreters add noise not unlike "hearsay," whether by design or by the very nature of the activity. They can distort meaning, not translate everything, or explain meanings beyond what a party has actually said or intended to disclose. They can choose to translate side comments or not, to explain or ignore emotional outbursts, and to convey fully or partially the intensity of words (as diplomats did for the Sultan's message to Queen Elizabeth). Importantly, interpreters are fully aware of their power, and often of the effects of their choice of words. They act on others' behalf and reflect on the art, science and ethics of their choices, as suggested by their intense discussions on these subjects at interpreter conferences.

Although generally perceived as having no personal stake in outcomes, interpreters may occasionally feel they do, or they may have an ideologically or identity-driven point of view and inclination to "help" one side. They may feel compelled to put a light finger on the scales, to tip them toward what they perceive as fair, all the while persuading themselves that it is the right thing to do (as I did during the business negotiation); this may even be seen as part of their job. The more specialized they are, such as professional interpreters working in high stakes contexts, the more knowledgeable of substantive issues they become, and the more able to intervene skillfully enough that their actions are difficult to detect. However, interpreters may also exercise their power when they can persuade themselves that stakes are low enough that their action only matters to their client, with no sizeable consequences for others. Instead of regarding interpretation as a neutral service, negotiators should be aware of its "dark side."

Negotiators need to be aware of interpreter effects beyond the lack of one-to-one correspondence between languages. Interpreters differ in their outlook on their profession, in skill, and in experience in specific contexts, so they are apt to render the same conversation differently. Communicating through interpreters amounts to letting them choose your words, a realization that might, and should, produce negotiator anxiety, especially when stakes are high. Both one-way and two-way interpreters are agents whom we entrust with our words while lacking full consent, quality control and trust—typical challenges in principal-agent relationships (e.g., Salacuse 1999; NDR: Nolan-Haley, *Agents*). I discuss next some aspects and implications of this relationship.

How Do Interpreters Interact with Their Clients?

> LANGUAGE, n. The music with which we charm the serpents guarding another's treasure.
> *Ambrose Bierce*, satirist (1842-1914): The Devil's Dictionary, 1911.

Context matters in the interpreter-client relationship. Even subtle context differences may result in different challenges for the effort to convey meaning. Several situational characteristics shape interpreters' role, including whether each party has its own interpreter, whether power and professionalism are in balance among parties, whether the situation is governed by rules and precedents and defines interpreting tasks precisely, and whether the interpreter is a "natural" stakeholder. Accordingly, interpreters are at times most like advocates, agents or interveners.

Advocate Roles

In situations of power and skill imbalance, the interpreter may end up advocating for the party for whom being misunderstood carries heavy consequences. Non-English-speaking clients may need help in communicating with service providers, to establish entitlements to assistance that hinge on an accurate understanding of needs. Then cultural interpretation is explicitly added to translation, whether volunteered by the interpreter or invited by the parties. The intervener switches then occasionally from translation to advocacy, and adds information to one party that does not come from the other, but is necessary for clarity. At such times, it helps to ask permission from each party, and explain what information is offered to the other. For example: Physicians talking to non-English speaking patients must understand their cultural attitudes toward illness or mental and physical handicaps, or risk fatal misunderstandings or a communication shutdown. For instance, to receive medical help, mentally ill patients have to accept it by recognizing their mental illness. I have had to translate physicians' requests for such recognition from people in whose culture this subject is taboo. Unable to bear the shame, one woman preferred to become homeless for two years, rather than agree that she had been mentally ill for years and needed treatment.

In turn, social services providers need interpreters to help educate clients on institutional arrangements, entitlements, and privacy issues. Some business negotiators used to practicing in other environments may have limited understanding of the consequences of misrepresenting the truth. Plaintiffs and defendants have similar difficulties in courts.

Lawyers' clients need assistance to overcome anxieties rooted in past experience, such as fear of authorities or feeling ashamed to find themselves in certain circumstances. One witness to a break-in at her neighbors' house had to explain why she had not called the police. The woman turned to me speechless, hoping I would understand and explain that, where she came from, calling the police was dangerous to the caller, and being seen talking to the police would cover the family in shame.

In many such asymmetrical power situations, interpreters mistakenly become the focus of attention of those with whom they share a native language. Assuming they share more than just language, clients seek and prize interpreters' understanding and approval, and any shame they feel is also relative to the interpreter. Misunderstandings about the interpreter role often crop up: during a deposition in a lawyer's office, a woman became annoyed with my asking her the clarification questions posed by the lawyer about a holiday custom, for which I clearly should have needed no explanation! In municipal court cases of drunk driving or spouse abuse, I am often treated to defendants' detailed disculpatory accounts, meant to improve my opinion of them. Despite my clarifications they often fail to register my role, my obligatory neutrality, the total lack of consequence of my opinions on the court, and the slim chance that we might ever meet again.

Agent and Intervener Roles

One-way interpreters (Figure 1) are comparable to agents, though formally at least, their representation of principals is limited to language and does not extend to interests. Jeswald Salacuse (1999: 158) has captured the principal-agent relationship through four key elements: (1) A fiduciary relationship between agent and principal; (2) Control by the principal over the agent; (3) Action by the agent on behalf of the principal; and (4) Consent by both principal and agent to the agency relationship. While element 3 is relatively clear for interpreters and their clients, the fiduciary aspect, the degree of control over agents, and the recognition of agency are problematic.

Two-way interpreters (Figure 1) fit Jeffrey Rubin's (1981) definition of a third party: "an individual who is in some way external to a dispute between two other parties, and who interposes (or is interposed) between them." In principle, interpreters should be indifferent among outcomes in a multi-lingual negotiation, especially since evaluation of service quality does not (or should not) hinge on outcome content. This reinforces expectations (though not perceptions) of their neutrality. However, unlike other interveners, they do not participate in process design or management. Their activities match closely those identified by Sanda Kaufman and George Duncan (1988) as central to mediation: information (supply and) transfers.

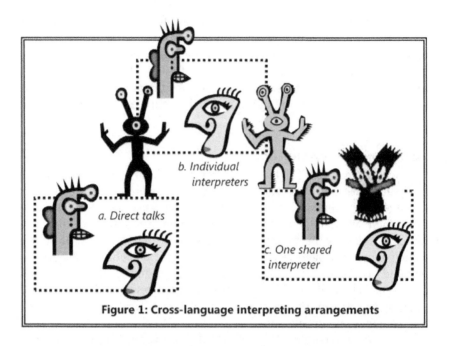

a. Direct talks

b. Individual interpreters

c. One shared interpreter

Figure 1: Cross-language interpreting arrangements

It is noteworthy that neither type of interpreter fits perfectly either the agent or the intervener role: each has both agency and intervention qualities. In general, the one-way interpreters may have no direct interest in outcomes, while the two-way interpreters may alternate as agents of each side.

Table 1 identifies some characteristics in which interpreters, agents, and interveners are comparable, since due to the interpreters' leeway in choosing words on behalf of others the impact of their activities exceeds their seemingly limited role in negotiations. The characteristics interact, so, for example, interpreters exercise their power because they can become invisible to the parties, and lack of control over the quality of their work is the source of trust problems. All three modes of intervention operate through language and can exercise more or less directly some form of power over process and outcomes. The extent to which interveners and agents have responsibility for the outcomes of negotiation depends on the specific cases, whereas interpreters are never held responsible for agreements and their content. The "invisible" quality and the neutrality expectation are mostly intervention qualities, whereas the fiduciary responsibility, relationship recognition and client control are mostly agency issues.

Mediators are supposed to feel successful when parties believe they did everything themselves. Ingratitude is a compliment of sorts for the mediator's skill in getting the parties to own their decisions. Interpreters prefer invisibility for a different, though also skill-related reason—creating for the parties the impression of unmediated conversation.

In contrast, as stakeholders themselves, agents are neither invisible nor do they seek to be. Invisibility, however, is the interpreters' ticket to their "dark side," as parties may forget they are not really hearing each other's words and are unable to control what the other hears.

Interpreters and interveners are expected to refrain from favoring a party through their actions. However, both negotiators perceive interpreters as having a special relationship with the party with whom they share a native language. Therefore, even in two-way interpretation, one party sees the interpreter as an agent of the other, who also perceives him or her to be "on their side" and to understand that side better. However, this relationship is assumed, rather than explicitly negotiated. The weaker the parties' ability to verify the interpreter's choices, the less wise is this assumption, as my business negotiation example illustrated. One-way situations stand in sharp contrast, because then interpreters can act like the agents they are perceived to be. Unlike interveners and agents, interpreters do not typically have process input, beyond modest requests about the length of time a party can speak before the interpreter takes a turn. This does not mean their presence does not affect the process. On the contrary, the periodic pauses give the natural flow a choppier quality, but they add to each party's time for reflection. Expression of emotions during negotiation is also impaired or somewhat misinterpreted. For instance, it is not uncommon for English, Americans or Scandinavians to interpret the Mediterranean (rather louder) interaction style as angry and unruly when they do not directly understand the content of exchanges. As the meaning is delayed through interpretation, the impressions linger even after the absence of anger becomes clear.

Interveners' and agents' input in negotiated outcomes is purposeful even when indirect, and it is mostly legitimate and visible to parties who understand the nature of each. Interpretation, on the other hand, is not supposed to affect negotiated outcomes, having a different avowed purpose. Nevertheless, interpreters may affect outcomes by their word choices, either inadvertently, or purposefully, as the translators did for Queen Elizabeth. As in that case, such actions are all the more insidious when consistent with expectations: the Queen had little reason to doubt a sign of friendship she expected. She might have been surprised had she received the original exhortation to subservience.

The fiduciary relationship described by Salacuse[6] as a component of agency also characterizes interpretation. Negotiators do expect their words to be conveyed to the other side. Unlike with agents though, their ability to exert control and evaluate the quality of service received is rather limited, as are their means of inducing alignment of interpreters' interests with their own. More problematic still, perceptions are not necessarily aligned with this reality given both parties' tendency to assume interpreter partiality to the side sharing a native language. Interpreters thus operate in a more weakly controlled space than agents or interveners. They alone have a "dark side"—the capability of giving free rein to biases or hidden agendas unless negotiators take steps to protect themselves, especially in high-stakes situations.

Mode / Characteristic	Intervention	Agency	Interpreta-tion
Language as key vehicle	Yes	Yes	Yes
Formal responsibility for outcome	Varies	Considerable	None
Power	Some (mainly over process)	Some (over process, content)	Some (over content)
Premium on being "invisible"	Yes	No	Yes
Parties' expectation of neutrality	Yes	No	Yes
Input in process	Yes	Some	None
Input in outcome	Indirect	Yes	Indirect
Fiduciary relationship	No	Yes	Partial
Recognition of the rela-tionship	Full	Full	Partial
Client ability to control/ supervise/evaluate	Strong	Variable	Very weak

(Left margin labels: rows 4–6 "Intervener-like"; rows 7–10 "Agent-like")

Table 1: Comparison Between Interveners, Agents and Interpreters

An Electronic Future?

One avenue for shedding some light on the "dark side" and giving principals a measure of control of their interpreters might be to use software to simultaneously translate back to a client the interpreter's rendering in a different language. Efforts to develop translation assistance date as far back as the middle of the 20th century (e.g., Hutchin 1978; Salus 2014). Eventually electronic translation combined with voice-to-text tools will reach the quality necessary for conducting in real time consequential exchanges among people speaking different languages. Already, those with some grasp of a language are able to use machine translation (MT) to assist them. There is also machine-aided human translation (MAHT) that entails different kinds of machine support for translations performed by professionals and nonprofessionals (Cole et al. 2010).

However, by many accounts the future is not today for negotiators, even with the most sophisticated devices. State-of-the-art software has yet to reach the precision or capture the nuances necessary for effective communication during negotiations (e.g. Kelly 2007). One extant reason among many is the difficulty of teaching machines to understand the meaning of words (e.g., Kakaes 2012; Rubens 2014) in context and precisely, a critical element of negotiations and one that is not yet threatening the livelihoods of interpreters. Even those who negotiate over the internet in their own language have experienced a measure of feedback loss that impedes their ability to assess the credibility of a counterpart who is neither seen nor heard. [See e.g. NDR: Ebner, *Email*] The loss of feedback and nuance deepens when parties negotiate in different languages and rely on machine assistance to understand each other. This leaves the translation task for the moment in the hands of human interpreters, warts and all.

Conclusion

> Between two beings there is always the barrier of words. Man has so many ears and speaks so many languages. Should it nevertheless be possible to understand one another? Is real communication possible if word and language betray us every time? Shall, in the end, only the language of tanks and guns prevail and not human reason and understanding?
> *Joost Merloo,* psychiatrist (1903-1976)

Interpreters, with their mixture of agent and intervener attributes, can affect the dynamics and outcomes of cross-language negotiations through communication, the very vehicle through which they are conducted. They alter nuances, tone, emotions, and even content of arguments, adding to, or subtracting from, offers, threats and promises, in amounts and ways that hinge on skill, values, identities, and sometimes interests. Parties can exert only limited control over interpreters, who may be more responsive to their professional peers' evaluations and ethics codes than to the parties.

What is a negotiator to do? Awareness of the nature of interpretation, of its agency and intervention dimensions, of what can and cannot be expected from it, and of some dangers inherent in the activity should help mitigate some of the pitfalls. Rather than viewing interpreting as a neutral, mechanical service, negotiators need to recognize its centrality to negotiations and invest an amount of scrutiny in the selection of interpreters commensurate with their potential impact on process and outcomes. They should also seek to enhance their ability to control quality and neutrality. For example, in high-stakes situations, bi-lingual observers (or a machine-translated version of what is being said) might provide a measure of control and even increased accuracy, given interpreters' sensitivity to peer opinions. Just as they prepare for negotiations, parties may consider preparing for the interpretation: meet with the interpreters before they encounter their counterparts, discuss expectations, process, ways of enhancing precision and reducing ambiguities, and any concerns with the agency aspects of the relationship. Depending on their trust level, negotiators may or may not disclose to interpreters whether they understand the others' language and to what extent. For repeated encounters, negotiators should debrief each session to fine-tune the process and check for any misunderstandings that could not be ironed out in real time. If uncomfortable with service quality or unable to develop a relationship of trust in their agency, negotiators should not hesitate to seek other interpreters even in midstream.

Back to the ceasefire: in English, it means a total end of any acts by one party that may be understood as aggressive toward the second party. In Hebrew, hafsakat esh means to Israelis that Palestinians must stop all attacks against them, but if Israelis have intelligence of a pending terror attack against them, they can and will act to prevent it. In Arabic, hudna means to Palestinians a temporary scaling down of hostilities against a true enemy until one can attack again. These differences are enough to torpedo any agreement after it is signed, and indeed we have already witnessed several rounds of just that. We learn the power and the weakness of words to be vehicles for understanding and barriers to it, at the same time. We also learn that people pursue doggedly their own interests rather than the words that represent them, so no unifying words can bridge real and persistent differences. Interpreters can only do so much.

Notes

[1] Translation of 1199 text of Maimonides to Shmuel ibn Tibbon, in Leo Schwartz, Memoirs of My People (1943).

[2] State-of-the-art machine translations (e.g., Google Translate) illustrate this point: Voltaire's "Better is the enemy of good" when translated from English into Russian, comes back into English as: "Better enemy of the good." Note the improvement from the older Babelfish: "The more best enemy it is good." Despite such advances, in 2014 the Malaysian government used Google Translate to boast that it had taken "drastic measures to increase the level of any national security threat" after the country's independence in 1957 (Rubens, 2014). In 2011, a machine translation of Occupy Wall Street's sign "No more corruption" yielded in Chinese "There is no corruption" (R.L.G. 2014). In 2014, the Spanish language version of the Healthcare.gov site was rife with examples of the perils of machine translation (Petri 2014).

[3] The translations of UN Resolution 242 from English are close to the verbatim end of the range, since the wording had been negotiated. Rendering its sense would have necessitated introducing or eliminating words, requiring further negotiations. The parties chose to allow the ambiguity rather than renew negotiations, with consequences that still impact today's Middle East (Rosenne 1971).

[4] Some interpreters believe their task to entail a literal translation of words or text. Others believe they should always contextualize by rewording to convey the precise meaning even if they have to use words or text other than the originator used (litera-

ture translators do that). Interpreters who make decisions in the moment place themselves at different points between these two extremes, having to ensure both precision and meaning.

[5] These negotiators perceived me as siding with them, on account of the shared native language. Therefore, they made comments they could not possibly have wanted understood by their American counterpart. For example, at one point they used a derogatory regionalism unfamiliar to me, to convey that their conversation with the American businessman was meant to accomplish nothing more than pass the time. After asking for clarification, I translated it. Having understood the futility of the negotiations, the businessman appealed to then-Secretary of Trade Ron Brown, present at the conference, who intervened successfully on his behalf.

References

Al-Ahram (Egypt), March 30, 2005. Translated in *MEMRI Special Dispatch* #894, April 19, 2005.

Avruch, K. and Z. Wang. 2005. Culture, Apology, and International Negotiation: The Case of the Sino-US "Spy Plane" Crisis. *International Negotiation* 10: 337-354.

Brett, J. M. 2007. *Negotiating Globally: How to Negotiate Deals, Resolve Disputes, and Make Decisions Across Cultural Boundaries*, 2d edn. San Francisco: John Wiley & Sons.

Cole, R. 2010. *Survey of the State of the Art in Human Language Technology.* Cambridge: Cambridge University Press.

Dateline NBC television broadcast 2005. Keith Morrison's report on Northern Uganda. Aug. 21.

Griffin, T. J. and W. R. Daggatt. 1990. *The Global Negotiator: Building Strong Business Relationships Anywhere in the World.* New York: Harper.

Halperin, M. D. 2003. *What You Need to Know About: Terror.* Jerusalem: Toby Press.

Hutchins, W. J. 1978. Machine Translation and Machine-Aided Translation. *Journal of Documentation* 34: 119-159.

Kakaes, K. 2012. Why Computers Still Can't Translate Languages Automatically. Accessed Sept. 9, 2015, http://www.slate.com/articles/technology/future_tense/2012/05/darpa_s_transtac_bolt_and_other_machine_translation_programs_search_for_meaning_.html.

Kaufman, S. and G. T. Duncan. 1988. The Role of Mandates in Third Party Intervention. *Negotiation Journal* 4: 403-412.

Kelly, N. "Why Machines Alone Cannot Solve the World's Translation Problem." Accessed Sept. 14, 2015. http://www.huffingtonpost.com/nataly-kelly/why-machines-alone-cannot-translation_b_4570018.html.

Lewicki, R. J., A. Hiam and K. W. Olander. 1996. *Think Before You Speak: A Complete Guide to Strategic Negotiation.* New York: John Wiley & Sons.

Lewis, B. 2004. *From Babel to Dragomans, Interpreting the Middle East.* London: Oxford University Press.

Nolan-Haley, J. 2006. Agents and Informed Consent. In *The Negotiator's Fieldbook: The Desk Reference for the Experienced Negotiator*, edited by A. K. Schneider and C. Honeyman. Washington, DC: American Bar Association.

Petri, A. 2014. Spanish version of Healthcare.gov apparently used computer translation? Accessed Sept. 14, 2015, https://www.washingtonpost.com/blogs/compost/wp/2014/01/13/spanish-version-of-healthcare-gov-apparently-used-computer-translation/.

Pinker, Steven. 2003. *The Blank Slate: The Modern Denial of Human Nature.* New York: Penguin.

Putnam, L. L. and M. E. Roloff, eds. 1992. *Communication and Negotiation.* Vol. 20. Newbury Park, CA: Sage Publications.

Putnam, L. 2006. Communication and Interaction Patterns. In *The Negotiator's Fieldbook: The Desk Reference for the Experienced Negotiator*, edited by A. K. Schneider and C. Honeyman. Washington, DC: American Bar Association.

Rosenne, S. 1971. On Multilingual Interpretation, *Israel Law Review* 6:360-366.

Rubens, P. Building Babel: Lost in Machine Translation. Accessed Sept. 14, 2015, http://www.bbc.com/future/story/20120306-lost-in-machine-translation.

Rubin, J. Z., ed. 1981. *Dynamics of Third Party Intervention: Kissinger in the Middle East*. New York: Praeger.

Salacuse, J. W. 1999. Law and Power in Agency Relationships. In *Negotiating on Behalf of Others: Advice to Lawyers, Business Executives, Sports Agents, Diplomats, Politicians and Everybody Else*, edited by R. Mnookin. New York: Sage.

Salus, P. H. *The History of Computer Language Translation*. Accessed May 13, 2016, http://blog.smartbear.com/testing/the-history-of-computer-language-translation/.

The Economist Johnson: The Rise of the Machine Translators. Accessed Sept. 14, 2015, http://www.economist.com/blogs/prospero/2014/06/computer-aided-translation.

❧ 101 ❧

The A is for Activism

Jennifer W. Reynolds

Editors' Note: Negotiation, mediation, and arbitration—the three major practice areas of ADR—have become so mainstream that many argue that the "A" of ADR, which historically has stood for "alternative," no longer applies. But modern ADR originally developed as a set of practices outside the mainstream, intended in large part to promote social transformation and empower individuals. Reynolds argues that these activist roots of ADR should not be forgotten, and in fact should spur new research and pedagogy around activism, community organizing, social movements, and other "extralegal" approaches to changing law and society.

Introduction

Two years ago, I met with a local activist group working for the rights of the homeless. They wanted help preparing for an upcoming meeting with the City Manager, who had announced plans to relocate one of the city's homeless encampments. The activists initially sought help from a local civil rights attorney, but she advised them that negotiation was likely their best option and referred them to me.

We met at the law school and spent two hours engaged in typical negotiation preparation activities: sorting through the history of this particular issue; developing realistic alternatives to negotiating, such as demonstrations and social media outreach; identifying the various stakeholders and interests at stake for each; assessing the current and desired status of relationships between the activists and these various stakeholders; and coming up with a preliminary set of options based on the

Jennifer Reynolds is an Associate Professor at the University of Oregon School of Law. She teaches civil procedure, conflict of laws, negotiation, and mediation. Her research interests include dispute systems design, problem-solving in multiparty scenarios, and cultural influences and implications of alternative processes. She serves as the Faculty Director of the nationally ranked, award-winning Oregon ADR Center, and is the co-chair of the Legal Education Policy Committee for the ABA Section on Dispute Resolution. Before law school, Reynolds worked as a systems analyst and associate director for information technology at the University of Texas at Austin.

interests at stake and the group's considerable knowledge of possible camping sites and resources. By the end of the meeting, we were able to distill the activists' interests and desired outcomes into a list of talking points for the proposed agreement. The group was pleased with the progress we had made, and we agreed to meet again to talk about process and strategy.

That second meeting did not happen. The activists' appointment with the City Manager ended up taking place sooner than expected, and there was no time to reconvene at the law school. The group brought its talking points to the meeting but ultimately the City Manager decided on a transition plan for the camp that not only was wholly repugnant to the activists but also, at least according to the activists, had been his plan all along. The activists felt worse than ignored; they felt humiliated by the interaction itself, sent packing after they tried to participate in constructive dialogue and provide input. After the meeting, my main contact with the activist group announced that she could not participate in the transition in good faith so instead would focus her energies on civil disobedience and on filing a civil rights lawsuit on behalf of the campers. She thanked me for my help and expressed hope that others would continue negotiating, but stated that she needed to pursue a more "radical" path and therefore would not negotiate anymore. The City Manager proceeded with his plan.

Why did the meeting with the City Manager go so poorly, given these facts? Possible answers to this question will depend largely on perspective. From the perspective of a negotiator, the meeting was a disaster because the preparation was insufficient, resulting in failure to develop a communications plan and strategy that could have highlighted the short- and long-term benefits of collaborative efforts around the camping agreement. This strategy also could have anticipated an early adverse result, like the one that actually happened, with contingencies in place for extending the negotiation process, changing the players, and drawing on alternatives to create short-term negative leverage. Additionally, the demanding and often unpredictable pace of the activists' work made it challenging for them to enlist resources from the law school, which itself had no real structure in place to provide ongoing support for these kinds of efforts. With better structural support and a more fully developed negotiation strategy, the activists would have stood a much better chance at reaching an acceptable negotiated outcome.

From the perspective of an activist, the meeting was never a negotiation in the first place. In fact, the group may have been lulled into a false sense of security by coming to the law school and adopting more mainstream approaches to dialogue, using the corporate-speak of "negotiate" and "interests" and "options," when in reality many activists believe that their power to effect change comes not from structural authority but instead from their principled positions, their capacity for mobilization, and their willingness to resist authority and decisions that they believe are unjust. On this view, an activist might conclude that working within the system and "negotiating" are not genuine opportunities to push for positive change, but instead simply sidetrack activists or, even worse, make them complicit with the perpetrators of injustice. Being or appearing complicit is of particular concern for activists, because it risks losing credibility with their constituents and the public, thus reducing the activists' overall effectiveness and ability to bring about major social reform. Negotiation, therefore, is an unappealing and high-risk approach for activists, because it implicates them as potentially complicit with oppressors and, because negotiated agreements are likely to contain compromises, does not often lead to significant or revolutionary paradigm shifts in the short term.

These two perspectives suggest very different ideas about what the act of negotiation is and should be within the larger dynamics of social movements and change. On the one hand, alternative dispute resolution (ADR) generally and negotiation specifically have become "part of the system," both state and corporate. Negotiation is central to the skillset of every competent person in law and business, and interest-based bargaining methods are widely taught at professional schools. Mediation and arbitration have become core practices and conventional sites of dispute processing within the civil legal system. Thousands of legal disputes currently are routed to mediation or arbitration as a matter of contract or of state or court rules. Indeed, legislatures and companies have become so enamored with the promise of privately determined tailor-made solutions to problems that they are funneling more and more specialized disputes to alternative forums. As such, the perception that ADR has become "the establishment" and part of the mainstream in modern dispute processing is undeniably correct.

On the other hand, it is also correct that ADR is fundamentally an expression of alterneity and even sub-alterneity,[1] intrinsically separate from and historically resistant to formalistic, disenfranchising mainstream processes. For many proponents of ADR, it is this difference that attracts them to the field. Not everyone comes to ADR, after all, because they are seeking to optimize their skillsets in settlement and deal-making so that they might better position themselves within conventional litigation and transactional contexts. And not everyone interested in ADR wants to be a mediator. Others are drawn to ADR because they want to learn more about negotiation and persuasion; cause lawyering, lobbying, and advocacy; influences on decision-making and the human capacity for judgment; small- or large-scale social change and access to justice; the elusive promise of individual self-determination; differing visions of community order and disorder; activism and change campaigns; and the potential and limits of human-made systems. For these people, focusing primarily on mainstream dispute resolution processes and the professional roles within those processes ignores the philosophical, theoretical, and practical priorities that they find compelling and important.

In other words, the "alternative" in "alternative dispute resolution" starts to pull apart into two senses of the word: as "additional or supplemental to formal process" and as "countercultural and perhaps motivated by unconventional priorities." The study of activism puts the unstable signifier of "alternative" at the center of analysis and thus provides an opportunity to examine both meanings of alternative in the context of dispute processing. How do activists create legal meaning within the system and established procedures? How do they promote alternative or anarchistic priorities and values? Can activism be described in ADR without being circumscribed by ADR? If activism rejects ADR, is that itself an expression of ADR? Activism as a subject of theory and practice, therefore, creates new avenues of inquiry around what constitutes alternative process, particularly when it comes to values and ideology, and how the field today might accommodate greater intellectual and practical diversity.

Such inquiries may help reconnect modern ADR practice with the historical progressive roots of ADR, which in turn could illuminate some potential gains of examining activism and ADR together. Regarding activism, for example, ADR could be an academic and practical resource for activists and others seeking social change. ADR can offer tools for advocacy and preparation; models of interaction, organization, and facilitation; interdisciplinary methods supported by case studies; and strategic perspectives on planning and executing campaigns. In return, activists bring substantive concerns and social meaning that, when considering negotiation strategies and examining conflict, promote greater ethical analysis and social relevance of negotiation process and cultural assumptions, which in turn may lead to new methods of practice and areas of research.

Roots and Divergence

Modern alternative dispute resolution (ADR) started as a social movement organized around three ideas: delivery of dispute resolution services; individual empowerment; and social transformation (Harringon and Merry 1988). The idea was that ADR could provide a legitimate and even better approach for disputants who either could not or did not want to address grievances through formal or traditional processes (Duffy and Thompson 1992). It was alternative not just in the sense of being different or other, but in the more expansive and revolutionary sense of reimagining the conventional approach to dispute resolution (that is, passive adversaries submitting to the coercive authority of the judge to impose a binary win-lose decision) as something new, namely as empowered participants working jointly to determine a resolution responsive to their interests and tailored to their needs (Cohen and Alberstein 2011).

In this way, community-based dispute resolution was a strong and perhaps even activist form of access to justice, even though it was not the same as access to courts. Justice on this view was achievable *because* it was outside the traditional legal system. Disputants sought to resolve their own disputes through dialogue, self-determination, and informed consent. If a third party was present, he or she generally played a neutral/impartial role that often, in the most classic formulation of the ideal, was facilitative and not directive or adjudicative (Reynolds 2012). Early ADR proponents were idealistic about process because they believed that fair process could give marginalized people voice and an authentic way to participate in their own lives, which could ultimately transform democratic society by way of more informed, more diverse, and more empowered members. Although we typically do not remember these early innovators as "activists," it is clear that they were pursuing a values-driven agenda that required a willingness to create and act outside the box. On this thinking, early ADR was an abundant site of activist energies and pragmatic reforms.

As the ADR movement progressed, the three original goals of delivery of dispute resolution services, individual empowerment, and social transformation were subsumed by focus on "consensus process" (Harrington and Merry 1988: 729) and subsequently by an increasing emphasis on related professions, such as ADR-skilled lawyers and mediators (Lande 1984). The original idealism of early ADR persisted for many ADR proponents but was largely recast as a belief in the general superiority of orderly dialogue-driven processes facilitated by neutral third parties (Reynolds 2012). Law schools facilitated these developments by teaching classes on the major ADR processes (mediation, arbitration, and negotiation), typically within the context of the legal system and thus focused on what certain professional roles, namely lawyers and mediators, needed to know about these major processes so that they might best represent or serve the interests of clients and parties. For example, many simulations in these classes mirror the basic structural assumptions of legal bargaining: bilateral exchange between (often professional) participants with some level of agreement authority, taking place in a single meeting or within a discrete set of meetings around a relatively stable issue or set of issues. These assumptions often define transactions within a generalized buyer-seller dynamic and are rarely questioned (Avruch 2006), despite the increased awareness of non-linearity and other complex dynamics within negotiation and conflict resolution processes (Honeyman and Coben 2010).

Narrowing ADR's expansive, visionary social prerogatives to a focus on process and profession has, on the whole, yielded tremendous dividends to the field. Today, negotiation is widely recognized as a core lawyering skill; mediation and arbitration are major, established process alternatives in a variety of dispute contexts; and the proliferation of hybrid procedures (e.g., med-arb) alongside the continuing development of related dispute management fields and competencies (e.g., dispute systems design) are testament to the demand for flexible and innovative approaches to disputes and deals. One way of interpreting this evolution is that ADR successfully followed through on its original activist agenda—transformation and empowerment—by assimilating into established institutions and creating more enlightened alternatives within those institutions. Yet in so doing, the movement detached itself from its original activist impulses and distanced itself from explicit commitments to social justice and radical change.[2] Such ideological divergence, along with ADR's successful assimilation into many corporate and judicial systems, may have contributed to the perception that ADR is not an affiliated practice or primary resource for modern activists.

Activism and ADR: Conflicting Assumptions

Accordingly, whether and how ADR can support activism depends in part on the fit between the fields. On first blush, it seems quite easy to define activism as entirely consistent with ADR. Activism is extralegal and "alternative" insofar as it involves people working for social change outside the established processes and power structures for making changes. Similarly, ADR provides theories and avenues for resolution outside the mainstream established processes (e.g., adversarial litigation) for resolution. Further, it seems relatively simple to define activism as an instance of negotiation, one of the major ADR processes, since activists are unable unilaterally to effectuate the change they want and so must engage in strategic campaigns intended to persuade. These campaigns may involve methods peculiar to activism (e.g., protests), but they are not especially unusual or different from other forms of leverage or alternatives one might see in negotiation.[3] As a definitional matter, therefore, activism seems congruent with theories and practices of alternative process and negotiation.

Yet activists often do not see themselves as negotiators or conflict resolvers. In fact, many activists may refuse to engage in civil discourse, reject overtures to negotiate, and even turn their energies to drumming up discord, all for strategic reasons. As Sharon Beder notes in the context of environmental activism:

> Good activism is designed to foster a sense of urgency and crisis so that people will cry out for change. Negotiation, however, can work against this by diffusing that sense of crisis and giving the impression that there is no need to worry since environmentalists are leading government in the right direction. This can be a false sense of confidence given the lack of power of negotiating environmentalists, particularly in times of recession (Beder 1991).

More recently, Stephan Sonnenberg and James Cavallaro (2012) have written that conflict resolution methods often do not resonate with activists and others who work for human rights. Human rights advocates recoil, for example, at the prospect of "accommodating all parties (including rights abusers)" within a neutral process and thus may believe that joint problem-solving and collaboration ultimately cannot serve the interests of justice (Sonnenberg and Cavallaro 2012: 264). Put another way, many activists think that cooperative piecemeal change and neutral process work to the benefit of entrenched interests and wrongdoers, and therefore they do not necessarily recognize incremental and inclusive reform strategies, such as negotiation, as the way forward.

Many activists, then, do not think of themselves as negotiators. The feeling is mutual, as it turns out, because many negotiators do not think of activists as negotiators, either. This is true even given the broad and inclusive approaches to negotiation teaching discussed above. Activism currently is not among the common negotiation contexts studied in negotiation courses. Even hostage negotiation involving pirates has become more central to the basic negotiation curriculum than has activism. If negotiators do think about activism, they are likely to think of activists as obstacles to negotiation, people who refuse to explore the issues in a constructive way. Or they might see activists as moving pieces or points of leverage in contentious complex negotiations. One could, for example, think of activists as (the human embodiments of) alternatives, in that they are people who stand ready to boycott, protest, burn things, and so on if some acceptable agreement is not reached. Or perhaps activists help generate interests, in that activists create cultural meaning through their highly visible public articulation of the values and concerns at stake, thus providing context to what shows up as interests in the negotiation. Or maybe activists serve as a type of criterion, in that their expected response to a negotiated outcome might provide an important benchmark for evaluating that outcome. Outside of these substantive and strategic considerations, however, many negotiators do not immediately think of activism as part of negotiation practice or ADR more generally.

How is it possible that activism and negotiation are the same and also not the same? The table below shows that some key assumptions about activism are inconsistent with some key assumptions about negotiation, which may explain in part why the two fields look different. Note that this is a table of general assumptions about both areas, meant to help interrogate why activism and negotiation appear so disparate; it does not depict the variety or nuances that shape practices and theories in both fields.

	(Typical) Assumptions about activism	(Typical) Assumptions about negotiation
Actors	Powerless members of the public coming together as a group; membership changing constantly	Empowered people with authority to negotiate; stable group during the period of the negotiation
Motivation	Primarily ideological or moral (based on conviction, values, and identity)	Primarily economic (often framed as a buyer-seller dynamic)
Primary goals	Awareness; major paradigm shift; revolution or radical change	Value creation (expanding the pie) and durable agreements
Typical setting	Multilateral (usually one of many entities, private and public, concerned with a given issue)	Bilateral (two-sided negotiated exchange that may have impacts on nonrepresented third parties)
Time horizon	Varies, but may go on for years or even generations	Typically confined to meeting or set of meetings
Bargaining style	Positional / distributive	Positional / distributive or integrative, depending on context
Leverage[4]	Primarily negative and normative	Primarily positive, then negative and normative
Primary mode of interaction	Protest	Dialogue
Stance in dialogue	Important to maintain "other" status for credibility	Important to build trust and rapport, if possible
Us/them mentality	Having an us/them mentality is important to avoid becoming or appearing complicit	Having an us/them mentality may serve strategic purposes but is generally not useful because it hinders trust building and value creation
Defining success	Did things change?	Did we come to agreement?

Table 1. Some typical assumptions about activism and negotiation.

Comparing some of the typical assumptions in activism and negotiation helps illuminate why the fields are often regarded as promulgating different or even opposite approaches to contentious issues. Activists take strong positions based on their values and then operate in relatively unstructured dialogic environments that may include, in varying degrees and at different times, governmental officials, local businesses, interested organizations, other activist groups, and members of the public. Because they are working within almost constant change, activists prize conviction and clarity—both of which are required to motivate volunteer members over time and in the midst of setbacks—and believe that negative and normative leverage are the best ways to move entrenched power structures. Negotiators, by contrast, know that positional bargaining often leads to impasse and so seek out the interests beneath those positions, typically working with decision-makers (though they may consult with outsiders, including activists) to generate multiple options and develop an agreement within a certain timeframe. They develop positive leverage such as concessions to promote cooperation and improve the chances of coming to agreement.

On closer inspection, however, these differences appear to be less about what activism and negotiation are, and more about what activism and negotiation *emphasize*. Prominent cultural images of activism (protestors outside the WTO in front of television cameras) are not the same as prominent cultural images of negotiation (suits in a paneled room, or maybe a prospective buyer at a car dealership), but this is not necessarily because they are different activities. They are, in truth, the same basic activity—an effort to persuade—only with different emphases in how participants come to be involved, the ways and settings in which they participate, the forms of exchange and communication they use, and what they believe counts for success in the short and long terms.

Both ADR and activism stand to gain from closer attention to these variations in emphasis, particularly given the broader historical context of ADR as a social movement. The normative aspirations of both fields may be otherwise unachievable, considering the complexities, gridlock, and capture that characterize much of the politico-legal environment today. Simply put, activists may find that alternative processes help them promote their causes more effectively. As Sonnenberg and Cavallaro (2012: 278) point out, achieving real "victories with regard to social, economic and cultural rights" may require "activists [to] weave together legal and conflict resolution strategies in their approach", which in turn will require innovative, diverse practices for activists to use. And for their part, ADR theorists may find that activism provides much-needed context on process design and implementation. Recent work on negotiation and "wicked problems," for example, highlights the pressing need for negotiation theorists to account for greater complexity in practice and pedagogy (Honeyman and Coben 2010; Chrustie et al. 2010); [see also NDR: Coleman et al., *Intractable 1 and 2*, and NDR: Coleman and Ricigliano, *Getting in Sync*]; activism provides an abundant source of "wicked problems" that strain the boundaries of typical assumptions and conventional understandings of parties, interests, options, and implementation. Moreover, as many scholars have argued, the "value neutrality" of ADR processes sometimes may disenfranchise weak parties and reify existing power disparities, and accordingly require greater content-based analysis and interrogation of process development and deployment to ensure that practices are consistent with, for example, ethical sensibilities around human rights (Cohen and Alberstein 2011; Sonnenberg and Cavallaro 2012). More intentional focus on activist-related negotiation and conflict resolution will undoubtedly introduce a host of fascinating policy and philosophical concerns, given the ADR field's longstanding commitment to neutrality.

In short, highlighting the intersection between ADR and activism represents an opportunity for those who believe that social justice, progressive reform, or any major sociopolitical change requires innovative, participatory, outside-the-box approaches. To capitalize on this opportunity, ADR scholars, professors, and practitioners must recognize some of the common emphases of activism and provide research and practical support for these emphases.

Activism = Negotiating with Emphasis

Carrie Menkel-Meadow (2002) famously observed that the modern lawyer must know more than the law; she must also how to build consensus among stakeholders with differing interests and values, in the absence of coercive state action. Doing so requires laying out "ethics for a new practice," that is, a set of normative priorities and practical skills for making possible these consensus-based agreements (2002).

Likewise, making the best use of potential synergies between ADR and activism requires the articulation of new or renewed commitments to ideas and practices that recognize and support the work of people who are not in positions of formal authority but nevertheless are working on often intractable problems featuring deep identity, and value-based concerns related to multiple changing constituencies within complex, shifting sociopolitical and economic landscapes, often over long periods of time. If activism is like "regular" negotiation only with different areas of emphasis, then those emphases need unpacking and support. Here are some activism-oriented areas of emphasis that would benefit from increased attention in ADR curriculum and scholarship. Within each area of interest, I have started listing ideas about who might undertake various kinds of scholarly or practical activities, as well as for whom these activities might provide benefit. These are not exhaustive lists, but are rather openings to further exploration and study in these areas.

Rethinking Compromise

Neither activists nor negotiators generally like the word "compromise." Activists do not like compromise because it sounds too much like selling out. Negotiators do not like compromise because it sounds like leaving money on the table, and may represent a failure to drill down past positions into interests. But compromise provides a valuable function of helping groups with divergent interests and/or values to come to an agreement that, although not wholly acceptable to each, represents a shared commitment in making some progress (Gutmann and Thompson 2012). [NDR: Menkel-Meadow, *Compromise*] In fact, the internal contradictions apparent in many political compromises may themselves be meaningful remnants of the disagreement and the mutual sacrifice that led to the compromise, which makes the compromise itself a symbol of an ongoing commitment to working together (Cohen forthcoming). Without a more nuanced understanding and appreciation of compromise, progress around contentious issues may be impossible.

Possible Action Items, by Whom and for Whom: Useful possible directions for scholars and scholar-practitioners include the following: developing a more rigorous methodology around compromise (how to make them and when); studying the historical uses of compromise in more depth, especially in political decision-making; exploring the identity- and value-based difficulties that compromise may present; and expanding theories of compromise to include, among other things, the performative value of compromise in intractable or otherwise complex, ongoing disputes. The theories and models coming out of this work could then be incorporated into negotiation teaching so that law students, graduate students, and activist communities undertaking training understand the benefits and tradeoffs of compromise, both as an end in itself and as part of a larger strategic plan.

Managing Multiple Constituencies, Internal and External

Most negotiation courses, modules, and simulations assume bilateral exchange. Even simulations that involve teams of people are usually allocated between two sides. This makes sense, because bilateral transactions are easier to teach and much easier to study, if only as a matter of experiment design and empirical data collection and analysis. Most activists, however, are not engaged in two-sided disputes but instead operate within complex multilateral settings. As Kathleen Blee (2012) observes, activists must not only organize their members internally, they must also mobilize their members to interact with a myriad of external parties, from other activist and citizen groups to city/state officials, neighboring businesses and organizations, the police, the public, and whatever other stakeholders might be concerned with the issues that the activists are championing.

Possible Action Items, by Whom and for Whom: With this in mind, and considering the increasing demand for multilateral skillsets in areas separate from activism, the legal academy needs more of everything when it comes to multilateral bargaining: more classes, more articles, more practical tools and trainings, more informed commentary on long-term or disordered disputes and coalition building, and more access to the excellent work being done in sociology, public dispute resolution, communications, and other areas that touch on the work of activists (Aslama and Napoli 2011; Blee 2012; Hanrie 2014).

Problem Definition in Short- and Long-Term Contexts

Determining the issues to be negotiated is the first step of any negotiation. Without a clear definition of the problem, the parties may waste time talking past one another, thus jeopardizing the possibility of agreement. Defining problems, however, may not be as straightforward as it sounds, especially for activist groups that build membership based on broad, aspirational calls for change. The social movement "Black Lives Matter," for example, has done an incredible job in a short period of time raising awareness of ongoing issues of racism and discriminatory treatment in the United States. Some have argued, however, that the movement does not provide sufficient problem definition in the short term and therefore cannot push for policy changes or legal reforms effectively. For some activists, raising awareness may be enough, because greater awareness spurs public discourse and creates social meaning, which hopefully eventually leads to paradigm shift. For other activists, of course, short-term change is imperative. Those working against the death penalty, for example, may be quite interested in methods that provide immediate relief to people awaiting execution. Regardless of short- or long-term orientation, activists must think about what is gained and what is lost by defining problems broadly or narrowly (Mayer 2009). And certainly intending to plan for both short- and long-term changes does not answer the question of how to prioritize activities or maintain long-term credibility when focusing on short-term goals.

Possible Action Items, by Whom and for Whom: Negotiation and clinical professors should consider developing specific training for activists around problem definition and tradeoffs. Groups that work regularly with public education and outreach (such as the National Lawyers Guild or "Know Your Rights" groups) may be useful resources in developing materials and pedagogical approaches that would resonate with audiences consisting of people who are not graduate students and who may be suspicious of "conventional" or "corporate" methods. That said, the benefits to having a mixed audience (graduate students and activists) would be considerable, from sharing of experiences to deepening of contextual awareness to networking and building relationships.

Imagining this mixed-audience course causes one to think further about the potential benefits of developing clinics or labs that provide an ongoing connection between the law school and one or more activist groups. Within this clinical setting, activists could consider the benefits and costs of spinning off certain issues into more digestible "problems," and the consequences of these decisions could also be studied, considered, and reconsidered over time. The clinic could go farther, bringing activists and students together to think through change campaigns and strategy. Julie Macfarlane has set forth a compelling vision of law school clinics that support "community and group organizing, individual and group rights assertions, partisan negotiation and conflict resolution, and lobbying for law reform and policy alternatives" (2009: 46). Over time, and depending on interests and needs, clinical faculty could work with activist leaders to anticipate and develop projects for students to work on, within the context of the group's goals and history. This kind of clinical offering may be challenging to pull off, given the difficult fit between the institutional machinery of the law school and the unpredictable, changeable nature of activist groups.[6]

Process Management and Dispute Systems Design

Considering that activists are operating in an ongoing and unstable multilateral context, they must learn how to handle communications and manage process. Some of these communications and processes may take place in formal settings, such as city council meetings, but many others will be less formal interactions, such as talking with the police or meeting with local businesses. Understanding basic communication frameworks (e.g., social media), process management (e.g., facilitation techniques), and dispute systems design (e.g., procedures for handling grievances between group members) are valuable competencies in activism, especially for large groups.

Possible Action Items, by Whom and for Whom: Scholars and instructors should find and describe actual case studies about processes and systems, external and internal, that activists develop and use, along with more data about how activists organize members, orchestrate activists, and manage the physical spaces in which they must operate. Though some may rightly point out the limits of anecdotal research, the benefits of illustrative examples are substantial in that they highlight strengths and weaknesses in existing theories and promote better, more relevant theorizing going forward. Relatedly, theory and practice around "capacity building" and restoring historically marginalized people will help ensure that conflict resolution processes are "rebalance[d]" and thus effective mechanisms for positive change (Sonnenberg and Cavallaro 2012: 271, 272). One practical possibility here is incorporating activism into dispute systems design courses. Students could map a historical, fictional, or actual/imminent story about activism as an exercise in assessment, design, implementation, and dealing with the inevitable and often unpredictable wrinkles that emerge in systems development.

Meaning, Memory, and Forgetting

Activist groups come together for many reasons. Sometimes they start fresh around a particular issue; sometimes they redirect themselves away from one issue and toward another; sometimes they undergo turnover that, by virtue of the changing membership, leads to shifts in priorities. Different members will recall the genesis of the group differently (and often strategically), and how the "birth" of the group is defined will "set in motion a trajectory of action" (Blee 2012: 17). Origin myths inform present values, and armed with those values, activists who are part of larger social movements "narrate new social meanings" that can ultimately "chang[e] the people who make the law and the landscape in which that law is made" (Guinier and Torres 2014: 2758, 2750).

Possible Action Items, by Whom and for Whom: ADR theorists must take into account these origin myths, both remembered and misremembered, when attempting to theorize what activists want, as a matter of negotiation. This is connected to the more basic emphasis in activism around values and identity, and ADR scholars and practitioners should continue developing refinements on interest-based theories to accommodate a more nuanced understanding of how values can and cannot be negotiated (Forester 2009). Moreover, theorists must grapple with the substantive challenge posed by participants who are not only expressing their own interests and values, but who may also be making social meaning and establishing the parameters for discourse around a particular subject.

Conclusion

Note that most of the possible action items listed above are not new, in that scholars and practitioners in negotiation and ADR have written about and produced pedagogical materials exploring values-based bargaining, multilateral scenarios, issue definition and wicked problems, dispute systems design, and all the other areas of emphasis that are characteristic of activism. We do not need new directions; we need more sustained commitment and depth in existing directions, incorporating relevant interdisciplinary research, intentionally developing both substantive/historical and practical/skills-intensive coursework, and contemplating diverse, interactive, hybrid student audiences that may include anti-university, anti-establishment types. Then we may better understand how activism—destabilized, decentralized, highly contingent and unpredictable, yet also a bulwark of democratic process and source of meaning, law, and social change—operates as a matter of negotiation and alternative process, as an A of ADR.

Notes

[1] I am using the term "subalterneity" in the postcolonial sense, generally as referring to that which is outside or underneath the colonial (i.e., central and imposed) power

structure. See, e.g., Spivak 1988 (providing fundamental theoretical work for the postcolonial studies movement.)

[2] To be clear, there are many negotiation and ADR professors and practitioners who strive for social justice in their life and work. The point here is simply that the most obvious and dominant development over time in ADR has been the advancements made in legal process and profession.

[3] And certainly many negotiation professors believe that the fundamental tenets of integrative bargaining are applicable across legal and non-legal practice areas. Basic negotiation courses often include, for example, simulations that allow students to practice negotiating in workplace, community, and interpersonal settings.

[4] Using here Richard Shell's definition of positive, negative, and normative leverage (Shell 1999).

[5] Bob Bordone's groundbreaking DSD clinic at Harvard Law School may provide an example for how to get past some of these structural challenges.

References

Aslama, M. and P. M. Napoli. 2011. Bridging Gaps, Crossing Boundaries. In *Communications Research in Action: Scholar-Activist Collaborations for a Democratic Public Sphere*, edited by P. M. Napoli and M. Aslama. New York: Fordham University Press.

Avruch, K. 2006. The Poverty of Buyer and Seller. In *The Negotiator's Fieldbook: The Desk Reference for the Experienced Negotiator*, edited by A. K. Schneider and C. Honeyman. Washington, DC: American Bar Association.

Beder, S. 1991. Activism versus Negotiation: Strategies for the Environment Movement. *Social Alternatives* 10, no. 4: 53-56.

Blee, K. 2012. *Democracy in the Making: How Activist Groups Form*. New York: Oxford University Press.

Chrustie, C., J. Docherty, L. Lira, J. Mahuad, H. Gadlin and C. Honeyman. 2010. Negotiating Wicked Problems: Five Stories. *Venturing Beyond the Classroom: Volume 2 of the Rethinking Negotiation Teaching Series*. St. Paul, MN: DRI Press.

Cohen, A. J. On Compromise, Negotiation, and Loss. *NOMOS LV: Compromise* (NYU Press forthcoming).

Cohen, A. J. 2009. Dispute Systems Design, Neoliberalism, and the Problem of Scale. *Harvard Negotiation Law Review* 14: 51-80.

Cohen, A. J. and M. Alberstein. 2011. Progressive Constitutionalism and Alternative Movements in Law. *Ohio State Law Journal* 72: 1083-1113.

Duffy, K. G. and J. Thomson. 1992. Community Mediation Centers: Humanistic Alternatives to the Court System: A Pilot Study. *Journal of Humanistic Psychology* 32, no. 2: 101-114.

Fischer, R., A. K. Schneider, E. Borgwardt and B. Ganson. 1996. *Coping with International Conflict: A Systematic Approach to Influence in International Negotiation*. New York: Pearson.

Forester, John. 2009. *Dealing with Differences: Dramas of Meeting Public Disputes*. New York: Oxford University Press.

Gayatui C. S. Can the Subaltern Speak? In *Marxism and the Interpretation of Culture* 271-313. C. Nelson and L. Lawrence eds. (1958) (Providing fundamental theoretical work for the postcolonial studies movement.)

Gutmann, A. and D. F. Thompson. 2012. *The Spirit of Compromise: Why Governing Demands It and Campaigning Undermines It*. New Jersey: Princeton University Press.

Guinier, L. and G. Torres. 2014. Changing the Wind: Notes toward a Demosprudence of Law and Social Movements. *Yale Law Journal* 123: 2740-2804.

Hanrie, H. 2014. *How Organizations Develop Activists: Civil Associations & Leadership in the 21st Century*. New York: Oxford University Press.

Harrington, C. B. and S. E. Merry. 1988. Ideological Production: The Making of Community Mediation. *Law & Society Review* 22: 709-736.

Honeyman, C. and J. R. Coben. 2010. Navigating Wickedness: A New Frontier in Teaching Negotiation. *Venturing Beyond the Classroom: Volume 2 of the Rethinking Negotiation Teaching Series*. St. Paul, MN: DRI Press.

Lande, J. 1984. Mediation Paradigms and Professional Identities. *Mediation Quarterly* 4: 19-47.

Macfarlane, J. 2009. Bringing the Clinic into the 21st Century. *Windsor Yearbook of Access to Justice* 27: 35-52.

Mayer, B. 2009. *Staying with Conflict: A Strategic Approach to Ongoing Disputes*. San Francisco: John Wiley & Sons.

Menkel-Meadow, C. 2002. The Lawyer as Consensus Builder: Ethics for a New Practice. *Tennessee Law Review* 70: 63-119.

Reynolds, J. 2012. Games, Dystopia, and ADR. *Ohio State Journal on Dispute Resolution* 27: 477-538.

Schneider, A. K. 1999. The Intersection of Therapeutic Jurisprudence, Preventive Law, and Alternative Dispute Resolution. *Psychology, Public Policy & Law* 5: 1084-1102.

Shell, G. R. 1999. *Bargaining for Advantage: Negotiation Strategies for Reasonable People*. New York: Viking.

Sonnenberg, S. and J. L. Cavallaro. 2012. Name, Shame, and Then Build Consensus? Bringing Conflict Resolution Skills to Human Rights. *Washington University Journal of Law & Policy* 39: 257-308.

Spivak, G. C. Can the Subaltern Speak? In *Marxism and the Interpretation of Culture* (Cary Nelson and Lawrence Grossberg eds.; U. of Illinois Press 1988, at 271-313.) (Providing fundamental theoretical work for the postcolonial studies movement).

Waltz, M. 2005. *Alternative and Activist Media*. Edinburgh: Edinburgh University Press.

Additions to the
Negotiator's Desk Reference

Index is now Search; Electronic Editions; Updates

The *Negotiator's Desk Reference* is part of a long-running project called the Canon of Negotiation Initiative. The rate of change in the Initiative has been high; for example, 60% of the chapters in this book are entirely new since our project's original book. (That was the first edition of *The Negotiator's Fieldbook*, published 2006 by the American Bar Association.) Every other chapter you see here, meanwhile, has been updated; and some of the updates have been extensive.

We now expect that rate of change to continue, and we have designed several features of this book to recognize that reality. These are offered without charge to anyone who has purchased the full print edition (i.e. both volumes), or the full Kindle edition. (Recognizing however that some people may take a course that specifies just one volume, as a courtesy we are making the two print volumes available separately.)

First, because many people now prefer to read in more than one format depending on where they happen to be, when you purchase the book as a whole (again, either as two print volumes, or as a Kindle book) you will receive complimentary access to the Web edition as well. Access instructions are below.

Second, we intend to use the Web edition of this book to make future updating both faster and more easily accessible for readers. Anticipated updates there (designated for convenience as "Volume 3") are also included in the price, for anyone who buys any full version, whether print, Kindle or Web. Finally, instead of a printed index, we are providing a customized search engine. This is designed to capture the latest updates as well as the original text.

If you have purchased the full book in hard copy or Kindle, please visit https://www.ndrweb.com/web-access-for-print-buyers.html and follow the registration and proof-of-purchase instructions. We have tried to make them as simple as possible. Your registration will also provide access to anticipated future "extras" such as interviews with contributors.

About the Editors:

Chris Honeyman is Managing Partner of Convenor Conflict Management, a consulting firm based in Washington, DC. (www.convenor.com) Chris has served as an adviser to numerous academic and practical conflict resolution programs in the U.S. and abroad, and as a mediator, arbitrator and in other neutral capacities in more than 2,000 disputes since the 1970s. From 2007-2013 he was co-director of Rethinking Negotiation Teaching, a major project to revamp the content and methods of negotiation teaching worldwide. From 2004-2009 he served as lead external consultant to ADR Center (Rome), the largest dispute resolution firm in continental Europe. And from 1990-2006 he was director of a succession of Hewlett Foundation-funded research-and-development programs, of national or international scale. Chris is co-editor of six books and author or co-author of more than 90 published articles, book chapters and monographs on dispute resolution ideas, infrastructure, quality control and ethics. He has held a variety of committee and advisory roles for the ABA, IMI and other organizations.

Andrea Kupfer Schneider is a Professor of Law at Marquette University Law School, where she has taught Dispute Resolution, Negotiation, Ethics, and International Conflict Resolution for over 20 years. She is the Director of Marquette's nationally-ranked dispute resolution program. She frequently publishes law review articles and book chapters on negotiation, gender, international conflict and dispute systems design, and has co-authored several leading legal textbooks on ADR, Negotiation and Mediation. Andrea gives negotiation trainings around the world to corporations, law firms, court systems, and, most recently, has focused on faculty in the STEM and medical fields, for which she has now received federal grants for software development and training. She is a founding editor of Indisputably, the blog for ADR law faculty, and started the Dispute Resolution Works-in-Progress Annual Conference in 2007. She was named 2009 Woman of the Year by the Wisconsin Law Journal and, in 2016, gave her first Tedx talk, entitled Women Don't Negotiate and Other Similar Nonsense. She was named the 2017 recipient of the ABA Section of Dispute Resolution Award for Outstanding Scholarly Work. Andrea received her A.B. cum laude from Princeton University and her J.D. cum laude from Harvard Law School.

Made in United States
North Haven, CT
23 August 2022

23113364R00437